Romantic Hearts

A Personal Reference
for Romance Readers

Third Edition

Peggy J. Jaegly

The Scarecrow Press, Inc.
Lanham, Md., & London
1997

SCARECROW PRESS, INC.

Published in the United States of America
by Scarecrow Press, Inc.
4720 Boston Way
Lanham, Maryland 20706

4 Pleydell Gardens, Folkestone
Kent CT20 2DN, England

British Cataloguing-in-Publication Information Available

Library of Congress Cataloging-in-Publication Data

Jaegly, Peggy J.
    Romantic hearts : a personal reference for romance for romance readers / Peggy
J. Jaegly. — 3rd ed.
        p.   cm.
    Includes bibliographical references and index.
    ISBN 0–8108–3002–7 (cloth : alk. paper). — ISBN 1–57886–000–8
(pbk. : alk. paper)
        1. Love stories, American—Bibliography.   2. Love stories,
English—Bibliography.   I. Title.
    Z1231.L68J34   1997
    [PS374.L6]
    016.813 ' 08508—dc21   96–37378
                                                                                        CIP

ISBN 0–8108–3002–7 (cloth : alk. paper)
ISBN 0–57886–000–8 (pbk. : alk. paper)

Dedicated to

Mary Kay Chelton,

an extraordinary woman

who made it happen.

CONTENTS

Elaine Barbieri, Jo Beverley, Jennifer Blake, Judith Bowen, Barbara
Bretton, Dixie Browning, Pamela Browning, Eileen Buckholtz, Linda Cajio,
Marisa Carroll, Barbara Cartland, Lori Copeland, Jasmine Cresswell, Emma
Darcy, Cassie Edwards, Marie Ferrarella, Judy Gill, Ruth Glick, Deborah Gordon,
Ginna Gray, Jennifer Greene, Patricia Hagan, Carole Halston, Shannon
Harper, Robin Lee Hatcher, Barbara Hazard, Sandra Heath/Sandra Wilson,
Emily Hendrickson, Tami Hoag, Susan Naomi Horton, Charlotte Hughes,
Arlene James, BJ James, Muriel Jensen, Jill Marie Landis, Ruth Ryan Langan,
Cathie Linz, Debbie Macomber, Ann Major, Sandra Marton, Connie Mason,
Curtiss Ann Matlock, Leigh Michaels, Linda Lael Miller, Helen Mittermeyer,
Vella Munn, Helen R. Myers, Carla Neggers, Sara Orwig, Laurie Paige,
Diana Palmer, Marilyn Pappano, Susan Elizabeth Phillips, Joan Elliot Pickart,
Mary Jo Putney, Patricia Rice, Emilie Richards, Eugenia Riley, Renee
Roszel, Sonia Simone-Rossney, Tracy Sinclair, Lass Small, Deborah Smith,
Joan Smith, Vicki Lewis Thompson, Carolyn Thornton, Pat Warren, Peggy
Webb, Joan Wolf, Sherryl Woods

ACKNOWLEDGMENTS

This new and improved third edition of *Romantic Hearts* has been possible through the contributions of many. I extend my gratitude to all the faithful romance readers who called or wrote since the last edition with their encouragement and excited anticipation for this third edition.

Special thanks and recognition go to Geraldine Bowman, who spent many otherwise days of leisure combing her books and catalogs for additional information. Carol DiTello of the Book Oasis in Ohio and Shirley Wexler also deserve special mention for their contributions. I can never thank enough my husband, Robert, nor our computer consultant, Ray Nettleship, who spent countless hours coaxing the computer to do what we wanted it to do, instead of the other way around.

Romantic Hearts wouldn't have been possible without all the willing assistance provided by the romance publishers themselves. To them, I express my heartfelt gratitude and appreciation. Most of all, I thank all the romance authors, whose work is intelligent, well-researched, and devoted. Each author has given blood, sweat, and tears to produce a product that gives us readers a few hours of escape and enjoyment. For all your sacrifices, authors, thank you.

Photographs of authors are courtesy of those authors. Additional credits are:

    p. 3 of Jo Beverley by Beninger Photography, Inc.
    p. 7 of Jennifer Blake by Bryan Rockett
    p. 13 of Dixie Browning by Deborah Armstrong
    p. 35 of Judy Gill by Lee
    p. 39 of Deborah Gordon by Bill Santos
    p. 47 of Carole Halston by Lemane's Photography Studio
    p. 59 of Tami Hoag courtesy of Bantam Books
    p. 63 of Charlotte Hughes by Johns Foto
    p. 67 of B. J. James by Robert M. Watkins
    p. 71 of Jill Marie Landis by Debbi de Mont
    p. 73 of Ruth Ryan Langan courtesy of Glamour Shots
    p. 87 of Leigh Michaels by Michael W. Lemberger
    p. 95 of Helen R. Myers by Randy Phillips Photography
    p. 97 of Carla Neggers by Parker Photography
    p. 101 of Laurie Paige by Firestone Photography
    p. 107 of Susan Elizabeth Phillips by Ron Stewart Portraiture
    p. 123 of Sonia Simone-Rossney courtesy of Terry Lorant
    p. 141 of Sherryl Woods by Teresa Salgado Photography

Dear Romance Readers:

No matter what type of romance story you enjoy--historical, contemporary, intrigue, regency, gothic, futuristic, or time-travel--this book has something to offer you. All types of romance novels are listed in our popular format.

Romantic Hearts is comprised of three sections for your easy use: "Author Profiles," "Author Pseudonym Index," and the "Author/Title Index."

Come visit with popular authors featured in the profile section. They candidly share their personal stories and provide you with a glimpse of what their lives are like as writers.

Over 10,000 titles have been added to this year's edition. Please note that authors' names are repeated at the top of each new column (unless they happen to begin there). Be sure to check the *preceding* column so as not to miss the starting point for any given author. Our new, larger format was done in an effort to keep the thickness of the book manageable and to maintain all the reference material in one book for your convenience. I have exhaustively researched all sources to ensure the accuracy and completeness of the information contained in this book. Any inaccuracies or omissions are unintentional.

Whet your appetite for forthcoming books by having future titles at your fingertips. Future titles listed are those planned at the time this book goes to press. Changes in editors, publication schedules, and other events can affect title decisions. Please understand if future books bear different titles.

Check the updated pseudonym index for your favorite authors' names and discover other enjoyable books they may have written under another name.

So many of you have written or called in the past year from all around the world. I love hearing from you! If you are a reader or writer and have titles you would like added to the next *Romantic Hearts* edition, please send them to me. As always, keep your letters, comments, and suggestions coming by sending them to: Peggy Jaegly; PO Box 285; Flagtown, NJ 08821-0285.

Keep reading!
Peggy J. Jaegly

KEY

AUTHOR/PSEUDONYM INDEX
   The author's real name is in bold and pseudonym in italics.

AUTHOR/TITLE INDEX
   Titles are usually listed in chronological order. Long titles have been
   abbreviated. Columns provide the following information:
   Author Pseudonym
      Series #   Title   Publication Date   Publisher/Line or Series

AUTHOR PROFILES

ELAINE BARBIERI

Readers: I started writing with simple purposes in mind. I hoped to touch my readers with the same impact with which I had been touched by my favorite authors. I wanted to write books that my readers would want to read over and again. My first love has always been historical romance and that's where I've concentrated my career.

My books are now published all over the world and I have received many awards, for which I am flattered and appreciative. My greatest personal reward, however, has come from the many readers I have met and the many letters I receive from readers who say they have read my books many times, and that my books have had a positive influence on their lives. For me, that response makes writing truly worthwhile.

Elaine Barbieri was born in the historic city of Paterson, New Jersey. The romance of history was bred into her as a child, but it was not until adulthood that she decided to put that background into the written word. In the time since, she has had twenty-five novels published. She has written for Berkley/Jove, Harlequin, Harper, Leisure, and Zebra Books, and she has over seven million books in print. Her titles have hit major bestseller lists all across the country and are published worldwide.

Elaine has received many awards for her work, including Storyteller of the Year, several Awards of Excellence, and Best Saga Awards from *Romantic Times Magazine*. Her book, *Dance Of The Flame*, has been nominated by *Romantic Times* as the Best Historical Fantasy Romance for 1994-1995. Her book, *Wings Of A Dove* was a Doubleday Book Club special selection.

Elaine was selected to be one of the launch authors for *Romance Alive Audio*. The release of *More Precious Than Gold* in January 1995, will be followed by the release of *Only For Love* at a later date.

2

Elaine's historical romance, entitled *Dangerous Virtues-Honesty*, was published in 1996 by Leisure Books.

JO BEVERLEY

Perhaps the most common question asked of any author is, "Where do you get your ideas?" It's an impossible question, of course, because mostly we just don't know. There we are, minding our own business, weeding the garden, fixing the car, or stirring a pot at the stove and ...

A story idea!

It isn't always welcome. Sometimes we mutter, "Take a number." Working authors generally have far more story ideas than time to write them.

Some ideas, however, are irresistible. Terrifying, but irresistible. I think of it as being mugged by my muse.

To me, my muse is like a guardian angel. She's been there all my life, most of the time tearing her hair out because I paid too little attention to my need to write.

As a child I scribbled stories, and as a teenager, I wrote a whole book--a historical romance, of course. Through college and a successful career, I kept scribbling but never did anything with my efforts.

Eventually, my muse got tough. She moved me and my husband from England to Canada. With no job, I finally wrote a book. At about this time, however, I also got pregnant and poured my energies into a local childbirth group. I put that book in a drawer and forgot about it.

Gnashing her teeth, my muse moved me, Ken, and our two children to a new place, and then arranged a talk at a local library on writing romances. When the speaker said she'd look at a first chapter, I ran home and wrote one.

And finally, the muse had won. I completed a second book, determined to make romance writing my career.

Three years later, *Lord Wraybourne's Betrothed* was published. Ten years later, my fourteenth book came out. Does that mean my muse is lazing on a beach in Acapulco? No. She's just hitting her stride.

Hitting. Mugging.

You see, every now and then, she pulls out this really outrageous idea and hits me over the head with it. "No!" I scream, cowering under the desk.

"Trust me," coos the muse, swinging a length of spiked chain. "You'll enjoy it."

And I do. I loved writing the schoolgirl and the rake, the adulterous heroine, and the childbirth-in-the-middle-of-battle stories.

In fact, though I'm working on a quite ordinary historical romance at the moment, I'm thinking of wandering into the darker alleys of my mind, hoping the muse is lurking there, outrageous idea in hand.

JENNIFER BLAKE

Jennifer Blake has been called one of the "grande dames" of romance fiction, and not without reason. She published her first book, a romantic mystery in the Gothic tradition, in 1970, and became a New York Times best selling author with *Love's Wild Desire* in 1977, more than three years before Romance Writers of America was formed. A charter member of RWA, she was one of the earliest recipients of the organization's Golden Treasure RITA for Lifetime Achievement. She was also among the first four authors to be inducted into the Affaire de Coeur Romance Hall of Fame in 1995.

Jennifer is a seventh-generation Louisianian, born on the land settled by her ancestors in the early 1800s, and delivered by her maternal grandmother who was a midwife. She was reared on a farm where she was a traditional tomboy who loved to run and romp, pick blackberries, climb trees--and who often disappeared into the woods for hours, book in hand, to avoid chores. When she was thirteen, she received a series of anonymous love poems. Two years later, she married her poet, and began a family that would eventually number two boys and two girls.

She started writing at twenty-one, while a housewife with three pre-schoolers under foot. A number of things contributed to that first endeavor: she had exhausted the stock of the local library, she had become disenchanted with the light reading she could find on the book racks, plus she wanted to record a story that had come to her one night in a dream. Putting words on paper was so much fun that she continued, spending the next six years perfecting her craft. Her first sale was a poem for the grand sum of one dollar, though it was quickly followed by articles, short stories, newspaper pieces, and more poems. Then came that first book sale. Some forty books later, she's still going strong.

While it's difficult to estimate the number of Jennifer Blake titles sold worldwide, a conservative estimate would be in excess of 22,000,000. European best seller lists and book clubs have carried the Blake name. Her growing international reputation has been bolstered vis translations into seventeen languages, including those of the Far East and Eastern Europe.

Jennifer and her husband live in the rolling hill country of north Louisiana in a home they designed themselves as a replica of a traditional Southern Planter's "Cottage." Known as Sweet Briar, it is a 4000 sq. ft., story-and-a-half house with dormers across the front, fanlighted entrance, white columns, and wide front porch or veranda. In her own words, she says: "Here I write my fantasies of love and adventure in the romantic South. And sometimes, when I sit in my porch swing with the sunlight falling across the lawn and the smells of magnolia, sweet olive, and antique roses wafting on the warm air, I live them."

JUDITH BOWEN

Ribald chuckwagon wake-up calls, melancholy ballads about good women gone bad, faithful ponies and ornery cows, the never-ending rigors of the weather. What is it about cowboy culture that fascinates me so?

My third book was a contemporary Western romance and I discovered I was doing something right when *Paper Marriage* won top honors in the first-ever National Readers' Choice Awards. It was a tremendous thrill to realize that readers loved my book enough to judge it the best traditional romance published in 1991.

A Home On The Range, my first long contemporary and also a Western romance, hit third spot on the Waldenbooks list, an unusual accomplishment, according to my editor, for a writer new to loyal readers of the longer lines. So I figured I still must be doing something right!

I dug deep into Old West lore researching the second in what had become a series planned about the Harlow family of Idaho, *High Country Rancher*, the story of Carson Harlow, a rambler and a prospector in southern Alberta. Again, the research process absorbed me completely.

Then I got to thinking about an old photo of my great-uncle Frank, a handsome, smiling, cocky-looking lad all decked out in chaps, wide-brimmed hat, the works ... courtesy, I'd always thought, of some turn of the century photographer's studio. Not so. Suddenly I remembered that Frank and my grandfather, Arthur, had left their home in New York State back around 1915 or so, two brothers who'd traveled West to make their fortunes. They'd become Arizona Rangers, after a spell catching and breaking wild horses to sell to ranchers and farmers, an interlude immortalized (according to family legend) in Zane Gray's book *Under Tonto Rim*.

I still had my grandfather's heavy, old-fashioned stock saddle. I'd learned to ride in that saddle. The Old West, it seemed, was in my blood, too.

Perhaps that's why I love the special challenge of writing a contemporary Western romance. To capture the feel and mood, the hopes and dreams of today's

Westerners--men, women, and children. To bring heroes and heroines to life on the pages of a book, people who owe everything to where they were born and the hardworking stock from which they sprang. To bring joy to readers as they weep and laugh and love along with my characters. That's my dream and my constant goal.

BARBARA BRETTON

The way I look at it, I had absolutely no choice but to become a writer. I can't sing. I can't dance. I can't operate heavy machinery. I'd pretty much exhausted my major job opportunities after I dusted buttons in the notions department at W.T. Grant's and made fried fish sandwiches beneath the Golden Arches. It was either become a writer or run for political office and since America probably isn't quite ready for a president who can quote passages from Kathleen Woodiwiss's *Shanna*, I think I made the right choice when I opted to become a romance writer.

The truth is, I never wanted to be anything but a writer. The hours are great, the working conditions are terrific, and I get paid to stay home and tell stories for a living.

I am proof that an average woman without a college degree or friends in the publishing business can write and sell a book. No, it's not easy but nothing worthwhile is ever easy. Writing a book takes drive, determination, and discipline... and more than a pinch of good luck. I was fortunate early on to recognize that my love of characterization and relationships lent itself to writing the romance so I focused all of my energies on doing exactly that.

And then one day I finally got "the call." Vivian Stephens, editor of Harlequin American Romance, phoned me on a snowy February afternoon and changed my life forever. With the words, "I want to buy your book," she turned me from a hopeful amateur into a published author. One year later my first book was on the shelves, one of the launch offerings from Harlequin American.

I've sold forty books since then; forty heroes and heroines have captured my heart and, I hope, a few readers' hearts as well. I've written about a princess, a policeman, a business tycoon, an orphan, a Revolutionary War hero, a little girl looking to find a new mommy. Without leaving my desk, I've walked 18th century streets and strolled the Rive Gauche. I've fallen in love with a renegade spy, a prize fighter, and a foreign correspondent and my husband never suspected a thing. And thanks to my heroines, I've been a beautiful blond, a ravishing redhead, and a stunning brunette and I never once had to worry about bad hair days, cellulite, or PMS.

Who says dreams can't come true?

You can write to me at:
Barbara Bretton
PO Box 482
Belle Mead NJ 08502

or via the Internet at: Bretton5@aol.com

DIXIE BROWNING

If I'd known I was going to be a writer, I would have learned how to write before I started writing. As it is, I've spent the past twenty years in on-the-job training. I simply decided to write one day, so I did it. And it got published. So did my next, and my next, and my next, etc., which has both a downside and an upside.

On the upside, there's the ego thing. I wrote a story and someone was willing to pay two hundred dollars for it. Wow! That was my reaction to my first two sales. And then, Silhouette Romances was born, and my time suddenly became more valuable. That's part of the upside. The largest part, however, is the incredible satisfaction of being immersed in people I love, and bringing their stories to life. There is nothing--NOTHING!--like the satisfaction of creating something that other people can share.

The downside is, since I didn't know how to write when I started, there are a lot of bad books out there with my name on them. Sorry about that, folks. I did the best I could at the time. Another handicap is that I never learned how to type. I use two or three fingers--arthritic ones, at that--on each hand, and spend more time cleaning up after myself than I do creating. The trouble is, once I got started, I never had the patience to go back and learn the basics. I was having too much fun.

I still am, by the way. I urge you--everyone who loves to read--to try your hand at writing. What do you have to lose?

PAMELA BROWNING

When I started writing romances, I thought of myself as an entertainer. Not any more. I'm an educator, and as such, I believe that every man should read a romance.

Why? Because of The Question!

Sigmund Freud asked it, though he wasn't the first man to do so and won't be the last. He asked with great frustration, "What do women want?" Well, if he'd read a romance, he'd have known.

What do women want? If today's romance novel is any indication, women want men who are strong without being macho and sexy without being pushy. They want men who will listen, men who aren't afraid to make a commitment, and men who will work just as hard as women do to make the relationship succeed. They want men who will actively help them attain their goals, just as the traditional woman has helped her man attain his goals in the past.

What do women want? We want a man who knows how to make love in a way that will please a woman. The stuff most men read in *Playboy* and *Hustler* was written by men and reflects their fantasies. If men want to know what women want, they should read a romance.

Recently, I moved from one house to another, and as the biggest burliest man in our moving crew was unloading boxes of books from the truck, I mentioned that I'm a writer and that's why I own so many books. His face lit up when I told him that I write romances. He ran back to his truck and returned with several romance novels which he keeps there to read on overnight trips. He offered thoughtful critiques and recommendations.

"And you know why I read romances?" he said. "Because they help me understand what my wife thinks. She likes to read them too."

As he hoisted yet another box of books on his shoulders, I thought to myself, *There's one fellow who will never have to ask The Question, "What do women want?"*

He's figuring it out all by himself--with a little help, of course.

So now you know why I consider myself an educator. Hey guys, anything I can do to help you out. I only wish I could have done something for Sigmund.

EILEEN BUCKHOLTZ

I'm Eileen Buckholtz and collaborate with Ruth Glick as Rebecca York. Currently, we are writing the 43 Light Street romantic suspense series set in Baltimore. So far, we've done twelve books in the series for Harlequin Intrigue, and this fall, lucky thirteen will be a single title release called *Face To Face*. And Harlequin has signed up to do more Light Street books after that.

I grew up in Warner Robins, a small town in Georgia. At the age of eleven, in our small, one-room library, I discovered the romance section and fell in love. By the time I'd left for college, I managed to read most of the books in the library and had a secret dream of being a romance writer. However, at Ohio State University, another discipline caught my imagination--the new field of computer science. I met my husband Howard in the computer center, and we were one of the first students in the U.S. to graduate with Computer and Information Science degrees. We got married, moved to Baltimore, and went to work. It would be ten years and two sons later until I'd get back to writing fiction. Now I often mix the areas by introducing new technology into our plots.

Probably the most influential event in my writing life was meeting Ruth Glick and getting involved with a local writer's support group. I thrived on the networking and the opportunities for collaboration. My first romance, *Love Is Elected* by Alyssa Howard, was written with Ruth and two women from the group. I introduced them to romances; they and I have written over fifty books together and won two lifetime achievement awards from Romantic Times in Romantic Suspense Series and Romantic Mystery.

People often ask me about collaboration. While it may not be for everyone, I've found a lot of advantages. Writing is more fun when you have someone with whom to share the experience. We can take on more ambitious projects together than we'd ever attempt alone. Our ideas feed off each other. There's someone to pick you up when you don't feel like writing. And instant feedback is a big plus.

For a collaboration to work well, you need to find a good partner. My tips on collaboration include: Pick a person who shares your view of the world. Make regular appointments to schedule work. Bring different and complementary skills to the process. Respect each other's contributions and ideas. Find someone you can trust.

I've recently created "Rebecca York's 43 Light Street Homepage" for the World Wide Web. Readers are invited to visit us at http://www.lightst.com.

LINDA CAJIO

I started writing to keep from robbing libraries. This seemed sensible to me, since I read books constantly. I read all types of books, except biographies. I don't know why I don't gravitate to them, I just don't. Anyway, I had reached a point where I was reading insurance policies, since I ran through everything else I could get my greedy little hands on. At that point, my brain suggested I write a book. I thought I was nuts. (I thought the same thing when it suggested children. I was right in that case.) The notion of creating my own stories lured me, however, and I started one. My brain said, "Linda, it's awful." I agreed with it and tried a second. This one I finished, which is a huge step in the writing process. Many, many wannabees never pass this crucial milestone. Third time's the charm, they say, and that book, *All Is Fair ...*, was published by Bantam Books for their Loveswept line. I've published twenty-two books thus far, including two historicals with Zebra Books. Number twenty-three is due out in the autumn of 1997.

Writers can take ideas from anything. I love having time on my hands in airports so I can play "Who's the spy?" That wonderful Carey Grant/Katherine Hepburn movie, *Bringing Up Baby*, inspired my first book, a screwball comedy. I've had books inspired by my children. (I hope they never recognize themselves or I'm in trouble.) Computer games inspired another, and a trip to England inspired three books, with number four in the works. I've even had a character, who refused to go away after a book, parley herself into five more. That was my Kitteridge series, about six cousins and their indomitable, matchmaking grandmother, Lettice Ketteridge. My latest historical, *Knight's Song*, got its start when a psychic told me I had been an abbess in another life. After I picked myself up from the floor, laughing, I begun to wonder what medieval women did and ran with it. All I ask is that the idea well never run dry. I think that's all any writer asks.

I'm grateful that readers have enjoyed my books and taken the time to write and let me know. I intend to write many more books--although I have to say that robbing libraries had to have been easier!

MARISA CARROLL
Carol Wagner
Marian Scharf

Marian and I have been asked numerous times how we can have co-authored more than twenty-five books for both Dell Publishing and Harlequin/Silhouette over the past thirteen years without getting "divorced".

That's easy. You can't divorce a sibling. We're sisters, seventeen months apart in age, and we got all our petty squabbles and knock-down, drag-out fights out of our systems growing up in a small northwestern Ohio farming community with four younger brothers and sisters.

Now we're grown women with children of our own and we don't argue anymore, well not much, anyway. Instead we concentrate on our writing, crafting emotional, reality-based stories that appeal to that part of all of us that longs to find the perfect soul-mate, the perfect career, and the perfect small town of our dreams.

It hasn't always been easy. Our vision of man/woman relationships and expression of small-town, traditional values didn't always mesh with market forces or editorial policy. Over the years we've garnered more rejection letters and suffered through the sting of more editorial brush-offs than we care to remember. But we didn't give up. Our parents, who built a successful business from the ground up and raised six children at the same time, instilled in us a fierce determination to achieve, and to succeed at whatever we attempted. Or, at least, to give it a damn good try.

Thankfully, eight years ago our work came to the attention of Debra Matteucci and Marsh Zinberg of Harlequin Books. The rest is history. Happily, the editorial staff at Harlequin/Sihouette continues to share our vision and our commitment to creating emotional, heart-warming stories filled with loyal, caring, occasionally flawed characters who are searching for the same thing that we all are, that perfect mate, career and family, home and hearth, in one word. Love.

And we plan to go "write" on doing just that.

20

BARBARA CARTLAND

Barbara Cartland, is known as the world's most famous romantic novelist. Today, her home is on the estate in Great Britain where Beatrix Potter wrote Peter Rabbit. She has written over 600 books and has sold approximately 600 million worldwide and Barbara is delighted that she is published in every country. *The Guiness Book of Records* says that she is the "Best Selling Author in the World."

Barbara, born in 1901, is one of three children of parents who came from a distinguished lineage. When she was seventeen, her father was killed in action after serving in the militia for four years during the Civil War with Ireland. Her mother was heart-broken and, since they had little money, asked Barbara where she would like to live. Barbara chose London and her mother moved her and her two younger brothers there. Barbara found the city so thrilling and exciting, she wrote her first novel, *We Danced All Night*. It was published in 1923 and was a huge success, going into six editions and being published in five languages. After that she began to write seriously to make money.

What matters to Barbara is that her romance novels bring happiness to people, for the simple reason that her heroines are the sweet, loving, genuine women who were first portrayed by Shakespeare in *Romeo and Juliet*.

It is they who evoke in a man the real love that is both spiritual and physical, and it is the woman in a marriage who stands for Morality, Compassion, Sympathy and Love.

This is the message she tries to impart to the world, her greatest compliment is when someone tells her that one of her books has made them happy.

In addition to sixteen historical works, she has also written books on Health, Sociology, Cookery, Philosophy, Cartoons, Poems, a Children's Pop-up book, a Book of Prayers, four autobiographies, and biographies of her mother and brother. Two of her stage plays have been performed, one on radio. In 1987 her book, *A Hazard of Hearts* was televised in the USA, followed by three more: *The Lady and the Highwayman, A Ghost In Monte Carlo,* and *A Duel of Hearts.* At the age of 77, she made a recording of love songs which she sang with The Royal Philharmonic Orchestra.

Barbara has been the recipient of many great honors in her country including being invested as Dame of the Order of St. John of Jerusalem for her efforts to better conditions and salaries for midwives and nurses. In 1991, the Queen at Buckingham Palace invested her as Dame of the Order of the British Empire for her contribution to literature.

LORI COPELAND

I have always been an avid reader of romance novels. I read them by the truckload. When I attempted to write one myself, I discovered it wasn't as easy as I thought, but I was determined to give it a try. I finally got the manuscript typed, proofread and sent off.

One day while running the sweeper, the phone rang and the lady on the other end said, "This is Dell Publishing Company." I thought they were selling magazines and told them I didn't want any. She said, "Oh, I think you'll want this. We would like to buy your story." The rest is history.

I sold my first romance, *Playing For Keeps*, which was published as a Dell Candlelight Ecstasy in April 1983. In the past thirteen years I have published over forty novels with houses including Harlequin, Bantam, Dell and Fawcett. Severn House, Random House and Dorchester Publishing have bought the rights to reprint my earlier novels.

Any who read my work know my love for laughter, and I'm often asked if I'm as crazy as my books. I'll have to say, sometimes I am. It helps to be a little crazy in this business of ups and downs. I'm thankful for my sense of humor.

I have been married to my high school sweetheart, Lance, for thirty-seven years and am proud mother to three boys and grandmother to three adorable grandsons. When not writing, I enjoy spending time with my family and traveling. My career has taken me to all parts of the United States and afforded me the opportunity to meet the very authors I so admired back in my "avid reading" days.

I've been the recipient of numerous awards, including Romantic Times Reviewer's Choice Award, Romantic Times Career Achievement Award, Affaire de Coeur Gold and Certificate Award and Waldenbooks Best Seller. I am a member of Novelists, Inc., Ozark Romance Authors, and Romance Writers of America.

Someone To Love, Fawcett Books, has been nominated for a Romantic Times Reviewer's Choice award this year. I was privileged to be a contributing author for

Leisure's *Love's Legacy* which debuted in January 1996, proceeds to go to the Literacy Foundation.

I love to write and I love to laugh. When I put the two together, only my computer knows what will come out. My fans seem to enjoy my craziness, and I love hearing from them. Write to me at 1736 E. Sunshine, Suite 200B, Springfield, Missouri 65804.

JASMINE CRESSWELL
Jasmine Craig

Jasmine's background is international: she was born in Wales, educated in London, England, graduated early from high school, and received a diploma in technical French and German from the Lycee Francaise in London before joining the British Foreign Office. Transferred to the British Embassy in Rio de Janeiro at the age of 20, she met and married Malcolm Candlish, a young British executive working for the Brazilian subsidiary of a British company. Jasmine accompanied her husband first to the States, then to Australia, and spent two years in Canada, before returning to Chicago in the United States, where Malcolm continued his high-speed climb to the top of the corporate ladder. She has a bachelor's degree with a double major in history and philosophy from Melbourne University in the Australian state of Victoria, an honor's degree in history from Macquarie University in the Australian state of New South Wales, as well as a Masters Degree in history and archival administration conferred by Case Western Reserve University in Ohio.

Experienced as a public speaker, Jasmine has conducted college seminars on writing the novel, addressed annual writers' conferences all over the country, and delivered general interest speeches to a variety of civic groups. Interviews and profiles have appeared in the Chicago *Tribune*, the Cleveland *Plain Dealer*, and the Denver *Post*, among many others. After a dozen or so interviews by local television stations, and more radio interviews that she can count, she considers herself a veteran of talk shows and news broadcasts.

Jasmine served for two years as the editor of the *Romance Writer's Report*, the national journal of the Romance Writers of America, and received RWA's Golden Rose Award for her efforts. She has also served as president of Rocky Mountain Fiction Writers, and is a founder and former president of Novelists, Inc., the nationwide association for writers of popular fiction. She also enjoys membership in England's Romantic Novelists Association, and the Author's Guild of America. She received the Colorado Authors League Award for Best Paperback Novel of the

26

Year, and she was voted Rocky Mountain Fiction Writer of the Year in both 1986 and 1989. In addition, her books have been nominated for RWA's Golden Medallion Award and for numerous awards given by *Romantic Times*.

EMMA DARCY
Wendy Brennan

Writing Romances has been the most wonderful journey of my life. It has taught me so much about caring and sharing and what is really meaningful, because to write these stories I had to learn to reach deep inside myself and bring out what I truly felt, what I truly thought, and I had to seek for a much greater understanding and compassion for why people do what they do.

Perhaps my life was always leading to this particular journey although becoming an author was never a conscious ambition. I was born in a small timber town in New South Wales, Australia. My father was a schoolteacher, appointed to a one-teacher school on an island in the Hastings River. I can't remember when I learnt to read but I certainly devoured all the books the small school had in its library at a very early age.

My family's trips to nearby towns followed a regular pattern. On Thursday afternoon when school hours ended, we went to Wauchope. The public library shut at four o'clock. It was a matter of desperate prayer that the car-ferry be waiting on our side of the river so we'd make it to the library on time.

On Saturdays, we went to Port Macquarie. My parents played golf. I and my two older brothers and younger sister went to the matinee at the movie theatre. I loved movies. I dreamed of becoming an actress.

My interest in books and drama led to my first career--English/French teacher. The Drama club at the schools where I taught invariably became my responsibility and pleasure. Directing and staging plays was meat and drink to me. Acting was pure cream.

My oldest brother had meanwhile become a computer programmer. He advised me to change careers--more money in programming and the future was computers. I was one of the first three females to be hired by IBM as a programmer in Australia.

Teaching taught me the importance of good communication skills. Computer programming focused more on problem-solving and the need for both lateral thinking and logical structure. Both careers were good training for writing, although I didn't know it then.

Marriage and motherhood came next.

My role changed from career-person to full-time wife and mother of three sons. This I would call the experience of the nitty-gritties of life, the reaching of full maturity with solidifying of values. It forms an integral part of what I now draw on as a writer.

As my boys grew up and became more independent, I cast around for activities which would give me personal satisfaction. Oil-painting and pottery filled many enjoyable hours. I also studied architecture and designed and sub-contracted the building of my present home. My pleasure in books was always a constant. I especially love Jane Austen's books, from which I eventually drew my pseudonym, Emma Darcy.

One day I read a romance which was highly unsatisfying. The hero didn't act as I thought a hero should. The heroine didn't respond as I would in various situations. The story didn't really deliver my concept of love.

I thought, "I could write a better book than that."

The question arose, Why not?

So it began.

To me, writing was like acting and directing only better. I could play every role, not just one character. Nor was I limited to what someone else had written. How I relished and revelled in creating dramatic scenes with great curtain lines! Immensely excited and enthused by this marvelous pastime of making up my own stories, I naturally shared it all with my husband who became very involved, contributing ideas and slants I would never have thought of myself.

Sadly, my husband died in 1995, yet in continuing to write the kind of stories we once shared together, I feel he is still very much with me. We wept and laughed and smiled with the characters we created, loved with them, fought with them, felt as passionately as they did. They were very real to us and the best part was we could give them the happiness we'd had, and the kind of relationship that answered all their needs.

It still is the best part.

CASSIE EDWARDS

Cassie Edwards got a late start in her writing career but that hasn't stopped her from delivering over 50 romance novels since beginning in 1982. She was inspired by the character of a rich and famous author from the soap opera *The Young and The Restless*. Her first book never made it to a publisher. Quickly completing that first book, she then thought it was so bad that she burned it. Turning to short stories, she rapidly found success. More than 350 poems and 50 short stories were published. The desire to write romance was rekindled on a trip to Cripple Creek, Colorado. The history of the little town inspired her to write a historical romance. Plotting the book on the plane home, she finished it in only six weeks and sold it to the first publisher to whom she submitted. Her effort resulted in an immediate offer for a six book contract.

Cassie has a wide range of writing with several publishing houses. She packs a lot into an uninterrupted three hour work day. That's three hours a day from her office overlooking a large deck near the backyard swimming pool. Surrounded by the lush grass and exquisite old trees of the Matton Golf and Country Club, the office in her home is the perfect place to create her romance novels. Success has generated the Cassie Edwards Fan Club; she answers boxes of mail every week. A musical group from Switzerland released a CD whose songs were written for and dedicated to Edwards. She takes great pride in her American Indian historical romances writing for Leisure and NAL and is thought of as the queen of American Indian romances. Detailed and accurate research on the tribes and customs and language create an authenticity that is often complimented by Native Americans. *Romantic Times*, a prominent magazine about romance books, awarded her a Lifetime Achievement Award for the best Indian series.

Cassie Edwards has a lot to offer from three hours a day. "I love what I do," says Edwards, "and [writing] just comes so naturally. I sit there and I don't struggle. It just happens...just like magic."

AUTHOR PROFILES

MARIE FERRARELLA

I was born with a pen in my hand and a plot in my head. It wasn't very well developed, but then, neither was I. I always wanted to be a writer. I began writing at a very early age because at the time, TV shows just didn't have enough red blooded women in them. If they were there at all, they were decorations, or worse, complete wimps who stood by while the hero did everything. I could never figure out why the heroes cared about these spineless creatures (no wonder cowboys used to kiss their horse, at least the horse came through when they needed them). So I began creating them. The Cartwrights of *Bonanza* had a sister, the detectives at *77 Sunset Strip* had a female detective who did *not* double as a secretary and so on. I wrote initially for my own entertainment. Then one day when I was in fifth grade, I discovered that I could entertain others as well. I began creating a historical using what I'd learned from my history lessons (and TV, bless it). I'd been a shy kid with a foreign accent up until then. Suddenly, I had friends. People were actually listening to what I had to say (a trick my husband has yet to manage) and coming back for more. I was hooked on story telling from that day forward.

The road from there to here hasn't been easy. I could redecorate my house in early rejection slips. But I hung in there because I believed in myself and because there wasn't anything else that I would have rather done than write (a Master's degree in Shakespeare qualifies you to philosophize, teach, or starve -- I wasn't good at any of that).

My one word of advice is that if you have a dream, if you really need to write, then do it and don't let anyone tell you that you can't. Perseverance does pay off. Look at me. Eighty books and still going (me and the over achieving battery operated rabbit).

AUTHOR PROFILES

JUDY GILL

I was born and raised in the wilderness at the tip of the Sunshine Coast of BC, in Canada. The only way in and out was by boat or seaplane, stores were few, and books were scarce but dearly cherished, read over and over. Hence, entertainment was something my siblings, cousins, and I provided for ourselves, the help of those books and the games of "let's pretend" they engendered. I've been playing "what if" for as long as I can remember, and writing when I had nothing to read.

Years later, while living in Germany with my then-soldier husband and two daughters, I discovered the same scarcity of books and entertained myself again by writing. In 1976, I sold my first manuscript to the second house to see it, and over the next four years, sold five more. No, I didn't know it wasn't supposed to be that easy.

After returning to BC in 1979, I stopped writing for many years while I worked in a book store, we built our home, and landscaped our piece of the Sunshine Coast wilderness.

Bantam Books published my first Loveswept in 1988. Now, I have over thirty books to my credit, the last two of which have been contracted by Harlequin's new Love and Laughter line. I also write Fantasy Romances and Science Fiction but am not yet published in those two genres.

When people ask if it's worth it, the answer is an emphatic *yes!* The commute is great. From bed, to coffee-maker, to computer. Nothing can beat that, except having the coffee and the laptop aboard our cruiser on an early morning in a quiet anchorage with bald eagles, blue herons, gulls and humming birds all around. Once, in a little gunkhole called Harmony Islands, a Townsend's Solitaire adopted our aft rail. Its feet couldn't find much purchase on the smooth, round stainless steel, so I gave it a towel to stand on and fed it cornmeal from my hand. When we finally pulled up the anchor, we shooed it away toward a nearby sailboat. Someday, you'll find him in a book, I'm sure.

AUTHOR PROFILES

I live in a little town called Sechelt (pronounced Sea-shelt) on a one-mile wide isthmus in the middle of the Sunshine Coast, northwest of Vancouver, with my husband, happily surrounded by water, family, books, and my growing collection of antique cobalt-glass artifacts.

RUTH GLICK

Back in High School, my sociology class was asked to research our future professions. Although I chose "writer," I assumed that there was no chance I could ever be one, because good grades in English class depended a great deal on spelling ability, a skill I didn't possess.

After college, marriage, graduate school, and two children--I still couldn't spell, and I hadn't picked a career. Then my local community college ran a workshop for women trying to define their occupational aspirations.

I came away with two strong convictions: I still wanted to be a writer. And part-time career opportunities were few and far between. So I called a local newspaper and asked if I could submit an article about the workshop. When they invited me to write it on speculation, I spent about 25 hours suffering over 2,000 words and asked my husband to check the spelling. The paper bought the piece and paid me the munificent sum of ten dollars. More assignments followed, and I also began submitting articles to larger papers and national magazines, some of which I actually sold. I also enrolled in a community college writing seminar, where participants read and critiqued each other's work. The thought of writing a whole novel was quite daunting, but as I listened to other people's fiction, I began to believe I could do it, too. In fact, I told myself, a chapter would be about the same length as a feature article. So I wrote *The Invasion of the Blue Lights*, a children's science fiction novel, got feedback from the group, and eventually sold the book to Scholastic. Later I asked some of the members to join me in a critique group. After almost twenty-five years, we're still going strong--with several of the original members plus new recruits. In that time, I've sold more than 65 books, many with Eileen Buckholtz, whom I met in the writing seminar; and computer spelling checkers have made life a lot easier for me.

Recently Eileen and I have been doing 43 Light Street, an ongoing romantic suspense series for Harlequin Intrigue. And I've also been lucky enough to keep selling non-fiction--primarily cookbooks, of which I've published seven, including *Skinny Soups* for Surrey Books. It's been a wonderful career for me, doing what I love. The only problem is that "part-time" has become a 60-hour-a-week job.

DEBORAH GORDON
Brooke Hastings

I'm often asked why I adopted the pseudonym Brooke Hastings (my middle name and my father's middle name) when I published my first book. For one thing, most romance writers were British in those days, and I thought the name sounded English and glamorous. Besides, romance novels, while challenging and delightful to write, weren't Serious Fiction. Since I was an honors graduate of a top university, I believed I should save my real name to use on the Great American Novel, which I fully intended to produce some day.

I've since realized two things. First, I'll never write the Great American Novel because I haven't led the Great American Life. I have wonderful parents. My childhood was largely happy. My college sweetheart and I have lived in the same house in beautiful California for almost all of our adult lives. Our two children have driven us only minimally crazy over the years, especially if one excludes their adolescence, and have given us infinite, incredible joy. In other words, though nobody escapes physical suffering and emotional pain in this life, I haven't endured the angst, the torment, the seeking, the bizarre and horrible experiences, that go into creating a Great American Author.

Second, I've come to understand that romance is what I do best, and that I genuinely love writing it. As I've said, life isn't always easy, and I believe it's an important and noble calling--to write novels that take people away from their problems for a time and leave them happier than when they began reading. I try to make each of my books unique, so even after almost thirty novels, I still get wrapped up in my characters and their individual stories.

And there's such range and flexibility in the romance genre! I've incorporated adventure, intrigue, murder, the supernatural, and even science fiction into my books. I've learned about everything from underwater archaeology to football, from big business to undercover police work, from filmmaking to Hawaiian mysticism. In my mind, I've traveled to pre-Revolutionary Boston and Gold Rush California,

38

post--Civil War Washington and Victorian Hong Kong, and places as exotic as Afghanistan and Madagascar. (Yes, I'm one of those writers who actually likes doing research.)

The romance genre has only two requirements--a love story and a happy ending-- and since I'm a sucker for such tales myself, I wouldn't want to write anything else. I'm finally doing so as Deborah Gordon, and it's a thrill to see that name on the bookstore shelves.

GINNA GRAY

I was born in Houston, Texas and lived there all my life until November 1993, when my husband and I moved to Durango, Colorado and built our dream home. Actually, we live about ten miles north of town on a small lake, where we're frequently privileged to see deer and elk and a variety of other wildlife.

Brad and I have two daughters. Beth, the oldest, is married and the mother of four (would you believe I was a *very* young bride) and Meghan is in her last year at Texas Tech and preparing to go to graduate school to get a PhD in Forensic Psychology.

I have been writing and painting in oils all my life. My parents gave me my first oil painting set before I started to school, and I began making up stories at about the same time. I did not, however, submit anything to a publisher until 1980. My first sale came in 1983, and I have been under contract to one publisher or another ever since.

The question writers are asked most often has to be, "Where do you get your ideas?" The answer is, everywhere.

It's really peculiar, the things that trigger an idea in a writer's brain. A casual remark, an observance, a sound, a color, a certain evocative smell, a piece in the newspaper or on the evening news, a conversation overheard in an airport or restaurant--anything, really--can set off a chain of memories and imaginings, feelings of deja vu or bubbly anticipation. Everything truly is grist for the mill.

Another question I am asked often is: "How much time do you spend writing?"

This usually comes from aspiring writers, and many times they are aghast at my reply. I work at least eight hours a day, everyday, Monday through Friday. At times, when I have a pressing deadline bearing down on me, I work seven days a week, twelve to eighteen hours a day until I get it done.

You can't wait for inspiration to strike. The key to success is to plant yourself in the chair in front of the computer (or typewriter, or pencil and pad--whatever works for you) and just do it.

Actually, that pretty much sums up my personal philosophy of life: If there is something that needs doing, a goal that I set for myself, if I have an unfulfilled talent or a dream ... I roll up my sleeves and give it all I've got.

JENNIFER GREENE
Alison Hart

I sold my first romance in 1980, and this year I hope to write my 50th book in the contemporary romance genre.

Growing up, I read the classics. Those were the only books that were allowed around our house. Scribbling stories was always a hobby, but I never anticipated writing as a career. My mom wasn't about to raise any impractical daughters who couldn't support themselves! I got degrees from Michigan State in Psychology and English, and then moved into the work force, first as a teacher, then as a manager in Labor Relations.

When I was pregnant with our first child, I quit work and planned to stay home (for as long as we could afford it) to raise our family. That was when I discovered my first romance. And fell in love with the field.

All my life I've been involved with womens' causes--still am. I was always a sucker for a good love story, but from that first romance, I discovered that the genre is more than that. Our books are by women, about women, and written to women. And my voracious reading 'bug' gradually turned into a writing 'bug' because the whole nature of the field inspired me to give it a try. Once I tried it, I'm afraid I never recovered from the addiction.

When I write a romance, I feel like I'm talking to a fellow sister. She is no stranger. I know her. She believes in love and commitment the way I do; she believes in families and healthy relationships... and she has the same problems I do as a woman living in the 90s, with all our conflicting and changing roles.

Possibly that caring between reader and writer is something that someone outside the romance field wouldn't understand. Romances are about us--our struggles, our hopes, our needs. I never had to 'work' to create a heroine...I find them all around me, women coping with the problems and trials of today, struggling to make the best life she can.

I've worked for three publishing houses since I began my writing career, and

42

accumulated the pseudonyms of Jeanne Grant and Jessica Massey before moving to Silhouette under "Jennifer Greene". Luck has followed me...there are 12 national writing awards on my walls, which is still a shock for someone who was never going to be a writer! The best part of writing, for me, though, has always been the connection to readers, and the nature of books I love to write best involve some kind of women's theme.

I sincerely believe that romances have the unique power to reach each other--and to help each other. That's always been my front line goal in writing. There is no other field I can imagine that has this hidden and incredibly satisfying reward.

PATRICIA HAGAN

I was born in Atlanta, Georgia and grew up all over the U.S. due to my father's position as a Federal attorney. I attended the University of Alabama, with a major in English.

Since childhood, I have been writing, filling notebooks with fantasy. I began my writing career while still in high school in Sylacauga, Alabama, where I worked part-time for a local radio station creating advertising copy. Since then I have worked as a Radio/TV motorsports journalist, a legal secretary, and an Emergency Medical Technician.

At this time, I am a full-time writer, having published over 2,500 short stories and 29 novels with over 12 millions copies in print. Some of my titles have been on the coveted *"New York Times Bestseller"* list and many have been selections of the Doubleday and Literary Guild books clubs.

Among my honors: Winner, "Romantic Times" Readers Choice; named to "Affaire de Coeur" magazine "Hall of Fame". 1st, 2nd, 3rd place honors in newspaper writing; 1st, 2nd, 3rd place honors in magazine writing, 2nd and 3rd place honors in Radio/TV--National Motorsports Press Association.

I live in western North Carolina, where I find the peace and tranquility of the mountains is conducive to creativity. In my spare time, I enjoy reading, painting, cooking, hiking, and spoiling my precious wire-haired fox terrier, Krystal.

I love telling stories and wish we could go back to the days when families sat on their porches in the evenings talking among themselves instead of gathering around the TV. We lose so much of our personal heritage by not sharing folklore and fantasy, and I like to feel that my books help preserve that art.

Having been all over the U.S. and Europe, I gave my heart to North Carolina over thirty years ago and can't imagine living anywhere else. I like to reflect North Carolina in my work as much as possible to share the beauty with my readers.

My favorite form is fiction, so that I can allow my mind, my creative talent, to flow freely.

To aspiring writers, I say, "Read! Learn as much as possible about the composition of life. Then write a little, at least every day."

I always cringe when I meet people who say, "I could write a book if I only had the time!" If they were born to write, they would make the time!

CAROLE HALSTON
Carolyn Hall

Writing romance novels is a great way to enjoy imaginative flings with handsome, sexy men and stay faithful to my husband of twenty-six years! Plus, I'm able to provide my readers the same pleasure. Yes, I fall in love with every hero I create, just like my heroine falls in love with him. Long before I write *the end* on the last page, the fictional world of my story has become as real as my actual world.

And during the final weeks, when the writing process is the most intense, it's actually an effort to drag myself back to everyday reality and the truly enjoyable lifestyle I'm lucky enough to have. I feel guilty because I experience difficulty carrying on conversations with my husband, my mother, my sisters, friends. My mind keeps inventing dialogue for my characters. It keeps developing their ongoing relationship instead of focusing on my important relationships.

Carried to this extreme, writing isn't the healthiest profession. Fortunately, my husband and family and friends are tolerant. They know I'll be back.

There's always a period, though, following the completion of a book when I suffer "separation pangs" from my characters. Leaving them to their own devices after I've brought them together in a "happily ever after" ending takes a few days.

I wish writing got easier with practice. For me, it hasn't. I work hard to breathe life into people I conjure up, to make them walk and talk and earn my affection and the affection of my readers. But the effort pays off when I'm proud of the end result and know I've written a heart-warming story.

With this bit of background, you can understand why I take offense when someone asks if I'm currently "cranking out" a romance novel. The creative process isn't that mechanical.

One wonderful benefit of my writing career is taking trips with my husband to many countries and to other regions in the United States to research settings.

Also, I'm a tennis player and I'm able to play competitive tennis with a women's league on Friday mornings, since I can arrange my own schedule. I love the

46

flexibility and rarely have to be rudely awakened by an alarm clock.

My greatest source of pride is the part I've played in expanding the parameters of romance fiction so that there are very few restrictions and only the loosest so-called "formula." I feel extremely fortunate that my publisher is Silhouette Books, whose editors give their writers leeway to write fresh, original, wonderful stories.

Readers can write me c/o Silhouette Books, 300 East 42nd Street, New York, NY 10017. Happy reading!

SHANNON HARPER
Anna James
Madeline Harper
Leigh Bristol
Taylor Brady

There are two things about my writing career that amaze me. The first is that I've survived! Somehow I've lasted for fifteen years and produced over forty books.

And I'm constantly surprised that my writing partner and I are still together. Madeline Porter, with whom I have coauthored over thirty books, lives in California and I live in Florida. We are good friends, but due to work, family, travel, deadlines, we rarely see each other and so must communicate by fax, phone, computer and the US Mail. The fact that only one manuscript has been lost in the mail is a miracle in itself. And maybe this long distance has contributed to the longevity of our partnership.

We began our career in romance as Anna James for Jove and Silhouette. It was as Anna James that we won the RWA first RITA award (then called the Golden medallion) for our saga, *Day Beyond Destiny*. Then for Harlequin Temptation we became Madeline Harper, and as Madeline Harper we wrote for Jove once more, winning a Silver Medallion in the mainstream category from RWA for *Love Dance*.

So that I could be thoroughly confused about my identity, I have also coauthored a dozen books with Donna Ball (a.k.a. Rebecca Flanders). We wrote eight books for Warner under the pen name Leigh Bristol and were lucky enough to win several *Romantic Times* awards, including a life time achievement for our 'Texas Trilogy'. *Legacy*, a Leigh Bristol book, also won honors as RT's Best North American historical. Under a new name, Taylor Brady, Donna and I created a western series for Avon. The 'Kincaids' featured a family of strong men and women who moved westward across America in the 19th century.

At present, Madeline Porter and I are concentrating on writing for Harlequin, romantic comedy for Temptation and romantic suspense for Intrigue. In 1993, *Affaire de Coeur* called "Madeline Harper" "A master of romantic comedy," and our 1995 Temptation, *The Trouble With Babies*, was cited as a "romantic romp" by *Romantic Times* and "Serious, hot, funny and precious," by *Rendezvous*, "the stuff that a good romance book should be."

Both of us enjoy travel--in fact, we crave it--and we've been lucky enough to weave our trips to Venice, Greece, Maine, Mexico and the Florida Keys into our books. Travel is a wonderfully creative stimulant for me, and I'm able to leave the mundane cares of homelife behind, allowing myself to relax and imagine and fantasize about what might be. And that's the way my books always begin, with that little question: *What if?* And if I'm lucky, that *what if* turns into characters and a plot and another romance is on the way. Who knows I may surprise myself and be around another fifteen years.

ROBIN LEE HATCHER

I began writing my first novel two months before my 30th birthday. I didn't own a typewriter, and computers were uncommon back then, even in offices, so I wrote my first two and half novels longhand on legal pads. A single mother, my creative time was after the kids were asleep at night. I would lie in bed and write. Then I would use the office typewriter during coffee breaks and lunch hours to type up my previous night's work. I sold my first book in 1983 and it was published in 1984. I haven't stopped writing since. In 1990, I quit my "day job" to write full-time. In 1996, my 22nd novel was published, and I plan to continue writing more novels for many years to come.

I like to write books that touch readers' hearts, and the responses I've received when I succeed have touched my heart in return. I know I'm one of the luckiest people in the world, to be able to do what I love and then to be rewarded for it in both tangible and intangible ways. Writing has broadened my world and brought so many wonderful people into my life, readers and writers alike. And ultimately, that's what really matters--other people.

In 1989, I married Jerry Neu, the man I call "my true soulmate," I'm mother to two lovely daughters who are now grown and mothers themselves. Being a young (*extremely* young, I might add) grandmother is fun. As I grow older, I plan to become an eccentric one, sort of like Auntie Mame. In the meantime, I love to travel, which I've had plenty of opportunity to do in recent years. In addition, Jerry and I have a lake cabin in the Central Idaho mountains where we can get away for a bit of peace and quiet.

BARBARA HAZARD

I consider myself one of the most fortunate people in the world because I am doing what I love, and that is, writing books! Knowing that people are reading stories I wrote, and hopefully enjoying them, is a wonderful feeling.

I think most authors are asked where they get their ideas and I imagine most of us have the same problem answering that question. It seems simplistic to say "they are just there in my head", but that is part of what happens. The stories come from my heart, too, and I believe there is more than a little magic involved in the process somehow. I have not thought of that too much, because I don't want to upset any applecarts. Remember the saying, "If it ain't broke, don't fix it?" Exactly!

When I finish a book, I try to take some time off. This is necessary to get the old characters out of my head and allow room for the new ones to move in. It's a bit like running a boarding house with tenants coming and going all the time. I admit I reread my books occasionally, to visit my old friends again.

In the future, although I intend to continue writing regencies, I want to write larger, more comprehensive historicals as well. I would like to try my hand at some regency mysteries, and I've several ideas for some romantic suspense set in the same period I've come to know and love so well.

I'm also fortunate because I have a wonderful husband, three handsome sons and now, three lovely daughters-in-law. I was born in New England and I live there still, in a college town with many libraries and too many things to do. I relish the changing seasons, especially autumn, my favorite, and deep winter snow storms. Then there's lobster and the shore in summer, and every spring thinking this is the year my garden is going to be a showcase.

What else can I tell you about me? I'm a Cancer, I'm 5'9" and the shortest girl in my family, and I've also been a musician and an artist along the way. I like traveling, especially to England, classical music, reading and quilting which I do while I'm watching my pro football team, the New York Giants.

Yes, indeed, God has blessed me in many ways. I am a very fortunate woman.

SANDRA HEATH/
SANDRA WILSON

My grandmother's house in the South Wales village of Cilfynydd (Kil-vun-ith) is still home to me. I was born toward the end of the war, and until marriage moved constantly to new towns or countries because my father was in the Royal Air Force. The only unchanging address was Nana's house, and when I was small I loved 'going home.' Nana's house meant gooseberry tarts, Welsh cakes, and walks on the mountainside to pick bilberries and drink from St. Patrick's Well, which got its name because the saint was said to have sipped its wonderful ice-cold water on his way to Ireland. Nana's house also meant seeing my Uncle Jack, who was the editor of the local newspaper and always seemed to have a paper and pencil in his hand. I wanted to be like him, although childish one-pagers about ponies were all I managed in those far-off days.

At eighteen, after moving to Germany from the Netherlands, I met my husband Robin. Ever since our marriage in 1967 we have lived in Royal Gloucestershire (the Prince and Princess of Wales, the Princess Royal, and Prince and Princess Michael of Kent all chose the same beautiful corner of England.) We have one daughter, Sarah, and two Siamese cats.

Historical novels of all kinds have always been favorites with me, and I eventually turned my hand to writing as a distraction when, at two, Sarah fell very ill with something akin to meningitis. At last I managed more than a one-pager, and the resulting medieval romance, *Less Fortunate Than Fair*, was published. I've been writing ever since--English Medieval Ancient Egyptian, Regency and Regency/Paranormal/Sensuous.

Romance fiction is a great escape for reader *and* writer, and historical romance somehow even more so. What pleasure there is in imagining oneself back in the days of carriages, gallant heroes, and beautiful heroines! What delights can one find in tales of grand houses, wonderful gowns, and tangled love affairs! To wander through the pages of such books is surely one of the best tonics in the world, and can be indulged in whenever the mood occurs. And if one should feel like a little sensuality as well, why, that too awaits between those same exciting pages.

A far cry indeed from Nana's house, Welsh cakes, walks on the mountainside to pick bilberries, cool drinks from St. Patricks' Well, and childish one-pagers...

EMILY HENDRICKSON
Dee Hendrickson

Not content to remain in my mid-west home, I headed east to design schools, first in Washington, D.C., then New York City. It was in New York I met and married my airline pilot husband. Through him I was later able to travel to England, developing my love for all things English.

Early on we moved to California where we raised our three children. My daughter proved to be the nose-in-a-book child that I'd been; we shared our love for the same sort of books and still do. Years later, desiring a change, my husband and I headed for the Sierra Nevada to build a home on the slopes above Lake Tahoe. Any setting further from Regency England I couldn't imagine. Our present home is located in Reno, unsurprisingly English Tudor-style.

I read Georgette Heyer and reread Jane Austen with new appreciation. After an attempt to write in another field, I tried writing a Regency since I loved to read them. That first Regency sold to Signet. That led to another and another and here I am, just finishing my twenty-sixth novel set in the world of lords and ladies of the Beau Monde, a glittering era full of charm and wit.

One of the frequent questions asked of me is how I do my research. This is followed by wondering where I find my plots. Actually, the two are intertwined. I delve into the books I've collected on the Regency and things English and I hunt in libraries and other sources for background information. It is while searching through books that I often happen on likely ideas for plots. Of course, there are the other instances when they merely pop into my mind. A solid grounding in the Regency period makes it possible to have a fair idea as to what is acceptable.

I insist upon historical accuracy in my novels when feasible. Readers are fond of descriptions of clothing and homes, the food served, and dances performed. I think they enjoy that almost as much as the developing romance between my hero and heroine. My daughter urges me to include those unusual bits and scraps of information I serendipitously happen on during my research. I find it a satisfying challenge to continually come up with new tidbits to include to intrigue my readers.

TAMI HOAG

People often ask me about the amount of research I do in preparing to write a new book, which is considerable. Occasionally, they ask me why I go to such trouble, after all, it's only fiction. I answer quite simply: that's my job. I believe it's my duty to create within the pages of a book a world that seems absolutely authentic to the reader.

My favorite mottos for research are "go to the source" and "learn by doing." For my 1996 court thriller, *Guilty As Sin* I was fortunate to have a guide into the world of a rural Minnesota legal system: a legal assistant to a criminal attorney in a nearby town, who was also a former clerk of court. Thrilled to help me with my research, she introduced me to everyone I needed to know, and all it took on my part to set that relationship in motion was a telephone call. I spent a day with a small-town defense attorney and another day with an assistant prosecuting attorney. I spent time in judge's chambers, watched a plea bargain get made, hung out in the hallway and listened to lots of deals get made, and, as a bonus, met a SWAT commander who can't wait for me to write a book about SWAT guys.

It has been my experience that people are almost always willing to talk about their professions and share their expertise. I recently had a Louisiana sheriff give me a whole day of his time. Not only did he grant me an interview, he hauled me all over his jurisdiction, showed me things I would not otherwise have gotten to see, introduced me to people I would never have met, told me great cop stories, and literally took me to where bodies had been dumped in the swamp. And all it took from me was a phone call. What I gained in insight, what I picked up in terms of details and nuances unique to that place will give my book a flavor as authentic as Pat Huval's crawfish ettouffee (something else the sheriff treated me to).

I've met many fascinating people in the course of doing my research, and the result has been books that draw the reader into a world as detailed and realistic as the one outside their door. Is it worth the effort? Absolutely.

SUSAN NAOMI HORTON

I was about nine when I wrote my first "novel". We'd had a long, cold Canadian prairie winter and I was tired of being stuck inside day after day, and had been driving my mother crazy because I didn't have anything to do. Her usual suggestion-- "and read a book"--didn't work, because I'd read them all. Four or five times. Finally, exasperated, she handed me a pad of yellow lined paper and a pencil and told me to sit down and write my own book.

I don't think she anticipated what happened next. Not only did I vanish from underfoot, I more or less disappeared for the rest of the winter. I'd curl up in the big armchair in the livingroom with a couple of cats for company, and I'd write. It was the closest thing to magic I'd ever experienced. I'd always loved stories. And right from the time I started to read, I could lose myself for hours in the depths of a good book. But this was different. These were my stories--I could invent whole worlds, and people them with characters out of my own imagination. My mother, bless her, had inadvertently turned another writer loose on the world.

Over the years, things changed. I studied engineering because I loved taking things apart to see what made them work almost as much as I loved writing, and I got married eventually, and worked at a variety of jobs all across the country. But always, I found time to write. I wrote for myself, mostly, but in the back of my mind I harbored the secret dream that one day there would be books on the racks in my favorite bookstore with my name on the covers. And then, finally, I decided to call my own bluff. It took three years and six full-length manuscripts, but then one day, the dream came true. An editor called me and told me that Silhouette wanted to buy my book. After almost three decades of writing I was, finally, a writer.

That book was *Dream Builder*, a Silhouette Desire published in 1984. There have been 22 others since then, but each one still holds that magic of that first book I ever wrote, the one when I was nine. I use a state-of-the-art computer now instead of pencils and lined yellow note pads, and the stories are longer and more complex, but writing is still as much fun as it was back then.

The people who come to me in my imagination are as real to me as anyone I meet on the street. They talk to me, and they tell me their dreams and their fears and their secrets. I may be the one who does the typing, but they are the ones who are telling the stories. What I hope is that my readers feel that magic right along with me, that these characters who spring to life in my heart are as real to everyone who reads about them as they are to me. Because that's what writing is all about--sharing a dream. And to all those readers who have shared my dreams over the year, I can only say thank you. And I hope we can share many more to come.

CHARLOTTE HUGHES

I published my first Bantam Loveswept in 1986, entitled *Too Many Husbands*, which hit #1 on the Waldenbooks' Best-Seller list. Fortunately, my titles consistently made the lists, including *USA Today's,* and I've developed a steady following of readers. I always enjoy hearing from fans how one of my stories made them laugh or cry. In this day and time, where stress plays such a big part of people's lives, I like knowing I'm able to get their minds off their troubles for a while.

Now, after almost two dozen romance novels, I am writing psychological thrillers for Avon Books as well. Since I often work late into the night, I sometimes get spooked writing about murder and mayhem. I find myself glancing over my shoulder constantly. My research can be grisly; I recently visited a morgue to interview a pathologist. I read books on poisons, guns, homicides, abnormal psychology, criminal behavior, coroners' reports, you name it. I'm not sure why I'm fascinated by this subject, but by the time I've finished delving into the darker side of the human psyche, I look forward to writing a sexy, humorous romance. So far, I've been able to balance writing for two houses.

As for my personal life, I've been married 19 years and have two teenage sons. (Talk about scary!) We live on one of several sea islands located 20 miles south of Beaufort, South Carolina. The area is rich with history and beautiful ante-bellum homes. A person would be hard-pressed to find a more beautiful place to live. Our island is a wildlife refuge where white-tail deer graze along the roadside and alligators swim in the lagoon behind our house and sunbathe on the two championship golf courses. We also have more raccoons than we need -- they're always getting into mischief!

My husband and I vacationed on Fripp Island for 11 years before we moved here and bought Johnson Creek Restaurant and Tavern on neighboring Harbor Island. One of our biggest thrills was being hired by Paramount Pictures for the kick-off party for *Forest Gump* when part of the movie was filmed in our locale. Another highlight was being invited to watch part of the filming itself! After that picture came *Lion King* and *Something to Talk About*. Two other movies made in our area were *The Big Chill* and *Prince of Tides*. We're now hoping that a portion of Pat Conroy's latest book, *Beach Music* will be filmed here as well. I suppose the folks in Hollywood are as impressed with our laid-back low country life-style and breathtaking surroundings as we are.

I hope my readers will follow me from romance to thrillers because I pour my heart and soul into both. I love hearing from you, and I try to respond to all your letters. You can write to me in care of Bantam Doubleday Dell, 1540 Broadway, New York, N.Y. 10036 or Avon Books, 1350 Ave of the Americas, New York, N.Y. 10019. And if you're ever out this way, please drop by our restaurant and say hello.

ARLENE JAMES
Deborah Rather

Writing, romance, and publishing in general have been very good to me. No other career could have so fulfilled my obsession with the written word, allowed me to make a living while staying home with my children, and given me time to indulge in the many other activities that fascinate me. I will admit that my marriage and children have come first, but I have tried very hard not to short-change my readers. It has not been easy, especially with a child whose health problems in years past have resulted in more than 40 hospitalizations and constant vigilance. But God has been good. That same child is now 18, one of the top runners in our district, and an honor student about to embark on the pathway to his own dreams.

It's empty nest time in my house. Oddly, for a woman who has so enjoyed her children, I am looking forward to it. I have told my husband for years that my most productive days would come after the children had left home. Soon I must prove it. Not that I've done so badly over the last 17 years, with 35 published books and three others making their way to the market now. If I have not been prolific, at least I've been steady, averaging three books a year in each of the last ten years.

I do manage to get myself embroiled in other things, however. I've been much involved in amateur theater and am currently directing my seventh or eighth play. (I refuse to stop and count them accurately. I may have dedicated more time to this "hobby" than I would care to admit.) I've worked extensively with young people through my local church. I sew a great deal, the current projects being my best friend's wedding dress and costumes for the play. And I love to entertain others in my home almost as much as my husband loves me to do it. I am a slightly better than decent cook, and my figure has reaped no benefit from it. Thank God for a husband who looks at me through a lens of love and acceptance. Now if only the man were not able to eat his weight three times a day and remain slim!

It's been a good life so far, and my readers have made it all possible. Thank you. Thank you. Thank you.

B J JAMES

How did I come to writing, what it is to me, and how has it changed my life? These questions are often asked of a writer. In many ways the answers are definition of self and individuality. Mine are contained, in part, in paraphrasing an author's note written for *Slade's Woman*, a Silhouette Desire.

The thought that I should write did not spring from discontent or disenchantment. No book was flung aside with the declaration that I could do better. Certainly, there were books I did not like or found of little merit. Some I struggled through, others I put aside, but never with the idea that I could write, for better, for worse, or at all. To some this must seem pitifully lacking in ambition. I prefer to think of it as an abiding respect for books, even the bad ones, and awe for those who wrote them.

So, I read. And for every book that did not enchant, there was one that was magic. In my constant search for the next good read, it was natural my friends would be readers, and that we would discuss what we read. Perhaps even natural that ideas burst vividly into life and refused to go away. That one day, on a dare, I would put them on paper and they would become a book.

The beginning! Setting me on the eternal quest for the mystery and the magic every writer hopes to give each story. Now books are more than entertaining companions. They are adventures to take, and imagination in flight. Dreams I dared not dream are at my fingertips, mine to make real for a while. Limited only by the measure of my own talent, there is opportunity to provoke excitement, drama, and passion. To paint with words a mood, an ambience, making it an integral force; to write with an intensity that has become my trademark.

Writing adds dimension to my life. Contrasts are more powerfully drawn, passions more exquisite. Characters become stronger, more human. They are my creations, my constant companions. From that exhilarating moment when a story is born, through the exciting and, sometimes, tedious complexity of turning inspiration into reality, they are a part of my life, a part of me. But more than

66

creations, they are my children, my friends. They live within me, involving and engaging me, and, I hope, the reader, as we go together into new worlds.

In these new worlds and the old, life is hectic, but never boring--and always the richer for what writing has brought to it.

MURIEL JENSEN

I am living proof that you *don't* have to suffer for your art. I had wonderful, functional parents, a loving husband with whom I raised three brilliant and beautiful children, and we're now enjoying the world's most precious grandchildren.

I have hilarious and supportive siblings, equally great in-laws, and the best friends anybody ever had.

So, what does one write with such a history? I wasn't sure, so I tried a few different things.

My husband was a journalist when we met, and was editor and/or publisher of several small newspapers in California and Oregon. I was often commandeered to help when he was understaffed, and learned quickly that journalism was not for me. Creative embroidery of the facts was frowned upon, even wept over. I found that no fun at all.

I turned to fiction, searching for a big and important idea. Then I realized I didn't really know anything big and important. But I was fascinated by relationships, and was sure there had to be some genre where I could explore this interest.

I tried writing a Gothic novel because I so enjoyed reading them, but soon discovered it required a more serious nature than I possessed. When I was supposed to be setting a somber, threatening mood, I was injecting humor and frivolity. It was time to look for another market.

That was when I discovered romance --- larger than life heroes, fearless heroines, adventure, excitement, *fun* --- and knew I'd come home.

In the thirteen years since, more blessings have been heaped upon me with a wonderful agent, many fine editors, and the support of warm and loyal readers who've taught me more about love and generosity than my books could have ever given them.

Thanks to all of you!

JILL MARIE LANDIS

Sunflower was my first published novel and it hit the stands in 1988. What a thrill to see a story that came out of my head on sale across America. Becoming a published novelist was a dream that came to me in the middle of a rewarding and satisfying career as an elementary teacher. Always a voracious reader, I had begun spending after school hours, summers and vacations unwinding with historical romances.

In 1983, my husband, Steve Landis, who was also a teacher at the time (he's now an actor) and I decided we would take a year off to live in California's High Sierras at a ski resort. Little did we know that would be a winter of constant snow storms. There were only eleven full days of sun on the mountain that season. Needless to say, I read so many romances I was saturated with them and decided that I was going to try to write one of my own.

After walking to the local book store through the snowy streets and looking up the publishers of my favorite authors, I began to send out a mass mailing of query letters, detailing the high points of my proposed novel, the setting and characters. Answers began to trickle in, editors wanting to look at three chapters and an outline. Of course, I didn't even have ten pages at that point, but that was all the inspiration I needed, believe me.

What followed were three magical years of learning, taking novel writing workshops, joining the Romance Writers of America, attending conferences, making friends and meeting people in the romance industry. In 1986, after winning a Golden Heart Award from Romance Writers for the best unpublished historical romance, I sold that manuscript, *Sunflower*, to Berkley Publishing Group.

Now, as I begin my eleventh novel for Berkley, I have to admit that each and every publication is still as thrilling. I can't wait to see the new covers before they arrive and am usually out the first day the book is on sale, haunting the bookstores at the mall or lurking behind stacks of grapefruit at the local market, waiting to see if anyone is going to pick up a copy of my book.

Writing for me is a joy, something I can do anywhere in the world, at home in Long Beach or in Hawaii, where I live part-time. My hope is that readers enjoy my books as much as I enjoy writing them.

RUTH RYAN LANGAN

In high school I was an honors student who wrote for the school paper, was editor of the yearbook, and was awarded a full college scholarship, where I hoped to pursue an English degree. My plans were changed by family financial conditions, and I joined the work force, becoming secretary to the vice-president of a large company.

I married my childhood sweetheart, Tom, and together we've raised five children. We're avid travelers and sports enthusiasts, who enjoy bowling, golfing, skiing, swimming, and jogging. Since my husband also loves boxing, we attend many boxing matches and have met many of the champions.

My writing career began when I gave a very special birthday present to myself--an hour a day to attempt a novel that had been spinning around in my mind. That novel, *Just Like Yesterday*, was published in 1981 by Silhouette Books. Since then I've been fortunate enough to lead a very busy, productive life doing what I always dreamed of--writing. To date, I've had forty-three novels, both contemporary and historical, published.

I think the nicest part of this career is the friends I've made. Writers are the warmest, most supportive people on earth. I cherish their friendship, and look forward each year to being with them, sharing a few laughs, a few tears, a few hugs.

Since I believe that a writer has no limitations, it was only natural that I would try other forms of writing. Along with two friends, I've completed four movie scripts. To date they haven't been optioned by a production company, but the experience was so enjoyable, I know we'll write more screenplays. And some day we hope to see our names on the big screen. And, as long as we're dreaming, we like to dream BIG. How about the lead title on the *New York Times*, an Oscar, and a Pulitzer?

The truth is, though those awards would be lovely, I'm already a winner, because I'm doing exactly what I've always dreamed of.

CATHIE LINZ

I'm often asked why I write romance novels. My answer throughout the fifteen years I've been published has always been that I write them because this is the genre I love to read. I've been an avid romance reader since my freshman year in high school when I picked up a Harlequin romance by Ann Mather. I still have that book, and a thousand others, on my keeper shelves of special romance novels. As for why I became a writer--I've been a writer even longer than high school. Back in the third grade we had a Knowledge Fair, where other kids did science projects mostly. I wrote a book. It was 4 pages, single-spaced and I typed it myself. I won second prize with that "book," and that early success spurred me on to continue my writing.

I write a fast-paced book with a lot of humorous dialogue. When I'm writing and it's going well, it's as if I'm taking down dictation from my characters. There are plenty of times when I don't know *what* they're going to say next!! I've often said that if I could only teach them how to type, I'd be in great shape. My characters are very real to me and I've been delighted to have readers tell me they become real to them, as well.

Working with new characters on a new story never fails to excite me. It can also terrify me, but I try and delegate as much anxiety as possible on to my characters. After all, we're all in this together! So when I received the *Romantic Times* Storyteller of the Year award, I was sure to thank my characters as well as the readers and booksellers!

I was also honored to be one of the contributing essayists to *Dangerous Men And Adventurous Women*. I am very proud to have been involved with this award-winning book about the strong appeal of romance novels and the way these stories empower women. As a result, I became more involved with the way romance novels are perceived, becoming Romance Writers of America's first every Library Liaison. One of the things I'm most excited about is the establishment of a

"Romance Fiction and Related Materials" collection at the Popular Culture Library at Bowling Green State University in Bowling Green, Ohio. Thanks to this collection, future generations will be able to understand and appreciate the various elements of romance novels--from writing to reading them.

DEBBIE MACOMBER

Dear Readers!

I'm delighted to be able to give you a greeting from the pages of *Romantic Hearts*.

I've always considered myself a storyteller. When I was a teenager I earned money by babysitting. I was in demand because I would tell my charges wonderful, made-up stories, using them as the main characters. I guess that's when my plotting skills got their fledgling start!

As a young mother I used to entertain myself and my friend Sharon during our evening walks by telling her plot ideas, and make up a story to go with them. Sharon was always supportive and would say, "Debbie, why don't you just write the story, instead of telling me?" I rejected her suggestion--I didn't have a college degree, I had four small children, too many responsibilities. I would do it later, when the kids were grown, when we had more money, when I had more time.

Well, as it happened, I found out that time is relative. Time had run out for my cousin David, someone I had grown up with, who was as close to me as a brother. When David died of Leukemia, I realized that if I had a dream to write, I better not put that dream on hold. Tomorrow holds no guarantees.

I grabbed hold of my dream and started writing. I wrote four manuscripts in five years, getting better with each one. Those years weren't easy, and I received lots of rejections, but in the end it was all worth it. I sold my first book in 1982.

I still dream, and I still have goals. My major goal as a writer is to pen uplifting books. When people finish a Debbie Macomber story I want them to feel better about life, about the future. I want to imbue my readers with enthusiasm and hope, to create characters they can identify with and care about. I'm not looking to change the world, but I consider it my duty to brighten someone's afternoon.

I recently joined the information age, and have my own Home Page on the Romance Authors Page. If you're hooked into the Internet and would like to read about my current activities, join me at http://www.nettrends.com/debbiemacomber.

If you prefer a more traditional form of communication, you can reach me at PO Box 1458, Port Orchard, WA 98366.

ANN MAJOR

There's no desperation quite like having to write an author profile.

I will start by answering the questions that people usually ask me.

First question: why is a nice girl like you writing *those* kinds of books?

The answer I have been known to give is that I do it for the money. The real reason is that I do it because they're fun.

Second question: when are you going to write a *real* book? (First, I think it's pointless to quibble over the definition of a *real* book with somebody rude enough to ask me this question.)

My answer is never. I like writing romance novels.

Third: why don't you write about nice men instead of dark brooding heroes?

I married a nice, stable guy who has an eight to five job. I'd rather read and write about unpredictable bad boys who live dangerous, exotic lives, men who aren't afraid to take risks.

Fourth: where do you get your ideas? As if they're weird and there's something a little wrong with my mind.

Answer: My madcap in-laws have given me my best ideas. Incidentally they are always asking me when I'm going to write a real book, but unlike my own family, my in-laws actually read my books.

Who am I really?

Ann Major is my pseudonym. Peggy Cleaves is my real name. I suppose somewhere between these two separate identities there is a perfectly normal human being. At least I hope so.

I was an imaginative child, and my father used to tease me by saying that a bad thought was the same as a bad deed. I've just about matured to the point where I can forgive him that one.

I was born and raised and still live in Corpus Christi, Texas. I have a Masters in English, and I am the mother of three children. I married a man I met when I was three although the romance didn't spark until I was sixteen. We have been happily married twenty-six years. I have four cats and each one thinks there are three other cats too many. I have a house, a yard, too many filing cabinets, and no time to cook. I like to sail and hike and climb mountains.

There are so many exciting things to do and so many interesting books to read, and yet my life goes by at such a hectic pace, I never get around to most of them.

My secret fantasy: Princess Di will be photographed on the cover of *The National Enquirer* in some delicious indiscretion while she is reading an ANN MAJOR novel.

I can dream, can't I?

SANDRA MARTON
Sandra Myles

At book signings--actually, almost everywhere I go--there's always someone who comes up and asks me, "How did you become a writer?"

The real question, I think, is how did I ever manage to spend so much of my life not being one?

There was never a time I didn't want to write. Even when I was a little girl, I spun fantasy lives for my toys. I cut out paper dolls and gave them not just paper dresses but paper lives of my own creation. Games of jump rope or ball were okay but it was really more fun to curl up in my favorite chair and lose myself in a world of fairy tales, where beautiful princesses locked away in dismal dungeons were rescued by gallant handsome princes who swept them off to a land called Forever After.

In junior high school, I joined every writing club there was. I wrote essays for the school magazine, articles for the school newspaper, and poetry for absolutely nobody but myself. I kept a diary and wrote in it endlessly. I read everything and anything I could get my hands on, including my mother's old copy of *Gone With the Wind*. I remember reading it almost non-stop and, when I was done, sensing that somehow, Margaret Mitchell had changed me forever.

In high school and college, I discovered Literature with a capital L. I read Shakespeare and Hemingway, Mailer and du Maurier. I took seminars in writing poetry, plays and short stories. Somehow--and this makes me smile today--I never got around to taking any courses in writing novels.

And then, all too suddenly, I was an adult. I had a husband and children. I had RESPONSIBILITIES. I was part of the Real World and there was no time for spinning fantasies. But the dream was still there, and it whispered to me in the dark of night, reminding me that there were adventures waiting and stories to be told, heroes and heroines eager for the breath of life.

One morning, I looked into the mirror and said, 'Sandra, it's now or never. Live the dream--or give it up.'

I dug out my old Royal portable, wrote a couple of short stories. When they sold, I wrote some more. Then I took a deep breath, settled in and wrote a novel. It sold, too, and suddenly the dream, the one that had been with me as far back as I can remember, was real.

I was--I am--a writer. I get to share my stories with readers around the world.

In other words, I am the luckiest woman I know.

CONNIE MASON

I have a tee shirt at home that says *Aged To Perfection* across the front. Wearing that shirt represents my own personal achievement.

Sixteen years ago my husband of forty-six years suggested that we sell our home in Michigan and retire to Florida. Great. While he enjoyed fishing I could concentrate on my untapped creativity.

I toyed with the idea of going to college but somehow the motivation was lacking. I was already a voracious reader, having discovered a passion for books the day Dick met Jane and saw Spot run. From the moment I read Rosemary Roger's first historical romance, I fell in love with the genre.

Time was marching on. If I was going to make my mark in life I'd better get moving. I wanted to do something I'd always dreamed of doing. I wanted to write. Shortly after our move to Clermont I began my first serious attempt at writing.

Arming myself with several reference books, a stack of legal pads and a gross of sharpened pencils, I wrote *Tender Fury*. It took six months to write my story. I found that I loved writing. Every lonely, time-consuming, frustrating, underpaid, often unrewarding minute.

In due time my story was completed. Now all I had to do was translate twelve legal pads of scribbling into neatly typed words. No problem. So what if I didn't own a typewriter and couldn't have used it even if I had one. I purchased a typewriter and enrolled in an adult typing class at the local high school. After six weeks I began typing my manuscript. It was more difficult than I thought, but it never occurred to me not to find a publisher.

While browsing the library one day, I discovered a book called *Literary Marketplace*. It listed all the U.S. publishers and their editors and told how to submit a manuscript. I prepared my cover letter, duplicated the first three chapters, wrote a synopsis and mailed multiple submissions. Three months later rejection slips began arriving daily. Undaunted, I submitted my manuscript to other publishers.

Briefly it occurred to me that I was incurably optimistic for thinking I could write at my age. Not that I considered myself doddering. I am moderately intelligent, possess a vivid imagination, am disciplined, and have experienced life in ways that come only with maturity. Miraculously, an editor expressed interest in my manuscript. Off it went by return mail and the rest is history. Leisure Books published *Tender Fury* in December 1984. A new dimension was added to my life that day. I have seen twenty-one full length historical romances and four Christmas novellas published by Leisure Books, and five historical romances from Avon Books. Currently there are over five million copies of my books in print, including translations in Chinese, Norwegian, Bulgarian and Polish.

On a more personal note. I have three grown children and eight grandchildren. I have lived in Europe and Asia and several states while my husband pursued an army career, and enjoyed every minute of it.

CURTISS ANN MATLOCK

When I first began writing, I struggled with fears of appearing foolish, of having my ideas ridiculed, of being disappointed in wild dreams, but most of all with the fear that I was wasting time, which to me would be the most foolish thing of all.

I was raised to be industrious and frugal--save those supper leftovers until they make penicillin and save all those slivers of soap until you can make a new bar in the microwave. The odds were great against selling what I wrote, and unless my writing earned money what good was it? We were not a rich family. I had a young son to clothe, struggled each month to pay the electric company, and canned garden vegetables to help with the grocery bill, too.

Over the past years I have heard all of my fears, and many others, voiced by beginning writers, with the concern over wasting time invariably topping the list. In the back of every beginning writer's mind are the questions: What if I don't publish? What if I don't write a blockbuster and become rich and famous? What then? All that time wasted!

Well, I have written a lot that never got published, and I have written and published twenty-one novels (none of them so-called blockbusters), and I can testify heartily that no time spent writing is ever wasted. What I have come to learn is that time spent writing is the greatest investment a person can make, because when a person writes, he begins to know exactly who he is. The struggling doesn't matter, how well the writing comes out doesn't matter. It is the thinking and the act of trying to get those thoughts put down. From this process comes the knowledge of the dreams and desires, the fears and foolishness and wisdom, too, that lies deep inside each of us.

How did you do it? some people ask. How did you keep on, even when you didn't know if you would publish? Well, I told myself what I tell those who ask: A person never knows what he can do, until he tries. So what if you never publish. Try and see what comes out of yourself. Get to know yourself on paper--and fiction is as viable a medium as fact, for even in the 'bad guys' we put a sliver of ourselves. Write first for yourself, then think of readers, then think of money. Learn all you can about the publishing business, but never, ever pay attention to the facts on your chances of publishing. My motto is to never, ever face facts. I haven't done so badly by following this line of thought.

LEIGH MICHAELS

I started creating stories before I could write, and the first romance novel I submitted was acquired by the first publisher to see it, with minimal revisions. But my path to publication wasn't as easy as it sounds. That book was a dozen years in the making; it took me that long to teach myself how to tell a story.

I finished my first novel--hand-written in stenographers' notebooks--when I was fifteen years old. Mercifully, I maintained enough detachment to realize that though it was a great learning experience it was a bad book, and I burned it. I also burned the next five manuscripts--more than a quarter of a million words.

I'm often asked whether I regret destroying those books. No--(except now and then when I could use a laugh). All the good ideas in those books remained in my mind, and most of them have been used in later published books. Even single good lines rattled around in my head--some for as long as twenty years--until I created a better setting for them. All that I destroyed was the poor plotting, inadequate characterization, and cliches which would have kept me trapped if I'd tried to revise instead of starting from scratch.

Writing for me is like tiptoeing into a world which sits off at a slight angle from the real one. In my special universe my characters--ones I've long ago finished with, ones I'm just discovering, ones I haven't yet met--are busily living their lives, dealing with their problems, and enjoying their happy endings. They're always there waiting for me, and all I have to do is watch and listen and report what they do.

I'm in awe of the ways in which my stories have touched the lives of my readers. I've heard from people who have been able to deal with painful past relationships because of a story I wrote, who can look more positively on lives full of sadness or illness because of the escape my characters offer. There's even a reader whose life may have been saved because my story about carbon monoxide poisoning prompted her to have her furnace checked. I am humbled and honored by the trust my readers put in me, and the fact that so many of them think of me as a friend.

I love to hear from readers, at PO Box 935, Ottumwa, Iowa, 52501-0935.

LINDA LAEL MILLER

The two questions writers are most often asked, at least in my experience, are: 1) Where do you get your ideas? 2) Who is your favorite author?

In reply to the first, I can honestly, unequivocally state that I don't know, but I do have one or two theories. As a child, pretending was my favorite game. When everybody else outgrew it, I didn't, so I started putting my scenarios on paper. I spent years learning to write, studying books and magazines on the subject, taking a correspondence course, and writing the same bad novel endlessly. Many ideas were woven from the mix of books and movies and paintings and sunsets and all the other impressions that pour into the human mind, I'm sure.

I also use various brainstorming techniques, more often to refine an idea than to create one. My favorite is to list twenty things that could happen in a book, chapter or scene, depending on the stage of the project, rapid-fire, without stopping to question any of them as I write. This has never failed to produce results for me.

In reply to question number two, there are many, many writers I admire and like all my ilk, I love to read. Among numerous romance authors I enjoy are: Debbie Macomber, Judith McNaught, LaVyrle Spencer, Nora Roberts and Jude Deveraux. These are all fantastically talented women.

There is one writer who, I feel, makes me better at my craft just by striving to reach her level, and that is the Scottish writer, Dorothy Dunnett. Several years ago, at the suggestion of my then-secretary, I read the first of Mrs. Dunnett's Lymond series, and I was hooked. I hunted the six novels down in hardcover and have several sets in paperback, as well. I have given away and loaned out many of the books to others who haven't discovered them, and am now reading the latest of the new series, *The House of Niccolo*, which I am enjoying just as much. Reading these wonderful books is an education in itself.

Several years ago, I was privileged to meet Mrs. Dunnett, in her home in Edinburgh and at a conference given there in her honor. She is, to me, a standard-bearer, a frame of reference. Everybody needs a role model, and she's mine, both as a person and as a writer. When I grow up, I want to be like her!

HELEN MITTERMEYER

Being able to trace your family back to 400AD doesn't mean you want to write historicals. It usually telegraphs you have an awesome number of miscreants in your background, capable of various and vicarious incidents that could make good copy. Some of those ancestors had a beguiling flair. Some you wouldn't invite into your parlor. I admit they intrigued me.

Born in a city in the Northeast, one of four children, I was raised on a strong work ethic. Educated by dedicated women from grade school to college, I never lost the desire to write. Thank God my teachers encouraged me. I liked my own company and writing and started doing it from the first moment I learned how to use a pencil.

I actually began to write an historical after I'd accrued a hefty pile of research on the family which I was going to give to an aunt, most interested in our genealogy. She died, and left me very sad, and with a hillock of research. My Scottish forebears would've been appalled had I wasted it, so I wrote my first historical after penning over forty contemporary novels.

It's been a never ending delight to write. When I was six my father informed me, when I asked if I could be a writer, I could be anything I wanted to be except a father. Life became a vast canvas. I began to write, married, had two boys and two girls, and allowed my imagination full rein in all I did. My heart pulls me to the plight of women and children. Thus they've become my crusade. To entertain as a writer doesn't abnegate the need to tell the truth. I shall spend my life writing and caring about the needs of women and children who could fall through the cracks so easily.

From my first novel titled *From The Torrid Past*, which won a National Bookseller's Award, through the next forty some of which were on the Waldenbooks Best Seller List, I've drowned in delight. I'm very proud of the volume and variety of my work, that they've sold all over the world in most languages and dialects. Winning a number of awards along the way has been fun and rewarding. Perhaps the greatest coup has been accruing the most loyal, the most friendly and knowledgeable group of fans anyone could have. I'm everlastingly grateful to them.

A city girl, born and bred, doesn't usually move to the Amish community in the center of New York State, but my husband and I have done that. If I hadn't already had a strong work ethic I would've learned it from my neighbors. They've intrigued me so much I've put them into a book, titled, *Divinity Brown* from Bantam. So taken with the area and its boundless story lines, I've gone another step and given the county a fictitious name. Our Seneca County has become Yokapa County. The prequel to *Divinity Brown* is the book that came out in September of 1995, titled *Dynasty Jones*.

I can't see doing anything but writing for the rest of my life. Of course, in between bouts with the computer, I will be doting on my one perfect granddaughter.

I love animals and children because of their crystal truthfulness, and I respect and revere my circle of friends. Books are the only weapons I need.

VELLA MUNN

Some people should never be taken out of the hills. Fortunately, I learned that about myself years ago and returned to the mountains and evergreens where my heart belongs, bringing my family with me. There's nothing I love more than looking out my office windows at birds, squirrels, and the occasional deer who jumps the fence into our back yard. Yes, living in a town of 2,000 has certain limitations, but I don't mind. Besides, if I want to go for a walk any time of the day or night or forget to lock a door, I can get away with it.

A sense of place has become essential in everything I write. If I can't visualize my character's roots and understand how they interact with whatever place they call home, I can't truly crawl into their heads and look at the world through their eyes. I firmly believe we're all shaped by our surroundings. My Silhouette editor calls my writing "atmospheric" and I'd be the last to disagree. However, my love of rural settings sometimes catches up with me since market research indicates that most readers are drawn to more populated areas (which explains why there are cities). I've gotten away with writing about forest fire fighters, grizzly bear researchers, back country canoeists, and search and rescue personnel in the Colorado mountains, but have also forged into towns and cities for stories about a world class power lifter and the woman attracted to him, a couple running from an evil Navajo ghost or "chinde", and most recently a social worker and the Apache owner of a construction company. As long as my characters feel passionately about their lives and explore relationships with every fiber of their being, I'll tell their stories.

My fondness for a simple life is part of what drew me into writing the Native American historical romances I'm doing for Tor books. The more I delve into the way Native Americans once lived, the more my respect for them grows. They might be "primitive" by present-day standards, but human emotions don't change with the ages. A man and woman who live off the land can love as completely and passionately as the most modern of couples, and the exploration for me, the writer,

92

remains the same whether I'm doing historicals or contemporaries. I hope my readers agree.

My first hardcover, *Spirit of the Eagle*, is on the stands and I just sold my thirty-second book.

HELEN R. MYERS

As one of the more privacy-loving members of the writing community, two frequently asked question I hear are, "How do you deal with loneliness?" and "Where do you get your ideas?" I usually groan because I'm always wondering how to squeeze another hour out of my day, and forever shuffling contract schedules to accommodate a captivating idea--only to see my projects stretching farther and farther into the future.

Loneliness doesn't exist for me as long as there's a life form on this planet. People, animals, plants... they're all fascinating. I can be entertained by watching birds discover a new feeder I've put out, a bee grow giddy over an unfolding blossom, a pet perform some trick or utterance I'd been teaching it. During breaks, strolls in the woods bring me upon signs of whom we share this land with: the print of a raccoon, and a kernel of corn stolen from where we feed deer; that of an opossum, deeper because she's carrying her young; the musky stench of a cottonmouth who doesn't want me in his territory. Danger, excitement, and beauty surround me every second of every day. The dilemma isn't loneliness, but to find the discipline to stay before the computer long enough to share what I experience with the reader.

In the same way I'm surrounded with hundreds of story ideas. Everyone, everything has a story. The challenge is to focus on one at a time. I tend to work thematically, and justice and principle are strong beacons in my books, as they are in my life. Even a basic comedy must hold some inner truth, otherwise I feel I've wasted my time and the reader's.

When looked at from a distance, the writing life seems exhausting. My days usually begin at three a.m. and rarely end before six that evening--longer if I'm under deadline pressure. I work every day that I'm not traveling somewhere, and more than once I've risen at one or two in the morning to finish a book in order to celebrate Christmas with family. Writers are born, I think, and they spend their entire lives trying to explain the world--but also to inspire it. There is no time for loneliness or absence of thought. There is no time to fulfill all of our dreams.

CARLA NEGGERS

I wrote my first book and mailed it off to an agent when I was twenty-four and so broke I had to rent a typewriter. I couldn't even afford photo-copying: I used carbon paper! My husband and I had just had our first child and watched every penny. The agent--Denise Marcil--was also just starting out. She took me on, even though she knew that first book wasn't going to be an easy sell. It was romantic suspense, written in the first-person, and the market for romantic suspense was dead. But I remember her enthusiasm when she called that first time, her words of encouragement--"I know you have a big book in you."

Denise tried to sell that first book--*The Venus Shoe*--for a year. We got great responses, but the market just wasn't there. Meanwhile I wrote a short romance and did a proposal for a historical romance...and she sold them both within a week. The historical she sold the same day she received the proposal! I ended up writing one of the six Bantam Loveswept launch books, and finally, three years later, Denise sold *The Venus Shoe*. It was a great victory for both of us.

Since then, my husband and I have moved several times, we've had another child, and I've sold dozens of books, won awards, made bestseller lists. I work on a computer now and have a laser printer, and while I'm still frugal, I don't have to watch every penny. But the things that were important to me when I sat down to my rented typewriter sixteen years ago are still important: making the characters in my head come to life on the page, writing the best book I possibly can, connecting with readers. So much has changed, but not that, not my commitment to each and every story I write.

I tell this story because it's so easy to get up in the trappings of writing. Equipment, agents, contracts, money, promotion, reviews. When I start getting a little crazy, I dip back into the past and remember the joy I felt sitting out on my front porch on a summer afternoon and putting pen to page. I knew nothing about the business. All I had was the desire and the drive--the dream--to write my story and have people read it, respond to it, and maybe want to read it again.

SARA ORWIG

With a minor in history, I find history fascinating, particularly the Old West. I collect books about the Old West and enjoy researching the history of the time.

My husband goes along with me on research trips. Last year we toured old Texas forts that formed the line of the frontier for so many years. After crossing the Red River, our first stop was Fort Richardson west of Fort Worth near Jacksboro, Texas. Then we went on to Fort Griffin which was part of the setting for an earlier historical of mine, *Sweet Desire*, New American Library/Onyx.

Part of Fort Griffin is preserved and visitors can walk around the grounds and see what is left of the crumbling, limestone buildings. The "MacKenzie Trail" leads from Fort Griffin, the first road going west across the Staked Plains.

We drove west to Palo Duro Canyon, scene of the last great battle of the Plains Indians when Randall MacKenzie attacked the Comanches and Kiowas in their winter campground in the deep canyon. It was a wild, beautiful place. This canyon is hidden from the eye as you look across the sweeping flat land that goes endlessly until the horizon blends with the sky.

Stand still on the edge of the canyon and you hear only the sigh of the wind. As a writer, it is easy for me to imagine the drama that unfolded on that site in the 1800s.

We traveled to the area where Fort Phantom Hill once stood. There is very little left now. We dropped south to Fort McKavett near Menard, Texas.

It is impossible to resist the Hill Country of texas in the springtime when bluebonnets carpet the fields. We went to San Antonio and visited old missions. These missions date back to the early eighteenth century and the first time I visited them, my imagination ran riot and the plot was born for the first book of my western trilogy, *San Antonio*, New American Library/Onyx.

Finally, it was home to Oklahoma, driving across land that is home to the Comanches and the Kiowas and part of the setting of my latest historical, *Warrior*

Moon.

Then it is back to my computer with dreams floating in my mind of these historic sites. I take too many pictures, but as I look at snapshots of rolling plains dotted by shimmering cottonwoods, in my mind, I can see the drama unfolding as a powerful warrior, wounded in battle, is found by a woman running away from an arranged marriage. Back to my magic world of books that I hope I can share with you!

LAURIE PAIGE
Olivia M. Hall

Readers frequently ask, "How do you get your ideas?" It's a question I love to answer. Magazine articles, newspapers, snatches of conversation--all spark ideas for stories. Once I read an article on how men acted when they met a woman. A lover was one who looked a woman in the eyes and talked to her face. A seducer was more interested in her body; his eyes would roam. Later, I watched a television program on a group of scientists at the South Pole. *South Of The Sun* was born. The heroine was a behavioral scientist. The hero was the leader...and the ultimate lover and husband to the heroine. The second-in-command was the seducer. My husband says I can get ideas from the fine print on a cracker box. (Now I know where to go if I ever get stuck.)

I was born on a small farm in Kentucky, the youngest of seven children. Reading was an early entertainment. Sitting around the fire on a winter's night, my mother and I read while my father and an older brother and sister took turns on the violin and guitar. We ate popcorn or apple turnovers. We had apple cider, too. In summer, we made ice cream with an old-fashioned, hand-crank freezer.

Those early memories carry through into my writing. All my stories center on the family, with the hero and heroine coming together to form this basic building block of civilization.

Many of my own experiences transmute in various ways into my stories. When my grandchildren were born, I was there with my daughter and son-in-law. My next book included an opening scene in which the hero's secretary goes into labor at the office. The heroine is there, waiting for her appointment with him. She gets to see the tough, quiet man she's known for years in an entirely new light. It was a revelation...and the start of a romance.

As Laurie Paige, I have written 35 books and still love a love story, whether my own or one of the authors I've come to know during my years of writing. Writing, like reading, has been an enriching experience for me. It's also rather awesome.

Just think--at any moment, anywhere in the world, someone might be sitting in the john reading one of my books.

DIANA PALMER
Susan Kyle
Diana Blayne
Katy Currie

It's a pleasure to have this opportunity to answer some frequently asked questions from my wonderful readers. I write for three publishing house (Silhouette, Warner, and Fawcett). I graduated in May 1995, from Piedmont College in Demorest, Georgia, with a B.A. in history (summa cum laude) after four years as a day student. I've had little time for mail, trying to write books under contract and study for finals all at once.

Thanks to my terrific niece Helen, some of my mail gets answered on time. But when she can't take dictation, I get behind. The lack of an SASE often prevents replies. I have severe arthritis in my hands and no typewriter, and I can't do envelopes properly on my laser printer. I have to address them by hand and it's very painful. If you want a quick reply, send me an addressed envelope, please.

I get so many questions on how to get published that I thought of doing a form letter about it, but that seemed too impersonal. Since I don't have time for detailed replies, here's my answer to that frequently asked question: Write what you like to read. Research the subject you're writing about. Never copy anyone else's style thinking that you will make a sale. Your own unique, individual voice is your best selling tool. Your own life experience is something no other writer has. Use it to good advantage when you write. And above all, be persistent.

There are lots of books on manuscript preparation, plotting, and addresses of specific markets. Go to your local library and check them out. How did I get published? I spent 16 years as a newspaper reporter and persisted until somebody bought one of my books. I didn't know anybody in New York. I didn't have an agent.

Another frequent question is: Do I have family in other states? I have "adopted" family all over the world--my wonderful readers. I have no blood relations except one sister and an uncle. I DO NOT HAVE A BROTHER. This fact is easily verified in any reference book that carries my biography.

I also get asked about future "Long, Tall Texans" in the Silhouette series. Yes, I will definitely be doing more of them.

Please keep writing to me. I love to keep in touch with the people who read my books, and I've been writing to some of you for fifteen years or more. I'd like to thank you all, again, for your kindness, your loyalty, your friendship and your prayers. You've made all the hard work worthwhile.

MARILYN PAPPANO

I've often been asked how I got into the business of writing. Truthfully, I can't remember a time when storytelling wasn't a major part of my life. Before I started school, according to my mother, I made up tales any time I found an audience. Once I learned to read and write, I began putting the stories on paper. It was a creative outlet, it kept me out of trouble, and it was just plain fun.

Even though a high school teacher urged me to continue writing, it never occurred to me that I could actually get published until an aspiring-author friend asked me to do some market research for her. It didn't take long at all to decide that this was what I wanted. After thousands of pages of "stories", I wrote my first full-length book and sent it off to New York. It whizzed back with a letter suggesting that I not submit to that editor again. My talent, it was apparent to her, lay elsewhere.

Until that day I'd never realized I couldn't say no to a challenge. Determined to prove her wrong, I finished the next book and mailed it off to Leslie Wainger at Silhouette, along with another three mainstream romances for Warner Books. I've had the pleasure of seeing my name on the bestseller lists and the honor of finding it on awards.

I can't conceive of a better job. I get to travel. I've met people who were my idols back when reading romances helped me through the week. I've made new friends through the reader mail I receive, and I've been honored to hear that something that gives me so much pleasure also gives them pleasure. It sounds silly to say that I would continue to write even it I didn't get paid for it, but that's exactly what I did all those years before I sold that first book, and it's exactly what I would do in the future if the career disappeared. I love to tell stories. I love to create characters as real as you and me, put them in difficult circumstances, and bring them through stronger and more secure than ever. Best of all, I love helping them fall in love. What could be better?

105

SUSAN ELIZABETH PHILLIPS

My writing career began in 1979 when a friend and I decided it would be fun to write a book together, even though neither of us had ever written a word of fiction. We sold this novel, a historical romance entitled *The Copeland Bride*, within three weeks to the first publisher who read it! Then the real work started.

My friend set off for law school and I discovered that writing a book alone wasn't nearly as much fun. Still, with the help of many gallons of vanilla chocolate fudge ice cream, I persevered and produced my first solo effort, a post-civil war romance entitled *Risen Glory*. For better or worse, I'd been firmly bitten by the writing bug.

After these two historical romances, I explored the world of women's fiction with my early eighties Glitz 'n' Glamour novel, *Glitter Baby*, and then moved on to *Fancy Pants*, my first *New York Times* bestseller. After several more of these larger women's fiction novels, I decided I wanted to write more focused romances with a very strong element of humor. *It Had To Be You*, Romance Writers' of America's Favorite Book of the Year for 1994, was the first of these romantic comedies, which I'm now writing with so much pleasure.

Many readers are curious about a writer's workday. I have an office on the second floor of our suburban Chicago home, where I write at a huge workstation I call the Starship Enterprise. When our sons were in school, I kept 9 a.m. to 3 p.m. office hours, but now that our youngest is in college and our oldest has graduated and joined the work force, I'm experimenting with a more flexible schedule. My husband Bill and I will celebrate our twenty-fifth wedding anniversary in 1996 and are still very much in love, despite a number of raging arguments on the golf course!

In addition to being a voracious reader, my other hobbies include low fat vegetarian cookery and trying to maintain a disciplined exercise schedule to compensate for my sedentary job. I'd much rather be reading, so this is an ongoing challenge for me!

My spiritual life is also important to me. Since I believe love is the most powerful force in the universe, is it any wonder that I feel so passionately about my profession?

JOAN ELLIOTT PICKART

I am the author of over seventy novels, including long and short contemporary romance, historicals, and mainstream women's fiction.

I received the Best New Series Author of the Year award from Romantic Times in 1985, and am a two-time Golden Medallion (Rita) award finalist of the National Romance Writers of America.

The Society of Southwestern Writers awarded me a Certificate of Award of Outstanding Achievement and a Certificate of Recognition for Notable Attainment as an Author.

I live in Prescott, Arizona, and in 1991 the Prescott Courier Newspaper selected me as one of Prescott's finest.

I am a frequent lecturer at conferences across the country, and have taught a writing class at Yavapai College in Prescott.

I am a co-founder of The Professional Writers of Prescott, a member of the National Romance Writers of America, The Phoenix Desert Rose Chapter of RWA, and a charter member and vice-president of Northern Arizona RWA.

I sold my first book in 1984, my manuscript having been found in the slush pile by Carolyn Nichols at Loveswept. Carolyn has since said that my manuscript was the last one selected before they shut down the slush pile at Bantam. A terrifying thought!

I am single and the mother of four daughters. My three "big" girls are in their twenties and out and about living their own wonderful lives.

In September of 1995, I traveled to China and adopted my fourth daughter, Autumn Joan Pickart, formerly Yang MengMeng. Three month old Autumn and I arrived safely home to begin our life together on September 27, 1995. I feel so blessed to be able to raise one more baby girl to womanhood. Autumn and I are a terrific team.

I am often asked what I feel is the most important quality a writer should have beyond their talent. The answer? Self-discipline. Unless you are working everyday, no matter what might be taking place in your personal life, you can't hope to make a successful career of your writing. It's the old "keep your bottom on the chair" cliche, and it works.

Like all writers, I love to read, enjoy working in my garden, knitting, watching football and basketball, and attending crafts shows on the town square. Once again a new mommy, I'm also enjoying reliving the fun and joy of watching a little one blossom like a beautiful flower.

MARY JO PUTNEY

I was born in Upstate New York with a reading addiction, a condition for which there is no cure. Though I adored all good stories and went around with my nose in a book, it never occurred to me that I could become a writer, a category that I placed somewhere up around the lesser angels. Then I bought a computer for my graphic design business, realized that I had the perfect tool to try to imply my vague fantasies of being a writer, and the rest is history.

My first book sold three months after I began writing, and I promptly went after a writing career like a lemming heading over a cliff. I'd finally found out what I wanted to do when I grew up. As a life-long Anglophile, it made sense to start writing Regencies. Soon I discovered that I would never be able to support myself with Regencies, my ideas were pretty subversive for the genre, and that I was too darned verbose anyhow. That made the progression to full-length historicals inevitable.

I love the hopefulness of writing romance, and I enjoy creating people who have the strength and wisdom to transform themselves during the course of the novel. My women are strong, my men are good-looking, and I try never to kill off anybody nice. I also like humor and firmly believe in happy endings. Sometimes I have trouble believing that I am lucky enough to be a writer. It's a great life. Almost perfect except for the fact that now and then we have to deliver books. Speaking of which, it's time I got back to the current story ....

PATRICIA RICE

One of the questions people ask most of me is how and when I first started writing. This question usually holds me stumped since I don't remember a time when I *didn't* write. Generally I tell them I started when I could first put crayon to the wall, and that's not much of an exaggeration.

As a transplant from New York to Kentucky when I was very young, I found myself in a spanking new subdivision (one of those horrible things with dirt lawns and two-foot trees and bare house frames everywhere) with no one my own age to play with. The culture shock left me scarcely able to speak to the few children who did live nearby. Try listening to a New Yorker and a Kentuckian say "pen" and "pin" sometime and you'll begin to get my meaning. Since I couldn't speak the same language as my neighbors, I retreated to my world of books, a world I'd discovered before I'd even started school.

Another problem with my new neighborhood was a serious lack of a library or nearby stores where I might purchase the latest Nancy Drew or Hardy Boys books. With no new reading material, I rapidly became desperate. So it was that, at the grand old age of nine, I first tried to write an entire book, just so I would have something new to read.

I never quite grew out of that stage. As a teenager, I wrote wildly romantic books about misunderstood teens who died tragically. I never thought to have any of my writing published. I did it for my own amusement and as a kind of self-therapy. I went on to marry, have children, and achieve a degree in accounting, all the while writing about anything that came into my head.

It was another move that propelled me into writing seriously. My husband accepted a job in a small town where I didn't know anyone and couldn't find a job. I was stuck in the country with a house full of small children, no transportation, and a driving need for adult conversation. Someone in a bookstore introduced me to the world of historical romance, and I delved into it with great joy, only to discover

112

there weren't enough good books at that time to satiate my driving need for more.
So, again, I sat down and wrote my own.

Perhaps, if you'll check my bibliography, you'll see if I succeeded!

EMILIE RICHARDS

I began my writing career with a baby on my lap, or so my Silhouette bio says. It's actually true. I even named my first hero Brendan, after the blond haired baby boy who was my constant companion that year. And later I named a hero after each of my other two sons and a heroine after my daughter.

Through the years my family has shown up in other ways in my books. My daughter is adopted, a "birth" that took place after a twenty-four hour flight from India. She emerged from that plane at age six, an instant addition to our family, and since then I've written several books about the trials and tribulations of adoption as well as its myriad rewards. Bratty Corey Haskins in *The Trouble With Joe* was patterned in some ways after our Jessie, who is now twenty-three. (And not bratty at all.)

Wayward teenage boys have walked through my books, just the way they seem to walk through my life. They always turn out well and luckily my own did, too. A twenty-seven year love affair with my minister husband convinced me that ministers could be heros too, and *Dragonslayer* was the result.

Through the years our family has moved from state to state. All of those places deserved and got at least one book. A four month sabbatical to Australia was good for four; stops along the way were good for four more. A vacation to Scotland became an Intimate Moments trilogy set in the Highlands. A trip to England and Paris was included in another.

Six years ago, when I was living in Louisiana, I traveled to Grand Isle. Before that trip I had heard about a hurricane that destroyed a village on a nearby peninsula in 1893. The trip was like going back in time. I saw the silver bell that had survived the storm, the graveyard where victims are memorialized. I began to spin a tale that grew more and more complex over the years until I realized I had to write the story. The finished product was two books, my first single titles. *Iron Lace*, was published by Mira in June of 1996, and the sequel, *Rising Tides*, in 1997.

I've learned that there are stories everywhere. I feel so privileged to put them on paper and so happy you enjoy reading them. Frustrations abound in this job, like any other, but at the end of the day, when a story is finally beginning to unfold, I still think I'm one of the luckiest people in the world.

EUGENIA RILEY

Eugenia Riley is proud to announce the August 1995 publication of her Avon Romantic Treasure, *Timeswept Bride*. It is the story of a modern, spirited woman who finds a note in an ancient bottle that washes up on the beach. She is then swept back in time to Victorian Galveston, to meet the rash, irresistibly sexy Irishman who sent her the message.

Timeswept Bride marks Ms. Riley's seventeenth published romance and her third time-travel romance; her first two, *A Tryst In Time* and *Tempest In Time*, were Waldenbooks romance bestsellers in mass-market paperback and have brought her over 1000 fan letters from locations all over the world. Ms. Riley's novels have earned numerous 4+ and 5 star ratings in publications such as *Romantic Times*, *Heartland Critiques*, and *Affaire de Coeur*; in *Popular Fiction News* reviewer Harriet Klausner calls Ms. Riley "One of the pioneers of the time-travel romance."

Ms. Riley is also proud to be the collaborator on Fabio's series of historical romance from Avon Books: *Pirate*; *Rogue*; *Viking*; *Comanche* (May 1995); and *Champion* (November 1995). Avon Books published Ms. Riley's time-travel romance, *Phantom In Time*, in July of 1996. She had a novella, *Tryst With An Angel*, in Love Spell's November 1995 anthology, *Christmas Angels*; Love Spell reissued *A Tryst In Time* in September 1995, and *Tempest In Time* in December 1996.

Ms. Riley is a magna cum laude graduate of Texas Wesleyan College in Fort Worth, a former English teacher and editor of *Touchstone Literary Quarterly*. She lives in Houston with her husband of twenty five years; they have two grown daughters.

AUTHOR PROFILES

RENEE ROSZEL
Renee Roszel Wilson

Boy, it's hard to write four hundred words about yourself. You try it and get back with me. Heck, I can write whole books about other people, their charms, their wit, their attractiveness and courage, sensitivity and humility. But as far as finding one, single thing to say about myself--well--*I'm thinking!*

Okay, I'm married. To a guy. An Engineer. When we were first married I asked him how much he loved me, and he said, "Fifty board feet."

Well, I was in heaven. I assumed that "fifty board feet." was something akin to fifty light years--you know the length of time it would take a board to travel to the sun or something--times fifty. Okay, I'm no math whiz. It took a lot of years before I found out that fifty board feet actually meant fifty feet of board. I confronted my husband with this knowledge, demanding, "You mean, when we were first married, and you were at your most passionate, your most obsessively horny, that was all you could come up with--YOU LOVED ME FIFTY BOARD FEET?"

But it was my own fault. When I was dating I specifically looked for a man who was good in math. I was so lousy in it, I had a horror of ever having to help children of my own with their arithmetic. So, once a man I dated let it slip that he couldn't multiply in his head, it was 'Goodbye sucker!'

If you want to know how my 'Looking for Mr. Sliderule' worked out, well, by the time my two sons were in the fifth grade, they were both better in math than either my husband or I. Besides that, they also *spelled* better. As it turned out, by marrying a smart man, I got an unexpected bonus! *Smart kids!* Who'da thought?

You many have already discovered one reason I love writing romances.

Yes, I can make up dialogue for the hero that bears no resemblance at all to 'I love you fifty board feet, darling.' One of these days, I'm going to print up--on big, glow-in-the-dark cards--the exact dialogue I want to hear from my engineer husband, then force him to real aloud during--well--you know...

Another reason I love writing romances is because they're Feel Good books.

118

They help women find better, stronger paths in life. Even I have become stronger due to writing spunky heroines. Once, when I was being belittled for what I wrote, I was preparing to be defensive, backing away flinching, when suddenly, in my mind, I screamed at myself, "*Good grief, Renee, your heroine wouldn't be doing this!*"

So I stood up to the woman who was disparaging me and told her what I *really* thought. Interestingly, instead of getting a scowling dressing down, she blinked, stuttered and disappeared into the crowd.

Ah, power! The power of having the courage of our convictions. That's what these books help us find--those of us who read them, as well as those of us who write them. So now you know who I am and why I love what I do. Oh, one other thing--I love you fifty board feet....

TRACY SINCLAIR

I began my career as a photojournalist, writing about murder, muggings and mayhem for the tabloids. Then someone gave me a romance novel to read, and suddenly crime lost its allure. Romance was a lot more fun than robbery. That was fifty three books and over fifteen years ago, and I still love to write romances.

People ask where I get my plots. They come from everywhere, an article in the newspaper, an overheard snatch of conversation in an airport, a broken engagement. Everybody has a story to tell if you're interested enough to listen.

Sometimes I start with, what if. What would happen if a beautiful high fashion model asked her twin sister to take her place for a month? Could they pull it off? And what if the twin fell in love with a gorgeous man who told her he could never forgive a woman who deceived him? That story became both a book and a C.B.S. made for television movie called, *A Change Of Place*.

When I'm not writing, I like to travel. It's fascinating to wander through castles in England, or to ride down the Grand Canal in Venice at night when the lights of the city are reflected in the dark water. I've also ridden a camel in Tangier, played bingo at two a.m. in Barcelona, and had other experiences too numerous to mention.

All of these locales end up in my books, but perhaps the most rewarding thing about travel is meeting the natives. Almost all of them have been friendly and helpful. They might laugh at my accent when I try to speak their language, but it brings us closer together. You really need a friend when you try to make a telephone call in a foreign country, or even if you just want to figure out what all those funny little coins are worth.

When I'm not writing or traveling, I like to give small dinner parties, where good conversation is more stimulating than the wine. I also like to putter around in the garden, even though I can only grow two things, weeds and orchids. And I can't take credit for either. In California where I live, both thrive in spite of well-meaning, but inept, gardeners like myself.

My first love, however, is writing. The characters I create are very real to me. I laugh and cry with them, and share in their happiness when they finally achieve it. I only hope my readers enjoy reading my books as much as I enjoy writing them.

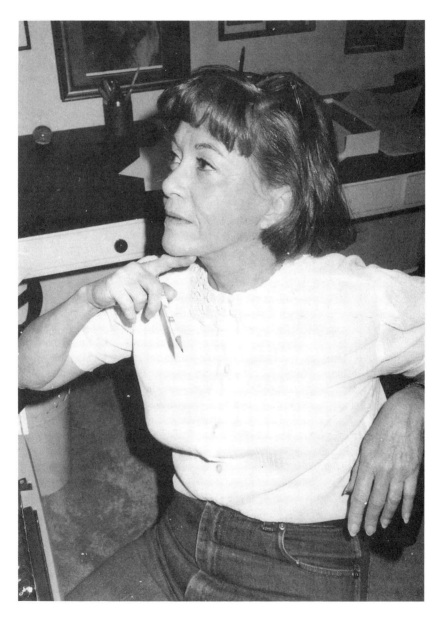

SONIA SIMONE-ROSSNEY

All my life, I've never quite fit in. Even by the standards of the eclectic sixties, my jazzman father and white witch mother were "different." In school, I was the one who wore hot turquoise when everyone else was wearing black, and black when flaming fuschia was *de rigueur*. As a lifelong misfit myself, I'm drawn to oddballs and outsiders. I majored in history, and loved reading about the groups of dreamers and flat-out crazies that have enriched America's history. Some of the most successful were idealistic firebrands who fought to end slavery--the abolitionists.

Scandalous is the story of painfully respectable former tomboy Liberty Brooks and an irascible, irresistible crusader named Zeke Malloy. Zeke is locked in deadly combat with a despicable slave trader, Captain Jack Blodgett, and the last thing he has time for is a distracting nuisance like Liberty. But her indomitable spirit and her gift for being in the wrong place at the wrong time are enough to disarm even the most dedicated grouch. As she leads him from the proper drawing rooms of Boston into the wild, dangerous swamps of Louisiana, poor Zeke finds that the only defense against the irrepressible Liberty is to fall in love.

My stories are driven first and foremost by my characters. Zeke and Liberty have been part of my life for three years, and I've grown to love them, for all their quirks and bad habits. Liberty's so caught up in her quest for an honorable life that she's confused honor with respectability. And Zeke is a thoroughly pigheaded, infuriating man. In fact, he'd be unbearable, if it weren't for the fact that he happens to have a heart the size of Texas. (That's big, folks.) They have a lot to teach one another. Fortunately, they have plenty of time, especially after Liberty gets kidnapped by the nefarious villain. You'll have to read the book to find out the rest!

Right now I'm living in Northern California with my husband, a wonderful man who may be an even bigger misfit than I am. My second book is a historical romantic suspense about another group of idealistic outcasts, the Shakers.

LASS SMALL

How delightful to have this opportunity to chat with you. My mother and teachers all told me that I should write. But I loved drawing, painting, and sculpture. When all our kids were in school, I had the opportunity of going to the School of Fine Arts when we lived in Fort Wayne, Indiana. It was a wonderful experience.

So the surprise came that I was pregnant! People asked, "Were you surprised?" We replied, "No. It was a SHOCK!" All of our children are just great and this tagalong was a delightful child, but he was allergic to everything. I had to again drop out of art school to care for him. And I began to write. I wrote short stories and novels for about seven or eight years.

Marie Burton who was in charge of the neighborhood Book Rack told me if I wanted to sell, I should write romances. And she sold me five. I read three and thought, 'I can do that.' And I sold my first book. The reason I sold it is because of the time.

Simon & Schuster had started the Desire line, which they later sold to Harlequin. Just about all the other American publishing houses joined the rush in a scramble for manuscripts. My first books went to Berkley Jove and that first published book won their award for best of that year! Two books went to Harlequin's Temptation, then Silhouette lured me. I've written for them since.

Apparently my mother and teachers were right in saying I ought to write. It is a pleasure. I laugh and cry over my books. Yeah. How dumb. But I really love them all. I wouldn't send them in if I didn't.

And I've been blessed with superb editors. They leave the text intact. They are kind, gentle and humorous. In the Fall of 1995, my 50th book was published. How amazing.

It is an honor to be included in this book. My writer's love to all readers. Here's to the next book you read--whose ever it is!

AUTHOR PROFILES

DEBORAH SMITH
Jackie Leigh
Jacquelyn Lennox

My ancestors kept General Sherman's feet dry. They didn't have much choice in the matter. The general--that infamous Civil War firebug--commandeered their river ferry during his notorious hike into Atlanta. Maybe that's why I love to write about modern-day southern families who have a dose of romantic conflict in their lives. If *only* we'd tipped the boat...

I began writing short stories in elementary school. My friend Janet was my only reader, and not a very discriminating fan. I gave up fiction when I majored in journalism at the University of Georgia. I spent several years as a reporter and editor for a suburban Atlanta newspaper, then worked for a medical newsletter company, writing clinical articles about back pain (not very romantic!) before I sold my first romance novel (Hurray! No more back pain!) in 1986. My pragmatic, electrical-engineer husband came home from work that day, heard the editor's message on our answering machine and spent the next hour dancing around the living room and calling every relative in both of our family trees. It takes a lot of excitement to make an electrical engineer dance around the living room.

Over the past ten years I published six contemporary series books with the Second Chance At Love line under my Jackie Leigh pen name and one Silhouette Desire under the name Jacquelyn Lennox, before moving to Bantam Books to write fifteen Loveswepts, a historical novel--*The Beloved Woman*--and three big contemporary novels--*Miracle, Blue Willow,* and *Silk and Stone*. My next contemporary will be published in hardcover in 1997. It's the story of Claire Maloney and Roan Sullivan, two people who grow up on opposite sides of the tracks in a small southern town, are separated by tragedy, but find their ways back to each other as adults.

Ten years and twenty-seven novels after trading back pain articles for romance novels, I've won many awards, been blessed with many loyal readers, watched my proud, supportive husband dance around the living room several more times, and almost redeemed my large, southern family, who still keep saying, *If only we'd tipped the boat...*

JOAN SMITH

I was born and grew up in Brockville, a small town in Ontario. After taking a B.A. at Queen's University in English, French and Art, I attended the Ontario College of Education in Toronto. I taught high school French and English in Ontario and Quebec, and English at St. Lawrence College in Cornwall, Ontario. When I married, I moved to Montreal and lived there for seven years, brushing up on my French.

I am still happily married. I have a daughter, two sons and three beautiful granddaughters. I live in Georgetown, near Toronto. My great pleasure, other than family and writing, is reading. I read five or six books a week, everything from the classics to mysteries, biographies and social history. My other hobbies are gardening, cooking and painting. During the winter, I grow exotic plants under grow lights.

I began writing twenty years ago and have published many, many novels. My first works were Regencies, which I still love. An era that could produce such different characters as Byron and Jane Austen provides an intriguing setting for fiction. The restrictions placed on women can lead to some harrowing adventures for headstrong heroines. England was beginning to industrialize, and the merchant class was rising in influence. England was also at war with Napoleon, which adds to the wealth of possible plot lines.

Recently, I have begun writing mysteries. I especially enjoy writing stories with some humor. I write every weekday morning from seven or eight until noon. In the afternoons I garden, swim in the summer, walk and cook. Some years ago I began using a word processor and love it. My goal as a writer is to keep writing as long as I can find readers.

VICKI LEWIS THOMPSON

I've always needed fantasy. As a young child I had an imaginary friend named Goatry and I insisted my mother set a place for him (I'm pretty sure he was a male friend) at the dinner table. I was the sort of kid who created grottos in weeping willows and labyrinths in fields of sugar cane. My bunk bed sailed the Seven Seas in search of treasure.

But I foolishly disregarded the advice of Peter Pan, listened to those older and wiser than me and Grew Up. For many years I buried my need for fantasy in the pursuit of adult goals such as A College Degree and A Decent Living. But my secret fantasy self waited for an opening, and finally it came in the form of romance novels. Whether I discovered them or they discovered me doesn't much matter now. All that matters is that I owe the romance genre a huge debt for putting me in touch with the imaginative child I once was. Romance novels have been my Tinker Bell.

Through writing and reading romance I've discovered a host of friends who also used to create grottos in weeping willows and labyrinths in fields of sugar cane. We talked to each other and swap stories about knights and ladies, pirates and princesses, warriors and captives.

Make no mistake. We all know the difference between fantasy and reality. None of us needs to be locked in a padded room or sent to a kindly yet condescending counselor. Yet oftentimes we're ridiculed for our fascination with the idyllic, the fantastic, the world of make-believe. We are told in no uncertain terms, with Wendy Darling shaking her finger at us, to Grow Up.

I like to think that acceptance of this imaginative side of our natures is the final stage in growing up. I like to think that an impulse toward play is a sign of a healthy, actualized adult. I've noticed that many of my fellow writers and readers of romance are some of the most well-adjusted people I know. Certainly they understand the meaning of fun.

Which brings me to the reason I've stayed at my keyboard for more than thirteen years and thirty books. Money wouldn't keep me here. Fame wouldn't keep me here. Fun, the wellspring of creativity, is the only thing powerful enough to hold me in my chair deadline after deadline.

And fun is the only reason people pick up a romance. The more stressful and obligatory our lives, the more important that impulse becomes. I didn't choose romance writing to help others; I chose it because the creation of love stories gives me great delight. Fortunately, delight is a highly contagious condition, spread easily through the printed word. I'm reminded of that each time a reader tells me they shared my fun.

As I once again creep beneath my willow-tree grotto, or explore the labyrinths of a sugar cane field, I relearn the wonder and renewing force of make-believe. As Goatry and I once more sail an imaginary pirate ship through dangerous seas in search of the greatest treasure of all, a life well and fully lived, I find the courage to stand firmly on the deck with hands on hips and declare with Peter--I won't grow up!

CAROLYN THORNTON

As Southern as grits and magnolias, native Mississippian Carolyn Thornton, has enjoyed multiple roles as a novelist, travel journalist, and photographer. Freelancing for newspapers and magazines (*The New York Daily News, London Free Press, Far East Traveler, Modern Bride,* and *TravelAmerica* to name a few), her journeys to the Far East, Europe, Central and South America, and throughout North America have provided inspiration for her romance novels.

While indulging a love for trains, she met her husband (and fellow train lover), Allan Nation, on a steam train excursion. For a number of years they had both ridden this particular train but kept missing each other. Carolyn would bake cookies for the crew, who would invite her to ride in the engine while Allan was relegated to riding the coaches. The year they met, both happened to be on the train. As Allan explained, "She had been hanging out the window waving all day long and turned to me with a face all sooty from coal smoke and said, 'Isn't this fun?' That's when I knew this was the woman for me." On a later train trip he asked her to marry him. Now they live in the piney woods of Mississippi where they are building a live steam garden railroad.

In addition to writing and photography, Carolyn is a publisher for Green Park Press, the book division of the *Stockman Grass Farmer,* an agricultural magazine where Allan is editor and publisher. They have adjoining offices in their home-- some 100 miles from the company office--where they both spend their mornings writing. Here, the family Bassett Hound makes certain their day includes ample interruptions and opportunities for walks in the woods and around the lake.

Since the publication of *The Search For Mr. Perfect* (an idea suggested by her husband and her favorite book), Carolyn has experimented with longer works of fiction containing elements of romance. She sums up her writing goals by saying, "One day I want to have someone write to me and say, 'You wrote exactly what I felt.' I want to touch people's hearts with my writing--make them laugh and cry."

PAT WARREN

I'm a dreamer, a person whose mind scurries off to a better place as I do mundane chores, or drive somewhere or fix dinner. I've been like this since childhood, going off in my own world, making up characters to people it, fantasizing heroic happenings, envisioning socko endings to each fairy tale. How could someone like that not turn out to be a writer?

I'm also a romantic from the first time I read about Heathcliff and saw Rhett Butler on the big screen. Heroes have changed since then, yet still we romantics continue to fantasize. We stop to see beauty in a rose, to hear joy in a song, to taste a snowflake on the tongue. In my imagination, wondrous things occur, things that rarely happen in real life. So, of course, my first books were romances.

But I have other yearnings. I'm a closet thrill-seeker, one who loves to be frightened without real risk. I conjure up ghosts strolling the hallways when I hear a step creak and I'm horribly fascinated by the criminal mind. What a great place to hide a body, I think as I drive down an overgrown country road. In my mind, I follow Jack the Ripper along his tortured path and wonder what he felt. Naturally, I had to try suspense novels.

From the time I could hold a book, I was a reader. Growing up in a small Ohio town, we lived near a library and I used to lug home armloads of books. The stories I read transported me all over the world, to the deep South, to Victorian England, to the jungles of Africa. Later, I married a travel agent who took me to most of those places. But the world of make-believe drew me like a magnet. I had to gain entry or die trying.

It took awhile. Several years writing for a newspaper, a few short stories, a couple of essays published. Seeing my name in print egged me on. Finally, as our four children grew more self-sufficient, I concentrated on a novel. The first one sold in 1986. May 1996, marked the tenth anniversary of that first sale, and the release of my fortieth book, *Beholden*, a mainstream romantic suspense from

Warner Books.

The nice thing about dreamers is that we get paid for doing what we do best, make up stories that we hope capture the imagination of readers just like us, people who find great pleasure in a world that comes alive only in our minds. There are no rules there, nothing holding us back, no limitations on our creative endeavors. We can stroll among kings and crooks and leprechauns with equal ease. Like Peter Pan, we need never grow up, nor grow old, nor go out of style.

Henry David Thoreau observed that most people "lead lives of quiet desperation." I consider myself a fortunate dreamer for there's nothing I'd rather do than write.

PEGGY WEBB

People are always asking me, "Where do your characters come from?" I wish I could say they came from Alabama or Arkansas or Pennsylvania, but I can't. I have to tell the truth: I don't know. The creative process is wonderfully mysterious, and characters are a part of that mystery.

Much of writing takes place in the unconscious mind. While the conscious mind is collecting and storing information, the unconscious mind is assimilating it, getting ready to release it at odd moments.

Some people call the writing process inspiration: I call it magic.

The magic began when I was child. I grew up in a large family (only two sisters, but dozens of aunts, uncles, and cousins), who elevated the Southern tradition of storytelling to an art. In our small Northeast Mississippi farming community, social life consisted of family reunions, funerals, and singings at the church with dinner on the ground (Although dinner was actually served from picnic tables, it was never described as anything except dinner on the ground). The major source of entertainment at these events was storytelling--even at the funerals, for somehow the stories that were told kept the memory of the deceased alive. There was always a bit of exciting or scandalous or nostalgic family history that got better with the telling.

By the time I was thirteen, I knew I would be a writer. I prepared for my career by listening to all the family stories and reading everything I could get my hands on. I took every opportunity to sneak away from household chores with a book. Much to my delight, I learned that reading was an acceptable excuse for not shelling peas, for Mama was a great lover of books and music. Books became my first love and music my second. The more I practiced the piano, the fewer peas I had to shell. I became an accomplished musician that way.

My dual love affair with books and music has endured through the years. As a child I fell in love with Mark Twain, and later, as I worked on my bachelor's and

136

master's degrees in English, I fell in love with Eudora Welty, John Steinbeck and Tennessee Williams. Now, of course, I'm writing books as well as reading them.

When I hit a brick wall with my writing, I turn to music for inspiration. Sometimes I put on a CD and listen to soaring opera or haunting blues, but usually I sit at my baby grand and make my own music. I like to think that the spirit of the jazz pianist who owned the 1929 piano is sitting in my quiet country home tapping his feet to the rhythm and nodding his head in approval.

JOAN WOLF

One of the questions I am most often asked by readers is what aspect of my life has had the greatest influence on my writing. The answer to that question is rather prosaic, I fear, but there is no doubt in my mind that my academic background is the factor that has had the greatest influence on me as a writer. In the course of earning several degrees in English and Comparative Literature, I necessarily did a tremendous amount of reading, and it is this reading, more than anything else, that has helped me to be the kind of writer that I am.

Anytime an aspiring writer asks me for advice, I always answer, "read good books." To my mind, there is nothing that can equal the value of exposure to fine writing. For it is not just the quantity of reading one does that is important, but the quality. The purity of the prose, the emotional validity of the characters, the resonance of the theme - these are what differentiate a good book from a mediocre one. In the end, after all, there are only so many stories in the world. It is the *way* they are told that makes the difference.

Character is the element of a novel that interests me most, which is why I chose to write romance. Romance is the genre where character reigns supreme. Action by itself and for itself I find supremely dull. It is the deeper motivations of the people who do the actions that interest me, and the thematic structure of a romance novel is perfectly set up for this kind of exploration of character. Most of the world's great novels incorporate a romance precisely because it is through the romantic entanglement that the writer is able to expose the deepest emotions of the novel's characters.

The other aspect of my academic background that has helped me with my writing was the experience I gained teaching creative writing to high school students. In fact, I actually taught writing before I tried to write myself! This might sound odd, but it worked out very well. I found that when I did sit down to try to write that first book, I was helped immeasurably by all the critical skills I had honed in

138

working with my students. You never learn anything so well as when you teach it. Over the course of the few years that I read and made suggestions for changes in the papers of confused teen-age poets and macho high-school football players, I probably learned more than they did about what makes writing work.

SHERRYL WOODS

I am not an easily intimidated human being. As a journalist, I covered presidential campaigns. I interviewed some of Hollywood's biggest and sometimes most difficult actors. As a hospital program coordinator, I worked with top executives and county officials, sometimes telling them what they were doing wrong. My boss declared me the most opinionated woman he'd ever met. I am.

However, faced with a blank piece of paper and the prospect of writing my first romance novel, I suffered a major crisis of confidence. Where were my interviews? Where were the lively quotations from well-informed sources? Where were the detailed descriptions of living, breathing people?

I might still be staring at that first blank page if someone hadn't pointed out, "You get to make it up."

There are still occasions when the journalist in me rebels at making it up, but after more than sixty books, I'm beginning to accept the concept.

I still do interviews. I still do research. My attention is still sparked by an overheard comment, a newspaper article, a TV talk show or a friend's anecdote.

But now my imagination takes over. *What if...* the story were to have taken this twist or that turn *What if...* this woman were to have met that man under those conditions? Romance blooms under the most outrageous circumstances and under the most ordinary.

Romance novels appeal to women not just because of the universal, timelessness of the stories, but because in the very best books we can identify with the heroine. We have experienced her plight, dealt with her tragedies and found the blessings that come with love and family.

The very best books bring recognition of the familiar and remind us of the essence of hope. When our heroines triumph and live happily ever after, we rediscover the possibilities in our own lives.

Readers and friends are often awed by the number of books, the bounty of ideas, but the truth is, the world is filled not just with ideas, but with romance. Sometimes all we need to do to find it is use our imagination.

AUTHOR PSEUDONYM INDEX

AUTHOR PSEUDONYM INDEX

Key: Actual names appear in bold. Pseudonyms appear in italics.

Aallyn, Alysse
Melissa Clark

Abbey, Anne Merton
See Janice Young Brooks, Jean Brooks Janowick

Abbey, Christina
See Nancy & John Sawyer

Abbey, Margaret
See Margaret Elizabeth York

Abbey, Ruth
See Ruth Pattison

Abbot, Laura
See Laura A. Shoffner

Abbott, Alice
See Kathryn Borland, & Helen Ross Speicher

Abbott, Francesca

Abbott, Jane Worth
See Stella Cameron, & Virginia Myers, & Linda Rice

Abbott, Jeanne
See Mary Jean Abbott

Abbott, Mary Jean
Jeanne Abbott, Elizabeth Hewitt

Abbott, Rose Marie

Abbott, Sandra

Abercrombie, Patricia
Patricia Barnes

Abrahamsen, Christine
Cristabel , Kathleen Westcott

Absalom, Stacy

Acaster, Linda

Adair, Cherry

Adams-Manson, Pat
Patricia Camden, Julia Howard

Adams, Alicia

Adams, Audra
See Marie Tracy

Adams, Candice
See Lois Arvin Walker

Adams, Daniel
See Leslie Arlen

Adams, Dorsey
See Dorsey Adams Kelley

Adams, F. Cleve

Adams, Joanna Z.

Adams, Jolene
See Olivia & Ken Harper

Adams, Joyce

Adams, Kasey
See Valerie Whisenand

Adams, Kat

Adams, Kelly

Adams, Melodie

Adams, Pepper
See Debrah Morris, & Pat Shaver

Adams, Tracy
See Lynn Williams

Adams, Tricia

Addison, Jayne

Adelson, Jean
Amanda Mack

Adelson, Sandra

Adkins, Cleo

Adler, Elizabeth

Adrian, Francis

Aeby, Jacquelyn
Jocelyn Carew, Vanessa Gray

Aghadjian, Mollie
Moeth Allison, Mollie Ashton

Ahearn, Pamela Gray
See Pat Ahearn

Ahearn, Pat
Pamela Gray Ahearn, Kate Fairchild, Caitlin Murray, Kate Meriwether

Aid, Frances

Aiken, Candice

Aiken, Ginny

Aiken, Joan

Aimes, Angelica
See Lita Scotti

Ainsley, Alix

Ainsworth, Harriet
Elizabeth Cadell

Key: Actual names appear in bold. Pseudonyms appear in italics.

Key: Actual names appear in bold. Pseudonyms appear in italics.

Allen, Robin
See Robin Lynette Hampton

Allen, Sheila Rosalynd
Sheila O' Hallion

Allen, T.D.

Allis, Sarah

Allison, Carlyle

Allison, Elizabeth
See Alice Harron Orr

Allison, Heather
See Heather Mac Allister

Allison, Moeth
See Mollie Aghadjian

Allison, Penny
See Carol Katz

Allister, Barbara
See Barbara Teer

Allyn, Ashley
See Susan Leslie

Allyn, Jennifer

Allyne, Kerry

Allyson, Kyn
See John M. Kimbro

Alpers, Mary Rose
Sarah Campion

Alred, Margaret
Anne Saunders

Alsobrook, Rosalyn
Gina Delaney, Jalynn Friends

Alvarez, Gloria

Amarillas, Susan

Amerski, Beth
Elizabeth Anderson, Beth Stanley

Ames, Jennifer
See Mary D. Warre

Ames, Laurel
See Barbara J. Miller

Ames, Leslie
See Dan Ross

Ames, Winter
See Phyllis Taylor Pianka

Amis, Breton
See Ray Bentinck

Amman, Marilyn M.
Marilyn Medlock, Amanda Stevens

Amo, Gary

Anders, Donna

Andersen, Catherine

Andersen, Jan

Andersen, Linda

Andersen, Lynda K.

Andersen, Susan

Anderson, Adeline Catherine
Catherine Anderson

Anderson, Ann

Anderson, Blaine

Anderson, Caroline

Anderson, Catherine
See Adeline Catherine Anderson

Anderson, Dana
Laura Pender

Anderson, Debra Mc Carthy
Debra Carroll, Carol Thomas, Rachel Vincer

Anderson, Elizabeth
See Beth Amerski

Anderson, Gail

Anderson, Jan

Anderson, Lee

Anderson, Marlene J.
Joan Lancaster

Anderson, Oliver

Anderson, Rachel
Rachel Bradby

Anderson, Roberta
Fern Michaels

Anderson, Shirley

Anderson, Susan M.
Lindsay Randall

Anderson, Virginia
Megan Ashe

Key: Actual names appear in bold. Pseudonyms appear in italics.

Andersson, Nina
Jane Archer, Asa Drake, Nina Romberg

Andre, Alix

Andresen, Julie Tetel
Julie Tetel, Julia Joyce

Andrew, Barbara
Pam Rock

Andrews, Alex
Caroline Charles, Cathy Christopher, Mary Christopher, Mary Mackie, Susan Stevens

Andrews, Beth

Andrews, Carolyn

Andrews, Elizabeth

Andrews, Felicia
See Charles L. Grant

Andrews, Jo

Andrews, Kristi
See Dorothy Renko

Andrews, Lucilla
Lucilla Crichton, Diana Gordon, Joanna Marcus

Andrews, Nicola
See Orania Papazoglou

Andrews, Roy Chapman

Andrews, Susan

Andrews, Sylvia

Anglin, Joyce

Ankrum, Barbara

Annabella,
See Charlotte Lowe

Annadale, Barbara
See Jean Bowden

Ansle, Dorothy P.
Margaret Campbell Barnes, Laura Conway, Hebe Elsna, Vicky Lancaster, Lyndon Snow

Anston, Linell
See Linell Evanston Nemeth

Anthony, Barbara
See Antonia Barber

Anthony, Diana
See Diane Antonio

Anthony, Evelyn

Anthony, Laura

Anthony, Page
See Page & Anthony Traynor

Antonio, Diane
Diana Anthony, Diana Lyndon

Anzelon, Robyn

Applegate, Katherine
Katherine Kendall

Arbor, Jane

Arch, E. L.
See Rachel Cosgrove Payes

Archer, Catherine

Archer, Jane
See Nina Andersson

Archery, Helen
See Helen Argyris

Arden, Jenny

Argers, Helen

Argo, Ellen
See Ellen Argo Johnson

Argyris, Helen
Helen Archery

Arkham, Candice
See Alice Ramirez

Arlen, Leslie
Daniel Adams, Robin Cade, Peter Grange, Mark Logan, Simon Mc Kay, Christopher Nicole, Christina Nicholson, Alison York, Andrew York

Armitage, Aileen
See Aileen Quigley

Armstrong, Charlotte
See Jo Valentine

Armstrong, Evelyn Stuart

Armstrong, John D.

Armstrong, Juliet

Armstrong, Lindsay

Armstrong, Thomas
Noreen O' Neill

Armstrong, Tilly
Kate Alexander, Tania Langley

Arness, Christine

AUTHOR PSEUDONYM INDEX

Key: Actual names appear in bold. Pseudonyms appear in italics.

Arnett, Caroline
See Lois Cole Taylor

Arnold, Elliot

Arnold, Judith
See Barbara Keiler

Arnold, Margo
See Petronella Cook

Arnout, Susan

Arnston, Harrison

Arthur, Katherine
See Barbara Eriksen

Arthur, Lee
See Lee & Arthur Browning

Arthur, William
See William Neubauer

Aruile, Cheryl
Sarah Temple

Arvonen, Helen
Margaret Worth

Ascani, Sparky

Ash, Kathleen
See Quenna Tilbury

Ash, Melissa
See June E. Casey

Ash, Pauline
See Quenna Tilbury

Ash, Rosalie

Ash, Sally

Ashby, Juliet
See Louise Lee Outlaw

Ashby, Kay

Ashcroft, Laura
Ashland Price, Laura Price, Janice Carlson

Ashe, Eugenia

Ashe, Megan
See Virginia Anderson

Ashe, Susan
See Marcia Wayne

Ashfield, Helen
See Pamela Bennetts

Ashford, Jane
See Jane Le Compte

Ashley, Amanda
See Madeline Baker

Ashley, Faye
Ashley Summers

Ashley, Jacqueline
See Jacqueline Casto

Ashley, Mellyora

Ashley, Rebecca
See Lois Arvin Walker

Ashley, Sarah

Ashley, Suzanne
See Susan Brown

Ashley, Veronica

Ashmore, April

Ashton, Andrea

Ashton, Ann
See John M. Kimbro

Ashton, Elizabeth
Rosemary Carter

Ashton, Fiona

Ashton, Kate
See Margaret Ball

Ashton, Katherine
See Katherine Talbot

Ashton, Laura

Ashton, Lorayne

Ashton, Mollie
See Mollie Aghadjian

Ashton, Sharon
See Helen Van Slyke

Ashton, Violet

Asquith, Nan
See Nancy Pattison

Astin, Cynthia

Astley, Juliet
See Peter Curtis

Astraham, Syrie Ann
Syrie James

Atkins, Jane
Sarah Keene

Attalla, Kathryn

Key: Actual names appear in bold. Pseudonyms appear in italics.

Atwood, Kathryn
See Kathy Ptacek

Aubert, Rosemary
Lucy Snow

August, Elizabeth
See Bettie Wilhite

Aumente, Joy
Joy Gardner, Joy Darlington

Austell, Diane

Austen, Carrie
See Janice Boies

Austen, Charlotte
See Adele Leone

Austin, Brett
See Will Watson

Austin, Cassandra

Austin, Deborah
Jacqueline Marshall

Austin, Marilyn
Lynne Loring

Austin, Sarah

Austin, Stephanie

Avallone, Micahel Angelo
Nick Carton, Troy Conway, Priscilla Dalton,
Mark Dane, Jean-Anne De Pre, Steve Michaels,
Dorothea Nile, Edwina Noone, Vance Stanton,
Sidney Stuart

Avery, Anne
See Anne Holmberg

Avery, Joan

Avery, Lynn
See Lois Cole Taylor

Avery, Ruby D.
Vicki Page

Awbrey, Elizabeth
See Elizabeth Awbrey Beach

Ayers, Rose

Ayers, Ruby M.

Aylesford, Susan

Ayre, Jessica

Ayres, Janet

Bacarr, Jina

Bacher, June Masters

Backus, Carol
Suzanne Barclay

Bacon, Cheryl
Lynnette Kent

Bacon, Nancy

Baczewski, Janice
Kay Barlett, Janice Kay Johnson, Kay Kirby,
Janice Stevens

Bade, Tom
Robin St. Thomas

Badger, Rosemary

Badgley, Anne V.

Baer, Judy
Judy Kaye

Baer, Tracy

Baggett, Nancy
Amanda Lee

Bagnara, Elsie Poe
Norah Hess

Bagnet, Joan

Bagwell, Stella

Bailey-Pratt, Cynthia
Lydia Browne

Bailey, Debbie

Bailey, Elizabeth

Bair, Ann

Baird, Jacqueline

Baird, Jaqui

Baker, Allison
See Alice Crumbaker

Baker, Anne
Nancy Cross

Baker, Betty
Elizabeth Renier

Baker, Christine
Christine West

Baker, Darlene
Heather Lang

Baker, Fran
Judith Baker, Cathlyn Mc Coy

AUTHOR PSEUDONYM INDEX

Key: Actual names appear in bold. Pseudonyms appear in italics.

Baker, Judith
  See Fran Baker, & Judith Noble

Baker, Lucinda

Baker, Madeline
  Amanda Ashley

Baker, Maggie

Baker, Marceil
  Marcia Miller

Baker, Marjorie
  Alison Mc Master

Baker, Mary Gladys
  Sheila Stuart

Baker, Sarah

Bakker, Kit

Baldwin, Ann

Baldwin, Anne

Baldwin, Cathryn
  See Cathryn La Dame

Baldwin, Cynthia

Baldwin, Faith
  See Faith Cuthrell

Baldwin, Rebecca
  Helen Chappell

Bale, Karen A.

Balkey, Rita
  See Rita Balkey Oleyar

Ball, Donna
  Leigh Bristol, Donna Carlisle, Rebecca Flanders,
  Taylor Brady

Ball, Margaret
  Kate Ashton, Kathleen Fraser, Catherine Lyndell

Balnshard, Audrey

Balogh, Mary

Balsee, Joan

Bamberger, Helen
  Helen Berger

Bamford, Susan

Bancroft, Iris May
  See Ingrid Nielson

Bane, Diana

Banis, V. J.
  Jan Alexander, Lynn Benedict, Elizabeth
  Monterey

Banks, Barbara

Banks, Leanne

Bannister, Patricia
  Gwyneth Moore, Patricia Veryan

Barber, Antonia
  Barbara Anthony

Barber, Brenda H.
  Brenda Hiatt

Barber, Lenora
  Janet Wing

Barbieri, Elaine
  Elaine Rome

Barbour, Anne
  See Barbara Yirka

Barbour, Jo Anne

Barclay, Alisha

Barclay, Ann
  See Mary D. Warre

Barclay, Suzanne
  See Carol Backus

Barclay, Vera C.
  Margaret Beech

Baricklow, Patti
  Patricia Burroughs

Barker, Becky

Barker, Margaret

Barker, Megan
  Ivor Drummond, Rosalind Erskine, Roger
  Longrigg

Barkin, Jill
  See Susan Johnson

Barkley, Jessica
  See Cori Deyoe

Barlett, Kay
  See Janice Baczewski, & Norma Tadlock

Barlett, Marie
  Rowena Lee, Valerie Rift

Barletta, Patricia
  Amy Christopher

AUTHOR PSEUDONYM INDEX

Key: Actual names appear in bold. Pseudonyms appear in italics.

Barlow, Linda

Barnard, Judith
Judith Michael

Barnes, Elizabeth

Barnes, Margaret Campbell
See Dorothy P. Ansle

Barnes, Patricia
See Patricia Abercrombie

Barnett, Jill

Barnett, Loraine

Barr, Elisabeth
See Irene Edwards

Barraclough, June

Barret, Helen
Justin Channing

Barrett, Elizabeth
Christine Collins, Cara Mc Lean

Barrett, Jean
See Lee Rogers, Robert Lee Rogers

Barrett, Karen Lawton

Barrett, Max
Maye Barrett

Barrett, Maye
See Max Barrett

Barrie, Monica
See David Wind

Barrie, Susan
See Ida Pollock

Barroll, Clare

Barron, Ann Forman
Annabel Erwin

Barron, Elizabeth
See Susan B. Twaddle

Barry, Andrea
See Annette Bartle

Barry, Eileen
See Quenna Tilbury

Barry, Jocelyn
See Jean Bowden

Barry, Joe

Barshon, Brenda Braxton

Bartell, Linda Lang

Bartholomew, Barbara

Bartholomew, Dale

Bartholomew, Jean
Patricia Beatty

Bartle, Annette
Andrea Barry

Bartlett, Janice

Bartlett, Kay

Bartlett, Lynn M.

Bartlett, Marie
See Valerie Rift

Bartlett, Stephanie

Barton, Beverly

Bashore, Vickie
Victoria Bruce

Basile, Gloria
Michaela Morgan

Basset, Aubriel

Bassett, Marjorie

Bassett, Sara Ware

Bates, Jenny
See Maura Seger

Batten-Carew, Elizabeth
Elizabeth Carew

Battyanyi-Petose, Laura
Nicole Grey

Battye, Gladys
Margaret Lynn

Bauer, Marsha

Bauer, Pamela
See Pamela Muelbauer

Bauling, Jayne

Bauman, Lauren

Baumann, Margaret
See Marguerite Lees

Baume, Eric

Baumgardner, Cathie
Cathie Linz

AUTHOR PSEUDONYM INDEX

Key: Actual names appear in bold. Pseudonyms appear in italics.

Baumgarten, Sylvia
Ena Halliday, Sylvia Halliday, Louisa Rawlings

Baumgartner, Lisa
Alicia Scott

Baxter, Elizabeth
Elizabeth Holland

Baxter, Judy
See June Haydon, Judith Simpson

Baxter, Mary Lynn

Baxter, Olive
Helen Eastwood, Fay Ramsay

Bayless, Anne Douglas
Anne Douglas

Beach, Elizabeth Awbrey
Elizabeth Awbrey, Elizabeth Stuart

Beach, Rex

Bear, Joan E.
Elizabeth Mayhew

Beard, Julie

Beatty, Patricia
Jean Bartholomew

Beaty, Betty

Beauchamp, Kathleen
Katherine Mansfield

Beauchamp, Margery

Beaudry, Antoinette

Beaufort, Jane
See Ida Pollock

Beaumann, Sally
Vanessa James

Beaumont, Anne
See Rosina Pyatt

Beaumont, Helen
See Jill Eckersley

Beaumont, Lisa

Beaumont, Marie

Beaumont, Nina
See Nina Gettler

Bechko, Peggy

Beck, K. K.

Beckford, Brania

Beckman, Patti
See Patti & Charles Boeckman

Beckwith, Lillian
See Lillian Comber

Becnel, Rexanne

Bedford, Debbie
See Deborah Lynn Bedford

Bedford, Deborah Lynn
Debbie Bedford

Beebe, Elswyth
Elswyth Thane

Beech, Jane

Beech, Margaret
See Vera C. Barclay

Bele, Karen A.

Bell, Anthea

Bell, Donna

Bell, Georgianna

Bell, Marguerite

Belle, Pamela

Bellem, Robert Leslie

Belmont, Kate
See Mary Jo Territo

Belmont, Kathryn
See Mary Jo Territo

Benedict, Barbara

Benedict, Lynn
See V. J. Banis

Benedict, Rachel
Jane Beverley, Doreen Stephens, Kay Stephens

Benet, Deborah
See Elaine Camp

Benjamin, Linda
See Linda H. Wallerich

Benjamin, Nikki
See Barbara Vosbein

Bennett, Barbara

Bennett, Cherie

Bennett, Christine
See William Neubauer

Bennett, Clarissa

Key: Actual names appear in bold. Pseudonyms appear in italics.

Bennett, Connie
  See Constance Bennett

Bennett, Constance
  Connie Bennett

Bennett, Corintha
  See Carolyn Wheat

Bennett, Dorothy
  Laura Kingsley

Bennett, Elizabeth

Bennett, Emma
  See Emma Merritt

Bennett, Janice
  See Eilleen Witton

Bennett, Laura Gilmou

Bennett, Rebecca
  See Ruby Frankel

Bennetts, Pamela
  Helen Ashfield, Margaret James

Bensen, Ronald
  Julia Thatcher

Bension, Margaret
  Maggie Shayne

Benson, Angela

Benson, Anne
  See Anne Kolaczak

Bentch, Kitty
  Dani Criss

Bentinck, Ray
  Breton Amis, Rayleigh Best, Leigh Haddow,
  Terrence Hughes, Desmond Roberts

Bentley, Barbara
  See Barbara B. Diamond

Bentley, Jayne
  See Jayne Ann Krentz

Bentley, Patricia
  See Julie Ellis

Bentley, Pauline

Benton, Darla
  Jessica Dare, Joanna Leslie

Benton, Elsie

Bercier, Leila

Berckman, Evelyn

Berensci, Susan

Berenson, Laurien
  Laurien Blair

Beresford, Elisabeth

Berg, M.D., Louis

Berg, Patti

Bergen, Fran
  See Frances De Talaver Berger

Berger, Daranna
  Caitlin Cross

Berger, Frances De Talaver
  Fran Bergen, Frances Flores

Berger, Helen
  See Helen Bamberger

Berger, Nomi
  Alyssa Welles

Bergstrom, Kay
  Cassie Miles

Bergstrom, Louise

Berk, Ariel
  See Barbara Keiler

Berland, Nancy
  Nancy Landon

Bernadette, Ann
  See D. H. Gadzak, & Karen Ray

Bernard, Dorothy Ann
  See Dorothy Weller

Berne, Karin
  See Sue Burrell, Michaela Karni

Berrisford, Mary
  Christianna Brand, Mary Lewis, China
  Thompson

Bertrand, Diane Gonzales

Best, Carol Ann
  See Marcia Wayne

Best, Rayleigh
  See Ray Bentinck

Betteridge, Anne
  See Margaret Neuman

Bevan, Gloria

Bevarly, Elizabeth

Key: Actual names appear in bold. Pseudonyms appear in italics.

Beverley, Jane
See Rachel Benedict

Beverly, Jo

Beyers, Cordia

Bianchi, Jacqui
Teresa Denys

Bianchin, Helen

Bickmore, Barbara

Bicos, Olga

Bidwell, J. S.
See Colleen Christie

Bidwell, Marjory
Mary Ann Gibbs

Bieber, Janet
Janet Joyce, Jenna Lee Joyce

Bierce, Jane

Bigg, Patricia N.
See Patricia Ainsworth

Biggs, Cheryl
Cheryln Jac

Billings, Buck

Bils, Sharon & Robert
Sarah Edwards

Bingham, Charlotte

Bingham, Lisa

Biondi, Diana
Diana Guest

Bird, Beverly
See Beverly Helland

Bird, Sara
Tory Cates

Birmingham, Sonya

Bishop, Carly
See Cheryl Mc Gonigle

Bishop, Cassandra
See Robin Latham

Bishop, Claudia
See Jane Feather

Bishop, Jamison
See Noreen Brownlie

Bishop, Leslie
Robin Tolivar

Bishop, Mary

Bishop, Natalie
See Nancy Bush

Bishop, Sandra

Bishop, Sheila

Bissell, Elaine
Whitney Faulkner

Bittner, Roseanne
Jessie Belle Sage

Black, Amanda

Black, Cheryl

Black, Dorothy
Kitty Black

Black, Hermina

Black, Irene Loyd

Black, Jackie
See Jacqueline Casto

Black, Kitty
See Dorothy Black

Black, Laura

Black, Maureen
See Maureen Peters

Black, Veronica
See Maureen Peters

Blackburn, Claire
See Linda C. Jacobs

Blackman, Lynne

Blackmon, Laura

Blackmore, Jane

Blackstock, Terri
Terri Herrington, Tracy Hughes

Blackstone, Alexandra

Blackstone, Charity
See Ursula Torday

Blacktree, Barbara
Barbara Coultry

Blackwell, Judith
See Judith Blackwell Myers

Key: Actual names appear in bold. Pseudonyms appear in italics.

Blair, Alison
See Janice Boies

Blair, Alma

Blair, Catherine

Blair, Clifford

Blair, Cynthia

Blair, Jennifer
See Adeline Mc Elfresh

Blair, Joan

Blair, Kathryn - #1
See Rosaline Brett, & Karen Blair Parker

Blair, Kathryn - #2
See Mary Kathryn Schamehorn

Blair, Laurien
See Laurien Berenson

Blair, Leona

Blaisdell, Anne
See Elizabeth Linigton

Blake, Andrea
See Anne Wilson

Blake, Antonia
See Mildred Juskevice

Blake, Jennifer
See Patricia Maxwell

Blake, Jillian

Blake, Karen

Blake, Laurel
See Elaine Fowler Palencia

Blake, Margaret Glaiser

Blake, Sally
See Jean Saunders

Blake, Stephanie
See Jack Pearl

Blake, Vanessa
See May Brown

Blake, Veronica

Blakelee, Alexandra
See Alexandra Hine

Blanchard, Angela Oritz
Rebecca Blanchard

Blanchard, Audrey

Blanchard, Rebecca
See Angela Oritz Blanchard

Blanford, Virginia
Sarah Crewe

Blayne, Diana
See Susan Kyle

Blayne, Sara

Blayney, Mary

Blinke, Katinka

Block, Nancy

Blocklinger, Betty
Jeanne Bowman, Peggy O' More

Blood, Marje
See Paige Mc Kenzie

Bloom, Jill

Bloom, Ursula
Sheila Burns, Mary Essex, Rachel Harvey,
Ursula Harvey, Deborah Mann, Lozania Prole

Blundell, Judith
Jude O' Neill

Blundell, V. R.
Kathleen Nixon

Blyth, Juliet
See Stella Riley

Blythe, Leonora
See Leonora Burton

Blythe, Megan
See Michalann Perry

Boatner, Patricia

Bobander, Jane

Bocardo, Claire

Bockoven, Georgia

Bode, Margo

Bodine, Sherill Lynn
Lynn Leslie, Leslie Lynn

Boeckman, C. V.

Boeckman, Patti & Charles
Patti Beckman

Boese, Dawn C.
Dawn Carroll

Bogard, Dale

AUTHOR PSEUDONYM INDEX

Key: Actual names appear in bold. Pseudonyms appear in italics.

Bogart, William

Bogolin, Carol

Boies, Janice
Carrie Austen, Alison Blair, Jan Bradford

Bolander, Judith

Bolt, Maxine

Bolton, Elizabeth
Catherine Chambers, Kate Chambers, Pamela Dryden, Lavinia Harris, Norma Johnston, Adrian Roberts, Nicole St. John

Bolton, Muriel Ray

Bonander, Jane

Bond-Smith, Sylvia

Bond, Evelyn
See Morris Herschman

Bond, Rebecca
See Rebecca Czuleger

Bonds, Parris Afton

Bonham, Barbara
See Sara North (Series)

Bonner, Elizabeth

Boon, August
Clare Breton-Smith, Elinor Caldwell, Claire Vernon, Hilary Wilde

Booth, Rosemary
Frances Murray

Borden, Leigh

Bordill, Judith

Borland, Kathryn
Alice Abbott

Borodin, George

Bosler, Colleen
Colleen Quinn

Bosna, Valerie
Valerie King, Sarah Montrose

Bostwick, Angela
Angela Welles

Boswell, Barbara
Betsy Osborne

Boucher, Rita

Boulet, Ada
Ada John

Bourne, Caroline

Bourne, Hester
Molly Troke

Bourne, Joanne Watkins

Bowden, Jean
Barbara Annadale, Jocelyn Barry, Avon Curry, Belinda Dell

Bowden, Susan
See Susan B. Twaddle

Bowe, Kate
See Mary Ann Taylor

Bowen, Alice
Alyce Bowen

Bowen, Alyce
See Alice Bowen

Bowen, Charlene

Bowen, Judith
See Judy E Corser

Bowen, Marjorie
Hilary Lang

Bowers, Terrell L.

Bowersock, Melissa

Bowes, Florence

Bowman, Jeanne
See Betty Blocklinger

Bowman, John Clark

Bowring, Mary

Boyard, Alexis

Boyd, Edmond
Esther Boyd

Boyd, Elizabeth
See Isabel Mac Call

Boyd, Esther
See Edmond Boyd

Boyd, Prudence
Lisette Garland, Nora Gibbs, Noelle Ireland, Lynne Merrill, Claire Ritchie, Dallas Romaine, Nina Shayne, Heather Wayne, Sara Whittingham

Boyer, Elizabeth

AUTHOR PSEUDONYM INDEX

Key: Actual names appear in bold. Pseudonyms appear in italics.

Boyle, Ann
Audrey Brent, Ann Bryan

Boynton, Judy

Bracale, Carla
Carla Cassidy

Bracho, Mary
Ana Seymour

Bradby, Rachel
See Rachel Anderson

Brader, Norma

Bradewyne, Rebecca

Bradford, Barbara Taylor
Sally Bradford, Barbara Siddon

Bradford, Debbie

Bradford, Jan
See Janice Boies

Bradford, Lily

Bradford, Sally
See Barbara Bradford, Sally Siddon

Bradford, Susannah

Bradley, Blythe

Bradley, Kate
See Kathleen Bryant

Bradley, Marion Zimmer

Bradley, Muriel

Bradley, Ramona

Bradshaw, Emily
See Emily Krokosz

Bradstreet, Valerie
See Mary Linn Roby

Brady, Taylor
See Donna Ball, & Shannon Harper

Braeme, Charlotte N.
Bertha M. Clay

Bramsch, Joan

Bramwell, Charlotte
See John M. Kimbro

Brand, Christianna
See Mary Berrisford

Brand, Debra
Suzanne Rand

Brand, Susan

Brandewyne, Rebecca
See Mary Rebecca Wadsworth Broc

Brandon, Alicia
See Virginia Myers

Brandon, Beatrice
See Robert W. Krepps

Brandon, Faith

Brandon, Jo Anna
See Olivia & Ken Harper

Brandon, Joyce

Brandon, Michelle
See Virginia Brown

Brandon, Sheila
See Claire Rayner

Brandon, William

Brandt, Cate

Brant, Kylie

Brantley, Paige

Brauer, Deanna
Dana Daniels, Dena Rhee

Braun, Matthew
Kandi Brooks

Braunstein, Binnie Syril
Binnie Syril

Braxton-Barshon, Brenna

Brayfield, Celia

Bremer, Joanne
Joellyn Carroll

Brendan, Mary

Brennan, Jan

Brennan, Lilla
See Alexandra Hine

Brennan, Wendy
Emma Darcy

Brent, Audrey
See Ann Boyle

Brent, Casey

Brent, Iris
See Ingrid Nielson

Brent, Madeleine

AUTHOR PSEUDONYM INDEX

Key: Actual names appear in bold. Pseudonyms appear in italics.

Breton-Smith, Clare
See August Boon

Brett, Austin
See Will Watson

Brett, Barbara

Brett, Katheryn
See Peg Robarchek

Brett, Rosalind
Kathryn Blair, Celine Conway

Bretton, Barbara

Brew, Cathleen

Brewster, Martha

Brewster, Paulette
Melody Morgan

Brian, Marilyn
See Jillian Dagg

Bride, Nadja
See Joi Nobisso

Bridge, Susan
Elizabeth Carey

Brier, Margaret

Bright, Elizabeth
See Robert Liston

Bright, Laurey
See Daphne De Jong

Brindel, June Rachuy

Brindley, Louise

Brisco, Gwen

Brisco, Patty
See Patricia Matthews

Brisken, Jacqueline

Bristol, Joanne

Bristol, Leigh
See Donna Ball, & Shannon Harper

Britt, Deborah
Brittany Colburn

Britt, Katrina
See Ethel Connell

Britton,

Britton, Vickie

Broadrick, Annette

Broc, Mary Rebecca Wadswort
Rebecca Brandewyne

Brocato, Kathryn

Brockman, Suzanne

Brockway, Connie

Brodeen, Melody

Brodeur, Diane & Greg
Diane Carey, Lydia Gregory

Brodnax, Elizabeth

Brody, Judith

Bromige, Iris
Ann Tracey

Brondos, Sharon

Bronson, Anita

Bronson, Antoinette
Maureen Bronson

Bronson, Maureen
See Antoinette Bronson, Maureen Woodstock

Bronte, Louisa
See Janet Louise Roberts

Brooke, Alice

Brooke, Anabel

Brookes, Beth
See Eileen Naumann

Brooks, Anne Tedlock
Ann Carter

Brooks, Betty

Brooks, Caroline

Brooks, Francesca
See Lynn Alden Kendall

Brooks, Helen

Brooks, Janet
See Janice Young Brooks, Jean Brooks Janowick

Brooks, Janice Young
Ann Merton Abbey, Janet Brooks, Jill Churchill, Valerie Vayle

Brooks, Kandi
See Matthew Braun

Brooks, Lynne

Brooks, Madeline

AUTHOR PSEUDONYM INDEX

Key: Actual names appear in bold. Pseudonyms appear in italics.

Broome, Susannah
  See Nancy Pattison

Brouder, Howard
  Melissa Hepburne, Lisa Lenore

Brouse, Barbara
  Araby Scott, Abra Taylor

Brown, Alyce

Brown, Amy Belding

Brown, Beth

Brown, Diana

Brown, Dora
  Dana Lindsey

Brown, Dr. Alan

Brown, Erin J.

Brown, Joy

Brown, Kitt
  See Aola Vadergriff

Brown, Leslie

Brown, Lisa G.
  Dana Warren Smith

Brown, Lois A.
  Jessica Elliot

Brown, Mandy
  See May Brown

Brown, May
  Vanessa Blake, Mandy Brown

Brown, Micki
  See Virginia Brown

Brown, Morna
  See Elizabeth Ferrars

Brown, Sandra
  Laura Jordan, Rachel Ryan, Erin St. Claire

Brown, Susan
  Suzanne Ashley

Brown, Virginia
  Micki Brown, Michelle Brandon, Virginia Lynn

Browne, Lizbie

Browne, Lydia
  See Cynthia Bailey-Pratt

Browning, Amanda

Browning, Diana
  See Florence Hershman

Browning, Dixie
  See Zoe Dozier

Browning, Lee & Arthur
  Lee Arthur

Browning, Pamela
  Pam Ketter, Melanie Rowe

Brownleigh, Eleanora
  See Rhonda Cohen

Brownley, Margaret
  Megan Brownley, Kate Damon

Brownley, Megan
  See Margaret Brownley

Brownlie, Noreen
  Jamisan Whitney, Jamison Bishop

Brubaker, Carolyn
  Carolyn Lampman

Bruce-Thomas, Carol
  Debra Carroll

Bruce, Victoria
  See Vickie Bashore

Brucker, Meredith
  Meredith Kingston, Meredith Lindley

Bruff, Nancy
  Nancy Gardner

Bruyere, Toni Marsh

Bryan, Ann
  See Ann Boyle

Bryan, Beth
  See Viola E. Long

Bryan, Beverley
  See Beverley Katz Rosenbaum

Bryan, Caitlin Adams

Bryan, Deborah
  See Deborah Bryson, & Joyce Porter

Bryan, Eileen
  See Ruth Alana Smith

Bryan, Jessica

Bryant, Arthur Herbert

Bryant, Erika
  See Anne Kolaczak

AUTHOR PSEUDONYM INDEX

Key: Actual names appear in bold. Pseudonyms appear in italics.

Bryant, Kathleen
See Kate Bradley

Bryant, La Ree

Bryant, Lynn Marie

Bryce, Debbie

Bryer, Judy
Brenna Drummond, Allison Lawrence, Eve O'
Brien

Bryson, Deborah
Deborah Bryan, Deborah Joyce

Buchan, Kate

Buchan, Stuart
Pamela Foxe, Becky Stuart

Buchanan, Laura
See Florence King

Bucheister, Patt
Patt Parrish

Buck, Carole
See Carole Buckland

Buck, Gayle

Buckholder, Marta
Marta Lloyd

Buckholtz, Eileen
Samantha Chase, Alyssa Howard, Amanda Lee,
Rebecca York

Buckingham, Nancy
See Nancy & John Sawyer

Buckland, Carole
Carole Buck

Budd, Carol

Bulk, Nancy Hardwood
Dee Holmes

Bull, Lois

Bullard, Ann Elizabeth
Casey Stuart

Bullinger, Maureen
Samantha Quinn

Bulock, Lynn

Burak, Linda
Alicia Meadowes

Burchell, Mary
See Ida Cook

Burford, Lolah

Burgess, Barbara

Burgess, Joanna
See Caroline Fireside

Burgess, Justine
Joanna Harris

Burgess, Mallory
See Mary Sandra Hingston

Burghley, Rose
See Ida Pollock

Burk, Ariel

Burke, Cinnamon
See Phoebe Conn Ingwalson

Burke, Diana
See Sue Burrell, Michaela Karni

Burke, Lydia

Burkhardt, Mary

Burn, Helen Jean

Burnes, Caroline
See Carolyn Haines

Burns, Carol
Samantha Holder

Burns, Patricia

Burns, Sheila
See Ursula Bloom

Burr, Kathaleen

Burrell, Sue
Karin Berne, Dianna Burke

Burroughs, Patricia
See Patti Baricklow

Burrows, Marjorie

Burtis, Thomas

Burton, Becky
Rebecca Winter

Burton, Katherine

Burton, Kristen
Susanna Christie

Burton, Leonora
Leonora Blythe

Burton, Rebecca
Rebecca Winters

AUTHOR PSEUDONYM INDEX

Key: Actual names appear in bold. Pseudonyms appear in italics.

Busbee, Shirlee

Bush, Christine
See Christine Matters

Bush, Kim
Kimberleigh Caitlin, Kimberly Cates

Bush, Nancy
Natalie Bishop

Bushyhead, Anne
Nicole Jordan

Butler, Gwendoline
Jennie Melville

Butler, Mary E.

Butler, Penelope

Butler, Rae
See Raymond Ragan Butler

Butler, Raymond Ragan
Rae Butler

Butler, Rose

Butterworth, William E.
Eden Hughes

Buxton, Anne
Anne Maybury, Katherine Troy

Byers, Cordia

Byfield, Sue

Byington, Deborah

Byington, Kaa
Sybil Le Grand, Octavia Street

Byrne, Beverly

Cade, Robin
See Leslie Arlen

Cadell, Elizabeth
See Harriet Ainsworth

Cail, Carol
See Kara Galloway

Caille, Julie

Caimi, Gina

Caine, Leslie

Caine, Rebecca
See Margery Woods

Caird, Janet

Caitlin, Kimberleigh
See Kim Bush

Caitlin, Miranda

Cajio, Linda

Caldwell-Wilson, Marolyn

Caldwell, Anne
See Jean Anne Caldwell

Caldwell, Elinor
See August Boon

Caldwell, Jean Anne
Anne Caldwell

Caldwell, Pamela

Caldwell, Taylor
See Max Renier

Callaghan, Margaret

Callahan, Elizabeth

Callan, Michaila

Callander, Shirley

Callender, Joan

Calloway, Jo

Calvin, June

Camden, Patricia
See Pat Adams-Manson

Cameron, Ann

Cameron, Barbara

Cameron, Blair
See Rosaline Brett, & Karen Blair Parker

Cameron, Caryn
See Karen Harper

Cameron, Charla
See Gloria Dale Skinner

Cameron, Claire

Cameron, Doug

Cameron, Elizabeth Jane
Jane Duncan

Cameron, Gay
See Gay Snell

Cameron, June
See Sharon Mac Iver

AUTHOR PSEUDONYM INDEX

Key: Actual names appear in bold. Pseudonyms appear in italics.

AUTHOR PSEUDONYM INDEX

Key: Actual names appear in bold. Pseudonyms appear in italics.

Carey, Verna
  Suzanne Carey

Carfax, Catherine

Carl, Lillian

Carleen, Sally

Carles, Riva
  See Irving Greenfield

Carleton, Cathleen
  See Kaye Wilson Klem

Carlisle, Amanda

Carlisle, Carris

Carlisle, Donna
  See Donna Ball, & Shannon Harper

Carlisle, Sara

Carlisle, Sarah

Carlson, Cathleen
  Kaye Wilson Kelm

Carlson, Elizabeth

Carlson, Janice
  See Ashland Price

Carlson, Nancy

Carlton, Kate
  See Linda Sinnott

Carlton, Lori

Carlyle, Tena
  See Carol Card Otten, Ellen Lyle Taber

Carmichael, Carol

Carmichael, Emily
  See Emily Krokosz

Carmichael, Jeanne
  See Carol Quinto

Carnell, Lois

Carol, Shana
  See Kerry Newcomb

Carpenter, Amanda

Carpenter, Brooke

Carpenter, Cyndy

Carpenter, Lynda Kay

Carr, Eleni
  See Helen Maragakis

Carr, Kerry
  See Ena Young

Carr, Lee

Carr, Leona

Carr, Madeleine

Carr, Philippa
  See Eleanor Hibbert

Carr, Roberta
  See Ivor Roberts

Carr, Robyn

Carr, Sally

Carr, Sherry
  See Sydney Ann Clary

Carras, Helen
  See Helen Maragakis

Carrington, Glenda
  Karen Glenn

Carro, Patricia
  See Patricia Markhan

Carrol, Kathleen
  See Kathleen Modrovich

Carrol, Shana
  See Frank Schaefer

Carroll, Dawn
  See Dawn C. Boese

Carroll, Debra
  See Debra Mc Carthy Anderson, & Carol Bruce-Thomas

Carroll, Enid

Carroll, Jay

Carroll, Joellyn
  See Jo Bremer, & Carol Wagner

Carroll, Joy
  Heather Hill

Carroll, Kathleen

Carroll, Lenore

Carroll, Lorraine

Carroll, Lynne
  See Carolyn Kleinsorge

Carroll, Malissa
  See Marian Scharf, & Carol Wagner

AUTHOR PSEUDONYM INDEX

Key: Actual names appear in bold. Pseudonyms appear in italics.

Carroll, Margaret

Carroll, Marissa
See Marian Scharf, & Carol Wagner

Carroll, Mary
See Annette Schorre Sanford

Carroll, Rosalynn
See Carol Katz

Carroll, Samantha

Carroll, Shirley
See Shirley Remes

Carsley, Anne

Carson, Angela
See Sue Peters

Carson, Christine

Carson, Rosalind
Margaret Chittendon

Carstens, Netta
See Martha Fortina

Carter, Ann
See Anne Tedlock Brooks

Carter, Ashley
See Harry Whittington

Carter, Helen
See Helen Maragakis

Carter, Janice
See Janice Hess

Carter, Marilyn
See Dan Ross

·Carter, Noel Vreeland

Carter, Rosemary
See Elizabeth Ashton

Cartier, Annee
See Annee Chartier

Cartier, Lynn

Cartland, Barbara
See Barbara Mc Corquodale

Carton, Nick
See Micahel Angelo Avallone

Cartwright, Jenny

Cartwright, Vanessa

Cary, Diane

Case, Barbra

Case, Jacqueline

Casey, June E.
Melissa Ash, Casey Douglas, Constance Ravenlock, June Trevor, June Triglia

Cass, Zoe
Dorothy Mackie Low, Lois Low, Lois Paxton

Cassidy, Becca
See Beverly Vines-Haines

Cassidy, Carla
See Carla Bracale

Cassidy, Kris
See Kathy Clark

Cassity, Jo Anne

Cassity, Joan

Casstevens, Jeanne Savery
Jeanne Savery

Castell, Megan
See Jeanne Williams

Castle, Brenda
See Georgina Ferrand

Castle, Jayne
See Jayne Ann Krentz

Castle, Jill
See Linda Neukrug

Castle, Linda
See Linda Crockett Gray

Castle, Philippa
See Marilyn Lowery

Casto, Jacqueline
Jacqueline Ashley, Jackie Black

Castoro, Laura
Laura Parker

Caswell, Anne
See Mary Orr

Caswell, Helen

Catalani, Victoria
See Carola Haas

Cateret, Cindy

Cates, Kimberly
See Kim Bush

Key: Actual names appear in bold. Pseudonyms appear in italics.

Key: Actual names appear in bold. Pseudonyms appear in italics.

Chartier, Annee
Annee Cartier

Chase, Carolyn

Chase, Elaine Raco

Chase, Isobel
See Elisie B. Rider

Chase, James Hadley

Chase, Lindsay
See Leslie O' Grady

Chase, Loretta
See Loretta Chekani

Chase, Marian
See Gary Provost

Chase, Samantha
See Nancy Baggett, Eileen Buckholtz, Ruth
Glick, Carolyn Males, & Louise Titchener

Chastain, Sandra
Jenna Darcy, Allie Jordan

Chater, Elizabeth
Lisa Moore

Chatfield, Susan
See Susan C. Fasshauer

Cheatham, Lillian

Chekani, Loretta
Loretta Chase

Cheney, Sally

Chenier, Blanche

Cheshire, Chloe
See Chloe Cheshire

Chesney, Marion
See Marion Scott-Gibbons

Chesnutt, Linda
Lindsey Hanks

Chester, Deborah

Chester, Sarah
See Marion Scott-Gibbons

Cheyney, Peter

Child, Judith
Juli Greene

Child, Maureen
Ann Carberry, Kathleen Kane

Childress, Susan
See Susan Wiggs

Chin, Charla
Charlotte Simms

Chisholm, Lilian
See Jane Alan

Chittendon, Margaret
See Rosalind Carson

Choate, Gwen
See Jeanne Williams

Christenberry, Judy
Judith Stafford

Christian, Jill
See Noreen Dilcock

Christie, Agatha

Christie, Colleen
J. S. Bidwell

Christie, Michelle
See Gerri O' Hara

Christie, Susanna
See Kristen Burton, Susan B. Ossana

Christina, Susan

Christopher, Amy
See Patricia Barletta

Christopher, Beth

Christopher, Cathy
See Alex Andrews

Christopher, Francine
See Francine Mandeville

Christopher, Honey
See Helen Cavanagh

Christopher, Jane
See Janet Clarke

Christopher, Mary
See Alex Andrews

Christopher, Paula
See Lynne Smith

Christy, Ann
See Helen Mittermeyer

Church, Emma
See E. Schattner

Churchill, Jill
See Janice Young Brooks, Jean Brooks Janowick

AUTHOR PSEUDONYM INDEX

Key: Actual names appear in bold. Pseudonyms appear in italics.

Chwedyk, Kathy M.
Cathryn Huntington Chadwick

Cichanth, Elaine
Elizabeth Shelley

Civil, Sue
Rachel Lee

Clague, Maryhelen
Ashley Snow

Clair, Daphne
See Daphne De Jong

Claire, Cathryn

Claire, Eve
See Claire De Long

Claire, Evelyn

Claire, Keith

Clamp, H.M.E.

Clare, Cathleen
See Catherine A. Toothman

Clare, Cathryn
See Cathy Stanton

Clare, Ellen
See Olga Daniels

Clare, Jane
See Dinah Shields

Clare, Samantha

Clare, Shannon
See Linda Harrel

Clark, Amanda

Clark, Blair
See Blair Foster

Clark, Cathy Gillen

Clark, Cecily

Clark, Christie
See Christie Craig

Clark, Dorothy
Dorothy Cork

Clark, Gail
See Maggie Mac Keever

Clark, Jean

Clark, Kathy
Kris Cassidy

Clark, Louise
See Roslyn Mac Donald, & Kay L. Mc Donald

Clark, Lydia
See Eloise Meaker

Clark, Marianne
See Marianne Willman

Clark, Mary Higgins

Clark, Melissa
See Alysse Aallyn

Clark, Norma Lee

Clark, Roberta

Clark, Sabina
See Marianne Willman

Clark, Sandra

Clark, Sylvia
See Blair Foster

Clarke, Brenda
See Brenda Honeyman

Clarke, Gail

Clarke, Janet
Jane Christopher, Joanna Kenyon, Nell Kincaid

Clarke, Marion
See Marion Schulz

Clarke, Pippa

Clary, Sydney Ann
Sherry Carr, Sara Chance

Clay, Bertha M.
See Charlotte N. Braeme

Clay, Rita
See Rita Estrada

Clay, Weston

Claybourne, Casey
Casey Mickle

Clayford, James
See Erolie Pearl Dern

Clayton, Donna
See Donna Fasano

Cleary, Gwen

Cleaver, Anastasia
See Natasha Peters

Cleaver, Julia

AUTHOR PSEUDONYM INDEX

Key: Actual names appear in bold. Pseudonyms appear in italics.

Cleaves, Margaret Major
Ann Major

Cleeve, Brian

Clemence, Ruth

Clemens-Fox, Carol
Alicia Fox

Clement, Ernest
Candance Connell

Clements, Abigail

Clements, Kaye L.
Caylin Jennings, Jeanne Kaye Triner

Clermont, Shana
See Dean Mc Elwain

Clifford, Kay

Clifton, Bonita

Clifton, Suzanne

Cloud, Patricia
See Pat Wallace Strother

Coan, La Verne
La Verne St. George

Coate, Evelyn

Coates, May

Coates, Sheila
See Sheila Holland

Coburn, Jean

Coburn, Walt

Cochrane, Kia

Cockcroft, Ann

Cocking, Ronald
Elsa Cook

Coddington, Lynn
Allison Hayes

Cody, Al

Cody, Joan A.
Nicola James

Cody, Pat

Coe, Phyllis

Coffaro, Katherine
See Katherine Kovacs

Coffman, Elaine

Coffman, Virginia
Kay Cameron, Victor Cross, Jeanne Duval,
Diana Saunders, Ann Stanfield

Coghlan, Peggie
Jessica Stirling

Cohen, Ellis

Cohen, Jean

Cohen, Rhonda
Eleanora Brownleigh, Diana Loy

Cohen, Sharron

Cohen, Susan
Elizabeth St. Clair

Colander, Valerie N.

Colburn, Brittany
See Rhonda Colburn

Colburn, Rhonda
Brittany Colburn

Coldenbaum, Sally

Cole, Hilary
See Valerie Miller

Cole, Jackson

Cole, Jennifer
See Mary Schultz, & Cheryl Zach

Cole, Justine
See Claire Kiehl, & Susan Elizabeth Phillips

Cole, Marianne
See Charlotte White

Cole, Sue Ellen
See Susan Cross

Cole, Victoria

Coleman, Clare
See Malcolm Easton

Coleman, Patricia

Coles, Janis

Colley, Barbara
Anne Logan

Collier, Leona

Collin, Marion Cripes

Collin, Marion
See Marion Smith

Collinge, Patricia

AUTHOR PSEUDONYM INDEX

Key: Actual names appear in bold. Pseudonyms appear in italics.

Collins, Christine
See Elizabeth Barrett

Collins, Kathryn

Collins, Laurel
See Linda C. Wiath

Collins, Marion Smith

Collins, Susanna
See Susan Cross

Collins, Toni

Collinson, Marie

Colt, Zandra
See Florence Stevenson

Colter, Cara

Colvin, Penny

Comber, Lillian
Lillian Beckwith

Combs, Becky

Combs, Iris

Combs, Susan

Comeaux, Donna

Comer, Linda
See Eileen Jackson

Comfort, Iris

Compton, Katherine

Conan, Christa
See Vickie Conan, & Christine Pacheco

Conan, Vickie
Christa Conan

Conant, Constance

Conarain, Alice
Elizabeth Hoy

Conaway, James
Leila Lyons, Vanessa Valcour

Conklin, Judith

Conlee, Jaelyn
See Fayrene Preston

Conn, Phoebe
Cinnamon Burke

Connell, Candance
See Ernest Clement

Connell, Ethel
Katrina Britt

Connell, Susan
Chloe Summers

Connolly, Vivian
See Susanna Rosse

Conrad, Constance
See Ruby Frankel

Conrad, Helen
Jena Hunt, Raye Morgan

Constant, Jan

Constantin-Weyer, M.

Conte, Charles
See Charles Roy Mac Kinnon

Converse, Jane
See Adela Maritano

Conway, Celine
See Rosalind Brett, & Karen Blair Parker

Conway, Jean

Conway, Laura
See Dorothy P. Ansle

Conway, Theresa

Conway, Troy
See Micahel Angelo Avallone

Conwell, Kent

Coogan, Beatrice
Claire Lorrimer, Patricia Robins

Cook, Barry
Jane Causeway

Cook, Bonna Lee
See Bonna Lee Du Bois

Cook, Deirde
Dorothy Cook

Cook, Dorothy
See Deirde Cook

Cook, Elsa
See Ronald Cocking

Cook, Eugenia

Cook, Ida
Mary Burchell

Cook, Petronella
Margo Arnold

AUTHOR PSEUDONYM INDEX

Key: Actual names appear in bold. Pseudonyms appear in italics.

Cook, Sally

Cook, Susan

Cooke, Deborah
Claire Delacroix

Cooke, Phyl

Cooke, Ronald J.

Cookson, Catherine
See Catherine Fawcett

Coombs, Ann
See Nina Combs Pykare

Coombs, Nina
See Nina Combs Pykare

Cooper, Ann

Cooper, Barbara A.

Cooper, Inglath
Inglath Caulder

Cooper, Jilly

Cooper, Lynna
See Gardiner Fox

Copeland, Lori

Copeland, Patricia Ann

Copeland, Patty

Copeland, Vivian
Vivian Keith

Coppula, Susan

Corathers, Annabel

Corbet, Colleen

Corbett, Paula

Corbin, Delinda

Corcoran, Barbara

Corcoran, Dottie
De Ann Patrick

Cord, Betty

Cordaire, Christina
See Chris Strong

Cores, Lucy

Corey, Gayle
See Elaine Havptman

Corey, Ryanne

Cork, Dorothy
See Dorothy Clark

Corren, Grace
See Robert Hoskins

Corrie, Jane

Corrigan, Mark

Corser, Judy E
Judith Bowen

Corson, Martha
Anne Lacey, Kristin Michaels

Cory, Caroline
See Mary Fitt

Cory, Diane

Cosgrove, Rachel R.
See Rachel Cosgrove Payes

Costain, Thomas

Cothran, Betty

Cotler, Julie
Julia Quinn

Cott, Christine Hella

Coughlin, Patricia
Liz Grady

Couillard, Beverlee
Beverlee Ross

Couldrey, Vivienne

Coulson, Juanita

Coulter, Catherine
See Jean Coulter

Coulter, Jean
Catherine Coulter

Coultry, Barbara
See Barbara Blacktree

Courcelles, Sandra
Samantha Day

Court, Katherine
See Elizabeth K. Schrempp

Courtland, Roberta
See Erolie Pearl Dern

Courtney, Caroline

Cousins, Margaret
See Mary Parrish

AUTHOR PSEUDONYM INDEX

Key: Actual names appear in bold. Pseudonyms appear in italics.

Covington, Linda
See Linda Windsor

Cowan, Debra S.

Cowdray, Rosalind

Cox, Eleanor Anne

Cox, Jane

Cox, Joan

Cox, Patricia
See Pat Warren

Coy, Stanlee Miller
Iona Charles, Cissie Miller

Craco, Catherine

Craen, Theresa

Craig, Christie
Christie Clark

Craig, Dolores
See Moira Lord

Craig, Georgia
See Erolie Pearl Dern

Craig, Jasmine
See Jasmine Cresswell

Craig, Mary Shura
Alexis Hill

Craig, Rebecca

Craig, Rianna
See Sharon & Rick Harrington

Craig, Vera
See Donald S. Rowland

Crain, Elley

Crampton, Helen
See Marion Scott-Gibbons

Crane, Caroline

Crane, Elizabeth

Crane, Leah
See Jean Hager

Crane, Teresa

Cranmer, Kathryn

Craven, Barbara Catlin
Barbara Catlin, Maranda Catlin

Craven, Sara

Crawford, Camille

Crawford, Diane Michele
See Georgette Livingston

Crawford, Elaine

Crawford, Lillian

Crawford, Rosemary

Crawley, Aileen

Crease, Gail
Gail Whitiker

Creasey, John

Crecy, Jeanne
See Jeanne Williams

Creekmore, Donna

Creel, Catherine

Creese, Bethea

Creighton, Kathleen
See Kathleen Modrovich

Crenshaw, Nadine Shearin
Nadine Crenshaw

Crenshaw, Nadine
See Nadine Shearin Crenshaw

Cresswell, Jasmine
Jasmine Craig

Cretenoid, Mary Ben
Mary-Ben Louis

Crewe, Sarah
See Virginia Blanford

Crews, Ethel Maxam
Mia Maxam

Crichton, Lucilla
Lucilla Andrews, Diana Gordon, Joanna Marcus

Crisp, Marty

Criss, Dani
See Kitty Bentch

Cristol, Jaymi

Criswell, Millie

Crockett, Christina
See Linda Crockett Gray

Croissant, Kay
Catherine Kay

Cromie, Alice

AUTHOR PSEUDONYM INDEX

Key: Actual names appear in bold. Pseudonyms appear in italics.

Crompton, Anne
Anne Eliot

Cromwell, Elsie
Elsie Lee, Jane Gordon, Lee Sheridan, Elsie
Sheridan

Crone, Alla

Crosby, Susan

Crosby, Tanya Anne

Crose, Susan
Lisa Jackson, Michelle Mathews

Cross, Caitlin
See Daranna Berger

Cross, Caroline

Cross, Charlene

Cross, Melinda

Cross, Nancy
Anne Baker

Cross, Peggy

Cross, Susan
Sue Ellen Cole, Susanna Collins, Susana De
Lyonne

Cross, Victor
See Virginia Coffman

Crosston, Pamela

Crowe, Cecily

Crowe, Evelyn A.

Crowleigh, Ann
See Barbara Cummings, & Jo-Ann Power

Crumbaker, Alice
Allison Baker

Crusie, Jennifer

Cruz, Joan Carroll

Cudlipp, Edythe
Julia Alcott, Edythe Lachlan, Bettina
Montgomery, Nicole Norman, Maureen Norris,
Rinalda Roberts

Cuevas, Judith

Cuevas, Judy

Culver, Carol
Carol Grace

Culver, Colleen
Colleen Faulkner

Cumberland, Patricia

Cummings, Barbara
Ann Crowleigh

Cummings, Monette

Cummins, Mary
Susan Taylor

Cunliffe, Corinna
See Corinna Wildman

Cunningham, Jan
See Chelsey Forrest

Cunningham, Madelyn

Cunningham, Marilyn

Currie, Anne Brook

Currie, Katy
See Susan Kyle

Curry, Avon
See Jean Bowden

Curry, Elissa
See Nancy Martin

Curtis, Jean

Curtis, Mary
Mary Haskell

Curtis, Peter
Juliet Astley, Norah Lofts

Curtis, Sharon & Tom
Robin James, Laura London

Curtis, Susannah
See Helen Upshall

Curtiss, Mary

Curwood, James Oliver

Curzon, Lucia
See Florence Stevenson

Cushing, Enid

Cust, Barbara
Caroline Fanshawe, Kate Ward

Cuthrell, Faith
Faith Baldwin

Czuleger, Rebecca
Rebecca Bond, Rebecca Forster

AUTHOR PSEUDONYM INDEX

Key: Actual names appear in bold. Pseudonyms appear in italics.

D'Arcy, Pamela
  See Mary Linn Roby

D'angelo, Christine

Dagg, Jillian
  Marilyn Brian, Jillian Fayre, Faye Wildman

Daheim, Mary

Dahlin, Betty

Dailey, Janet

Dair, Christina
  See Louzana Kaku

Daish, Elizabeth

Dakers, Elaine
  Jane Lane

Dale, Jennifer
  See Charlotte White

Dale, Ruth Jean
  See Betty Duran, & Jean Stribling

Daley, Kathleen
  See Patti Moore

Daley, Kit
  See Patti Moore

Daley, Margaret
  See Patti Moore

Dallmayr, Ilse
  Heidi Strasser

Dalton, Emily
  See Danice Jo Allen

Dalton, Gena
  See Genell Dellin Smith

Dalton, Jenifer
  See David Wind

Dalton, Margot

Dalton, Pamela
  See Pamela Johnson

Dalton, Pat

Dalton, Priscilla
  See Micahel Angelo Avallone

Daly, Kathleen
  See Patti Moore

Daly, Kit
  See Patti Moore

Daly, Margaret
  See Patti Moore

Daly, Saralyn

Dalzell, Helen

Damon, Kate
  See Margaret Brownley

Damon, Lee
  See Jane H. Look

Dana, Erin
  See Nancy Elliott

Dana, Rose
  See Dan Ross

Danbury, Iris

Dancer, Lacey

Dane, Eva
  See Edna Dawes

Dane, Lisa
  See Beth Henderson

Dane, Mark
  See Micahel Angelo Avallone

Daniel, Elaine

Daniel, Megan
  See Donna Meyer

Daniels, B.J.
  See Barbara Johnson Smith

Daniels, Carol
  See Carol Viens

Daniels, Dana
  See Deanna Brauer

Daniels, Dorothy
  See Helen Gray Weston

Daniels, Elizabeth
  See Beth Henderson

Daniels, Faye

Daniels, Joleen
  See Gayle Malon Schimek

Daniels, Jordanna

Daniels, Judith
  See Judy Pelfrey

Daniels, Kayla
  See Karin Hofland

Daniels, Laura

AUTHOR PSEUDONYM INDEX

Key: Actual names appear in bold. Pseudonyms appear in italics.

Daniels, Leigh
See Lisbeth Chance

Daniels, Maggie
See Maggie Davis

Daniels, Max
See Roberta Gellis

Daniels, Melanie

Daniels, Olga
Ellen Clare, Olga Sinclair

Daniels, Rebecca

Daniels, Rhett
See Judy Pelfrey

Daniels, Val
See Alfie Thompson

Daniels, Zoe
See Connie Laux

Dansby, Lee Ann

Danson, Sheryl

Danton, Rebecca
See Janet Louise Roberts

Darby, Catherine
See Maureen Peters

Darcy, Clare

Darcy, Emma
See Wendy Brennan

Darcy, Jenna
See Sandra Chastain, & Nancy Knight

Darcy, Lilian

Dare, Jessica
Darla Benton, Joanna Leslie

Dark, Sandra

Darke, Hilary

Darling, Joan
See Ellen Searight

Darlington, Con
See Marcia Wayne

Darlington, Joy
See Joy Aumente

Darnell, Berde

Darrell, Elizabeth
See Edna Dawes

Darrington, Paula
Paula Williams

Darty, Peggy

Darwin, Jeanette
See Candance Schuler

Dauost, Pamela
Katharine Kincaid

Davenport, Kathryn
See Keller Graves

Daveson, Mons

David, Cay
See Carla Luan

Davids, Marilyn
See David Wind

Davidson, Andrea
See Susan Lowe

Davidson, Carolyn

Davidson, Diane Mott

Davidson, Sandra

Davies, Frances
See Leone Lewesohn

Davies, Iris
See Iris Gower

Davis, Berrie

Davis, Deborah

Davis, Diane Wicker
Delaney Devers

Davis, Elinor

Davis, Elizabeth
See Lou Ellen Davis

Davis, Genevieve

Davis, Julie
Juliana Davison

Davis, Justine
See Justine Davis Smith

Davis, Katherine
See Mildred Davis

Davis, Kathryn Lynn

Davis, Kathryn

Davis, Leslie
See Leslie D. Guccione

AUTHOR PSEUDONYM INDEX

Key: Actual names appear in bold. Pseudonyms appear in italics.

Davis, Lou Ellen
Elizabeth Davis

Davis, Madeline
See Madeline Garry

Davis, Maggie
Katherine Deauxville, Maggie Daniels

Davis, Mary
Rosemary Jordan

Davis, Melanie
See Claudette Williams

Davis, Mildred
Katherine Davis

Davis, Suzanne

Davis, Wendi
See Nancy Holder

Davison, Juliana
See Julie Davis

Dawes, Edna
Eva Dane, Elizabeth Darrell, Eleanor Drew,
Emma Drummond

Dawson, Elizabeth

Dawson, Geralyn

Dawson, Helena

Dawson, Saranne
See Saranne Hoover

Day, Adrienne

Day, Dianne

Day, Elyn

Day, Jocelyn
See Lorena Mc Courtney

Day, Lucinda
See Marie Flasschoen, & Marian Scheirman

Day, Samantha
See Sandra Courcelles

Dayton, Lily
See Linda Hampton

De Benedetto, Theresa

De Bets, Julie
Maura Mc Giveny

De Blassis, Celeste

De Boer, Marjorie Rockwell

De Boer, Marjorie

De Borde, Sherry
Kristal Leigh Scott

De Coto, Jean

De Coursey, Virginia

De Covarrubias, Barbara Faith
Barbara Faith

De Genaro, Mary Jane
See Mary Jane Lloyd

De Guise, Elizabeth
See Elisie B. Rider

De Jarnette, Harriette

De Jong, Daphne
Laurey Bright, Daphne Clair, Claire Lorel

De Jong, Linda Renee

De Jourlet, Marie
See Paul Little

De La Fuente, Patricia
Patricia Oliver, Olivia Fontayne

De Lancey, Elizabeth
See Elizabeth Tunis

De Lange, Anneke

De Lauer, Marjel

De Lazzari, Jo Ann

De Leeuw, Cateau W.
Kay Hamilton, Jessica Lyon

De Leon, Ana Lisa
Celina Mullan, Rachel Scott, Marisa De Zavala

De Long, Claire
Eve Claire, Claire Evans

De Lyn, Nicole
Nicole Lindsay, Eva Woodland

De Lyonne, Susana
See Susan Cross

De Nore, Rochelle
See Roberta Denmore

De Paul, Edith
See Edith Delatush

De Pre, Jean-Anne
See Micahel Angelo Avallone

De Sha, Sandra
Sandra Donovan

Key: Actual names appear in bold. Pseudonyms appear in italics.

De St. Jeor, Owanna

De Vere, Jane
See Julia Fitzgerald

De Vincent, Eleanora

De Vita, Sharon

De Voe, Lily

De Vore, Mary
Madelyn Dohrn

De Winter, Danielle
See Keith Timson

De Wolfe, Adrienne
See Adrienne M. Sobolak

De Zavala, Marisa
See Ana Lisa De Leon

Dean, Alyssa

Dean, Carole

Dean, Diane

Dean, Dinah
See Marjorie May

Dean, Nell Marr
See Nell Dean Ratzlaff

Dean, Rena

Deauxville, Katherine
See Maggie Davis

Decoto, Jean

Dee, Sherry
See Sheryl Hines Flournoy

Dees, Catherine
Catherine Kay

Deiterle, Robin

Deka, Connie

Delacorte, Shawna
Shawn Dennison

Delacroix, Claire
See Deborah Cooke

Delancey, Elizabeth

Delaney, Gina
See Rosalyn Alsobrook, & Patricia Walls

Delatour, Elise

Delatush, Edith
Alyssa Morgan, Edith St. George, Edith De Paul

Delinsky, Barbara
Bonnie Drake, Billie Douglass

Delk, Karen Jones

Dell, Belinda
See Jean Bowden

Dellamere, Wanda

Dellin, Genell

Delmore, Diana
See Lois Nollett

Demetropoulos, Nicholas
Jean Evans, Marianne Evans

Denmore, Roberta
Rochelle De Nore

Dennis, Roberta

Dennis, Stacey
See Esther Morris

Dennison, Shawn
Shawna Delacorte

Denny, Roz
See Roz Fox

Dent, Roxanne
Melissa Masters

Dentinger, Jane

Denton, Kate
See Carolyn Hake, & Jeanie Lambright

Denys, Teresa
See Jacqui Bianchi

Deobold, Sue

Dern, Erolie Pearl
James Clayford, Roberta Courtland, Georgia Craig, Peggy Dern, Peggy Gaddis, Gail Jordan, Perry Lindsay, Joan Sherman

Dern, Peggy
See Erolie Pearl Dern

Des Jardien, Teresa

Desmond, Hilary
See Lee Hays

Deveraux, Jude
See Jude Gilliam White

Devers, Delaney
See Diane Wicker Davis

Devin, Flanna
See Karen Juneman

Devine, Angela

Devine, Carol

Devine, Thea

Devlin, Dianna
See Dianna Hannah

Devlin, Mary

Devoe, Lily

Devon, Alexandra
See Joan Dial

Devon, Anne
See Marian Pope Rettke

Devon, Georgina
See Alison J. Hentges, & Amber Kay

Devon, Lynn

Devon, Marian
See Marian Pope Rettke

Devon, Sara
See Quenna Tilbury

Dewar, Sandra

Deyoe, Cori
Jessica Barkley

Di Benedetto, Theresa
Theresa Michaels, Raine Cantrell

Di Donato, Georgia

Di Francesco, Phyllis
Anne Harmon, Phyllis Herrmann

Dial, Joan
Alexandra Devon, Katherine Kent, Katherine Sinclair, Amanda York

Diamond, Barbara B.
Barbara Bentley

Diamond, Graham
Rochelle Leslie

Diamond, Jacqueline
See Jackie Hyman

Diamond, Petra
See Judith Sachs

Dickerson, Marilyn

Dier, Debra

Diespecker, Dick

Difrancesco, Phyllis

Dilcock, Noreen
Jill Christian, Norrey Ford, Christian Walford

Dillard, Polly Hargis
Pauline Hargis, Polly Hargis

Dillon, Catherine

Dillon, Eiles

Dillon, Patricia

Dilmore, Diana

Dimick, Cherylle Lindsey
Dawn Lindsey

Dingley, Sally G.
Sally Garrett

Dingwell, Joyce
Kate Starr

Dion, Paula

Dix, Dorothy
See Elizabeth Meriwether Gilmer

Dix, Isabel

Dixon, Debra

Dixon, Diana

Dixon, Lesley
See Kathleeen Vernon

Dixon, Rhonda

Dobarganes, Patricia
Annette Summers

Dobkin, Kaye

Dobravolsky, Barbara

Dobson, Margaret

Dodd, Christina

Dohrn, Madelyn
See Joan Dornbusch

Dolan, Charlotte Louise

Dominque, Meg
See Annette Schorre Sanford

Domning, Denise

Domning, Joan J.

Donald, Robyn

Key: Actual names appear in bold. Pseudonyms appear in italics.

Donald, Vivian
See Charles Roy Mac Kinnon

Donick, Catherine Lee
Catherine Leigh

Donnelly, Jane

Donner, Katherine

Donohue, Mary Irene
Irene Michaels

Donovan, Sandra
See Sandra De Sha

Donthan, Jean Ann

Dooley, Janet M.
Liz Henley

Dore, Christy
See Jim Plagakis

Dornbusch, Joan
Madelyn Dohrn

Dors, Alexandra
See Dorothy Mc Kittrick

Dorset, Ruth
See Dan Ross

Dorsett, Danielle
See Helen Gray Weston

Dorsey, Christine
Christine Elliott

Douglas, Alyssa
See Anne Canadeo

Douglas, Anne
See Anne Douglas Bayless

Douglas, Barbara
See Barbara Ovstedahl

Douglas, Billie

Douglas, Carole Nelson

Douglas, Casey
See June E. Casey

Douglas, Charlotte
Anne Penney, Marina Malcolm

Douglas, Elizabeth
See Bettie Wilhite

Douglas, Gail

Douglas, Gloria
See Gloria Upper

Douglas, Jessica

Douglas, Kate
See Kathryn Ewing

Douglas, Kathryn
See Kathryn Ewing

Douglas, La Lette
Lafayette Hammett

Douglas, Mary
See Mary Tew

Douglas, Monica

Douglas, Sheila

Douglass, Amanda Hart

Douglass, Billie
See Barbara Delinsky

Douglass, Jessica
See Linda H. Wallerich

Dowdell, Dorothy

Dowling, Shirley

Downes, Deirde
Kathleen Downes

Downes, Kathleen
See Deirde Downes

Downie, Jill

Doyle, Amanda

Doyle, Barbara

Doyle, Emily
See Betty L. Henrichs

Doyle, Richard J.

Doyle, Sir Arthur Conan

Dozier, Zoe
Dixie Browning, Bronwyn Williams

Drake, Asa
See Nina Andersson

Drake, Bonnie
See Barbara Delinsky

Drake, Connie

Drake, H.B.

Drake, Shannon
See Heather Graham Pozzessere

Drake, Susan

Key: Actual names appear in bold. Pseudonyms appear in italics.

Key: Actual names appear in bold. Pseudonyms appear in italics.

Dureau, Lorena

Durham, Anne

Dustin, Sandra
See Hannah Howell

Dustin, Sarah
See Hannah Howell

Duval, Jeanne
See Virginia Coffman

Duval, Justine

Duval, Nicole

Duvall, Aimee
See Aimee Thurlo

Dwight, Allan
See Lois Cole Taylor

Dworman, Brenda
Brenda Joyce

Dwyer-Joyce, Alice

Dyal, Gloria

Dyer, Lois Faye

Dyne, Michael
Evelyn Hanna

Eady, Carol Maxwell

Eagle, Kathleen

Eagle, Sarah
See Sarah Hawkes

Earley, Fran
See Bob Whearley

Early, Margot

Earnest, Jeanette
See Judy Martin

Easton, M. Coleman
See Malcolm Easton

Easton, Malcolm
Clare Coleman, M. Coleman Easton

Eastvale, Margaret

Eastwood, Gail
See Gail Eastwood Stokes

Eastwood, Helen
See Olive Baxter

Eatock, Margaret

Eatock, Marjorie

Eaton, Evelyn

Eaton, Laura

Ebel, Kelly Varner
Kelly R. Stevens

Eberhardt, Anna
Tiffany White

Eberhart, Mignon Good

Eccles, Lark Eden
Lark Eden

Echols, Allan K.

Eckersley, Jill
Helen Beaumont, Denise Emery, Jill Sanderson,
Anna Stanton

Eckert, Roberta

Eden, Dorothy
Mary Paradise

Eden, Lark
See Lark Eden Eccles, & Sandra Scarpa

Eden, Laura
See Claire Harrison

Edgar, Josephine
See Mary Mussi

Edgehill, Rosemary

Edgeworth, Ann

Edgley, Leslie

Edmonds, Janet

Edouard, Dianne

Edward, Ann
See Anna West

Edwards, Adrienne
See Anne Kolaczak

Edwards, Andrea
See Anne Kolaczak

Edwards, Cassie

Edwards, Claudia

Edwards, Emily Ruth

Edwards, Estelle
Mollie Gregory

Edwards, Irene
Elisabeth Barr

AUTHOR PSEUDONYM INDEX

Key: Actual names appear in bold. Pseudonyms appear in italics.

Edwards, Jane
Jane Campbell

Edwards, Jaroldeen

Edwards, Judi

Edwards, Kathryn

Edwards, Marian
See Marian Jastrzembski

Edwards, Patricia

Edwards, Paula

Edwards, Rachelle

Edwards, Samuel
See Noel B. Gerson

Edwards, Sara
See Sharon & Robert Bils

Egan, Lesley
See Elizabeth Linigton

Eirls, Sandra Lynn

Elder, Catherine

Elgin, Betty
Kate Kirby

Elgin, Mary

Elgin, Suzette

Eliot, Anne
See Anne Crompton

Eliot, Carolyn

Eliot, Jessica

Eliot, Winslow
Ellie Winslow

Elizabeth, Suzanne

Elkins, Charlotte
Emily Spenser

Ellerbeck, Rosemary
See Anna L' Estrange

Ellingham, Marnie

Elliot, Anne
Christine Elliot

Elliot, Christine
See Anne Elliot, Christine Dorsey

Elliot, Emily
See Emily Mims

Elliot, Jessica
See Lois A. Brown, Barbara Levy

Elliot, Lucy
See Nancy Greenman

Elliot, Rachel

Elliott, Christine
See Christine Dorsey

Elliott, Joan

Elliott, Nancy
Erin Dana, Ellen Langtry

Elliott, Rachel

Elliott, Robin
See Joan Elliott Pickart

Ellis, Alexandra
See Carmel B. Reingold

Ellis, Audrey

Ellis, Delia

Ellis, Janine

Ellis, Joan
See Julie Ellis

Ellis, Julie
Patricia Bentley, Joan Ellis, Marilyn Ellis,
Allison Lord, Jeffery Lord, Susan Marino,
Richard Marvin, Susan Marvin, Linda Michaels,
Jill Monte, Susan Richard

Ellis, Kathy

Ellis, Leigh
See Anne & Louisa Rudeen

Ellis, Louise

Ellis, Lyn

Ellis, Marilyn
See Julie Ellis

Ellis, Patricia
See Valerie Mangrum

Ellison, Marjorie
See Marjorie Norton

Ellison, Suzanne Pierson

Ellswort, Kelly Ferjutz
Kelly Ferjutz

Elmblad, Mary

Elroy, Edwina

Key: Actual names appear in bold. Pseudonyms appear in italics.

Elsna, Hebe
See Dorothy P. Ansle

Elver, Rose

Elward, James
Rebecca James

Emerson, Cheryl

Emerson, Kathy Lynn
Kaitlyn Gordon

Emery, Denise
See Jill Eckersley

Emery, Lynn
See Margaret Hubbard

Emm, Catherine
Kay Mc Mahon

Engels, Mary Tate
Corey Keaton, Cory Kenyon, Tate Mc Kenna

Englander, Cronshi

Engles, Mary Tate

English, Genevieve
See Sarah Patton

English, Judith
Judith Kelly

Engren, Edith
See Edith Mc Caig

Ensley, Clare
Clare Plummer

Erickson, Lynn
See Carla Peltonen

Eriksen, Barbara
Katherine Arthur

Ernenwein, Leslie

Ernest, Francine

Erskine, Andra
See Judy Martin

Erskine, Barbara

Erskine, Helen
See Helen Santori

Erskine, Rosalind
See Megan Barker

Erwin, Annabel
See Ann Forman Barron

Esler, Anthony

Esmond, Harriet

Essenmacher, Eugenia Riley
Eugenia Riley

Essex, Marianna
See Joan Van Nuys

Essex, Mary
See Ursula Bloom

Essig, Terry

Estrada, Rita Clay
Rita Clay, Tira Lacy

Etheridge, Christine

Evanick, Marcia

Evanovich, Janet
Steffie Hall

Evanovich, Janey

Evans, Ann

Evans, Claire
See Claire De Long

Evans, Constance M.
See Mairi O' Nair

Evans, Jean
See Nicholas Demetropoulos

Evans, John

Evans, Laurel
See Ellen Wilson

Evans, M.
See Flora Speer

Evans, Margaret
See Margaret Neuman

Evans, Marianne
See Nicholas Demetropoulos

Evans, Patricia Gardner

Evanston, Linell

Everest, Francine

Everett, Gail
See Lynn Williams

Everitt, Marjorie

Ewing, Kathryn
Kate Douglas, Kathryn Douglas

Eyre, Annette
See Anne Worboys

Key: Actual names appear in bold. Pseudonyms appear in italics.

Fabian, Erika

Fabian, Robert

Fabian, Ruth
See Aileen Quigley

, Fabio
See Fabio Lanzoni

Faid, Mary
Mary Dunn

Fain, Michael
Judith Maxwell

Fairchild, Kate
See Pat Ahearn

Fairchilde, Sarah

Faire, Zabrina
See Florence Stevenson

Fairfax, Ann
See Marion Scott-Gibbons

Fairfax, Gwen
See Mary Jo Territo

Fairfax, Kate
See Irene Ord

Fairfax, Lynn

Fairman, Paul W.
Paula Fairman, Janet Lovesmith, Paulette Warren

Fairman, Paula
See Paul W. Fairman, Robert Vaughan

Faith, Barbara
See Barbara Faith De Covarrubias

Falcon, Debra
Carol Finch

Falcon, Sally
See Sarah Hawkes

Fanshawe, Caroline
Barbara Cust, Kate Ward

Farland, Kathryn
See Kathryn Fladland

Farmer, Joan

Farnes, Eleanor

Farraday, Alicia
See Sharon M. Rose

Farrant, Sarah

Farrell, Marjorie

Fasano, Donna
Donna Clayton

Fasshauer, Susan C.
Susan Chatfield

Faulkner, Colleen
See Colleen Culver

Faulkner, Whitney
See Elaine Bissell

Faure, Jean
See Nancy Richards-Akers, & Mary Kilchenstein

Favor, Erika

Favors, Jean
Elizabeth Morris

Fawcett, Catherine
Catherine Cookson, Catherine Marchant

Faye, Shirley

Fayre, Jillian
See Jillian Dagg

Fearn, John Russell

Feather, Jane
Claudia Bishop

Fecher, Constance
See George Fleming

Feddersen, Connie
Gina Roberts, Gina Robins, Carol Finch

Felber, Edith
Edith Layton

Feldman, Gilda
Louisa Gillette, Madeline Hale

Felice, Cynthia

Felix, Jenny

Felldin, Jeanne

Fellows, Catherine

Fenton, Julia

Fenwick, Patricia

Ferguson, Jo Ann
Rebecca North

Ferguson, Maggie

Ferjutz, Kelly
See Kelly Ferjutz Ellswort

Key: Actual names appear in bold. Pseudonyms appear in italics.

Fernald, Abby

Ferrand, Georgina
Brenda Castle

Ferrarella, Marie R.
Marie Charles, Anne Hunter Lowell, Marie Michael, Marie Nicole, Marie Rydzynski

Ferrari, Ivy

Ferrars, E. X.
See Elizabeth Ferrars

Ferrars, Elizabeth
Morna Brown, E. X. Ferrars

Ferrell, Olivia

Ferris, Gina
Gina Wilkins

Ferris, Rose Marie
Robin Francis, Valerie Ferris, Michelle Roland

Ferris, Valerie
See Rose Marie Ferris

Fetzer, Amy J.

Field, Karen

Field, Penelope
See Dorothy Giberson

Field, Sandra
See Jill Mc Lean

Fielding, Liz

Finch, Carol
See Debra Falcon, Connie Feddersen, & Gina Robins

Findley, Ferguson

Finkelstein, Roni
Janine French

Finlay, Fiona

Finley, Glenna

Finnigan, Karen
Karen Straford, Karen Lockwood

Fiorotto, Christine
Lucy Gordon

Fireside, Caroline
Joanna Burgess

Firth, Suzanne

Fish, Mildred T.
Megan Alexander

Fisher, Dorothea
Dorothy Canfield, Miriam Canfield, Dorothy Fletcher

Fisher, Gene Louis
See Gene Lancour

Fitt, Mary
Caroline Cory, Kathleen Freeman

Fitzcharles, Mara

Fitzgerald, Amber
See Nancy Smith

Fitzgerald, Arlene

Fitzgerald, Barbara
Mona Newman, Jean Stewart

Fitzgerald, Catherine
See Mary Sandra Hingston

Fitzgerald, Ellen
See Florence Stevenson

Fitzgerald, Julia
Jane De Vere, Julia Hamilton, Julia Watson

Fitzgerald, Maeve
See Maura Seger

Fitzgerald, Nancy

Fitzgerald, Rosemary

Fitzgerald, Sara

Fitzjames, Phoebe

Fladland, Kathryn
Kathryn Farland

Flanders, Rebecca
See Donna Ball, & Shannon Harper

Flannery, Constance O' Day

Flasschoen, Marie
Lucinda Day

Fleming, Cardine
See Mildred Grieveson

Fleming, Caroline
See Mildred Grieveson

Fleming, Danielle
See Nancy Morse

Fleming, George
Constance Fecher, Constance Heaven, Christina Merlin

AUTHOR PSEUDONYM INDEX

Key: Actual names appear in bold. Pseudonyms appear in italics.

Fleming, Kate
Jenny Mcguire

Fleming, Lee
Ginny Haymond

Fletcher, Aaron

Fletcher, Donna

Fletcher, Dorothy
See Dorothea Fisher

Fletcher, Ellen

Fletcher, Leigh

Fletcher, Margaret

Fletcher, Verne

Fletcher, Violet

Fleury, Jacqueline

Fleury, Jane
See Pauline A. Kjellberg

Flindt, Dawn
See Vella Munn

Flixton, Katherine

Floren, Lee
See Will Watson

Flores, Frances
See Frances De Talaver Berger

Flores, Janis
Risa Kirk, April Thorne

Flournoy, Sheryl Hines
Sherry Dee

Fluery, Jacqueline
See Pauline A. Kjellberg

Flynn-Alexander, Connie
Casey Roberts

Flynn, Christine

Flynn, Margaret
Margaret Livingston

Flynn, Mary
See Margaret Livingston

Flynn, Veronica
Jacqueline Lyons

Flynt, Catriona

Foley, Rae

Fontayne, Olivia
See Patricia De La Fuente

Foote, Victoria

Forbes, Elaine

Ford, Bette

Ford, Elbur
See Eleanor Hibbert

Ford, Elizabeth
Hilary Ford

Ford, Hilary
See Elizabeth Ford

Ford, Jessie
See Jessie Osborne

Ford, Lila

Ford, Marcia

Ford, Marti Ann
See Julianna Morris

Ford, Norrey
See Noreen Dilcock

Ford, Rachel

Forest, Regan

Forrest, Chelsey
Jan Cunningham

Forrest, Pamela Kae

Forrester, Helen

Forster, Rebecca
See Rebecca Czuleger

Forster, Suzanne

Forstot, Marilyn

Forsyth, Travis

Forsythe, Melissa

Forsythe, Patricia
Patrica Knoll, Charlotte Nichols

Fortina, Martha
Netta Carstens, Christina Laffeaty

Foster, Blair
Blair Clark, Sylvia Clark

Foster, Delia
See Quenna Tilbury

Foster, Jeanne
See Jeanne Williams

Key: Actual names appear in bold. Pseudonyms appear in italics.

Foster, John T.

Foster, Lawrence & Pauline
Jessica Logan

Fowler, Peggy & Dennis
Lauren Fox

Fowlkes, Mary

Fox, Alicia
See Carol Clemens-Fox

Fox, Caroline

Fox, Diana

Fox, Gardiner
Lynna Cooper

Fox, Lauren
See Peggy & Dennis Fowler

Fox, Natalie

Fox, Norman A.

Fox, Roz
Roz Denny

Fox, Susan

Foxe, Pamela
See Stuart Buchan

Foxx, Rosalind
See June Haydon, Judith Simpson

Frances, Robin

Franchon, Lisa
See Will Watson

Francis, Dorothy
See Ellen Goforth

Francis, Emily

Francis, Marina

Francis, Robin
See Rose Marie Ferris

Francis, Sara

Francis, Sharon
See Maureen Wartski

Frank, Ethel
Evelyn Hanna

Frank, Kate

Frankel, Emily

Frankel, Ruby
Rebecca Bennett, Constance Conrad, Lillian Marsh

Franklin, Edwina

Franklin, Janet

Franz, Carol

Fraser, Alison

Fraser, Anthea

Fraser, Jane
See Rosamunde Pilcher

Fraser, Kathleen
See Margaret Ball

Fraser, Sylvia

Frazier, Amy

Frazier, Pamela
See Florence Stevenson

Frederick, Kate

Frederick, Thea
See Barbara Keiler

Freed, Jan

Freed, Mary Kay
Mary Kay Simmons

Freeman, Cynthia

Freeman, Jayne

Freeman, Joy

Freeman, Kathleen
See Mary Fitt

Freethy, Barbara
Kristina Logan

Freiman, Kate

French, Ashley
See Julia Kane

French, Emily

French, Janine
See Roni Finkelstein, & Antonia Van-Loon

French, Judith E.

French, Marilyn

Friend, Oscar J.

Friends, Jalynn
See Rosalyn Alsobrook, & Jean Haught

AUTHOR PSEUDONYM INDEX

Key: Actual names appear in bold. Pseudonyms appear in italics.

Frisbie, R.D.

Fritch, Elizabeth
Eleanor Frost

Frost, Eleanor
See Elizabeth Fritch

Frost, Joan Van Emery

Fruchey, Deborah

Fulford, Paula

Fulford, Stephanie James

Fullbrook, Gladys
See Patricia Hutchinson

Fuller, Kathleen
See Theodore Mark Gottfried

Fuller, Samuel Michael

Fyfe, Sheila

Gabaldon, Diana

Gabhart, Ann

Gabriel, Mary

Gabriel, Tonya

Gacy, Linda M.

Gaddis, Peggy
See Erolie Pearl Dern

Gadzak, D. H.
Ann Bernadette

Gaeddert, Lou Ann

Gaetlin, Kimberleigh

Gaffney, Patricia

Gage, Carol
See Renee Shann

Gage, Elizabeth

Gage, Elsie

Gainer, Kathleen
See Kathleen Orr

Gaines, Diana

Gair, Diana

Gale, Adela
See Adela Maritano

Gale, Shannon

Gallagher, Patricia

Gallagher, Rita

Gallant, Felicia

Gallant, Jennie
See Joan Smith

Galloway, Kara
See Carol Cail

Galloway, Laura

Galt, Serena

Gamble, M. L.
See Marsha Nuccio

Gamel, Nona

Garcia, Nancy
Kate O' Donnell

Gardner, Joy
See Joy Aumente

Gardner, Kit
See Kit Garland

Gardner, Maria
Jillian Hunter

Gardner, Nancy
See Nancy Bruff

Gardner, Toni

Garfield, Patrice
See Marie Duess

Garland, Blanche
See Ruth Lesko

Garland, Kit
Kit Gardner

Garland, Lisette
See Prudence Boyd

Garland, Sherry
Lynn Lawrence

Garlock, Dorothy
Dorothy Glenn, Dorothy Phillips, Johanna Phillips

Garnar, Pauline

Garner, Kathleen
See Kathleen Orr

Garner, Phyllis A.
Phyllis Whitney

Garner, Sharon

Garratt, Maria

AUTHOR PSEUDONYM INDEX

Key: Actual names appear in bold. Pseudonyms appear in italics.

Garratt, Mary A.

Garrett, Sally
See Sally G. Dingley

Garrett, Sara

Garrett, Sibylle

Garrett, Wendy
Wendy Haley

Garrison, Joan
See William Neubauer

Garrod, Rene J.

Garry, Madeline
Madeline Davis

Garth, Will

Garvice, Charles
Caroline G. Hart, Carolyn Hart

Garwood, Julie

Gaskin, Catherine

Gasparotti, Elizabeth
Elizabeth Seifert

Gaston, Pat

Gates, Natalie

Gaud, Priscilla

Gault, Cinda

Gauthier, La Florya

Gaver, Jessica

Gay, Valerie

Gay, Virginia

Gayle, Emma

Gayle, Margaret
See Gail Hamilton

Gayle, Pamela

Gayle, Susan

Gaynor, Anne

Geach, Christine
Anne Lowing, Christine Wilson

Gedney, Mona K.

Gee, Evelyn
Constance O' Banyon, Micah Leigh

Gelles, Sandi
Nicole Raine

Gellis, Roberta
Max Daniels, Priscilla Hamilton, Leah Jacobs

Gentry, Georgina
See Lynne Murphy

Gentry, Jane
Jane Malcolm

Gentry, Peter
See Kerry Newcomb

George, Catherine

George, Mary
Elizabeth Thornton

George, Peter

George, Rebecca

Gerard, Cindy

Gerber, Ruth

Gergich, Millie
Millie Grey

Germany, Jo
Josie King

Gerritsen, Terry
Tess Gerritsen

Gerritsen, Tess
See Terry Gerritsen

Gerrond, Carol Blake

Gerson, Noel B.
Samuel Edwards, Paul Lewis, Dana Fuller Ross, Phillip Vail, Carter Vaughan

Gettler, Nina
Nina Beaumont

Gibbs, Mary Ann
See Marjory Bidwell

Gibbs, Nora
See Prudence Boyd

Giberson, Dorothy
Penelope Field

Gibert, Jacqueline

Gibeson, Jacqueline
Jacqueline La Tourette

Gibson, Hanna

AUTHOR PSEUDONYM INDEX

Key: Actual names appear in bold. Pseudonyms appear in italics.

Gibson, Jacqueline
Sabrina Grant

Gibson, Madelaine
See Madelaine G. Duckett

Gibson, Robin

Gibson, Rosemary

Giddings, Lauren
See Nancy Gideon

Gideon, Nancy
Lauren Giddings, Dana Ransom

Gideon, Robin
See K.D. Severson

Giencke, Jill

Gilbert-Lewis, Jeane

Gilbert, Anna
See Marguerite Lazarus

Gilbert, Jacqueline

Gilbert, Kate

Gilbert, Nan
See Mildred Gilbertson

Gilbert, Therese

Gilbertson, Mildred
Nan Gilbert, Jo Mendel

Giles, Raymond

Gill, Judy Griffith

Gillen, Cathy
See Cathy Gillen Thacker

Gillen, Lucy
Rebecca Stratton

Gillenwater, Sharon

Gilles, Katherine
See Katherine Gilles Sidel

Gillespie, Jane

Gillette, Louisa
See Gilda Feldman, & Leslie Rugg

Gilliland, Alexis

Gillis, Jacquelyn

Gillman, Olga

Gilman, Dorothy

Gilman, Hilary

Gilmer, Donna

Gilmer, Elizabeth Meriwether
Dorothy Dix

Gilmor, Ann
See Dan Ross

Gilmore, Cecile

Gilmour, Ann
See Anne Boyce Mc Naught

Gilmour, Barbara

Gilpen, Joanna
See Joanna Mc Gauran

Gilzean, Elizabeth
Elizabeth Houghton, Mary Hunton

Gimbel, Joan

Ginnes, Judith S.
Paige Mitchell

Giscard, Valerie
Emily Mesta

Gladden, Theresa

Gladstone, Arthur
Maggie Gladstone, Lisabet Norcross, Margaret Se Bastian, Cilla Whitmore

Gladstone, Eve
See Herma Werner

Gladstone, Maggie
See Arthur Gladstone

Glass, Amanda
See Jayne Ann Krentz

Glay, George Albert

Gleit, Joyce
Eve Gladstone

Glenn, Dorothy
See Dorothy Garlock

Glenn, Elizabeth
See Martha Gregory

Glenn, Karen
See Glenda Carrington

Glenn, Victoria

Glick, Ruth
Samantha Chase, Alyssa Howard, Alexis Hill Jordan, Amanda Lee, Tess Marlowe, Rebecca York

190

AUTHOR PSEUDONYM INDEX

Key: Actual names appear in bold. Pseudonyms appear in italics.

Glover, Judith

Gluyas, Constance

Godwin, Elizabeth

Goff, Jacqueline
Jenna Ryan

Goforth, Ellen
Dorothy Francis, Pat Louis

Goldenbaum, Sally
Natalie Stone

Goldie, Patricia

Golding, Morton J.
Patricia Morton

Goldman, James

Goldreich, Gloria

Goldrick, Elizabeth & Bob
Emma Goldrick

Goldrick, Emma
See Elizabeth & Bob Goldrick

Golon, Sergeanne

Gonzales, Deborah Martin
Deborah Martin, Deborah Nicholas

Good, Susanna

Goodchild, George

Gooding, Katherine

Goodis, David

Goodman, Irene
Diana Morgan

Goodman, Jo

Goodman, Liza

Goodman, Ruth
Meagan Mc Kinney

Goodwin, Hope
Linda Lee

Goold, Christine R.
Christine Robb

Gordon, Anita
Anne Merton Abbey

Gordon, Deborah
Brooke Hastings

Gordon, Diana
Lucilla Andrews, Lucilla Crichton, Joanna Marcus

Gordon, Emma

Gordon, Ethel E.

Gordon, Jane
See Elsie Cromwell

Gordon, Kaitlyn
See Kathy Lynn Emerson

Gordon, Katharine

Gordon, Laura

Gordon, Lucy
See Christine Fiorotto, & Christine Sparks

Gordon, Martha
Martha Starr

Gordon, Susan
See Susan G. Carboni

Gordon, Victoria

Goring, Anne

Gosling, Paula

Gottfried, Theodore Mark
Kathleen Fuller, Harry Gregory, Ted Mark, Katherine Tobias

Gottlieb, Irene Hannon
Irene Hannon

Goudge, Eileen

Goulart, Ron
Jillian Kearny

Gould, Judith

Gower, Iris
Iris Davies

Gowland, J.S.

Grace, Alicia
See Irving Greenfield

Grace, Anita
See Irving Greenfield

Grace, Carol
See Carol Culver

Grace, Janet

Grace, Rosemary

AUTHOR PSEUDONYM INDEX

Key: Actual names appear in bold. Pseudonyms appear in italics.

Grady, Liz
See Pat Coughlin

Graham, Elizabeth
See E. Schattner

Graham, Heather
See Heather Graham Pozzessere

Graham, Lewis

Graham, Lynne

Graham, Marteen D.

Grahame, Lucia

Graihan, Deborah

Grames, Selwyn Anne

Gramm, Nancy

Granau, Mary Ellen

Granbeck, Marilyn

Grand, Natalie
Susannah Hart

Grandower, Elissa
See Hillary Waugh

Grandville, Louise
See Daniel Streib

Grange, Peter
See Leslie Arlen

Granger, George
See Georgia Granger

Granger, Georgia
George Granger

Granger, Katherine
See Mary Sederquest

Grant, Anna
Anthea Malcolm

Grant, Charles L.
Felicia Andrews, Deborah Lewis

Grant, Hilda
Kay Grant, Jan Hilliard

Grant, Jeanne
See Alison Hart

Grant, Joan & Tracy
Anthea Malcolm

Grant, Kathryn
Kathleen Maxwell

Grant, Kay
See Hilda Grant

Grant, Laurie
See Laurie Chappelyear, Laurie Miller

Grant, Natalie

Grant, Sabrina
See Jacqueline Gibson

Grant, Sara
See Marianne Irwin

Grant, Tracy
Anthea Malcolm

Grant, Vanessa

Grasso, Patricia

Graversen, Pat

Graves, Keller
Kathryn Davenport, Evelyn Rogers

Graves, Tricia

Gray, Alison
See Alma Moser

Gray, Angela
See Helen Gray Weston

Gray, Evelyn
See Susan Leslie

Gray, Georgina

Gray, Ginna

Gray, Harriet
Ashley French, Julia Kane, Denise Robins, Francesca Wright

Gray, Jane
See Mairi O' Nair

Gray, Janet
See Sybil Russell

Gray, Janice

Gray, Juliet

Gray, Kerrie

Gray, Linda Crockett
Christina Crockett, Linda Castle

Gray, Lori
Marcy Gray

Gray, Marcy
See Lori Gray

AUTHOR PSEUDONYM INDEX

Key: Actual names appear in bold. Pseudonyms appear in italics.

Gray, Samantha

Gray, Suzanna

Gray, Valerie

Gray, Vanessa
  See Jacquelyn Aeby

Grayson, Elizabeth
  See Karyn Witmer-Gow

Grayson, Leanne
  See Robin Wiete

Grazia, Theresa
  Therese Alderton, Alberta Sinclair

Greco, Margaret

Green, Anne

Green, Billie June

Green, Elaine

Green, Grace
  Grace Reid

Green, Iris

Green, Judith

Green, Lois

Green, Maria

Green, Sharon

Greenaway, Gladys
  See Julia Manners

Greenberg, Jan
  See Jillian Karr

Greene, Carolyn
  Carolyn Monroe

Greene, Jennifer
  See Alison Hart

Greene, Juli
  See Judith Child, & Lisa Neher

Greene, Maria

Greenfield, Irving
  Riva Carles, Alicia Grace, Anita Grace, Gail St. John

Greenlea, Denice

Greenleaf, Jeanne M.

Greenleigh, Denice

Greenman, Nancy
  Lucy Elliot

Greenwood, Leigh
  See Harold Lowery

Greer, Francesca
  See Frankie-Lee Janas

Gregg, Margo

Gregg, Meredith

Gregor, Carol

Gregory, Harry
  See Theodore Mark Gottfried

Gregory, Jeri

Gregory, Jessica

Gregory, Jill
  See Jan Greenberg

Gregory, Kay

Gregory, Lisa
  See Kristen James

Gregory, Lydia
  See Diane & Greg Brodeur

Gregory, Martha
  Elizabeth Glenn, Marty Gregory

Gregory, Marty
  See Martha Gregory

Gregory, Mollie
  See Estelle Edwards

Gregory, Veronica

Greig, Christine

Greig, Maysie
  See Mary D. Warre

Greiman, Lois

Grey, Belinda

Grey, Charlotte

Grey, Evelyn
  See Ashley Allyn

Grey, Georgina
  See Mary Linn Roby

Grey, Gillian

Grey, Kitty
  See Mary Elizabeth Allen

AUTHOR PSEUDONYM INDEX

Key: Actual names appear in bold. Pseudonyms appear in italics.

Grey, Millie
    See Millie Gergich

Grey, Naidra

Grey, Nicole
    See Laura Battyanyi-Petose

Grey, Shirley

Greyland, Valerie
    See Valerie Seibond

Greyle, Katherine
    See Katherine Grill

Grice, Julia
    See Julia Haughey

Grieg, Sylvia

Grierson, Linden

Grieveson, Mildred
    Cardine Fleming, Caroline Fleming, Anne
    Mather

Griffin, Anne
    See Arthur Griffin

Griffin, Arthur
    Anne Griffin

Griffin, Chery
    Victoria Alexander

Griffin, Jocelyn
    See Laura Halford

Griffith, Kathryn Meyer

Griffith, Roslynn

Grijalva, Lucy

Grill, Katherine
    Katherine Greyle

Grimstead, Hettie
    Marsha Manning

Grinstead, J.E.

Grisanti, Mary Lee
    Perdita Shepherd

Gronau, Mary Ellen

Gross, Martha

Grove, Donna

Grove, Joan

Grundman, Donna

Guccione, Leslie Davis
    Leslie Davis

Guest, Diana
    See Diana Biondi

Guhrke, Laura Lee

Gumbley, Lynne
    Lynne Wilding

Gunn, Tom

Gunn, Virgina

Guntrum, Suzanne Simmons
    Suzanne Simmons, Suzanne Simms

Guss, Linda

Haaf, Beverly T.
    Beverly Terry

Haas, Carola
    Victoria Catalani

Habersham, Elizabeth
    See Shannon Harper, & Madeline Porter

Hacsi, Jacqueline
    Jacqueline Hope, Jacqueline Louis

Hadary, Simone

Haddow, Leigh
    See Ray Bentinck

Haddrill, Marilyn

Hadley, Liza

Hagan, Lorinda

Hagan, Patricia

Hagar, Jean
    Jeanne Stephens

Hagar, Judith
    See Judith Anne Polley

Hage, Lorinda
    See Elizabeth Lorinda Du Breuill

Hager, Jean
    Amanda Mc Allister, Leah Crane, Marlaine
    Kyle, Sarah North, Jeanne Stephens

Hahn, Lynn L.
    Lynn Lowery

Hailey, Johanna
    See Marcia Y. Howl, Sharon Jarvis

Hailstock, Shirley

AUTHOR PSEUDONYM INDEX

Key: Actual names appear in bold. Pseudonyms appear in italics.

Haines, Carolyn
Caroline Burnes

Haines, Pamela

Hake, Carolyn
Kate Denton

Haldeman, Linda

Hale, Antoinette
See Terri Harrington, & Antoinette Stockenberg

Hale, Arlene
See Lynn Williams

Hale, Dorothea
See Dorothy Weller

Hale, Katherine

Hale, Madeline
See Gilda Feldman, & Leslie Rugg

Hale, Mary
See Lynn Williams

Haley, Andrea
See Irene M. Pascoe

Haley, Jocelyn
See Jill Mc Lean

Haley, Wendy
See Wendy Garrett

Halford, Laura
Jocelyn Griffin, Laura Sparrow

Hall, Carolyn
Carole Halston, Caroline Halter

Hall, Claudia
See Will Watson

Hall, Diana
See Diane Holloway

Hall, Gillian

Hall, Gimane

Hall, Libby
See Olivia M. (Libby) Hall

Hall, Olivia M.
Libby Hall, Laurie Paige

Hall, Steffie
See Janet Evanovich

Halldorson, Phyllis Taylor

Halleran, E.E.

Halliday, Dorothy
Dorothy Dunnett

Halliday, Ena
See Sylvia Baumgarten

Hallin, Emily
Elaine Harper

Hallquist, F. Jacquelyn

Halsall, Penny
Penny Jordan

Halston, Carole
See Carolyn Hall

Halter, Caroline
See Carolyn Hall

Hamilton, Brenda
Brenna Todd

Hamilton, Celeste
See Jan Hamilton Powell

Hamilton, Daphne

Hamilton, Diana

Hamilton, Gail
Margaret Gayle

Hamilton, Julia
See Julia Fitzgerald

Hamilton, Katrina

Hamilton, Kay
See Cateau W. De Leeuw

Hamilton, Lucy
See Julia Rhyne

Hamilton, Paula

Hamilton, Priscilla
See Roberta Gellis

Hamilton, Steve
Linda Stevens, Linda Vail

Hamilton, Violet

Hamilton, Wade

Hamlett, Christina

Hamlin, Dallas
See Dallas Schulze

Hammett, Lafayette
See La Lette Douglas

Hammond, Ann

Key: Actual names appear in bold. Pseudonyms appear in italics.

AUTHOR PSEUDONYM INDEX

Key: Actual names appear in bold. Pseudonyms appear in italics.

Harper, Karen
Caryn Cameron

Harper, Madeline
See Shannon Harper, & Madeline Porter

Harper, Olivia & Ken
Jolene Adams, Jo Anna Brandon

Harper, Shannon
Madeline Harper, Elizabeth Habersham, Anna James, Taylor Brady, Leigh Bristol

Harrel, Linda
Shannon Clare

Harrell, Anne
See Carla Neggers

Harrell, Janice

Harrington, Alexis

Harrington, Emma
See Virginia Brown, Jane Harrison

Harrington, Kathleen

Harrington, Sharon & Rick
Rianna Craig

Harrington, Terri
See Antoinette Hardy

Harris, Andrea
See Irma Walker

Harris, Cindy M.
Bess Willingham

Harris, Elizabeth
Anne Merton Abbey

Harris, Ellen
Laura Eden, Claire St. John

Harris, Joanna
See Justine Burgess

Harris, Lane
Monica Harris

Harris, Lavinia
See Elizabeth Bolton

Harris, Leann

Harris, Lisa

Harris, Louise

Harris, Marilyn

Harris, Melinda
See Melinda Snodgrass

Harris, Monica
See Lane Harris

Harris, Sandra
See Sandra Young

Harris, Vivian
See Vivian H. Tichenor

Harrison, Allie

Harrison, Barbara

Harrison, Claire
Laura Eden

Harrison, Claudia

Harrison, Elizabeth
See Elizabeth Headley

Harrison, Jane
Emma Harrington

Harrison, Janis

Harrison, Leann

Harrison, Sarah

Harrison, Whit

Harrod-Eagles, Cynthia

Harrowe, Fiona
See Florence Hurd

Hart, Alison
Jeanne Grant, Jennifer Greene, Jessica Massey

Hart, Caroline G.
See Charles Garvice

Hart, Carolyn
See Charles Garvice

Hart, Carrie
See Carolyn Joyner

Hart, Catherine
See Diane Tidd

Hart, Elizabeth

Hart, Jessica

Hart, Joan Mary

Hart, Mallory Dorn

Hart, Neesa
See Mandalyn Kaye

Hart, Pam

Hart, Samantha

197

AUTHOR PSEUDONYM INDEX

Key: Actual names appear in bold. Pseudonyms appear in italics.

Hart, Susannah
  See Natalie Grand

Hart, Teresa

Hart, Virginia L.

Harte, Samantha

Hartman, Jane & Lorie
  Susannah Lawrence

Hartwig, Daphne

Harvey, Judy

Harvey, Marianne
  Mary Williams

Harvey, Rachel
  See Ursula Bloom

Harvey, Samantha

·Harvey, Ursula
  See Ursula Bloom

Harwell, Connie

Haskell, Leigh
  See Leigh Shaheen

Haskell, Mary
  See Mary Curtis

Hastings, Brooke
  See Deborah Gordon

Hastings, Charlotte
  See Charlotte Wisely

Hastings, Julia

Hastings, Laura

Hatcher, Robin Lee
  Robin Leigh

Hathaway, Jan
  See William Neubauer

Hatton, Pamela

Hauber, Josephine C.
  Josephine Charlton

Haughey, Julia
  Julia Grice

Haught, Jean
  Jalynn Friends, Patricia Pellicane

Haviland, Diana
  See Florence Hershman

Haviland, Meg
  See Helen Ketcham

Havptman, Elaine
  Gayle Corey

Hawkes, Sally
  See Sarah Hawkes

Hawkes, Sarah
  Sarah Eagle, Sally Falcon, Sally Hawkes

Hawley, S. R.

Hawthorne, Alaine
  See Alaine Richardson

Hawthorne, Violet
  See Christopher Rainone

Hay, Suzanne

Haycraft, Molly Costain

Hayden, Laura

Haydon, June
  Judy Baxter, Rosalind Foxx, Taria Hayford, Sara
  Logan

Haye, Jan
  Juliet Shore, Anne Vinton

Hayes, Allison
  See Lynn Coddington

Hayes, M.R.

Hayes, Morgan
  See Katrina Hamilton

Hayes, Sally Tyler

Hayford, Taria
  See Pat Rutherford

Hayle, Felicity

Haymond, Ginny
  See Lee Fleming

Haynes, Sally Tyler
  See Teresa Hill

Haynesworth, Susan
  See Susan E. Robertson

Hays, Lee
  Hilary Desmond, Sara Nichols

Hazard, Barbara
  Lillian Lincoln

Headley, Elizabeth
  Betty Cavanna, Elizabeth Harrison

Key: Actual names appear in bold. Pseudonyms appear in italics.

Healy, Catherine
Erin Yorke

Healy, Eugene

Healy, Letitia

Heath, Edith

Heath, Lorraine

Heath, Sandra
See Sandra Wilson

Heathcott, Mary
Mary Constance Keegan, Mary Raymond

Heaven, Constance
See George Fleming

Hecht, Ben
Veronica Heley

Hecklemann, Charles N.

Hedley, Catherine

Heggan, Christiane

Hehl, Eileen

Heidel, Kim
Kiz Von Robin

Heland, Victoria
See Josephine James

Held, G. N.

Heley, Veronica
See Ben Hecht

Helland, Beverly
Beverly Bird

Heller, Arnie
Eve O' Brian

Helm, Georgia

Hely, Sara

Hemmings, Lauren

Henaghan, Rosalie

Henchman, Jane

Henderson, Beth
Lisa Dane, Elizabeth Daniels

Henderson, George C.

Hendrickson, Doris E.
Emily Hendrickson

Hendrickson, Emily
See Doris E. Hendrickson

Hendrickson, Margaret

Hendrix, Lisa

Hendryx, James B.

Heneghan, Rosalie

Henke, Courtney

Henke, Shirl
See Shirl Henke, & Carol Reynard

Henley, Liz
See Janet M. Dooley

Henley, Virginia

Henrichs, Betty L.
Emily Doyle, Amanda Kent

Henry, Anne
See Judith Wall

Henry, Elizabeth

Hentges, Alison J.
Georgina Devon

Hepburne, Melissa
See Howard Brouder

Herbert, A. P.

Herbert, Julia

Herbert, Kathleen

Hermann, Nancy
Jessica Jeffries, Renee Russell, Samantha Scott

Hermann, Phyllis
See Phyllis DiFrancesco, Nira Hermann

Hern, Candice

Herres, Anne

Herrick, Susannah

Herring, Christina

Herrington, Terri
Tracy Hughes

Herrmann, Nira
Phyllis Hermann

Herrmann, Phyllis
See Phyllis Di Francesco, Nira Herrmann

Herschman, Morris
Evelyn Bond, Ian Kavanaugh, Sara Roffman, Janet Templeton, Lionel Webb

AUTHOR PSEUDONYM INDEX

Key: Actual names appear in bold. Pseudonyms appear in italics.

Herschner, Judith

Hershman, Florence
Diana Browning, Diana Haviland

Herter, Loretta M.
Lori Herter

Herter, Lori
See Loretta M. Herter

Hervey, Evelyn

Hess, Janice
Janice Carter

Hess, Norah
See Elsie Poe Bagnara

Hewitt, Elizabeth
See Mary Jean Abbott

Heydron, Vicki Ann

Heyer, Georgette
See Georgette Rougier

Heywood, Phillippa

Heywood, Sally

Hiatt, Brenda
See Brenda H. Barber

Hibbert, Eleanor
Philippa Carr, Elbur Ford, Victoria Holt,
Kathleen Kellow, Jean Plaidy, Ellalice Tate

Hicks, Daisy
See M. S. Roe

Hicks, Helen B.

Hicks, Joan Wilson
Kay Wilding, Kit Windham

Hicks, Martha
See Barbara Catlin Craven, Martha Rand Hix

Higgins, Joyce

High, Monique Raphael

Highet, Helen
Helen Mac Innes

Hill, Alexis - #1
See Ruth Glick, Carolyn Males, & Louise
Titchener

Hill, Alexis-#2
See Mary Shura Craig

Hill, Anne
See Netta Muskett

Hill, Deborah

Hill, Donna

Hill, Fiona
See Ellen Pall

Hill, Grace Livingston
See Grace Livingston Hill Lutz

Hill, Heather
See Joy Carroll

Hill, Johanna

Hill, Judith

Hill, Pamela

Hill, Rosa

Hill, Sandra

Hill, Teresa
Sally Tyler Haynes

Hillary, Anne
See Anne Kolaczak

Hiller, Flora
See Florence Hurd

Hilliard, Jan
See Hilda Grant

Hilliard, Nerina

Hills, Ida

Hilton, Linda

Hilton, Margery
See Margery Woods

Himrod, Brenda
Megan Lane, Brenda Trent

Hinchman, Jane

Hine, Alexandra
Alexandra Blakelee, Lilla Brennan

Hines, Charlotte
See Judith Mc Williams

Hines, Jeanne
See Rosamond Royal

Hingle, Metsy

Hingston, Mary Sandra
Mallory Burgess, Catherine Fitzgerald

Hinkemeyer, Michael T.
Vanessa Royall

Hintze, Naomi

Key: Actual names appear in bold. Pseudonyms appear in italics.

AUTHOR PSEUDONYM INDEX

Key: Actual names appear in bold. Pseudonyms appear in italics.

Hood, Ann

Hood, Gwenyth

Hooper, Kay
Kay Robins

Hoos, Suzanne
Anne Merton Abbey

Hoover, Saranne
Saranne Dawson, Pamela Lind

Hope, Amanda

Hope, Daphne

Hope, Jacqueline
See Jacqueline Hacsi

Hope, Margaret
See Alanna Knight

Hoppe, Stephanie

Hopson, William

Horler, Sydney

Horsman, Jennifer

Horton, Marian L.
Marian Lorraine

Horton, Naomi
See Susan Naomi Horton

Horton, Susan Naomi
Naomi Horton

Hoskins, Robert
Grace Corren, Susan Jennifer

Houghton, Elizabeth
See Elizabeth Gilzean

Houseman, Jennifer

Houseman, Phyllis

Houston, Henrietta
See Prudence Bingham Lichte

Houston, James

Howard, Alyssa
See Nancy Baggett, Eileen Buckholtz, Ruth Glick, Carolyn Males, & Louise Titchener

Howard, Don M.
Andrea St. John

Howard, Eleanor
See Eleanor Hodgson

Howard, Jessica
See Schere Monroe

Howard, Joy

Howard, Julia
See Pat Adams-Manson

Howard, Lesley

Howard, Linda
See Linda Howington

Howard, Linden
See Audrie Manley-Tucker

Howard, Lynde
See Lynette Howard

Howard, Lynette
Lynde Howard, Lynsey Stevens

Howard, Mary
See Mary Mussi

Howard, Stephanie

Howard, Teresa

Howard, Veronica

Howatch, Susan

Howe, Doris
See Mary Munro

Howe, Susannah
See Bree Thomas

Howell, Dorothy
Kit Prate

Howell, Elizabeth

Howell, Hannah
Sarah Dustin, Sandra Dustin

Howell, Jean

Howington, Linda
Linda Howard

Howl, Marcia Y.
Johanna Hailey, Pauline York

Hoy, Charlotte
Scotney St. James

Hoy, Elizabeth
See Alice Conarain

Hoyle, Coral
See Coral Hoyle Titus

Hrimak, Denise
Denise Mathews

AUTHOR PSEUDONYM INDEX

Key: Actual names appear in bold. Pseudonyms appear in italics.

Hubbard, Charlotte

Hubbard, Margaret
Lynn Emery

Hudson, Anna
See Jo Ann Algermissen

Hudson, Harriet L.
See Leigh Shaheen

Hudson, Jan
See Janece O. Hudson

Hudson, Janece O.
Jan Hudson, Jan Oliver

Hudson, Janis Reams

Hudson, Meg
See Carole Standish

Huff, Tom E.
Beatrice Parker, Katherine St. Clair, Edwina Marlow, Jennifer Wilde

Hufford, Susan
Samantha Hughes

Hughes, Cally
See Lass Small

Hughes, Charlotte

Hughes, Dorothy B.

Hughes, Eden
See William E. Butterworth

Hughes, Linda

Hughes, Rose

Hughes, Samantha
See Susan Hufford

Hughes, Terrence
See Ray Bentinck

Hughes, Tracy
See Terri Herrington

Hughesdon, Beverly

Hull, Beverly Wilcox

Hulme, Anne

Humphrey, Aileen

Hungengerg, Kristin

Hunt, Angela Elweel

Hunt, Beverly
Beverly Allen

Hunt, Charlotte
See Doris Marjorie Hodges

Hunt, Howard

Hunt, Jena
See Helen Conrad

Hunter, Diane

Hunter, Elizabeth
See Elisie B. Rider

Hunter, Hillary

Hunter, Jillian
See Maria Gardner

Hunter, Joan
See Jeanne Yarde

Hunter, Julia

Hunter, Margaret
See Ron Singer

Hunter, Susan
Marina Malcolm

Hunter, Valancy
See Eloise Meaker

Hunton, Mary
See Elizabeth Gilzean

Hurd, Florence
Flora Hiller, Fiona Harrowe

Hurley, Ann
See Ann Salern

Hurt, Terri

Husted, Darrell

Hutchinson, Bobby

Hutchinson, Nancy

Hutchinson, Patricia
Gladys Fullbrook

Huxley, Donna

Hyatt, Betty Hale

Hylton, Sara

Hyman, Ann

Hyman, Jackie
Jacqueline Diamond, Jacqueline Jade, Jacqueline Topaz

Hynnes, Lucetta
Caroline Light

AUTHOR PSEUDONYM INDEX

Key: Actual names appear in bold. Pseudonyms appear in italics.

Ibbotson, Eva

Ihle, Sharon
   See Sharon Mac Iver

Imboden, Durant
   Cheryl Durant

Ingram, Grace

Ingwalson, Phoebe C.
   Phoebe Conn, Cinnamon Burke

Innes, Jean
   See Jean Saunders

Ireland, Jane
   See Jackie Potter

Ireland, Liz

Ireland, Noelle
   See Prudence Boyd

Irwin, Margaret

Irwin, Marianne
   Sara Grant

Ison, Dorothy

Issacs, Susan

Ives, Averil

Jac, Cheryln
   See Cheryl Biggs

Jackson, Angela
   Lisa Sanders

Jackson, Betty

Jackson, Eileen
   Linda Comer, Helen May

Jackson, Elizabeth

Jackson, Helen Hunt

Jackson, Lisa
   See Susan Crose

Jacobs, Leah
   See Roberta Gellis

Jacobs, Linda C.
   Claire Blackburn

Jacobs, Lynn

Jade, Jacqueline
   See Jackie Hyman

Jaegly, Peggy
   Meg Miley

Jaffre, Susanne

Jagger, Brenda

Jakes, John
   Jay Scotland

James, Amalia
   See Carla Neggers

James, Anna
   See Shannon Harper, & Madeline Porter

James, Arlene
   See Deborah Rather

James, B. J.

James, Dana

James, Deana

James, Deborah

James, Ellen

James, Josephine
   Victoria Heland

James, Kristen
   Candace Camp, Lisa Gregory, Sharon Stephens

James, Kristin

James, Leigh Franklin
   See Paul Little

James, Livia

James, Margaret
   See Pamela Bennetts

James, Melanie

James, Nicola
   See Joan A. Cody

James, Rebecca
   See James Elward

James, Robin
   See Sharon & Tom Curtis

James, Sally
   Joyce Wilson

James, Samantha

James, Sandra
   See Sandra Kleinschmit

James, Sarah
   See Mildred Juskevice

James, Stephanie
   See Jayne Ann Krentz

Key: Actual names appear in bold. Pseudonyms appear in italics.

James, Susannah

James, Syrie
See Syrie Ann Astraham

James, Vanessa
See Sally Beaumann

Jameson, Claudia

Jamison, Amelia
See Sally M. Singer

Jamison, Ellen
See Jane Toombs

Jamison, Janelle
Tracie Peterson

Jamison, Kelly

Janas, Frankie-Lee
Francesca Greer, Saliee O' Brien

Janes, Josephine

Janeway, Harriet

Janeway, Judith

Janke, James A.

Jannet, Anna

Janney, Kate

Janowick, Jean Brooks
Anne Merton Abbey

Janssen, Krista
See Rhoda Poolle

Jansson, Georgeann
Joey Light

Jantz, Caroline

Jarette, Harriettade

Jarman, Rosemary Hawley

Jarrett, Bella
Belle Thorne

Jarrett, Miranda
See Susan Holloway Scott

Jarrett, Roxanne
See Herma Werner

Jarvis, Sharon
Johanna Hailey

Jason, Veronica
See Velda Johnston

Jastrzembski, Marian
Marian Edwards

Jay, Amanda Moor
Laura Kinsale

Jeal, Tim

Jean Brooks, Janowick
Anne Merton Abbey

Jefferies, Jessica

Jeffrey, Elizabeth

Jeffries, Jessica
See Nancy Hermann

Jeffries, Julia
See Lynda Ward

Jekel, Pamela

Jenkins-Nuttig, Linda
Kate Jenkins

Jenkins, Beverly

Jenkins, Kate
See Linda Jenkins-Nuttig

Jenkins, Linda

Jenkins, Sara Lucille
Joan Sargent

Jenkins, Vivian Knight

Jenner, Suzanne
See Gretchen Johnson, & Sally Netzel

Jennet, Anna

Jennifer, Susan
See Robert Hoskins

Jennings, Caylin
See Jeanne Triner

Jennings, Sara
See Maura Seger

Jensen, Muriel

Jensen, Shirl

Jerina, Carol

Jerome, Owen Fox

Jerrold, Pamela
See Pamela Muelbauer

Jeske, Colleen
Colleen Shannon

AUTHOR PSEUDONYM INDEX

Key: Actual names appear in bold. Pseudonyms appear in italics.

Jessup, Kathryn
  See Anne Kolaczak

Jett, Judith

Jewel, Carolyn

Joel, Barbara

Johansen, Iris

John, Ada
  See Ada Boulet

John, Nancy
  See Nancy & John Sawyer

Johns, Avery
  Margaret Cousins, Mary Parrish, William Masters

Johns, Karen
  See Karen Kimpel-Johns

Johnson, Barbara Ferry

Johnson, Betsy

Johnson, Claire

Johnson, Ellen Argo
  Ellen Argo

Johnson, Gretchen
  Suzanne Jenner

Johnson, Janice Kay
  See Janice Baczewski, & Norma Tadlock

Johnson, Katrina

Johnson, Martha P.

Johnson, Mary
  M. J. Rodgers

Johnson, Maud

Johnson, Norma Tadlock
  Kay Kirby

Johnson, Pamela
  Pamela Dalton

Johnson, Renate
  Ellen Tanner Marsh

Johnson, Susan
  Jill Barkin

Johnson, Velda

Johnston, Coleen L.

Johnston, Corinne

Johnston, Joan

Johnston, Norma
  See Elizabeth Bolton

Johnston, Velda
  Veronica Jason

Jones-Wolf, Gloria

Jones, Annabel

Jones, Beth Carsley

Jones, Deborah
  Samantha Holder

Jones, Diane Mc Clure
  Phoebe Matthews

Jones, Elinor

Jones, H. Bedford

Jones, Jan
  Caron Welles

Jones, Jill

Jones, Kathy

Jones, Kit O' Brien

Jones, Marian

Jones, Melissa Lynn

Jones, Minka

Jones, Nancy
  See Nancy Holder

Jones, Sandy

Jones, Veda Boyd

Jong, Erica

Jordan, Alexis Hill
  See Ruth Glick, Carolyn Males, & Louise Titchener

Jordan, Allie
  See Sandra Chastain, & Nancy Knight

Jordan, Carrie

Jordan, Debbie

Jordan, Gail
  See Erolie Pearl Dern

Jordan, Gale

Jordan, Janeane
  See Janeane Sena

Jordan, Joanna
  See Debrah Morris, & Pat Shaver

AUTHOR PSEUDONYM INDEX

Key: Actual names appear in bold. Pseudonyms appear in italics.

Jordan, Laura
  See Sandra Brown

Jordan, Madeleine

Jordan, Nicole
  See Anne Bushyhead

Jordan, Penny
  See Penny Halsall

Jordan, Rosemary
  See Mary Davis

Jordon, Joanna
  See Deborah Morris, Pat Shaver

Jordon, Laura

Joscelyn, Archie

Joseph, Joan

Joseph, Marie

Joseph, Robert
  Robin Joseph

Joseph, Robin
  See Robert Joseph

Joseph, Sarah G.

Joyce, Brenda
  See Brenda Dworman

Joyce, Deborah
  See Deborah Bryson, & Joyce Porter

Joyce, Jane
  See Ena Young

Joyce, Janet
  See Janet Bieber, Joyce Thies

Joyce, Janey

Joyce, Jenna Lee
  See Janet Bieber, Joyce Thies

Joyce, Julia
  See Julia Andresen

Joyce, Marianne

Joyce, Marie

Joyner, Carolyn
  Carrie Hart, Jackie Merritt

Judd, Catherine

Julien, Isobel
  Carola Salisbury

June, Dianna

Juneman, Karen
  Flanna Devin

Jurin-Reid, Barbara

Juskevice, Mildred
  Antonia Blake, Sarah James

Justice, Ann
  See Jo Horne Schmidt

Justin, Jennifer
  Jennifer West

Kachelmeier, Glenda Sanders
  Glenda Sanders, Glenda Sands

Kahn, Mary
  Miranda Cameron, Amanda Troy

Kaiser, Janice

Kaku, Louzana
  Christina Dair

Kalman, Yvonne

Kalmes, Susan

Kalpakian, Laura

Kamada, Annalise

Kamaroff, Alex
  Diana Morgan

Kamien, Marcia
  Marcia Rose

Kandel, Aben

Kane, Andrea

Kane, Carol

Kane, Elaine

Kane, Frank
  Gayle Kaye

Kane, Julia
  Ashley French, Harriet Gray, Denise Robins,
  Francesca Wright

Kane, Kathleen
  See Maureen Child

Kane, Valerie

Karni, Michaela
  Karin Berne, Diana Burke

Karr, Jillian
  Jan Greenberg, Karen Katz

AUTHOR PSEUDONYM INDEX

Key: Actual names appear in bold. Pseudonyms appear in italics.

Karr, Lee
  Leona Karr

Karr, Leona
  See Lee Karr

Karr, Phyllis Ann

Karron, Kris
  See Carol Norris

Kary, Elizabeth
  See Karyn Witmer-Gow

Kasey, Michelle
  See Kathie Seidick

Kasper, Gayle

Katz, Carol
  Penny Allison, Rosalynn Carroll

Katz, Karen
  See Jillian Karr

Katz, Molly

Kauffman, Donna

Kaukas, Bevlyn M.
  Bevlyn Marshall

Kavaler, Rebecca

Kavanaugh, Cynthia
  See Helen Gray Weston

Kavanaugh, Ian
  See Morris Herschman

Kay, Amber
  Georgina Devon

Kay, Catherine
  See Kay Croissant, & Catherine Dees

Kay, Karen

Kay, Patricia
  Trisha Alexander, Ann Patrick

Kaye, Amber

Kaye, Barbara
  See Barbara Kaye Walker

Kaye, Gayle
  See Frank Kane

Kaye, Joanne
  See Rachel Cosgrove Payes

Kaye, Judy
  See Judy Baer

Kaye, M. M.

Kaye, Mandalyn
  See Neesa Hart

Kayle, Hilary

Keane, Lucy

Kearny, Jillian
  See Ron Goulart

Kearsley, Susanna

Keast, Karen
  See Sandra Canfield

Keaton, Corey
  See Mary Tate Engels, & Vicki Lewis Thompson

Keegan, Mary Constance
  Mary Heathcott, Mary Raymond

Keelyn, Patricia
  See Pat Van Wie

Keene, Day

Keene, Sarah
  See Jane Atkins

Keiler, Barbara
  Judith Arnold, Ariel Berk, Thea Frederick

Keinzley, Francis

Keith, Vivian
  See Vivian Copeland

Keller, Barbara

Keller, Kathy

Kelley, Dorsey Adams
  Dorsey Adams, Dorsey Kelley

Kelley, Dorsey
  See Dorsey Adams Kelley

Kelley, Thomas P.

Kellman, Ellen
  Leonora Woodbury

Kellow, Kathleen
  See Eleanor Hibbert

Kells, Sabine

Kells, Susannah

Kelly, Carla

Kelly, Ellen

Kelly, Judith
  See Judith English

Kelly, Susan

Key: Actual names appear in bold. Pseudonyms appear in italics.

Kelm, Kaye Wilson
See Cathleen Carlson

Kelrich, Victoria

Kemp, Shirley

Kendall, Julia Jay
Katherine Kingsley

Kendall, Katherine
See Katherine Applegate

Kendall, Lynn Alden
Francesca Brooks

Kendyl, Sharice

Kennealy, Patricia
See Patricia Morrison

Kennedy, Marilyn

Kennedy, Nancy

Kenner, Laura

Kent, Amanda
See Betty L. Henrichs

Kent, Andrea

Kent, Fortune
See John Toombs

Kent, Helen
See Judith Anne Polley

Kent, Jean Salter
Kathryn Kent

Kent, Jean

Kent, Katherine
See Joan Dial

Kent, Kathryn
See Jean Salter Kent

Kent, Lynnette
See Cheryl Bacon

Kent, Pamela
See Ida Pollock

Kenyon, Bruce

Kenyon, Cory
See Mary Tate Engels, & Vicki Lewis Thompson

Kenyon, Joanna
See Janet Clarke

Kenyon, Theda

Keppel, Charlotte
See Ursula Torday

Ker, Madeleine

Kerr, Katharine

Kersh, Gerald

Kerstan, Lynn

Ketcham, Helen
Meg Haviland

Ketter, Pam
See Pamela Browning

Key, Alexander

Keyes, Francis Parkinson

Keyworth, Anne

Kichline, Linda
Allyson Ryan, Carin Rafferty

Kidd, Elizabeth
See Linda Jeannette Triegel

Kidd, Flora

Kidd, Lucy

Kidder, Jane
Katharine Charles

Kidwell, Jane

Kiehl, Claire
Justine Cole

Kihlstrom, April

Kilchenstein, Mary
Jean Faure, Mary Alice Kirk, Mary Kirk

Kilgore, Katherine

Kilgore, Kay

Kilmer, Wendela P
Karen Van Der Zee, Moran Van Wieren

Kimbro, Jean
See John M. Kimbro

Kimbro, John M.
Kyn Allyson, Ann Ashton, Charlotte Bramwell, Jean Kimbro, Katheryn Kimbrough

Kimbrough, Colleen
See Kay Porterfield

Kimbrough, Katheryn
See John M. Kimbro

Key: Actual names appear in bold. Pseudonyms appear in italics.

AUTHOR PSEUDONYM INDEX

Key: Actual names appear in bold. Pseudonyms appear in italics.

Knight, Alicia
Lucretia Wright

Knight, Allison
See Martha Krieger

Knight, Barbara

Knight, Joan Giezey
Iris Summers

Knight, Kristie
See Nancy Knight

Knight, Nancy
Jenna Darcy, Kristie Knight

Knoll, Anne

Knoll, Patrica
See Patricia Forsythe, & Barbara Williams

Knowles, Mabel Winnifred
Wynne May

Koehler, Margaret Hudson
Maggi Charles, Meg Hudson, Russell Mead,
Carole Standish

Koehler, Margaret
See Carole Standish

Koen, Karleen

Kohake, Rosanne

Kohl, Candice

Kohman, Catherine
Anne Merton Abbey

Kolaczak, Anne
Anne Benson, Erika Bryant, Adrienne Edwards,
Andrea Edwards, Anne Hillary, Kathryn Jessup

Kolaski, Barbara Reeves
Barbara Reeves

Koontz, Dean
Leigh Nichols

Koppel, Lillian
Lillian Shelley

Korbel, Kathleen
See Eileen Dryer

Koskinen, Sue

Kossoff, Harriet
Harriet Klass

Kotselas, Janet

Koumalats, Jodi
Jodi Thomas

Kovack, Teri
Tess Holloway, Tess Oliver, Teri Shapiro

Kovacs, Katherine
Katherine Coffaro

Kovats, Nancy

Krahn, Betina M.

Kramer, Katherine
Katherine Vickery

Kramer, Kathryn

Krause, Kathleen

Krentz, Jayne Ann
Jayne Bentley, Jayne Castle, Amanda Glass,
Stephanie James, Amanda Quick, Jayne Taylor

Krentz, Joan

Krepps, Robert W.
Beatrice Brandon

Kreps, Penelope

Krieger, Martha
Allison Knight

Krinard, Susan

Kriske, Anne

Kroeger, Kelly

Krokosz, Emily
Emily Bradshaw, Emily Carmichael

Krueger, Elizabeth

Kruger, Mary
Mary Kingsley

Kuczir, Mary
Fern Michaels, Iris Summers

Kuether, Eidth Lyman
Margaret Malcolm

Kuhlin, Suzanne J.
Jennifer Mikels

Kuhn, Phyllis

Kurr, Maureen

Kwock, Laureen
Clarice Peters

Kyle, Marlaine
See Jean Hager

Key: Actual names appear in bold. Pseudonyms appear in italics.

Kyle, Susan
Diana Blayne, Katy Currie, Diana Palmer

L' Estrange, Anna
Rosemary Ellerbeck, Nicola Thorne, Katherine Yorke

La Barre, Harriet

La Dame, Cathryn
Cathryn Baldwin, Cathryn Ladd

La Foy, Leslie Marie

La Rosa, Linda

La Rue, Brandy

La Tourette, Jacqueline
See Jacqueline Gibeson

Lacey, Anne
See Martha Corson

Lachlan, Edythe
See Edythe Cudlipp

Lacy, Tira
See Rita Estrada

Ladd, Cathryn
See Cathryn La Dame

Ladd, Linda
Jillian Roth

Laden, Janis
See Janis Shiffman

Ladley, Anne

Laffeaty, Christina
Netta Carstens, Martha Fortina

Lahey, Karen
Elizabeth Albright

Laine, Annabel

Laity, Sally

Lake, Patricia

Lake, Rozella
Roumelia Lane, Roberta Leigh, Rachel Lindsay, Janey Scott

Laker, Rosalind
See Barbara Ovstedahl

Lakso, Elaine
Laine Allen

Lamb, Arnette

Lamb, Charlotte
See Sheila Holland

Lambert, Bill
Willa Lambert

Lambert, Elizabeth

Lambert, Willa
See Bill Lambert

Lambright, Jeanie
Kate Denton

Lammert, Charlotte

Lamont, Marianne
Alexandra Manners, Joanne Marshall

Lampman, Carolyn
See Carolyn Brubaker

Lancaster, Bruce

Lancaster, Joan
See Marlene J. Anderson

Lancaster, Lisa
Elizabeth Lane

Lancaster, Lydia
See Eloise Meaker

Lancaster, Sheila
See Sheila Holland

Lancaster, Vicky
See Lyndon Snow

Lance, Leslie
See Irene Mossop, Charles & Irene Swatridge

Lancour, Gene
Jeanne Lancour, Gene Louis Fisher

Lancour, Jeanne
See Gene Lancour

Land, Jane

Landers, Dawn

Landers, Lynda Stowe

Landers, Mary Anne
Rima Saret

Landis, Jill Marie

Landon, Nancy
See Nancy Berland

Lane, Allison
See Susan Pace

Lane, Beverly

AUTHOR PSEUDONYM INDEX

Key: Actual names appear in bold. Pseudonyms appear in italics.

Lane, Elizabeth
Lisa Lancaster

Lane, Jane
See Elaine Dakers

Lane, Kami
See Elaine C. Smith

Lane, Megan
See Brenda Himrod, & B.L. Wilson

Lane, Roumelia
See Rozella Lake

Lang, Eve
See Ruth Ryan Langan

Lang, Frances

Lang, Grace
See Will Watson

Lang, Heather
See Darlene Baker

Lang, Hilary
See Marjorie Bowen

Lang, Maud

Lang, Miriam
Margot Leslie

Langan, Ruth Ryan
Eve Lang

Lange, Emma

Langford, Sandra
See Olivia Sinclair

Langley, Tania
See Tilly Armstrong

Langtry, Ellen
See Nancy Elliott

Lanham, Cheryl

Lanigan, Catherine
Joan Wilder

Lansdale, Nina
See Marilyn Meeske Sorel

Lansing, Jessica
See David Ritz

Lanzoni, Fabio
Fabio

Larkin, Elinor
See Diane Lefer

Larkin, Kara

Larkin, Rochelle

Larson, Shirley

Larson, Susan
Suzanne Michelle

Latham, Robin
Cassandra Bishop, Robin Lynn

Lattin, Anne
See Lois Cole Taylor

Laurence, Anne

Laurens, Stephanie

Laurenson, R.M.
Elizabeth Law

Laux, Constance
Zoe Daniels

Laven, Marti
See Marti L. O' Laimhin

Lavender, Gwyn

Laverentz, Liana

Law, Elizabeth
See R.M. Laurenson

Law, Susan Kay

Lawrence, Allison
See Judy Bryer

Lawrence, Jacqueline

Lawrence, Juliet

Lawrence, Kathy

Lawrence, Katy
See Kathleen Kelly Martin, & Larry Jay Martin

Lawrence, Lynn
Sherry Garland

Lawrence, Mary Margaret

Lawrence, Mary Terese
Terry Lawrence

Lawrence, Nancy
See Nancy Stack

Lawrence, Susannah
See Jane Hartman

Lawrence, Terry
See Mary Terese Lawrence

AUTHOR PSEUDONYM INDEX

Key: Actual names appear in bold. Pseudonyms appear in italics.

Lawson, Christine
   See Quenna Tilbury

Lawton, Lynna

Laye, Patricia

Layle, Emmey

Laymon, Carla

Layton, Andrea
   See Ingrid Nielson

Layton, Edith
   See Edith Felber

Lazarus, Marguerite
   Anna Gilbert

Le Butt, Paul

Le Clair, Laurie

Le Claire, Day

Le Compte, Jane
   Jane Ashford

Le Grand, Sybil
   See Kaa Byington

Le Mon, Lynn
   Lynette Wert

Le Roy, Irene
   See Sally Svee

Le Varre, Deborah
   See Deborah Varlinsky

Leabo, Karen

Lear, Caty

Lebedeff, Ivan

Lebourdais, D.M.

Lechleidner, Mary L.
   Delia Parr

Ledbetter, Suzann

Lee, Adrienne

Lee, Alice Chetwynd

Lee, Alyssa

Lee, Amanda
   See Nancy Baggett, Eileen Buckholtz, Ruth
   Glick, Carolyn Males, & Louise Titchener

Lee, Devon
   See Robert Warren Pohle

Lee, Doris

Lee, Elsie
   See Elsie Cromwell

Lee, Joyce

Lee, Katherine

Lee, Linda Francis

Lee, Linda
   See Hope Goodwin

Lee, Lucy
   See Charlene Talbot

Lee, Lydia
   See Rose Marie Lima

Lee, Maureen

Lee, Miranda

Lee, Rachel
   See Sue Civil

Lee, Rebecca Hagen

Lee, Rowena
   Marie Bartlett, Valerie Rift

Lee, Sandra
   See Sandra Lee Smith

Lee, Sharon

Lee, Sherry

Lees, Marguerite
   Margaret Baumann

Lefer, Diane
   Elinor Larkin

Lehman, Paul Evan

Lehr, Helene
   Helene Sinclair

Leiber, Vivian

Leigh, Ana

Leigh, Barbara

Leigh, Bristol
   See Donna Ball, & Shannon Harper

Leigh, Catherine
   See Catherine Lee Donick

Leigh, Cynthia

Leigh, Elizabeth
   See Debbie Hancock

AUTHOR PSEUDONYM INDEX

Key: Actual names appear in bold. Pseudonyms appear in italics.

Leigh, Helena

Leigh, Jackie
See Deborah Smith

Leigh, Jo

Leigh, Lori

Leigh, Meredith

Leigh, Micah
See Evelyn Gee

Leigh, Olivia
Helen Champ

Leigh, Petra
See Peter Ling

Leigh, Roberta
See Rozella Lake

Leigh, Robin
See Robin Lee Hatcher

Leigh, Susannah

Leigh, Tamara

Leigh, Victoria

Leinster, Murray

Leitfred, Robert H.

Lemberger, Le Ann
Leigh Michaels

Lemery, Alysse
See Alysse S. Rasmussen

Lenke, Gail

Lennox, Jacqueline
See Deborah Smith

Lennox, Marion

Lenore, Lisa
See Howard Brouder

Leonard, Lila

Leonard, Phyllis G.
Isabel Ortega

Leone, Adele
Charlotte Austen

Leone, Laura
See Laura Resnick

Leosing, Jan

Lesko, Ruth
Blanche Garland

Leslie, Alice

Leslie, Doris

Leslie, Joanna
See Jessica Dare

Leslie, Lynn
See Sherill Lynn Bodine, & Elaine Leslie Sima

Leslie, Margot
Miriam Lang

Leslie, Miriam
See Dan Ross

Leslie, Rochelle
See Graham Diamond

Leslie, Susan
Ashley Allyn, Evelyn Gray

Lesoing, Jan

Lester, Jane
See Quenna Tilbury

Lester, Samantha
See Lester Roper

Levitt, Dianne

Levy, Barbara
Jessica Elliot

Lewellyn, Caroline

Lewesohn, Leone
Frances Davies

Lewis, Deborah
See Charles L. Grant

Lewis, Hilda

Lewis, Kim
Anne Merton Abbey

Lewis, Mary
See Mary Berrisford

Lewis, Maynah

Lewis, Paul
See Noel B. Gerson

Lewis, Sherry

Lewis, Susan

Lewty, Marjorie

Ley, Alice Chetwynd

Leyton, Sophie
Sheila Wash

AUTHOR PSEUDONYM INDEX

Key: Actual names appear in bold. Pseudonyms appear in italics.

Lichte, Prudence Bingham
Henrietta Houston, Prudence Martin

Lide, Mary

Liggett, Walter W.

Light, Caroline
See Lucetta Hynnes

Light, Joey
See Georgeann Jansson

Liholm, Molly

Lima, Rose Marie
Lydia Lee

Limber, Jill

Lin, Belle

Lincoln, Lillian
See Barbara Hazzard

Lind, Judi

Lind, Pamela
See Saranne Hoover

Linden, Catherine

Linden, Deanna
See Dana Rae Pugh

Lindley, Erica
See Aileen Quigley

Lindley, Meredith
See Meredith Brucker

Lindsay, Dawn

Lindsay, Devon
See Cynthia Wright

Lindsay, Nicole
See Nicole De Lyn

Lindsay, Norman

Lindsay, Perry
See Erolie Pearl Dern

Lindsay, Phillip

Lindsay, Rachel
See Rozella Lake

Lindsey, Betina

Lindsey, Dana
See Dora Brown

Lindsey, Dawn
See Cherylle Lindsey Dimick

Lindsey, Devon

Lindsey, Johanna

Lindsey, Patrice
See Patricia Pinianski, & Linda Sweeney

Lindsey, Terri
See Terri Lynn Wilhelm

Ling, Peter
Petra Leigh

Lingard, Joan

Linigton, Elizabeth
Anne Blaisdell, Lesley Egan, Egan O' Neill, Dell Shannon

Link, Gail

Linley, Elinor

Linz, Cathie
See Cathie Baumgardner

Lippencott, Dorothy

Lisle, Mary
See Marylyle Rogers

Liston, Robert
Elizabeth Bright

Little, Paul
Marie De Jourlet, Leigh Franklin James, Paula Little, Paula Minton

Little, Paula
See Paul Little

Litton, Pamela

Livingston, Alice

Livingston, Georgette
Diane Crawford

Livingston, Margaret
Margaret Flynn, Mary Flynn

Lloyd, Adrien

Lloyd, Frances

Lloyd, Levanah
See Maureen Peters

Lloyd, Marta
See Marta Buckholder

Lloyd, Mary Jane
Mary Jane De Genaro

Lobb, Charlotte
Charlotte Moore

AUTHOR PSEUDONYM INDEX

Key: Actual names appear in bold. Pseudonyms appear in italics.

Lockhart, Lynn

Lockwood, Karen
  See Karen Finnigan

Lofts, Norah
  See Peter Curtis

Logan, Anne
  See Barbara Colley

Logan, Cait
  See Lois Kleinsasser Testerman

Logan, Daisy
  See Sara Orwig

Logan, Jessica
  See Lawrence Foster

Logan, Kate

Logan, Kristina
  See Barbara Freethy

Logan, Leandra
  See Mary Schultz

Logan, Mark
  See Leslie Arlen

Logan, Sara
  See June Haydon, Judith Simpson

Loghry, Lizabeth

London, Anne
  See Ann Miller

London, Cait
  See Lois Kleinsasser Testerman

London, Hilary
  See Nancy & John Sawyer

London, Laura
  See Sharon & Tom Curtis

London, Victoria

Long, Amelia Reynolds

Long, Jean M.

Long, Manning

Long, Viola E.
  Beth Bryan

Long, William Stuart
  See Violet Vivian Mann

Longford, Lindsay
  See Jimmie Morel

Longrigg, Roger
  See Megan Barker

Look, Jane H.
  Lee Damon

Lopez, Dee
  Dee Norman

Loraine, Connie
  Colleen L. Reece

Lord, Alexandra
  See Patricia Williams

Lord, Allison
  See Julie Ellis

Lord, Bette Bao

Lord, Jeffery
  See Julie Ellis

Lord, Moira
  Dolores Craig, Miriam Lynch, Claire Vincent

Lord, Vivian
  See Pat Wallace Strother

Lorel, Claire
  See Daphne De Jong

Lorimer, Claire

Lorin, Amii
  See Joan M. Hohl

Loring, Emilie

Loring, Jane
  See Lee Sawyer

Loring, Jenny
  Lee Sawyer, Martha Sans

Loring, Lynne
  See Marilyn Austin

Lorraine, Anne
  See Jane Alan

Lorraine, Marian
  See Marian L. Horton

Lorrimer, Claire
  See Beatrice Coogan

Lough, Loree
  Cara Mc Cormack

Louis, Jacqueline
  See Jacqueline Hacsi

Louis, Mary-Ben
  See Mary Ben Cretenoid

AUTHOR PSEUDONYM INDEX

Key: Actual names appear in bold. Pseudonyms appear in italics.

Louis, Pat
See Ellen Goforth

Lovan, Thea
Christine King

Lovelace, Jane
See Dixie Mc Keone

Lovelace, Merline

Lovesmith, Janet
See Paul Fairman

Low, Dorothy Mackie
Zoe Cass, Lois Low, Lois Paxton

Low, Lois
See Dorothy Mackie Low

Lowe, Charlotte
Annabella

Lowe, Susan
Andrea Davidson, Elise Randolph

Lowell, Anne Hunter
See Marie Ferrarella

Lowell, Elizabeth
See Ann Maxwell

Lowell, Lydia

Lowery, Harold
Leigh Greenwood

Lowery, Lynn
See Lynn L. Hahn

Lowery, Marilyn
Philippa Castle

Lowewengard, Heidi
Martha Albrand, Katrin Holland

Lowing, Anne
See Christine Geach

Loy, Diana
See Rhonda Cohen

Lozana, Wendy

Luan, Carla
See Cay David

Lucas, Mary Mayo

Luellan, Valentina
See Judith Anne Polley

Lutyens, Mary
Esther Wyndham

Lutz, Grace Livingston Hill
Grace Livingston Hill

Lyle, Elizabeth

Lynch, Frances

Lynch, Miriam
Delores Craig, Moira Lord, Claire Vincent

Lyndell, Catherine
See Margaret Ball

Lyndon, Diana
See Diane Antonio

Lynley, Elinor

Lynn, Anita

Lynn, Ann
See Karen Paradiso

Lynn, Karen
See Lynn Taylor

Lynn, Leslie
See Sherill Lynn Bodine, & Elaine Leslie Sima

Lynn, Margaret
See Gladys Battye

Lynn, Mary
See Elizabeth Neibor

Lynn, Robin
See Robin Latham

Lynn, Sheryl

Lynn, Terri
See Terri Lindsey

Lynn, Virginia
See Virginia Brown

Lynne, Deborah

Lynne, Suzanna

Lynnford, Janet

Lynson, Jane

Lynton, Anne
Sheila Brandon, Ruth Martin, Claire Rayner

Lyon, Jessica
See Cateau W. De Leeuw

Lyon, Mary

Lyons, Jacqueline
See Veronica Flynn

Key: Actual names appear in bold. Pseudonyms appear in italics.

Lyons, Leila
See James Conaway

Lyons, Maggie

Lyons, Mary

Ma Caffree, Sharon

Mac Allister, Heather
Heather Allison

Mac Call, Isabel
Elizabeth Boyd

Mac Carthy, Dorothy

Mac Donald, Elisabeth
Sabrina Ryan

Mac Donald, Roslyn
Louise Clark

Mac Donald, Sue

Mac Donnell, Megan
See Serita Stevens

Mac Gregor, Miriam

Mac Innes, Helen
See Helen Highet

Mac Iver, Sharon
June Cameron, Sharon Ihle

Mac Keever, Maggie
Gail Clark, Grace Scott, Grace South

Mac Kenzie, Maura

Mac Kinnon, Charles Roy
Charles Conte, Vivian Donald, Rory Macalpin,
Graham Montrose, Hilary Rose, Charles Stuart,
Iain Torr

Mac Lean, Anne
Jan Mac Lean

Mac Lean, Jan
See Anne Mac Lean

Mac Leod, Charlotte

Mac Leod, Jean S.
Catherine Airlie

Mac Leod, Laura

Mac Millan, Don

Mac Neill, Anne
See Maura Seger

Mac Pherson, A. D. L.

Mac Pherson, Selina

Mac Williams, Margaret

Macalpin, Rory
See Charles Roy Mac Kinnon

Macaluso, Pamela

Mace, Merlda

Machin, Meredith Land

Macias, Stacie

Macias, Susan
Susan Mallery

Mack, Amanda
See Jean Adelson

Mack, Dorothy
See Dorothy Mc Kittrick

Mackenzie, Myrna

Mackey, Leonora
Dorothy Rivers, Leonora Starr

Mackey, Mary

Mackie, Mary
See Alex Andrews

Mackintosh, May

Maclay, Charlotte

Maclean, Jan

Macomber, Debbie

Madden, Anne Wakefield

Madden, Mickee

Maderich, Robin

Madl, Linda

Magner, Laura
See Laura Parris

Magner, Lee

Mahon, Kay

Mahoney, Irene
Angela Simon

Maitland, Margaret
See Elizabeth Lorinda Du Breuill

Maitland, Pamela

Major, Ann
See Margaret Major Cleaves

AUTHOR PSEUDONYM INDEX

Key: Actual names appear in bold. Pseudonyms appear in italics.

Makepeace, Joanna
  See Margaret Elizabeth York

Makewell, Kathleen

Malcolm, Aileen
  Aleen Malcolm

Malcolm, Aleen
  See Aileen Malcolm

Malcolm, Anthea
  See Joan & Tracy Grant

Malcolm, Jane
  See Jane Gentry

Malcolm, Margaret
  See Eidth Lyman Kuether

Malcolm, Marina
  See Charlotte Douglas, & Susan Hunter

Maleckar, Nicolette
  Jane Shore

Malek, Doreen Owens
  Faye Morgan

Males, Carolyn
  Alyssa Howard, Clare Richards

Malina, Fred

Malkind, Margaret
  Kate Nevins

Mallery, Susan
  See Susan Macias

Mallin, Gail

Mallory, Kathryn

Malmont, Valerie S.

Malone, Bev

Malone, Margaret Gay

Maloy, Donna
  See Donna Saucier

Malteree, Elona

Mandeville, Francine
  Francine Christopher

Manger, Lee
  See Ellen M. Tatara

Mangrum, Valerie
  Patricia Ellis

Manley-Tucker, Audrie
  Linden Howard

Manley, Edna Maye

Mann, Deborah
  See Ursula Bloom

Mann, Margaret

Mann, Violet Vivian
  Barbara Allen, Alex Stuart, Robyn Stuart, Vivian Stuart, William Stuart Long

Manners, Alexandra
  See Marianne Lamont

Manners, Julia
  Gladys Greenaway

Manning, Jo
  Irene Robinson

Manning, Lisa

Manning, Marilyn

Manning, Marsha
  See Hettie Grimstead

Manning, Mary Louise
  Lou Cameron

Mansell, Joanna

Mansfield, Elizabeth
  See Paula Reibel

Mansfield, Katherine
  Kathleen Beauchamp

Maragakis, Helen
  Eleni Carr, Helen Carter, Helen Carras

Marath, Laurie
  Suzanne Roberts

March, Jessica

March, Lindsay

March, Stella
  Marguerite Mooers Marshall

Marchant, Catherine
  See Catherine Fawcett

Marchant, Jessica

Marcus, A.A.

Marcus, Joanna
  Lucilla Andrews, Lucilla Crichton, Diana Gordon

Mardon, Deirdre

Marie, Susan

AUTHOR PSEUDONYM INDEX

Key: Actual names appear in bold. Pseudonyms appear in italics.

Marino, Susan
See Julie Ellis

Marion, Carolyn

Maritano, Adela
Jane Converse, Adela Gale, Kay Martin

Mark, Ted
See Theodore Mark Gottfried

Markhan, Patricia
Patricia Carro

Markowiak, Linda

Marks, Joanna
See Ellen Tanner Marsh

Marlin, Marcia

Marliss, Deanna
Diana Mars, Diana Moore

Marlow, Edwina
See Tom E. Huff

Marlowe, Ann

Marlowe, Delphine
See Ron Singer

Marlowe, Katharine

Marlowe, Tess
See Ruth Glick, Carolyn Males, & Louise Titchener

Marnay, Jane

Marr, Anne
See Nell Dean Ratzlaff

Marrs, Pauline Draper

Mars, Diana
See Deanna Marliss

Marsh, Ellen Tanner
See Renate Johnson

Marsh, Lillian
See Ruby Frankel

Marsh, Rebecca
See William Neubauer

Marsh, Valerie

Marshall, Bevlyn
See Bevlyn M. Kaukas

Marshall, Edison

Marshall, Jacqueline
Deborah Austin

Marshall, Joanne
See Marianne Lamont

Marshall, Marguerite Mooers
See Stella March

Marshall, Marilyn

Marshall, Paula

Marshall, Raymond

Martel, Aimee
See Aimee Thurlo

Marten, Jacqueline

Martin, Ann
See Marcia Wayne

Martin, Caroline

Martin, Chuck

Martin, Deborah
See Deborah Martin Gonzales

Martin, Ione

Martin, Judy
Jeanette Earnest, Andra Erskine

Martin, Kat
See Kathleen Kelly Martin, & Larry Jay Martin

Martin, Kathleen Kelly
Katy Lawrence, Kat Martin

Martin, Kay
See Adela Maritano

Martin, Larry Jay
Katy Lawrence

Martin, Lee

Martin, Marcia

Martin, Margaret

Martin, Marian

Martin, Mary

Martin, Monica

Martin, Nancy
Elissa Curry

Martin, Patricia

Martin, Prudence
See Prudence Bingham Lichte

Martin, Rhona

221

AUTHOR PSEUDONYM INDEX

Key: Actual names appear in bold. Pseudonyms appear in italics.

Martin, Ruth
  See Claire Rayner

Martin, Sally

Martin, W.

Martini, Teri
  Alison King, Theresa Martini, Wendy Martini

Martini, Theresa
  See Teri Martini

Martini, Wendy
  See Teri Martini

Marton, Sandra
  Sandra Myles

Marton, Suzanne
  See Selina Mac Pherson

Martyn, Norma

Marvin, Richard
  See Julie Ellis

Marvin, Susan
  See Julie Ellis

Mason, A.E.W.

Mason, Amelia

Mason, Connie
  Cara Miles

Mason, F. Van Wyke

Mason, Felicia

Mason, Hilary
  See Barbara Roddick

Mason, Lois

Mason, Van Wyck

Mass, Donald
  Stephanie St. Clair

Massey, Ellen Gray

Massey, Jessica
  See Alison Hart

Massie, Charlotte

Massie, Sonja

Masters, Melissa
  See Roxanne Dent

Masters, William
  See Mary Parrish

Masterton, Graham

Mather, Anne
  See Mildred Grieveson

Mather, Carole

Mather, Melissa

Mathews, Denise
  See Denise Hrimak

Mathews, Laura

Mathews, Michelle
  See Susan Crose

Mathews, Pat

Mathieu, Marilyn

Matlock, Curtiss Ann

Matters, Christine
  Christine Bush

Matthewman, Phyllis
  See Kathryn Surrey

Matthews, Bay
  See Sandra Canfield, & Penny Richards

Matthews, Brenda

Matthews, Carolyn
  See Carolyn Seabaugh

Matthews, Jan
  See Jan Milella

Matthews, Laura
  See Elizabeth Neff Walker

Matthews, Patricia
  Patty Brisco, Laura Wiley

Matthews, Phoebe
  See Diane Mc Clure Jones

Mattingly, Joan

Maugham, W. Somerset

Max, Barbara
  Justina Valenti, Vanessa Victor

Maxam, Mia
  See Ethel Maxam Crews

Maxfield, Karen
  Karen Lynn

Maxwell, A.E.
  See Ann Maxwell

Maxwell, Ann
  A.E. Maxwell, Elizabeth Lowell, Analise Sunn

AUTHOR PSEUDONYM INDEX

Key: Actual names appear in bold. Pseudonyms appear in italics.

Maxwell, Cathy

Maxwell, Emily

Maxwell, Judith
See Michael Fain

Maxwell, Kathleen
Kathryn Grant

Maxwell, Mary

Maxwell, Patricia
Jennifer Blake, Maxine Patrick, Patricia Ponder,
Elizabeth Trehearne

Maxwell, Vicky
See Anne Worboys

May, Helen
See Eileen Jackson

May, Janis Susan

May, Margaret

May, Marjorie
Dinah Dean

May, Susan

May, Wynne
See Mabel Winnifred Knowles

Maybury, Anne
See Anne Buxton

Mayfield, Anne
See Kathy Ptacek

Mayhar, Ardath

Mayhew, Elizabeth
See Joan E. Bear

Mayhew, Margaret

Mayne, Cora
See Quenna Tilbury

Mayne, Elizabeth

Mayne, Sharon

Maynell, Laurence

Mayo, Margaret

Mayson, Marina
Marina Rosemary

Mc Allister, Amanda
See Jean Hager

Mc Allister, Anne
See Barbara Schenck

Mc Allister, Heather

Mc Allister, Patricia

Mc Andrew, Cass
See Mary Ann Taylor

Mc Aneny, Marjorie

Mc Arthur, A.

Mc Bain, Laurie

Mc Bride, Caitlin

Mc Bride, Harper
See Judith Weaver

Mc Bride, Jule

Mc Bride, Kate

Mc Bride, Mary
See Mary Myers

Mc Cafferty, Jeanne

Mc Caffree, Sharon
See Victoria Shakarjian

Mc Caffrey, Anne

Mc Caig, Edith & Robert
Edith Engren

Mc Call, Dinah
See Sharon Sala

Mc Call, Kathleen
See Kathleen Drymon

Mc Call, Virginia
See Virginia Nielsen

Mc Callum, Kristy

Mc Candless, Pat
Pat Montana

Mc Cann, Heather

Mc Carrick, Marsha

Mc Carry, Charles

Mc Carthy, Betsy

Mc Carthy, Candace

Mc Carthy, Susanne

Mc Cartney, Brenna

Mc Cary, Reed

Mc Cauley, Barbara

AUTHOR PSEUDONYM INDEX

Key: Actual names appear in bold. Pseudonyms appear in italics.

Mc Clure, Anna
  See Roy Sorrels

Mc Clure, Holly S.

Mc Cluskey, Sally
  Bethany Campbell

Mc Comas, Mary Kay

Mc Conachie, Audrey

Mc Connell, Lisa
  See Lorena Mc Courtney

Mc Connell, Margaret S.

Mc Cord, Joseph

Mc Cormack, Cara
  See Loree Lough, & Una Mc Manus

Mc Cormick, Claudia

Mc Cormick, Marsha

Mc Corquodale, Barbara
  Barbara Cartland

Mc Courtney, Lorena
  Jocelyn Day, Lisa Mc Connell, Rena Mc Kay

Mc Coy, Cathlyn
  See Fran Baker, & Judith Noble

Mc Coy, Cathryn

Mc Coy, Susan Hatton

Mc Cray, Judy

Mc Cue, Noelle Berry
  Nicole Monet

Mc Culley, Johnson

Mc Culloch, Sara
  See Jean Ure

Mc Cullough, Helen

Mc Cullough, Karen G.

Mc Cutcheon, Pam

Mc Daniel, Jan

Mc Daniel, Laraine

Mc Daniel, Lurlene

Mc Dermid, Terry Zahniser

Mc Donald, Kay L.
  Louise Clark

Mc Donnell, Margie
  Margie Michaels

Mc Dowell, Donna

Mc Elfresh, Adeline
  Jennifer Blair, Jane Scott, Elizabeth Wesley

Mc Elhaney, Carole

Mc Elwain, Dean
  Shana Clermont

Mc Fadden, Corey
  See Harriet Pilger

Mc Father, Nelle

Mc Gauran, Joanna
  Joanna Gilpen, Christa Merlin, Jan Mc Gown

Mc Gee, Emilie
  Emilie Richards

Mc Gee, Gwen
  Eboni Snoe

Mc Gill, Joyce

Mc Giveny, Maura
  See Julie De Bets

Mc Glamry, Beverly

Mc Gonigle, Cheryl
  Carly Bishop

Mc Gorian, Gladys
  See Gladys Dressler

Mc Gown, Jan
  See Joanna Mc Gauran

Mc Grath, Kay

Mc Grath, Laura

Mc Graw, Terry

Mc Guire, Jenny
  See Nancy Morgan

Mc Guire, Molly

Mc Guire, Sarah

Mc Intyre, Hope
  See Ruth B. Tucker

Mc Kay, Rena
  See Lorena Mc Courtney

Mc Kay, Simon
  See Leslie Arlen

Mc Kean, Margarett

Mc Kee, Jan
  See Janice Mc Kee

AUTHOR PSEUDONYM INDEX

Key: Actual names appear in bold. Pseudonyms appear in italics.

Mc Kee, Janice
Jan Mc Kee

Mc Kee, Lynn Armistead

Mc Kenna, Lindsay
See Eileen Naumann

Mc Kenna, Tate
See Mary Tate Engels, & Vicki Lewis Thompson

Mc Kenzie, Kate

Mc Kenzie, Melinda
See Melinda Snodgrass

Mc Kenzie, Paige
See Marje Blood

Mc Keone, Dixie
Jane Lovelace, Lee Mc Keone

Mc Keone, Lee
See Dixie Mc Keone

Mc Kinney, Georgia
See Ardia Poteet

Mc Kinney, Meagan
See Ruth Goodman

Mc Kinney, Megan
See Patricia Mc Linn

Mc Kittrick, Dorothy
Alexandra Dors, Dorothy Mack

Mc Knight, Carolyn

Mc Knight, Jane

Mc Knight, Jenna
See Ginny Schweiss

Mc Laughlin, Patricia
Patricia Mc Linn

Mc Lean, Cara
See Elizabeth Barrett

Mc Lean, Jan
See Jill Mc Lean

Mc Lean, Jill
Sandra Field, Jocelyn Haley, Jan Mc Lean

Mc Lean, Joyce

Mc Leary, Rena

Mc Leay, Alison

Mc Leod, Ken

Mc Linn, Patricia
See Patricia Mc Laughlin

Mc Mahon, Barbara

Mc Mahon, Kay
See Catherine Emm

Mc Manus, Una
Cara Mc Cormack

Mc Master, Alison
Marjorie Baker

Mc Millan, Maxine

Mc Millan, Terry

Mc Minn, Suzanne

Mc Naught, Anne Boyce
Ann Gilmour

Mc Naught, Judith

Mc Neil, Anne

Mc Neill, Elisabeth

Mc Nicholas, Betty

Mc Pherren, Charlotte

Mc Rae, Melinda

Mc Reynolds, Glenna

Mc Shane, Mary
Margo Owen

Mc Williams, Judith
Charlotte Hines

Mcguire, Jenny
See Kate Fleming

Mcleary, Rena
See Rochelle Alers

Meacham, Leila

Mead, Russell
See Margaret Hudson Koehler

Meadowes, Alicia
See Linda Burak, & Joan Zeig

Meadows, Alice

Meaker, Eloise
Lydia Clark, Valancy Hunter, Lydia Lancaster

Meaney, Dee Morrison

Medeiros, Teresa

Medlock, Marilyn
See Marilyn M. Amman

Meeks, Dianna

Key: Actual names appear in bold. Pseudonyms appear in italics.

Meier, Susan

Meinhardt, Shelly Thacker
Shelly Thacker

Melahn, Martha

Melbourne, Alix

Mellings, Rose

Melville, Anne
See Margaret Neuman

Melville, Jennie
See Gwendoline Butler

Mendel, Jo
See Mildred Gilbertson

Mengell, Lois J.

Menitt, Jackie

Menzel, Lois

Mercer, June

Mercer, Peggy

Meredith, Jane

Meriwether, Kate
See Pat Ahearn

Merkt, Frankie
Ann Richards

Merlin, Christa
See Joanna Mc Gauran

Merlin, Christina
See George Fleming

Mernit, William
See Lee Williams

Merrill, Jean

Merrill, Lynne
See Prudence Boyd

Merrit, William

Merritt, Elizabeth

Merritt, Emma
Emma Bennett, Micah Leigh

Merritt, Jackie
See Carolyn Joyner

Mertz, Barbara
Barbara Michaels, Elizabeth Peters

Merwin, Lucy

Merwin, Sam Jr.

Messman, Jon
Colleen Moore, Claudette Nicole, Claudia Nicole, Pamela Windsor

Mesta, Emily
See Valerie Giscard

Metcalf, Jill

Metzger, Barbara

Meyer, Anita

Meyer, Donna
Megan Daniel

Meyer, Suzanne

Meyers, Barrie
Jeanne Sommers

Meyers, Helen R.

Meyers, Julie

Meyers, Virginia
See Stella Cameron, & Virginia Myers, & Linda Rice

Meyrick, Polly

Michael, Judith
See Judith Barnard

Michael, Marie
See Marie R. Ferrarella

Michaels, Barbara
See Barbara Mertz

Michaels, Carol
See Carol Quinto

Michaels, Elizabeth Ann
See Marie Sproull

Michaels, Fern - #1
See Roberta Anderson

Michaels, Fern - #2
See Mary Kuczir

Michaels, Irene
See Mary Irene Donohue

Michaels, Jan
See Jan Milella

Michaels, Kasey - # 2
See Kathie Seidel

Michaels, Kasey
See Kathie Seidick

Key: Actual names appear in bold. Pseudonyms appear in italics.

Michaels, Kristin
See Sue Long Turner, & Jeanne Williams

Michaels, Laura

Michaels, Leigh
See Le Ann Lemberger

Michaels, Linda
See Julie Ellis

Michaels, Lorna
Thelma Zirkelbach

Michaels, Lynn
See Lynne Smith

Michaels, Margie
See Margie Mc Donnell

Michaels, Michelle
See Gerri O' Hara

Michaels, Sharry C.

Michaels, Steve
See Micahel Angelo Avallone

Michaels, Susan

Michaels, Theresa
See Theresa Di Benedetto

Michel, Freda

Michel, M. Scott

Michelle, Suzanne
See Susan Larson, & Barbara Michels

Michels, Barbara
Suzanne Michelle

Michels, Christine
Sharry Michels

Michels, Sharry
See Christine Michels

Mickle, Casey
See Casey Claybourne

Mickles, Linda

Miesel, Sandra

Mikels, Jennifer
See Suzanne J. Kuhlin

Milan, Angel
See Elizabeth Neibor

Milella, Jan
Jan Matthews, Jan Michaels

Miles, Cara
See Connie Mason

Miles, Cassie
See Kay Bergstrom

Miles, Cynthia

Miles, Deborah

Miley, Meg
See Peggy Jaegly

Miller, Ann
Anne London, Leslie Morgan

Miller, Barbara
Laurel Ames

Miller, Bill

Miller, Cissie
See Stanlee Coy Miller, & Carolyn Nichols

Miller, Helen Topping

Miller, Kathy

Miller, Laurie
Laurie Grant

Miller, Linda Lael

Miller, Marcia
See Marceil Baker

Miller, Nadine

Miller, Stanlee Coy
Iona Charles, Cissie Miller

Miller, Sue

Miller, Valerie
Hilary Cole

Millhiser, Marlys

Mills, Anita

Mills, Catherine

Mills, Frances

Milne, Rosaleen

Mims, Emily
Emily Elliot

Minger, Elda

Minger, Miriam

Minton, Paula
See Paul Little

Mireles, Sandra

AUTHOR PSEUDONYM INDEX

Key: Actual names appear in bold. Pseudonyms appear in italics.

Mitchell, Allison

Mitchell, Ann

Mitchell, Erica

Mitchell, Jay
  See Jennifer O' Green

Mitchell, Joseph

Mitchell, Margaret

Mitchell, Paige
  See Judith S. Ginnes

Mittermeyer, Helen
  Ann Christy, Hayton Moneith, Danielle Paul

Mixon, Veronica
  See Nigella Weston

Modean, Mary
  See Modean Moon

Modrovich, Kathleen
  Kathleen Creighton, Kathleen Carrol

Moeller, Laurie
  Laura Anthony

Moffett, Julie

Moffett, Paula
  Vanessa Richards

Molay, Mollie

Moneith, Hayton
  See Helen Mittermeyer

Monet, Nicole
  See Noelle Berry Mc Cue

Monroe, Carolyn
  See Carolyn Greene

Monroe, Schere
  Jessica Howard, Jean K. Schere, Abigail Winter

Monson, Christine

Montague, Jeanne
  See Jeanne Yarde

Montague, Lisa
  See Sandra Dawn Shulman

Montana, Pat
  See Pat Mc Candless

Monte, Jill
  See Julie Ellis

Monterey, Elizabeth
  See V. J. Banis

Montgomery, Bettina
  See Edythe Cudlipp

Montgomery, Marianne
  D.H. Allen

Montrose, David

Montrose, Graham
  See Charles Roy Mac Kinnon

Montrose, Sarah
  See Valerie Bosna

Moody, Susan

Moon, Arthur

Moon, Modean
  Mary Modean

Mooney, Martin

Mooney, Mary Alice

Moor, Amanda Jay
  Laura Kinsale

Moore, Amos

Moore, Anne

Moore, Brian

Moore, Caro Olson
  See Estella Wold

Moore, Charlotte
  See Charlotte Lobb

Moore, Colleen
  See Jon Messman

Moore, Diana
  See Deanna Marliss

Moore, Ellen

Moore, Emily

Moore, Gwyneth
  See Patricia Bannister

Moore, Jill

Moore, Kate

Moore, Lisa
  See Elizabeth Chater

Moore, Margaret
  See Margaret Wilkins

Moore, Marjorie

Moore, Mary Ellen

AUTHOR PSEUDONYM INDEX

Key: Actual names appear in bold. Pseudonyms appear in italics.

Moore, Mary

Moore, Miriam
Miriam Morton

Moore, Patti
Kathleen Daley, Kit Daley, Margaret Daley,
Margaret Ripy

Moore, Paula
See Paul W. Fairman, Robert Vaughan

Moore, Rayanne

Moore, Sandra

Moore, Susan

Moorhouse, Catherine
See Catherine Allen

Morel, Angela

Morel, Jimmie
Lindsay Longford

Moreland, Peggy
See Peggy B. Morse

Moren, Sally
Jane Morgan

Morgan, Alice

Morgan, Alyssa
See Edith Delatush

Morgan, Diana
See Alex Kamaroff

Morgan, Elizabeth

Morgan, Faye
See Doreen Owens Malek

Morgan, Jane
See Sally Moren

Morgan, Kathleen

Morgan, Kristin
See Barbara Lantier Veillon

Morgan, Leslie
See Ann Miller

Morgan, Marley

Morgan, Melody
See Paulette Brewster

Morgan, Meredith

Morgan, Michaela
See Gloria Basile

Morgan, Nancy
Jenny Mc Guire

Morgan, Peggy J.

Morgan, Raye
See Helen Conrad

Morgan, Tracy

Morgan, Virginia

Moritmer, Carole

Morland, Lynette
Karen O' Connell

Morrell, Karen

Morris, Debrah
Pepper Adams, Joanna Jordan, Dianne Thomas,
Jo Ann Stacey

Morris, Elizabeth
See Jean Favors

Morris, Esther
Stacey Dennis

Morris, Gilbert

Morris, Ira J.

Morris, Janet

Morris, Julianna
Marti Ann Ford, Carole Mortimer

Morris, Kathleen

Morris, Suzanne

Morrison, Jo

Morrison, Patricia
Patricia Kennealy

Morrison, Roberta
See Jean Francis Webb

Morrow, Vicky

Morrow, Victoria

Morse, Nancy
Danielle Fleming

Morse, Peggy B.
Peggy Morehead

Morsi, Pamela

Mortimer, Carole
See Julianna Morris

Morton, Miriam
Miriam Moore

AUTHOR PSEUDONYM INDEX

Key: Actual names appear in bold. Pseudonyms appear in italics.

Morton, Patricia
See Morton J. Golding

Morton, Tommye
Thomasina Ring

Mosco, Maise

Moser, Alma
Alison Gray

Moss, Jan

Moss, W. Stanley

Mossop, Irene
See Fay Chandos

Motheral, Nancy
Laura Shaw

Motley, Annette

Moulton, Nancy

Mountjoy, Roberta
See Jerry Sohl

Moyer, Florence

Muelbauer, Pamela
Pamela Bauer, Pamela Jerrold

Muir, Jean

Muir, Lucy

Mulford, Clarence E.

Mulholland, Judith
Judith Duncan

Mullan, Celina
See Ana Lisa De Leon

Mullen, Dore
Dorothy Mullen

Mullen, Dorothy
See Dore Mullen

Mulvihill, Rochelle A.
Rochelle Wayne

Munn, Vella
Dawn Flindt, Heather Williams

Munro, Mary
Doris Howe, Newlyn Nash

Munson, Sheryl Mc Danel

Murphy, Lynne
Georgina Gentry

Murray, Annabel
See Marie Murray

Murray, Beatrice
See Richard Posner

Murray, Caitlin
See Pat Ahearn

Murray, E. P.

Murray, Edna
See Donald S. Rowland

Murray, Frances
See Rosemary Booth

Murray, Jill
See Quenna Tilbury

Murray, Julia

Murray, Marie
Annabelle Murray

Murray, Rachel

Murrey, Jeneth

Musgrave, David
Jacqueline Musgrave

Musgrave, Jacqueline
See David Musgrave

Muskett, Netta
Anne Hill

Mussi, Mary
Josephine Edgar, Mary Howard

Mutch, Karen

Myers, Eve

Myers, Helen R.

Myers, Judith Blackwell
Judith Blackwell, Julie Myers

Myers, Judy

Myers, Julie
See Judith Blackwell Myers

Myers, Katherine

Myers, Mary Ruth

Myers, Mary
Mary Mc Bride

Myers, Peggy
Ann Williams

AUTHOR PSEUDONYM INDEX

Key: Actual names appear in bold. Pseudonyms appear in italics.

Myers, Virginia
Jane Worth Abbott, Alicia Brandon

Myles, Frances

Myles, Sabrina
See Lois Arvin Walker

Myles, Sandra
Sandra Marton

Myrus, Joyce

Naismith, Marion

Napier, Priscilla

Napier, Susan

Nash, Jean
See Jean Sutherland

Nash, Newlyn
See Mary Munro

Nash, Noreen

Nash, Petra

Naughton, Lee

Nauman, Eileen
Beth Brookes, Lindsay Mc Kenna

Nazworth, Lenora H.

Neal, Hilary
See T. R. Noon

Neale, Linda

Neels, Betty

Neggers, Carla
Anne Harrell, Amalia James

Neggers, Dorothy

Neher, Lisa
Juli Greene

Neibor, Elizabeth
Mary Lynn, Angel Milan, Elizabeth Nelson

Neil, Barbara
See Barbara Sherrod

Neil, Joanna

Neilan, Sarah

Neilson, Virginia

Nel, Stella Frances

Nelson, Elizabeth
See Elizabeth Neibor

Nelson, Judith

Nelson, Louella

Nelson, Marguerite
See Will Watson

Nelson, Rachelle
Shelli Nelson

Nelson, Shelli
See Rachelle Nelson

Nelson, Valerie K.

Nemeth, Linell Evanston
Linell Anston

Neri, Penelope

Netzel, Sally
Suzanne Jenner

Neubauer, William
William Arthur, Christine Bennett, Joan
Garrison, Jan Hathaway, Rebecca Marsh, Norma
Newcomb

Neukrug, Linda
Jill Castle

Neuman, Margaret
Anne Betteridge, Margaret Evans, Margaret
Potter, Anne Melville

Neville, Anne
See Jane Viney

Nevins, Kate
See Margaret Malkind

Newcomb, Kerry
Shana Carol, Peter Gentry, Christina Savage

Newcomb, Norma
See William Neubauer

Newell, Rosemary

Newman, Holly

Newman, Mona
Barbara Fitzgerald, Jean Stewart

Newsome, Muriel

Nicholas, Deborah
See Deborah Martin Gonzales

Nicholas, Robin

Nichols, Carolyn
Iona Charles, Cissie Miller

AUTHOR PSEUDONYM INDEX

Key: Actual names appear in bold. Pseudonyms appear in italics.

Nichols, Charlotte
See Patricia Forsythe, & Barbara Williams

Nichols, Leigh
See Dean Koontz

Nichols, Margaret

Nichols, Mary

Nichols, Sarah
Lee Hays

Nichols, Suzanne
See Marlys Staplebrock

Nicholson, Christina
See Leslie Arlen

Nicholson, Peggy

Nickels, Meryl

Nickens, Catherine A.
Catherine Reynolds

Nickson, Hilda

Nickson, Jeanne

Nicole, Christopher
See Leslie Arlen

Nicole, Claudette
See Jon Messman

Nicole, Claudia
See Jon Messman

Nicole, Marie
See Marie R. Ferrarella

Nielsen, Virginia
Virginia Mc Call

Nielson, Ingrid
Iris May Bancroft, Iris Brent, Andrea Layton

Nigro, Deborah

Nile, Dorothea
See Micahel Angelo Avallone

Nixon, Kathleen
See V. R. Blundell

Nobisso, Joi
Nadja Bride, Nuria Wood

Noble, Judith
Judith Baker, Cathlyn Mc Coy

Noel, Angela

Nolan, Frederick

Nolan, Jenny
See Mary Jo Young

Nollet, Lois
Diana Delmore, Lois Stewart

Noon, T. R.
Hilary Neal, Olive Norton, Bess Norton, Kate Norway

Noone, Edwina
See Micahel Angelo Avallone

Norcross, Lisabet
See Arthur Gladstone

Norman, Colleen

Norman, Dee
See Dee Lopez, Norma Williams

Norman, Diana

Norman, Elizabeth

Norman, Nicole
See Edythe Cudlipp

Norman, Yvonne
See Norma Yvonne Seely

Norrell, Marjorie
See Marjorie Norton

Norris, Carol
Kris Karron

Norris, Maureen
See Edythe Cudlipp

North, Andrew
See Alice Mary Norton

North, Jessica
See Robert Somerlott

North, Miranda

North, Rebecca
See Jo Ann Ferguson

North, Sara
Barbara Bonham, Leah Crane, Jean Hager, Marlaine Kyle, Amanda Mc Allister, Jeanne Stephens

Northan, Irene

Norton, Alice Mary
Andre Norton, Andrew North

Norton, Andre
See Alice Mary Norton

AUTHOR PSEUDONYM INDEX

Key: Actual names appear in bold. Pseudonyms appear in italics.

Norton, Bess
See T. R. Noon

Norton, Marjorie
Marjorie Ellison, Marjorie Norrell

Norton, Olive
See T. R. Noon

Norway, Kate
See T. R. Noon

Nottingham, Poppy
See Pattie Dunaway

Novak, Rose
Marcia Rose

Nowasky, Jan

Nowinson, Marie

Noyes, Patricia Ann

Nuccio, Marsha
M. L. Gamble

Nuelle, Helen

Nunn, Rebecca

Nusser, Lynda

Nye, Nelson C.

Nye, Valerie

O' Banyon, Constance
See Evelyn Gee

O' Brian, Eve
See Arnie Heller

O' Brian, Gayle

O' Brian, Soliee

O' Brien, Eve
See Judy Bryer

O' Brien, Judith

O' Brien, Kathleen
See Kathleen Pynn

O' Brien, Maryann

O' Brien, Saliee
See Frankie-Lee Janas

O' Bryan, Sofi

O' Caragh, Mary

O' Connell, June

O' Connell, Karen
See Lynette Morland

O' Connell, Shannon

O' Day-Flannery, Constance

O' Dell, Amanda

O' Donnell, Bernard

O' Donnell, Jodi

O' Donnell, Kate
See Nancy Garcia

O' Donoghue, Maureen

O' Grady, Leslie
Lindsay Chase

O' Grady, Rohan
See June Skinner

O' Green, Jennifer
Jay Mitchell, Jennifer Roberson

O' Hallion, Sheila
See Sheila Rosalynd Allen

O' Hara, Gerri
See Michelle Michaels

O' Hara, Kate

O' Laimhin, Marti L.
Marti Laven

O' Meill, Suzannah

O' More, Peggy
See Betty Blocklinger

O' Nair, Mairi
Constance M. Evans, Jane Gray

O' Neal, Katherine

O' Neal, Reagan
See James O. Rigney

O' Neil, Olivia

O' Neill, Dorothy P.

O' Neill, Egan
See Elizabeth Linigton

O' Neill, Jude
See Judith Blundell

O' Neill, Noreen
See Thomas Armstrong

O' Neill, Olivia

O' Neill, Suzannah

AUTHOR PSEUDONYM INDEX

Key: Actual names appear in bold. Pseudonyms appear in italics.

O' Rourke, Frank

O' Sullivan, Ellen

Oaks, Marian

Oakson, Pat C.
Robin Tolivar

Ocork, Shannon

Offord, Lenore Glen

Ogan, George
Rosetta Stowe

Ogilvie, Charlot

Ohlrogge, Anne Kristine Stuart
Anne Stuart

Oldfield, Elizabeth

Oleyar, Rita Balkey
Rita Balkey

Oliver, Amy Roberta
See Berta Onions

Oliver, Jan
See Janece O. Hudson

Oliver, Marina

Oliver, Patricia
See Patricia De La Fuente

Oliver, Tess
See Teri Kovack

Olshaker, Thelma

Oltmann, Vanessa

Onions, Berta
Amy Roberta Oliver, Berta Ruck

Oppenheim, E. Phillips

Oppenheimer, Joan

Ord, Irene
Kate Fairfax

Ormsby, Patricia

Orr, Alice Harron
Elizabeth Allison, Morgana Starr

Orr, Kathleen
Kathleen Gainer, Kathy Orr, Catherine Spencer

Orr, Kathy
See Kathleen Orr

Orr, Mary
Anne Caswell

Orr, Zelma

Ortega, Isabel
Phyliss G. Leonard

Orvis, Kenneth

Orwig, Sara
Daisy Logan

Osborn, Elane

Osborne, Betsy
See Barbara Boswell

Osborne, Helena

Osborne, Jessie
Jessie Ford

Osborne, Maggie
Margaret St. George

Osler, E.B.

Ossana, Susan B.
Susanna Christie

Ostrander, Kate

Ott, Patricia

Otten, Carol Card
Tena Carlyle

Oust, Gail
Elizabeth Turner

Outlaw, Louise Lee
Juliet Ashby, Lee Canady

Overfield, Joan

Ovstedahl, Barbara
Barbara Douglas, Rosalind Laker, Barbara Paul

Owen, Ann

Owen, Margo
See Mary Mc Shane

Owen, Ruth

Owen, Wanda

Owens, Marissa

Owens, Ruth

Oxley, Gillian
See Kerry Vine

Pace, A.

Pace, De Wanna

Key: Actual names appear in bold. Pseudonyms appear in italics.

Pace, Laurel
See Barbara Wohjoski

Pace, Miriam

Pace, Susan
Allison Lane

Pacheco, Christine
Christa Conan

Pacotti, Pamela

Pacter, Trudi

Pade, Victoria

Page, Betsy
See Bettie Wilhite

Page, Laurel

Page, Vicki
See Ruby D. Avery

Paige, Laurie
See Olivia M. Hall

Paige, Natalie

Paisley, Rebecca
See Rebecca Boado Rosas

Palencia, Elaine Fowler
Laurel Blake

Pall, Ellen
Fiona Hill

Palmer, Catherine

Palmer, Diana
See Susan Kyle

Palmer, Gail

Palmer, Linda Varner
Scotney St. James, Linda Varner

Palmer, Rachel
See Ruth Potts

Palmieri, Marina
See Marilyn Campbell

Papazoglou, Orania
Nicola Andrews, Ann Paris

Pape, Sharon

Pappano, Marilyn

Paquin, Ethel

Paradise, Mary
See Dorothy Eden

Paradiso, Karen
Ann Lynn

Parageter, Margaret

Parenteau, Shirley

Pargeter, Margaret

Paris, Ann
See Orania Papazoglou

Parker, Barbara Jeanne

Parker, Beatrice
See Tom E. Huff

Parker, Cynthia

Parker, Elizabeth

Parker, Garda

Parker, Karen Blair
Blair Cameron, Kathryn Blair - #1

Parker, Laura
See Laura Castoro

Parker, Norah
See Eleanor Hodgson

Parker, Una-Mary

Parkes, Patricia

Parkin, Bernadette

Parkinson, Cornelia
Day Taylor

Parmett, Doris

Parnell, Andrea

Parr, Delia
See Mary L. Lechleidner

Parris, Laura
Laura Magner

Parrish, Mary
Margaret Cousins, Avery Johns

Parrish, Patt
See Patt Bucheister

Parv, Valerie

Pascoe, Irene M.
Andrea Haley

Patrick, Ann
See Patricia Kay

Patrick, De Ann
See Dottie Corcoran, & Mary Ann Slokowski

AUTHOR PSEUDONYM INDEX

Key: Actual names appear in bold. Pseudonyms appear in italics.

Patrick, Lynn
See Nancy Elaine Pindrus

Patrick, Maxine
See Patricia Maxwell

Patrick, Natalie

Patrick, Roslynn

Patten, Darlene

Patterson, Betty Ann
Vickie York

Patterson, Morgan

Pattison, Nancy
Nan Asquith, Susannah Broome

Pattison, Ruth
Ruth Abbey

Patton, Sarah
Genevieve English

Paul, Barbara
See Barbara Ovstedahl

Paul, Danielle
See Helen Mittermeyer

Paul, Paula

Paul, Sandra

Paul, Susan

Paul, Wynne

Pauley, Barbara Anne

Paulos, Sheila

Pavlik, E. M.
Adora Sheridan

Paxton, Diane

Paxton, Jean
See Martha Jean Powers

Paxton, Lois
Zoe Cass, Dorothy Mackie Low, Lois Low

Payes, Rachel Cosgrove
E. L. Arch, Rachel R. Cosgrove, Joanne Kaye

Payne, Tiffany

Peacock, Max

Peak, Caroline

Peake, Kay

Peake, Lillian

Peake, Lynsey

Peale, Constance F.
See Whitney Stine

Pearl, Esther E.
See David Ritz

Pearl, Jack
Stephanie Blake

Peart, Jane

Peck, Maggie
See Marjorie Price

Pedersen, Gloria

Pega, Bonnie

Pelfrey, Judy
Judith Daniels, Rhett Daniels

Pelham, Howard

Pellicane, Patricia
See Jean Haught

Pelton, Sonya T.

Peltonen, Carla
Lynn Erickson

Pemberton, Margaret

Pemberton, Nan
See Nina Combs Pykare

Pence, Joanne

Pender, Laura
See Dana Anderson

Pendleton, Grace

Penney, Anne
See Charlotte Douglas, & Susan Hunter

Pepper, Joan
Joan Alexander

Perch, Jane
Margaret Campion

Percival, Lloyd

Percy, Karen

Perez-Venero, Mirna
Mima Pierce

Perkins, Barbara

Perry, Anne

Perry, Carol Duncan
Carol S. Duncan

AUTHOR PSEUDONYM INDEX

Key: Actual names appear in bold. Pseudonyms appear in italics.

Perry, Michalann
Megan Blythe

Pershall, Mary
Susan Shelley

Pershing, Diane

Pershing, Karen
Kerry Price

Pershing, Marie
See Pearle Henriksen Schultze

Peters, Anne
See Anne Hanson

Peters, Clarice
See Laureen Kwock

Peters, Elizabeth
See Barbara Mertz

Peters, Louise

Peters, Maureen
Maureen Black, Veronica Black, Catherine Darby, Levanah Lloyd, Sharon Whitby

Peters, Natasha
See Anastasia Cleaver

Peters, Sue
Angela Carson

Petersen, Herman

Peterson, Carrie

Peterson, Tracie
See Janelle Jamison

Petkus, Peggy Murphy

Petratur, Joyce
Joyce Verrette

Petrie, Glen

Petty, Mary Eileen
See Eileen Van Kirk

Phelps, Lauren M.

Phillips, Alan

Phillips, Barbara

Phillips, Dorothy
See Dorothy Garlock

Phillips, Johanna
See Dorothy Garlock

Phillips, Laura

Phillips, Michael

Phillips, Patricia
Sonia Phillips

Phillips, Sonia
See Patricia Phillips

Phillips, Susan Elizabeth
Justine Cole

Phillips, Susan Leslie

Phillips, Tori
See Mary Schaller

Pianka, Phyllis Taylor
Winter Ames

Pickart, Joan Elliott
Robin Elliott

Picker, Rita
Martina Sultan

Pierce, Georgia
Lindsey Hanks

Pierce, Mima
See Mirna Perez-Venero

Pilcher, Rosamunde
Jane Fraser

Pilger, Harriet
Corey Mc Fadden

Pindrus, Nancy Elaine
Lynn Patrick, Patricia Rosemoor

Pinianski, Patricia
Patrice Lindsey

Pinnell, Bill

Pizzey, Erin

Pizzuti, Carolyn
Carolyn Zane

Plagakis, Jim
Christy Dore

Plaidy, Jean
See Eleanor Hibbert

Plante, Edmund

Playfair, Helen

Plowman, Mary Sharon

Plummer, Clare
Clare Ensley

Poenbeck, Pat

AUTHOR PSEUDONYM INDEX

Key: Actual names appear in bold. Pseudonyms appear in italics.

Pohle, Robert Warren
Devon Lee

Polk, Dora

Pollero, Rhonda Harding
Kelsey Roberts

Polley, Judith Anne
Judith Hagar, Helen Kent, Valentia Luellan, Judith Stewart

Pollock, Ida
Susan Barrie, Jane Beaufort, Rose Burghley, Anita Charles, Pamela Kent, Barbara Rowan, Mary Whistler

Pollock, Rosemary

Ponder, Patricia
See Patricia Maxwell

Poolle, Rhoda
Krista Janssen

Poore, Dawn Aldridge

Pope, Ann
See Ann Zavala

Pope, Lee
See Ann Zavala

Pope, Pamela

Porter, Jessica

Porter, Joyce
Deborah Joyce

Porter, Madeline
Madeline Harper, Elizabeth Habersham, Anna James

Porter, Margaret Evans

Porter, Nina
See Nina Coombs Pykare

Porterfield, Kay
Colleen Kimbrough

Porterfield, Marie

Posner, Richard
Beatrice Murray

Poteet, Ardia
Georgia Mc Kinney

Potter, Allison

Potter, Jackie
Jane Ireland

Potter, Margaret
See Margaret Neuman

Potter, Patricia

Potts, Ruth
Rachel Palmer

Powell, Jan Hamilton
Celeste Hamilton, Neely Powell

Powell, Neely
See Jan Hamilton Powell

Power, Elizabeth

Power, Jo Ann
Ann Crowleigh

Powers, Anne
See Anne Schwartz

Powers, Martha Jean
Jean Paxton

Powers, Nora
See Nina Combs Pykare

Powers, Tom

Pozzessere, Heather Graham
Shannon Drake, Heather Graham

Prate, Kit
See Dorothy Howell

Pratt, Rosina

Preble, Amand
See Christine Tayntor

Prentice, Wendy

Prentiss, Charlotte

Pressley, Hilda

Preston, Fayrene
Jaelyn Conlee

Preston, Hilary

Prewitt-Parker, Jolene

Price, Ashland
Laura Ashcroft, Janice Carlson, Laura Price

Price, Dianne

Price, Eugenia

Price, Kerry
See Karen Pershing

Price, Laura
See Laura Ashcroft

AUTHOR PSEUDONYM INDEX

Key: Actual names appear in bold. Pseudonyms appear in italics.

Price, Laurel

Price, Lynn
See Cheryl Lynn Purviance

Price, Marjorie
Maggie Peck, Margot Prince

Price, Melinda

Prince, Margot
See Marjorie Price

Prine, Linda

Prior, Mollie
Janet Roscoe

Pritchard, Pat

Pritchett, Ariadne

Procter, Kate

Proctor, Carol

Proctor, Kate

Prole, Lozania
See Ursula Bloom

Provost, Gary
Marian Chase

Pryce, Melinda
See Linda Shertzel

Pryor, Natalie
See Nina Combs Pykare

Pryor, Pauline
See Mary Linn Roby

Pryor, Vanessa
See Chelsea Quinn Yarbro

Ptacek, Kathy
Kathryn Atwood, Anne Mayfield

Pugh, Dana Rae
Deanna Linden

Purviance, Cheryl Lynn
Lynn Price, Cheryl Spencer

Putnam, Alice

Putnam, Eileen
See Eileen Winwood

Putney, Mary Jo

Puyear-Alerding, Kathy
Kathy Alerding

Pyatt, Rosina
Anne Beaumont

Pykare, Nina Coombs
Ann Coombs, Nina Coombs, Nan Pemberton, Nina Porter, Nora Powers, Natalie Pryor

Pynn, Kathleen
Kathleen O' Brien

Quentin, Dorothy

Quest, Erica
See Nancy & John Sawyer

Quick, Amanda
See Jayne Ann Krentz

Quigley, Aileen
Aileen Armitage, Ruth Fabian, Erica Lindley

Quin-Harkin, Janet

Quinn, Alison

Quinn, Colleen
See Colleen Bosler

Quinn, Julia
See Julie Cotler

Quinn, Samantha
See Maureen Bullinger

Quinn, Tara Taylor
See Tara Lee Reames

Quinto, Carol
Jeanne Carmichael, Carol Michaels

Rabe, Sheila

Rabl, S.S.

Radcliff, Janette
See Janet Louise Roberts

Raddall, Thomas H.

Raddon's, Charlene

Rade, Sheila

Radke, Nancy

Radko, Karren

Rae, Doris

Rae, Patricia
See Patricia Walls

Raeschild, Sheila

Raffell, Elizabeth & Burton

AUTHOR PSEUDONYM INDEX

Key: Actual names appear in bold. Pseudonyms appear in italics.

Rafferty, Carin
See Linda Kichline

Ragosta, Millie J.
Melanie Randolph

Ragsdale, Clyde B.

Raine, Nicole
See Sandi Gelles

Rainone, Christopher
Violet Hawthorne

Raintree, Lee
Con Sellers

Rainville, Rita

Ramey, J.J.R.

Ramin, Teresa
See Terese Daly Ramin Vita

Ramirez, Alice
Serena Alexander, Candice Arkham

Ramirez, Jeanette

Ramsay, Eileen

Ramsay, Fay
See Olive Baxter

Ramsey, Eileen Ainsworth

Rand, Erika

Rand, Suzanne
See Debra Brand

Randal, Jude

Randall, Caitlin

Randall, Diana
See Dan Ross

Randall, Lindsay
See Susan M. Anderson

Randall, Rona
See Rona Shambrook

Randolph, Elise
See Susan Lowe

Randolph, Ellen
See Dan Ross

Randolph, Melanie
See Millie J. Ragosta

Rangel, Doris

Rangel, Kimberly
Kimberly Ray

Ransom, Dana
See Nancy Gideon

Ransom, Katherine
See Mary Sederquest

Rasky, Frank

Rasley, Alicia Todd
Elizabeth Todd, Michelle Venet

Rasley, Alicia

Rasmussen, Alysse S.
See Alysse Lemery

Rather, Deborah
Arlene James

Ratzlaff, Nell Dean
Nell Marr Dean, Anne Marr, Virginia Roberts

Rau, Margaret

Ravenlock, Constance
See June E. Casey

Rawlings, Cynthia

Rawlings, Ellen

Rawlings, Louisa
See Sylvia Baumgarten

Rawlins, Debbi

Ray, Angie

Ray, Francis

Ray, Jane

Ray, Karen
Ann Bernadette

Ray, Kimberly
See Kimberly Rangel

Raye, Linda
See Linda Ray Turner

Raymer, Kimberly

Raymond, Mary
Mary Heathcott, Mary Constance Keegan

Rayner, Claire
Sheila Brandon, Ann Lynton, Ruth Martin

Raynes, Jean

Read, Lorna
Caroline Standish

AUTHOR PSEUDONYM INDEX

Key: Actual names appear in bold. Pseudonyms appear in italics.

Reading, Margot

Reames, Tara Lee
Tara Taylor Quinn

Reavin, Sara

Reavis, Cheryl
Cinda Richards

Rebuth, Jeanette

Receveur, Betty Layman

Redd, Joanne
Lauren Wilde

Reddin, Joan

Reding, Jaclyn

Redmond, Marilyn

Redmond, Shirley-Raye

Reece, Colleen L.
See Connie Loraine

Reece, Jean
See Mary Kistler

Reed, Anne

Reed, Blair

Reed, Leslie

Reed, Melody

Reed, Miriam

Reeger, Jacki

Reep, Diane
See Diane Reep

Reep, Dianna
See Emily Ann Allen, Diane Reep

Rees, Eleanor

Rees, Joan

Reeve, Elaine

Reeves, Barbara
See Barbara Reeves Kolaski

Reeves, Joan L. A.

Reibel, Paula
Elizabeth Mansfield, Paula Schwartz

Reid, Grace
See Grace Green

Reid, Henrietta

Reid, Margaret Ann

Reid, Michelle

Reingold, Carmel B.
Alexandra Ellis

Reisser, Anne N.

Rellas, Dorothy

Remes, Shirley C.
Shirley Carroll

Remington, Eleanor

Renceveur, Betty Layman

Renick, Jeane
See Melody Reed

Renier, Elizabeth
See Betty Baker

Renier, Max
Taylor Caldwell

Renko, Dorothy
Kristi Andrews

Rennie, George Murdock

Reno, Marie R.

Renshaw, Lisa M.
Malori Winters

Renwick, Gloria

Resnick, Laura
Laura Leone

Rettke, Marian Pope
Anne Devon, Marian Devon

Reynard, Carol
Shirl Henke

Reynolds, Anne
See Anne E. Steinke

Reynolds, Catherine
See Catherine A. Nickens

Reynolds, Elizabeth
See Anne E. Steinke

Reynolds, Maureen

Rhee, Dena
See Deanna Brauer

Rhoades, Knight
See Sandra K. Rhoades

AUTHOR PSEUDONYM INDEX

Key: Actual names appear in bold. Pseudonyms appear in italics.

Rhoades, Sandra K.
Knight Rhoades

Rhodes, Karen

Rhome, Adah
Ada Steward, Ada Summer

Rhyne, Julia
Lucy Hamilton

Rice, Darcy

Rice, Linda
Alicia Brandon, Linda Walters

Rice, Molly

Rice, Patricia

Rich, Mary Lou

Rich, Sue

Richard, Susan
See Julie Ellis

Richards-Akers, Nancy

Richards, Ann
See Frankie Merkt

Richards, Bay
See Sandra Canfield, & Penny Richards

Richards, Celia Gardner

Richards, Cinda
See Cheryl Reavis

Richards, Claire

Richards, Clare
See Ruth Glick, Carolyn Males, & Louise Titchener

Richards, Denise
See Hope Richardson

Richards, Emilie
See Emilie Mc Gee

Richards, Jessica

Richards, Leigh

Richards, Penny
Bay Matthews, Bay Richards, Sandi Shane

Richards, Serena

Richards, Stephanie

Richards, Vanessa
See Paula Moffett

Richardson, Alaine
Alaine Hawthorne

Richardson, Evelyn

Richardson, Hope

Richardson, Mozelle

Richardson, Susan

Richey, Cynthia

Richmond, Clare
See Ruth Glick, Carolyn Males, & Louise Titchener

Richmond, Emma

Ricks, Patricia
Patricia Wynn

Rider, Elisie B.
Isobel Chase, Elizabeth De Guise, Elizabeth Hunter

Ridley, Sheila

Riefe, A. R.
See Alan Riefe

Riefe, Alan
A. R. Riefe, Barbara Riefe

Riefe, Barbara
See Alan Riefe

Rieger, Catherine

Rift, Valerie
Marie Bartlett, Rowena Lee

Rigg, Jennifer
Genevieve Scott

Riggs, Paula Detmer

Rigney, James O.
Reagan O' Neal

Riker, Leigh

Riley, Eugenia
See Eugenia Riley Essenmacher

Riley, Judith Merkle

Riley, Mildred E.

Riley, Stella
Juliet Blyth

Rimmer, Christine

Rinehold, Connie

242

Key: Actual names appear in bold. Pseudonyms appear in italics.

Ring, Thomasina
See Tommye Morton

Ripley, Alexandra

Ripy, Margaret
See Patti Moore

Risku, Cillay

Ritchie, Claire
See Prudence Boyd

Ritter, Margaret

Ritz, David
Jessica Lansing, Esther E. Pearl

Rivers, Dorothy
See Leonora Mackey

Rivers, Francine

Rivers, Georgina

Rivers, Kendall

Rivers, Nikki

Robarchek, Peg
Katheryn Brett

Robards, Karen

Robb, Christine
See Christine R. Goold

Robb, Jo Ann
See Jo Ann Ross

Robb, John

Robb, Sandra

Robbe, Michele
See Lucy Seaman

Robbin, Jo Ann
See Jo Ann Ross

Robbins, Andrea
See Peter Albano

Robbins, Denise

Robbins, Gina
See Connie Feddersen

Robbins, Joann

Robbins, Kay
See Kay Hooper

Robbins, Rebecca

Robbins, Serena

Roberson, Jennifer
See Jennifer O' Green

Roberta, Phyllis

Roberts, Adrian
See Elizabeth Bolton

Roberts, Alina

Roberts, Ann Victoria

Roberts, Annie Sims

Roberts, Casey
See Connie Flynn-Alexander

Roberts, Desmond
See Ray Bentinck

Roberts, Doreen

Roberts, Gina
See Connie Fedderson

Roberts, Irene
See Ivor Roberts

Roberts, Ivor
Roberta Carr, Elizabeth Harle, Irene Roberts,
Iris Rowland, Irene Shaw

Roberts, Jacqueline

Roberts, Janet Louise
Louisa Bronte, Rebecca Danton, Janette Radcliff

Roberts, Kelsey
See Rhonda Harding Pollero

Roberts, Kenneth

Roberts, L.M.
Meg Lynn Roberts

Roberts, Leigh
See Lora R. Smith

Roberts, Meg Lynn
See L.M. Roberts

Roberts, Nora
See Ellie Wilder

Roberts, Paula
See Joan M. Hohl

Roberts, Peggy
See Peggy Hanchar

Roberts, Phyllis

Roberts, Rinalda
See Edythe Cudlipp

Key: Actual names appear in bold. Pseudonyms appear in italics.

AUTHOR PSEUDONYM INDEX

Key: Actual names appear in bold. Pseudonyms appear in italics.

Roper, Lester
Samantha Lester

Rosas, Rebecca Boado
Rebecca Paisley

Roscoe, Janet
Mollie Prior

Rose, Hilary
See Charles Roy Mac Kinnon

Rose, Jeanne

Rose, Jennifer
See Nancy Webber

Rose, Kathryn

Rose, Marcia
See Marcia Kamien, & Rose Novak

Rose, Sharon M.
Alicia Farraday

Roseberry, Sherry

Rosemary, Marina
See Marina Mayson

Rosemoor, Patricia
See Nancy Elaine Pindrus

Rosenbaum, Beverly Katz
Beverly Bryan

Ross, Beverlee
See Beverlee Couillard

Ross, Clarissa
See Dan Ross

Ross, Dan
Leslie Ames, Marilyn Carter, Rose Dana, Ruth Dorset, Ann Gilmor, Miriam Leslie, Diana Randall, Ellen Randolph, Clarissa Ross, Dana Ross, Marilyn Ross, Rose Williams

Ross, Dana Fuller
See Noel B. Gerson

Ross, Erin
See Shirley Tallman

Ross, Helaine
See Helen Gray Weston

Ross, Jo Ann
Jo Ann Robb, Jo Ann Robbin

Ross, Kathryn

Ross, Marilyn
See Dan Ross

Ross, Regina

Rosse, Susanna
Vivian Connolly

Rossiter, Clare

Roszel, Renee
See Renee Roszel Wilson

Roth, Jillian
See Linda Ladd

Roth, Pamela
See Pamela Toth

Rothman, Marcy Elias

Rothwell, Una

Rotter, Elizabeth
See Elizabeth Neff Walker

Rougier, Georgette
Georgette Heyer

Rouverol, Jean

Rowan, Barbara
See Ida Pollock

Rowan, Deirdre
See Jeanne Williams

Rowan, Hester

Rowe, Margaret

Rowe, Melanie
Pam Ketter, Melanie Rowe

Rowe, Myra

Rowland, Donald S.
Vera Craig, Edna Murray

Rowland, Iris
See Ivor Roberts

Rowland, Susannah

Rowland, V. M. D.

Royal, Diane

Royal, Rosamond
Jeanne Hines, Valerie Sherwood

Royall, Vanessa
See Michael T. Hinkemeyer

Ruck, Berta
See Berta Onions

Rudeen, Anne
Leigh Ellis

Key: Actual names appear in bold. Pseudonyms appear in italics.

AUTHOR PSEUDONYM INDEX

Key: Actual names appear in bold. Pseudonyms appear in italics.

Sandstrom, Eve K.
Elizabeth Storm

Sandys, Elspeth

Sanford, Annette Schorre
Mary Carroll, Lisa St. John, Meg Dominque

Sans, Martha
Jenny Loring, Lee Sawyer

Santore, Sue

Santori, Helen
Helen Erskine

Saret, Rima
See Mary Anne Landers

Sargent, Joan
See Sara Lucille Jenkins

Sargent, Katherine

Sargent, Nancy

Sark, Sylvia

Satinwood, Deborah

Satran, Pamela Redmond

Sattler, Veronica

Saucier, Donna
See Donna Schomberg

Saunders, Amy Elizabeth

Saunders, Anne
See Margaret Alred

Saunders, Bree

Saunders, Diana
See Virginia Coffman

Saunders, Diane

Saunders, Glenda

Saunders, Irene

Saunders, Jaroldine

Saunders, Jean
Sally Blake, Jean Innes, Rowena Summers

Saunders, Jeraldine

Savage, Christina
See Kerry Newcomb

Savery, Jeanne
See Jeanne Savery Casstevens

Savoy, Suzanne
See Susan Stern

Sawyer, Lee
Jane Loring, Martha Sans

Sawyer, Meryl
See Martha Unickel

Sawyer, Nancy & John
Christina Abbey, Nancy Buckingham, Nancy John, Hilary London, Erica Quest

Sawyer, Susan

Saxe, Coral Smith

Saxon, Antonia

Sayers, Jessica

Scantlin, Bea

Scariano, Margaret M.

Scarpa, Sandra
Lark Eden

Schaal, Elizabeth
Elizabeth Shelley

Schaefer, Frank
Shana Carrol, Peter Gentry, Christina Savage

Schaller, Mary
Tori Phillips

Schamehorn, Mary Kathryn
Blair Cameron, Kathryn Blair - #2

Scharf, Marian
Malissa Carroll, Marissa Carroll, Joellyn Carroll

Schattner, E.
Emma Church, Elizabeth Graham

Scheirman, Marian
Lucinda Day

Schenck, Barbara
Anne Mc Allister

Schere, Jean K.
See Schere Monroe

Schimek, Gayle Malon
Joleen Daniels

Schmidt, Anna
Anne Shorr

Schmidt, Jo Horne
Ann Justice

Key: Actual names appear in bold. Pseudonyms appear in italics.

Schmidt, Ruth
Lee Scofield

Schneider, Rosemary

Schoder, Judith
Lacey Shay

Schofield, William G.

Schomberg, Donna
Donna Saucier

Schoonover, Lawrence

Schrempp, Elizabeth K.
Katherine Court

Schuler, Candace
Jeanette Darwin

Schultz, Jane
See Janet Schultz

Schultz, Janet
Tracy Sinclair, Jan Stuart

Schultz, Mary
Jennifer Cole, Leandra Logan

Schultze, Pearle Henriksen
Marie Pershing

Schulz, Marion
Marion Clarke

Schulze, Dallas
Dallas Hamlin

Schulze, Hertha
Kate Wellington

Schulze, Julie

Schwartz, Anne
Anne Powers

Schwartz, Paula
See Paula Reibel

Schweiss, Ginny
Jenna Mc Knight

Scofield, Carin

Scofield, Lee
See Ruth Schmidt

Scotch, Cheri

Scotland, Jay
See John Jakes

Scott-Drennan, Lynne
Amanda Scott

Scott-Gibbons, Marion
Marion Chesney, Sarah Chester, Helen Crampton, Ann Fairfax, Jennie Tremain

Scott, Adrienne
See Laurie Williams

Scott, Alexandra

Scott, Alicia
See Lisa Baumgartner

Scott, Amanda
See Lynne Scott-Drennan

Scott, Araby
See Barbara Brouse

Scott, Barbara A.

Scott, Bradford

Scott, Celia

Scott, Christine

Scott, De Loras
See Lisa Scott

Scott, Fela Dawson

Scott, Genevieve
See Jennifer Rigg

Scott, Grace
See Maggie Mac Keever

Scott, Isobel

Scott, Jane
See Adeline Mc Elfresh

Scott, Janey
See Rozella Lake

Scott, Joanna

Scott, Kristal Leigh
See Sherry De Borde

Scott, Lisa
De Loras Scott

Scott, Melissa
See Joyce Thies

Scott, Rachel
See Ana Lisa De Leon

Scott, Samantha
See Nancy Hermann

Scott, Susan Holloway
Miranda Jarrett

Scott, Theresa

AUTHOR PSEUDONYM INDEX

Key: Actual names appear in bold. Pseudonyms appear in italics.

AUTHOR PSEUDONYM INDEX

Key: Actual names appear in bold. Pseudonyms appear in italics.

Shaw, Irene
See Ivor Roberts

Shaw, Laura
See Nancy Motheral

Shaw, Linda

Shay, Lacey
See Judith Schoder, & Sharon Sigmond Shebar

Shayne, Maggie
See Margaret Bension

Shayne, Nina
See Prudence Boyd

Shebar, Sharon Sigmond
Lacey Shay

Sheehan, Michael

Sheehan, Nancy

Shelbourne, Cecily

Sheldon, Sidney

Shellabarger, Samuel

Shelley, Elizabeth
See Elaine Cichanth

Shelley, Lauren

Shelley, Lillian
See Lillian Koppel

Shelley, Susan
See Mary Pershall

Shepherd, Perdita
See Mary Lee Grisanti

Sheridan, Adora
See J.F. Hong, & E.M. Pavlik

Sheridan, Anne-Marie

Sheridan, Elsie
See Elsie Cromwell

Sheridan, Jane
Pauline Glin Winslow

Sheridan, Lee
See Elsie Cromwell

Sheridan, Theresa

Sherill, Suzanne
See Sherryl Ann Woods

Sherman, Joan
See Erolie Pearl Dern

Sherman, Jory

Sherrell, Carl

Sherrill, Suzanne
See Sherryl Woods

Sherrod, Barbara
Barbara Neil

Shertzel, Linda
Melinda Pryce

Sherwood, Deborah

Sherwood, Valerie
See Rosamond Royal

Shields, Dinah
Jane Clare

Shiffman, Janis
Janis Laden

Shimer, Ruth H.

Shiplett, June Lund

Shock, Marianne

Shoebridge, Marjorie

Shoffner, Laura A.
Laura Abbot

Shore, Anne
See Annette Sandford

Shore, Edwina

Shore, Francine
See Maureen Wartski

Shore, Jane
See Nicolette Maleckar

Shore, Juliet
Jan Haye, Anne Vinton

Shorr, Anne
See Anna Schmidt

Shott, Abel

Shreffler, Kim

Shuler, Linda Lay

Shulman, Sandra Dawn
Lisa Montague

Siddon, Barbara
See Barbara Bradford, Sally Siddon

Siddon, Sally
Sally Bradford, Barbara Siddon

AUTHOR PSEUDONYM INDEX

Key: Actual names appear in bold. Pseudonyms appear in italics.

Siddons, Anne Rivers

Sidney, Sidney
See Micahel Angelo Avallone

Siegenthal, Deb
Deborah Simmons

Silber, Diana

Silverlock, Anne
See Ruth Glick, Carolyn Males, & Louise
Titchener

Silverwood, Jane
See Ruth Glick, Carolyn Males, & Louise
Titchener

Sima, Elaine
Leslie Lynn, Lynn Leslie

Simake, Clifford

Simmons, Deborah
See Deb Siegenthal

Simmons, Mary Kay
See Mary Kay Freed

Simmons, Suzanne
See Suzanne Guntrum

Simmons, Trana Mae

Simms, Charlotte
See Charla Chin

Simms, Suzanne
See Suzanne Guntrum

Simon, Angela
See Irene Mahoney

Simon, Joann
Joanna Campbell

Simon, Laura

Simone-Rossney, Sonia
Sonia Simone

Simone, Sonia
See Sonia Simone-Rossney

Simons, Renee

Simonson, Sheila

Simpson, Carla

Simpson, Judith
Judy Baxter, Rosalind Foxx, Taria Hayford, Sara
Logan

Simpson, Maggie

Simpson, Pamela

Simpson, Patricia

Simpson, Rosemary

Sims, Lavonne

Sinclair, Alberta
See Theresa Grazia

Sinclair, Brooke

Sinclair, Cynthia
See Maureen Wartski

Sinclair, Elizabeth
See Marguerite Smith

Sinclair, Gordon

Sinclair, Heather

Sinclair, Helene
See Helene Lehr

Sinclair, Joanne

Sinclair, Katherine
See Joan Dial

Sinclair, Olga
See Olga Daniels

Sinclair, Olivia
Sandra Langford

Sinclair, Rebecca
See Patricia Viall

Sinclair, Tracy
See Janet Schultz

Sinclaire, Francesca

Singer, Kurt

Singer, Ron
Margaret Hunter, Delphine Marlowe

Singer, Sally M.
Amelia Jamison

Singleton, Linda Joy

Sinnott, Linda
Kate Carlton

Sites, Elizabeth

Sizemore, Susan

Skillern, Christine

Skinner, Gloria Dale
Charla Cameron

AUTHOR PSEUDONYM INDEX

Key: Actual names appear in bold. Pseudonyms appear in italics.

Skinner, June
Rohan O' Grady

Sky, Kathleen

Skye, Christina
See Roberta Stahlberg

Slattery, Sheila
Roseanne Williams

Slide, Dorothy

Slokowski, Mary Ann
Mary Ann Hammond, De Ann Patrick

Small, Bertrice

Small, Elaine

Small, Lass
Cally Hughes

Smith-Ware, Sandra
Gabrielle Du Pree

Smith, Alana
See Ruth Alana Smith

Smith, Arnold

Smith, Barbara Dawson

Smith, Barbara Johnson
B. J. Daniels

Smith, Bobbi
See Bobbi S. Walton

Smith, Carol Sturm

Smith, Christine

Smith, Dana Warren
See Lisa G. Brown

Smith, Deborah
Jackie Leigh, Jacquelyn Lennox

Smith, Doris E.

Smith, Elaine C.
Kami Lane

Smith, Genell Dellin
Gena Dalton

Smith, George

Smith, Harvey

Smith, Hazel

Smith, Jeri

Smith, Joan
Jennie Gallant

Smith, Justine Davis
Justine Davis

Smith, Karen Rose
Kari Sutherland

Smith, Lois
Cleo Chadwick

Smith, Lora R.
Leigh Roberts

Smith, Lynne
Paula Christopher, Lynn Michaels

Smith, Marcine

Smith, Marguerite
Elizabeth Sinclair

Smith, Marion
Marion Collin

Smith, Nancy
Amber Fitzgerald

Smith, Ruth Alana
Eileen Bryan, Alana Smith

Smith, Sandra Lee
Sandra Lee

Smith, Taylor

Smith, Veronica

Smith, Wynne
See Winifred Witton

Snell, Gay
Gay Cameron

Snelling, Lauraine

Snodgrass, Melinda
Melinda Harris, Melinda Mc Kenzie

Snoe, Eboni
See Gwen Mc Gee

Snow, Ashley
See Maryhelen Clague

Snow, Charles H.

Snow, Lucy
See Rosemary Aubert

Snow, Lyndon
See Dorothy P. Ansle

Snyder, Vicki

Sobolak, Adrienne M.
Adrienne De Wolfe

Sohl, Jerry
Roberta Mountjoy

Solerno, Ann

Soliman, Patricia B.

Somerlott, Robert
Jessica North

Somers, Suzanne
See Helen Gray Weston

Somerset, Rose

Sommars, Colette

Sommerfield, Sylvie F.

Sommers, Beverly

Sommers, Elda Minger

Sommers, Jeanne
See Barrie Meyers

Sommers, Justine

Sommers, Lilah

Sommerset, Judith

Sorel, Marilyn Meeske
Nina Lansdale

Sorrels, Roy
Anna Mc Clure

Soule, Maris
Samantha Seymour, Barbara Stephens

South, Barbara
Samantha Seymour

South, Grace
See Maggie Mac Keever

Southwick, Teresa

Spark, Natalie

Sparks, Christine
Lucy Gordon

Sparrow, Laura
See Laura Halford

Spearman, Stephanie L.

Speas, Jan Cox

Speer, Flora
M. Evans

Speicher, Helen Ross
Alice Abbott

Spencer, Anne

Spencer, Candace
See Candace Schuler

Spencer, Catherine
See Kathleen Orr

Spencer, Cheryl
See Cheryl Lynn Purviance

Spencer, Emma Jane

Spencer, La Vyrle

Spencer, Mary

Spenser, Emily
See Charlotte Elkins

Spenser, Emma Jane

Spindler, Erica

Spitfire, Rosemary

Sprenger, Terri

Spring, Marianne

Springer, Lacey

Sproull, Marie
Elizabeth Ann Michaels

St. Bastian, Margaret

St. Clair, Elizabeth
See Susan Cohen

St. Clair, Jessica

St. Clair, Joy

St. Clair, Katherine
See Tom E. Huff

St. Clair, Stephanie
See Donald Mass

St. Claire, Erin
See Sandra Brown

St. Claire, Jessica

St. Claire, Madeline

St. David, Joy
Ellen Du Pont

St. George, Edith
See Edith Delatush

St. George, La Verne
See La Verne Coan

AUTHOR PSEUDONYM INDEX

Key: Actual names appear in bold. Pseudonyms appear in italics.

Key: Actual names appear in bold. Pseudonyms appear in italics.

Steele, Jessica

Steele, Linda
See Linda Steele Uzquiano

Steele, Marianne

Steen, Sandy

Steffen, Sandra

Stegman, Michele

Steiner, Irene Hunter

Steiner, Susan

Steinfeld, Ann

Steinke, Anne E.
Anne Reynolds, Elizabeth Reynolds, Anne Williams

Stephens, Barbara
See Maris Soule

Stephens, Blythe

Stephens, Casey
See Sharon Wagner

Stephens, Donna

Stephens, Doreen
See Rachel Benedict

Stephens, Jeanne
See Jean Hagar

Stephens, Kay
See Rachel Benedict

Stephens, Sharon
See Kristen James

Stephens, Suzanne
See Harry Whittington

Sterling, Elaine K.

Sterling, Jessica
See Tracy Stern

Sterling, Maria S.
See Will Watson

Stern, Susan
Susan Sackett, Suzanne Savoy

Stern, Tracy
See Jessica Sterling

Stevens, Amanda
See Marilyn M. Amman

Stevens, Blaine
See Harry Whittington

Stevens, Blythe
See Sharon Wagner

Stevens, Diane

Stevens, Janice
See Janice Baczewski, & Norma Tadlock

Stevens, Jennifer
See Peggy Hanchar

Stevens, Kelley R.
See Kelly Varner Ebel

Stevens, Kimberly

Stevens, Linda
See Steve Hamilton

Stevens, Lucille

Stevens, Lynsey
See Lynette Howard

Stevens, Serita
Megan Mac Donnell, Shira Stevens

Stevens, Shira
See Serita Stevens

Stevens, Susan
See Alex Andrews

Stevenson, Anne

Stevenson, Florence
Zandra Colt, Lucia Curzon, Zabrina Faire, Pamela Frazier, Ellen Fitzgerald

Stevenson, Kate

Stevenson, Robin
Robin St. Thomas

Steward, Ada
See Adah Rhome

Stewardson, Dawn

Stewart, Barbara

Stewart, Isobell
See Edward Stanley

Stewart, Jean
See Mona Newman

Stewart, Judith
See Judith Anne Polley

Stewart, Kathryn

Stewart, Leigh

AUTHOR PSEUDONYM INDEX

Key: Actual names appear in bold. Pseudonyms appear in italics.

Stewart, Lois
  See Lois Nollett

Stewart, Lucy Phillips

Stewart, Mary

Stewart, Rosaline

Stewart, Ruth

Stewart, Sally

Stine, Whitney
  Constance F. Peale

Stirling, Elaine K.

Stirling, Jessica
  See Peggie Coghlan

Stirling, Jocelyn

Stockenberg, Antoinette
  Antoinette Hale, Antoinette Hardy

Stoddard, Charles

Stokes, Gail Eastwood
  Gail Eastwood

Stokes, Manning Lee

Stoks, Peggy

Stone, Charlotte

Stone, Elisa
  See Elaine Stancliffe

Stone, Gillian

Stone, Karen
  Karen Young

Stone, Katherine

Stone, Natalie
  See Sally Goldenbaum, & Adrienne Staff

Stone, Sally

Stone, Sharon

Stone, Thomas
  Caroline Stafford

Storm, Elizabeth
  See Eve K. Sandstrom

Storm, Virginia
  See Irene Mossop, Charles & Irene Swatridge

Stover, Deb

Stowe, Rosetta
  See George Ogan

Stowe, Tanya

Straford, Karen
  See Karen Finnigan

Strasser, Heidi
  See Ilse Dallmayr

Stratford, Karen

Stratham, Frances Patton

Strather, Patricia

Stratton, Rebecca
  See Lucy Gillen

Street, Kelly
  See Joy Tucker

Street, Octavia
  See Kaa Byington

Streib, Daniel
  Louise Grandville

Stribling, Jean
  Ruth Jean Dale

Strickland, Laura

Stringer, Arthur

Stromeyer, Carolyn
  Carolyn Thornton

Strong, Chris
  Christina Cordaire

Strother, Pat Wallace
  Patricia Cloud, Vivian Lord, Pat Wallace, Pat West

Strutt, Sheila

Stuart, Alex
  See Violet Vivian Mann

Stuart, Anne
  See Anne Kristine Stuart Ohlrogge

Stuart, Becky
  See Stuart Buchan

Stuart, Casey
  See Ann Elizabeth Bullard

Stuart, Charles
  See Charles Roy Mac Kinnon

Stuart, Dee
  See Ellen Searight

Stuart, Diana
  See Jane Toombs

Key: Actual names appear in bold. Pseudonyms appear in italics.

Key: Actual names appear in bold. Pseudonyms appear in italics.

Key: Actual names appear in bold. Pseudonyms appear in italics.

Terry, Beverly
See Beverly T. Haaf

Testerman, Lois Kleinsasser
Cait Logan, Cait London

Tetel, Julie
See Julia Andresen

Tew, Mary
Mary Douglas

Thacker, Cathy Gillen
Cathy Gillen

Thacker, Shelly
See Shelly Thacker Meinhardt

Thane, Elswyth
See Elswyth Beebe

Thatcher, Julia
See Ronald Bensen

Thatcher, Phyllis
Catherine Hardcastle

Thayer, Geraldine
See Helen Gray Weston

Thayer, Patricia

Thian, Valerie

Thiels, Kathryn Gorsha

Thies, Joyce
Janet Joyce, Jenna Lee Joyce, Melissa Scott

Thimblethorpe, J. S.
Sylvia Thorpe

Thomas, Alexandra

Thomas, Bree
Susannah Howe

Thomas, Carol
See Debra McCarthy Anderson

Thomas, Dianne
See Deborah Morris, Pat Shaver

Thomas, Jodi
See Jodi Koumalats

Thomas, Kate

Thomas, Lee
See Will Watson

Thomas, Leslie

Thomas, Lorelei

Thomas, Martha Lou

Thomas, Michele Y.

Thomas, Molly
See Myrna Temte

Thomas, Nicola

Thomas, Patricia

Thomas, Penelope

Thomas, Rosie

Thomas, Victoria

Thompson, Alfie
Val Daniels

Thompson, Aline

Thompson, Anne Armstrong

Thompson, China
See Mary Berrisford

Thompson, Christene

Thompson, Jonathan
See M. S. Roe

Thompson, Marcella
Pamela Thompson

Thompson, Pamela
See Marcella Thompson

Thompson, Sydney

Thompson, Trudy

Thompson, Vicki G.

Thompson, Vicki Lewis
Corey Keaton, Cory Kenyon

Thompson, Victoria

Thomson, Christina

Thomson, Daisy
See M. S. Roe

Thorne, Alexandra

Thorne, April
See Janis Flores

Thorne, Avery

Thorne, Belle
See Bella Jarrett

Thorne, Nicola
See Anna L' Estrange

Thorne, Victoria

Key: Actual names appear in bold. Pseudonyms appear in italics.

AUTHOR PSEUDONYM INDEX

Key: Actual names appear in bold. Pseudonyms appear in italics.

Trent, Dan
Danielle Trent, Lynda Trent

Trent, Danielle
See Dan Trent

Trent, Jessica

Trent, Lynda
See Dan Trent

Tresillian, Richard

Trevor, June
See June E. Casey

Trevor, Meriod

Triegel, Linda Jeannette
Elizabeth Kidd

Triglia, June
See June E. Casey

Triner, Jeanne Kaye
See Jeanne Triner

Triner, Jeanne
Caylin Jennings, Jeanne Kaye Triner

Troke, Molly
See Hester Bourne

Troutman, Jackie

Troy, Amanda
See Mary Kahn

Troy, Katherine
See Anne Buxton

Truesdell, June

Tucker, Delaine
See Elaine Camp

Tucker, Elaine
See Elaine Camp

Tucker, Helen

Tucker, Joy
Kelly Street

Tucker, Ruth B.
Hope Mc Intyre

Tunis, Elizabeth
Elizabeth De Lancey

Turner, Barbara Kay

Turner, Elizabeth
See Gail Oust

Turner, Joan

Turner, Judy

Turner, Len
See Will Watson

Turner, Linda Ray
Linda Raye

Turner, Lynn
See Mary Watson

Turner, Mary

Turner, Sue Long
Kristin Michaels

Turney, C. Dell

Turney, Catherine

Twaddle, Susan B.
Elizabeth Barron, Susan Bowden

Tyler, Alison
See Elise Title

Tyler, Antonia
See Susan Whittlesey Wolf

Tyre, Robert

Ullman, Albert E.

Unickel, Martha
Meryl Sawyer

Upper, Gloria
Gloria Douglas

Upshall, Helen
Susannah Curtis

Ure, Jean
Sara Mc Culloch

Uzquiano, Linda Steele
Linda Steele

Vadergriff, Aola
Kitt Brown

Vail, Linda
See Steve Hamilton

Vail, Phillip
See Noel B. Gerson

Valcour, Vanessa
See James Conaway

Valenti, Justina
See Barbara Max

Valentine, Jo
Charlotte Armstrong

261

AUTHOR PSEUDONYM INDEX

Key: Actual names appear in bold. Pseudonyms appear in italics.

Valentine, Terri

Valentino, Donna

Valley, Lorraine

Van Der Zee, Karen
  See Wendela Kilmer

Van Kirk, Eileen
  Mary Eileen Petty

Van Nuys, Joan
  Marianna Essex

Van Slyke, Helen
  Sharon Ashton

Van Vogt, A.E.

Van Wie, Pat
  Patricia Keelyn

Van Wieren, Moran
  See Wendela Kilmer

Van-Loon, Antonia
  Janine French

Vandergriff, Aola

Vandervelde, Isabel

Vann, Suzette

Vanner, Lynn

Vargas, Deborah

Varley, John

Varlinsky, Deborah
  Deborah Le Varre

Varner, Linda
  See Charlotte Hoy, Linda Varner Palmer

Varner, Lynda
  Scotney St. James

Vasilopoulos, Freda
  Freda Vasilos, Tina Vasilos

Vasilos, Freda
  See Freda Vasilopoulos

Vasilos, Tina
  See Freda Vasilopoulos

Vaughan, Carter
  See Noel B. Gerson

Vaughan, Jane
  Vivian Vaughan

Vaughan, Louise

Vaughan, Robert
  Paula Moore, Paula Fairman

Vaughan, Vivian
  See Jane Vaughan

Vaughn, Dona

Vaughn, Evelyn

Vaughten, Carolyn

Vayle, Valerie
  See Janice Young Brooks, Jean Brooks Janowick

Veillon, Barbara Lantier
  Kristen Morgan

Vendresha, Vita

Venet, Michelle
  See Alicia Todd Rasley

Verge, Lisa Ann
  Lisann St. Pierre

Vermandel, Janet Gregory

Vernon, Claire
  See August Boon

Vernon, Dorothy

Vernon, Kathleen R.
  Lesley Dixon, Kay Vernon

Vernon, Kay
  See Kathleeen Vernon

Veronese, Gina

Verrette, Joyce
  See Joyce Petratur

Veryan, Patricia
  See Patricia Bannister

Vest, Jo Ann
  See Joanna Wayne

Viall, Patricia
  Rebecca Sinclair

Vickery, Katherine
  See Katherine Kramer

Victor, Cindy

Victor, Kathleen

Victor, Vanessa
  See Barbara Max

Viens, Carol
  Carol Daniels

AUTHOR PSEUDONYM INDEX

Key: Actual names appear in bold. Pseudonyms appear in italics.

Vincent, Claire
Delores Craig, Moira Lord, Miriam Lynch

Vincent, Heather
See Quenna Tilbury

Vincent, Honor
See Quenna Tilbury

Vincent, Joan

Vincentnathan, Lyn
Sally Du Bois

Vincenzi, Penny

Vincer, Rachel
See Debra Mc Carthy Anderson

Vine, Kerry
Gillian Oxley

Vines-Haines, Beverly
Becca Cassidy, Jamie West

Vinet, Lynette

Viney, Jane
Anne Neville

Vinton, Anne
Jan Haye, Juliet Shore

Vita, Terese Daly Ramin
Teresa Daly Ramin, Teresa Ramin

Vitek, Donna Kimel
Donna Alexander

Vivian, Angela

Vivian, Daisy

Voeller, Sydell

Von Robin, Kiz
See Kim Heidel

Von Stroheim, Erich

Vosbein, Barbara
Nikki Benjamin

Wade, Elizabeth Evelyn

Wade, Jennifer

Wade, Suzanne
See Susan Kirby

Wagner, Carol
Malissa Carroll, Marisa Carroll, Joellyn Carroll

Wagner, Kimberli

Wagner, Nancy

Wagner, Sharon
Blythe Stevens, Casey Stephens

Wainscott, Tina Ritter

Wake, Vivien Fiske

Wakefield, Maureen

Wakeley, Dorothy

Walden, Luanne

Walford, Christian
See Noreen Dilcock

Walker, Barbara Kaye
Barbara Kaye

Walker, Constance

Walker, Dorothy Pierce

Walker, Elizabeth Neff
Laura Matthews, Elizabeth Rotter

Walker, Emily
See Quenna Tilbury

Walker, Irma Ruth
Andrea Harris, Ruth Walker

Walker, Joan

Walker, Kate

Walker, Laurie

Walker, Linda

Walker, Lois Arvin
Candice Adams, Rebecca Ashley, Sabrina Myles

Walker, Lucy
Dorothy Sanders

Walker, Margaret
Margaret Alexander

Walker, Margie

Walker, Ruth
See Irma Walker

Wall, Judith
Anne Henry

Wallace, Claire

Wallace, Edgar

Wallace, Pamela
Dianne King

Wallace, Pat
See Pat Wallace Strother

AUTHOR PSEUDONYM INDEX

Key: Actual names appear in bold. Pseudonyms appear in italics.

Wallerich, Linda H.
Linda Benjamin, Jessica Douglass

Walls, Patricia
Gina Delaney, Patricia Rae

Walsh, Alida

Walsh, Kelly
V. P. Walsh

Walsh, Penelope

Walsh, Sheila

Walsh, V. P.
See Kelly Walsh

Walters, Jade

Walters, Janet Lane

Walters, Linda
See Linda Rice

Walters, Shelly

Walton, Bobbi S.
Bobbi Smith

Walton, Kay

Walz, Jay & Audrey

Warady, Phylis Ann

Ward, Kate
Barbara Cust, Caroline Fanshawe

Ward, Lynda
Julia Jeffries

Ward, Rebecca

Ware, Ciji

Ware, Edouard

Ware, Joyce C.

Ware, Lynch W.

Warfield, Teresa

Warre, Mary D.
Jennifer Ames, Ann Barclay, Maysie Greig

Warren, Betsy

Warren, Beverly C.

Warren, Linda
Frances West

Warren, Norma

Warren, Pat
Patricia Cox

Warren, Paulette
See Paul Fairman

Wartski, Maureen
Sharon Francis, Evelyn Shannon, Francine Shore, Cynthia Sinclair

Wash, Sheila
See Sophie Leyton

Washburn, Jan

Washington, Elsie
Rosalind Welles

Watson, Julia
See Julia Fitzgerald

Watson, Ken

Watson, Margaret

Watson, Mary
Lynn Turner

Watson, Will
Brett Austin, Lee Floren, Lisa Franchon, Claudia Hall, Matt Harding, Grace Lang, Marguerite Nelson, Maria Sterling, Lee Thomas, Len Turner

Watters, Patricia

Waugh, Hillary
Elissa Grandower

Waverly, Kathleen
Shannon Waverly

Waverly, Shannon
See Kathleen Waverly

Way, Margaret

Wayne, Heather
See Prudence Boyd

Wayne, Joanna
Jo Ann Vest

Wayne, Marcia
Susan Ashe, Carol Ann Best, Con Darlington, Ann Martin

Wayne, Rachel

Wayne, Rochelle
See Rochelle A. Mulvihill

Weale, Anne
Andrea Blake, Anne Wilson

Weaver, Ingrid

AUTHOR PSEUDONYM INDEX

Key: Actual names appear in bold. Pseudonyms appear in italics.

Weaver, Judith
Ashley Chapel, Harper Mc Bride

Webb, Jean Francis
Roberta Morrison

Webb, Lionel
See Morris Herschman

Webb, Peggy

Webber, Nancy
Jennifer Rose

Webster, Elizabeth

Webster, Jan

Webster, M. Coates

Wees, Frances Shelly

Weger, Jackie

Weinbaum, Stanley G.

Weir, Theresa

Weldon, Susan

Welks, Alyssa

Weller, Dorothy
Dorothy Ann Bernard, Dorothea Hale

Welles, Alyssa
See Nomi Berger

Welles, Angela
See Angela Bostwick

Welles, Caron
Jan Jones

Welles, Elisabeth
See Mary Linn Roby

Welles, Patricia
See Patricia Rogers

Welles, Rachel
See Patricia Rogers

Welles, Rosalind
See Elsie Washington

Wellington, Kate
See Hertha Schulze

Wells, Angela

Welsh, Jeanette

Wender, Ruth

Wendt, Jo Ann

Wentworth, Julia

Wentworth, Sally

Werner, Hazeldell

Werner, Herma
Eve Gladstone, Roxanne Jarrett

Werner, Patricia

Wert, Lynette
See Lynn Le Mon

Wesley, Caroline

Wesley, Elizabeth
See Adeline Mc Elfresh

Wesolowsky, Joan
Ann Edward

West, Angela

West, Anna
See Ann Edward

West, Cara

West, Christine
See Christine Baker

West, Frances
See Linda Warren

West, Jamie
See Beverly Vines-Haines

West, Jennifer
Jennifer Justin

West, Nicola

West, Pat
See Pat Wallace Strother

West, Sara Ann

Westcott, Jan

Westcott, Kathleen
See Christine Abrahamsen

Westhaven, Margaret
Peggy M. Hansen

Westland, Lynn

Weston, Garnett

Weston, Helen Gray
Dorothy Daniels, Danielle Dorsett, Angela Gray, Cynthia Kavanaugh, Helaine Ross, Suzanne Somers, Geraldine Thayer

Weston, Nigella
Veronica Mixon

Weston, Sophie

Westweed, Hillary

Westwood, Gwen

Weyrich, Becky Lee

Whaley, Frances

Whearley, Bob
Fran Earley

Wheat, Carolyn
Corintha Bennett

Wheeler, Amanda

Wherlock, Julia

Whindham, Eleanor

Whisenand, Valerie
Kasey Adams, Isabel Whitfield

Whistler, Mary
See Ida Pollock

Whitby, Sharon
See Maureen Peters

White, Ann Howard

White, Charlotte
Marianne Cole, Jennifer Dale

White, Frances

White, Jude Gilliam
Jude Deveraux

White, Linda

White, Patricia

White, Tiffany
See Anna Eberhardt

White, William C.

Whitehead, Barbara

Whitfield, Donna

Whitfield, Isabel
See Valerie Whisenand

Whitiker, Gail
See Gail Crease

Whitmee, Jeanne

Whitmore, Cilla
See Arthur Gladstone

Whitmore, Loretta

Whitney, Diana
See Diana Hinz

Whitney, Jamisan
See Noreen Brownlie

Whitney, Phyllis
See Phyllis A. Garner

Whittaker, Charlotte Amalie

Whittal, Yvonne

Whitten, Judy

Whittenburg, Karen Toller

Whittingham, Sara
See Prudence Boyd

Whittington, Harry
Ashley Carter, Suzanne Stephens

Whitworth, Karen

Wiath, Linda C.
Laurel Collins

Wibberley, Anna

Wibberley, Mary

Widmer, Mary Lou

Wieselberg, Helen

Wiete, Robin Leanne
Leanne Grayson

Wiggs, Susan
Susan Childress

Wilbee, Brenda

Wilby, Jane
See Anne Hampson

Wilde, Hilary
See August Boon

Wilde, Jennifer
See Tom E. Huff

Wilde, Jocelyn
See John Toombs

Wilde, Lauren
See Joanne Redd

Wilde, Leslie
See Ray Bentinck

Wilder, Ellie
Nora Roberts

AUTHOR PSEUDONYM INDEX

Key: Actual names appear in bold. Pseudonyms appear in italics.

Wilder, Joan
See Catherine Lanigan

Wilder, Quinn

Wilding, Kay
See Joan Wilson Hicks

Wilding, Lynne
See Lynne Gumbley

Wildman, Corinna
Corinna Cunliffe

Wildman, Faye
See Jillian Dagg

Wiley, Ann

Wiley, Laura
See Patricia Matthews

Wilhelm, Terri Lynn
Terri Lindsey, Terri Lynn

Wilhite, Bettie Marie
Elizabeth August, Elizabeth Douglas

Wilkins, Barbara

Wilkins, Gina
Gina Ferris

Wilkins, Margaret
Margaret Moore

Wilkinson, Lee

William, Cathy

Williams, Ann - #1
See Peggy Myers

Williams, Ann - #2
See Cathy Williams

Williams, Anne
See Anne E. Steinke

Williams, Barbara
Charlotte Nichols

Williams, Ben Ames

Williams, Bronwyn
See Zoe Dozier, Mary Williams

Williams, Cathy
Ann - #2 Williams

Williams, Claudette
Melanie Davis

Williams, Frances
See Frances Hardier

Williams, Heather

Williams, Jeanne
Megan Castell, Gwen Choate, Jeanne Crecy,
Jeanne Foster, Kristin Michaels, Deirdre Rowan,
Megan Stuart

Williams, Jennifer

Williams, Laurie
Adrienne Scott

Williams, Lee
Leigh Anne Williams, William Mernit

Williams, Leigh Anne
See Lee Williams

Williams, Lynn
Tracy Adams, Gail Everett, Arlene Hale, Mary
Hale, Mary Tate

Williams, Mary - #2
Bronwyn Williams

Williams, Mary - #1
See Marianne Harvey

Williams, Norma
Dee Norma, Wynn Williams

Williams, Patricia
Alexandra Lord

Williams, Paula
See Paula Darrington

Williams, Rose
See Dan Ross

Williams, Roseanne
See Sheila Slattery

Williams, Stephanie

Williams, Wynn
See Norma Williams

Williamson, Penelope

Willingham, Bess
See Cindy M. Harris

Willis, Kathy

Willis, Ted

Willman, Marianne
Sabina Clark, Marianne Clark

Willoughby, Lee Davis-Series N

Willow, Shannon

Wills, Ann Meredith

AUTHOR PSEUDONYM INDEX

Key: Actual names appear in bold. Pseudonyms appear in italics.

Wills, Maralys

Wilroy, Jan

Wilsen, Marolyn

Wilson-Harris, Crystal

Wilson, Abigail
  See Sandra Young

Wilson, Alanna

Wilson, Anne
  Andrea Blake, Anne Weale

Wilson, B. L.
  Brenda Trent

Wilson, Caryl

Wilson, Christine
  See Christine Geach

Wilson, Ellen
  Laurel Evans

Wilson, Fran

Wilson, Frances Engle

Wilson, Gayle

Wilson, Jean

Wilson, Joyce
  See Sally James

Wilson, Marilyn Caldwell

Wilson, Mary Anne

Wilson, Mary
  See Mary Linn Roby

Wilson, Pamela
  Margaret Summerville

Wilson, Patricia

Wilson, Renee Roszel
  Renee Roszel

Wilson, Rowena

Wilson, Sandra
  Sandra Heath

Wimberly, Clara

Wind, Barbara
  See Barbara Samuel

Wind, David
  Monica Barrie, Jenifer Dalton, Marilyn Davids

Wind, Ruth
  See Barbara Samuel

Windham, Kit
  See Joan Wilson Hicks

Windham, Susannah

Windsor, Kathleen

Windsor, Linda
  Linda Covington

Windsor, Pamela
  See Jon Messman

Wing, Janet
  Lenora Barber

Wingo, Helen

Winn, Bonnie

Winslow, Eliot
  Ellie Winslow

Winslow, Ellie
  See Eliot Winslow

Winslow, Laurel
  See Maura Seger

Winslow, Pauline Glin
  See Jane Sheridan

Winsor, Kathleen

Winspear, Violet

Winstead, Linda

Winston, Anne Marie
  See Anne Marie Rodgers

Winston, Donna

Winter, Abigail
  See Schere Monroe

Winter, Pat

Winters, Malori
  See Lisa M. Renshaw

Winters, Rebecca
  See Rebecca Burton

Winwood, Eileen
  Eileen Putman

Wisdom, Linda Randall
  Linda Wisdom

Wisdom, Linda
  See Linda Randall Wisdom

AUTHOR PSEUDONYM INDEX

Key: Actual names appear in bold. Pseudonyms appear in italics.

Wisdom, Penelope
Penelope Stuart

Wisely, Charlotte
Charlotte Hastings

Witmer-Gow, Karyn
Elizabeth Grayson, Elizabeth Kary

Witton, Eileen
Janice Bennett

Witton, Winifred
Wynne Smith

Wohjoski, Barbara
Laurel Pace

Wold, Estella
Caro Olson Moore

Wolf, Bernice

Wolf, Joan

Wolf, Susan Whittlesey
Antonia Tyler

Wolfe, Gene

Wolfe, Lois
Gillian Wyeth

Wood, Barbara

Wood, Deborah

Wood, Nuria
See Joi Nobisso

Wood, Sally

Wood, Sara

Wood, Tonya
Courtney Ryan

Woodbury, Leonora
See Ellen Kellman

Woodhouse, Sarah

Woodiwiss, Kathleen E.

Woodland, Eva
See Nicole De Lyn

Woods, Eleanor
See Eleanor Rogers

Woods, Margery
Rebecca Caine, Margery Hilton

Woods, Sherryl Ann
Alexandra Kirk, Suzanne Sherill

Woodstock, Maureen
Maureen Bronson

Woodward, Daphne

Woolf, Victoria
See Sheila Holland

Worboys, Anne
Annette Eyre, Vicky Maxwell

Worley, Dorothy

Worth, Margaret
See Helen Arvonen

Worthington, Avis

Wren, P.C.

Wright, Cynthia
Devon Lindsay

Wright, Don

Wright, Francesca
Ashley French, Harriet Gray, Julia Kane, Denise Robins

Wright, Lucretia
Alicia Knight

Wright, Patricia

Wright, Watkins E.

Wyatt, Catherine

Wyatt, Stephanie

Wyckoff, Julie

Wyeth, Gillian
See Lois Wolfe

Wyland, Amanda

Wyndham, Esther
See Mary Lutyens

Wynn, Patricia
See Patricia Ricks

Wynne, Annabel

Yansick, Susan
Erin Yorke

Yapp, Kathleen

Yarbro, Chelsea Quinn
Vanessa Pryor

Yarde, Jeanne
Joan Hunter, Jeanne Montague

AUTHOR PSEUDONYM INDEX

Key: Actual names appear in bold. Pseudonyms appear in italics.

Yates, Judith
See Judith Yoder

Yerby, Frank

Yirka, Barbara A.
Anne Barbour

Yoder, Judith
Judith Yates

York, Alison
See Leslie Arlen

York, Amanda
See Joan Dial

York, Andrew
See Leslie Arlen

York, Elizabeth
See Margaret Elizabeth York

York, Georgia

York, Helen

York, Margaret Elizabeth
Margaret Abbey, Joanna Makepeace, Elizabeth York

York, Pauline
See Marcia Y. Howl

York, Rebecca
See Nancy Baggett, Eileen Buckholtz, Ruth Glick, Carolyn Males, & Louise Titchener

York, Vickie
See Betty Ann Patterson

Yorke, Erin
See Christine Healy, Susan Yansick

Yorke, Katherine
See Anna L' Estrange

Young, Brittany
See Sandra Young

Young, Cassandra

Young, Ena
Kerry Carr, Jane Joyce

Young, Karen
See Karen Stone

Young, Mary Jo
Jenny Nolan

Young, Maryann

Young, Rena

Young, Sandra
Sandra Harris, Brittany Young, Abigail Wilson

Young, Selwyn Marie

Young, W.J.

Youngblood, Ila Dell

Zach, Cheryl
Jennifer Cole

Zachary, Elizabeth

Zane, Carolyn
See Carolyn Pizzuti

Zaroulis, Nancy

Zavala, Ann
Ann Pope, Lee Pope

Zayne, Valerie
See Leigh Shaheen

Zeig, Joan
Alicia Meadowes

Zide, Donna Comeaux

Ziobro, Marie

Zirkelbach, Thelma
See Lorna Michaels

AUTHOR/TITLE INDEX

Adams, Faye
    Rosebud   05/94   Pocket
    The Goodnight Loving Trail   02/95   Pocket Historical

Adams, Joanna Z.
    Intimate Connections   Warner

Adams, Jolene
  38   From This Day Forward   /82   Berkley Second Chance At Love

Adams, Joyce
    Gambler's Lady   05/94   Zebra Heartfire

Adams, Kasey
    Purely Physical   07/84   Nal Rapture Romance
  35   Untamed Desire   Nal Rapture Romance

Adams, Kat
  773   Thursday's Child   03/93   Silhouette Desire
  463   Love Bug   10/86   Silhouette Romance
  788   The Ace Of Hearts   04/91   Silhouette Romance
  810   The Price Of Paradise   08/91   Silhouette Romance
  811   Irresistible Force   08/91   Silhouette Romance

Adams, Kelly
  47   Bittersweet Revenge   /82   Berkley Second Chance At Love
  265   Wildfire   /85   Berkley Second Chance At Love
  292   Sunlight And Silver   /85   Berkley Second Chance At Love
  455   Storm Fire   Berkley Second Chance At Love
  461   The Silent Heart   Berkley Second Chance At Love
  473   Tender Nights   Berkley Second Chance At Love

Adams, Melodie
  137   Return Of The Drifter   Harlequin Superromance
  265   I'll Fly The Flags   12/83   Silhouette Romance
  516   A Dangerous Proposition   07/87   Silhouette Romance
  647   The Medicine Man   05/89   Silhouette Romance
  722   In The Family Way   05/90   Silhouette Romance
  934   What About Charlie?   06/93   Silhouette Romance
  152   Gentle Possession   03/84   Silhouette Special Edition

Adams, Pepper
    Spring Fancy - "Out Of The Dark"   02/94   Harlequin Anthology
  48   Taking Savannah   10/96   Harlequin Here Come The Grooms
    Silhouette Spring Fancy Collection   03/94   Silhouette Anthology
  486   Heavenly Bodies   02/87   Silhouette Romance
  504   In Hot Pursuit   05/87   Silhouette Romance
  600   Taking Savannah   09/88   Silhouette Romance
  724   Cimarron Knight   06/90   Silhouette Romance
  740   Cimarron Glory   08/90   Silhouette Romance
  753   Cimarron Rebel   10/90   Silhouette Romance
  805   Hunter At Large   07/91   Silhouette Romance
  842   The Old Black Magic   01/92   Silhouette Romance
  862   Rookie Dad   05/92   Silhouette Romance

Adams, Pepper

897	Wake Up Little Susie	10/92	Silhouette Romance
964	Mad About Maggie (Fabulous Father)	10/93	Silhouette Romance
983	Lady Willpower	01/94	Silhouette Romance
1003	The Bachelor Cure	04/94	Silhouette Romance

Adams, Tracy

86	The Moth And The Flame	06/81	Silhouette Romance

Adams, Tricia

20	Between The Sheets	/84	Berkley To Have And To Hold

Addison, Jayne

888	You Made Me Love You	09/92	Silhouette Romance
944	Something Blue	06/93	Silhouette Romance
980	A Precious Gift (Under The Mistletoe)	12/93	Silhouette Romance
1034	Temporary Groom (Hasty Weddings)	09/94	Silhouette Romance
1117	Wild West Wife	11/95	Silhouette Romance

Adkins, Cleo

479	The Case Of The Ebony Queen	/59	Harlequin

Adler, Elizabeth

	The Secret Of The Villa Mimosa	11/95	Delacorte
	Legacy Of Secrets	07/94	Dell
	Leonie		Dell
	Peach		Dell
	The Rich Shall Inherit		Dell
	The Property Of A Lady		Dell
	Fortune Is A Woman		Dell

Aeby, Jacquelyn

	Wait For Dawn		Dell Candlelight
	Linnet's Folly		Dell Candlelight
173	Serena		Dell Candlelight
176	Diary Of Danger		Dell Candlelight
177	The Trillium Cup		Dell Candlelight
184	Counterfeit Love		Dell Candlelight
191	Cottage On Catherina Cay		Dell Candlelight
193	Falconer's Hall		Dell Candlelight
199	The Storm		Dell Candlelight
202	The Sign Of The Blue Dragon		Dell Candlelight
205	Never Look Back		Dell Candlelight

Ahearn, Pamela

	All Our Yesterdays		Knightsbridge
	Love No Other	/88	Paperjacks

Aiken, Candice

	Wayward Angel	Pocket Richard Gallen Books

Aiken, Ginny

	Love Evergreen	12/93	Jove Historical

Aiken, Joan

	Castle Barebane	Gothic

AUTHOR/TITLE INDEX

Algermissen, Jo Ann

276	Challenge The Fates	04/86	Silhouette	Desire
300	Serendipity Samantha	08/86	Silhouette	Desire
318	Hank's Woman	11/86	Silhouette	Desire
361	Made In America	07/87	Silhouette	Desire
409	Lucky Lady	03/88	Silhouette	Desire
486	Butterfly	03/89	Silhouette	Desire
539	Bedside Manner	12/89	Silhouette	Desire
559	Sunshine	04/90	Silhouette	Desire
706	Hometown Man	04/92	Silhouette	Desire
374	Purple Diamonds	04/87	Silhouette	Special Edition
455	Blue Emeralds	05/88	Silhouette	Special Edition
542	Paper Stars	08/89	Silhouette	Special Edition
607	Best Man	07/90	Silhouette	Special Edition
655	Would You Marry Me Anyway?	03/91	Silhouette	Special Edition
692	Family Friendly	09/91	Silhouette	Special Edition
702	Hometown Man		Silhouette	Special Edition
20	I Do?	05/96	Silhouette	Yours Truly

Allan, Bette

308	Doctor Paul	/54	Harlequin

Allan, Jeanne

2875	The Waiting Heart		Harlequin Romance
2899	The Game Is Love		Harlequin Romance
2935	Trust In Love		Harlequin Romance
2989	One Reckless Moment		Harlequin Romance
3121	No Angel		Harlequin Romance
3175	Rancher's Bride	02/92	Harlequin Romance
3217	From The Highest Mountain	09/92	Harlequin Romance
3286	The Cowboy Next Door	10/93	Harlequin Romance
3384	Charlotte's Cowboy	11/95	Harlequin Romance
3408	Moving In With Adam	05/96	Harlequin Romance

Allan, Tony

480	Grey Cup Cavalcade	/59	Harlequin
622	Football Flashbacks	/61	Harlequin
694	Football Today And Yesteryear	/62	Harlequin

Allardyce, Paula

Miss Philadelphia Smith
Eliza
Legacy Of Pride
Gentleman's Rogue
Paradise Row
Emily
The Carradine Affair
My Dear Miss Emma
The Rebel Lover
The Vixen's Revenge

AUTHOR/TITLE INDEX

Allardyce, Paula
    The Rogue's Lady
    Haunting Me   Period Romance
    Lonely Stranger   Regency

Allen, Barbara
  416 Doctor Lucy   /58 Harlequin
 1159 The Gay Gordons   /67 Harlequin
 1186 Someone Else's Heart   /68 Harlequin

Allen, Beverly
    Keeper Of The Dawn   Crown

Allen, Charlotte Vale
    Danger Zones   05/96 Fawcet
    Painted Lives   08/92 Ivy
    Dreaming In Color   04/95 Mira
    Somebody's Baby   07/95 Mira
    Running Away   07/96 Mira
    Claudia's Shadow   05/96 Mira
    Illusions   /94 Wings
    Dream Train   /94 Wings
    Night Magic   /94 Wings

Allen, Danice
    Arms Of A Stranger   01/95 Avon Historical
    Arms Of A Stranger   01/95 Avon Historical
    Beloved Rivals   01/93 Diamond
    Beauty And The Beastie 10/91 Harlequin Regency
    A Heavenly Housequest 02/92 Harlequin Regency

Allen, Elizabeth Evelyn
    Bright Destiny   Warner
    Freedom Fire   Warner
    Rebel   Warner
    To Fortune Born   Warner
    The Lady Anne   Warner
    Witch Woman   Warner

Allen, Jeanne
 2665 Peter's Sister   Harlequin Romance
 2845 When Love Flies By   Harlequin Romance
 3073 Bluebirds In The Spring Harlequin Romance

Allen, Laine
  276 Undercover Kisses   /85 Berkley Second Chance At Love
  445 Friendly Persuasion   Berkley Second Chance At Love

Allen, Mary Elizabeth
    All Hallow's Eve   10/92 Walker Regency

Allen, Ralph
  706 Peace River Country   /62 Harlequin

Allen, Robin
    Breeze   09/95 Genesis Press

AUTHOR/TITLE INDEX

Allen, Sheila Rosalynd

The Meddlesome Ghost	/89	Walker
The Reluctant Ghost	/89	Walker
The Passionate Ghost	/91	Walker
The Helpful Ghost	/91	Walker

Allen, T.D.

251	Doctor In Buckskin	/53	Harlequin

Allison, Carlyle

453	The Corner Cupboard	/59	Harlequin

Allison, Elizabeth

24	Dance Of Desire		Nal Rapture Romance

Allison, Heather

3091	Deck The Halls	/91	Harlequin Romance
3157	Pulse Points	11/91	Harlequin Romance
3218	Jack Of Hearts	09/92	Harlequin Romance
3269	Ivy's League	06/93	Harlequin Romance
3284	Haunted Spouse	10/93	Harlequin Romance
3309	Couterfeit Cowgirl	04/94	Harlequin Romance
3341	The Santa Sleuth (Kids & Kisses Christmas)	12/94	Harlequin Romance
3386	Undercover Lover	11/95	Harlequin Romance
3421	Temporary Texan	08/96	Harlequin Romance

Allison, Moeth

8	Love Everlasting	06/83	Silhouette Intimate Moments
43	Russian Roulette	03/84	Silhouette Intimate Moments
102	Every Other Weekend	07/85	Silhouette Intimate Moments
111	Soft Touch	09/85	Silhouette Intimate Moments

Allison, Penny

20	King Of Diamonds	10/82	Silhouette Desire
65	Reckless Venture	05/83	Silhouette Desire
143	North Country	06/84	Silhouette Desire
271	Night Train To Paradise	01/84	Silhouette Romance

Allistair, Barbara

An Amiable Arrangement	07/94	Nal Signet Regency

Allister, Barbara

A Love Match	08/91	Nal Regency
Frustrated Bridegroom	08/90	Nal Regency
The Captivated Countess	04/86	Nal Regency
A Temporary Husband	03/87	Nal Regency
The Prudent Partnership	01/89	Nal Regency
The Mischievous Matchmaker		Nal Regency
The Midnight Bride	/89	Nal Penguin Regency
The Impulsive Governess	01/93	Penguin Regency

Allyn, Ashley

Channing Hall

Allyne, Kerry

254	Summer In Paradise	10/95	Harlequin

AUTHOR/TITLE INDEX

Allyne, Kerry

2019	Summer Rainfall	/76	Harlequin
2094	Bound For Marandoo	/77	Harlequin
2184	Tuesday's Jillaroo	/78	Harlequin
2205	The Wool King	/78	Harlequin
361	Bindaburra Outstanding		Harlequin Presents
513	Coral Cay		Harlequin Presents
743	Legally Bound		Harlequin Presents
783	Tropical Eden		Harlequin Presents
2248	West Of The Waminda		Harlequin Romance
2283	The Plains Of Promise		Harlequin Romance
2323	Across The Great Divide		Harlequin Romance
2341	Sweet Harvest		Harlequin Romance
2389	The Challenge		Harlequin Romance
2407	Reunion At Pitereeka		Harlequin Romance
2479	Mixed Feelings		Harlequin Romance
2515	Valley Of Lagoons		Harlequin Romance
2527	Spring Fever		Harlequin Romance
2593	Somewhere Call Home		Harlequin Romance
2647	Time To Forget		Harlequin Romance
2725	Mierringanne Bluff		Harlequin Romance
2737	Return To Wallaby Creek		Harlequin Romance
2761	Stranger In Town	05/86	Harlequin Romance
2809	Tullagindi Rodeo		Harlequin Romance
2869	Carpentaria Moon		Harlequin Romance
2929	Losing Battle		Harlequin Romance
2947	Beneath Wimmera Skies		Harlequin Romance
2990	Man Of The High Plains		Harlequin Romance
3037	Dark Memories		Harlequin Romance
3145	Disastrous Encounter	09/91	Harlequin Romance
3235	Cause For Love	12/92	Harlequin Romance

Alsobrook, Rosalyn

63	A Tiny Flaw	07/84	Harlequin American
103	All Or Nothing	05/85	Harlequin American
412	Questing Heart	10/91	Harlequin American
	Time Storm	07/93	Pinnacle Time Travel
	Seascape: The Perfect Stranger	07/96	St. Martin's
	Thorn Bush Blooms	12/91	Tower Books Historical
	Brazen Heart	06/91	Zebra
	Desire's Gamble	11/89	Zebra
	Elusive Caress	04/89	Zebra
	Emerald Storm	08/86	Zebra
	Mail-Order Mistress	12/91	Zebra
	Wanton Bride	05/89	Zebra
	Wild Western Bride	10/90	Zebra
	Ecstasy's Fire	07/88	Zebra
	Runaway Bride	12/87	Zebra

Andersen, Susan

	Present Danger	/93	Zebra	Contemporary
	Exposure	04/96	Zebra	Romantic Suspense
	On Thin Ice	08/95	Zebra	Suspense

Anderson, Blaine

	Destiny's Kiss		Warner	
	Heartspell		Warner	
	Love's Sweet Captive		Warner	

Anderson, Caroline

281	Taken For Granted	05/96	Harlequin	
242	A Gentle Giant	07/95	Harlequin	Direct
	Coming Up Roses	08/93	Harper	
	Indigo Blue	09/92	Harper	

Anderson, Catherine

	Three Weddings & A Kiss	/95	Anthology	
	Keegan's Lady	07/96	Avon	
92	Reasonable Doubt		Harlequin	Intrigue
114	Without A Trace		Harlequin	Intrigue
135	Switchback	04/90	Harlequin	Intrigue
206	Cry Of The Wild	02/93	Harlequin	Intrigue
	Cheyenne Amber	03/94	Harper	
	Tall, Dark & Dangerous	08/95	Harper	Anthology
1	Comanche Heart	12/91	Harper	Comanche Trilogy
2	Comanche Moon	07/93	Harper	Comanche Trilogy
3	Indigo Blue	10/92	Harper	Comanche Trilogy
	Coming Up Roses	/94	Harper	Monogram
	Comanche Magic	10/94	Harper	Monogram

Anderson, Gail

272	Orchid Moon		Harlequin	Superromance

Anderson, Lee

	The Reluctant Heir	/91	Avalon	
	Dangerous Bequest	10/92	Avalon	

Anderson, Oliver

243	School For Love	/53	Harlequin	

Anderson, Susan

	Stolen Dreams		Diamond	
	Shadow Dance		Warner	
	Obsessed	10/94	Zebra	

Andrew, Sylvia

	Dalliance & Deception - "Serena"	10/95	Harlequin	Anthology
	Reluctant Bridegrooms	05/95	Harlequin	Promotion
95	Perdita	04/93	Harlequin	Regency

Andrews, Barbara

176	Passionate Deceiver	/83	Dell	Candlelight Ecstasy
405	Seduced By A Stranger	/86	Dell	Ecstasy Romance

Andrews, Beth

AUTHOR/TITLE INDEX

Andrews, Beth
    The Marplot Marriage   Lion Hearted Historical
Andrews, Carolyn
  498   C.J.'s Defense   07/94   Harlequin Temptation
  528   Service With A Smile   02/95   Harlequin Temptation
  581   The Marriage Curse   04/96   Harlequin Temptation
Andrews, Felecia
    The Velvet Heart   Berkley
    Moonwitch   Berkley
    Mountainwitch   Berkley
    Riverrun   Berkley
    Silver Huntress   Berkley
    Seacliff   Berkley
Andrews, Jo
  514   Gale Force   08/89   Silhouette Desire
Andrews, Kristi
    Love Lights   /88   Bantam Young Adult
Andrews, Nicola
  180   Reckless Desire   /84   Berkley Second Chance At Love
  200   Head Over Heels   /84   Berkley Second Chance At Love
Andrews, Roy Chapman
  291   Heart Of Asia   /54   Harlequin
Andrews, Susan
  206   Fair Game   Harlequin American
Angel, Defiant
    Stephanie Stevens
Anglin, Joyce
  373   Feeling The Flame   01/90   Bantam Loveswept
  544   Old Devil Moon   05/92   Bantam Loveswept
Ankrum, Barbara
    Renegade Bride   07/92   Zebra Heartfire
    Chase The Fire   Zebra Heartfire
    Passion's Prize   Zebra Heartfire
Anston, Linell
  26   Lady Elizabeth   05/90   Harlequin Regency
Anthony, Diana
    Once A Lover
Anthony, Evelyn
    Silver Falcon   Suspense
    The Scarlett Thread   09/91   Harper
    House Of Vandekar   Harper
Anthony, Laura
  1092   Raleigh And The Rancher   07/95   Silhouette Romance
  1119   Second Chance Family   11/95   Silhouette Romance
  1166   Undercover Honeymoon   07/96   Silhouette Romance

AUTHOR/TITLE INDEX

Anzelon, Robyn

49	The Forever Spell		Harlequin Superromance
120	Sandcastle Dreams		Harlequin Superromance
198	Searching		Harlequin Superromance

Arbor, Jane

3	House Of Discord		Harlequin
8	Flash Of Emeralds (Premiere)		Harlequin
423	City Nurse (Nurse Greve)	/58	Harlequin
454	Such Frail Armor	/59	Harlequin
474	Towards The Dawn	/59	Harlequin
482	Nurse Harlowe	/59	Harlequin
489	Consulting Surgeon	/59	Harlequin
498	The Eternal Circle (Nurse Atholl Returns)	/59	Harlequin
513	Far Sanctuary	/60	Harlequin
524	Queen's Nurse	/60	Harlequin
576	Sandflower	/61	Harlequin
646	Nurse In Waiting	/62	Harlequin
690	Nurse Of All Work	/62	Harlequin
701	Strange Loyalties (Doctor's Love)	/62	Harlequin
780	Jasmine Harvest	/63	Harlequin
801	Desert Nurse	/64	Harlequin
832	No Silver Spoon	/64	Harlequin
858	No Lease For Love	/64	Harlequin
887	Lake Of Shadows	/65	Harlequin
919	Dear Intruder	/65	Harlequin
950	Kingfisher Tide	/65	Harlequin
1000	A Girl Named Smith	/66	Harlequin
1048	High Master Of Clere	/66	Harlequin
1108	Summer Every Day	/67	Harlequin
1157	Yesterday's Magic	/67	Harlequin
1182	Golden Apple Island	/68	Harlequin
1277	Stranger's Trespass	/69	Harlequin
1336	The Cypress Garden	/69	Harlequin
1406	Walk Into The Wind	/70	Harlequin
1443	The Feathered Shaft	/70	Harlequin
1480	The Linden Leaf	/71	Harlequin
1544	The Other Miss Donne	/71	Harlequin
1582	Wildfire Quest	/72	Harlequin
1665	The Flower On The Rock	/73	Harlequin
1740	Roman Summer	/73	Harlequin
1789	The Velvet Spur	/74	Harlequin
1832	Meet The Sun Halfway	/74	Harlequin
1896	The Wide Fields Of Home	/75	Harlequin
1963	Smoke Into Flame	/76	Harlequin
2033	Tree Of Paradise	/77	Harlequin
2066	Two Pins In A Fountain	/77	Harlequin
2108	A Growing Moon	/77	Harlequin

AUTHOR/TITLE INDEX

Arbor, Jane

2231	Return To Silbersee		Harlequin Romance
2251	Late Rapture		Harlequin Romance
2299	Pact Without Desire		Harlequin Romance
2342	Devil Drives		Harlequin Romance
2396	Where The Wolf Leads		Harlequin Romance
2419	One Brief Sweet Hour		Harlequin Romance
2467	Invisible Wife		Harlequin Romance
2509	The Price Of Paradise		Harlequin Romance
2545	Handmaid To Midas		Harlequin Romance
	By Yet Another Door		Mills & Boon

Archer, Catherine

136	Rose Among Thorns	08/92	Harlequin Historical
282	Velvet Bond	08/95	Harlequin Historical
322	Velvet Touch	06/96	Harlequin Historical

Archer, Ellen

	Under His Spell	09/95	Zebra Anthology

Archer, Jane

	Satin And Silver		Nal Penguin
1	Tender Torment	/78	Pinnacle
2	Wild Wind!	02/93	Pinnacle
	Bayou Passion		Zebra
	Captive Desire	/90	Zebra Heartfire
	Captive Dreams		Zebra Heartfire
	Hidden Passions		Zebra Heartfire
	Rebel Seduction		Zebra Heartfire

Archery, Helen

	The Age Of Elegance		Fawcett
	The Season Of Loving	12/92	Harper Monogram
	Lady Adventuress	01/94	Harper Regency
	Duel Of Hearts	10/94	Harper Regency

Arden, Jenny

1063	To The Victor, The Spoils		Harlequin Presents
1215	Friend Of Foe		Harlequin Presents
1311	This Time, Forever		Harlequin Presents
1399	Running Scared	10/91	Harlequin Presents
2995	Some Enchanted Evening		Harlequin Romance
3055	Intense Involvement		Harlequin Romance
3115	Arrogant Invader		Harlequin Romance

Argers, Helen

	An Unlikely Lady	11/92	Diamond Regency
	A Captain's Lady	11/91	Diamond Regency
	A Scandalous Lady		Diamond Regency
	Noblesse Oblige	11/94	St. Martin's Historical

Argo, Ellen

	Yankee Girl

AUTHOR/TITLE INDEX

Arguile, Cheryl
182   Independent Angel   11/93 Meteor

Arkham, Candice
     Wayward Angel
536   Embers Of The Heart   Dell Candlelight

Armstrong, John D.
     The Return Of Jericho Pike   /92 Avalon

Armstrong, Juliet

681	I'll Never Marry!	/62	Harlequin
689	Nurse In India	/62	Harlequin
892	The House Of The Swallows	/65	Harlequin
938	The Doctor Is Indifferent	/65	Harlequin
1066	Nurse At Ste. Monique	/66	Harlequin
1136	The Pride You Trampled	/67	Harlequin
1220	Isle Of The Hummingbird	/68	Harlequin
1322	Wind Through The Vineyards	/69	Harlequin
1493	Orange Blossom Island	/71	Harlequin
1585	The Flowering Valley	/72	Harlequin
1694	The Tideless Sea	/73	Harlequin

Armstrong, Lindsay

559	Melt A Frozen Heart		Harlequin Presents
607	Enter My Jungle		Harlequin Presents
806	Saved From Sin		Harlequin Presents
871	Finding Out		Harlequin Presents
887	Love Me Not		Harlequin Presents
927	An Elusive Mistress		Harlequin Presents
951	Surrender My Heart		Harlequin Presents
983	Standing On The Outside		Harlequin Presents
1039	The Shadow Of Moonlight		Harlequin Presents
1071	Reluctant Wife		Harlequin Presents
1095	When You Leave Me		Harlequin Presents
1183	Heat Of The Moment		Harlequin Presents
1295	One More Night		Harlequin Presents
1327	A Love Affair		Harlequin Presents
1439	The Director's Wife	03/92	Harlequin Presents
1487	Leave Love Alone	09/92	Harlequin Presents
1546	A Dangerous Lover	04/93	Harlequin Presents
1569	Dark Captor	07/93	Harlequin Presents
1593	An Unusual Affair	10/93	Harlequin Presents
1626	The Seduction Stakes	02/94	Harlequin Presents
1693	A Difficult Man	10/94	Harlequin Presents
1713	An Unsuitable Wife	01/95	Harlequin Presents
1770	A Masterful Man	10/95	Harlequin Presents
1798	Trial By Marriage	03/96	Harlequin Presents
1656	Unwilling Mistress	06/94	Harlequin Presents Plus
2443	Spitfire		Harlequin Romance

AUTHOR/TITLE INDEX

Armstrong, Lindsay

2497	My Dear Innocent		Harlequin	Romance
2582	Perhaps Love		Harlequin	Romance
2653	Don't Call It Love		Harlequin	Romance
2785	Some Say Love		Harlequin	Romance
2876	The Heart To The Matter	12/87	Harlequin	Romance
2893	When The Night Grows		Harlequin	Romance
3013	The Marrying Game		Harlequin	Romance

Armstrong, Patricia

665	Kate	10/95	Harlequin	Superromance

Arness, Christine

	Rosemary For Remembrance	08/91	Harper

Arnett, Caroline

Theodora		Regency
Claudia		Regency
Stephanie		Regency
Clarissa		Ballantine Regency
Melinda		Ballantine Regency
Christina		Ballantine Regency

Arnold, Elliot

175	The Commandos	/52	Harlequin

Arnold, Judith

104	Come Home To Love		Harlequin	American
120	A Modern Man		Harlequin	American
130	Flowing To The Sky		Harlequin	American
139	Jackpot		Harlequin	American
149	Special Delivery		Harlequin	American
163	Man And Wife	08/86	Harlequin	American
189	Best Friends	03/87	Harlequin	American
201	Keeping The Faith: Promises		Harlequin	American
205	Keeping The Faith: Commitments		Harlequin	American
209	Keeping The Faith: Dreams		Harlequin	American
225	Comfort And Joy	12/87	Harlequin	American
240	Twilight		Harlequin	American
255	Going Back		Harlequin	American
259	Harvest The Sun		Harlequin	American
281	One Whiff Of Scandal		Harlequin	American
304	Independence Day		Harlequin	American
330	Survivors		Harlequin	American
342	Lucky Penny		Harlequin	American
362	Change Of Life		Harlequin	American
378	One Good Turn		Harlequin	American
389	A Loverboy		Harlequin	American
405	Safe Harbor	09/91	Harlequin	American
431	Trust Me	03/92	Harlequin	American
449	Opposing Camps	08/92	Harlequin	American

AUTHOR/TITLE INDEX

Arnold, Judith

467	Sweet Light	12/92	Harlequin	American
482	Just Like Romeo And Juliet	04/93	Harlequin	American
496	Oh, You Beautiful Doll	07/93	Harlequin	American
524	Private Lies	02/94	Harlequin	American
553	The Marrying Type	10/94	Harlequin	American
460	Raising The Stakes	07/91	Harlequin	Superromance
509	The Woman Downstairs	07/92	Harlequin	Superromance
559	Flashfire	08/93	Harlequin	Superromance
581	The Parent Plan	01/94	Harlequin	Superromance
611	Alessandra & The Archangel	09/94	Harlequin	Superromance
634	Cry Uncle (Family Man)	03/95	Harlequin	Superromance
684	Married To The Man	03/96	Harlequin	Superromance
122	On Love's Trail	09/86	Harlequin	Temptation
561	The Lady In The Mirror	11/95	Harlequin	Temptation
565	Timeless Love	12/95	Harlequin	Temptation

Arnston, Harrison

	Act Of Passion	Harper

Arthur, Katherine

	Listen To Your Heart		My Valentine 1991	
2755	Cinderella Wife		Harlequin	Romance
2821	Road To Love		Harlequin	Romance
2905	Forecast Of Love		Harlequin	Romance
2948	Send Me No Flowers		Harlequin	Romance
2971	Remember In Jamaica		Harlequin	Romance
2991	Through Eyes Of Love		Harlequin	Romance
3014	Loving Deceiver		Harlequin	Romance
3043	Mountain Lovesong		Harlequin	Romance
3061	One More Secret		Harlequin	Romance
3103	To Tame A Cowboy		Harlequin	Romance
3146	Never Doubt My Love	09/91	Harlequin	Romance
3181	Keep My Heart Forever	03/92	Harlequin	Romance
3229	Signs Of Love	11/92	Harlequin	Romance
3282	Reluctant Lover	09/93	Harlequin	Romance

Ash, Pauline

833	Seaside Hospital	/64	Harlequin
916	Doctor Vannard's Patients	/65	Harlequin
970	A Challenge To Nurse Honor	/65	Harlequin
1033	With Love From Dr. Lucien	/66	Harlequin
1065	Student Nurse At Swale	/66	Harlequin
1113	Bequest For Nurse Barbara	/67	Harlequin
1161	Doctor Napier's Nurse	/67	Harlequin
1249	Doctor Arnold's Ambition	/68	Harlequin
1289	The Much-Loved Nurse	/69	Harlequin

Ash, Rosalie

55	Melting Ice		Harlequin Direct

AUTHOR/TITLE INDEX

Ash, Rosalie

87	Unsafe Harbor		Harlequin Direct
94	Private Property	09/91	Harlequin Direct
111	The Gypsy's Bride	06/92	Harlequin Direct
119	Love By Design	10/92	Harlequin Direct
129	Law Of The Circle	03/93	Harlequin Direct
157	The Witch's Wedding	10/93	Harlequin Direct
174	Hostile Inheritance	02/94	Harlequin Direct
16	Calypso's Island	09/95	Harlequin Presents
24	Vengeful Bride	01/96	Harlequin Presents
1723	Original Sin (Secrets...)	02/95	Harlequin Presents
	Ghost Bride	10/95	Worldwide Libr. Stolen Moments

Ash, Sally

| | Hedge Of Thorns | 04/94 | Goodfellow |

Ashby, Juliet

162	One Man Forever	07/82	Silhouette Romance
258	Midnight Lover	11/83	Silhouette Romance
279	Dream Of Passion	02/84	Silhouette Romance

Ashcroft, Laura

| | Heart Of Fire | | Zebra Historical & Family Sagas |

Ashe, Megan

| 46 | A Mountain Man | | Nal Rapture Romance |

Ashe, Rebecca

| | Masque Of The Swan | 01/96 | Pinnacle Denise Little Presents |

Ashfield, Helen

	Crystal		Regency
	Sapphire		St. Martin's
	Pearl		St. Martin's
	Garnet		St. Martin's
	Ruby		St. Martin's
	Opal		St. Martin's
	Topaz		St. Martin's
	Regency Rogue		St. Martin's
	Beau Baron's Lady		St. Martin's
	Emerald		St. Martin's
	The Michaelmas Tree		St. Martin's
	The Loving Highwayman		St. Martin's
	The Marquis And Miss Jones		St. Martin's
	Midsummer Morning		St. Martin's

Ashford, Jane

	The Reluctant Rake	05/87	Nal Regency
	Meddlesome Miranda	01/89	Nal Regency
	The Repentent Rebel		Nal Penguin Regency
	A Radical Arrangement		Nal Penguin Regency
	The Marchington Scandal		Nal Penguin Regency
	The Three Graces		Nal Penguin Regency

AUTHOR/TITLE INDEX

Ashford, Jane

	The Irresolute Rivals		Nal Penguin Regency
	First Season		Nal Penguin Regency
	The Headstrong Ward		Nal Penguin Regency
	Gwendeline		Warner
	Man Of Honour		Warner
	Bluestocking		Warner
	The Impetuous Heiress		Warner
32	Rivals Of Fortune		Warner Regency

Ashley, Amanda

	Embrace The Night	08/95	Leisure Fantasy

Ashley, Faye

167	Besieged	08/87	Harlequin Temptation

Ashley, Jacqueline

20	Love's Revenge		Harlequin American
40	Hunting Season		Harlequin American
78	Other Half Of Love		Harlequin American
136	In The Name Of Love		Harlequin American
157	Spring's Awakening	05/86	Harlequin American
182	Long Journey Home		Harlequin American
208	A Question Of Honor		Harlequin American
299	The Gift	06/89	Harlequin American
316	Love Thy Neighbor	10/89	Harlequin American
4	Secrets Of The Heart		Harlequin Intrigue

Ashley, Mellyora

	A Lady In Disguise		Zebra Regency

Ashley, Rebecca

	The Right Suitor		Ballantine Regency
	Lady Fair		Ballantine Regency
	Feuds And Fantasies		Ballantine Regency
	A Lady's Lament		Ballantine Regency
	A Suitable Arrangement		Ballantine Regency
	A Miss With A Purpose	04/93	Ballantine Regency
695	The Arrogant Aristocrat		Candlelight Regency
707	Intrepid Encounter		Candlelight Regency
621	An Intriguing Innocent		Dell Candlelight Regency
638	A Season Of Surprises		Dell Candlelight Regency
677	The Willful Widow		Dell Candlelight Regency
	Ruins And Romance	11/91	Fawcett Crest Regency
	An Awkward Arrangement	10/92	Fawcett Crest Regency

Ashley, Suzanne

556	Bittersweet Betrayal	10/89	Silhouette Special Edition

Ashley, Veronica

	Sea Siren		Zebra Pinnacle/Historical

Ashmore, April

	Autumn's Tender Fire		Zebra Heartfire

AUTHOR/TITLE INDEX

Ashmore, April

    Tender Texas Touch   Zebra Heartfire

Ashton, Elizabeth

13	The Gilded Butterfly (Premiere)		Harlequin
1373	The Pied Tulip	/70	Harlequin
1421	Parisian Adventure	/70	Harlequin
1453	The Benevolent Despot	/70	Harlequin
1534	Cousin Mark	/71	Harlequin
1636	Flutter Of White Wings	/72	Harlequin
1659	A Parade Of Peacocks	/73	Harlequin
1713	Alpine Rhapsody	/73	Harlequin
1741	Moorland Magic	/73	Harlequin
1762	Sigh No More	/74	Harlequin
1788	Errant Bride	/74	Harlequin
1810	The Rocks Of Arachenza	/74	Harlequin
1835	Dark Angel	/74	Harlequin
1853	The Road To The Border	/75	Harlequin
1869	The House Of The Eagles	/75	Harlequin
1891	Scorched Wings	/75	Harlequin
1918	The Player King	/75	Harlequin
1933	Miss Nobody From Nowhere	/75	Harlequin
1946	Crown Of Willow	/76	Harlequin
1972	Lady In The Limelight	/76	Harlequin
1989	My Lady Disdain	/76	Harlequin
2044	Mountain Heritage	/77	Harlequin
2076	Aegean Quest	/77	Harlequin
2093	Voyage Of Enchantment	/77	Harlequin
2116	Green Harvest	/77	Harlequin
2172	Breeze From The Bosphorus	/78	Harlequin
2179	The Questing Heart	/78	Harlequin
2192	The Golden Girl	/78	Harlequin
2200	Rendezvous In Venice	/78	Harlequin
179	Sanctuary In The Desert	/77	Harlequin Presents
2247	The Willing Hostage		Harlequin Romance
2256	Garden Of The Gods		Harlequin Romance
2300	Moonlight On The Nile		Harlequin Romance
2311	Joyous Adventure		Harlequin Romance
2312	Return To Devil's View		Harlequin Romance
2324	Reluctant Partnership		Harlequin Romance
2347	Rekindled Flame		Harlequin Romance
2395	Borrowed Plumes		Harlequin Romance
2401	Sicilian Summer		Harlequin Romance
2425	Silver Arrow		Harlequin Romance
2444	Rebel Against Love		Harlequin Romance
2503	White Witch		Harlequin Romance
2863	Bride Upon Approval		Harlequin Romance

Ashton, Laura

AUTHOR/TITLE INDEX

AUTHOR/TITLE INDEX

August, Elizabeth

	Jingle Bells, Wedding Bells	11/94	Silhouette Anthology
554	Author's Choice	01/88	Silhouette Romance
590	Truck Driving Woman	07/88	Silhouette Romance
626	Wild Horse Canyon	01/89	Silhouette Romance
668	Something So Right	08/89	Silhouette Romance
719	The Nesting Instinct	05/90	Silhouette Romance
749	Joey's Father	10/90	Silhouette Romance
771	Ready-Made Family	01/91	Silhouette Romance
790	The Man From Natchez	05/91	Silhouette Romance
809	A Small Favor	08/91	Silhouette Romance
833	The Cowboy And The Chauffeur	12/91	Silhouette Romance
857	Like Father, Like Son	04/92	Silhouette Romance
881	The Wife He Wanted	08/92	Silhouette Romance
921	The Virgin Wife	02/93	Silhouette Romance
922	Haunted Husband	03/93	Silhouette Romance
945	Lucky Penny	06/93	Silhouette Romance
953	A Wedding For Emily	08/93	Silhouette Romance
989	The Seeker	02/94	Silhouette Romance
1019	The Forgotten Husband	07/94	Silhouette Romance
1054	Ideal Dad (Fabulous Fathers)	01/95	Silhouette Romance
1067	A Husband For Sarah (Where The Heart Is)	03/95	Silhouette Romance
1091	The Bridal Shower (Always A Bridesmaid)	07/95	Silhouette Romance
1126	A Father's Vow	01/96	Silhouette Romance
1157	A Handy Man To Have Around	06/96	Silhouette Romance
871	One Last Fling! (That Special Woman!)	03/94	Silhouette Special Edition

Austell, Diane

	Lights Along The Shore	02/92	Bantam Fanfare

Austen, Charlotte

	Love Everlasting		Warner

Austin, Cassandra

190	Wait For The Sunrise	09/93	Harlequin Historical
279	Trusting Sarah	08/95	Harlequin Historical

Austin, Neffetiti

	Eternity	08/95	Pinnacle Arabesque

Autin, Amelia

666	Gideon's Bride	09/95	Silhouette Intimate Moments

Avery, Anne

	Enchanted Crossings	09/94	Leisure Anthology
	A Distant Star	09/93	Love Spell
	All's Fair	03/94	Love Spell
	Far Star	/95	Love Spell
	Hidden Heart	07/96	Love Spell

Avery, Joan

	Angel Of Passage	05/93	Harper

Awbray, Elizabeth

AUTHOR/TITLE INDEX

Awbray, Elizabeth
    Reckless Angel
Aylworth, Susan
    Ride The Rainbow Home   11/95   Avalon
Ayre, Jessica
  2504   Not To Be Trusted   Harlequin Romance
  2599   Hard To Handle   Harlequin Romance
  2641   New Discovery   Harlequin Romance
Ayres, Janet
    26   Odyssey Of Love   Harlequin Superromance
Bacher, June Masters
    No Time For Tears   /93   Harvest House Heartland Heritage Series
    Songs In The Whirlwind   /93   Harvest House Heartland Heritage Series
    Where Lies Our Hope   /93   Harvest House Heartland Heritage Series
    Return To The Heartland   /93   Harvest House Heartland Heritage Series
    1   Journey To Love   /93   Harvest House Journey To Love Series
    2   Dreams Beyond Tomorrow   /93   Harvest House Journey To Love Series
    3   Seasons Of Love   /93   Harvest House Journey To Love Series
    4   My Heart's Desire   /93   Harvest House Journey To Love Series
    5   The Heart Remembers   /93   Harvest House Journey To Love Series
    6   From This Time Forth   /93   Harvest House Journey To Love Series
    1   Love's Soft Whisper   /93   Harvest House Love's Soft Whisper Series
    2   Love's Beautiful Dream   /93   Harvest House Love's Soft Whisper Series
    3   When Hearts Awaken   /93   Harvest House Love's Soft Whisper Series
    4   Another Spring   /93   Harvest House Love's Soft Whisper Series
    5   When Morning Comes Again   /93   Harvest House Love's Soft Whisper Series
    6   Gently Love Beckons   /93   Harvest House Love's Soft Whisper Series
    1   Love Is A Gentle Stranger   /93   Harvest House Love/Gentle Stranger Series
    2   Love's Silent Song   /93   Harvest House Love/Gentle Stranger Series
    3   Diary Of A Loving Heart   /93   Harvest House Love/Gentle Stranger Series
    4   Love Leads Home   /93   Harvest House Love/Gentle Stranger Series
    5   Love Follows The Heart   /93   Harvest House Love/Gentle Stranger Series
    6   Love's Enduring Hope   /93   Harvest House Love/Gentle Stranger Series
Badger, Rosemary
   289   The Hero Trap   07/96   Harlequin
   165   Dancing With Shadows   12/93   Harlequin Direct
   228   Sweet Desire   04/95   Harlequin Direct
  2617   Corporate Lady   Harlequin Romance
  2629   A Girl Called Andy   Harlequin Romance
  2695   A Time Of Deception   Harlequin Romance
  2749   A Matter Of Marnie   Harlequin Romance
  2773   Shadows Of Eden   Harlequin Romance
  2827   Time To Trust   Harlequin Romance
  2864   The Good Time Guy   Harlequin Romance
Bagnet, Joan
    The Sturbridge Dynasty   Warner

Bagwell, Stella

9	Cactus Rose	04/96	Harlequin	Here Come The Grooms
39	Madeline's Song	09/96	Harlequin	Here Come The Grooms
469	Golden Glory	11/86	Silhouette	Romance
485	Moonlight Bandit	02/87	Silhouette	Romance
510	A Mist On The Mountain	06/87	Silhouette	Romance
543	Madeline's Song	11/87	Silhouette	Romance
560	The Outsider	02/88	Silhouette	Romance
587	The New Kid In Town	07/88	Silhouette	Romance
621	Cactus Rose	12/88	Silhouette	Romance
634	Hillbilly Heart	03/89	Silhouette	Romance
657	Teach Me	06/89	Silhouette	Romance
674	The White Night	09/89	Silhouette	Romance
699	No Horsing Around	01/90	Silhouette	Romance
723	That Southern Touch	05/90	Silhouette	Romance
748	Gentle As A Lamb	10/90	Silhouette	Romance
789	A Practical Man	04/91	Silhouette	Romance
812	Precious Pretender	08/91	Silhouette	Romance
836	Done To Perfection	12/91	Silhouette	Romance
878	Rodeo Rider	07/92	Silhouette	Romance
903	Their First Thanksgiving	11/92	Silhouette	Romance
909	The Best Christmas Ever	12/92	Silhouette	Romance
915	New Year's Baby	01/93	Silhouette	Romance
954	Hero In Disguise	08/93	Silhouette	Romance
991	Corporate Cowgirl	02/94	Silhouette	Romance
1020	Daniel's Daddy	07/94	Silhouette	Romance
1052	A Cowboy For Christmas	12/94	Silhouette	Romance
1085	Daddy Lessons	06/95	Silhouette	Romance
1140	Wanted: Wife	03/96	Silhouette	Romance
1049	Found: One Runaway Bride	08/96	Silhouette	Special Edition

Bailey, Debbie

	Tender Outlaw	09/94	Berkley Wildflower

Bailey, Elizabeth

94	Sweet Sacrifice	03/93	Harlequin Regency

Bailey-Pratt, Cynthia

	Gentlemen's Folly	12/91	Jove Regency
	The Temporary Bride	09/91	Jove Regency
	Queen Of Hearts	08/92	Jove Regency
	A Lady In Love	02/93	Jove Regency
	A Lady In Disguise	07/93	Jove Regency
	Summertime Splendor	07/92	Jove Regency Collection

Baird, Jacqueline

1079	Dark Desiring		Harlequin Presents
1359	Shattered Trust		Harlequin Presents
1431	Passionate Betrayal	02/92	Harlequin Presents
1558	Dishonorable Proposal	06/93	Harlequin Presents

Baird, Jacqueline

1627	Guilty Passion	02/94	Harlequin Presents
1683	Master Of Passion	09/94	Harlequin Presents
1726	Gamble On Passion	03/95	Harlequin Presents
1757	Nothing Changes Love (Wedlocked!)	08/95	Harlequin Presents
1795	The Valentine Child	02/96	Harlequin Presents
1827	A Devious Desire	08/96	Harlequin Presents

Baker, Fran

161	Seeing Stars	10/86	Bantam Loveswept
246	The Widow And The Wildcatter	04/88	Bantam Loveswept
363	King Of The Mountain	11/89	Bantam Loveswept
474	San Antonio Rose	06/91	Bantam Loveswept

Baker, Judith

5	When Last We Loved	06/82	Silhouette Desire
21	Love In The China Sea	10/82	Silhouette Desire

Baker, Madeline

Enchanted Crossings	09/94	Leisure Anthology
A Wilderness Christmas	11/93	Leisure Anthology
Love's Legacy: "To Love Again"	01/96	Leisure Anthology
Beneath A Midnight Moon	09/94	Leisure Fantasy
Midnight Fire	09/92	Leisure Historical
Forbidden Fires	10/92	Leisure Historical
A Frontier Christmas	11/92	Leisure Historical
First Love, Wild Love		Leisure Historical
Lacey's Way		Leisure Historical
Love Forevermore	07/91	Leisure Historical
Love In The Wind	09/91	Leisure Historical
Prairie Heat		Leisure Historical
Reckless Desire		Leisure Historical
Reckless Heart		Leisure Historical
Reckless Love	11/95	Leisure Historical
Comanche Flame	03/92	Leisure Historical
The Spirit Path	03/93	Leisure Historical
A Whisper On The Wind	05/93	Leisure Historical
Warrior's Lady	09/93	Leisure Historical
Cheyenne Surrender	02/94	Leisure Historical
Apache Runaway	03/95	Leisure Historical
Lakota Renegade	08/95	Leisure Historical
The Angel And The Outlaw	03/96	Leisure Historical
Secrets Of The Heart	/94	Topaz Anthology

Baker, Maggie

339	A Man For The Night	03/91	Harlequin Temptation

Bakker, Kit

14	Sea Treasure		Harlequin Intrigue
387	Julianne's Song		Harlequin Superromance

Baldwin, Anne

Baldwin, Anne
   First Season   07/92 Zebra Regency
Baldwin, Rebecca
   A Gentleman From Philadelphia   Regency
   The Cassandra Knot   Regency
   Lady Scandal   Regency
   A Sandition Quadrille   Ballantine Regency
   A Season Abroad   Ballantine Regency
   A Matter Of Honor   Ballantine Regency
 201 The Dollar Duchess   Coventry
  14 The Matchmakers   Coventry Regency
  30 Peerless Theodosia   Coventry Regency
 173 A Very Simple Scheme   Coventry Regency
   A Lady Of Fashion   06/94 Harper
   Dartwood's Daughter   St. Martin's
   Annabella And The Beast   St. Martin's
Bale, Karen A.
   Bold Montana Bride   Zebra
   Desperado Dream   Zebra
   Apache's Angel   09/92 Zebra Lovegram Romance
  1 Sun Dancer's Passion   Zebra Sweet Medicine's Prophecy
  2 Little Flower's Desire   Zebra Sweet Medicine's Prophecy
  3 Winter's Lovesong   Zebra Sweet Medicine's Prophecy
  4 Savage Fury   Zebra Sweet Medicine's Prophecy
  5 Sun Dancer's Legacy   Zebra Sweet Medicine's Prophecy
  6 Cheyenne Surrender   Zebra Sweet Medicine's Prophecy
  7 Winter Wolf's Woman   Zebra Sweet Medicine's Prophecy
Balkey, Rita
   Passion's Disguise   Zebra
   Midnight Ecstasy   Zebra Heartfire
   Passion's Fury   Zebra Heartfire
   Glorious Conquest   Zebra Historical & Family Sagas
   Silk And Steel   Zebra Historical & Family Sagas
Balnshard, Audrey
   Affair Of Dishonor   Regency
Balogh, Mary
   Tempting Harriet   07/94
   Gentle Conquest   Regency
   Heartless   10/95 Berkley Historical
   Truly   05/96 Berkley Historical
   Timeswept Brides   07/96 Jove Anthology
   Love's Legacy   11/95 Leisure Anthology
   Regency Christmas   11/93 Nal
   A Certain Magic   Nal
   The Devil's Web   Nal
   The Double Wager   Nal

Balogh, Mary

The Gilded Web		Nal
The Incurable Matchmaker		Nal
A Masked Deception		Nal
The Red Rose		Nal
A Regency Christmas 2		Nal
Secrets Of The Heart		Nal
An Unacceptable Offer		Nal
An Unlikely Duchess		Nal
Web Of Love		Nal
Regency Valentine		Nal
Courting Julia	11/93	Nal
Beyond The Sunrise	11/92	Nal Onyx
The Ideal Wife	10/91	Nal Regency
Christmas Beau	12/91	Nal Regency
A Counterfeit Betrothal	06/92	Nal Regency
The Notorious Rake	08/92	Nal Regency
A Christmas Promise	12/92	Nal Regency
The Trysting Place	06/86	Nal Regency
The First Snowdrop	09/86	Nal Regency
The Wood Nymph	01/87	Nal Regency
The Constant Heart	07/87	Nal Regency
Lady Of Property	04/88	Nal Regency
The Ungrateful Governess	10/88	Nal Regency
A Gift Of Daisies	02/89	Nal Regency
The Obedient Bride	05/89	Nal Regency
A Chance Encounter	05/89	Nal Regency
Lady With A Black Umbrella	09/89	Nal Regency
A Promise Of Spring	02/90	Nal Regency
Christmas Belle	11/94	Nal Regency
The Secret Pearl	09/91	Nal Super Regency
A Regency Valentine 2	01/92	Nal Super Regency
A Regency Summer	06/92	Nal Super Regency
A Regency Christmas 4	11/92	Nal Super Regency
Tokens Of Love	12/92	Nal Super Regency
Full-Moon Magic	09/92	Nal Super Signet Historical
Snow Angel	06/91	Nal Penguin
The Secret Pearl		Nal Penguin Regency
Christmas Bean		Nal Penguin Regency
The Rogue & The Runaway		Nal Penguin Regency
The Would-Be Widow		Nal Penguin Regency
A Promise Of Spring		Nal Penguin Regency
Daring Masquerade		Nal Penguin Regency
Dancing With Clara	01/94	Nal Signet
From The Heart	01/94	Nal Signet Anthology
Dark Angel	08/94	Nal Signet Regency
Blossoms	03/95	Onyx Anthology

AUTHOR/TITLE INDEX

Barbieri, Elaine

Dangerous Virtues - Honesty	09/96	Leisure
Love's Legacy - "Loving Charity"	01/96	Leisure Anthology
Tattered Silk	09/91	Zebra
Untamed Captive	09/87	Zebra
Defiant Mistress	06/86	Zebra
Ecstasy's Trail	01/87	Zebra
Love's Fiery Jewel	/82	Zebra
Captive Ecstasy	/80	Zebra
Sweet Torment	06/84	Zebra
Passion's Dawn	09/85	Zebra
Midnight Rogue	08/95	Zebra
Amber Fire	/81	Zebra Amber Trilogy
Amber Passion	01/85	Zebra Amber Trilogy
Amber Treasure	/83	Zebra Amber Trilogy
To Love A Stranger	10/93	Zebra Historical
Only For Love	08/94	Zebra Historical
More Precious Than Gold	09/92	Zebra Super Special

Barbour, Anne

Lady Liza's Luck	07/94	
A Dangerous Charade		
A Talent For Trouble	08/92	Nal Regency
A Pressing Engagement	11/92	Nal Regency
Lord Glenraven's Return	06/94	Nal Regency
From The Heart	01/94	Nal Signet Anthology
Kate And The Soldier	05/93	Penguin Regency
My Cousin Jane	07/95	Signet Regency
A Dangerous Charade	02/95	Signet Regency

Barbour, Jo Anne

46	One On One	06/91	Meteor

Barclay, Suzanne

141	Knight Dreams	09/92	Harlequin Historical
162	Knight's Lady	02/93	Harlequin Historical
184	Knight's Honor	08/93	Harlequin Historical
272	Lion Of The North	06/95	Harlequin Historical
252	Lion's Heart (#1)	01/95	Harlequin Lion Trilogy
272	Lion Of The North (#2)	06/95	Harlequin Lion Trilogy
304	Lion's Legacy (#3)	02/96	Harlequin Lion Trilogy
483	Man With A Mission	03/93	Silhouette Initmate Moments

Barker, Becky

	Captured By A Cowboy		Dell
50	Renegade Texan	07/91	Meteor
57	Back In His Arms	09/91	Meteor
76	Sassy Lady	02/92	Meteor
114	Impossible Match	11/92	Meteor
141	Bedroom Eyes	04/93	Meteor

AUTHOR/TITLE INDEX

Barrie, Susan

792	Gates Of Dawn	/64	Harlequin
831	Hotel At Treloan	/64	Harlequin
904	Moon At The Full	/65	Harlequin
926	Mountain Magic	/65	Harlequin
967	The Wings Of The Morning	/65	Harlequin
997	Castle Thunderbird	/66	Harlequin
1020	No Just Cause	/66	Harlequin
1043	Marry A Stranger	/66	Harlequin
1078	Royal Purple	/67	Harlequin
1099	Carpet Of Dreams	/67	Harlequin
1128	The Quiet Heart	/67	Harlequin
1168	Rose In The Bud	/67	Harlequin
1189	Accidental Bride	/68	Harlequin
1221	Master Of Melincourt	/68	Harlequin
1259	Wild Sonata	/68	Harlequin
1311	The Marriage Wheel	/69	Harlequin
1359	Return To Tremarth	/69	Harlequin
1428	Night Of The Singing Birds	/70	Harlequin
1526	Bride In Waiting	/71	Harlequin
2	Air Ticket		Harlequin Petite
2240	Victoria & Nightingale		Harlequin Romance

Barroll, Clare

	The Iron Crown	Ballantine

Barron, Ann

	Windswept

Barron, Elizabeth

	The Viscount's Wager	Warner
	Miss Drayton's Crusade	Warner
	The Elusive Countess	Warner
	An Amicable Arrangement	Warner

Barry, Andrea

194	African Enchantment	12/82	Silhouette Romance

Barry, Joe

43	The Clean-Up	/50	Harlequin
83	Fall Guy	/50	Harlequin
84	The Triple Cross	/50	Harlequin
101	Three For The Money	/51	Harlequin

Barshon, Brenda Braxton

	Southern Oaks	07/93	Harper Collins

Bartell, Linda Lang

	Alyssa	Avon
	Brianna	Avon
	Marisa	Avon
	Brittany	Avon
	Caressa	Avon

Bartell, Linda Lang

	Tender Pirate		Zebra
	Traitor's Kiss		Zebra
	Tender Rogue	10/94	Zebra
	Tender Warrior	11/92	Zebra
	Tender Marauder	01/94	Zebra
	Tender Scoundrel	01/96	Zebra

Bartholomew, Barbara

428	A Man Of Character	04/86	Silhouette Romance
457	The Romantic & The Realist	09/86	Silhouette Romance

Bartlett, Janice

61	Home Field Advantage	10/91	Meteor
87	All Through The House	04/92	Meteor
142	Lifesaver	04/93	Meteor Kismet

Bartlett, Kay

254	A Shiver Of Rain	09/88	Silhouette Intimate Moments
275	Family Ties	02/89	Silhouette Intimate Moments

Bartlett, Lynn

207	Defy The Eagle	02/94	Harlequin Historical
290	The Price Of Glory	06/89	Silhouette Intimate Moments
376	Heart And Soul	03/91	Silhouette Intimate Moments

Bartlett, Stephanie

	Highland Rebel	02/92	Bantam Fanfare
	Highland Flame	10/92	Bantam Fanfare
	Under His Spell	09/95	Zebra Anthology
	Golden Rapture	11/94	Zebra Historical
	Dearest Enemy	11/95	Zebra Lovegram

Barton, Beverly

580	Yankee Lover	07/90	Silhouette Desire
628	Lucky In Love	03/91	Silhouette Desire
662	Out Of Danger	09/91	Silhouette Desire
687	Sugar Hill		Silhouette Desire
711	Talk Of The Town	05/92	Silhouette Desire
766	The Wanderer	02/93	Silhouette Desire
799	Cameron	07/93	Silhouette Desire
831	The Mother Of My Child	03/94	Silhouette Desire
881	Nothing But Trouble	09/94	Silhouette Desire
453	This Side Of Heaven	10/92	Silhouette Intimate Moments
515	Paladin's Woman	08/93	Silhouette Intimate Moments
557	Lover And Deceiver	03/94	Silhouette Intimate Moments
614	The Outcast (Romantic Traditions)	01/95	Silhouette Intimate Moments
670	Defending His Own	10/95	Silhouette Intimate Moments
688	Guarding Jeannie	01/96	Silhouette Intimate Moments
707	Blackwood's Woman	04/96	Silhouette Intimate Moments

Bassett, Marjorie

538	Strange Request	/60	Harlequin

AUTHOR/TITLE INDEX

Baumann, Margaret

842	Nurse Barby's Secret Love	/64	Harlequin
947	A Woman Alone	/65	Harlequin
1366	Design For Loving	/70	Harlequin
1962	Debt Of Honour	/76	Harlequin

Baume, Eric

296	Half-Caste	/54	Harlequin

Baxter, Mary Lynn

	A Day In April	07/92	Harlequin	
	Undercover Lovers	06/94	Harlequin	Anthology
4	Another Kind Of Love	07/93	Harlequin	Men Made In America
	Moonbeams Aplenty	08/95	Harlequin	Western Lovers
	Too Hot To Handle	07/95	Silhouette	Anthology
24	Shared Moments	10/82	Silhouette	Desire
527	Added Delight	10/89	Silhouette	Desire
542	Winter Heat	01/90	Silhouette	Desire
571	Slow Burn	06/90	Silhouette	Desire
660	Tall In The Saddle	08/91	Silhouette	Desire
679	Marriage, Diamond Style	12/91	Silhouette	Desire
727	And Baby Makes Perfect	08/92	Silhouette	Desire
781	Mike's Baby	05/93	Silhouette	Desire
822	Dancler's Woman	11/93	Silhouette	Desire
991	Saddle Up	04/96	Silhouette	Desire
19	Another Kind Of Love	09/83	Silhouette	Intimate Moments
52	Memories That Linger	05/84	Silhouette	Intimate Moments
74	Everything But Time	11/84	Silhouette	Intimate Moments
117	A Handful Of Heaven	11/85	Silhouette	Intimate Moments
130	Price Above Rubies	02/86	Silhouette	Intimate Moments
156	When We Touch	08/86	Silhouette	Intimate Moments
197	Fool's Music	07/87	Silhouette	Intimate Moments
217	Moonbeams Aplenty	12/87	Silhouette	Intimate Moments
272	Knight Sparks	01/89	Silhouette	Intimate Moments
296	Wish Giver	07/89	Silhouette	Intimate Moments
9	All Our Tomorrows	03/82	Silhouette	Special Edition
31	Tears Of Yesterday	07/82	Silhouette	Special Edition
96	Autumn Awakening	05/83	Silhouette	Special Edition
360	Between The Raindrops	01/87	Silhouette	Special Edition
	Sweet Justice	02/94	Warner	
	Priceless	03/95	Warner	

Bayless, Anne Douglas

	The Fourth Season	01/95	Signet

Beach, Rex

241	Son Of The Gods	/53	Harlequin

Beard, Julie

	Lady And The Wolf	07/94	Diamond Historical
	A Dance In Heather	06/96	Jove Historical

AUTHOR/TITLE INDEX

Beaty, Betty

737	Maiden Flight	/63	Harlequin
790	South To The Sun	/64	Harlequin
824	Amber Five	/64	Harlequin
1004	The Path Of The Moonfish	/66	Harlequin
.1155	Miss Miranda's Walk	/67	Harlequin
1941	Love And The Kentish Maid	/76	Harlequin
2004	Head Of Chancery	/76	Harlequin
2069	Fly Away, Love	/77	Harlequin
2166	Master At Arms	/78	Harlequin
	Atlantic Sky		Mills & Boon
	The Swallows Of San Fedora		Mills & Boon
	Doctor On Board		Mills & Boon

Beaufort, Jane

1149	A Nightingale In The Sycamore	/67	Harlequin
1181	Dangerous Love	/68	Harlequin
	Love In High Places		Mills & Boon

Beauman, Sally

	Destiny		Fawcett Crest
	Lovers And Liars	03/95	Fawcett Crest

Beaumont, Anne

139	Feelings Of Love		Harlequin Direct
1231	That Special Touch		Harlequin Presents
1391	Secret Whispers	09/91	Harlequin Presents
3049	Another Time, Another Love		Harlequin Romance
3199	A Cinderella Affair	06/92	Harlequin Romance
3241	Images Of Desire	01/93	Harlequin Romance

Beaumont, Lisa

	Flames Of Tourney		Ballantine Regency

Beaumont, Marie

391	Catherine's Song		Harlequin Superromance
538	Halfway Home	03/93	Harlequin Superromance

Beaumont, Nina

101	Sapphire Magic	11/91	Harlequin Historical
153	Promises To Keep	02/93	Harlequin Historical
203	Across Time	01/94	Harlequin Historical
246	Tapestry Of Fate	11/94	Harlequin Historical
278	Tapestry Of Dreams	07/95	Harlequin Historical
303	Twice Upon A Time	02/96	Harlequin Historical

Bechko, Peggy

47	Dark Side Of Love		Harlequin Superromance

Beck, K. K.

	Young Mrs. Cavendish & The Kaiser's Men	/88	Walker

Beckman, Patti

8	Captive Heart	05/80	Silhouette Romance
37	The Beachcomber	10/80	Silhouette Romance

AUTHOR/TITLE INDEX

Beckman, Patti

54	Louisiana Lady	01/81	Silhouette	Romance
72	Angry Lover	04/81	Silhouette	Romance
96	Love's Treacherous Journey	08/81	Silhouette	Romance
124	Spotlight To Fame	01/82	Silhouette	Romance
154	Daring Encounter	06/82	Silhouette	Romance
179	Mermaid's Touch	10/82	Silhouette	Romance
227	Forbidden Affair	06/83	Silhouette	Romance
273	Time For Us	01/84	Silhouette	Romance
348	On Stage	03/85	Silhouette	Romance
571	Someday My Love	04/88	Silhouette	Romance
13	Bitter Victory	04/82	Silhouette	Special Edition
61	Tender Deception	12/82	Silhouette	Special Edition
85	Enchanted Surrender	04/83	Silhouette	Special Edition
109	Thunder At Dawn	08/83	Silhouette	Special Edition
169	Storm Over The Everglades	06/84	Silhouette	Special Edition
212	Nashville Blues	01/85	Silhouette	Special Edition
226	The Movie	03/85	Silhouette	Special Edition
270	Odds Against Tomorrow	10/85	Silhouette	Special Edition
278	Dateline: Washington	12/85	Silhouette	Special Edition
321	Summer's Storm	07/86	Silhouette	Special Edition
370	Danger In His Arms	03/87	Silhouette	Special Edition

Becnel, Rexanne

	The Christmas Wish	12/93	
	Where Magic Dwells	07/94	
	The Rose Of Blacksword	06/92	Dell
	Christmas Journey	12/92	Dell
	My Gallant Enemy	07/90	Dell
	Thief Of My Heart	05/91	Dell
	A Dove At Midnight	06/93	Dell

Bedford, Debbi

187	Blessing	09/93	Harlequin	Historical
154	Touch The Sky		Harlequin	Superromance
239	A Distant Promise	07/95	Harlequin	Superromance
333	Passages		Harlequin	Superromance
384	To Weaver Tomorrow		Harlequin	Superromance
522	Just Between Us	11/92	Harlequin	Superromance
546	After The Promise	05/93	Harlequin	Superromance
	Chickadee	06/95	Harper	

Bedford, Deborah

	A Child's Promise	01/95	Harper
	Timberline	04/96	Harper

Beech, Jane

575	The Year Of Waiting (Doctor Standing)	/61	Harlequin
1215	Soft Is The Music	/68	Harlequin

Bele, Karen A.

Bele, Karen A.
    Apache's Angel   Zebra
Bell, Ann
   3 Inspired Love   02/95 Barbour & Co. Rocky Bluff Chronicles
Bell, Anthea
    A London Season   St. Martin's
    The Floral Companion   St. Martin's
Bell, Donna
    All's Fair   Jove Regency
    The Scandalous Miss   Pageant
    An Improper Pursuit   06/94 Zebra
    Flowers For The Bride   04/95 Zebra Anthology
    The Valentine's Day Ball   Zebra Regency
    The Bluestocking's Beau   05/96 Zebra Regency
Bell, Marguerite
   3 A Rose For Danger   Mills & Boon
   8 The Devil's Daughter   Mills & Boon
Belle, Pamela
    The Chains Of Fate   Berkley
Bellem, Robert Leslie
  106 The Window With The Sleeping Nude   /51 Harlequin
Belmont, Kate
    That Certain Smile   04/82 Richard Gallen
Belmont, Kathryn
   74 Mission Of Mercy   04/91 Harlequin Historical
 222 The Fugitive Heart   05/94 Harlequin Historical
  39 Dark Side Of The Moon   02/84 Silhouette Intimate Moments
  40 A Time To Sing   02/84 Silhouette Intimate Moments
  72 Night Music   01/83 Silhouette Special Edition
 112 From The Beginning   08/83 Silhouette Special Edition
 173 From The Flames   06/84 Silhouette Special Edition
Belvedere, Lee
    Meet A Dark Stranger   Dell Candlelight
Benedict, Barbara
    Golden Dreams
    Catch Of The Season   Jove Regency
    Love And Honor   02/94 Jove Regency
    Lovestorm   Leisure
    A Taste Of Heaven   09/93 Zebra Heartfire
    Destiny   11/94 Zebra Lovegram
    Always   09/95 Zebra Lovegram
Benet, Deborah
    Riptide   07/84 Nal Rapture Romance
  23 Midnight Eyes   Nal Rapture Romance
  44 Winter Flame   Nal Rapture Romance
  64 Wrangler's Lady   Nal Rapture Romance

Benjamin, Linda

	Ecstasy's Fury		Zebra	
	Midnight Chase		Zebra	
	Texas Wildcat		Zebra	
	Beloved Outlaw		Zebra	
	Wild For Love		Zebra	

Benjamin, Nikki

359	A Man To Believe In	11/90	Silhouette	Intimate Moments
519	Restless Wind	09/93	Silhouette	Intimate Moments
645	The Wedding Venture	06/95	Silhouette	Intimate Moments
729	The Lady And Alex Payton	08/96	Silhouette	Intimate Moments
663	On The Whispering Wind	04/91	Silhouette	Special Edition
716	The Best Medicine	01/92	Silhouette	Special Edition
782	It Must Have Been The Mistletoe	12/92	Silhouette	Special Edition
880	My Baby, Your Child	04/94	Silhouette	Special Edition
928	Only St. Nick Knew	12/94	Silhouette	Special Edition

Bennett, Cherie

	Sunset Island		Berkley	
	Sunset Kiss		Berkley	
	Sunset Dreams		Berkley	
	Sunset Farewell		Berkley	
	Sunset Reunion		Berkley	
	Sunset Secrets		Berkley	
	Sunset Paradise	12/92	Berkley	

Bennett, Connie

547	Fifty Ways To Be Your Lover	08/94	Harlequin	American
311	Suspicions	02/95	Harlequin	Intrigue
293	Share My Tomorrow		Harlequin	Superromance
294	A Wild Wind		Harlequin	Superromance
327	Thinking Of You		Harlequin	Superromance
364	When I See Your Face		Harlequin	Superromance
373	Changes In The Wind		Harlequin	Superromance
416	Playing By The Rules		Harlequin	Superromance
436	Believe In Me		Harlequin	Superromance
513	Tourist Attraction	08/92	Harlequin	Superromance
562	Windstorm (Women Who Dare)	09/93	Harlequin	Superromance
586	Single... With Children	03/94	Harlequin	Superromance
695	Married To A Stranger	06/96	Harlequin	Superromance

Bennett, Constance

	The Pirate's Vixen			
	Pirate's Pleasure			
	Morning Sky			
	Moonsong	11/92	Diamond	
	Blossom		Diamond	

Bennett, Elizabeth

| | Changes Of Heart | 02/92 | Jove | |

AUTHOR/TITLE INDEX

Bennett, Elizabeth
Heart And Soul   05/94   Jove

Bennett, Emma
167   Beneath The Willow Tree   /83   Dell Candlelight Ecstasy

Bennett, Esther Wingert
The Unseemly Woman   12/94   Dorrance Historical

Bennett, Janice
Across Forever   06/94   Pinnacle Time Travel
A Dangerous Intrigue   /92   Zebra
A Lady's Champion   04/94   Zebra
An Eligible Bride   /87   Zebra Regency
Forever In Time   /90   Zebra Regency
An Intriguing Desire   /89   Zebra Regency
A Logical Lady   /91   Zebra Regency
Midnight Masque   /88   Zebra Regency
A Mysterious Miss   /91   Zebra Regency
Tangled Web   /88   Zebra Regency
A Tempting Miss   /89   Zebra Regency
A Timely Affair   /90   Zebra Regency
A Touch Of Forever   /92   Zebra Regency
A Christmas Keepsake   11/91   Zebra Regency
Christmas Holiday   /90   Zebra Zebra Short Stories

Bennett, Laura Gilmou
By All That Is Sacred   Avon

Bennetts, Pamela
23   Dear Lover England   Mills & Boon

Benson, Angela
Dreams   01/95   Pinnacle
Bands Of Gold   11/94   Pinnacle
Choices   09/95   Pinnacle
Between The Lines   05/96   Pinnacle Arabesque
For All Time   08/95   Pinnacle Arabesque
Holiday Cheer   11/95   Zebra Arabesque

Benson, Anne
Escape To Love   Playboy Press
The Tangled Web   Playboy Press
Love's Gentle Smile   Playboy Press

Bentley, Jayne
A Moment Past Midnight   /79   Mcfadden
Turning Towards Home   /79   Mcfadden
Maiden Of The Morning   /79   Mcfadden

Bercier, Leila
Style
Vanities
My Life To Live   12/93   Starlog Moonlight Contemporary

Berckman, Evelyn

Berckman, Evelyn
    Heir Of Staravelings   Gothic

Berenson, Laurien

109	Come As You Are	09/85	Bantam Loveswept
210	Winner Take All		Harlequin American
255	Lucky In Love	06/89	Harlequin Temptation
310	Talisman	08/90	Harlequin Temptation
368	The Sweetheart Deal	10/91	Harlequin Temptation
	Night Cries		Harper
	A Pedigree To Die For	02/95	Kensington
	Deep Cover	09/94	Zebra

Beresford, Elisabeth
    Veronica

Berg, M.D., Louis

191	Prison Doctor	/52	Harlequin
258	World Behind Bars	/53	Harlequin

Berg, Patti
    Enchanted   11/94   Jove Contemporary

Bergen, Fran

191	Capitol Affair	02/85	Silhouette Desire
29	Yearning Of Angels	06/82	Silhouette Special Edition
77	Prelude To Passion	02/83	Silhouette Special Edition
101	Golden Impulse	06/83	Silhouette Special Edition
142	Dream Feast	01/84	Silhouette Special Edition
214	Perfect Harmony	01/85	Silhouette Special Edition

Berger, Nomi
    Dreams To Keep   06/91   Bantam Fanfare

Bergstrom, Kay

	Tomorrow's Dreams	09/95	Pinnacle
34	Love's Awakening	04/94	Zebra Lucky In Love

Bergstrom, Louise

	South Sea Serenade		
	Second Spring	/92	Avalon
	The Lucia Bride	/91	Avalon
	Sing Me A Love Song	10/92	Avalon
178	House Of The Sphinx		Dell Candlelight

Berk, Ariel

93	Silent Beginnings	10/83	Silhouette Desire
154	Promise Of Love	08/84	Silhouette Desire
180	Remedies Of The Heart	12/84	Silhouette Desire
194	Hungry For Love		Silhouette Desire
216	Breaking The Ice	06/85	Silhouette Desire
239	False Impression	10/85	Silhouette Desire
250	Teacher's Pet	12/85	Silhouette Desire
305	No Plan For Surrender	09/86	Silhouette Desire
335	Game, Set, Match	02/87	Silhouette Desire

Bevarly, Elizabeth

908	A Dad Like Daniel (From Here To Maternity	02/95	Silhouette Desire
920	The Perfect Father (From Here To Maternity	04/95	Silhouette Desire
933	Dr. Daddy (From Here To Maternity)	06/95	Silhouette Desire
993	Father Of The Brat	04/96	Silhouette Desire
1005	Father Of The Brood	06/96	Silhouette Desire
1016	Father On The Brink	08/96	Silhouette Desire
557	Destinations South	10/89	Silhouette Special Edition
590	Close Range	04/90	Silhouette Special Edition
639	Donovan's Chance	12/90	Silhouette Special Edition
676	Moriah's Mutiny	06/91	Silhouette Special Edition
737	Up Close	04/92	Silhouette Special Edition
803	Hired Hand	03/93	Silhouette Special Edition
844	Return Engagement	10/93	Silhouette Special Edition

Beverley, Jo

A Christmas Angel	11//92	Co. Of Rogues
Married At Midnight: "The Desperate Bride"	08/96	Avon Anthology
My Lady Notorious	03/93	Avon Georgian Romance
Lord Of My Heart	08/92	Avon Medieval Romance
Dark Champion	10/93	Avon Medieval Romance
Deirdre And Don Juan	12/93	Avon Traditional Regency
The Christmas Cat: "A Gift Of Light"	11/96	Berkley Anthology
Moonlight Lovers: "The Demon's Bride"	10/93	Nal Anthology
Winter Heart	05/96	Pocket
A Regency Christmas: "A Mummer's Play"	10/95	Signet Anthology
Emily And The Dark Angel	05/91	Walker
The Fortune Teller	10/91	Walker
The Stolen Bride	/90	Walker
The Fortune Hunter	10/91	Walker
All Hallow's Eve: "Lord Samhain's Night"	10/92	Walker Halloween Anthology
The Lord Of Elphindale	/93	Walker Lords & Fairies Anth.
The Stanforth Secrets	/89	Walker Traditional Regency
Lord Wraybourne's Betrothed	/88	Walker Traditional Regency
If Fancy Be The Food Of Love	03/91	Walker Valentine
Dangerous Joy	11/95	Zebra
Something Wicked	01/97	Zebra
A Christmas Delight	12/91	Zebra Anthology
A Spring Bouquet: "Forbidden Affections"	05/96	Zebra Anthology
Twelfth Night	12/91	Zebra Christmas Anthology
An Arranged Marriage	07/91	Zebra Co. Of Rogues
An Unwilling Bride	02/92	Zebra Co. Of Rogues
Forbidden	03/94	Zebra Co. Of Rogues
Tempting Fortune	03/95	Zebra Georgian Romance
The Shattered Rose	05/96	Zebra Medieval Romance

Beyers, Cordia

Desire And Deceive		Ballantine

Bianchin, Helen

Bianchin, Helen

	The Willing Heart (Premiere)		Harlequin
2010	Bewildered Haven	/76	Harlequin
2084	Avenging Angel	/77	Harlequin
2175	The Hills Of Home	/78	Harlequin
271	Vines Of Splendour		Harlequin Presents
289	Stormy Possession		Harlequin Presents
409	Devil In Command		Harlequin Presents
415	Edge Of Spring		Harlequin Presents
457	The Savage Touch		Harlequin Presents
527	Wildfire Encounter		Harlequin Presents
695	Yesterday's Shadow		Harlequin Presents
720	Savage Pagan		Harlequin Presents
744	Sweet Tempest		Harlequin Presents
751	Dark Tyrant		Harlequin Presents
839	Bitter Encore		Harlequin Presents
975	Dark Enchantment		Harlequin Presents
1111	An Awakening Desire		Harlequin Presents
1240	Touch The Flame		Harlequin Presents
1383	The Tiger's Lair	08/91	Harlequin Presents
1423	The Stefanos Marriage	01/92	Harlequin Presents
1527	No Gentle Seduction	02/93	Harlequin Presents
1561	Stormfire	06/93	Harlequin Presents
1601	Reluctant Captive	11/93	Harlequin Presents
1741	Dangerous Alliance	05/95	Harlequin Presents
1809	Forgotten Husband	05/96	Harlequin Presents
1704	Passion's Mistress	12/94	Harlequin Presents Plus
2378	Master Of Uluru		Harlequin Romance

Bickmore, Barbara

	East Of The Sun	/87	
	The Moon Below		Bantam
	Homecoming	09/95	Kensington
	The Back Of Beyond	04/94	Zebra

Bicos, Olga

	White Tigers	10/91	Dell
	Santana Rose	12/92	Dell
	By My Heart Betrayed		Dell
	More Than Magic	08/95	Pinnacle Denise Little Presents
	Sweeter Than Dreams	05/95	Pinnacle Denise Little Presents

Bieber, Janet

250	Let's Do It Again	04/88	Bantam Loveswept
470	Montana's Treasure	01/89	Silhouette Desire
533	Seeing Is Believing	11/89	Silhouette Desire
646	The Family Plan	06/91	Silhouette Desire

Bierce, Jane

| 15 | Building Passion | | Harlequin American |

Bittner, Rosanne

Montana Woman	/90	Bantam	
Embers Of The Heart	/90	Bantam	
Tender Betrayal	10/93	Bantam	
Wildest Dreams	09/94	Bantam	
The Forever Tree	03/95	Bantam	
Chase The Sun	09/95	Bantam	
In The Shadow Of The Mountains	07/91	Bantam	Fanfare
Song Of The Wolf	03/92	Bantam	Fanfare
Thunder On The Plains	08/92	Bantam	Fanfare
Cherished Moments	04/95	St. Martin's	Anthology
Oregon Bride		Warner	
This Time Forever	/89	Warner	
Destiny's Dawn		Warner	Blue Hawk Series
Savage Horizons		Warner	Blue Hawk Series
Frontier Fires	/87	Warner	Blue Hawk Series
Tennessee Bride	/88	Warner	Bride Series
Texas Bride	/88	Warner	Bride Series
Arizona Bride		Zebra	
Arizona Ecstasy		Zebra	
Comanche Sunset	11/91	Zebra	
Ecstasy's Chains		Zebra	
Hearts Surrender		Zebra	
Lawless Love		Zebra	
Prairie Embrace		Zebra	
Rapture's Gold		Zebra	
Sioux Splendor		Zebra	
Lawless Love		Zebra	
Sweet Mountain Magic		Zebra	
Unforgettable	01/94	Zebra	
Indian Summer	05/94	Zebra	
Until Tomorrow	08/95	Zebra	
Full Circle	09/94	Zebra	Historical
1 Sweet Prairie Passion		Zebra	Savage Destiny
2 Ride The Free Wind		Zebra	Savage Destiny
3 River Of Love		Zebra	Savage Destiny
4 Embrace The Wild Land		Zebra	Savage Destiny
5 Climb The Highest Mountain		Zebra	Savage Destiny
6 Meet The New Dawn		Zebra	Savage Destiny
Caress	07/92	Zebra	Special Release

Black, Cheryl

Comanche Caress		Zebra	
Comanche Lovesong		Zebra	Heartfire

Black, Irene Loyd

My Sweet Valentine	07/94		
The Duke's Easter Lady		Regency	
A Determined Lady	/96	Regency	

AUTHOR/TITLE INDEX

Black, Irene Loyd

	Tattered Valentine		Valentines Day Treasure
	A Charmed Betrothal		Zebra Regency
	A Husband For The Countess	08/90	Zebra Regency
	A Mischievous Miss		Zebra Regency
	Lady Sarah's Fancy	11/94	Zebra Regency
	A Touch Of Merry	12/95	Zebra Regency

Black, Jackie

	Winter Winds		Dell Candlelight Ecstasy
	Crimson Morning		Dell Candlelight Ecstasy
	Autumn Fires		Dell Candlelight Ecstasy
	Promises In The Night		Dell Candlelight Ecstasy
	A Time To Love		Dell Candlelight Ecstasy
	Romantic Roulette		Dell Candlelight Ecstasy
	Catch Of The Season		Dell Candlelight Ecstasy
	Island Of Illusions		Dell Candlelight Ecstasy
	The Vixen's Kiss		Dell Candlelight Ecstasy
	Charlie's Chance		Dell Candlelight Ecstasy
85	A Little Bit Of Warmth	/86	Dell Candlelight Ecstasy
152	Autumn Fires	/83	Dell Candlelight Ecstasy
170	Promises In The Night	/83	Dell Candlelight Ecstasy
	Wayfaring Stranger	02/89	Dell Romantic Suspense
16	Payment In Full		Ecstasy Supreme
28	Fascination		Ecstasy Supreme
56	From This Day Forward		Ecstasy Supreme
85	A Little Bit Of Warmth		Ecstasy Supreme
157	Dark Paradise		Ecstasy Supreme

Black, Laura

	Ravenburn		Warner
	Gendraco	/77	Warner

Blackmore, Jane

524	Tears In Paradise		Dell Candlelight

Blackstone, Alexandra

	Texas Kiss	06/95	Jove Wildflower

Blair, Alma

	Of Shadow And Substance	11/88	Abbey Press
	Beyond Legal Limits	/92	Avalon
	The Dark Side Of Paradise		Avalon Mystery Romance
	The Unwitting Witness	01/90	Avalon Mystery Romance
	Web Of Danger	11/88	Avalon Mystery Romance

Blair, Catherine

89	Devil Wind	08/91	Harlequin Historical

Blair, Clifford

	Trouble Town	/92	Avalon
	Guns On Fossil Ridge	/91	Avalon
	Ghost-Town Gold	/91	Avalon

320

AUTHOR/TITLE INDEX

Blair, Jennifer

	Danger At Olduvai		Dell Candlelight	
182	Dangerous Assignment		Dell Candlelight	
195	The Long Shadow		Dell Candlelight	

Blair, Joan

648	Gray's Hospital	/62	Harlequin	
672	Gregor Lothian, Surgeon	/62	Harlequin	
703	Course Of True Love	/62	Harlequin	
811	The Way To The Wedding	/64	Harlequin	
907	Two For The Doctor	/65	Harlequin	

Blair, Kathryn - #1

633	Children's Nurse	/61	Harlequin	
650	The Golden Rose	/62	Harlequin	
667	Nurse Laurie	/62	Harlequin	
682	Plantation Doctor	/62	Harlequin	
700	Tamarisk Bay	/62	Harlequin	
717	The House At Tegwani	/63	Harlequin	
749	Wild Crocus	/63	Harlequin	
766	The Enchanting Island	/63	Harlequin	
785	The Surgeon's Marriage	/64	Harlequin	
805	Love This Enemy	/64	Harlequin	
823	Dear Adversary	/64	Harlequin	
843	A Summer At Barbazon	/64	Harlequin	
861	Bewildered Heart	/64	Harlequin	
878	This Kind Of Love	/64	Harlequin	
893	Sweet Deceiver	/65	Harlequin	
920	The Man At Mulera	/65	Harlequin	
941	Mayenga Farm	/65	Harlequin	
954	Doctor Westland	/65	Harlequin	
972	Barbary Moon	/65	Harlequin	
988	The Primrose Bride	/66	Harlequin	
1012	No Other Haven	/66	Harlequin	
1038	Battle Of Love	/66	Harlequin	
1059	The Tulip Tree	/66	Harlequin	
1083	Dearest Enemy	/67	Harlequin	
1107	They Met In Zanzibar	/67	Harlequin	
1148	Flowering Wilderness	/67	Harlequin	

Blair, Kathryn - #2

285	Home Is The Sailor		Harlequin	American
328	Dancing In The Aisles		Harlequin	American
403	Shadows Of The Past	08/91	Harlequin	American

Blair, Laurien

105	Sweet Temptation	12/83	Silhouette	Desire
130	Between The Covers	04/84	Silhouette	Desire
210	That Special Magic	05/85	Silhouette	Desire
243	Taken By Storm	11/85	Silhouette	Desire

Blair, Leona
>   Privilege
Blake, Andrea

755	September In Paris	/63	Harlequin
864	Now And Always	/64	Harlequin
944	Whisper Of Doubt	/65	Harlequin
974	Night Of The Hurricane	/65	Harlequin

Blake, Jennifer

Tender Heart		Sweet & Savage
Storm At Midnight	/73	Ace
Stardust	09/94	Avon Anthology
The Quilting Circle: "Pieces Of Dreams"	/96	Berkley Anthology
Royal Passion	/86	Fawcett
Joy And Anger	/91	Fawcett
Wildest Dreams	07/92	Fawcett
Prisoner Of Desire	/86	Fawcett
Surrender In The Moonlight	/84	Fawcett
Bride Of A Stranger	/74	Fawcett
Dark Masquerade	/74	Fawcett
Embrace And Conquer	/81	Fawcett
Fierce Eden	/85	Fawcett
Golden Fancy	/80	Fawcett
Louisiana Dawn	/87	Fawcett
Love And Smoke	/89	Fawcett
Night Of The Candles	/78	Fawcett
The Notorious Angel	/77	Fawcett
Perfume Of Paradise	/88	Fawcett
Royal Seduction	/83	Fawcett
Southern Rapture	/87	Fawcett
Spanish Serenade	/90	Fawcett
The Storm And The Splendour	/79	Fawcett
Sweet Piracy	/78	Fawcett
Midnight Waltz	/85	Fawcett
Arrow To The Heart	07/93	Fawcett
Shameless	06/94	Fawcett
Secret Of Mirror House	/70	Fawcett
Stranger At Plantation Inn	/71	Fawcett
Silver-Tongued Devil	/96	Fawcett
Tigress	07/96	Fawcett
A Purrfect Romance: "Out Of The Dark"	08/95	Harper Anthology
Haven Of Fear	/77	Manor Books
Murder For Charity	/77	Manor Books
The Bewitching Grace	/73	Popular Library
Court Of The Thorn Tree	/73	Popular Library
Love's Wild Desire	/77	Popular Library
Tender Betrayal	/79	Popular Library
The Abducted Heart	/78	Signet

Blayne, Diana
  110 Tangled Destinies   02/86 Dell Ecstasy Supreme

Blayne, Sara
      A Christmas Delight   /91 Zebra Anthology
      Sea Witch   Zebra Heartfire
      Sweet Abandon   Zebra Heartfire
      Duel Of The Heart   Zebra Regency
      A Nobleman's Bride   Zebra Regency
      Passion's Lady   Zebra Regency
      An Elusive Guardian   10/94 Zebra Regency
      An Easter Courtship   10/95 Zebra Regency

Blayney, Mary
  448 True Colors   09/88 Silhouette Desire
  688 Father Christmas   12/89 Silhouette Romance

Block, Nancy
      Once Upon A Pirate   04/95 Harper Monogram

Bloom, Jill
   57 Playing With Fire   Harlequin Intrigue
   37 Two Of A Kind   12/84 Harlequin Temptation
  105 The Sky's The Limit   05/86 Harlequin Temptation

Blyth, Juliet
      The Parfit Knight   St. Martin's

Blythe, Leonora
      Helene   Ballantine Regency

Blythe, Megan
      Satin Chains   Zebra Heartfire

Bobander, Jane
      Secrets Of A Midnight Moon 11/91 St. Martin's
      Magic Of The Wolf   01/93 St. Martin's

Bocardo, Claire
      Maybe Later, Love   09/92 Zebra Special Over 45 Release

Bockoven, Georgia
   82 Restless Tide   Harlequin Superromance
  102 After The Lightning   Harlequin Superromance
  138 Little By Little   Harlequin Superromance
  179 Today, Tomorrow, Always   Harlequin Superromance
  222 The Long Road Home   Harlequin Superromance
  246 Love Songs   Harlequin Superromance
   14 Tracings On A Window   06/84 Harlequin Temptation
   57 A Gift Of Wildflowers   05/85 Harlequin Temptation
   94 A Week From Friday   02/86 Harlequin Temptation
  161 Tomorrow's Love Song   07/87 Harlequin Temptation
      Tracings On A Window   08/95 Harlequin Western Lovers
      Moments   03/94 Harper
      The Way It Should Have Been 03/93 Harper
      A Marriage Of Convenience 02/91 Harper

Bockoven, Georgia
    Alone In A Crowd   03/95 Harper
    Far From Home   05/96 Harper
Bode, Margo
    Jasmine Splendor   Richard Gallen
Boeckman, C. V.
    House Of Secrets   /92 Avalon
    Remember Our Yesterdays   /91 Avalon
Bogard, Dale
  147 Pardon My Body   /51 Harlequin
Bogart, William
  57 Murder Man   /50 Harlequin
  68 The Queen City Murder Case   /50 Harlequin
  114 Johnny Saxon   /51 Harlequin
Bogolin, Carol
  143 Heavenly   04/93 Meteor Kismet
Bolander, Judith
  264 The Best Of Yesterday   Harlequin Superromance
Bolt, Maxine
    A Dream To Build On   Avalon Career Romance
    Hard Hats And Roses   Avalon Career Romance
    The Silver Swan   Avalon Mystery Romance
    Whispers From The Past   Avalon Mystery Romance
Bolton, Muriel Ray
    The Golden Porcupine   Avon
Bonander, Jane
    To Have And To Hold   06/94 Avon Anthology
    A Christmas Together   10/94 Avon Anthology
    The Bedroom Is Mine   10/95 Longmeadow Pres Anthology
  1 Wild Heart   09/95 Pocket Heart Trilogy
  2 Winter Heart   05/96 Pocket Heart Trilogy
  3 Warrior Heart   10/97 Pocket Heart Trilogy
    Secrets Of A Midnight Moon   11/91 St. Martin's
    Forbidden Moon   04/94 St. Martin's
    Fires Of Innocence   12/94 St. Martin's Historical
Bond, Evelyn
    The Heart's Intrigue   Zebra Regency
Bond, Rebecca
  92 In Passion's Defense   Harlequin American
  109 Bed And Board   Harlequin American
  172 Open Channels   10/86 Harlequin American
  31 The Matthias Ring   /85 Harlequin Intrigue
Bonds, Parris Afton
    Snow And Ice   Ballantine
    Sweet Enchantress   11/91 Bantam
    Deep Purple   Fawcett

AUTHOR/TITLE INDEX

Bonds, Parris Afton

	Lavender Blue		Fawcett
	Blue Moon		Fawcett
	Mood Indigo		Fawcett
	For All Time	11/92	Harper Monogram
	Tame The Wildest Heart	11/94	Harper Monogram
	Dream Time	05/93	Harper Monogram
	The Savage	/95	Leisure
	Spinster's Song	08/92	Leisure Comtemporary Romance
	A Valentine Sampler	01/93	Leisure Contemporary
	The Captive	09/93	Leisure Historical
5	Windsong	06/83	Silhouette Intimate Moments
41	Widow Woman	03/84	Silhouette Intimate Moments
77	Spinter's Song	01/85	Silhouette Intimate Moments
113	Midsummer Midnight	10/85	Silhouette Intimate Moments
153	Man For Hire	08/86	Silhouette Intimate Moments
189	Wanted Woman	05/87	Silhouette Intimate Moments
218	Renegade Man	12/87	Silhouette Intimate Moments
241	That Mc Kenna Woman	06/88	Silhouette Intimate Moments
70	Made For Each Other	04/81	Silhouette Romance
526	Run To Me	09/87	Silhouette Romance
	Ravished!	/89	Silhouette Summer Sizzlers

Bonham, Barbara

	Proud Passion		Playboy Press

Bonner, Elizabeth

	A Vow To Keep	11/93	Diamond Historical

Borchardt, Alice

	Devoted	12/95	Dutton

Borodin, George

208	Pillar Of Fire	/53	Harlequin

Boswell, Barbara

	Magic Slippers	07/96	Avon Anthology
53	Little Consequences	07/84	Bantam Loveswept
78	Sensuous Perception	01/85	Bantam Loveswept
95	Darling Obstacles	06/85	Bantam Loveswept
117	Landslide Victory	11/85	Bantam Loveswept
142	Trouble In Triplicate	05/86	Bantam Loveswept
158	Always, Amber	09/86	Bantam Loveswept
160	Beside Manners	10/86	Bantam Loveswept
164	Whatever It Takes	11/86	Bantam Loveswept
183	Tangles	03/87	Bantam Loveswept
194	Not A Marrying Man	06/87	Bantam Loveswept
207	Playing Hard To Get	09/87	Bantam Loveswept
236	Sharing Secrets	02/88	Bantam Loveswept
242	Intimate Details	03/88	Bantam Loveswept
261	Baby, Baby	06/88	Bantam Loveswept

Boswell, Barbara

272	And Tara, Too	08/88	Bantam Loveswept
313	Ms. Fortune's Man	03/89	Bantam Loveswept
334	Simply Irresistible	06/89	Bantam Loveswept
359	One Step From Paradise	10/89	Bantam Loveswept
444	The Last Brady	01/91	Bantam Loveswept
486	Strong Temptation	08/91	Bantam Loveswept
582	Private Lessons	12/92	Bantam Loveswept
7	The Bridal Price	04/96	Harlequin Here Come The Grooms
	Wicked Games	11/94	Jove
	Red Velvet	11/95	Jove
	Jingle Bells, Wedding Bells	11/94	Silhouette Anthology
558	Rule Breaker	03/90	Silhouette Desire
583	Another Whirlwind Courtship	08/90	Silhouette Desire
609	The Bridal Price	12/90	Silhouette Desire
651	The Baby Track	07/91	Silhouette Desire
685	License To Love	01/92	Silhouette Desire
749	Double Trouble	11/92	Silhouette Desire
787	Triple Treat	06/93	Silhouette Desire
821	The Best Revenge	11/93	Silhouette Desire
877	Family Feud (Man Of The Month)	09/94	Silhouette Desire
932	The Engagement Party	06/95	Silhouette Desire
943	The Wilde Bunch (Man Of The Month)	08/95	Silhouette Desire

Boucher, Rita

	Miss Gabrielle's Gambit	07/94	
	A Misbegotten Match	11/94	Avon Regency
	Scandalous Schoolmistress		Avon Regency Romance

Bourne, Caroline

	Wild Southern Rose		
	Falcon's Lady		
	Texas Conquest		
	Texas Fire		
	Riverboat Seduction		Zebra
	Allegheny Captive		Zebra
	Allegheny Ecstasy		Zebra
	On Rapture's Wing		Zebra
	Riverboat Seduction		Zebra
	Love's Perfect Dream	05/93	Zebra
	A Bride's Passion	05/93	Zebra Anthology
	Edge Of Heaven	10/94	Zebra Historical
	White Lace	08/95	Zebra Lovegram

Bourne, Joenna Watkins

| | The Ladyship's Companion | | Avon Regency |

Bowden, Susan

| | In The Shadow Of The Crown | /87 | Bantam |
| | Touched By Thorns | 04/92 | Bantam Fanfare |

Bradford, Barbara Taylor

	Angel	05/92	Random House
	Remember	10/90	Random House
	Hold The Dream	/94	Wings
	To Be The Best	/94	Wings
	Act Of Will	/94	Wings

Bradford, Debbie

| 546 | After The Promise | 06/93 | Harlequin Superromance |

Bradford, Lily

| 11 | Moonfire Melody | /81 | Berkley Second Chance At Love |
| 17 | Heart Of The Glen | /81 | Berkley Second Chance At Love |

Bradford, Sally

281	The Arrangement		Harlequin Superromance
365	Spring Thaw		Harlequin Superromance
518	Out On A Limb	10/92	Harlequin Superromance
263	When Fortune Smiles	08/89	Harlequin Temptation
	Deceive Me Darling	/88	Pageant

Bradford, Susannah

| | Blind Trust | | M. Evans |

Bradley, Blythe

| 129 | To Love A Stranger | 02/93 | Meteor Kismet |

Bradley, Kate

231	Ancient Secrets	03/88	Silhouette Intimate Moments
346	Sheep's Clothing	08/90	Silhouette Intimate Moments
901	Beginning With Breakfast	11/92	Silhouette Romance
951	Almost Innocent	07/93	Silhouette Romance

Bradley, Marion Zimmer

| | Mists Of Avalon | | Pocket |
| | The Firehand | | Pocket |

Bradley, Muriel

	Tanya		Richard Gallen
	The Sudden Summer		Richard Gallen
28	Waltz In Scarlet	11/83	Silhouette Intimate Moments
66	Island Man	09/84	Silhouette Intimate Moments
	Ecstasy's Wings		Zebra Heartfire

Bradley, Ramona

| 411 | Hot Arctic Nights | 09/92 | Harlequin Temptation |

Bradshaw, Emily

	Heart's Journey	11/92	Dell
	Cactus Blossom	11/91	Dell
	Midnight Dancer	11/94	Dell Historical
	Country Christmas	11/93	Nal Anthology

Bradstreet, Valerie

| | The Fortune Wheel | | Avon |
| | The Ivory Fan | | Avon |

Brady, Taylor

Brady, Taylor

Raging River	10/92	Avon	The Kincaids
Prairie Thunder	/93	Avon	The Kincaids
Mountain Fury	/93	Avon	The Kincaids
Westward Winds	/93	Avon	The Kincaids

Bramsch, Joan

41	The Sophisticated Mountain Gal	04/84	Bantam	Loveswept
64	A Kiss To Make It Better	10/84	Bantam	Loveswept
81	The Light Side	02/85	Bantam	Loveswept
88	At Nightfall	04/85	Bantam	Loveswept
119	The Stallion Man	12/85	Bantam	Loveswept
200	With No Reservations	07/87	Bantam	Loveswept

Brandewyne, Rebecca

	Night Magic	09/93	Avon	Anthology
	New Year's Resolution: Husband	01/96	Harlequin	Anthology
	Hired Husband	11/96	Harlequin	Fortune's Children
	Dust Devil	03/96	Mira	
	Beyond The Starlit Frost		Pocket	
	Passion Moon Rising		Pocket	
	Abduction And Seduction	03/95	Silhouette	Anthology
955	Wildcat	10/95	Silhouette	Desire
	Desperado	11/92	Warner	
	Across A Starlit Sea		Warner	
	And Gold Was Ours		Warner	
	Desire In Disguise		Warner	
	Forever My Love		Warner	
	Heartland		Warner	
	Love, Cherish Me		Warner	
	No Gentle Love		Warner	
	The Outlaw Hearts		Warner	
	Rainbow's End		Warner	
	Rose Of Rapture		Warner	
	Upon A Moon-Dark Moor		Warner	
	Swan Road	01/94	Warner	
	Rapture's Beef	03/95	Warner	
	The Jacardia Tree	10/95	Warner	
	A Spring Bouquet	05/96	Zebra	Anthology

Brandon, Alicia

121	Love Beyond Question		Harlequin American
40	Full Circle		Harlequin Intrigue

Brandon, Joyce

After Eden		Preston House	
The Lady And The Outlaw		Preston House	
The Lady And The Lawman		Preston House	
Adobe Palace	/90	Preston House	
The Lady And The Robber Baron	/90	Preston House	

AUTHOR/TITLE INDEX

Brandon, Michelle
    Touch Of Heaven   09/92   Diamond
    Heaven On Earth   09/93   Diamond
Brandon, William
  63   The Dangerous Dead   /50   Harlequin
Brandt, Cate
    Silken Chains   Zebra
    Colorado Jewel   Zebra Heartfire
    Texas Glory   Zebra Heartfire
Brant, Kylie
  528 Mclain's Law (Premiere)   10/93   Silhouette Intimate Moments
  552 Rancher's Choice   02/94   Silhouette Intimate Moments
  622 An Irresistible Man   02/95   Silhouette Intimate Moments
  693 Guarding Raine   02/96   Silhouette Intimate Moments
Brantley, Paige
    Heart's Awakening   12/95   Zebra
    Captive To His Kiss   Zebra Heartfire
Brauer, Deanna
  599 Simply Sam   09/88   Silhouette Romance
Braun, Matthew
    This Loving Promise   Zebra Hist. & Family Sagas
Braxton-Barshon, Brenna
    Southern Oaks   05/91   Harper
    Through All Eternity   05/92   Harper
Brayfield, Celia
    The Princess   07/92   Bantam Fanfare
Bremer, Joanne
  106 To Love A Thief   /86   Dell Candlelight Ecstasy Supr.
  302 It's All In The Game   Harlequin Superromance
Brendan, Mary
    Beloved Avenger   11/91   Zebra Regency
    A Gentleman's Mistress   Zebra Regency
Brent, Audrey
  63   Snowflakes In The Sun   02/81   Silhouette Romance
Brent, Madeleine
    The Long Masquerade
    Golden Urchin   Ballantine
    Tregaron's Daughter   Doubleday
    Stormswift   Doubleday
    A Heritage Of Shadows   Doubleday
    The Capricorn Stone   Doubleday
    Merlin's Keep   Doubleday
    Stranger At Wildings   Doubleday
    Moonraker's Bride   Doubleday
Brett, Katheryn

331

AUTHOR/TITLE INDEX

Brett, Katheryn

195	The Genuine Article	06/87	Silhouette Intimate Moments

Brett, Rosalind

656	Stormy Haven	/62	Harlequin
693	Towards The Sun	/62	Harlequin
731	Whispering Palms	/63	Harlequin
740	Nurse On Holiday	/63	Harlequin
760	Fair Horizon	/63	Harlequin
773	Winds In The Wilderness	/63	Harlequin
783	Portrait Of Susan	/63	Harlequin
800	Sweet Waters	/64	Harlequin
815	Young Tracy	/64	Harlequin
839	Tangle In Sunshine	/64	Harlequin
856	Too Young To Marry	/64	Harlequin
869	The Reluctant Guest	/64	Harlequin
877	Dangerous Waters	/64	Harlequin
908	Elizabeth Browne, Children's Nurse	/65	Harlequin
952	A Cottage In Spain	/65	Harlequin
989	Hotel Mirador	/66	Harlequin
1101	The Girl At White Drift	/67	Harlequin
1131	The Bolambo Affair	/67	Harlequin
1176	Winds Of Enchantment	/68	Harlequin
1319	Brittle Bondage	/69	Harlequin
43	They Came To Valeira	/74	Harlequin Presents
55	Love This Stranger	/74	Harlequin Presents
71	And No Regrets	/74	Harlequin Presents

Bretton, Barbara

	One And Only	09/94	Berkley
	Royal Privilege	09/94	Berkley
	The Long Way Home	/95	Berkley
	Maybe This Time	05/95	Berkley
	Sleeping Alone	04/97	Berkley
	Always	/98	Berkley
	Home For The Holidays	12/96	Berkley Anthology
	Fire's Lady	/89	Crown
	Operation: Baby	/97	Harlequin American
	Operation: Family	/97	Harlequin American
3	Loves Changes		Harlequin American
49	Sweetest Of Debts		Harlequin American
91	No Safe Place		Harlequin American
138	The Edge Of Forever		Harlequin American
161	Promises In The Night	08/86	Harlequin American
175	Shooting Star		Harlequin American
211	Second Harmony		Harlequin American
230	Nobody's Baby		Harlequin American
305	Mother Knows Best		Harlequin American
322	Mrs. Scrooge		Harlequin American

AUTHOR/TITLE INDEX

Bretton, Barbara

365	Sentimental Journey		Harlequin American
369	Stranger In Paradise		Harlequin American
393	Bundle Of Joy		Harlequin American
441	Daddy's Girl	06/92	Harlequin American
493	Renegade Lover	07/93	Harlequin American
554	The Invisible Groom	10/94	Harlequin American
193	Playing For Time		Harlequin American Pax
251	Honeymoon Hotel		Harlequin American Pax
274	A Fine Madness		Harlequin American Pax
355	All We Know Of Heaven		Harlequin American Pax
505	The Bride Came C.O.D.	10/93	Harlequin American Pax
581	Operation: Husband	05/95	Harlequin American Pax
	American Romance 10th Anniversary	08/93	Harlequin Anthology
	Love And Laughter	09/94	Harlequin Anthology
14	Bundle Of Joy	05/96	Harlequin Here Come The Grooms
	The Perfect Wife	/97	Harlequin Historical
135	The Reluctant Bride	08/92	Harlequin Historical
18	Starfire		Harlequin Intrigue
28	Nobody's Baby	11/94	Harlequin Men Made In America
	I Do, I Do	04/92	Harlequin To Have And To Hold
	No Safe Place	06/95	Mira
	Shooting Star	12/95	Mira
	Starfire	03/96	Mira
	Guilty Pleasures	09/96	Mira
1	Somewhere In Time	03/94	Mira Time Travel
2	Tomorrow And Always	04/94	Mira Time Travel
3	Destiny's Child	09/95	Mira Time Travel
	Midnight Lover	07/89	Pocket

Brian, Marilyn

19	Passion's Glow	/84	Berkley To Have And To Hold

Bright, Elizabeth

	Passion's Heirs		Richard Gallen
	Reap The Wild Harvest		Richard Gallen
	My Beloved Enemy	05/93	Starlog Rhapsody Historical

Bright, Laurey

470	Summers Past	01/93	Silhouette Intimate Moments
621	A Perfect Marriage	02/95	Silhouette Intimate Moments
107	Tears Of Morning	10/81	Silhouette Romance
125	Sweet Vengeance	01/82	Silhouette Romance
356	Long Way From Home	04/85	Silhouette Romance
525	The Rainbow Way	08/87	Silhouette Romance
568	Jacinth	04/88	Silhouette Romance
62	Deep Waters	12/82	Silhouette Special Edition
143	When Morning Comes	01/84	Silhouette Special Edition
213	Fetters Of The Past	01/85	Silhouette Special Edition
516	A Sudden Sunlight	03/89	Silhouette Special Edition

Bright, Laurey

564	Games Of Chance	11/89	Silhouette Special Edition
586	A Guilty Passion	03/90	Silhouette Special Edition
761	The Older Man	08/92	Silhouette Special Edition
820	The Kindness Of Strangers	06/93	Silhouette Special Edition
916	An Interrupted Marriage	10/94	Silhouette Special Edition

Brindley, Louise

Forever Roses		Pinnacle Press

Brisco, Gwen

Calico Palace		Historical

Brisken, Jacqueline

Dreams Are Not Enough

Bristol, Leigh

Angel	/92	Warner	
Twice Blessed	/91	Warner	
Sunswept	/90	Warner	
Hearts Of Fire	/89	Warner	
Legacy	04/93	Warner	
1	Scarlet Sunrise	/87	Warner Texas Trilogy
2	Amber Skies	/87	Warner Texas Trilogy
3	Silver Twilight	/87	Warner Texas Trilogy

Britt, Katrina

1300	A Kiss In A Gondola	/69	Harlequin
1393	Healer Of Hearts	/70	Harlequin
1490	The Fabulous Island	/71	Harlequin
1525	The Unknown Quest	/71	Harlequin
1626	A Spray Of Edelweiss	/72	Harlequin
1679	The Gentle Flame	/73	Harlequin
1703	Reluctant Voyager	/73	Harlequin
1727	Strange Bewilderment	/73	Harlequin
1760	The Guarded Gates	/74	Harlequin
1793	The King Of Spades	/74	Harlequin
1866	The Greater Happiness	/75	Harlequin
1892	The House Called Sakura	/75	Harlequin
1906	Take Back Your Love	/75	Harlequin
1969	The Spanish Grandee	/76	Harlequin
2017	The Emerald Garden	/76	Harlequin
2039	If Today Be Sweet	/77	Harlequin
2070	The Villa Faustino	/77	Harlequin
2121	The Faithful Heart	/77	Harlequin
2143	The Silver Tree	/78	Harlequin
2171	The Enchanted Woods	/78	Harlequin
2212	Open Not The Door	/78	Harlequin
207	Girl In Blue	/77	Harlequin Presents
2238	The Hills Beyond		Harlequin Romance
2269	The Midnight Sun		Harlequin Romance

AUTHOR/TITLE INDEX

Britt, Katrina

2305	The Man On The Peak	Harlequin	Romance
2343	Flowers For My Love	Harlequin	Romance
2371	Island For Dreams	Harlequin	Romance
2397	The Wrong Man	Harlequin	Romance
2449	Hotel Jacarandas	Harlequin	Romance

Britton, Vickie

Path Of The Jaguar	Avalon	Mystery Romance
The Seven Sapphires Of Mardi Gras	Zebra	Gothic

Broadrick, Annette

	Undercover Lovers	06/94	Harlequin	Anthology
13	Circumstantial Evidence	05/96	Harlequin	Here Come The Grooms
27	Married?!	07/96	Harlequin	Here Come The Grooms
	California Deceptions	09/93	Harlequin	Men Made In America
5	Deceptions	09/93	Harlequin	Men Made In America
25	Choices	10/94	Harlequin	Men Made In America
	Hunter's Prey	08/95	Harlequin	Western Lovers
	Return To Yesterday	10/95	Harlequin	Western Lovers
	Where There Is Love	05/92	Silhouette	
	Silhouette Summer Sizzlers	06/94	Silhouette	Anthology
	Wanted: Mother - "What's A Dad To Do?"	05/96	Silhouette	Anthology
	Christmas Magic	/88	Silhouette	Christmas Stories
185	Hunter's Prey	01/85	Silhouette	Desire
219	Bachelor Father	07/85	Silhouette	Desire
242	Hawk's Flight	11/85	Silhouette	Desire
272	Deceptions	04/86	Silhouette	Desire
283	Choices	06/86	Silhouette	Desire
314	Heat Of The Night	11/86	Silhouette	Desire
336	Made In Heaven	02/87	Silhouette	Desire
360	Return To Yesterday	06/87	Silhouette	Desire
367	Adam's Story	08/87	Silhouette	Desire
414	Momentary Marriage	03/88	Silhouette	Desire
433	With All My Heart	07/88	Silhouette	Desire
464	A Touch Of Spring	12/88	Silhouette	Desire
499	Irresistible	06/89	Silhouette	Desire
552	A Loving Spirit	02/90	Silhouette	Desire
577	Candlelight For Two	07/90	Silhouette	Desire
666	Lone Wolf	09/91	Silhouette	Desire
714	Where There Is Love	05/92	Silhouette	Desire
734	Love Texas Style!	09/92	Silhouette	Desire
739	Courtship Texas Style!	10/92	Silhouette	Desire
745	Marriage Texas Style!	11/92	Silhouette	Desire
793	Zeke	07/93	Silhouette	Desire
883	Temptation Texas Style!	10/94	Silhouette	Desire
925	Mysterious Mountain Man	05/95	Silhouette	Desire
979	Megan's Marriage	02/96	Silhouette	Desire
992	The Groom, I Presume?	04/96	Silhouette	Desire

AUTHOR/TITLE INDEX

Broadrick, Annette

329	Circumstantial Evidence	11/84	Silhouette Romance
359	Provocative Peril	05/85	Silhouette Romance
412	Sound Of Summer	02/86	Silhouette Romance
442	Unheavenly Angel	07/86	Silhouette Romance
501	Strange Enchantment	04/87	Silhouette Romance
533	Mystery Lover	10/87	Silhouette Romance
544	That's What Friends Are For	12/87	Silhouette Romance
609	Come Be My Love	10/88	Silhouette Romance
676	A Love Remembered	10/89	Silhouette Romance
742	Married?!	09/90	Silhouette Romance
796	The Gemini Man	06/91	Silhouette Romance
976	Daddy's Angel	12/93	Silhouette Romance
1018	Impromptu Bride (Celebration 1000!)	07/94	Silhouette Romance
1139	Instant Mommy	03/96	Silhouette Romance
877	Mystery Wife (That Special Woman!)	04/94	Silhouette Special Edition

Brocato, Kathryn

8	Storm Warning	08/90	Meteor

Brockman, Suzanne

365	No Ordinary Man	04/96	Harlequin Intrigue
168	Future Perfect	08/93	Meteor Kismet
575	Hero Under Cover	06/94	Silhouette Intimate Moments
647	Not Without Risk	06/95	Silhouette Intimate Moments

Brockmann, Suzanne

787	Kiss And Tell	05/96	Bantam Loveswept
180	Love Scenes	09/93	Meteor
681	A Man To Die For	12/95	Silhouette Intimate Moments
720	Prince Joe	06/96	Silhouette Intimate Moments

Brockway, Connie

	Promise Me Heaven	02/94	Avon
	Mirage	06/95	Avon
	Heaven In Your Eyes	06/95	Avon
	Anything For Love	10/94	Avon Historical
	A Dangerous Man	07/96	Dell

Brodnax, Elizabeth

	A Splendid Scheme	07/94	Jove Regency
	The Marquis Of Carabas	/91	Walker

Brondos, Sharon

4	White Lightning	06/93	Harlequin Crystal Creek
50	Special Touches	05/95	Harlequin Men Made In America
32	Kiss Of Darkness	05/94	Harlequin Shadows
153	A Magic Serenade	02/85	Harlequin Superromance
183	Partners For Life	10/85	Harlequin Superromance
215	A Primitive Affair	06/86	Harlequin Superromance
228	Give And Take	09/86	Harlequin Superromance
266	Search For The Rainbow	07/87	Harlequin Superromance

AUTHOR/TITLE INDEX

Brondos, Sharon

328	Special Touches	10/88	Harlequin	Superromance
353	Special Treasures	04/89	Harlequin	Superromance
459	A Place To Land	07/91	Harlequin	Superromance
505	East Of The Moon	06/92	Harlequin	Superromance
527	Southern Reason, Western Rhymes	02/93	Harlequin	Superromance
554	The Marriage Ticket	07/93	Harlequin	Superromance
574	Doc Wyoming (Women Who Dare)	12/93	Harlequin	Superromance
588	Luck Of The Irish	03/94	Harlequin	Superromance
657	The West Virginian	08/95	Harlequin	Superromance
70	In Perfect Harmony	08/85	Harlequin	Temptation
6	Change Of Pace	08/90	Meteor	

Bronson, Maureen

32	Delta Pearl		Harlequin	Historical
96	Ragtime Dawn	10/91	Harlequin	Historical
149	Tender Verdict		Harlequin	Superromance
496	Blind Faith	04/92	Harlequin	Superromance

Brooke, Alice

242	No Guarantee	08/83	Silhouette	Romance
320	Harbor Lights	09/84	Silhouette	Romance

Brookes, Beth

36	Hold Fast Til Morning	/82	Berkley	Second Chance At Love
53	Untamed Desire	/82	Berkley	Second Chance At Love
183	Torrid Nights	/84	Berkley	Second Chance At Love

Brooks, Betty

	Comanche Passion		Zebra
	Apache Sunset		Zebra
	Heart Of The Mountains		Zebra
	Love's Endless Flame		Zebra
	Savage Flame		Zebra
	Passion's Siren	/88	Zebra
	Warrior's Destiny	/95	Zebra
	Apache Captive		Zebra Heartfire
	Comanche Embrace		Zebra Heartfire
	Warrior's Embrace		Zebra Heartfire
	Wild Texas Magnolia		Zebra Heartfire
	Passion's Angel	/87	Zebra Heartfire
	Viking Mistress	09/94	Zebra Historical

Brooks, Caroline

	Marchman's Lady	02/86	Nal Regency
	The Runaway Princess	04/87	Nal Regency
	A Sea Change	12/87	Nal Regency
	Regency Rose	09/88	Nal Regency
	An Old Scandal		Nal Penguin Regency

Brooks, Helen

262	Stone Angel	12/95	Harlequin

337

Brooks, Helen
   23   Deceitful Lover   01/96 Harlequin Presents
3350 And The Bride Wore Black   02/95 Harlequin Romance
3378 Angels Do Have Wings   09/95 Harlequin Romance
       The Sultan's Favourite   10/95 Worldwide Libr. Stolen Moments

Brooks, Janice Young
       In Love's Own Time   Playboy Press

Brooks, Kandi
  472 The Real World   08/88 Silhouette Special Edition

Browing, Dixie
    5 Best Man For The Job   03/96 Harlequin Here Come The Grooms

Brown, Amy Belding
       Island Summer Love   07/92 St. Martin's
       Strawberry Lace   10/94 St. Martin's

Brown, Beth
  224 Lady Hobo   /53 Harlequin

Brown, Diana
       A Debt Of Honour   03/87 Nal Regency
       Come Be My Love   Nal Penguin Regency
       The Sandalwood Fan   Nal Penguin Regency
       St. Martin's Summer   Nal Penguin Regency
       The Sandalwood Fan   St. Martin's
       Come Be My Love   St. Martin's
       The Emerald Necklace   St. Martin's
       The Blue Dragon   St. Martin's

Brown, Dr. Alan
  415 The Normal Child   /58 Harlequin

Brown, Joy
   72 Night Of Terror   /50 Harlequin

Brown, Leslie
       Golden Dolly   Pageant

Brown, Lisa G.
       Crazy For Lovin' You   04/94 Harper
       Billy Bob Walker Got Married 04/93 Harper

Brown, Micki
       Once A Rebel   01/92 St. Martin's

Brown, Sandra
       Another Dream   Bantam
       Texas! Lucky   02/91 Bantam Fanfare
       Texas! Chase   08/91 Bantam Fanfare
       Texas! Sage   03/92 Bantam Fanfare
    1 Heaven's Price   05/83 Bantam Loveswept
   22 Breakfast In Bed   11/83 Bantam Loveswept
   51 Send No Flowers   07/84 Bantam Loveswept
   66 In A Class By Itself   10/84 Bantam Loveswept
   79 Thursday's Child   02/85 Bantam Loveswept

AUTHOR/TITLE INDEX

Brown, Sandra

115	Riley In The Morning	11/85	Bantam	Loveswept
136	The Rana Look	04/86	Bantam	Loveswept
154	22 Indigo Place	08/86	Bantam	Loveswept
185	Sunny Chandler's Return	03/87	Bantam	Loveswept
197	Demon Rumm	06/87	Bantam	Loveswept
217	Fanta C	11/87	Bantam	Loveswept
229	Tidings Of Great Joy	01/88	Bantam	Loveswept
252	Adam's Fall	05/88	Bantam	Loveswept
263	Hawk O' Tolle's Hostage	06/88	Bantam	Loveswept
300	Long Time Coming	01/89	Bantam	Loveswept
336	Temperatures Rising	07/89	Bantam	Loveswept
366	A Whole New Light	12/89	Bantam	Loveswept
1	Tomorrow's Promise		Harlequin	American
	The Devil's Own	11/94	Mira	
	Tomorrow's Promise	03/95	Mira	
	Led Astray	03/95	Mira	
	The Thrill Of Victory	03/95	Mira	
	Tiger Prince	03/95	Mira	
	Honor Bound	03/95	Mira	
	The Thrill Of Victory	03/95	Mira	
	A Secret Splendor	08/95	Mira	
	Two Alone	06/95	Mira	
	A Secret Splendor	05/96	Mira	
	A Treasure Worth Seeking	09/92	Warner	
	French Silk	04/93	Warner	
	Another Dawn		Warner	
	Best Kept Secrets	02/94	Warner	
	Breath Of Scandal		Warner	
	Mirror Image		Warner	
	Sunset Embrace		Warner	
	Shadows Of Yesterday	02/92	Warner	
	Hidden Fires	11/94	Warner	
	Where There's Smoke	05/93	Warner	
	The Silken Web	10/93	Warner	
	Eloquent Silence	01/95	Warner	
	Prime Time	09/95	Warner	
	Love Beyond Reason	08/94	Warner	
	Slow Heat In Heaven	02/94	Warner	
	Charade	02/95	Warner	
	The Witness	07/95	Warner	
	Prime Time	08/95	Warner	

Brown, Virginia Lynn

Defy The Thunder
Storm Of Passion
Desert Dreams
Moonflower

AUTHOR/TITLE INDEX

Brown, Virginia Lynn

The Moonrider	06/94	Bantam	
Jade Moon	12/95	Jove	
Timeswept Brides	07/96	Jove Anthology	
The Veiled Vixen	/92	Walker	
Wildfire		Warner	
Emerald Nights		Zebra	
Hidden Touch		Zebra	
Renegade Embrace		Zebra	
Wildest Heart	04/94	Zebra	
Commanche Moon	04/93	Zebra Historical	

Browne, Lydia

Passing Fancy	10/94	Diamond A Town Called Harmony	
Heart Strings	09/93	Diamond Homespun	
Wedding Bells	01/94	Diamond Homespun	
Heart's Desire	02/95	Diamond Love Potion Collection	
Love Potion	02/95	Jove Anthology	
Autumn Fires	08/96	Jove Historical	
Summer Lightning	07/95	Jove Homespun	
Honeysuckle Song	01/96	Jove Homespun	

Browning, Amanda

1055	Perfect Strangers		Harlequin Presents	
1329	Web Of Deceit		Harlequin Presents	
1400	Something From The Heart	10/91	Harlequin Presents	
1432	A Promise To Repay	02/92	Harlequin Presents	
1566	A Time For Love	06/93	Harlequin Presents	
1566	A Time For Love	06/93	Harlequin Presents	
1677	An Old Enchantment	08/94	Harlequin Presents	
1724	Savage Destiny (Too Hot To Handle)	02/95	Harlequin Presents	
1742	Trail Of Love	05/95	Harlequin Presents	
1789	The Bitter Price Of Love	01/96	Harlequin Presents	
1750	Enemy Within	07/95	Harlequin Presents Plus	
3031	The Asking Price		Harlequin Romance	

Browning, Diana

All The Golden Promises		Fawcett

Browning, Dixie

	Spring Fancy - "Grace & The Law"	02/94	Harlequin Anthology	
	Bad Boys	09/93	Harlequin By Request: Anthology	
	White Witch		Harlequin Historical	
	Dandelion		Harlequin Historical	
	Stormwalker		Harlequin Historical	
	Gideon's Fall		Harlequin Historical	
	The Mariner's Bride		Harlequin Historical	
	A Promise Kept		Harlequin Historical	
20	The Love Thing	07/94	Harlequin Men Made In America	
33	The Security Man	02/95	Harlequin Men Made In America	

Browning, Dixie

	The Hawk And The Honey	04/95	Harlequin	Western Lovers
	Silhouette Spring Fancy Collection	03/94	Silhouette	Anthology
	Henry The Ninth	/87	Silhouette	Christmas Stories 1987
68	Shadow Of Yesterday	06/83	Silhouette	Desire
91	Image Of Love	10/83	Silhouette	Desire
111	The Hawk And The Honey	01/84	Silhouette	Desire
121	Late Rising Moon	03/84	Silhouette	Desire
169	Stormwatch	11/84	Silhouette	Desire
188	The Tender Barbarian	02/85	Silhouette	Desire
212	Matchmaker's Moon	06/85	Silhouette	Desire
234	A Bird In Hand	09/85	Silhouette	Desire
264	In The Palm Of Her Hand	02/86	Silhouette	Desire
324	A Winter Woman	12/86	Silhouette	Desire
337	There Once Was A Lover	03/87	Silhouette	Desire
403	Fate Takes A Holiday	02/88	Silhouette	Desire
427	Along Comes Jones	06/88	Silhouette	Desire
474	Thin Ice	01/89	Silhouette	Desire
517	Beginner's Luck	09/89	Silhouette	Desire
541	Ships In The Night	01/90	Silhouette	Desire
588	Twice In A Blue Moon	08/90	Silhouette	Desire
637	Just Say Yes	05/91	Silhouette	Desire
678	Not A Marrying Man	11/91	Silhouette	Desire
691	Gus And The Nice Lady	02/92	Silhouette	Desire
720	Best Man For The Job	06/92	Silhouette	Desire
780	Hazards Of The Heart	04/93	Silhouette	Desire
801	Kane's Way	08/93	Silhouette	Desire
820	Keegan's Hunt (Outer Banks)	11/93	Silhouette	Desire
853	Lucy And The Stone	05/94	Silhouette	Desire
890	Two Hearts, Slightly Used.	11/94	Silhouette	Desire
949	Alex And The Angel	09/95	Silhouette	Desire
985	The Beauty, The Beast And The Baby	03/96	Silhouette	Desire
1011	The Baby Notion	07/96	Silhouette	Desire
12	Unreasonable Summer	06/80	Silhouette	Romance
38	Tumbled Wall	10/80	Silhouette	Romance
53	Chance Tomorrow	01/81	Silhouette	Romance
73	Wren Of Paradise	04/81	Silhouette	Romance
93	East Of Today	07/81	Silhouette	Romance
113	Winter Blossom	11/81	Silhouette	Romance
142	Renegade Player	04/82	Silhouette	Romance
164	Island On The Hill	07/82	Silhouette	Romance
172	Logic Of The Heart	09/82	Silhouette	Romance
191	Loving Rescue	12/82	Silhouette	Romance
203	A Secret Valentine	02/83	Silhouette	Romance
221	Practical Dreamer	05/83	Silhouette	Romance
275	Visible Heart	02/84	Silhouette	Romance
292	Journey To Quiet Waters	05/84	Silhouette	Romance

Browning, Dixie

305	The Love Thing	07/84	Silhouette	Romance
323	First Things Last	10/84	Silhouette	Romance
381	Something For Herself	08/85	Silhouette	Romance
460	Reluctant Dreamer	09/86	Silhouette	Romance
527	A Matter Of Timing	09/87	Silhouette	Romance
747	The Homing Instinct	09/90	Silhouette	Romance
50	Finders Keepers	10/82	Silhouette	Special Edition
110	Reach Out To Cherish	08/83	Silhouette	Special Edition
181	Just Deserts	08/84	Silhouette	Special Edition
205	Time And Tide	12/84	Silhouette	Special Edition
228	By Any Other Name	03/85	Silhouette	Special Edition
314	The Security Man	06/86	Silhouette	Special Edition
414	Belonging	10/87	Silhouette	Special Edition
	Grace And The Law	04/94	Silhouette	Spring Fancy Trilogy
7	Single Female Reluctantly Seeks ...	11/95	Silhouette	Yours Truly
	The Warfield Bride		Topaz	Historical
	Bedeviled		Topaz	Historical
	Slow Surrender		Topaz	Historical
	Halfway Home	08/96	Topaz	Historical

Browning, Pamela

	Simple Gifts	/88	Harlequin	American
	Fly Away	/88	Harlequin	American
	Harvest Home	/88	Harlequin	American
101	Cherished Beginnings	/85	Harlequin	American
116	Handyman Special	/85	Harlequin	American
123	Through Eyes Of Love	/85	Harlequin	American
131	Interior Designs	/85	Harlequin	American
140	Ever Since Eve	/86	Harlequin	American
150	Forever Is A Long Time	/86	Harlequin	American
170	To Touch The Stars	10/86	Harlequin	American
181	Flutterby Princess	01/87	Harlequin	American
194	Ice Crystals	/87	Harlequin	American
227	Kisses In The Rain	12/87	Harlequin	American
237	Heartland Trilogy: Simple Gifts	03/88	Harlequin	American
241	Heartland Trilogy: Fly Away	04/88	Harlequin	American
245	Heartland Trilogy: Harvest Home	05/88	Harlequin	American
287	Feathers In The Wind	/89	Harlequin	American
297	Until Spring	/89	Harlequin	American
354	Humble Pie	/90	Harlequin	American
384	A Man Worth Loving	/91	Harlequin	American
420	For Auld Lang Syne	12/91	Harlequin	American
439	Sunshine And Shadows	05/92	Harlequin	American
451	Morgan's Child	08/92	Harlequin	American
516	Merry Christmas, Baby	12/93	Harlequin	American
565	The World's Last Bachelor	01/95	Harlequin	American
600	Angel's Baby	09/95	Harlequin	American

AUTHOR/TITLE INDEX

Bucheister, Patt

614	Stroke By Stroke	05/93	Bantam Loveswept
650	Tame A Wildcat	11/93	Bantam Loveswept
688	Strange Bedfellows	05/94	Bantam Loveswept
728	Hot Southern Nights	02/95	Bantam Loveswept
750	Wild In The Night	08/95	Bantam Loveswept
773	Tilt At Windmills	10/92	Silhouette Special Edition
899	Unpredictable	07/94	Silhouette Special Edition
953	Instant Family	04/95	Silhouette Special Edition

Buck, Carole

	Magic Slippers	07/96	Avon Anthology
	Love And Laughter	06/89	Berkley Second Chance At Love
269	Love Play	/85	Berkley Second Chance At Love
289	Fallen Angel	/85	Berkley Second Chance At Love
	Summer Sizzlers	06/93	Harlequin Anthology
46	Make Believe Marriage	10/96	Harlequin Here Come The Grooms
565	Time Enough For Love	05/90	Silhouette Desire
614	Paradise Remembered	01/91	Silhouette Desire
644	White Lace Promises	06/91	Silhouette Desire
677	Red-Hot Satin	11/91	Silhouette Desire
699	Knight And Day	03/92	Silhouette Desire
750	Blue Sky Guy	11/92	Silhouette Desire
808	Sparks	09/93	Silhouette Desire
899	Dark Intentions	12/94	Silhouette Desire
934	Annie Says I Do (Wedding Belles)	06/95	Silhouette Desire
976	Peachy's Proposal	01/96	Silhouette Desire
989	Zoe And The Best Man	03/96	Silhouette Desire
752	Make-Believe Marriage	10/90	Silhouette Romance

Buck, Gayle

	The Desperate Viscount	07/94	
	Regency Christmas		Nal
	Hearts Betrayed		Nal
	Willowswood Match		Nal
	The Waltzing Widow	07/91	Nal Regency
	The Hidden Heart	05/92	Nal Regency
	Lord Rathbone's Flirt	12/94	Nal Regency
	Full-Moon Magic	09/92	Nal Super Signet Historical
	Mutual Consent	04/91	Nal Penguin
	A Chance Encounter	11/91	Nal Penguin
	Lord John's Lady	03/88	Nal Penguin Regency
	The Demon Rake		Nal Penguin Regency
	The Righteous Rakehill	11/88	Nal Penguin Regency
	Love's Masquerade	06/86	Nal Penguin Regency
	Honor Beseiged	02/90	Nal Penguin Regency
	Miss Dower's Paragon	07/93	Penguin Regency
	Willowswood Match	/89	Signet Regency
	Lady Althea's Bargain	08/95	Signet Regency

AUTHOR/TITLE INDEX

Buckingham, Nancy
  192   Quest For Alexis   Dell Candlelight

Budd, Carol
        Scarlet Scandals   Pocket

Bull, Lois
  314   Forbidden   /54   Harlequin

Bullard, Anne
   15   A Matter Of Time   10/90 Meteor
  157   Fire On The Mountain   07/93 Meteor Kismet

Bulock, Lynn
        Kisses Worth Waiting For   /91   Avalon
        Leave Yesterday Behind   /90   Avalon
        The Promise Of Summer   /90   Avalon
        Roses For Caroline   /89   Avalon
        Tallie's Song   /89   Avalon
        Heart Games   /91   Avalon Career Romance
  108   In Your Dreams   09/92 Meteor
 1053 Surprise Package (Under The Mistletoe) 12/94 Silhouette Romance
 1154 And Mommy Makes Three   05/96 Silhouette Romance

Bunkley, Anita
        Black Gold   05/94 Dutton

Burcell, Robin
        When Midnight Comes   12/95 Harper Monogram

Burchell, Mary
  409   Hospital Corridors   /58   Harlequin
  422   Then Come Kiss Me   /58   Harlequin
  461   For Ever And Ever   /59   Harlequin
  468   Surgeon Of Distinction   /59   Harlequin
  478   Dear Trustee   /59   Harlequin
  494   Love Is My Reason   /59   Harlequin
  521   On The Air   /60   Harlequin
  528   Wife By Arrangement   /60   Harlequin
  533   Over The Blue Mountains   /60   Harlequin
  546   Choose The One You'll Marry /60   Harlequin
  565   Paris--And My Love   /61   Harlequin
  603   Across The Counter   /61   Harlequin
  605   Dear Sir   /61   Harlequin
  616   Love Him Or Leave Him   /61   Harlequin
  627   With All My Worldly Goods   /61   Harlequin
  658   Reluctant Relation   /62   Harlequin
  686   Stolen Heart   /62   Harlequin
  712   House Of Conflict   /63   Harlequin
  746   Nurse Marika, Loyal In All (Loyal In All) /63   Harlequin
  782   Inherit My Heart   /63   Harlequin
  813   The Wedding Dress   /64   Harlequin
  837   Away Went Love   /64   Harlequin

Burchell, Mary

844	Meet Me Again (Nurse Alison's Trust)	/64	Harlequin
871	Yours To Command	/64	Harlequin
895	And Falsely Pledge My Love	/65	Harlequin
915	The Strange Quest Of Nurse Anne	/65	Harlequin
956	Take Me With You	/65	Harlequin
980	A Song Begins	/66	Harlequin
1003	The Heart Cannot Forget	/66	Harlequin
1029	Choose Which You Will	/66	Harlequin
1052	Meant For Each Other	/66	Harlequin
1075	Cinderella After Midnight	/67	Harlequin
1100	The Broken Wing	/67	Harlequin
1117	Dearly Beloved	/67	Harlequin
1138	Loving Is Giving	/67	Harlequin
1165	Ward Of Lucifer	/67	Harlequin
1187	Sweet Adventure	/68	Harlequin
1214	The Marshall Family	/68	Harlequin
1244	When Love Is Blind	/68	Harlequin
1270	Though Worlds Apart	/69	Harlequin
1298	Missing From Home	/69	Harlequin
1330	A Home For Joy	/69	Harlequin
1354	When Love's Beginning	/69	Harlequin
1382	To Journey Together	/70	Harlequin
1405	The Curtain Rises	/70	Harlequin
1431	The Other Linding Girl	/70	Harlequin
1455	Girl With A Challenge	/70	Harlequin
1474	My Sister Celia	/71	Harlequin
1508	Child Of Music	/71	Harlequin
1543	But Not For Me	/71	Harlequin
1567	Do Not Go, My Love	/72	Harlequin
1587	Music Of The Heart	/72	Harlequin
1632	One Man's Heart	/72	Harlequin
1655	It's Rumoured In The Village	/73	Harlequin
1704	Except My Love	/73	Harlequin
1733	Call And I'll Come	/73	Harlequin
1767	Unbidden Melody	/74	Harlequin
1792	Pay Me Tomorrow	/74	Harlequin
1811	Strangers May Marry	/74	Harlequin
1834	Song Cycle	/74	Harlequin
1871	The Brave In Heart	/75	Harlequin
1890	Tell Me My Fortune	/75	Harlequin
1919	Just A Nice Girl	/75	Harlequin
1936	Remembered Serenade	/75	Harlequin
1947	The Girl In The Blue Dress	/76	Harlequin
1964	Under The Stars Of Paris	/76	Harlequin
2043	Elusive Harmony	/77	Harlequin
2061	Honey	/77	Harlequin

Burke, Lydia

594	The Devil And Jessie Webster	09/94	Silhouette Intimate Moments

Burkhardt, Mary

	The Panther And The Rose	12/93	Zebra
	Highland Ecstasy	04/93	Zebra
	Midnight Heat	11/91	Zebra Heartfire
	Forbidden Hearts		Zebra Heartfire

Burnes, Caroline

86	A Deadly Breed	03/88	Harlequin Intrigue
100	Measure Of Deceit		Harlequin Intrigue
115	Phantom Filly		Harlequin Intrigue
134	Fear Familiar		Harlequin Intrigue
154	The Jaguar's Eye		Harlequin Intrigue
155	Shattered Vows	02/91	Harlequin Intrigue
186	Deadly Currents	05/92	Harlequin Intrigue
204	Fatal Ingredients	11/92	Harlequin Intrigue
215	Too Familiar	02/93	Harlequin Intrigue
229	Hoodwinked	06/93	Harlequin Intrigue
241	Flesh And Blood	09/93	Harlequin Intrigue
256	Thrice Familiar	12/93	Harlequin Intrigue
267	Cutting Edge	03/94	Harlequin Intrigue
277	Shades Of Familiar	06/94	Harlequin Intrigue
293	Familiar Remedy	10/94	Harlequin Intrigue
322	Familiar Tale (Fear Familiar Mystery)	05/95	Harlequin Intrigue
343	Bewitching Familiar	10/95	Harlequin Intrigue
	The Deadly Breed	09/95	Harlequin Western Lovers

Burr, Kathaleen

	Rainbow Dreams	/92	Avalon
	Wintersong	/91	Avalon
	Home Is The Heart	/91	Avalon

Burroughs, Patricia

421	Some Enchanted Season	09/90	Bantam Loveswept
495	Scandalous	09/91	Bantam Loveswept
447	Razzmatazz	09/88	Silhouette Desire
490	Beguiled Again	04/89	Silhouette Desire
	What Wild Ecstasy		Zebra Heartfire

Burrows, Marjorie

	The Winter Hearts		Avon
77	The Loving Swords	05/91	Harlequin Historical

Burtis, Thomas

312	The Seeker	/54	Harlequin
315	The Black Eagle	/54	Harlequin

Burton, Katherine

292	Sweet Summer Heat		Harlequin Superromance
346	Calloway Corners: Tess	09/93	Harlequin Superromance

Busbee, Shirlee

Busbee, Shirlee

Each Time We Love	05/93	Avon
Deceive Not My Heart	/84	Avon Historical
Gypsy Lady		Avon Historical
Lady Vixen	/80	Avon Historical
Midnight Masquerade	/88	Avon Historical
Spanish Rose	/86	Avon Historical
Tiger Lily	/85	Avon Historical
While Passion Sleeps	/83	Avon Historical
Whisper To Me Of Love	/91	Avon Historical
Love A Dark Rider	07/94	Avon Historical
Lovers Forever	05/96	Warner

Bush, Christine

Where The Heart Belongs	/91	Avalon
Deadline For Danger	05/93	Avalon

Bush, Kim

A Gift Of Love	11/95	Pocket Anthology

Bush, Nancy

Scandal's Darling	07/94	
Lady Sundown		Pocket
Danner's Lady	08/90	Pocket
Jesse's Renegade		Pocket

Butler, Gwendoline

Albion Walk	Suspense
Sarsen Place	Ballantine
Olivia	Ballantine

Butler, Mary

Wolf's Lady

Butler, Mary E.

The Genuine Article	Diamond Regency
The Gallant Heiress	Warner

Butler, Penelope

660	Doctor Raoul's Romance	/62	Harlequin

Byers, Cordia

Eden	01/92	Fawcett
An Affair Of Interest		Fawcett
Heather	/79	Fawcett
Callista	/83	Fawcett
Nicole La Bell	/84	Fawcett
Silk And Steel	/85	Fawcett
Love Storm	/86	Fawcett
Priate Royale	/86	Fawcett
Star Of The West	/87	Fawcett
Ryan's Gold	/88	Fawcett
Lady's Fortune	/89	Fawcett
Desire And Deceive	/90	Fawcett

AUTHOR/TITLE INDEX

Byers, Cordia

Devon	/92	Fawcett
The Hawk And The Falcon	/90	Fawcett
The Black Angel	06/93	Fawcett Gold Medal
Midnight Surrender	10/94	Fawcett Historical

Byfield, Sue

2529	To Be Or Not To Be		Harlequin Romance

Byington, Deborah

Alone Together	08/93	Starlog Moonlight Contemporary
Stranded	/93	Starluck Press

Byrne, Beverly

A Lasting Fire	07/91	Bantam Fanfare
Flames Of Vengeance	12/91	Bantam Fanfare
The Morgan Woman		Bantam Fanfare 2 Trilogy
The Firebirds	05/92	Bantam Fanfare 3 Trilogy

Byron, Eve

Tempt Me Not	05/95	Avon

Cadell, Elizabeth

448	Bridal Array	/59	Harlequin
473	The Cuckoo In Spring	/59	Harlequin

Cail, Carol

116	Ivory Lies	11/92	Meteor

Caille, Julie

	The Rake And His Lady	/95	
966	A Family For Ronnie	06/95	Silhouette Special Edition
	Change Of Heart		Zebra Regency
	Impetuous Bride		Zebra Regency
	The Scandalous Marquis	04/90	Zebra Regency
	A Valentine's Day Fancy		Zebra Regency
	Lessons In Love	08/94	Zebra Regency

Caimi, Gina

125	Passionate Awakening	03/84	Silhouette Desire
174	A Wilder Enchantment	11/84	Silhouette Desire
218	Hearts Are Wild	07/85	Silhouette Desire
270	Unfinished Rhapsody	03/86	Silhouette Desire
308	Branded	10/86	Silhouette Desire
338	Forbidden Fantasies	03/87	Silhouette Desire
	Betrayals		Warner

Caine, Leslie

10	Bridge Of Love	06/80	Silhouette Romance

Caine, Rebecca

2045	Child Of Tahiti	/77	Harlequin
84	That Summer Of Surrender	/75	Harlequin Presents
107	Pagan Heart	/75	Harlequin Presents

Caitlin, Kimberleigh

Nightwynde

AUTHOR/TITLE INDEX

Caitlin, Kimberleigh
      Sky Of Ashes, Sea Of Flames
      Wild Witch   Berkley

Caitlin, Miranda
  303 Prisoner Of Love   04/86 Silhouette Special Edition

Cajio, Linda

145	All Is Fair	06/86	Bantam Loveswept
177	Hard Habit To Break	01/87	Bantam Loveswept
201	Rescuing Diana	07/87	Bantam Loveswept
224	Double Dealing	12/87	Bantam Loveswept
247	Silk On The Skin	04/88	Bantam Loveswept
268	Strictly Business	07/88	Bantam Loveswept
298	At First Sight	12/88	Bantam Loveswept
337	Desperate Measures	07/89	Bantam Loveswept
367	Unforgettable	12/89	Bantam Loveswept
403	Just One Look	06/90	Bantam Loveswept
447	Nights In White Satin	01/91	Bantam Loveswept
471	Earth Angel	05/91	Bantam Loveswept
505	Night Music	11/91	Bantam Loveswept
559	The Reluctant Prince	08/92	Bantam Loveswept
609	Dancing In The Dark	04/93	Bantam Loveswept
624	Me And Mrs. Jones	07/93	Bantam Loveswept
664	He's So Shy	01/94	Bantam Loveswept
721	Irresistible Stranger	12/94	Bantam Loveswept
735	The Perfect Catch	03/95	Bantam Loveswept
759	Hot And Bothered	10/95	Bantam Loveswept
	Golden Masquerade	/97	Zebra
	Knight's Song	01/96	Zebra Historical
	Colorado Gold	08/93	Zebra Lovegram

Caldwell, Anne
      Scandal's Darling   04/91 Avon Romance
      Pirates And Promises   03/94 Jove Tea Rose Romance

Caldwell, Carol
      Fields Of Fire   01/95 Kensington Denise Little Presents

Caldwell, Jean Anne
      Summer Magic   07/93 Jove Anthology
      Swept Away   08/93 Jove Brides Of The West

Caldwell, Pamela
      Knight's Beloved   12/93 Zebra
      Desire's Song   07/94 Zebra
      Passion's Bold Caress   02/91 Zebra Heartfire
      Stormswept Caress   01/92 Zebra Heartfire
      Scandalous   03/93 Zebra Heartfire

Caldwell, Taylor
      Glory And The Lightening   Historical

Caldwell-Wilson, Marolyn

Caldwell-Wilson, Marolyn
    Whirlwind   /86   Walker
Callaghan, Margaret
  121   Substitute Husband   11/92   Harlequin Direct
  131   Passing Strangers   04/93   Harlequin Direct
Callan, Michaila
  167   Playing Love's Odds   08/93   Meteor Kismet
Callander, Shirley
    The Reluctant Heir   Diamond Regency
Callender, Joan
  873   Nurse Julie Of Ward Three   /64   Harlequin
Calloway, Jo
  150   One Of A Kind   /83   Dell Candlelight Ecstasy
  164   Illusive Lover   /83   Dell Candlelight Ecstasy
Calvin, June
    The Jilting Of Baron Pelham   12/94   Nal Regency
    The Baron And The Bookseller   11/94   Signet
    Miss Henderson's Secret   08/95   Signet Regency
    The Duke's Desire   03/96   Signet Regency
Camden, Patricia
    Surrender In Scarlett   08/91   Avon
    Scarlett Kisses   12/92   Avon
    Promise Me Magic   04/95   Bantam
Cameron, Barbara
  66   Star Ride   07/85   Harlequin Temptation
  158   Rapture Of The Days   09/84   Silhouette Desire
Cameron, Blair
  98   Million-Dollar Lover   /86   Dell Candlelight Ecstasy
Cameron, Caryn
    A Season Of Joy   /91   Harlequin Hist. Christmas Stories
  11   Dawn's Early Light   Harlequin Historical
  27   Silver Swords   Harlequin Historical
  39   Liberty's Lady   Harlequin Historical
  49   Freedom Flame   Harlequin Historical
  61   Braden's Brides   01/91   Harlequin Historical
  70   Wild Lily   03/91   Harlequin Historical
  106   King's Man   12/91   Harlequin Historical
Cameron, Charla
  396   Diamond Days   Harlequin American
  433   A Man For Easter   Harlequin American
    Glory Nights   05/93   Pinnacle Magnolia Road
    Sultry Nights   Zebra Pinnacle/ Magnolia Road
Cameron, Doug
  92   Dig Another Grave   /51   Harlequin
Cameron, Gay

AUTHOR/TITLE INDEX

Cameron, Gay
264 His Brother's Keeper   02/94 Harlequin Intrigue

Cameron, June
Gypsy Jewel   10/92 Diamond

Cameron, Kate
The Legend Makers   11/95 Ballantine
Orenda   12/91 Ballantine Historical Fiction

Cameron, Kay
Passion's Rebel   Nal Penguin

Cameron, Miranda
The Dissolute Duke   09/86 Nal Penguin Regency
The Undaunted Bride   03/87 Nal Penguin Regency
The Meddlesome Heiress   Nal Penguin Regency
A Scandalous Bargain   Nal Penguin Regency
The Reluctant Abigail   Nal Penguin Regency
Lord Cleary's Revenge   Nal Penguin Regency

Cameron, Peta
868 This Starry Stranger   /64 Harlequin

Cameron, Stella
His Magic Touch   03/93 Avon
To Love And To Honor   04/93 Avon Anthology
Only By Your Touch   08/92 Avon Romantic Treasures
Breathless   06/94 Avon Suspense
1 Fascination   11/93 Avon Trilogy
2 Charmed   02/95 Avon Trilogy
153 Shadows   Harlequin American
195 No Stranger   Harlequin American
226 Second To None   12/87 Harlequin American
243 A Party Of Two   Harlequin American
268 The Message   Harlequin American
306 Friends   Harlequin American
360 Risks   Harlequin American
391 Mirror, Mirror   Harlequin American
419 An Angel In Time   12/91 Harlequin American
433 A Man For Easter   04/92 Harlequin American
460 Mad About The Man   10/92 Harlequin American
50 All That Sparkles   Harlequin Intrigue
83 Some Die Telling   Harlequin Intrigue
107 A Death In The House   02/89 Harlequin Intrigue
123 The Late Gentleman   Harlequin Intrigue
185 Moontide   Harlequin Superromance
340 One And For Always   Harlequin Superromance
448 Undercurrents   Harlequin Superromance
448 One Summer   Harlequin Superromance
451 One Winter   Harlequin Superromance
457 Snow Angels   Harlequin Superromance

Cameron, Stella

	Pure Delights	12/94	Kensington
3	Bride	12/95	Warner Trilogy
	Sheer Pleasure	09/95	Zebra

Camp, Candace

	Flame Lily	07/94	
	Rain Lily		
	Analise	07/91	Harper
	Light And Shadow	08/91	Harper
	Rosewood	07/91	Harper
	Bonds Of Love	03/92	Harper
	Bitterleaf	07/92	Harper
	Evensong	03/95	Harper
	Heirloom	09/92	Harper Monogram
	Crystal Heart	09/92	Harper Monogram
	Suddenly	02/96	Mira

Camp, Candance

	The Black Earl	04/95	Harper Regency

Camp, Deborah

	Blazing Embers		Avon
	Belle Starr		Avon
	Master Of Moonspell	08/93	Avon
	Too Tough To Tame	02/96	Avon
	Cheyenne's Shadow	03/94	Avon Historical
	Lonewolf's Woman	03/95	Avon Historical
	Black-Eyed Susan	05/92	Avon Romance
	Fire Lily	08/91	Avon Romance
	Primrose	11/90	Avon Romance
	My Wild Rose	11/92	Avon Romantic Treasure
	Lady Legend	05/92	Avon Romantic Treasures

Camp, Delayne

	Black-Eyed Susan	05/90	Avon
	Fallen Angel	07/89	Avon Historical
598	Taming The Wild Man	09/95	Harlequin American
289	A Newsworthy Affair	03/90	Harlequin Temptation
335	Oklahoma Man	02/91	Harlequin Temptation
403	The Butler Did It	07/92	Harlequin Temptation

Camp, Elaine

207	Love Letters	05/85	Silhouette Desire
251	Hook, Line And Sinker	12/85	Silhouette Desire
298	Destiny's Daughter	08/86	Silhouette Desire
419	The Second Mr. Sullivan	04/88	Silhouette Desire
99	To Have, To Hold	08/81	Silhouette Romance
173	Devil's Bargain	09/82	Silhouette Romance
270	This Tender Truce	01/84	Silhouette Romance
113	For Love Or Money		Silhouette Special Edition

355

Camp, Elaine

159	In A Pirate's Arms	04/84	Silhouette	Special Edition
263	Just Another Pretty Face	09/85	Silhouette	Special Edition
285	Vein Of Gold	01/86	Silhouette	Special Edition
301	Right Behind The Rain	04/86	Silhouette	Special Edition
316	After Dark	06/86	Silhouette	Special Edition

Campbell, Bethany

	Gentle On My Mind	10/94	Harlequin	Crystal Creek
	Lone Star State Of Mind	02/95	Harlequin	Crystal Creek
3	Amarillo By Morning	05/93	Harlequin	Crystal Creek
8	The Thunder Rolls	10/93	Harlequin	Crystal Creek
527	Rhinestone Cowboy	05/94	Harlequin	Crystal Creek
532	Gentle On My Mind	12/94	Harlequin	Crystal Creek
65	Pros And Cons		Harlequin	Intrigue
116	Roses Of Constant		Harlequin	Intrigue
151	Dead Opposite		Harlequin	Intrigue
196	Child's Play	09/92	Harlequin	Intrigue
21	Pros And Cons	08/94	Harlequin	Men Made In America
2726	After The Stars Fall		Harlequin	Romance
2779	Only A Woman		Harlequin	Romance
2803	A Thousand Roses		Harlequin	Romance
2815	Sea Promises		Harlequin	Romance
2852	The Long Way Home		Harlequin	Romance
2877	Heartland	12/87	Harlequin	Romance
2911	Flirtation River		Harlequin	Romance
2949	The Diamond Trap		Harlequin	Romance
3000	The Lost Moon Flower	/89	Harlequin	Romance
3019	The Snow Garden		Harlequin	Romance
3045	The Heart Of The Sun		Harlequin	Romance
3062	Dancing Sky		Harlequin	Romance
3079	The Ends Of The Earth		Harlequin	Romance
3109	Every Woman's Dream		Harlequin	Romance
3133	The Cloud Holders	07/91	Harlequin	Romance
3163	Every Kind Of Heaven	12/91	Harlequin	Romance
3187	Spellbinder	04/92	Harlequin	Romance
3211	Sand Dollar	08/92	Harlequin	Romance
3230	Only Make-Believe	11/92	Harlequin	Romance
3260	Add A Little Spice	04/93	Harlequin	Romance
3277	The Lady And The Tomcat	08/93	Harlequin	Romance
3293	The Man Who Came For Christmas	12/93	Harlequin	Romance

Campbell, Caroline

Love Masque		Walker

Campbell, Colleen

Castaway Heart		Zebra Heartfire

Campbell, Diana

Kissing Cousins	05/86	Nal Regency

AUTHOR/TITLE INDEX

Campbell, Diana

The Earl's Invention	10/86	Nal Regency
A Breath Of Scandal	10/87	Nal Regency
The Late Lord Latimer	11/88	Nal Regency
A Marriage Of Inconvenience	10/91	Nal Regency
The Reluctant Cyprian		Nal Penguin Regency
Lord Margrave's Deception		Nal Penguin Regency
Payment In Kind		Nal Penguin Regency
Family Affairs		Nal Penguin Regency
The Counterfeit Countess		Nal Penguin Regency

Campbell, Drucilla

The Frost And The Flame		Richard Gallen

Campbell, Laurie

990	And Father Makes Three	10/95	Silhouette Special Edition

Campbell, Marilyn

	Pyramid Dreams	03/92	Leisure
	Topaz Dreams	12/92	Leisure Futuristic Romance
124	No Competition	01/93	Meteor
	Daydreams		Nal
	Stardust Dreams	11/93	Nal Topaz
	Pretty Maids In A Row	01/95	Onyx
	Stolen Dreams	06/94	Penguin Topaz
	Just In Time	07/96	Topaz
	A Dreamspun Christmas	11/94	Topaz Anthology
	Worlds Apart	12/94	Topaz Dreamspun
	Gateway To Glory	12/94	Topaz Futuristic
	Pretty Maids In A Row	03/94	Villard Books Suspense
	See How They Run		Zebra
	Come Into My Parlor	10/92	Zebra Suspense

Campbell, Patricia

35	Lush Valley	/50	Harlequin

Campion, Margaret

	Crystal's Passion	/95	Contemporary
	Angel Bride	/94	Contemporary

Canavan, Jean

Midwinter's Night		Pocket
Highland Tryst		Tapestry

Cane, Nancy

	Keeper Of The Rings	01/96	Leisure Love Spell
1	Moonlight Rhapsody	09/94	Leisure Love Spell
2	Circle Of Light	01/95	Leisure Love Spell
3	Starlight Child	04/95	Leisure Love Spell

Canfield, Sandra

	Dark Journey	06/94	Bantam Contemporary
213	Cherish This Moment		Harlequin Superromance
252	Voice On The Wind		Harlequin Superromance

AUTHOR/TITLE INDEX

Canfield, Sandra

278	Night Into Day		Harlequin Superromance
338	Calloway Corners: Mariah	09/93	Harlequin Superromance
419	Tigers By Night		Harlequin Superromance
519	Star Song	10/92	Harlequin Superromance
545	Snap Judgement	04/93	Harlequin Superromance
568	Proof Positive	10/93	Harlequin Superromance
702	Jericho	08/96	Harlequin Superromance
	The Loving	06/92	Harper
469	One Lavender Evening	08/88	Silhouette Special Edition

Canham, Marsha

	Bound By The Heart		Avon
	China Rose		Avon
	The Wind And The Sea		Avon
	Through A Dark Mist	11/91	Dell
	Under The Desert Moon	10/92	Dell
	In The Shadow Of Midnight	07/93	Dell
	Straight For The Heart	04/95	Dell
386	Dark And Dangerous	03/92	Harlequin Temptation

Cannam, Helen

	The Last Ballad	11/91	St. Martin's

Canning, Victor

41	Panther's Moon	/50	Harlequin
393	A Forest Of Eyes	/57	Harlequin

Canon, Mary

	Wild Rose		
38	How The Game Is Played	12/84	Harlequin Temptation

Cantrell, Raine

	Desert Sunrise	05/92	Diamond
	Calico	07/93	Diamond Historical
	Country Christmas	11/93	Nal Anthology
	Tarnished Hearts	02/94	Penguin Topaz
	Emerald Enchantment	02/95	St. Martin's Anthology
	For The Love Of Chocolate	05/96	St. Martin's Anthology
	The Bride's Gift	03/95	St. Martin's Anthology
	Whisper My Name	05/95	Topaz
	Darling Annie	09/94	Topaz Western Trilogy

Capron, Jean F.

	Just Good Friends		
	Perilous Plot	/92	Avalon
	Puzzle From The Past		Avalon Mystery Romance
	The Reluctant Heir		Avalon Mystery Romance

Carberry, Ann

1	Maggie And The Gambler	05/95	Avon Four Roses Series
2	Frannie And The Charmer	01/96	Avon Four Roses Series
	Frontier Bride	08/92	Diamond Wildflower

AUTHOR/TITLE INDEX

Carberry, Ann

	Nevada Heat	07/93	Diamond Wildflower
	Runaway Bride	04/94	Diamond Wildflower
	Shotgun Bride	11/93	Diamond Wildflower Historical
	Summer Magic	07/93	Jove Anthology
	The Scoundrel	09/95	Jove Historical

Cardwell, Ann

22	Crazy To Kill	/49	Harlequin

Carew, Dan

163	Guntown	/52	Harlequin

Carew, Jocelyn

	Pavilion Of Passion		Avon
	Crown Of Passion		Avon
	The Golden Sovereigns		Avon

Carey, Suzanne

	Summer Sizzlers	06/93	Harlequin Anthology
44	Most Convenient Marriage	10/96	Harlequin Here Come The Grooms
4	Kiss And Tell	06/82	Silhouette Desire
69	Passion's Portrait	06/83	Silhouette Desire
92	Mountain Memory	10/83	Silhouette Desire
126	Leave Me Never	03/84	Silhouette Desire
176	Counterparts	12/84	Silhouette Desire
206	Angel In His Arms	05/85	Silhouette Desire
268	Confess To Apollo	03/86	Silhouette Desire
310	Love Medicine	10/86	Silhouette Desire
368	Any Pirate In A Storm	08/87	Silhouette Desire
330	Never Say Goodbye	04/90	Silhouette Intimate Moments
392	Strangers When We Met	07/91	Silhouette Intimate Moments
435	True To The Fire	06/92	Silhouette Intimate Moments
518	Eleanora's Ghost	09/93	Silhouette Intimate Moments
715	Whose Baby?	06/96	Silhouette Intimate Moments
633	A Most Convenient Marriage	02/89	Silhouette Romance
682	Run, Isabella	11/89	Silhouette Romance
736	Virgin Territory	08/90	Silhouette Romance
777	The Baby Contract	02/91	Silhouette Romance
825	Home For Thanksgiving	10/91	Silhouette Romance
855	Navajo Wedding	03/92	Silhouette Romance
880	Baby Swap	08/92	Silhouette Romance
928	Dad Galahad	04/93	Silhouette Romance
1001	Marry Me Again (Celebration 1000!)	04/94	Silhouette Romance
1025	The Male Animal	08/94	Silhouette Romance
1072	The Daddy Project (Bundles Of Joy)	04/95	Silhouette Romance
1120	Father By Marriage	12/95	Silhouette Romance

Carleen, Sally

46	Shaded Leaves Of Destiny	12/94	Harlequin Shadows
1101	An Improbable Wife	08/95	Silhouette Romance

AUTHOR/TITLE INDEX

Carleen, Sally

Carlisle, Donna

Carlisle, Sara

Carlow, Joyce

Carlson, Elizabeth

Carlson, Nancy

Carlton, Kate

Carlyle, Tena

Carmichael, Carol

Carmichael, Emily

Carmichael, Jeanne

Carr, Phillippa

The Lion Triumphant		Period Romance
The Adulteress		Ballantine
The Changeling		Ballantine
The Love Child		Ballantine
The Pool Of St. Branock		Ballantine
Voices In A Haunted Room		Ballantine
Will You Love Me In September?		Ballantine
The Black Swan	07/91	Fawcett Gold Medal

Carr, Robyn

The Everlasting Covenant		
The Braiswod Tapestry		
The Bellrose Bargain		
The Black Swan		
The Troubador's Romance		Pocket
517 Informed Risk	04/89	Silhouette Special Edition
Backward Glance	/91	Silhouette To Mother With Love
Woman's Own	/90	St. Martin's

Carr, Sally

257 Deceptive Desire	11/95	Harlequin
246 A Captive Heart	08/95	Harlequin Direct

Carras, Helen

84 Fair Winds	03/92	Meteor
By Love's Command	04/95	Zebra Lovegram

Carro, Patricia

234 Deja Vu	04/88	Silhouette Intimate Moments

Carroll, Dawn

268 Code Name Casanova	09/89	Harlequin Temptation
354 Naughty Thoughts	07/91	Harlequin Temptation
423 Beguiled	02/93	Harlequin Temptation

Carroll, Debra

530 Obsession (Secret Fantasies)	03/95	Harlequin Temptation
568 Man Under The Mistletoe	12/95	Harlequin Temptation
578 To Catch A Thief	03/96	Harlequin Temptation
597 An Inconvenient Passion	08/96	Harlequin Temptation

Carroll, Jay

Proud Blood		Bantam

Carroll, Joellyn

131 Run Before The Wind	04/83	Dell Candlelight Ecstasy
159 A Flight Of Splendor	07/83	Dell Candlelight Ecstasy
281 Match Made In Heaven	10/84	Dell Candlelight Ecstasy

Carroll, Kathleen

151 Angel's Walk		Harlequin American

Carroll, Lenore

The Heart Remembers	11/93	Harper
Love With A Warm Cowboy	02/93	Harper

Carroll, Lenore

	Abduction From Ft. Union	/88	Walker
	Annie Chambers	/90	Watermark Press

Carroll, Lorraine

670	Lead With Your Heart	05/91	Silhouette	Special Edition
705	The Ice Princess	11/91	Silhouette	Special Edition
1020	Playing Daddy	03/96	Silhouette	Special Edition

Carroll, Margaret

| | Montana Sunrise | 04/92 | Harper |
| | Prairie Light | 01/94 | Harper |

Carroll, Marisa

	Untitled	05/97	Harlequin	#3 Hurricane Beach Trilogy
127	Natural Attraction	11/85	Harlequin	American
160	Jenna's Choice	07/86	Harlequin	American
190	Tomorrow's Vintage	03/87	Harlequin	American
256	Come Home To Me	07/88	Harlequin	American
286	Ties That Bind	03/89	Harlequin	American
	My Valentine 1994	02/94	Harlequin	Anthology
	Baby Beat	02/96	Harlequin	By Request
	Yours, Mine & Ours	02/97	Harlequin	By Request
29	Natural Attraction	12/94	Harlequin	Men Made In America
13	Unexpected Son	08/96	Harlequin	Return To Tyler
24	Mission: Kids	02/97	Harlequin	Return To Tyler
	It's A Wonderful Life	12/96	Harlequin	Superromance
268	Remembered Magic	07/87	Harlequin	Superromance
318	Gathering Place	08/88	Harlequin	Superromance
418	Saigon Legacy: Rescue From Yesterday	09/90	Harlequin	Superromance
426	Saigon Legacy: Refuge From Today	11/90	Harlequin	Superromance
437	Saigon Legacy: Return To Tomorrow	01/91	Harlequin	Superromance
515	One To One	09/92	Harlequin	Superromance
529	Keeping Christmas	12/92	Harlequin	Superromance
565	Hawk's Lair	09/93	Harlequin	Superromance
598	Wedding Invitation (Weddings, Inc.)	06/94	Harlequin	Superromance
635	Marry Me Tonight (Weddings, Inc.)	03/95	Harlequin	Superromance
655	Peacekeeper (4 Strong Men)	08/95	Harlequin	Superromance
10	Crossroads	12/92	Harlequin	Tyler
12	Loveknot	02/93	Harlequin	Tyler

Carroll, Mary

2	Shadow And Sun	05/80	Silhouette	Romance
45	Too Swift The Morning	11/80	Silhouette	Romance
75	Divide The Wind	04/81	Silhouette	Romance
120	Take This Love	12/81	Silhouette	Romance
204	Midnight Sun	02/83	Silhouette	Romance
222	Two Faces Of Love	05/83	Silhouette	Romance
246	Where Tomorrow Waits	09/83	Silhouette	Romance

Carroll, Rosalynn

AUTHOR/TITLE INDEX

Carroll, Rosalynn
  67 Enchanted Encore   Nal Rapture Romance

Carroll, Samantha
  26 Silken Caresses   /81 Berkley Second Chance At Love

Carroll, Shirley
 174 Simple Pleasures   09/93 Meteor

Carroll, Susan
     Miss Prentiss And The Yankee   07/94
     The Bishop's Daughter   Ballantine
     The Sugar Rose   Ballantine Regency
     Rosemary Edghill   Ballantine Regency
     Turkish Delight   Ballantine Regency
     The Painted Veil   09/95 Ballantine Regency
     The Lady Who Hated Shakespeare   Fawcett Regency
     Brighton Road   Fawcett Regency
     Valentine's Day Ball   02/94 Fawcett Regency
     Christmas Belles   11/92 Fawcett Crest Regency
     The Wooing Of Miss Masters   11/91 Fawcett Crest Regency Romance
     Mistress Mischief   09/92 Fawcett Crest Regency Romance
 840 Black Lace And Linen   02/94 Silhouette Desire
 876 Love Power (Centerfolds)   08/94 Silhouette Desire

Carsley, Anne
     Lady Defiant

Carson, Angela
 2317 The Vital Spark   Harlequin Romance
 2619 Face Of The Stranger   Harlequin Romance
 2853 Gathering Of Eagles   Harlequin Romance
 3044 Sweet Illusion   Harlequin Romance
 3067 Another Man's Ring   Harlequin Romance

Carson, Christine
     Canadian Kiss   Zebra Heartfire

Carson, Rosalind
  16 This Dark Enchantment   Harlequin Superromance
  40 Song Of Desire   Harlequin Superromance
  91 Such Sweet Magic   Harlequin Superromance
 123 Love Me Tomorrow   Harlequin Superromance
 175 To Touch The Moon   Harlequin Superromance
 214 Close To Home   Harlequin Superromance
 310 The Moon Gate   06/88 Harlequin Superromance
  40 Lovespell   12/84 Harlequin Temptation
 156 The Marrying Kind   05/87 Harlequin Temptation
     Beyond The Rainbow   /86 Worldwide Lib.
     Forever Love   /88 Worldwide Lib.

Carter, Ashley
     Master Of Blackoakes   Ballantine Regency
     Secret Of Blackoakes   Ballantine Regency

Carter, Ashley

    Sword Of The Golden Stud   Ballantine Regency

Carter, Helen

  194   Touched By Lightning   /84   Berkley Second Chance At Love

Carter, Janice

   63   Double Jeopardy   Harlequin Intrigue

  593   Ghost Tiger   04/94 Harlequin Superromance

  671   A Christmas Baby   12/95 Harlequin Superromance

Carter, Noel Vreeland

  656   Miss Hungerford's Handsome Hero   Dell Candlelight Regency

Carter, Rosemary

  247   Captive Bride   09/95 Harlequin

  264   Games Lovers Play   01/96 Harlequin

 1986   Man Of The Wild   /76   Harlequin

  122   Certain Of Nothing   11/92 Harlequin Direct

  263   Adam's Bride   /78   Harlequin Presents

  283   Sweet Imposter   Harlequin Presents

  290   Bush Doctor   Harlequin Presents

  301   The Awakening   Harlequin Presents

  362   Kelly's Man   Harlequin Presents

  397   Desert Dream   Harlequin Presents

  410   Face In The Portrait   Harlequin Presents

  439   Safari Encounter   Harlequin Presents

  469   Another Life   Harlequin Presents

  560   Daredevil   Harlequin Presents

  575   Master Of Tinarua   Harlequin Presents

  615   Lion's Domain   Harlequin Presents

  664   Serpent In Paradise   Harlequin Presents

  752   Letter From Bronze Man   Harlequin Presents

  831   Impetuous Marriage   Harlequin Presents

  855   A Forever Affair   Harlequin Presents

  880   Pillow Portraits   Harlequin Presents

 2312   Return To Devil's View   Harlequin Romance

 2380   Man In The Shadows   Harlequin Romance

 2816   Walk Into Tomorrow   Harlequin Romance

 2965   No Greater Joy   Harlequin Romance

 3050   Partners In Passion   Harlequin Romance

         Night Of The Scorpion   10/95 Worldwide Libr. Stolen Moments

Cartier, Annee

         Tradewinds   02/95 Pinnacle Denise Little Presents

         Surrender To The Dawn 03/96 Pinnacle Denise Little Presents

Cartland, Barbara

    1   The Daring Deception   Bantam

    2   No Darkness For Love   Bantam

    3   The Little Adventure   Bantam

    4   Lessons In Love   Bantam

Cartland, Barbara

AUTHOR/TITLE INDEX

Cartland, Barbara

51	The Proud Princess	Bantam
52	Hungry For Love	Bantam
53	The Heart Triumphant	Bantam
54	The Dream And The Glory	Bantam
55	The Taming Of Lady Lorinda	Bantam
56	The Disgraceful Duke	Bantam
57	Vote For Love	Bantam
58	The Mysterious Maid-Servant	Bantam
59	The Magic Of Love	Bantam
60	Kiss The Moonlight	Bantam
61	The Rhapsody Of Love	Bantam
62	The Marquis Who Hated Women	Bantam
63	Look, Listen And Love	Bantam
64	A Duel With Destiny	Bantam
65	The Curse Of The Clan	Bantam
66	Punishment Of A Vixen	Bantam
67	The Outrageous Lady	Bantam
68	A Touch Of Love	Bantam
69	The Dragon And The Pearl	Bantam
70	The Love Pirate	Bantam
71	The Temptation Of Torilla	Bantam
72	Love And The Loathsome Leopard	Bantam
73	The Naked Battle	Bantam
74	The Hell-Cat And The King	Bantam
75	No Escape From Love	Bantam
76	The Castle Made For Love	Bantam
77	The Sign Of Love	Bantam
78	The Saint And The Sinner	Bantam
79	A Fugitive From Love	Bantam
80	The Twists And Turns Of Love	Bantam
81	The Problems Of Love	Bantam
82	Love Leaves At Midnight	Bantam
83	Magic Of Mirage	Bantam
84	Love Locked In	Bantam
85	Lord Ravenscar's Revenge	Bantam
86	The Wild, Unwilling Wife	Bantam
87	Love, Lords, And Lady-Birds	Bantam
88	A Runaway Star	Bantam
89	The Passion And The Flower	Bantam
90	A Princess In Distress	Bantam
91	The Judgement Of Love	Bantam
92	The Race Of Love	Bantam
93	Lovers In Paradise	Bantam
94	The Irresistible Force	Bantam
95	The Chieftain Without A Heart	Bantam
96	The Duke And The Preacher's Daughter	Bantam

AUTHOR/TITLE INDEX

Cartland, Barbara

97	The Ghost Who Fell In Love	Bantam
98	The Drums Of Love	Bantam
99	Alone In Paris	Bantam
100	The Prince And The Pekinese	Bantam
101	The Serpent Of Satan	Bantam
102	The Treasure Of Love	Bantam
103	Light Of The Moon	Bantam
104	The Prisoner Of Love	Bantam
105	Flowers For The God Of Love	Bantam
106	A Voice In The Dark	Bantam
107	The Duchess Disappeared	Bantam
108	Love Climbs In	Bantam
109	Love Climbs In	Bantam
110	Terror In The Sun	Bantam
111	Who Can Deny Love	Bantam
112	Love Has His Way	Bantam
113	The Explosion Of Love	Bantam
114	Only Love	Bantam
115	Women Have Hearts	Bantam
116	A Gentleman In Love	Bantam
117	Love In The Clouds	Bantam
118	The Power And The Prince	Bantam
119	Imperial Splendor	Bantam
120	Free From Fear	Bantam
121	Little White Doves Of Love	Bantam
122	The Perfection Of Love	Bantam
123	Bride To The King	Bantam
124	Punished With Love	Bantam
125	The Dawn Of Love	Bantam
126	Lucifer And The Angel	Bantam
127	Olga And The Sea Wolf	Bantam
128	The Prude And The Prodigal	Bantam
129	Love For Sale	Bantam
130	The Goddess And The Gaiety Girl	Bantam
131	Signpost To Love	Bantam
132	Lost Laughter	Bantam
133	From Hell To Heaven	Bantam
134	Pride And The Poor Princess	Bantam
135	The Lioness And The Lily	Bantam
136	The Kiss Of Life	Bantam
137	Afraid	Bantam
138	Love In The Moon	Bantam
139	Waltz Of Hearts	Bantam
140	Dollars For The Duke	Bantam
141	Dreams Do Come True	Bantam
142	A Night Of Gaiety	Bantam

Cartland, Barbara

143	Enchanted		Bantam
144	Winged Magic		Bantam
145	A Portrait Of Love		Bantam
146	The River Of Love		Bantam
147	Gift Of The Gods		Bantam
148	An Innocent In Russia		Bantam
149	A Shaft Of Sunlight		Bantam
150	Love Wins		Bantam
151	Sweet Harbour		Bantam
152	Looking For Love		Bantam
153	The Vibrations Of Love		Bantam
154	Lies For Love		Bantam
155	Love Rules		Bantam
156	Moments Of Love		Bantam
157	Music From The Heart		Bantam
158	The Call Of The Highlands		Bantam
159	Kneel For Mercy		Bantam
160	Wish For Love		Bantam
161	Mission To Monte Carlo		Bantam
162	Caught By Love		Bantam
163	Love At The Helm		Bantam
164	Pure And Untouched		Bantam
165	A Marriage Made In Heaven		Bantam
166	From Hate To Love		Bantam
167	Love On The Wind		Bantam
168	The Duke Comes Home		Bantam
169	A King In Love		Bantam
170	Journey To A Star		Bantam
171	Love And Lucia		Bantam
172	The Unwanted Wedding		Bantam
173	Gypsy Magic		Bantam
174	Help From The Heart		Bantam
175	A Duke In Danger		Bantam
176	Tempted To Love		Bantam
177	Lights, Laughter And A Lady		Bantam
178	Riding To The Moon		Bantam
179	The Unbreakable Spell		Bantam
180	Diona And A Dalmation		Bantam
181	Fire In The Blood		Bantam
182	The Scots Never Forget		Bantam
183	A Rebel Princess		Bantam
118	The Angel And The Rake	06/93	Berkley Camfield Romance
119	The Queen Of Hearts	07/93	Berkley Camfield Romance
1	The Poor Governess		Berkley/Jove Camfield Romance
2	Winged Victory		Berkley/Jove Camfield Romance
3	Lucky In Love		Berkley/Jove Camfield Romance

AUTHOR/TITLE INDEX

Cartland, Barbara

4	Love And The Marquis	Berkley/Jove	Camfield Romance
5	A Miracle In Music	Berkley/Jove	Camfield Romance
6	Light Of The Gods	Berkley/Jove	Camfield Romance
7	Bride To A Brigand	Berkley/Jove	Camfield Romance
8	Love Comes West	Berkley/Jove	Camfield Romance
9	A Witch's Spell	Berkley/Jove	Camfield Romance
10	Secrets	Berkley/Jove	Camfield Romance
11	The Storm Of Love	Berkley/Jove	Camfield Romance
12	Moonlight On The Sphinx	Berkley/Jove	Camfield Romance
13	White Lilac	Berkley/Jove	Camfield Romance
14	Revenge Of The Heart	Berkley/Jove	Camfield Romance
15	The Island Of Love	Berkley/Jove	Camfield Romance
16	Theresa And A Tiger	Berkley/Jove	Camfield Romance
17	Love Is Heaven	Berkley/Jove	Camfield Romance
18	Miracle For A Madonna	Berkley/Jove	Camfield Romance
19	A Very Unusual Wife	Berkley/Jove	Camfield Romance
20	The Peril And The Prince	Berkley/Jove	Camfield Romance
21	Alone And Afraid	Berkley/Jove	Camfield Romance
22	Temptation Of A Teacher	Berkley/Jove	Camfield Romance
23	Royal Punishment	Berkley/Jove	Camfield Romance
24	The Devilish Deception	Berkley/Jove	Camfield Romance
25	Paradise Found	Berkley/Jove	Camfield Romance
26	Love Is A Gamble	Berkley/Jove	Camfield Romance
27	A Victory For Love	Berkley/Jove	Camfield Romance
28	Look With Love	Berkley/Jove	Camfield Romance
29	Never Forget Love	Berkley/Jove	Camfield Romance
30	Helga In Hiding	Berkley/Jove	Camfield Romance
31	Safe At Last	Berkley/Jove	Camfield Romance
32	Haunted	Berkley/Jove	Camfield Romance
33	Crowned With Love	Berkley/Jove	Camfield Romance
34	Escape	Berkley/Jove	Camfield Romance
35	The Devil Defeated	Berkley/Jove	Camfield Romance
36	The Secret Of The Mosque	Berkley/Jove	Camfield Romance
37	A Dream In Spain	Berkley/Jove	Camfield Romance
38	The Love Trap	Berkley/Jove	Camfield Romance
39	Listen To Love	Berkley/Jove	Camfield Romance
40	The Golden Cage	Berkley/Jove	Camfield Romance
41	Love Casts Out Fear	Berkley/Jove	Camfield Romance
42	A World Of Love	Berkley/Jove	Camfield Romance
43	Dancing On A Rainbow	Berkley/Jove	Camfield Romance
44	Love Joins The Clans	Berkley/Jove	Camfield Romance
45	An Angel Runs Away	Berkley/Jove	Camfield Romance
46	Forced To Marry	Berkley/Jove	Camfield Romance
47	Bewildered In Berlin	Berkley/Jove	Camfield Romance
48	Wanted: A Wedding Ring	Berkley/Jove	Camfield Romance
49	The Earl Escapes	Berkley/Jove	Camfield Romance

Cartland, Barbara

50	Starlight Over Tunis	Berkley/Jove	Camfield Romance
51	The Love Puzzle	Berkley/Jove	Camfield Romance
52	Love And Kisses	Berkley/Jove	Camfield Romance
53	Sapphires In Siam	Berkley/Jove	Camfield Romance
54	A Caretaker Of Love	Berkley/Jove	Camfield Romance
55	Secrets Of The Heart	Berkley/Jove	Camfield Romance
56	Riding In The Sky	Berkley/Jove	Camfield Romance
57	Lovers In Lisbon	Berkley/Jove	Camfield Romance
58	Love Is Invincible	Berkley/Jove	Camfield Romance
59	The Goddess Of Love	Berkley/Jove	Camfield Romance
60	An Adventure Of Love	Berkley/Jove	Camfield Romance
61	The Herb For Happiness	Berkley/Jove	Camfield Romance
62	Only A Dream	Berkley/Jove	Camfield Romance
63	Saved By Love	Berkley/Jove	Camfield Romance
64	Little Tongues Of Fire	Berkley/Jove	Camfield Romance
65	A Chieftain Finds Love	Berkley/Jove	Camfield Romance
66	A Lovely Liar	Berkley/Jove	Camfield Romance
67	The Perfume Of The Gods	Berkley/Jove	Camfield Romance
68	A Knight In Paris	Berkley/Jove	Camfield Romance
69	Revenge Is Sweet	Berkley/Jove	Camfield Romance
70	The Passionate Princess	Berkley/Jove	Camfield Romance
71	Solita And The Spies	Berkley/Jove	Camfield Romance
72	The Perfect Pearl	Berkley/Jove	Camfield Romance
73	Love Is A Maze	Berkley/Jove	Camfield Romance
74	A Circus For Love	Berkley/Jove	Camfield Romance
75	The Temple Of Love	Berkley/Jove	Camfield Romance
76	The Bargain Bride	Berkley/Jove	Camfield Romance
77	The Haunted Heart	Berkley/Jove	Camfield Romance
78	Real Love Or Fake	Berkley/Jove	Camfield Romance
79	Kiss From A Stranger	Berkley/Jove	Camfield Romance
80	A Very Special Love	Berkley/Jove	Camfield Romance
81	The Necklace Of Love	Berkley/Jove	Camfield Romance
82	A Revolution Of Love	Berkley/Jove	Camfield Romance
83	The Marquis Wins	Berkley/Jove	Camfield Romance
84	Love Is The Key	Berkley/Jove	Camfield Romance
85	Love At First Sight	Berkley/Jove	Camfield Romance
86	The Taming Of A Tigress	Berkley/Jove	Camfield Romance
88	The Earl Rings A Belle	Berkley/Jove	Camfield Romance
89	The Queen Saves The King	Berkley/Jove	Camfield Romance
90	No Disguise For Love	Berkley/Jove	Camfield Romance
91	Love Lifts The Curse	Berkley/Jove	Camfield Romance
92	Beauty Or Brains	Berkley/Jove	Camfield Romance
93	Too Precious To Lose	Berkley/Jove	Camfield Romance
94	Hiding	Berkley/Jove	Camfield Romance
95	Tangled Web	Berkley/Jove	Camfield Romance
96	Just Fate	Berkley/Jove	Camfield Romance

Cartland, Barbara

97	A Miracle In Mexico		Berkley/Jove	Camfield Romance
98	Warned By A Ghost		Berkley/Jove	Camfield Romance
99	Two Hearts In Hungary		Berkley/Jove	Camfield Romance
100	A Theatre Of Love		Berkley/Jove	Camfield Romance
101	A Dynasty Of Love		Berkley/Jove	Camfield Romance
102	Magic From The Heart		Berkley/Jove	Camfield Romance
103	The Windmill Of Love		Berkley/Jove	Camfield Romance
104	Love Strikes A Devil		Berkley/Jove	Camfield Romance
105	Love And War		Berkley/Jove	Camfield Romance
106	Seek The Stars		Berkley/Jove	Camfield Romance
108	A Wish Comes True		Berkley/Jove	Camfield Romance
109	Loved For Himself		Berkley/Jove	Camfield Romance
110	A Kiss In Rome		Berkley/Jove	Camfield Romance
111	Hidden By Love		Berkley/Jove	Camfield Romance
112	Born Of Love		Berkley/Jove	Camfield Romance
113	Walking To Wonderland		Berkley/Jove	Camfield Romance
114	Terror From The Throne		Berkley/Jove	Camfield Romance
115	The Cave Of Love		Berkley/Jove	Camfield Romance
116	The Peaks Of Ecstasy		Berkley/Jove	Camfield Romance
117	Lucky Logan Finds Love		Berkley/Jove	Camfield Romance
118	The Angel And The Rake		Berkley/Jove	Camfield Romance
119	The Queen Of Hearts		Berkley/Jove	Camfield Romance
120	The Wicked Widow	07/93	Berkley/Jove	Camfield Romance
121	To Scotland With Love	09/93	Berkley/Jove	Camfield Romance
122	Love At The Ritz	10/93	Berkley/Jove	Camfield Romance
123	The Dangerous Marriage	11/93	Berkley/Jove	Camfield Romance
124	Good Or Bad	12/93	Berkley/Jove	Camfield Romance
125	This Is Love		Berkley/Jove	Camfield Romance
126	Running Away To Love	02/94	Berkley/Jove	Camfield Romance
127	Look With The Heart	03/94	Berkley/Jove	Camfield Romance
128	Safe In Paradise	04/94	Berkley/Jove	Camfield Romance
129	The Duke Finds Love	05/94	Berkley/Jove	Camfield Romance
130	The Wonderful Dream	06/94	Berkley/Jove	Camfield Romance
131	A Royal Rebuke	07/94	Berkley/Jove	Camfield Romance
132	The Dare-Devil Duke	08/94	Berkley/Jove	Camfield Romance
133	Never Lose Love	09/94	Berkley/Jove	Camfield Romance
134	The Spirit Of Love	10/94	Berkley/Jove	Camfield Romance
135	The Eyes Of Love	11/94	Berkley/Jove	Camfield Romance
136	Saved By A Saint	12/94	Berkley/Jove	Camfield Romance
137	The Incomparable	01/95	Berkley/Jove	Camfield Romance
138	The Innocent Imposter	02/95	Berkley/Jove	Camfield Romance
139	The Loveless Marriage	03/95	Berkley/Jove	Camfield Romance
140	A Magical Moment	04/95	Berkley/Jove	Camfield Romance
141	The Patient Bridegroom	05/95	Berkley/Jove	Camfield Romance
142	The Protection Of Love	06/95	Berkley/Jove	Camfield Romance
143	Running From Russia	07/95	Berkley/Jove	Camfield Romance

Cartland, Barbara

144	Someone To Love	08/95	Berkley/Jove	Camfield Romance
145	Beyond The Stars	09/95	Berkley/Jove	Camfield Romance
146	Love In The Ruins	10/95	Berkley/Jove	Camfield Romance
147	Passage To Love	11/95	Berkley/Jove	Camfield Romance
148	An Icicle In India	12/95	Berkley/Jove	Camfield Romance
149	Fascination In France	01/96	Berkley/Jove	Camfield Romance
150	Three Days To Love	02/96	Berkley/Jove	Camfield Romance
	The Cave Of Love	03/93	Jove	
1	Desire Of The Heart		Jove	
2	A Hazard Of Hearts		Jove	
3	Coin Of Love		Jove	
4	Love In Hiding		Jove	
5	The Enchanting Evil		Jove	
6	The Unpredictable Bride		Jove	
7	The Secret Heart		Jove	
8	A Duel Of Hearts		Jove	
9	Love Is The Enemy		Jove	
10	The Hidden Heart		Jove	
11	Love To The Rescue		Jove	
12	Love Holds The Cards		Jove	
13	Love Is Contraband		Jove	
14	Love Me Forever		Jove	
15	The Innocent Heiress		Jove	
16	Debt Of Honor		Jove	
17	Sweet Adventure		Jove	
18	The Royal Pledge		Jove	
19	The Little Pretender		Jove	
20	The Golden Gondola		Jove	
21	Stars In My Heart		Jove	
22	Messenger Of Love		Jove	
23	The Secret Fear		Jove	
24	An Innocent In Paris		Jove	
25	The Wings Of Love		Jove	
26	The Enchanted Waltz		Jove	
27	The Hidden Evil		Jove	
28	Elizabethan Lover		Jove	
29	The Unknown Heart		Jove	
30	A Kiss Of Silk		Jove	
31	Love Is Dangerous		Jove	
32	The Kiss Of The Devil		Jove	
33	Lost Love		Jove	
34	The Reluctant Bride		Jove	
35	The Pretty Horse-Breakers		Jove	
36	Again This Rapture		Jove	
37	Open Wings		Jove	
38	The Kiss Of Paris		Jove	

AUTHOR/TITLE INDEX

Cartland, Barbara

39	Love Under Fire	Jove
40	The Enchanted Moment	Jove
41	The Audacious Adventuress	Jove
42	No Heart Is Free	Jove
43	Love Is Mine	Jove
44	Stolen Halo	Jove
45	Sweet Punishment	Jove
46	Lights Of Love	Jove
47	Wings On My Heart	Jove
48	A Ghost In Monte Carlo	Jove
49	Love Is An Eagle	Jove
50	Love On The Run	Jove
51	Love Forbidden	Jove
52	Lost Enchantment	Jove
53	The Complacent Wife	Jove
54	Blue Heather	Jove
55	A Halo For The Devil	Jove
56	A Light To The Heart	Jove
57	The Irresistible Buck	Jove
58	Sweet Enchantress	Jove
59	The Odious Duke	Jove
60	Out Of Reach	Jove
61	The Price Is Love	Jove
62	The Dream Within	Jove
63	The Thief Of Love	Jove
64	Armour Against Love	Jove
65	Passionate Pilgrim	Jove
66	A Heart Is Broken	Jove
67	Theft Of A Heart	Jove
68	Against The Stream	Jove
69	The Runaway Heart	Jove
70	The Leaping Flame	Jove
71	Where Is Love?	Jove
72	Towards The Stars	Jove
73	Desperate Defiance	Jove
74	An Innocent In Mayfair	Jove
75	A Rainbow To Heaven	Jove
76	The Bitter Winds Of Love	Jove
77	Love And Linda	Jove
78	Broken Barriers	Jove
79	Love Is Pity	Jove
80	Dance On My Heart	Jove
81	Love At Forty	Jove
82	This Time It's Love	Jove
83	The Adventurer	Jove
84	Escape From Passion	Jove

Cassidy, Carla

856	Whatever Alex Wants	04/92	Silhouette Romance
884	Fire And Spice	08/92	Silhouette Romance
905	Homespun Hearts	02/93	Silhouette Romance
924	Golden Girl	03/93	Silhouette Romance
942	Something New	06/93	Silhouette Romance
958	Pixie Dust (Fabulous Father)	09/93	Silhouette Romance
978	The Littles Matchmaker	12/93	Silhouette Romance
996	The Marriage Scheme	03/94	Silhouette Romance
1048	Anthing For Danny	12/94	Silhouette Romance
1141	Deputy Daddy	03/96	Silhouette Romance
1147	Mom In The Making	04/96	Silhouette Romance
1152	An Impromptu Proposal	05/96	Silhouette Romance
1158	Daddy On The Run	06/96	Silhouette Romance
4	Swamp Secrets	03/93	Silhouette Shadows
61	Mystery Child	02/96	Silhouette Shadows

Cassidy, Kris

| 12 | Born To Be Wild | 09/90 | Meteor |

Cassity, Jo Anne

	Holding Hands	02/95	Berkley A Town Called Harmony
	The Quilting Circle	/96	Berkley Anthology
	Lover's Cove	10/93	Berkley Historical
	Tender Wishes	08/93	Diamond Homespun
	Courting Season	08/94	Diamond Homespun
	Harvest Hearts	11/93	Jove Historical Anthology

Cassity, Joan

| | Now And Again | | Avon |

Casstevens, Jeanne

	A Reformed Rake	03/94	
	A Springtime Affair		
	All Hallow's Eve	/92	Walker Anthology
	A June Betrothal	06/93	Zebra Anthology

Castle, Jayne

	Double Dealing	/84	Dell
	Trading Secrets	/85	Dell
	Gentle Pirate	/80	Dell Candlelight Ecstasy
	Wagered Weekend	/81	Dell Candlelight Ecstasy
	Right Of Possession	/81	Dell Candlelight Ecstasy
	Bargain With The Devil	/81	Dell Candlelight Ecstasy
	A Man's Protection	/82	Dell Candlelight Ecstasy
	Relentless Adversary	/82	Dell Candlelight Ecstasy
	Affair Of Risk	/82	Dell Candlelight Ecstasy
	A Negotiated Surrender	/82	Dell Candlelight Ecstasy
	Power Play	/82	Dell Candlelight Ecstasy
	Spellbound	/82	Dell Candlelight Ecstasy
	Conflict Of Interest	/83	Dell Candlelight Ecstasy

Castle, Jayne

2	The Gentle Pirate		Dell	Candlelight Ecstasy
17	Wagered Weekend		Dell	Candlelight Ecstasy
1	The Desperate Game	/86	Dell	Guinevere Jones Series
2	The Chilling Deception	/86	Dell	Guinevere Jones Series
3	The Sinister Touch	/86	Dell	Guinevere Jones Series
4	The Fatal Fortune	/86	Dell	Guinevere Jones Series
	Vintage Of Surrender	/79	Mcfadden	
	Queen Of Hearts	/79	Mcfadden	

Castle, Jill

660	It Happened One Morning	07/89	Silhouette Romance

Castle, Linda

261	Fearless Hearts (March Madness)	03/95	Harlequin Historical
321	Abbie's Child	06/96	Harlequin Historical

Castle, Philippa

651	The Reluctant Bride		Dell Candlelight Regency
	The Dandy's Deception		Warner
	The Reluctant Duke		Warner

Casto, Jackie

Daughter Of Destiny	/95	Leisure
The New Frontier	12/95	Leisure Futuristic Romance

Cates, Kim

550	Uncertain Angels	02/94	Silhouette Intimate Moments
580	A Father's Claim	07/94	Silhouette Intimate Moments
687	The Wishing Tree	08/91	Silhouette Special Edition
777	A Sky Full Of Miracles	11/92	Silhouette Special Edition

Cates, Kimberly

The Raider's Bride	07/94	
Only Forever	04/92	Pocket
Restless Is The Wind		Pocket
To Catch A Flame		Pocket
Crown Of Dreams	/94	Pocket
The Raider's Daughter	10/94	Pocket
Stealing Heaven	04/95	Pocket

Cates, Tory

65	Handful Of Sky	12/82	Silhouette Special Edition
125	Where Aspens Quake	10/83	Silhouette Special Edition
196	Cloud Waltzer	10/84	Silhouette Special Edition
236	Different Dreams	05/85	Silhouette Special Edition
310	A Passionate Illusion	05/86	Silhouette Special Edition

Catlin, Barbara

488	Smoky's Bandit	11/88	Silhouette Special Edition
519	Mr. Right	04/89	Silhouette Special Edition
724	Shotgun Wedding	02/92	Silhouette Special Edition

Cato, Nancy

Forefathers	Nal Penguin

Cato, Nancy
    All The River's Run   Nal Penguin

Caulder, Inglath
  609   Truths And Roses   08/94   Harlequin Superromance

Cavaliere, Anne
  328   Perfect Timing   01/87   Silhouette Desire
  512   Squeeze Play   08/89   Silhouette Desire
  693   Private Lessons   02/92   Silhouette Desire

Cavanagh, Helen
    Second Best   Scholastic Young Adult
    Honey   Silhouette

Cave, Emma
    Cousin Henrietta   St. Martin's
    Little Angie   St. Martin's

Caviliere, Anne
  512   Squeeze Play   08/89   Silhouette Desire

Chace, Isobel
  725   The Song And The Sea   /63   Harlequin
  821   The Wild Land   /64   Harlequin
  935   A House For Sharing   /65   Harlequin
  976   Flamingoes On The Lake   /65   Harlequin
 1040   The Rhythm Of Flamenco   /66   Harlequin
 1053   The Japanese Lantern   /66   Harlequin
 1152   A Garland Of Marigolds   /67   Harlequin
 1216   Oranges And Lemons   /68   Harlequin
 1250   The Saffron Sky   /68   Harlequin
 1306   A Handful Of Silver   /69   Harlequin
 1334   The Damask Rose   /69   Harlequin
 1390   Sugar In The Morning   /70   Harlequin
 1436   The Day That The Rain Came Down /70   Harlequin
 1477   The Land Of The Lotus-Eaters /71   Harlequin
 1506   The Flowering Cactus   /71   Harlequin
 1561   Home Is Goodbye   /72   Harlequin
 1586   To Marry A Tiger   /72   Harlequin
 1618   The Wealth Of The Islands   /72   Harlequin
 1653   The Tartan Touch   /73   Harlequin
 1673   A Pride Of Lions   /73   Harlequin
 1698   Cadence Of Portugal   /73   Harlequin
 1721   The Flamboyant Tree   /73   Harlequin
 1750   The House Of The Scissors /74   Harlequin
 1773   A Man Of Kent   /74   Harlequin
 1795   The Edge Of Beyond   /74   Harlequin
 1829   The Dragon's Cafe   /74   Harlequin
 1849   The Hospital Of Fatima   /75   Harlequin
 1904   The Cornish Hearth   /75   Harlequin
 1945   The Desert Castle   /76   Harlequin

Chambers, Ginger

71	Passion's Prey		Harlequin	American
107	In Love's Shadow		Harlequin	American
169	When Hearts Collide	10/86	Harlequin	American
238	Firefly In The Night		Harlequin	American
254	Call My Name Softly		Harlequin	American
288	Passages Of Gold		Harlequin	American
335	Nightshade		Harlequin	American
395	Bird In A Mirror		Harlequin	American
411	Eagle On The Wind	10/91	Harlequin	American
601	Till September	06/94	Harlequin	Superromance
647	Father Takes A Wife (Family Man)	06/95	Harlequin	Superromance
680	A Match Made In Texas	02/96	Harlequin	Superromance
8	Bachelor's Puzzle	10/92	Harlequin	Tyler
11	Courthouse Steps	01/93	Harlequin	Tyler

Chambers, Pamela Quint

	Family Recipe	04/95	Jove Homespun

Chance, Lisbeth

	Baja Run	/86	Walker

Chance, Megan

	A Candle In The Dark	09/93	Dell
	After The Frost	10/94	Dell
	The Portrait	09/95	Dell

Chance, Sara

46	Her Golden Eyes	02/83	Silhouette	Desire
83	Home At Last	08/83	Silhouette	Desire
107	This Wildfire Magic	12/83	Silhouette	Desire
183	A Touch Of Passion	01/85	Silhouette	Desire
244	Look Beyond Tomorrow	11/85	Silhouette	Desire
357	Where The Wandering Ends	06/87	Silhouette	Desire
388	Double Solitaire	11/87	Silhouette	Desire
406	Shadow Watch	02/88	Silhouette	Desire
430	To Tame The Wind	06/88	Silhouette	Desire
467	New Orleans: Southern Comfort	12/88	Silhouette	Desire
485	New Orleans: Woman In The Shadows	03/89	Silhouette	Desire
500	New Orleans: Eye Of The Storm	06/89	Silhouette	Desire
524	With A Little Spice	10/89	Silhouette	Desire
299	Fire In The Night	08/89	Silhouette	Intimate Moments

Chancellor, Victoria

	All My Dreams	11/92	Harper Monogram
	Forever & A Day	/95	Leisure Fantasy
188	Escorting Alicia	12/93	Meteor

Chandler, Laurel

30	Heart's Victory		Nal Rapture Romance
59	Boundless Love		Nal Rapture Romance

Chandler, Lauryn

Charles, Maggi

575	The Love Expert	01/90	Silhouette Special Edition
599	Strictly For Hire	05/90	Silhouette Special Edition
647	Shadows On The Sand	01/91	Silhouette Special Edition
771	As The Moon Rises	10/92	Silhouette Special Edition
795	The Other Side Of The Mirror	02/93	Silhouette Special Edition

Charles, Marie

65	Smoldering Embers	/82	Berkley Second Chance At Love
	Scenes From The Heart	03/83	Jove Second Chance At Love
	Claimed By Rapture	09/83	Jove Second Chance At Love

Charles, Riva

Thrall Of Love   Berkley

Charlton, Ann

857	An Irresistible Force		Harlequin Presents
912	Titan's Woman		Harlequin Presents
967	The Deception Trap		Harlequin Presents
1008	Street Song		Harlequin Presents
1319	Love Spin		Harlequin Presents
1777	Hot November	11/95	Harlequin Presents
1782	Steamy December	12/95	Harlequin Presents
2660	Place Of Wild Honey		Harlequin Romance
2684	No Last Song		Harlequin Romance
2701	Winter Sun, Summer Rain		Harlequin Romance
2762	The Driftwood Dragon	05/86	Harlequin Romance
2977	Ransomed Heart		Harlequin Romance

Charlton, Josephine

135	Table For Two	05/84	Silhouette Desire

Charlton, Madeline

1686	Alpenrose	/73	Harlequin
2055	A Sense Of Words	/77	Harlequin

Chartier, Danette

	Midnight Promises	07/94	Zebra
	Stolen Fire	05/93	Zebra Heartfire

Chase, Carolyn

	Renegade Hearts		Bantam
	Frontier Rogue		Bantam
5	Rebel's Kiss		Dell 13 Colonies Series
6	Seafaring Stranger		Dell 13 Colonies Series

Chase, Elaine Raco

19	Tender Yearnings		Dell Candlelight Ecstasy
162	Video Vixen	/83	Dell Candlelight Ecstasy
	Dare The Devil/ Special Delivery		Leisure
	The Best Of Elaine Raco Chase	/94	Leisure
	A Dream Come True/ No Easy Way Out	11/92	Leisure Contemporary
	Designing Woman/ Video Vixen	07/91	Leisure Contemporary
	Double Occupancy/ Rules Of The Game		Leisure Contemporary

AUTHOR/TITLE INDEX

Chase, Elaine Raco

104	Calculated Risk	12/83	Silhouette Desire
138	Lady Be Bad	05/84	Silhouette Desire

Chase, James Hadley

95	You're Lonely When You're Dead	/51	Harlequin
108	No Orchids For Miss Blandish	/51	Harlequin
111	The Flesh Of The Orchid	/51	Harlequin
124	The Dead Stay Dumb	/51	Harlequin
130	Figure It Out For Yourself	/51	Harlequin
135	Lay Her Among The Lilies	/51	Harlequin
160	Twelve Chinks And A Woman	/52	Harlequin
197	Strictly For Cash	/52	Harlequin
199	The Double Shuffle	/52	Harlequin
206	You Never Know With Women	/53	Harlequin
245	The Soft Touch	/53	Harlequin
267	I'll Bury My Dead	/54	Harlequin
316	This Way For A Shroud	/54	Harlequin
323	Tiger By The Tail	/55	Harlequin
385	Eve	/57	Harlequin
413	I'll Get You For This	/58	Harlequin

Chase, Lindsay

The Oath	07/91	Diamond
The Vow		Diamond
Honor	02/94	Diamond

Chase, Loretta

Three Weddings & A Kiss	/95	Anthology
Captives Of The Night	02/94	Avon
A Christmas Present	12/94	Avon Anthology
The Lion's Chase	09/92	Avon Historical
The Lion's Daughter	10/92	Avon Regency
Isabella		Avon Regency Romance
Lord Of Scoundrels	01/95	Avon Romantic Treasure
Isabella	/88	Walker
The Devil's Delilah	/89	Walker
The Sandalwood Princess	/90	Walker
The English Witch		Walker
Viscount Vagabond		Walker
Knave's Wager	08/91	Walker

Chase, Marian

267	Share The Dream	12/83	Silhouette Romance

Chase, Mary

A Sparkling Affair	04/93	Zebra

Chase, Samantha

Postmark		Tudor Books
Needlepoint	10/89	Tudor Books

Chastain, Sandra

Chastain, Sandra

	Rebel In Silk	05/94	Bantam	
	The Redhead And The Preacher	10/95	Bantam	
	Raven And The Cowboy	07/96	Bantam	
	My Guardian Angel	02/95	Bantam	Anthology
	Southern Nights	07/92	Bantam	Fanfare
	Scandal In Silver	11/94	Bantam	Fanfare
	Dance With The Devil	12/92	Bantam	Loveswept
	The Morning After	09/93	Bantam	Loveswept
	The Judge And The Gypsy	12/91	Bantam	Loveswept
235	Too Hot To Handle	02/88	Bantam	Loveswept
262	For Love Of Lacey	06/88	Bantam	Loveswept
277	Showdown At Lizard Rock	09/88	Bantam	Loveswept
320	The Silver Bullet Affair	04/89	Bantam	Loveswept
344	Joker's Wild	08/89	Bantam	Loveswept
374	Penthouse Suite	01/90	Bantam	Loveswept
391	Adam's Outlaw	04/90	Bantam	Loveswept
410	Run Wild With Me	07/90	Bantam	Loveswept
454	Danny's Girl	02/91	Bantam	Loveswept
459	Firebrand	03/91	Bantam	Loveswept
479	Silver Bracelets	06/91	Bantam	Loveswept
512	The Judge And The Gypsy	12/91	Bantam	Loveswept
531	Love And A Blue-Eyed Cowboy	03/92	Bantam	Loveswept
546	Lean Mean Loving Machine	06/92	Bantam	Loveswept
571	Scarlett Butterfly	10/92	Bantam	Loveswept
592	Night Dreams	01/93	Bantam	Loveswept
610	Hannah's Hunk	04/93	Bantam	Loveswept
636	The Morning After	09/93	Bantam	Loveswept
672	Gabriel's Outlaw	03/94	Bantam	Loveswept
717	Imaginary Lover	11/94	Bantam	Loveswept
758	Mac's Angels: Midnight Fantasy	09/95	Bantam	Loveswept
156	Jasmine And Silk	01/93	Harlequin	Historical
198	Sunshine And Satin	11/93	Harlequin	Historical
	Sweetwater		Warner	
	This Fiery Splendor		Warner	

Chater, Elizabeth

Angela	Ballantine	Regency
The Duke's Dilemma	Ballantine	Regency
The Earl And The Emigree	Ballantine	Regency
Gallant Lady	Ballantine	Regency
The King's Doll	Ballantine	Regency
Lady Dearborne's Debut	Ballantine	Regency
The Marriage Mart	Ballantine	Regency
Milford's Leigewoman	Ballantine	Regency
The Reformed Rake	Ballantine	Regency
The Runaway Debutante	Ballantine	Regency
A Season For The Heart	Ballantine	Regency

AUTHOR/TITLE INDEX

Chater, Elizabeth

	Milady Hot-At-Hand	Ballantine Regency
	The Gamester	Ballantine Regency
	The Elsingham Portrait	Ballantine Regency
	A Delicate Situation	Ballantine Regency
	A Time To Love	Ballantine Regency
	A Place For Elfreda	Ballantine Regency
	Miss Cayley's Unicorn	Ballantine Regency

Chatfield, Susan

6	Leaves Of Fire, Flames Of Love	Dell Candlelight Ecstasy

Cheatham, Lillian

549	The Runaway Heiress	Dell
4	The Shadowed Reunion	Dell Candlelight Ecstasy
549	The Runaway Heiress	Dell Candlelight Regency
808	Lady With A Past	Harlequin Presents
888	The Winter Heart	Harlequin Presents
2683	Island Of Dolphins	Harlequin Romance
	The Secret Of Saramount	Playboy Press

Cheney, Sally

36	Game Of Hearts		Harlequin Historical
112	Thief In The Night	02/92	Harlequin Historical
148	Tender Journey	11/92	Harlequin Historical
192	Tapestry	10/93	Harlequin Historical

Chenier, Blanche

	Summer Masquerade		Ballantine Regency
	Regency Row		Ballantine Regency
	The Defiant Heart		Ballantine Regency
19	Lucinda	02/90	Harlequin Regency
37	The Wayward Heiress	11/90	Harlequin Regency

Cheshire, Chloe

	A Gypsy At Almack's	04/94	Harper Regency

Chesney, Marion

Penelope
My Lords, Ladies And Marjorie
Love And Lady Lovelace
The Ghost And Lady Alice
The Duke's Diamonds
Lady Lucy's Lover
The French Affair
Sweet Masquerade
Those Endearing Young Charms
To Dream Of Love
At The Sign Of The Golden Pineapple
Milady In Love
Lessons In Love
The Paper Princess

Chesney, Marion

	The Perfect Gentleman		
	The Flirt		
	Henrietta		
	Poor Relation		
	The Education Of Miss Patterson		
	The Original Miss Honeyford		
	The Viscount's Revenge		
	Silken Bonds		
	The Highland Countess		
	Pretty Polly		
	Annabelle		
	The Constant Companion		
	Lady Margery's Intrigues		
	Quadrille		
	Silken Bonds #2		
	The Scandalous Bride		
	The Scandalous Lady Wright		
	Regency Gold		
	Daisy		
	Colonel Sandhurst To The Rescue	07/94	
	Lady Fortescue Steps Out	07/94	
	Sir Philip's Folly	07/94	
1	Miser Of Mayfair		A House For All Seasons
2	Plain Jane		A House For All Seasons
3	The Wicked Godmother		A House For All Seasons
4	Rake's Progress		A House For All Seasons
5	The Adventuress		A House For All Seasons
1	Minerva		Six Armitage Sisters Series
2	The Taming Of Annabelle		Six Armitage Sisters Series
3	Deirde And Desire		Six Armitage Sisters Series
4	Diana The Huntress		Six Armitage Sisters Series
5	Daphne		Six Armitage Sisters Series
6	Frederica In Fashion		Six Armitage Sisters Series
1	Refining Felicity		The School Of Manners
2	Perfecting Fiona		The School Of Manners
3	Enlightening Delilah		The School Of Manners
4	Finessing Clarissa		The School Of Manners
5	Animating Maria		The School Of Manners
6	Marrying Harriet		The School Of Manners
1	The First Rebellion		The Waverly Women
4	The Love Match		The Waverly Women
	His Lordship's Pleasure		Ballantine
	The Duke's Diamonds/Ghost And Lady	02/95	Ballantine Regency
	The Sins Of Lady Dacey	04/94	Fawcett Regency
	Her Grace's Passion	08/91	Fawcett Crest Regency
	The Scandalous Marriage	02/92	Fawcett Crest Regency

Chesney, Marion

Marriage Of Inconvenience	06/92	Fawcett Crest	Regency
Governess Of Distinction	12/92	Fawcett Crest	Regency
The Glitter And The Gold		Fawcett Crest	Regency Romance
The Desirable Duchess		Fawcett Crest	Regency Romance
Miss Davenport's Christmas	11/93	Fawcett Crest	Regency Romance
Summertime Splendor	07/92	Jove	Regency Collection
The Marquis Takes A Bride	01/87	Nal	Regency
Miss Fiona's Fancy	07/87	Nal	Regency
My Dear Duchess	09/87	Nal	Regency
The Highland Countess	12/87	Nal	Regency
The Savage Marquess	03/88	Nal	Regency
The Marquis Takes A Bride	04/95	Signet	Regency
Emily Goes To Exeter	09/91	St. Martin's	
Belinda Goes To Bath	12/91	St. Martin's	
Penelope Goes To Portsmouth	03/92	St. Martin's	
Beatrice Goes To Brighton	06/92	St. Martin's	
Deborah Goes To Dover	09/92	St. Martin's	
Yvonne Goes To York	12/92	St. Martin's	
Beatrice Goes To Brighton	11/91	St. Martin's	

Chester, Deborah

22	Captured Hearts		Harlequin Historical

Cheyney, Peter

354	Dark Bahama	/56	Harlequin

Child, Maureen

Run Wild My Heart	03/92	Diamond	
Loving Hearts	02/92	Diamond	
The Bandit's Lady	12/95	Harper Monogram	

Chisholm, Lilian

601	Love Without Ending (Nurse Nicky)	/61	Harlequin
610	Doctor At Hilltops	/61	Harlequin
652	Diana Drake, M.D.	/62	Harlequin
677	The Doctor Next Door	/62	Harlequin
708	Calling Nurse Grant	/63	Harlequin
739	When The Heart Is Young	/63	Harlequin
851	A Song For Tommorow	/64	Harlequin
866	Hearts Go Singing	/64	Harlequin
889	A Friend Of The Family	/65	Harlequin

Chittenden, Margaret

	Marriage By Design	04/94	Harlequin Anthology
183	The Wainright Secret	04/92	Harlequin Intrigue
242	Shadow Of A Doubt	09/93	Harlequin Intrigue
366	Until October		Harlequin Superromance
444	The Scent Of Magic		Harlequin Superromance
531	Double Take	01/93	Harlequin Superromance
575	When The Spirit Is Willing	12/93	Harlequin Superromance

AUTHOR/TITLE INDEX

Chittenden, Margaret
666 As Years Go By   11/95 Harlequin Superromance
Christain, Zita
Just A Miracle   05/96 Harper Monogram
Christenberry, Judith
Moonlight Charade   Jove Regency
Christenberry, Judy
Sweet Remembrance   02/92 Diamond Regency
555 Finding Daddy   10/94 Harlequin American
579 Who's The Daddy? (New Arrival)   04/95 Harlequin American
612 Wanted: Christmas Mommy   12/95 Harlequin American
626 Daddy On Demand   04/96 Harlequin American
Susannah's Secret   03/93 Jove Regency
5 A Little Inconvenience   08/90 Meteor
27 Goldilocks   01/91 Meteor
113 I'll Be Home   11/92 Meteor
The Notorious Widow   Pageant
Mama's Disappointment   06/91 Walker Regency
Christian, Jill
621 Nurse To Captain Andy   /61 Harlequin
713 Harvest Of The Heart (Nurse Of My Heart)   /63 Harlequin
1651 A Scent Of Lemons   /73 Harlequin
Christian, Zita
First And Forever   11/94 Harper Monogram
Christie, Agatha
242 The Murder On The Links   /53 Harlequin
359 The Secret Adversary   /56 Harlequin
377 The Secret Of Chimneys   /57 Harlequin
441 The Murder On The Links   /58 Harlequin
Christie, Colleen
558 A Kiss Is Still A Kiss   02/88 Silhouette Romance
Christie, Susanna
143 The Find Of A Lifetime   05/86 Silhouette Intimate Moments
186 Eden's Temptation   04/87 Silhouette Intimate Moments
203 Close Encounters   08/87 Silhouette Intimate Moments
Christina, Susan
Lord Darver's March   Lion Hearted Time Travel
Christopher, Amy
Captive Kiss   02/92 Zebra Heartfire
Ecstasy's Gamble   Zebra Heartfire
Rebel's Captive   Zebra Heartfire
Christopher, Francine
191 Hold On To Forever   Harlequin Superromance
235 Sweet Tomorrows   Harlequin Superromance
Midnight In Paris   Zebra Lucky In Love
Church, Emma

388

AUTHOR/TITLE INDEX

Church, Emma

7	The Heart Remembers		Harlequin	Superromance
167	Sapphire Secrets		Harlequin	Superromance

Clague, Mary Helen

1	Beside The Still Waters		Berkley
2	Beyond The Shining River		Berkley

Clair, Daphne

	Wilde Heart	07/96	Harelquin	Wedding By Dewilde
2197	A Streak Of Gold	/78	Harlequin	
355	Darling Deceiver		Harlequin	Presents
367	Something Less Than Love		Harlequin	Presents
385	A Wilder Shore		Harlequin	Presents
458	Dark Remembrance		Harlequin	Presents
481	Promise To Pay		Harlequin	Presents
506	The Loving Trap		Harlequin	Presents
679	A Ruling Passion		Harlequin	Presents
687	Marriage Under Fire		Harlequin	Presents
711	Take Hold Of Tomorrow		Harlequin	Presents
881	Dark Dream		Harlequin	Presents
1056	No Escape		Harlequin	Presents
1096	No Winner		Harlequin	Presents
1271	The Wayward Bride		Harlequin	Presents
1586	And Then Came Morning	09/93	Harlequin	Presents
1730	Infamous Bargain	03/95	Harlequin	Presents
1648	Flame On The Horizon	05/94	Harlequin	Presents Plus
1688	Dark Mirror	10/94	Harlequin	Presents Plus
1749	Edge Of Deception	07/95	Harlequin	Presents Plus
2292	The Sleeping Fire		Harlequin	Romance
2329	The Jasmine Bride		Harlequin	Romance
2420	Never Count Tomorrow		Harlequin	Romance
2516	Pacific Pretence		Harlequin	Romance

Claire, Cathryn

399	To The Highest Bidder	01/88	Silhouette	Desire

Claire, Eva

149	Appalachian Summer	02/84	Silhouette	Special Edition
240	Star Attraction	05/85	Silhouette	Special Edition

Claire, Keith

	The Otherwise Girl		Berkley

Clamp, H.M.E.

65	Bridewell Beauty	/50	Harlequin

Clare, Cathleen

	Felicia		Avon	
	Clarissa		Avon	
	Tournament Of Hearts	01/94	Avon	Regency
	A Delectable Dilemma	08/95	Avon	Regency
	Mistress Of Mishap	07/92	Avon	Regency Romance

Clare, Cathleen

	Letitia	07/94	Avon Regency Romance
	Midwinter's Bliss	01/95	Avon Regency Romance

Clare, Cathryn

	To The Highest Bidder	/88	Silhouette Desire
508	Blind Justice	07/89	Silhouette Desire
550	Lock, Stock, Barrel	02/90	Silhouette Desire
591	Five By Ten	09/90	Silhouette Desire
663	The Midas Touch	09/91	Silhouette Desire
688	Hot Stuff	01/92	Silhouette Desire
503	Chasing Destiny	06/93	Silhouette Intimate Moments
558	Sun And Shadow	03/94	Silhouette Intimate Moments
599	The Angel And The Renegade	10/94	Silhouette Intimate Moments
629	Gunslinger's Child	03/95	Silhouette Intimate Moments
702	The Wedding Assignment	03/96	Silhouette Intimate Moments
714	The Honeymoon Assignment	05/96	Silhouette Intimate Moments
726	The Baby Assignment	07/96	Silhouette Intimate Moments

Clare, Jane

26	Old Love, New Love	11/83	Silhouette Intimate Moments
70	Traces Of Dreams	01/83	Silhouette Special Edition

Clare, Shannon

43	Sweet Temptation		Harlequin Superromance
78	Snow Bride		Harlequin Superromance
113	Wake The Moon		Harlequin Superromance

Clark, Amanda

3007	Blueprint For Love		Harlequin Romance
3104	City Girl, Country Girl		Harlequin Romance
3219	A Neighborly Affair	09/92	Harlequin Romance
3321	Early Harvest	07/94	Harlequin Romance
3333	Sullivan's Law (Kids & Kisses)	10/94	Harlequin Romance
640	First Love, Second Chance (Family Man)	04/95	Harlequin Superromance

Clark, Cathy Gillen

367	It's Only Temporary		Harlequin American

Clark, Christie

1041	Two Hearts Too Late (Premiere)	10/94	Silhouette Romance

Clark, Dorothy

1668	Summer Mountain	/73	Harlequin
2242	Forget & Forgive		Harlequin Romance
148	Reluctant Deceiver	05/82	Silhouette Romance
188	No More Regrets	11/82	Silhouette Romance
238	Outback Dreaming	08/83	Silhouette Romance
286	The Man From The Past	04/84	Silhouette Romance
304	Chosen Wife	07/84	Silhouette Romance
397	With Marriage In Mind	11/85	Silhouette Romance

Clark, Gail

	Dulcie Bligh		G.P. Putnam's

Clark, Kathy

	No Satisfaction	/89	Crown Pageant
	Golden Days		Dell
	A Private Affair		Dell
	Another Sunny Day		Dell
	Carousel Of Love		Dell Candlelight Ecstasy
	Destiny's Lady		Dell Candlelight Ecstasy
	Passion And Possession		Dell Candlelight Ecstasy
	A Hint Of Splendor		Dell Candlelight Ecstasy
224	Sweet Anticipation		Harlequin American
282	Kissed By An Angel		Harlequin American
333	Sight Unseen		Harlequin American
348	Phantom Angel		Harlequin American
366	Angel Of Mercy		Harlequin American
383	Starting Over		Harlequin American
428	Good Morning, Miss Greene	02/92	Harlequin American
442	Cody's Last Stand	06/92	Harlequin American
461	Count Your Blessings	02/93	Harlequin American
481	Good-Bye, Desperado	04/93	Harlequin American
536	Groom Unknown	06/94	Harlequin American
571	Stroke Of Midnight	02/95	Harlequin American
	Hearts Against The Wind	09/93	Harlequin Crystal Creek
10	Stand By Your Man	12/93	Harlequin Crystal Creek

Clark, Louise

	Lover's Knot	06/94	Love Spell
	Dangerous Desires	10/93	Lovespell

Clark, Marianne

33	Apache Tears		Nal Rapture Romance

Clark, Norma Lee

	Kitty Quinn		Ballantine Regency
	Megan		Ballantine Regency
	Zandra		Ballantine Regency
	Mallory		Ballantine Regency
	The Infamous Rake		Nal
	The Marriage Mart		Nal
	The Impulsive Miss Pymbrook		Nal
	Cupid's Calendar	07/92	Nal Regency
	Miss Holland's Betrothal	08/86	Nal Regency
	Pippa	11/87	Nal Regency
	The Daring Duchess	08/88	Nal Regency
	The Infamous Rake	02/90	Nal Regency
	The Perfect Match	03/90	Nal Regency
	The Impulsive Miss Pymbroke	04/90	Nal Regency
	The Marriage Mart	08/90	Nal Regency
	Lady Jane		Walker Regency
	The Tyndale Daughters		Walker Regency

AUTHOR/TITLE INDEX

Clayton, Donna
 1066 Nanny And The Professor   03/95 Silhouette Romance
 1118 Fortune's Bride   11/95 Silhouette Romance
 1162 Daddy Down The Aisle   07/96 Silhouette Romance

Cleary, Gwen
   Passion's Bold Caress
   Tender Heart   08/94 Kensington
   Colorado Temptation   Zebra
   Dream's Desire   Zebra
   Missouri Flame   Zebra
   Nevada Temptation   Zebra
   Ecstasy's Masquerade   Zebra Heartfire
   Passionate Possession   Zebra Heartfire
   Victoria's Ecstasy   Zebra Heartfire
   Riverboat Temptation   08/92 Zebra Lovegram Romance

Cleaver, Julia
   Morning Glory

Cleaves, Margaret Major
   Midnight Surrender   Dell Candledlight Tudor Special

Cleeve, Brian
   Kate   Historical
   Sara   Regency

Clemence, Ruth
 1063 The Man From Rhodesia   /66 Harlequin
 1195 Spread Your Wings   /68 Harlequin
 1418 A Cure With Kindness   /70 Harlequin
 1619 Happy With Either   /72 Harlequin
 1697 Healing In The Hills   /73 Harlequin
 1814 A Time To Love   /74 Harlequin
 1985 Wife Made To Measure   /76 Harlequin
 2158 Man With A Mission   /78 Harlequin

Clermont, Shana
   Memphis   Zebra
   Natchez   Zebra

Cleves, Margaret Major
 603 Midnight Surrender   Dell Candlelight Regency

Clifford, Kay
 2468 No Time For Love   Harlequin Romance
 2505 A Temporary Affair   Harlequin Romance
 2611 Heart Of Gold   Harlequin Romance
 2881 Dream Of Love   Harlequin Romance
 2912 Recipe For Love   Harlequin Romance

Clifton, Bonita
   Time Of The Rose   Leisure
   Journey Of The Rose   01/94 Leisure Love Spell

Cloud, Patricia

AUTHOR/TITLE INDEX

Cloud, Patricia
    This Willing Passion   Berkley

Coates, May
 1357   Ripples In The Lake   /69   Harlequin
 1677   Stranger At The Door   /73   Harlequin

Coburn, Walt
  350   The Renegade   /56   Harlequin

Cochrane, Kia
  600   Married By A Thread (Premiere)   10/94   Silhouette Intimate Moments

Cockcroft, Ann
    Pirate's Promise   Pocket
  294   Beloved Pirate   05/84   Silhouette Romance
    River Jewel   Tapestry

Cocking, Ronald
  233   Die With Me Lady   /53   Harlequin

Cody, Al
   93   Empty Saddles   /51   Harlequin
  153   Outlaw Valley   /52   Harlequin
  274   Lost Valley   /54   Harlequin
  285   Texas Outlaw   /54   Harlequin
  325   Satan's Range   /55   Harlequin
  343   Gun Thunder Valley   /55   Harlequin
  345   The Gunman   /55   Harlequin

Cody, Pat
    A Dangerous Dandy   12/94   Harper
    A Risky Rogue   07/95   Harper

Coe, Phyllis
    The Basket Bride   12/92   Harper Monogram

Coffaro, Katherine
    Promo: Gently Into Night   Harlequin American
   44   A Logical Passion   Harlequin American
   70   No Other Love   Harlequin American
   81   Sunward Journey   Harlequin American

Coffman, Elaine
    Captive Angel
    To Have And To Hold   06/94   Avon Anthology
    For All The Right Reasons   10/91   Dell
    Somewhere Along The Way 09/92   Dell
    Angel In Marble   Dell
    Escape Not My Love   Dell
    If My Love Could Hold You   Dell
    My Enemy, My Love   Dell
    Heaven Knows   03/94   Fawcett
    So This Is Love   07/93   Fawcett Gold Medal
    Outlaw Brides - "The Bride Of Blackness C 06/96   Harlequin Anthology
    Midsummer Night's Madness   06/95   St. Martin's Anthology

AUTHOR/TITLE INDEX

Coffman, Elaine
    When Love Comes Along   11/95   Warner
Coffman, Virginia
    Moura
    Dark Winds
    Gaynor Woman   Historical
    Jeweled Darkness   Severn House
    Dark Desire   Warner
Cohen, Christy
    Whispered Lies   09/94   Bantam
Cohen, Sharron
  1015   High Country   Harlequin Presents
  2839   Odd Man Out   Harlequin Romance
Coldenbaum, Sally
   206   A Dream To Cling To   09/87   Bantam Loveswept
Cole, Hilary
   290   The Sweetheart Trust   /85   Berkley Second Chance At Love
Cole, Jackson
   100   Black Rider   /51   Harlequin
Cole, Sue Ellen
    7   A Distant Castle   06/83   Silhouette Intimate Moments
   30   Race Against The Wind   12/83   Silhouette Intimate Moments
  103   Head Over Heels   07/85   Silhouette Intimate Moments
  119   Critic's Choice   11/85   Silhouette Intimate Moments
Cole, Victoria
  510   Mind Reader   07/93   Silhouette Intimate Moments
Coleman, Clare
    Daughter Of The Reef   12/92   Jove Historical
    Sister Of The Sun   09/93   Jove Historical
    Child Of The Dawn   03/94   Jove Historical
Coleman, Patricia
    Daring Deceptions   12/90   Fawcett Regency
Collier, Leona
    Change Of Heart   Tiara Regency
Collier, Susan
    Time Heals   06/95   Leisure Love Spell
Collin, Marion
  860   Nurse At The Top   /64   Harlequin
  913   Doctors Three   /65   Harlequin
 1169   The Doctor's Delusion   /68   Harlequin
Collinge, Patricia
   43   Duet   05/91   Meteor
Collins, Kathryn
   97   The Wings Of Night   Harlequin Superromance
  156   Windy Fire   Harlequin Superromance

AUTHOR/TITLE INDEX

Collins, Kathryn

  207   Dreams Gather   Harlequin Superromance

Collins, Laurel

        Silver Eyes

        Dark Surrender

        The Jade Garden   04/92   Diamond

        Magic Nights   11/91   Diamond

        Desert Enchantress   St. Martin's

        Dream Weaver   05/95   Zebra Lovegram

Collins, Marion Smith

134	Out Of The Clear Blue	03/86	Bantam Loveswept
5	By Mutual Consent	04/84	Harlequin Temptation
22	By Any Other Name	08/84	Harlequin Temptation
35	This Thing Called Love	11/84	Harlequin Temptation
49	On The Safe Side	03/85	Harlequin Temptation
63	This Time, This Moment	06/85	Harlequin Temptation
86	Without A Hitch	12/85	Harlequin Temptation
114	For Love Or Money	07/86	Harlequin Temptation
211	Foxy Lady	07/88	Harlequin Temptation
179	Another Chance	02/87	Silhouette Intimate Moments
252	Better Than Ever	08/88	Silhouette Intimate Moments
320	Catch Of The Day	01/90	Silhouette Intimate Moments
383	Shared Ground	05/91	Silhouette Intimate Moments
452	Baby Magic	10/92	Silhouette Intimate Moments
514	Fire On The Mountain	08/93	Silhouette Intimate Moments
610	Surrogate Dad	12/94	Silhouette Intimate Moments
773	Home To Stay	02/91	Silhouette Romance
849	Every Night At Eight	02/92	Silhouette Romance

Collins, Susanna

1	Flamenco Nights	/81	Berkley Second Chance At Love
14	Hard To Handle	/81	Berkley Second Chance At Love
19	Destiny's Spell	/81	Berkley Second Chance At Love
62	On Wings Of Magic	/82	Berkley Second Chance At Love
201	Brief Enchantment	/84	Berkley Second Chance At Love

Collins, Toni

686	Immoral Support	01/92	Silhouette Desire
687	Sugar Hill	01/92	Silhouette Desire
664	Ms. Maxwell And Son	08/89	Silhouette Romance
893	Letters From Home	10/92	Silhouette Romance
941	Something Old	06/93	Silhouette Romance
1008	Miracle Dad	05/94	Silhouette Romance
1050	Miss Scrooge (Under The Mistletoe)	12/94	Silhouette Romance
1159	Willfully Wed	06/96	Silhouette Romance
6	Unhappily Unwed	10/95	Silhouette Yours Truly

Colt, Zandra

   40   Cactus Rose   /82   Berkley Second Chance At Love

Colter, Cara
  491   Dare To Dream   03/87 Silhouette Romance
  1161 Baby In Blue   06/96 Silhouette Romance
Colvin, Penny
      Blood And Wine   Pocket
Combs, Becky
  23   Taking Savannah   11/83 Bantam Loveswept
Combs, Iris
  24   The Reluctant Lark   11/83 Bantam Loveswept
Combs, Susan
  23   A Perfect Match   12/90 Meteor
Comeaux, Donna
      Lost Splendour   Sweet & Savage
Compton, Katherine
      The Lady And The Outlaw   04/94 Avon Historical
      Whispers In The Wind   02/95 Avon Historical
      Blue Moon Bayou   08/92 Avon Romance
      Brazen Whispers   12/90 Avon Romance
      Outlaw Bride   06/91 Avon Romance
      Eden's Angel   07/90 Avon Romance
Comstock, Mary Chase
      A Midsummer's Magic   07/94 Zebra
Conan, Christa
  678 All I Need   11/95 Silhouette Intimate Moments
Conant, Constance
  1   Star Trilogy: Southern Star   Leisure Historical
  2   Star Trilogy: Falling Star   Leisure Historical
  3   Star Trilogy: Star Of The West   Leisure Historical
Conklin, Judith
      Mistress Of The Moors   Leisure Gothic Romance
Conlan, Margaret
      Abilene Gamble   08/95 Jove Wildflower
Conlee, Jaclyn
  71   Satin And Steele   /83 Berkley Second Chance At Love
Conn, Phoebe
      Hearts Of Gold   Warner
      Beyond The Stars   02/88 Warner Poplar
      By Love Enslaved   11/89 Warner Poplar
      In Passion's Wake   11/90 Warner Poplar
      Arizona Angel   Zebra
      Captive Heart   Zebra
      Emerald Fire   Zebra
      Love Me 'til Dawn   Zebra
      Loving Fury   Zebra
      No Sweeter Ecstasy   07/90 Zebra

Conn, Phoebe

	Starlit Ecstasy		Zebra
	Tempt Me With Kisses		Zebra
	Tender Savage		Zebra
	Love's Elusive Flame	10/83	Zebra
	Savage Fire	06/84	Zebra
	Ecstasy's Paradise	10/84	Zebra
	Savage Storm	10/84	Zebra
	No Sweeter Ecstasy	07/90	Zebra
	Swept Away	02/94	Zebra
	Beloved	12/94	Zebra
	Tangled Hearts		Zebra
	Paradise	08/95	Zebra
	To Love And To Honor	05/95	Zebra Anthology
	A Groom For Holly: "To Love And Honor"	06/95	Zebra Anthology

Connell, Candace

551	Dark Legacy		Dell Candlelight

Connell, Susan

543	Glory Girl	05/92	Bantam Loveswept
606	Some Kind Of Wonderful	04/93	Bantam Loveswept
638	Trouble In Paradise	09/93	Bantam Loveswept
671	Looks Like Love	02/94	Bantam Loveswept
697	Captain's Orders	07/94	Bantam Loveswept
725	Rings On Her Fingers	01/95	Bantam Loveswept
752	Pagan's Paradise	08/95	Bantam Loveswept
981	Reese: The Untamed	02/96	Silhouette Desire: Sons & Lovers #2

Connolly, Vivian

10	I Know My Love	/84	Berkley To Have And To Hold
21	Moonlight And Magnolias	/84	Berkley To Have And To Hold
30	Promises To Keep	/84	Berkley To Have And To Hold
63	Love In Exile		Harlequin Superromance

Conrad, Constance

27	On Wings Of Night	11/82	Silhouette Desire

Conrad, Helen

8	Temptation's Sting	06/83	Bantam Loveswept
68	Undercover Affair	11/84	Bantam Loveswept
2731	Tears Of Gold		Harlequin Romance
322	Desperado		Harlequin Superromance
544	Joe's Miracle	04/93	Harlequin Superromance
617	Jake's Promise	10/94	Harlequin Superromance
3	Everlasting	03/84	Harlequin Temptation
118	Diamond In The Rough	08/86	Harlequin Temptation
	Desperado	09/95	Harlequin Western Lovers
	Silver Linings		Harper
	Stranger's Embrace	08/92	Zebra Heartfire

Constant, Jan

Constant, Jan

| | The Only Hope | 06/94 | Fawcett |
| | The Beringer Heiress | 07/92 | Fawcett Crest Regency Romance |

Constantin-Weyer, M.

| 318 | The Half-Breed | /54 | Harlequin |

Converse, Jane

129	Moonlit Path	01/82	Silhouette Romance
5	Paradise Postponed	02/82	Silhouette Special Edition
40	Heartstorm	08/82	Silhouette Special Edition
64	Mist Of Blossoms	12/82	Silhouette Special Edition
117	The Coral Sea	09/83	Silhouette Special Edition

Conway, Celine

620	White Doctor	/61	Harlequin
675	Wide Pastures	/62	Harlequin
721	Ship's Surgeon	/63	Harlequin
736	The Tall Pines	/63	Harlequin
754	The Rancher Needs A Wife	/63	Harlequin
807	Full Tide	/64	Harlequin
826	Doctor's Assistant	/64	Harlequin
863	The Blue Caribbean	/64	Harlequin
885	At The Villa Massina	/65	Harlequin
911	The Return Of Simon	/65	Harlequin
934	My Dear Cousin	/65	Harlequin
965	Came A Stranger	/65	Harlequin
996	Perchance To Marry	/66	Harlequin
1019	Flower Of The Morning	/66	Harlequin
1046	Three Women	/66	Harlequin

Conway, Laura

| | Take Heed Of Loving Me | | Suspense |

Conway, Theresa

	A Passion For Glory		
	Seeds Of Destiny		
	Crimson Glory		Ballantine Regency
	Gabrielle		Ballantine Regency
	Silver Clouds, Golden Dreams		Berkley
	Paloma		Berkley
	Love Chase		Tapestry

Conwell, Kent

| | Cattle Drive To Dodge | /92 | Avalon |
| | Panhandle Gold | /91 | Avalon |

Cook, Elsa

| | To Pluck A Rose | | Pocket |

Cook, Sally

1223	Deep Harbour		Harlequin Presents
1287	Belonging		Harlequin Presents
1320	Hijacked Heart		Harlequin Presents

AUTHOR/TITLE INDEX

Cook, Sally

1407	Tiger's Tail	11/91	Harlequin Presents
1440	Inherit Your Love	03/92	Harlequin Presents
1495	Spring Sunshine	10/92	Harlequin Presents

Cooke, Ronald J.

7	The House On Craig Street	/49	Harlequin
56	The Mayor Of Cote St. Paul	/50	Harlequin

Cookson, Catherine

The Dwelling Place
The Parson's Daughter
The Girl
The Banneman Legacy
Rooney
The Menagerie
The Mallen Lot
The Mallen Girl
The Mallen Streak
Feather's In The Fire
Love Child
The Harrogate Secret
The Wingless Bird
The Black Velvet Gown
The Moth
The Black Candle
The Bailey Chronicles
Fenwick Houses
The Fifteen Streets
The Glass Virgin
Kate Hannigan
Kate Mulholland
Our Kate
Pure As A Lily
The Whip

Tilly		Historical
The Maltese Angel	12/94	Simon & Schuste

Coombs, Nina

32	Forbidden Joy		Nal Rapture Romance
56	Sun Spark	/84	Nal Rapture Romance

Cooper, Ann

295	Battle With Desire	Harlequin Presents
2383	Fool's Paradise	Harlequin Romance
2384	Island Fiesta	Harlequin Romance
2630	Maelstrom	Harlequin Romance

Copeland, Lori

	Someone To Love	04/95	Ballantine
387	Darling Deceiver	03/90	Bantam Loveswept

AUTHOR/TITLE INDEX

Copeland, Lori

Corbet, Colleen
    Dark Eyes   04/95   Avon Historical
Corbett, Paula
    156   Maid In Boston   08/84   Silhouette Desire
Cord, Betty
    254   Mesquite Johnny   /53   Harlequin
Cordaire, Christina
    Forgiving Hearts   10/94   Diamond Homespun
    Spring Enchantment   06/96   Jove Haunting Hearts
    Loving Honor   08/95   Jove Homespun
    Winter Longing   02/96   Jove Homespun
    Heart's Deception   10/92   Jove Regency
    Love's Triumph   05/93   Jove Regency
    Pride's Folly   09/93   Jove Regency
    Daring Illusion   04/94   Jove Regency
    Beloved Stranger   02/95   Jove Regency
Cordaire, Christine
    The Quilting Circle   /96   Berkley Anthology
Cores, Lucy
    Fatal Passion   /89   Walker
    Destiny's Passion   Zebra
Corey, Gayle
    200   Top Marks   04/88   Harlequin Temptation
Corey, Ryanne
    615   The Valentine Street Hustle   01/91   Silhouette Desire
    657   Leather And Lace   08/91   Silhouette Desire
    764   The Stranger   02/93   Silhouette Desire
    950   When She Was Bad   09/95   Silhouette Desire
Cork, Dorothy
    1511 Where Black Swans Fly   /71   Harlequin
    1549 A Night For Possums   /71   Harlequin
    1644 Wayaway   /72   Harlequin
    1692 Butterfly Montane   /73   Harlequin
    1714 Spirit Of The Sun   /73   Harlequin
    1757 The Girl At Saltbush Flat   /74   Harlequin
    1784 The Red Plains Of Jounima   /74   Harlequin
    1812 A Promise To Keep   /74   Harlequin
    1876 Gate Of The Golden Gazelle   /75   Harlequin
    1894 Quicksilver Summer   /75   Harlequin
    1927 Wandalilli Princess   /75   Harlequin
    1966 Red Diamond   /76   Harlequin
    1978 The Eye Of The Sun   /76   Harlequin
    2057 Dreamtime At Big Sky   /77   Harlequin
    2115 Breakers On The Beach   /77   Harlequin
    2139 Outback Rainbow   /78   Harlequin
    2199 A Thousand Miles Away   /78   Harlequin

Cork, Dorothy

6	The Kurranulla Round		Harlequin Premiere Edition
2253	Heart Of The Whirlwind		Harlequin Romance
2259	Island Of Escape		Harlequin Romance
2288	Walkabout Wife		Harlequin Romance
2372	Outback Runaway		Harlequin Romance
2390	Barefoot Bride		Harlequin Romance
103	Be Honour Bound	09/81	Silhouette Romance
219	Island Spell	04/83	Silhouette Romance
365	Wildest Dreams	06/85	Silhouette Romance

Cornelius, Kay

	Sign Of The Spirit	07/95	Barbour & Co.
	A Matter Of Security	07/95	Barbour & Co.

Cornwell, Patricia

	All That Remains	06/93	Avon
	The Body Farm		Scribners

Corrie, Jane

1956	The Impossible Boss	/76	Harlequin
2020	Rainbow For Megan	/76	Harlequin
2038	Sinclair Territory	/77	Harlequin
2053	Green Paddocks	/77	Harlequin
2072	The Bahamian Pirate	/77	Harlequin
2087	Dangerous Alliance	/77	Harlequin
2098	Rimmer's Way	/77	Harlequin
2159	Rafferty's Legacy	/78	Harlequin
2167	Patterson's Island	/78	Harlequin
2194	The Texan Rancher	/78	Harlequin
2209	Peacock's Walk	/78	Harlequin
2257	The Island Bride		Harlequin Romance
2285	Caribbean Cocktail		Harlequin Romance
2313	The Spanish Uncle		Harlequin Romance
2335	Tasmanian Tangle		Harlequin Romance
2365	The Station Boss		Harlequin Romance
2413	Pirate's Lair		Harlequin Romance
2431	Bride For Sale		Harlequin Romance
2521	Ross's Girl		Harlequin Romance
2551	Man With Two Faces		Harlequin Romance
2743	Cartier's Strike		Harlequin Romance

Corrigan, Mark

187	Shanghai Jezebel	/52	Harlequin
277	Lady Of China Street	/54	Harlequin

Cory, Diane

	A Token Of Jewels		Pocket
	High Society	07/90	Pocket

Costain, Thomas

	Black Rose		Historical

AUTHOR/TITLE INDEX

Cothran, Betty

Over The Moon	06/94	Zebra	To Love Again
Blue Moon	11/94	Zebra	To Love Again

Cott, Christine Hella

22	Midnight Magic		Harlequin Superromance
30	A Tender Wilderness		Harlequin Superromance
50	Dangerous Delight		Harlequin Superromance
98	Perfume And Lace		Harlequin Superromance
144	Riches To Hold		Harlequin Superromance
168	Seaspun Magic		Harlequin Superromance
178	Strawberry Kiss		Harlequin Superromance
220	Cinnamon Hearts		Harlequin Superromance

Coughlin, Patricia

	Wild Paradise		
39	The Bargain	/95	Harlequin Men Made In America
83	Message For Jesse	11/85	Harlequin Temptation
632	Love In The First Degree	04/95	Silhouette Intimate Moments
722	Borrowed Bride	07/96	Silhouette Intimate Moments
	Love Child	12/92	Silhouette Special Edition
438	Shady Lady		Silhouette Special Edition
485	The Bargain	10/88	Silhouette Special Edition
523	Some Like It Hot	05/89	Silhouette Special Edition
602	The Spirit Is Willing	06/90	Silhouette Special Edition
726	Her Brother's Keeper	02/92	Silhouette Special Edition
786	Gypsy Summer	12/92	Silhouette Special Edition
804	The Awakening	03/93	Silhouette Special Edition
837	My Sweet Baby	09/93	Silhouette Special Edition
867	When Stars Collide	02/94	Silhouette Special Edition
919	Mail Order Cowboy (That Special Woman!)	11/94	Silhouette Special Edition
982	Joyride (Congratulations!)	09/95	Silhouette Special Edition
	Easy Come ...	/90	Silhouette Summer Sizzlers

Coulter, Catherine

	Night Fire		Avon
	Night Shadow		Avon
	Night Storm	08/95	Avon
	The Cove	02/96	Berkley
	The Valentine Legacy	07/96	Berkley Legacy Trilogy
	The Nightingale Legacy	01/95	G P Putnam
	The Sherbrook Bride	04/92	Jove
	The Hellion Bride	10/92	Jove
	The Heiress Bride	11/92	Jove
	Lord Of Hawkfell Island	11/93	Jove
	Lord Of Raven's Peak	03/94	Jove
2	The Nightingale Legacy	07/95	Jove Legacy Trilogy
1	The Wyndham Legacy	09/94	Jove Legacy Triology
3	Lord Of Falcon Ridge	02/95	Jove Viking Saga
	Chandra		Nal

404

AUTHOR/TITLE INDEX

Craig, Jasmine

	Imprisoned Heart	/83	Berkley/Jove
	Stormy Reunion	/83	Berkley/Jove
	Runaway Love	/82	Berkley/Jove
	Tender Triumph	/82	Berkley/Jove

Craig, Mary Shura

	Pirate's Landing		Berkley
	Lyon's Pride		Berkley

Craig, Rebecca

	Gentle Thunder	04/95	Jove Wildflower

Craig, Rianna

56	Love Match		Harlequin American
39	On Executive Orders		Harlequin Intrigue

Craig, Vera

	Glen Hall		Dell Candlelight
	Now And Forever		Dell Candlelight

Crain, Elley

478	Deep In The Heart	02/93	Silhouette Initmate Moments
533	New Year's Resolution	11/93	Silhouette Intimate Moments

Crampton, Helen

	The Marquis Takes A Bride		Pocket Cotillion Regency
	The Highland Countess		Pocket Cotillion Regency

Crane, Caroline

	Whispers From Oracle Falls	/91	Avalon

Crane, Elizabeth

	Time Remembered	07/94	Leisure
	Reflections In Time	09/93	Leisure Historical

Crane, Leah

66	Dark Ecstasy		Harlequin Superromance

Crane, Teresa

	A Dream Of Spring	10/91	Dell

Cranmer, Kathryn

2517	Passionate Enemies		Harlequin Romance
2620	Pas De Deux		Harlequin Romance
2719	Wrecker's Bride		Harlequin Romance

Craven, Sara

1943	The Garden Of Dreams	/76	Harlequin
191	Strange Adventure	/77	Harlequin Presents
195	A Gift For A Lion	/77	Harlequin Presents
199	Wild Melody	/77	Harlequin Presents
215	Temple Of The Moon	/77	Harlequin Presents
235	A Place Of Storms	/78	Harlequin Presents
243	Past All Forgetting	/78	Harlequin Presents
251	The Devil At Archangel	/78	Harlequin Presents
255	Dragon's Lair	/78	Harlequin Presents
291	High Tide At Midnight		Harlequin Presents

Craven, Sara

307	Moth To Flame		Harlequin	Presents
331	Flame Of Diablo		Harlequin	Presents
368	Fugitive Wife		Harlequin	Presents
398	Shadow Of Desire		Harlequin	Presents
411	Moon Of Aphrodite		Harlequin	Presents
440	Summer Of The Raven		Harlequin	Presents
459	Witching Hour		Harlequin	Presents
487	Dark Summer Dawn		Harlequin	Presents
551	Unguarded Moment		Harlequin	Presents
561	Counterfeit Bride		Harlequin	Presents
599	Sup With The Devil		Harlequin	Presents
616	Pagan Adversary		Harlequin	Presents
647	A Bad Enemy		Harlequin	Presents
704	Dark Paradise		Harlequin	Presents
815	Alien Vengeance		Harlequin	Presents
832	Act Of Betrayal		Harlequin	Presents
856	Promise Of The Unicorn		Harlequin	Presents
872	Escape Me Never		Harlequin	Presents
920	A High Price To Pay		Harlequin	Presents
1010	The Marriage Deal		Harlequin	Presents
1032	Night Of The Condor		Harlequin	Presents
1072	Outsider		Harlequin	Presents
1097	Witch's Harvest		Harlequin	Presents
1119	Comparative Stranger		Harlequin	Presents
1143	Devil And The Deep Sea		Harlequin	Presents
1176	Kind Of Swords		Harlequin	Presents
1241	Island Of The Heart		Harlequin	Presents
1279	Flawless		Harlequin	Presents
1330	Storm Force		Harlequin	Presents
1471	When The Devil Drives	07/92	Harlequin	Presents
1503	Desperate Measures	11/92	Harlequin	Presents
1549	Dark Ransom	04/93	Harlequin	Presents
1708	Tower Of Shadows	12/94	Harlequin	Presents
1786	Dark Apollo	01/96	Harlequin	Presents
1640	Dawn Song	04/94	Harlequin	Presents Plus
1761	Thunder Of The Reef	09/95	Harlequin	Presents Plus

Crawford, Camille

The Emerald Paradise	07/93	Avalon	

Crawford, Claudia

A Dangerous Gift	05/96	Signet	

Crawford, Diane

27	Sapphire Island	/82	Berkley	Second Chance At Love
158	Season Of Marriage	/84	Berkley	Second Chance At Love

Crawford, Diane Michele

Comedy Of Errors	10/92	Bantam	Sweet Dreams

Crawford, Elaine

	Timeless	05/94	Berkley Anthology
	Captive Angel	09/92	Diamond Wildflower
	River Temptress	03/93	Diamond Wildflower
	Love Potion	02/95	Jove Anthology
	Love So Wild	04/94	Jove Historical
	A Perfect Gentleman	04/96	Jove Historical

Crawford, Rosemary A.

529	Image Of Evil		Dell Candlelight

Crease, Gail

	Letters To A Lady	07/93	Harlequin Regency

Creasey, John

116	Kill The Toff	/51	Harlequin

Crecy, Jeanne

	Hands Of Terror	/72	Berkley
	The Lightning Tree	/73	Berkley
	The Evil Among Us	/75	Nal Signet
	My Face Beneath The Stone	/75	Nal Signet
	The Winter Keeper	/75	Nal Signet
	The Night Hunter	/82	Nal Signet

Creekmore, Donna

528	The Coachman's Daughter		Dell Candlelight

Creel, Catherine

	Texas Bride		
	Breathless Passion		
	Surrender To Desire		
	Golden Obsession		
	Rapture's Rogue		
	Scoundrel's Bride		
	Texas Spitfire		
	The Yankee And The Belle		Belmont Tower
	Wild Texas Rose	12/93	Fawcett
	Westward Angel	12/95	Fawcett
	Lady Alex	10/94	Fawcett Historical
	Captive Flame		Zebra
	Cimarron Bride		Zebra
	Nevada Captive		Zebra
	Passion's Chains		Zebra
	Texas Flame		Zebra
	Texas Torment		Zebra
	Wild Texas Loving		Zebra

Creese, Bethea

697	Glorious Haven (Patient In Love)	/62	Harlequin
859	Irish Rose (Nurse In Ireland)	/64	Harlequin
1413	The Family Face	/70	Harlequin

Creighton, Kathleen

AUTHOR/TITLE INDEX

Creighton, Kathleen

139	Delilah's Weakness	05/86	Bantam Loveswept
163	Still Waters	11/86	Bantam Loveswept
208	Katie's Hero	09/87	Bantam Loveswept
239	The Prince And The Patriot	02/88	Bantam Loveswept
279	Winter's Daughter	09/88	Bantam Loveswept
299	The Sorcerer's Keeper	12/88	Bantam Loveswept
	Men In Uniform	04/94	Harlequin Anthology
12	Rogue's Valley	03/94	Harlequin Men Made In America
	The Mysterious Gift	/90	Silhouette Christmas Stories
584	The Heart Mender	08/90	Silhouette Desire
654	In From The Cold	07/91	Silhouette Desire
84	Demon Lover	02/85	Silhouette Intimate Moments
157	Double Dealings	09/86	Silhouette Intimate Moments
196	Gypsy Dancer	06/87	Silhouette Intimate Moments
216	In Defense Of Love	11/87	Silhouette Intimate Moments
240	Rogue's Valley	05/88	Silhouette Intimate Moments
289	Tiger Dawn	06/89	Silhouette Intimate Moments
322	Love And Other Surprises	02/90	Silhouette Intimate Moments
417	Wolf And The Angel	02/92	Silhouette Intimate Moments
547	A Wanted Man (American Heroes)	02/94	Silhouette Intimate Moments
616	Eyewitness	01/95	Silhouette Intimate Moments
639	One Good Man	05/95	Silhouette Intimate Moments
677	Man Of Steel	11/95	Silhouette Intimate Moments
	A Christmas Love	12/92	St. Martin's

Crenshaw, Nadine

	Destiny And Desire	/92	Pinnacle
	For The Love Of Chocolate	05/96	St. Martin's Anthology
	Spellbound	/90	Zebra
	Edin's Embrace	/88	Zebra
	Captive Melody	/88	Zebra Heartfire
	Mountain Mistress	11/87	Zebra Heartfire

Cresswell, Jasmine

	I Do, Again	03/97	Harlequin
	Marriage By Design	04/94	Harlequin Anthology
30	Love For Hire	07/96	Harlequin Here Come The Grooms
51	Undercover	/86	Harlequin Intrigue
77	Chase The Past	/87	Harlequin Intrigue
105	Free Fall	/89	Harlequin Intrigue
124	Charades	/89	Harlequin Intrigue
182	House Guest	03/92	Harlequin Intrigue
194	Nowhere To Hide	09/92	Harlequin Intrigue
245	Keeping Secrets	01/94	Harlequin Intrigue
297	Edge Of Eternity (Weddings, Inc.)	11/94	Harlequin Intrigue
913	Hunter's Prey	/86	Harlequin Presents
	Rakes And Rascals	08/95	Harlequin Promotion
3176	Love For Hire	02/92	Harlequin Romance

AUTHOR/TITLE INDEX

Cresswell, Jasmine

3270	The Perfect Bride	06/93	Harlequin Romance
574	Midnight Fantasy	02/96	Harlequin Temptation
	Shattered Vows	04/96	Harlequin Weddings By Dewilde
	Tarrisbroke Hall		Mills & Boon
	The Moreton Scandal	/86	Mills & Boon
	Traitor's Heir	/84	Mills & Boon
	Lord Rutherford's Affair	/84	Mills & Boon
	Desires & Deceptions	05/95	Mira
	Chase The Past	05/95	Mira
	No Sin Too Great	05/96	Mira
	Charades	06/96	Mira
	Timeless	04/94	Penguin Topaz
	To Catch The Wind	09/93	Penguin Topaz
	Prince Of The Night	06/95	Penguin Topaz
	The Abducted Heiress	/78	Robert Hale
	The Blackwood Bride	/79	Robert Hale
	The Princess	/82	Robert Hale
	Caroline	/80	Robert Hale
	The Rossiter Arrangement	/79	Robert Hale
	The Substitute Bride	/78	Robert Hale
	Forgotten Marriage	/77	Robert Hale
	The Reluctant Viscountess	/82	Robert Hale Regency
	The Danewood Legacy	/81	Robert Hale Regency
113	Mixed Doubles	01/84	Silhouette Desire

Crewe, Sarah

195	Night Flame	/84	Berkley Second Chance At Love
281	Windflame	/85	Berkley Second Chance At Love

Crisp, Marty

	At Your Own Risk	03/93	Avalon

Criss, Dani

1065	Family In The Making	02/95	Silhouette Romance
1112	Family Ties	10/95	Silhouette Romance
490	Sheriff's Lady	04/93	Silhouette Special Edition

Cristol, Jaymi

28	Three Wishes	03/93	Zebra Lucky In Love

Cristy, Ann

	Enthralled		
	Mystique		
49	Form The Torrid Past	/82	Berkley Second Chance At Love
60	Torn Asunder	/82	Berkley Second Chance At Love
3	Tread Softly	/84	Berkley To Have And To Hold
24	Homecoming	/84	Berkley To Have And To Hold

Criswell, Mille

	Desperate	10/97	Warner #1 Lawmen Trilogy

Criswell, Millie

Criswell, Millie

	Diamond In The Rough	01/94	Harper Historical
	Phantom Lover	05/93	Harper Monogram
	Mail-Order Outlaw	07/94	Harper Monogram
	Sweet Laurel	03/96	Warner Flowers Of West Trilogy
1	Wild Heather	07/95	Warner Flowers Of West Trilogy
	Brazen Virginia Bride	12/90	Zebra Heartfire
	California Temptress	06/91	Zebra Heartfire
	Desire's Endless Kiss	12/91	Zebra Heartfire
	Temptation's Fire	06/92	Zebra Heartfire

Crockett, Christina

55	To Touch A Dream		Harlequin Superromance
103	A Moment Of Magic		Harlequin Superromance
146	Song Of The Seabird		Harlequin Superromance
171	Windward Passage		Harlequin Superromance

Crockett, Linda

| | Carousel | 04/95 | St. Martin's |

Crook, Elizabeth

| | Promised Lands | 06/94 | Doubleday |

Crosby, Susan

888	The Mating Game (Premiere)	10/94	Silhouette Desire
952	Almost A Honeymoon	09/95	Silhouette Desire
1018	Baby Fever	08/96	Silhouette Desire

Crosby, Tanya Anne

	Out Of Wedlock	06/93	Avon
	Kissed	12/95	Avon
	A Christmas Together	10/94	Avon Anthology
	Viking's Prize	04/94	Avon Historical
	Sagebrush Bride	05/93	Avon Historical
	Once Upon A Kiss	02/95	Avon Historical
	Angel Of Fire	04/92	Avon Romance

Crose, Susan Lynn

264	The Brass Ring	07/88	Bantam Loveswept
	Kiss Of The Moon	07/94	Pocket
	Outlaw	11/95	Pocket

Cross, Caitlin

272	High Risk	11/85	Silhouette Special Edition
341	Catch The Wind	10/86	Silhouette Special Edition
380	Shadow Of Doubt	05/87	Silhouette Special Edition
413	A Natural Woman	10/87	Silhouette Special Edition

Cross, Caroline

810	Dangerous	09/93	Silhouette Desire
851	Rafferty's Angel	04/94	Silhouette Desire
910	Truth Or Dare	02/95	Silhouette Desire
939	Operation Mommy	07/95	Silhouette Desire
1013	Gavin's Child	07/96	Silhouette Desire

Cunliffe, Corinna

	Play Of Hearts	02/86	Nal Regency
	The Unsuitable Chaperone	02/88	Nal Regency
	Hand Of Fortune	09/90	Nal Regency

Cunningham, Marilyn

	The Women Of Liberty Creek	04/93	Harper Monogram
334	Someone To Turn To	05/90	Silhouette Intimate Moments
355	Enchanted Circle	10/90	Silhouette Intimate Moments
411	Long White Cloud	12/91	Silhouette Intimate Moments
527	On The Edge	10/93	Silhouette Intimate Moments

Curland, Lynn

	Stardust Of Yesterday	04/96	Berkley Haunted Hearts

Currie, Anne Brook

	Natalya		Ballantine

Currie, Katy

5	Blind Promises	03/84	Silhouette Inspirational

Curry, Elisa

18	Playing For Keeps	/84	Berkley To Have And To Hold

Curry, Elissa

178	Winter Wildfire	/84	Berkley Second Chance At Love
193	Lady With A Past	/84	Berkley Second Chance At Love
263	Gentleman At Heart	/85	Berkley Second Chance At Love
287	Sophisticated Lady	/85	Berkley Second Chance At Love
23	Kiss Me, Cait	/84	Berkley To Have And To Hold

Curtis, Jean

1204	This Was Love	/68	Harlequin
1285	Out Of A Dream	/69	Harlequin

Curtis, Mary

424	Love Lyrics	12/87	Silhouette Special Edition
526	Cliffhanger	05/89	Silhouette Special Edition
730	Loving Arms Of The Law	03/92	Silhouette Special Edition

Curtis, Sharon

	The Golden Touch	10/92	Bantam Fanfare
25	Lightning That Lingers	12/83	Bantam Loveswept

Curtis, Tom & Sharon

	The Windflower	11/94	Bantam

Curtiss, Mary

699	Top Of The Mountain	10/91	Silhouette Special Edition

Curwood, James Oliver

162	The River's End	/52	Harlequin
176	The Valley Of Silent Men	/52	Harlequin
380	The River's End	/57	Harlequin
383	The Valley Of Silent Men	/57	Harlequin
406	The Flaming Forest	/57	Harlequin
429	Steele Of The Royal Mounted	/58	Harlequin

Dailey, Janet

223	The Indy Man	/78	Harlequin Presents
227	Darling Jenny	/78	Harlequin Presents
231	Reilly's Woman	/78	Harlequin Presents
236	To Tell The Truth	/78	Harlequin Presents
239	Sonora Sundown	/78	Harlequin Presents
244	Big Sky Country	/78	Harlequin Presents
248	Something Extra	/78	Harlequin Presents
252	Master Fiddler	/78	Harlequin Presents
256	Beware Of The Stranger	/78	Harlequin Presents
259	Giant Of Mesabi	/78	Harlequin Presents
264	The Matchmakers	/78	Harlequin Presents
267	For Bitter Or Worse		Harlequin Presents
272	Green Mountain Man		Harlequin Presents
275	Six White Horses		Harlequin Presents
279	Summer Mahagony		Harlequin Presents
284	Bride Of Delta Queen		Harlequin Presents
292	Tidewater Lover		Harlequin Presents
296	Strange Bedfellow		Harlequin Presents
302	Low Country Liar		Harlequin Presents
308	Sweet Promise	10/89	Harlequin Presents
313	For Mike's Sake		Harlequin Presents
319	Sentimental Journey		Harlequin Presents
326	Land Called Deseret		Harlequin Presents
332	Kona Winds		Harlequin Presents
338	That Boston Man		Harlequin Presents
343	Bed Of Grass		Harlequin Presents
349	The Thawing Of Mara		Harlequin Presents
356	The Mating Season		Harlequin Presents
363	Lord Of High Lonesome		Harlequin Presents
369	Southern Nights		Harlequin Presents
373	Enemy In Camp		Harlequin Presents
386	Difficult Decision		Harlequin Presents
391	Heart Of Stone		Harlequin Presents
399	One Of The Boys		Harlequin Presents
416	Wild And Wonderful		Harlequin Presents
421	A Tradition Of Pride		Harlequin Presents
427	The Travelling Kind		Harlequin Presents
428	Seduction		Harlequin Presents
445	Dakota Dreaming		Harlequin Presents
475	Northern Magic		Harlequin Presents
482	With A Little Luck		Harlequin Presents
488	That Carolina Summer		Harlequin Presents
	Marry Me, Cowboy!	04/95	Harlequin Promotion
	Rivals	/89	Little Brown Co
	Tangled Vines	06/93	Little Brown Co
	Masquerade	/90	Little Brown Co

Dailey, Janet

	The Best Way To Lose		Pocket	
	For The Love Of God		Pocket	
	Foxfire Light		Pocket	
	The Glory Game		Pocket	
	The Great Alone		Pocket	
	The Hostage Bride		Pocket	
	The Lancaster Men		Pocket	
	Leftover Love	/86	Pocket	
	Nightway		Pocket	
	The Pride Of Hannah Wade	/88	Pocket	
	Ride The Thunder	/88	Pocket	
	The Rogue		Pocket	
	The Second Time		Pocket	
	Separate Cabins		Pocket	
	Silver Wings, Santiago Blue		Pocket	
	Terms Of Surrender		Pocket	
	Touch The Wind		Pocket	
	Western Man		Pocket	
	Calder Born, Calder Bred		Pocket	The Calder Saga
	Stands A Calder Man		Pocket	The Calder Saga
	This Calder Range		Pocket	The Calder Saga
	This Calder Sky		Pocket	The Calder Saga
	Santa's Little Helpers - "The Healing Touch"	11/95	Silhouette	Anthology
	Mistletoe And Holly	12/91	Silhouette	Christmas Magic 1991
82	The Hostage Bride	06/81	Silhouette	Romance
106	The Lancaster Men	10/81	Silhouette	Romance
118	For The Love Of God	12/81	Silhouette	Romance
153	Wildcatter's Woman	05/82	Silhouette	Romance
177	The Second Time	09/82	Silhouette	Romance
195	Mistletoe And Holly	12/82	Silhouette	Romance
213	Separate Cabins	03/83	Silhouette	Romance
231	Western Man	06/83	Silhouette	Romance
1	Terms Of Surrender	02/82	Silhouette	Special Edition
36	Foxfire Light	07/82	Silhouette	Special Edition
132	The Best Way To Lose	11/83	Silhouette	Special Edition
150	Leftover Love	02/84	Silhouette	Special Edition
	Aspen Gold	03/92	Warner	
	Masquerade		Warner	
	The Proud And The Free	08/95	Warner	
	A Spring Bouquet	05/96	Zebra	Anthology

Dair, Christina

	Deadly Desires	07/94	Harper	
666	A Will Of Her Own	04/91	Silhouette	Special Edition
917	Hesitant Hero	10/94	Silhouette	Special Edition

Dale, Jennifer

	Frostfire		Nal Rapture Romance
27			

AUTHOR/TITLE INDEX

Dale, Ruth Jean

	Friends, Family & Lovers	10/93	Harlequin	Anthology
2	A Million Reasons Why	03/96	Harlequin	Here Come The Grooms
168	Legend	04/93	Harlequin	Historical
3097	Society Page	01/91	Harlequin	Romance
3205	Fireworks!	07/92	Harlequin	Romance
3242	Showdown!	01/93	Harlequin	Romance
3313	Wild Horses (Back To The Ranch)	05/94	Harlequin	Romance
3413	Runaway Wedding	06/96	Harlequin	Romance
678	Kids, Critters And Cupid	02/96	Harlequin	Superromance
687	The Cupid Chronicles	04/96	Harlequin	Superromance
244	Extra! Extra!	03/89	Harlequin	Temptation
286	Together Again	02/90	Harlequin	Temptation
315	One More Chance	09/90	Harlequin	Temptation
380	A Million Reasons Why	01/92	Harlequin	Temptation
413	The Red-Blooded Yankee	10/92	Harlequin	Temptation
579	The Cupid Conspiracy	03/96	Harlequin	Temptation
	Honeymoon Suite	05/95	St. Martin's	Anthology

Daley, Kit

	Sweeter Tomorrows	/86	Dell Candlelight Ecstasy
97			

Dalton, Emily

	Make Room For Daddy	06/95	Harlequin	American
586				
31	A Country Chit	08/90	Harlequin	Regency
44	An Infamous Sea Bath	02/91	Harlequin	Regency
59	Beauty And The Beastie	10/91	Harlequin	Regency
68	A Heavenly Houseguest	02/92	Harlequin	Regency
85	Lily And The Lion	02/93	Harlequin	Regency

Dalton, Gena

69	Sorrel Sunset	01/83	Silhouette	Special Edition
147	April Encounter	02/84	Silhouette	Special Edition
201	Wild Passions	11/84	Silhouette	Special Edition
307	Cherokee Fire	05/86	Silhouette	Special Edition

Dalton, Jennifer

	Whispers Of Destiny		Pocket Richard Gallen Books

Dalton, Margot

	My Valentine 1994	02/94	Harlequin	Anthology
	The Heart Won't Lie	01/95	Harlequin	Crystal Creek
	Southern Nights	04/94	Harlequin	Crystal Creek
	Never Givin' Up On Love	09/94	Harlequin	Crystal Creek
2	Cowboys And Cabernet	04/93	Harlequin	Crystal Creek
5	Even The Nights Are Better	07/93	Harlequin	Crystal Creek
11	New Way To Fly	01/94	Harlequin	Crystal Creek
13	Mustang Heart	03/94	Harlequin	Crystal Creek
19	Never Givin' Up On Love	08/94	Harlequin	Crystal Creek
23	The Heart Won't Lie	01/95	Harlequin	Crystal Creek
527	Southern Nights	06/94	Harlequin	Crystal Creek

Dalton, Margot

530	Never Givin' Up On Love	09/94	Harlequin	Crystal Creek
	Another Woman	10/94	Harlequin	Promotion
401	Under Prairie Skies		Harlequin	Superromance
425	Sagebrush And Sunshine		Harlequin	Superromance
431	Magic And Moonbeams		Harlequin	Superromance
451	Ask Me Anything		Harlequin	Superromance
480	Three Waifs And A Daddy	12/91	Harlequin	Superromance
502	Sunflower	06/92	Harlequin	Superromance
508	Tumbleweed	07/92	Harlequin	Superromance
511	Juniper	08/92	Harlequin	Superromance
533	Daniel And The Lion	01/93	Harlequin	Superromance
558	Another Woman	08/93	Harlequin	Superromance
576	Angels In The Light	12/93	Harlequin	Superromance
622	Kim & The Cowboy (Class Of '78)	12/94	Harlequin	Superromance
638	The Secret Years (Showcase)	04/95	Harlequin	Superromance
664	Man Of My Dreams	10/95	Harlequin	Superromance
693	The Hiding Place	05/96	Harlequin	Superromance
	Sagebrush And Sunshine	12/95	Harlequin	Western Lovers
	Tangled Lives	02/96	Mira	

Dalton, Pamela

957	The Prodigal Husband	08/93	Silhouette	Romance
1100	Second Chance At Marriage	08/95	Silhouette	Romance

Dalzell, Helen

2570	Not Marrying Kind		Harlequin	Romance

Damon, Kate

	Napa Lynx	02/89

Damon, Lee

16	Lady Laughing Eyes	/84	Berkley	To Have And To Hold
133	Summer Sunrise		Harlequin	Superromance
	Again The Magic	08/82	Richard Gallen	

Danbury, Iris

1137	Doctor At Drumlochan	/67	Harlequin
1178	Rendezvous In Lisbon	/68	Harlequin
1211	Bride Of Kylsaig	/68	Harlequin
1257	Doctor At Villa Ronda	/68	Harlequin
1301	Hotel By The Loch	/69	Harlequin
1331	Hotel Belvedere	/69	Harlequin
1372	Isle Of Pomegranates	/70	Harlequin
1398	Feast Of The Candles	/70	Harlequin
1439	Serenade At Santa Rosa	/70	Harlequin
1461	Island Of Mermaids	/71	Harlequin
1485	Chateau Of Pines	/71	Harlequin
1519	Summer Comes To Albarosa	/71	Harlequin
1558	Legend Of Roscano	/72	Harlequin
1620	Jacaranda Island	/72	Harlequin

AUTHOR/TITLE INDEX

Danbury, Iris

1671	Mandolins Of Montori	/73	Harlequin
1771	The Silver Stallion	/74	Harlequin
1804	The Fires Of Toretta	/74	Harlequin
1837	The Amethyst Meadows	/74	Harlequin
1873	A Pavement Of Pearl	/75	Harlequin
2011	The Windmill Of Kalakos	/76	Harlequin
2042	The Scented Island	/77	Harlequin
2122	The Painted Palace	/77	Harlequin

Dancer, Lacey

7	Silent Enchantment	08/90	Meteor
35	Diamond On Ice	03/91	Meteor
49	Sunlight On Shadows	07/91	Meteor
59	13 Days Of Luck	09/91	Meteor
77	Flight Of The Swan	02/92	Meteor
98	Baby Makes Five	07/92	Meteor
169	Many Faces Of Love	09/93	Meteor
127	Forever Joy	02/93	Meteor Kismet
133	Lightning Strikes Twice	03/93	Meteor Kismet
163	His Woman's Gift	08/93	Meteor Kismet

Dane, Lisa

1	Diamonds And Denim	06/92	Berkley Different Worlds
2	Ribbons And Rawhide	12/92	Berkley Different Worlds
3	Silk And Stone	06/93	Berkley Different Worlds

Daniel, Megan

A Time-Travel Christmas	11/95	Leisure Anthology
All The Time We Need		Leisure Time-Travel
Queen Of Hearts	08/86	Nal Penguin Regency
An American Bride		Nal Penguin Regency
The Unlikely Rivals		Nal Penguin Regency
The Sensible Courtship		Nal Penguin Regency
The Reluctant Suitor		Nal Penguin Regency
Amelia		Nal Penguin Regency

Daniels, B.J.

312	Stand By Your Man	02/95	Harlequin Intrigue
353	Outlawed!	01/96	Harlequin Intrigue

Daniels, Dana

302	Unspoken Longings	/85	Berkley Second Chance At Love

Daniels, Dorothy

The Cormac Legend		Nal Penguin
A Mirror Of Shadows	/77	Warner
The Magic Ring	/77	Warner
Perrine	/77	Warner

Daniels, Elizabeth

Paradise In His Arms		
Bird Of Paradise		Leisure

Daniels, Joleen

891	The Ideal Wife	09/92	Silhouette Romance
939	Inheritance	05/93	Silhouette Romance
990	Jilted!	02/94	Silhouette Romance
1043	Long Lost Husband	11/94	Silhouette Romance
507	The Reckoning	02/89	Silhouette Special Edition
645	Against All Odds	01/91	Silhouette Special Edition

Daniels, Judith

389	The Sun Always Rises	06/87	Silhouette Special Edition

Daniels, Kayla

474	Spitting Image	08/88	Silhouette Special Edition
578	Father Knows Best	02/90	Silhouette Special Edition
654	Hot Prospect	02/91	Silhouette Special Edition
707	Rebel To The Rescue	11/91	Silhouette Special Edition
790	From Father To Son	01/93	Silhouette Special Edition
814	Heiress Apparent	05/93	Silhouette Special Edition
911	Miracle Child	09/94	Silhouette Special Edition

Daniels, Leigh

106	On The Run	01/89	Harlequin Intrigue
166	The Basque Swallow	07/91	Harlequin Intrigue

Daniels, Maggie

	A Christmas Romance	12/91	St. Martin's
	Moonlight & Mistletoe	12/94	St. Martin's

Daniels, Megan

	All The Time We Need		Leisure
	A Time-Travel Christmas		Leisure

Daniels, Melanie

	The River Queen		Diamond

Daniels, Rebecca

431	L. A. Midnight	05/92	Silhouette Initmate Moments
467	Fog City	12/92	Silhouette Initmate Moments
369	L.A. Heat	02/91	Silhouette Intimate Moments
563	Lawyers, Guns And Money	04/94	Silhouette Intimate Moments
654	Tears Of The Shaman	07/95	Silhouette Intimate Moments
696	Father Figure	02/96	Silhouette Intimate Moments
7	Way Of The Wolf	02/95	Silhouette Montana Mavericks
987	Loving The Enemy	01/94	Silhouette Romance

Daniels, Rhett

184	Overtures Of The Heart	08/84	Silhouette Special Edition

Daniels, Stephanie

192	Broken Vows	12/93	Meteor

Daniels, Val

3092	Silver Bells		Harlequin Romance
3377	Forever Isn't Long Enough	09/95	Harlequin Romance
3418	A Ranch, A Ring And Everything	07/96	Harlequin Romance
42	Between Dusk And Dawn (Premiere)	10/94	Silhouette Shadows

Daniels, Zoe
   1   The Dream   04/95 Berkley Year Of The Cat Trilogy
   3   The Amulet   08/95 Berkley Year Of The Cat Trilogy

Dansby, Lee Ann
     Beyond Forever   Lion Hearted Historical

Danson, Sheryl
  434 Always A Fiancee   03/93 Harlequin Temptation
  479 The Spy Who Loved Her   02/94 Harlequin Temptation
  503 The Ranger Man   08/94 Harlequin Temptation

Danton, Rebecca
     French Jade   Ballantine Regency
     The Ruby Heart   Ballantine Regency
     Fire Opals   Ballantine Regency

Danvers, Dennis
     Time And Time Again   10/94 Simon & Schuste

Darcy, Clare
     Lady Pamela
     Allegra
     Victoria
     Cressida
     Carolina And Julia
     Gwendolyn
     Letty
     Lydia
     Cecily Or A Young Lady Of Quality   Zebra Pinnacle
     Elyza   Zebra Pinnacle
     Eugenia   Zebra Pinnacle
     Georgina   Zebra Pinnacle
     Regina   Zebra Pinnacle
     Rolande   Zebra Pinnacle

Darcy, Emma
     Blind Date   /88   Harlequin
     Pattern Of Deceit   /90   Harlequin
     Father Of Her Child   /96   Harlequin
     Their Wedding Day   /96   Harlequin
  648 Twisting Shadows   Harlequin Presents
  680 Tangle Of Torment   Harlequin Presents
  823 Don't Play Games   Harlequin Presents
  840 Fantasy   Harlequin Presents
  864 Song Of A Wren   Harlequin Presents
  882 Point Of Impact   Harlequin Presents
  903 Man In The Park   Harlequin Presents
  921 A World Apart   Harlequin Presents
  935 The Impossible Woman   Harlequin Presents
  960 Woman Of Honour   Harlequin Presents
  984 Don't Ask Me Now   Harlequin Presents

AUTHOR/TITLE INDEX

AUTHOR/TITLE INDEX

Dark, Sandra
- 44 Sleeping Tigers — 11/94 Harlequin Shadows
- 63 Old Flames — 04/96 Silhouette Shadows

Darke, Hilary
- 569 Wife To Doctor Dan — /61 Harlequin

Darnell, Berde
- Passion's Whisper — Zebra

Dart, Iris Rainer
- ' Til The Real Thing Comes Along — 09/95 Warner

Darty, Peggy
- The Crimson Roses Of Fountain Court — Zebra Gothic
- The Precious Pearls Of Cabot Hall — Zebra Gothic
- The Wailing Winds Of Juneau Abbey — Zebra Gothic
- The Widowed Bride Of Raven Oaks — 09/92 Zebra Regency Romance

Davenport, Kathryn
- Nevada Loving — Zebra Heartfire
- Pirate's Mistress — Zebra Heartfire

Daveson, Mons
- 1415 The House In The Foothills — /70 Harlequin
- 1456 This Too I'll Remember — /70 Harlequin
- 91 Desert Interlude — 08/91 Harlequin Direct
- 103 Master Of Namangilla — 02/92 Harlequin Direct
- 2461 Land Of Tomorrow — Harlequin Romance
- 2534 My Lord Kasseem — Harlequin Romance
- 2575 Mac Kenzie Country — Harlequin Romance
- 2756 Girl Of Mystery — 04/86 Harlequin Romance

David, Berrie
- 576 Dark Paradise — Dell Candlelight

David, Cay
- 67 Crystal Clear — 11/91 Meteor
- 102 Swept Away — 08/92 Meteor
- 184 The Heat Of The Night — 11/93 Meteor
- 624 Desperate — 02/95 Silhouette Intimate Moments

David, Kay
- 706 Baby Of The Bride — 04/96 Silhouette Intimate Moments
- 725 Hero In Hiding — 07/96 Silhouette Intimate Moments

Davids, Marilyn
- 50 A Love So Fresh — Nal Rapture Romance

Davidson, Andrea
- 16 Music In The Night — Harlequin American
- 21 Untamed Possession — Harlequin American
- 45 Treasures Of Heart — Harlequin American
- 122 An Unexpected Gift — Harlequin American
- 324 The Best Gift Of All — Harlequin American
- 371 The Light On Willow Lane — Harlequin American
- 25 A Siren's Lure — Harlequin Intrigue

Davis, Suzannah

	Outlaw Heart	06/91	Avon Romance
	Dance Of Deception	03/92	Avon Romantic Treasures
359	Airwaves		Harlequin Superromance
455	Evening Star		Harlequin Superromance
903	A Christmas Cowboy	01/95	Silhouette Desire
947	The Rancher And The Redhead	08/95	Silhouette Desire

Davison, Juliana

	Velvet Ribbons		Warner
	Petals Of The Rose		Warner
	The Pink Phaeton		Warner

Dawson, Elizabeth

1878	Isle Of Dreams	/75	Harlequin
2306	The Bending Reed		Harlequin Romance

Dawson, Geralyn

	The Texan's Bride	04/93	Bantam Fanfare
	Tempting Morality	05/95	Bantam Fanfare
	The Bad Luck Wedding Dress	04/96	Bantam Fanfare

Dawson, Helena

294	A Trusting Heart	08/96	Harlequin
89	Portrait Of A Stranger	07/91	Harlequin Direct
104	Right Conclusions	02/92	Harlequin Direct
120	Shadows On The Sea	10/92	Harlequin Direct
133	Web Of Fate	05/93	Harlequin Direct
137	Web Of Fate	05/93	Harlequin Direct
3008	Heart Of Marble		Harlequin Romance

Dawson, Saranne

· 180	Intimate Strangers		Harlequin American
222	Summer's Witness	09/87	Harlequin American
364	A Talent For Love		Harlequin American
448	Bewitched	07/92	Harlequin American
480	Deception And Desire	03/93	Harlequin American
504	Twilight Magic	09/93	Harlequin American
286	In Self Defense	08/94	Harlequin Intrigue
307	Her Other Half	01/95	Harlequin Intrigue
356	Expose	01/96	Harlequin Intrigue
	The Enchanted Land	11/91	Leisure
	Awakenings		Leisure
	Heart Of The Wolf		Leisure
	Crystal Enchantment	/95	Leisure Futuristic
	From The Mist		Leisure Futuristic Romance
	Greenfire		Leisure Futuristic Romance
	On Wings Of Love	06/94	Leisure Lovespell
	Star-Crossed	11/94	Lovespell Futuristic

Day, Adrienne

	Rebellious Bride	09/95	Avon

AUTHOR/TITLE INDEX

AUTHOR/TITLE INDEX

De La Fuente, Patricia
    The Reluctant Duchess   06/93   Jove Regency
De Lancey, Elizabeth
    Sea Of Dreams   04/92   Berkley Diamond
    The Defiant Bride   06/93   Berkley Diamond
    Touch Of Lace   06/93   Diamond Historical
    Meant To Be   06/94   Diamond Historical
De Lange, Anneke
  173   Anna   /52   Harlequin
De Lazzari, Jo Ann
    Scoundrel's Captive   07/91   Avon
    Scoundrel's Desire   02/93   Avon
De Leon, Ana Lisa
  61   Kiss Good Night And Say Goodbye   Harlequin American
De Paul, Edith
  672   The Viscount's Witch   Dell Candlelight Regency
De Vita, Sharon
  475   Heavenly Match   12/86   Silhouette Romance
  498   Lady And The Legend   04/87   Silhouette Romance
  545   Kane And Mabel   12/87   Silhouette Romance
  573   Baby Makes Three   04/88   Silhouette Romance
  593   Sherlock's Home   08/88   Silhouette Romance
  610   Italian Knights   11/88   Silhouette Romance
  693   Sweet Adeline   12/89   Silhouette Romance
 1013   Child Of Midnight   02/96   Silhouette Special Edition
De Vries, Laura Lee
    Gambler's Daughter   03/96   Dell Historical
De Wolfe, Adrienne
  1   Texas Outlaw   12/95   Bantam Rawlings Brothers Trilogy
Dean, Alyssa
  524   Mad About You (Dreamscape)   01/95   Harlequin Temptation
  551   The Last Hero (Rebels & Rogues)   08/95   Harlequin Temptation
Dean, Carole
  89   Just One Kiss   05/92   Meteor
  111   California Man   10/92   Meteor
  178   Dreams Don't Wait   10/93   Meteor
  121   One Tough Cookie   01/93   Meteor Kismet
Dean, Diane
    Unauthorized Access   12/92   Avalon
Dean, Dinah
    The Country Gentleman   /86   Harlequin Regency
  7   The Cockermouth Mail   08/89   Harlequin Regency
  24   Flight From The Eagle   Mills & Boon
Dean, Rena
  319   Public Secret   Harlequin American

AUTHOR/TITLE INDEX

AUTHOR/TITLE INDEX

Dell, Belinda

1407	Next Stop Gretna	/70	Harlequin
1475	The Vermilion Gateway	/71	Harlequin
1623	Flowers For The Festival	/72	Harlequin
1749	Lovely Is The Rose	/74	Harlequin
1797	The Darling Pirate	/74	Harlequin
1846	Lake Of Silver	/75	Harlequin

Dellamere, Wanda

24	Call Of The Heart	Harlequin Superromance

Dellin, Genell

Cherokee Dawn	06/92	Avon
Cherokee Nights	04/92	Avon
Cherokee Sundown	06/92	Avon
Comanche Flame	06/94	Avon
Comanche Wind	05/93	Avon
Comanche Rain	04/95	Avon

Delmore, Diana

Chance Encounter	09/91	Diamond Regency
The Substitute Bride	03/93	Diamond Regency
Anthea	/88	Walker
Leonie	/88	Walker

Denison, Janelle

Heaven's Gift	10/95	Leisure

Dennis, Roberta

60	Between The Lines	04/83	Silhouette Desire

Dennis, Stacey

Merry Christmas My Love	11/93	Zebra Anthology
Repeat Performance	05/93	Zebra Anthology
Full Bloom	12/94	Zebra To Love Again
Sealed With A Kiss	09/93	Zebra To Love Again
Remember Love	12/92	Zebra To Love Again

Denny, Roz

3032	Red Hot Pepper		Harlequin Romance
3122	Romantic Notions		Harlequin Romance
3169	The Cinderella Coach	01/92	Harlequin Romance
3276	Stubborn As A Mule (Back To The Ranch)	08/93	Harlequin Romance
3320	Island Child (Kids & Kisses)	07/94	Harlequin Romance
3336	Some Like It Hotter	11/94	Harlequin Romance
	Trouble At Lone Spur	11/96	Harlequin Superromance
	Starr Of Wonder	12/95	Harlequin Superromance
649	Major Attraction (4 Strong Men)	06/95	Harlequin Superromance
672	Christmas Star	12/95	Harlequin Superromance
686	The Water Baby	04/96	Harlequin Superromance

Dent, Roxanne

Sweetwater Saga	Nal Penguin

Denton, Jamie Ann

Diamond, Jacqueline

239	The Cinderella Dare		Harlequin	American
270	Capers And Rainbows		Harlequin	American
279	A Ghost Of A Chance		Harlequin	American
315	Flight Of Magic		Harlequin	American
351	By Leaps And Bounds		Harlequin	American
406	Old Dreams, New Dreams	09/91	Harlequin	American
446	The Trouble With Terry	07/92	Harlequin	American
491	A Dangerous Guy	06/93	Harlequin	American
583	The Runaway Bride (In Name Only)	05/95	Harlequin	American
615	Yours, Mine And Ours	01/96	Harlequin	American
642	One Husband Too Many	08/96	Harlequin	American
14	A Lady's Point Of View	11/89	Harlequin	Regency
	The Day-Dreaming Lady	/88	Walker	
	The Forgetful Lady	/88	Walker	
	Lady In Disguise		Walker	
	A Lady Of Letters		Walker	
	Song For A Lady		Walker	

Diamond, Petra

275	Night Of A Thousand Stars	/85	Berkley	Second Chance At Love
31	Confidentially Yours	/84	Berkley	To Have And To Hold

Dier, Debra

	Christmas Angels	11/95	Leisure	Anthology
	Angel Christmas: "Trouble With Hannah"	11/95	Leisure	Anthology
	Surrender The Dream	03/93	Leisure	Historical
	Deceptions & Dreams		Leisure	Historical
	A Quest Of Dreams	/95	Leisure	Historical
	Scoundrel	/95	Leisure	Historical
	The Sorcerer's Lady	06/95	Leisure	Love Spell

Diespecker, Dick

234	Rebound	/53	Harlequin	
235	General Duty Nurse	/53	Harlequin	

Dille, Mary Lynn

179	City Girl	10/93	Meteor	

Dillon, Eiles

	Wild Geese		Ballantine	Regency
	Blood Relations		Ballantine	Regency

Dilmore, Diana

	Anthea		Warner
	Cassandra		Warner
	Dorinda		Warner
	Leonie		Warner

Dingwell, Joyce

476	Nurse Jess	/59	Harlequin	
512	Australian Hospital	/60	Harlequin	
626	Nurse Trent's Children	/61	Harlequin	

Dingwell, Joyce

AUTHOR/TITLE INDEX

Dingwell, Joyce

2123	A Drift Of Jasmine	/77	Harlequin
2164	Year Of The Dragon	/78	Harlequin
2189	Remember September	/78	Harlequin
2216	All The Days Of Summer	/78	Harlequin
2225	The Boss's Daughter		Harlequin Romance
2318	The Angry Man		Harlequin Romance
2402	Come Back To Love		Harlequin Romance
2432	The All The Way Man		Harlequin Romance
2600	Brother Wolf		Harlequin Romance

Dix, Isabel

2491	Cast A Tender Shadow		Harlequin Romance

Dixon, Debra

655	Tall, Dark, And Lonesome	12/93	Bantam Loveswept
682	Midnight Hour	04/94	Bantam Loveswept
706	Mountain Mystic	09/94	Bantam Loveswept
723	Doc Holiday	01/95	Bantam Loveswept
757	Hot As Sin	09/95	Bantam Loveswept
774	Bad To The Bone	02/96	Bantam Loveswept
781	Slow Hands	03/96	Bantam Loveswept

Dixon, Diana

98	Lucifer's Playground	06/85	Silhouette Intimate Moments
30	Return Engagement	09/80	Silhouette Romance
377	Enter With A Kiss	08/85	Silhouette Romance
3	Mexican Rhapsody	02/82	Silhouette Special Edition
24	Gamble Of Desire	05/82	Silhouette Special Edition
87	Jessica: Take Two	04/83	Silhouette Special Edition
99	Quest For Paradise	06/83	Silhouette Special Edition
120	Lia's Daughter	09/83	Silhouette Special Edition
174	No Strings	06/84	Silhouette Special Edition

Dobson, Margaret

173	Restless Wind	/83	Dell Candlelight Ecstasy

Dodd, Christina

	Candle In The Window	/92	Harper
	Treasure Of The Sun	09/91	Harper
	Priceless	08/92	Harper
	Outrageous	04/94	Harper
	Castles In The Air	07/93	Harper
	Tall, Dark & Dangerous	08/95	Harper Anthology
	The Greatest Lover In All England	12/94	Harper Monogram
	Move Heaven And Earth	07/95	Harper Monogram
	Once A Knight	04/96	Harper Monogram
128	The Lady In Black	02/93	Meteor Kismet

Dodge, Alice M.

	Girl Of The Far Country		Dell Candlelight

Dohrn, Madelyn

Dohrn, Madelyn

523	The Best Defense	08/87	Silhouette Romance
501	Labor Of Love	01/89	Silhouette Special Edition
616	Two For The Price Of One	08/90	Silhouette Special Edition
633	One For One	11/90	Silhouette Special Edition

Dolan, Charlotte Louise

	Three Lords For Lady Anne	10/91	Nal Regency
	The Resolute Runaway	02/92	Nal Regency
	The Unofficial Suitor	07/92	Nal Regency
	The Black Widow	10/92	Nal Regency
	The Substitute Bridegroom	02/91	Nal Regency
	A Regency Summer	06/92	Nal Super Regency
	Full-Moon Magic	09/92	Nal Super Signet Historical
	A Scandalous Suggestion	10/91	Nal Penguin
	Fallen Angel	02/93	Penguin Regency
	The Counterfeit Gentleman	/94	Signet Regency

Dominique, Meg

2774	Sand Castles		Harlequin Romance
2775	Age Of Consent		Harlequin Romance
2	When Stars Fall Down	03/84	Harlequin Temptation
27	Rebel Heart	09/84	Harlequin Temptation
43	Yes, With Love	01/85	Harlequin Temptation
71	As Love Would Have It	08/85	Harlequin Temptation

Domning, Denise

	Winter's Heat	02/94	Penguin Topaz
	Summer's Storm	08/94	Penguin Topaz
	Spring's Fury	03/95	Topaz

Domning, Joan J.

12	Hunter's Payne	07/83	Bantam Loveswept
13	Tiger Lady	08/83	Bantam Loveswept
19	Pfarr Lake Affair	10/83	Bantam Loveswept
39	Kirsten's Inheritance	04/84	Bantam Loveswept
54	The Gypsy And The Yachtsman	07/84	Bantam Loveswept
63	Lahti's Apple	10/84	Bantam Loveswept
488	Rainy Day Man	08/91	Bantam Loveswept
519	Stormy's Man	01/92	Bantam Loveswept
598	The Forever Man	02/93	Bantam Loveswept
657	Fever	12/93	Bantam Loveswept

Donald, Robyn

232	Bride At Whangatapu	/78	Harlequin Presents
260	Dilemma In Paradise	/78	Harlequin Presents
285	Summer At Awakopu		Harlequin Presents
303	Wife In Exchange		Harlequin Presents
320	Shadow Of The Past		Harlequin Presents
441	The Interloper		Harlequin Presents
500	The Dark Abyss		Harlequin Presents

Donald, Robyn

567	Mansion For My Love		Harlequin	Presents
623	The Guarded Heart		Harlequin	Presents
631	Return To Yesterday		Harlequin	Presents
649	An Old Passion		Harlequin	Presents
665	Gates Of Rangitatau		Harlequin	Presents
696	A Durable Fire		Harlequin	Presents
904	An Unbreakable Bond		Harlequin	Presents
936	Long Journey Back		Harlequin	Presents
952	Captives Of The Past		Harlequin	Presents
976	A Willing Surrender		Harlequin	Presents
1040	Country Of The Heart		Harlequin	Presents
1064	A Late Loving		Harlequin	Presents
1104	Smoke In The Wind		Harlequin	Presents
1128	The Sweetest Trap		Harlequin	Presents
1233	Love's Reward		Harlequin	Presents
1263	A Bitter Homecoming		Harlequin	Presents
1303	No Guarantees		Harlequin	Presents
1343	A Matter Of Will		Harlequin	Presents
1376	The Darker Side Of Paradise	07/91	Harlequin	Presents
1408	A Summer Storm	11/91	Harlequin	Presents
1434	No Place Too Far	02/92	Harlequin	Presents
1464	Some Kind Of Madness	06/92	Harlequin	Presents
1505	Storm Over Paradise	11/92	Harlequin	Presents
1537	The Golden Mask	06/93	Harlequin	Presents
1565	Once Bitten, Twice Shy	06/93	Harlequin	Presents
1565	Once Bitten, Twice Shy	06/93	Harlequin	Presents
1577	The Stone Princess (Year Down Under)	08/93	Harlequin	Presents
1611	Such Dark Magic	12/93	Harlequin	Presents
1666	Paradise Lost	07/94	Harlequin	Presents
1699	Island Enchantment	11/94	Harlequin	Presents
1714	The Colour Of Midnight (Secrets...)	01/95	Harlequin	Presents
1735	Dark Fire	04/95	Harlequin	Presents
1783	Prince Of Lies	12/95	Harlequin	Presents
1794	Indiscretions	02/96	Harlequin	Presents
1803	Element Of Risk	04/96	Harlequin	Presents
1639	Paga Surrender	04/94	Harlequin	Presents Plus
1755	Tiger Eyes	08/95	Harlequin	Presents Plus
2391	Bay Of Stars		Harlequin	Romance
2437	Iceberg		Harlequin	Romance

Donley, Dorothea

	The Beaux Of Bayley Dell	03/95	Zebra Regency

Donnelly, Jane

249	Shadow Of A Tiger	09/95	Harlequin
278	Sleeping Beauty	04/96	Harlequin
1227	A Man Apart	/68	Harlequin
1332	Don't Walk Alone	/69	Harlequin

AUTHOR/TITLE INDEX

Donnelly, Jane

1376	Shadows From The Sea	/70	Harlequin
1432	Take The Far Dream	/70	Harlequin
1462	The Man In The Next Room	/71	Harlequin
1483	Never Turn Back	/71	Harlequin
1548	Halfway To The Stars	/71	Harlequin
1592	The Mill In The Meadow	/72	Harlequin
1660	A Stranger Came	/73	Harlequin
1681	The Long Shadow	/73	Harlequin
1723	Rocks Under Shining Water	/73	Harlequin
1859	The Man Outside	/75	Harlequin
1882	Ride Out The Storm	/75	Harlequin
1929	Collision Course	/75	Harlequin
1993	Dark Pursuer	/76	Harlequin
2027	The Silver Cage	/76	Harlequin
2064	The Intruder	/77	Harlequin
2090	Dear Caliban	/77	Harlequin
2124	Four Weeks In Winter	/77	Harlequin
2150	Touched By Fire	/78	Harlequin
2187	The Black Hunter	/78	Harlequin
2195	Love For A Stranger	/78	Harlequin
2217	Spell Of The Seven Stones	/78	Harlequin
105	Once A Cheat	03/92	Harlequin Direct
132	The Trespasser	04/93	Harlequin Direct
173	Hold Back The Dark	02/94	Harlequin Direct
237	Cover Story	06/95	Harlequin Direct
2255	Forest Of The Night		Harlequin Romance
2270	Behind A Closed Door		Harlequin Romance
2293	A Savage Sanctuary		Harlequin Romance
2325	A Man To Watch		Harlequin Romance
2373	No Way Out		Harlequin Romance
2408	When Lightning Strikes		Harlequin Romance
2456	Flash Point		Harlequin Romance
2510	Diamond Cut Diamond		Harlequin Romance
2552	Call Up The Storm		Harlequin Romance
2576	Face The Tiger		Harlequin Romance
2635	A Fierce Encounter		Harlequin Romance
2649	Moon Lady		Harlequin Romance
2654	The Frozen Heart		Harlequin Romance
2702	Ring Of Crystal		Harlequin Romance
2738	To Cage A Whirlwind		Harlequin Romance
2810	Ride A Wild Horse		Harlequin Romance
2871	Force Field		Harlequin Romance
2906	No Place To Run		Harlequin Romance
2954	Fetters Of Gold		Harlequin Romance
3033	When We're Alone		Harlequin Romance
3128	The Jewels Of Helen		Harlequin Romance

AUTHOR/TITLE INDEX

Douglas, Carole Nelson
  Irene's Last Waltz   10/94 Tor
  Angel Christmas: "Catch A Falling Angel"   11/95 Zebra Anthology
Douglas, Casey
   25 Infidel Of Love   Harlequin Superromance
   56 Proud Surrender   Harlequin Superromance
   75 Dance Away Lover   Harlequin Superromance
  107 Edge Of Illusion   Harlequin Superromance
  131 Taste Of A Dream   Harlequin Superromance
  194 Kentucky Woman   Harlequin Superromance
  271 Season Of Enchantment   Harlequin Superromance
Douglas, Charlotte
  591 It's About Time (Rising Star)   07/95 Harlequin American
  623 Bringing Up Baby   03/96 Harlequin American
       Jacaranda Bend   05/93 Harper Monogram
       Lady In The Shadows   02/93 Leisure
       Darkness At Fair Winds   02/93 Leisure Gothic
       Relative Danger   12/95 Zebra
Douglas, Elizabeth
       An Exquisite Deception
       Virginia Bride   12/91 Diamond
Douglas, Gail
  283 On Wings Of Flame   10/88 Bantam Loveswept
  302 Flirting With Danger   01/89 Bantam Loveswept
  327 Lost In The Wild   05/89 Bantam Loveswept
  442 It Had To Be You   12/90 Bantam Loveswept
  451 Banned In Boston   02/91 Bantam Loveswept
  463 The Best Laid Plans   04/91 Bantam Loveswept
  511 After Hours   12/91 Bantam Loveswept
  553 All The Way   07/92 Bantam Loveswept
  574 The Lady Is A Scamp   10/92 Bantam Loveswept
  633 Stormy Weather   08/93 Bantam Loveswept
  355 Swashbuckling Lady   10/89 Bantam Loveswept: Dreamweavers
  361 Gambling Lady   10/89 Bantam Loveswept: Dreamweavers
  379 Sophisticated Lady   02/90 Bantam Loveswept: Dreamweavers
  385 Bewitching Lady   03/90 Bantam Loveswept: Dreamweavers
Douglas, Gloria
   88 Winning Hearts   12/85 Harlequin Temptation
Douglas, Jessica
       Snowfire
       All My Heart Can Hold
Douglas, Kate
       Pirate's Wild Paradise   Zebra
       Prairie Paradise   Zebra
Douglas, Kathryn
       Cavendish Square   Ballantine

444

Douglas, Monica

1706	Shadow Of The Past	/73	Harlequin

Douglas, Sheila

1729	The Young Doctor	/73	Harlequin
1897	Westhampton Royal	/75	Harlequin
2015	Sherrington Hall	/76	Harlequin
2097	The Reluctant Neighbour	/77	Harlequin
2336	Return To Lanmore		Harlequin Romance
2392	The Girl Between		Harlequin Romance
2518	The Uncertain Heart		Harlequin Romance

Douglass, Amanda Hart

	Christabel		Belmont Tower

Douglass, Billie

38	Sweet Serenity	01/83	Silhouette Desire
56	Flip Side Of Yesterday	04/83	Silhouette Desire
74	Beyond Fantasy	07/83	Silhouette Desire
6	Search For A New Dawn	02/82	Silhouette Special Edition
32	A Time To Love	07/82	Silhouette Special Edition
80	Fast Courting	03/83	Silhouette Special Edition
123	An Irrestible Impulse	10/83	Silhouette Special Edition
133	The Carpenter's Lady	12/83	Silhouette Special Edition

Douglass, Charlotte

380	Dream Maker	07/96	Harlequin Intrigue

Douglass, Jessica

	Angel Of Fire	07/94	
	All My Heart Can Hold	09/91	Dell
	Wish Me A Rainbow	10/92	Dell
	Snowfire		Dell
665	Montana Rogue	09/95	Silhouette Intimate Moments

Dowdell, Dorothy

	The Allerton Rose		Dell Candlelight
	Strange Rapture		Dell Candlelight

Downes, Kathleen

49	The Man Next Door	06/84	Bantam Loveswept
93	Practice Makes Perfect	05/85	Bantam Loveswept
151	Char's Webb	08/86	Bantam Loveswept
211	Evenings In Paris	10/87	Bantam Loveswept

Downie, Jill

	Mistress Of Moon Hill		

Doyle, Amanda

1036	The Outback Man	/66	Harlequin
1085	A Change For Clancy	/67	Harlequin
1116	Play The Tune Softly	/67	Harlequin
1190	The Shadow And The Sun	/68	Harlequin
1239	This Wish I Have	/68	Harlequin
1308	A Mist In Glen Torran	/69	Harlequin

AUTHOR/TITLE INDEX

Doyle, Amanda

1351	The Girl For Gillgong	/69	Harlequin
1448	The Year At Yattabilla	/70	Harlequin
1486	The Post At Gundooee	/71	Harlequin
1527	Dilemma At Dullora	/71	Harlequin
1562	Kookaburra Dawn	/72	Harlequin
1630	Escape To Koolonga	/72	Harlequin
1960	Return To Tuckarimba	/76	Harlequin

Doyle, Barbara

519	Search For Yesterday		Dell Candlelight
559	The Midnight Embrace		Dell Candlelight

Doyle, Emily

95	A Matter Of Trust	05/83	Silhouette Special Edition

Doyle, Richard J.

213	The Royal Story	/53	Harlequin

Doyle, Sir Arthur Conan

238	The Lost World	/53	Harlequin

Drake, Bonnie

3	The Passionate Touch		Dell Candlelight Ecstasy
9	Surrender By Moonlight		Dell Candlelight Ecstasy
18	Sweet Ember		Dell Candlelight Ecstasy
146	Passion And Illusion	/83	Dell Candlelight Ecstasy

Drake, Connie

	Angel's Fire		

Drake, H.B.

190	Slave Ship	/52	Harlequin

Drake, Shannon

Ondine		
Bride Of The Wind	09/92	Avon
Damsel In Distress		Avon
No Other Man	/96	Avon
No Other Woman	/96	Avon
No Other Love	/96	Avon
Christmas Love Stories	/91	Avon Anthology
Night Magic	09/93	Avon Anthology
Under The Mistletoe	10/93	Avon Christmas Anthology
Knight Of Fire	12/93	Avon Historical
Branded Hearts	02/95	Avon Historical
Lie Down In Roses		Berkley
Blue Heaven, Black Night		Berkley
Princess Of Fire	/89	Charter
Emerald Embrace		Jove
Tomorrow The Glory	02/94	Pinnacle
Blue Heaven, Black Night	08/95	Pinnacle
Hearts In Hiding		Pinnacle Press

Drake, Susan

Drake, Susan
  588   Hear No Evil   08/94 Silhouette Intimate Moments
Drew, Jennifer
  1040 Turn Back The Night   10/94 Silhouette Romance
Dreyer, Eileen
        Uncharitable Acts   07/91 Harper
        If Looks Could Kill   10/92 Harper
        A Man To Die For   /92 Harper
        Nothing Personal   Harper
        Bad Medicine   06/95 Harper
Druett, Joan
        Abigail
        A Promise Of Gold
Drummond, Brenna
  42   Proud Vintage   08/82 Silhouette Special Edition
Drummond, June
        The Imposter   12/94 Avon Regency Romance
Drury, Rebecca
        Blue Glory   /82 Dell Historical
        Savage Beauty   /82 Dell Historical
Drymon, Kathleen
        Castaway Angel   11/91 Zebra
        Gentle Savage   Zebra
        Midnight Bride   Zebra
        Velvet Savage   Zebra
        Kimberly's Kiss   /87 Zebra
        Destiny's Splendor   /89 Zebra
        Warrior Of The Sun   Zebra
        Time's Angel   04/94 Zebra
        A Rebel Christmas   Zebra A Christmas Kiss Coll.
Du Bay, Sandra
        Crimson Conquest
        Fidelity's Flight
        In Passion's Shadow
        Scarlett Surrender
        Where Passion Dwells   Leisure
        Flame Of Fidelity   Leisure
        Burn On, Sweet Fire   Leisure Historical
        By Love Beguiled   Leisure Historical
        Mistress Of The Sun King   Leisure Historical
        Nightrider   Leisure Historical
        Quicksilver   Leisure Historical
        Tempest   Leisure Historical
        Whispers Of Passion   Leisure Historical
        Wilder Shores Of Love   Leisure Historical
        By Love Betrayed   05/93 Leisure Historical

Du Bois, Dixie
   42   True Colors   05/91   Meteor
  118   Home Fires   12/92   Meteor
Du Pont, Diane
      The French Passion   Ballantine Regency
Dubois, Bonna Lee
      Long Ago Love   /86   Walker
Dubois, Sally
   13   The Marriage Season   Dell Candlelight Ecstasy
Ducoty, Lyn
   33   A Pocketful Of Dreams   11/84   Harlequin Temptation
Dudley, Charlotte
      Promise Me Forever   05/93   Avalon
Duke, Elizabeth
  284   To Catch A Playboy   06/96   Harlequin
  127   Whispering Vines   02/93   Harlequin Direct
  161   Outback Legacy   11/93   Harlequin Direct
  180   Bogus Bride   04/94   Harlequin Direct
  220   Shattered Wedding   02/95   Harlequin Direct
 2833   Softly Flits A Shadow   Harlequin Romance
 3034   Island Deception   Harlequin Romance
 3110   Fair Trial   Harlequin Romance
 3200   Wild Temptation   06/92   Harlequin Romance
Dumbrille, Dorothy
  718   All This Difference   /63   Harlequin
Dunaway, Diane
      Desert Hostage   /83   Dell
  158   Desire And Conquer   /83   Dell Candlelight Ecstasy
Dunbar, Inga
      Rose Royale   08/86   Harlequin Historical
Dunbar, Jean
 1358   Home To White Wings   /69   Harlequin
 1468   Yesterday, Today And Tommorrow   /71   Harlequin
 1537   The Summer Nights   /71   Harlequin
 1606   The Quiet Veld   /72   Harlequin
Duncan, Carol
  270   Stranger On The Shore   01/89   Silhouette Intimate Moments
Duncan, Dorian
      Castle Of Dolls   05/93   Avalon
Duncan, Judith
      Father Knows Last!   05/94   Harlequin Anthology
   51   Tender Rhapsody   Harlequin Superromance
   77   Hold Back The Dawn   Harlequin Superromance
  114   Reach The Splendor   Harlequin Superromance
  143   When Morning Comes   Harlequin Superromance

Duncan, Judith

196	Into The Light		Harlequin	Superromance
251	All That Matters		Harlequin	Superromance
291	Beginnings		Harlequin	Superromance
407	Streets Of Fire		Harlequin	Superromance
	All That Matters	05/95	Harlequin	Western Lovers
400	A Risk Worth Taking	09/91	Silhouette	Intimate Moments
421	Better Than Before	03/92	Silhouette	Intimate Moments
536	Beyond All Reason	12/93	Silhouette	Intimate Moments
577	That Same Old Feeling	07/94	Silhouette	Intimate Moments
651	The Return Of Eden Mc Call	07/95	Silhouette	Intimate Moments
704	Driven To Distraction	04/96	Silhouette	Intimate Moments

Dunkel, Elizabeth

	Every Woman Loves A Poet		Harper

Dunn, Carola

	His Lordship's Reward	07/94		
25	A Susceptible Gentleman	05/90	Harlequin	Regency
39	A Poor Relation	12/90	Harlequin	Regency
52	A Lord For Miss Larkin	06/91	Harlequin	Regency
63	The Fortune-Hunters	12/91	Harlequin	Regency
73	The Road To Gretna	05/92	Harlequin	Regency
86	My Lord Winter	02/93	Harlequin	Regency
98	Thea's Marquis	05/93	Harlequin	Regency
98	Thea's Marquis	05/93	Harlequin	Regency
108	Ginnie Come Lately	10/93	Harlequin	Regency
	Lord Iverbrook's Heir	/86	Walker	
	The Man In The Green Coat	/87	Walker	
	Smuggler's Summer	/88	Walker	
	Two Corinthians	/89	Walker	
	The Black Sheep's Daughter	/89	Walker	
	Byron's Child	/91	Walker	
	Polly And The Prince	/91	Walker	
	Lavender Lady	/83	Walker	
	The Miser's Sister	/84	Walker	
	Miss Hartwell's Dilemma	/88	Walker	
	A Maid At Your Window	/91	Walker	A Regency Valentine
	The Frog Earl	03/92	Walker	Regency
	Miss Jacobson's Journey	09/92	Walker	Regency
	Lady In The Briars	/90	Walker	Regency
	Toblethorpe Manor	/81	Warner	
	Angel	/85	Warner	
	Gabrielle's Gamble	/89	Warner	
	Smuggler's Summer	/89	Warner	
	Flowers For The Bride	04/95	Zebra	Anthology
	The Captain's Inheritance	08/94	Zebra	Regency
	The Lady And The Rake	03/95	Zebra	Regency

Dunnett, Dorothy

Dyer, Lois Faye
  1038 Lonesome Cowboy   06/96 Silhouette Special Edition

Eady, Carol Maxwell
      Her Royal Destiny

Eagle, Kathleen

	This Time Forever	11/92	Avon
	Fire And Rain	01/94	Avon
	Sunrise Song	03/96	Avon
	Heat Lightning	/89	Crown Pageant "Now And Forever"
	Mistletoe Marriages	11/94	Harlequin Anthology
	Friends, Families, Lovers	10/93	Harlequin Anthology
	Historical Christmas Collection 1994	11/94	Harlequin Anthology
2	Private Treaty	07/88	Harlequin Historical
30	Medicine Woman	/89	Harlequin Historical
50	Heaven And Earth		Harlequin Historical
34	A Class Act	02/95	Harlequin Men Made In America
41	For Old Times' Sake	/95	Harlequin Men Made In America
	Dream Catchers	01/96	Harlequin Two Novels
	Carved In Stone	07/95	Harlequin Western Lovers
	Men Of Summer: "All-Around Cowboy Blu	07/96	Silhouette Anthology
	Brave Hearts	10/94	Silhouette By Request: Anthology
	Surrender	09/95	Silhouette By Request: Anthology
	The Twelfth Moon	/88	Silhouette Christmas Stories
428	To Each His Own	04/92	Silhouette Initmate Moments
451	Black Tree Moon	10/92	Silhouette Initmate Moments
457	A Walk On The Wild Side	11/92	Silhouette Initmate Moments
480	Diamond Willow	02/93	Silhouette Initmate Moments
148	For Old Time's Sake	06/86	Silhouette Intimate Moments
242	More Than A Miracle	06/88	Silhouette Intimate Moments
257	But That Was Yesterday	10/88	Silhouette Intimate Moments
284	Paintbox Morning	04/89	Silhouette Intimate Moments
412	Bad Moon Rising	12/91	Silhouette Intimate Moments
589	Defender (American Hero)	09/94	Silhouette Intimate Moments
204	Someday Soon	11/84	Silhouette Special Edition
274	A Class Act	11/85	Silhouette Special Edition
304	Georgia Nights	04/86	Silhouette Special Edition
359	Something Worth Keeping	01/87	Silhouette Special Edition
396	Carved In Stone	07/87	Silhouette Special Edition
437	Candles In The Night	02/88	Silhouette Special Edition
576	' Til There Was You	01/90	Silhouette Special Edition
848	Broomstick Cowboy	11/93	Silhouette Special Edition
	Sentimental Journey	/91	Silhouette Summer Sizzlers

Eagle, Sarah

A Reluctant Suitor		Berkley
The Marriage Gamble	02/92	Jove Regency
A Regency Holiday		Jove Regency
The Reluctant Bridegroom		Jove Regency

AUTHOR/TITLE INDEX

Eckert, Roberta

	The Duke's Gambit	01/87	Nal Regency
	My Lady Adverturess	06/87	Nal Regency
	Heir To Vengeance	03/90	Nal Regency
	Lady Angel	07/90	Nal Regency

Eden, Dorothy

	Whistle For The Crows		Gothic
	Millionaire's Daughter		Historical
	Shadow Wife		Suspense

Eden, Lark

	Flames Of Rapture	01/96	Leisure Love Spell

Eden, Laura

105	Mistaken Identity	09/81	Silhouette Romance
210	Flight Of Fancy	03/83	Silhouette Romance
44	Summer Magic	09/82	Silhouette Special Edition

Edgar, Josephine

	Margaret Normandy		Nal Penguin
	Duchess		St. Martin's
	Bright Young Things		St. Martin's
	Countess		St. Martin's
	Margaret Normanby		St. Martin's

Edgehill, Rosemary

	The Ill-Bred Bride		Ballantine
	Two Of A Kind		St. Martins Regency
	Turkish Delight		St. Martins Regency

Edgeworth, Ann

39	Runaway Maid		Mills & Boon

Edghill, Rosemary

	Fleeting Fancy

Edgley, Leslie

132	False Face	/51	Harlequin

Edmonds, Janet

	Mischief & Mayhem	03/95	Harlequin Promotion
	Rivers Of Gold	12/91	St. Martin's
	Turn Of The Dice		St. Martin's

Edouard, Dianne

	Sacred Lies	05/93	Bantam
	Mortal Sins	05/91	Bantam Fanfare

Edwards, Andrea

645	Starting Over	06/91	Silhouette Desire
291	Above Suspicion	06/89	Silhouette Intimate Moments
363	Rose In Bloom	02/87	Silhouette Special Edition
428	Say It With Flowers	01/88	Silhouette Special Edition
490	Ghost Of A Chance	11/88	Silhouette Special Edition
550	Violets Are Blue	09/89	Silhouette Special Edition
591	Places In The Heart	04/90	Silhouette Special Edition

AUTHOR/TITLE INDEX

Edwards, Andrea

618	Fly Away Home	08/90	Silhouette	Special Edition
706	Home Court Advantage	11/91	Silhouette	Special Edition
740	Sweet Knight Times	05/92	Silhouette	Special Edition
770	Father: Unknown	10/92	Silhouette	Special Edition
809	Man Of The Family	04/93	Silhouette	Special Edition
856	The Magic Of Christmas	12/93	Silhouette	Special Edition
883	Just Hold On Tight! (That Special Woman!)	05/94	Silhouette	Special Edition
932	A Ring And A Promise (This Time, Forever)	01/95	Silhouette	Special Edition
944	A Rose And A Wedding Vow	03/95	Silhouette	Special Edition
956	A Secret And A Bridal Pledge	05/95	Silhouette	Special Edition
981	Kisses And Kids (Congratulations!)	09/95	Silhouette	Special Edition
1029	On Mother's Day	05/96	Silhouette	Special Edition
1046	A Father's Gift	08/96	Silhouette	Special Edition

Edwards, Andrienne

29	Honorable Intentions	/84	Berkley	To Have And To Hold

Edwards, Cassie

5	Passion In The Wind		Harlequin Historical
17	A Gentle Passion		Harlequin Historical
42	Passion's Embrace		Harlequin Historical
	Savage Bliss		Jove
	Savage Dance		Jove
	Savage Dream		Jove
	Savage Eden	06/96	Jove
	Savage Splendor	07/96	Jove
	Savage Surrender		Jove
	Savage Whispers		Jove
	Savage Mists	08/92	Leisure
	Eden's Promise	/89	Leisure
	Roses After Rain		Leisure
	Savage Persuasion		Leisure
	Island Rapture		Leisure
	Savage Promise	/95	Leisure
	When Passion Calls	/90	Leisure
	Velvet Fire	/90	Leisure
	Savage Sunrise	02/93	Leisure
	An Old-Fashioned Valentine	02/93	Leisure
	Secrets Of My Heart	06/93	Leisure
	Savage Illusion	08/93	Leisure
	Touch The Wild Wind	09/93	Leisure
	Savage Spirit	08/94	Leisure
	Savage Embers		Leisure
	Savage Pride		Leisure
	Savage Secrets	07/95	Leisure
	Island Rapture	/95	Leisure
	Savage Passions	02/96	Leisure
	Savage Shadows	08/96	Leisure

Edwards, Cassie

Savage Whispers	09/96	Leisure
Love's Legacy	11/95	Leisure Anthology
Savage Surrender	05/96	Leisure Lovespell
Wild Ecstasy	05/92	Nal Onyx
Wild Rapture	10/92	Nal Onyx
Wild Embrace	06/93	Nal Topaz
Wild Desire	05/94	Nal Topaz
Wild Splendor	/94	Nal Topaz
Wild Abandon	11/94	Topaz
Wild Bliss	05/95	Topaz
Wild Whispers	/96	Topaz
Wild Thunder	12/95	Topaz
Wild Whispers	05/96	Topaz
Rolling Thunder	11/96	Topaz
Beloved Embrace		Zebra
Desire's Blossom		Zebra
Enchanted Enemy		Zebra
Passion's Fire		Zebra
Passion's Web		Zebra
Savage Obsession		Zebra
Eugenia's Embrace		Zebra
Portrait Of Desire		Zebra
Rapture's Rendezvous		Zebra
Forbidden Embrace		Zebra
Silken Rapture		Zebra
Elusive Ecstasy		Zebra
Savage Heart		Zebra
Savage Paradise		Zebra
Savage Innocence		Zebra
Savage Torment		Zebra

Edwards, Emily Ruth

2791	Hunter's Snare		Harlequin Romance

Edwards, Estelle

21	Moonslide		Nal Rapture Romance
47	The Knave Of Hearts		Nal Rapture Romance

Edwards, Jane

	Tangled Heritage	/92	Avalon
	Terror By Design		Avalon Mystery Romance
90	Listen With Your Heart	01/86	Harlequin Temptation
39	Impersonation	05/93	Zebra Lucky In Love

Edwards, Judi

471	For Encores, A Kiss	08/88	Silhouette Special Edition
658	Step From A Dream	03/91	Silhouette Special Edition
765	Nobody's Bride	09/92	Silhouette Special Edition

Edwards, Marian

AUTHOR/TITLE INDEX

Edwards, Marian
>A Year And A Day
>Hearts Victorious 06/96 Zebra

Edwards, Marissa
>The Scandalous Masquerade 07/94
>A June Betrothal 04/93 Zebra Anthology

Edwards, Patricia
>446 Sweet Promised Land Harlequin Superromance

Edwards, Paula
>23 Bewitching Grace 08/80 Silhouette Romance

Edwards, Rachelle
>Lord Trenton's Proposal Ballantine
>Runaway Bride Ballantine Regency
>Fortune's Child Ballantine Regency
>The Marriage Bargain Ballantine Regency
>The Scoundrel's Daughter Ballantine Regency
>Dangerous Dandy Ballantine Regency
>An Unequal Match Ballantine Regency
>Regency Masquerade Ballantine Regency
>The Ransom Inheritance Ballantine Regency
>Lady Of Quality Ballantine Regency
>Marylebone Park Ballantine Regency
>The Rake's Revenger Ballantine Regency
>The Highwayman And The Lady Ballantine Regency
>Lucifer's Lady Ballantine Regency
>Sweet Hoyden Ballantine Regency
>The Outrageous Lady Caroline Ballantine Regency
>The Merchant's Daughter Ballantine Regency
>Lord Heathbury's Revenge Ballantine Regency
>Debt Of Love Ballantine Regency
>Love Finds A Way Ballantine Regency
>Brighton Beau 05/94 Fawcett Regency
>The Devilish Earl 10/94 Fawcett Regency
>Bath Revels 09/91 Fawcett Crest Regency Romance
>The Duke's Dilemma 06/92 Fawcett Crest Regency Romance

Edwards, Sara
>Fire And Sand St. Martin's
>Crystal Rapture St. Martin's

Edwards, Susan
>White Wind 03/96 Leisure #1 White Series

Eliot, Jessica
>550 Home To The Highlands Dell Candlelight

Elizabeth, Suzanne
>When Destiny Calls Harper
>Kiley's Storm 02/94 Harper
>Destiny Awaits 02/95 Harper

456

AUTHOR/TITLE INDEX

Elizabeth, Suzanne

| | Fan The Flame | 09/93 | Harper Historical |
| | Destined To Love | 09/94 | Harper Monogram |

Ellingham, Marnie

| | Dolly Blanchard's Fortune | | Walker |
| | The Wicked Marquis | | Walker |

Ellingson, Marnie

| 572 | Double Folly | Dell Candlelight Regency |
| 588 | Jessica Windom | Dell Candlelight Regency |

Ellinson, Marnie

| 579 | Unwilling Bride | Dell Candlelight Regency |

Elliot, Christine

	Traitor's Embrace
	Wild Virginia Nights
	Bold Rebel Love
	Captain's Captive
	Kansas Kiss
	The Pirate

Elliot, Kathleen

| | A Special License | 03/95 | Harper Regency |

Elliot, Lucy

8	Shared Passions		Harlequin Historical
24	Frontiers Of The Heart		Harlequin Historical
44	Summer's Promise		Harlequin Historical
64	Contraband Desire	02/91	Harlequin Historical
79	Private Paradise	06/91	Harlequin Historical
95	Passionate Alliance	10/91	Harlequin Historical
129	The Claim	06/92	Harlequin Historical
146	The Conquest	10/92	Harlequin Historical
	A Cinderella Christmas	/89	Sil. Hist. Christmas Stories

Elliot, Rachel

123	Winter Challenge	12/92	Harlequin Direct
176	Unwanted Legacy	03/94	Harlequin Direct
1207	Journey Back To Love		Harlequin Presents
1415	Fantasy Of Love	12/91	Harlequin Presents

Elliott, Christine

| | Captain's Conquest | | Zebra |

Elliott, Elizabeth

| | Scoundrel | 02/96 | Bantam Fanfare |

Elliott, Emily

	Tomorrow's Promise		
88	The Best Reason Of All	/86	Dell Candlelight Ecstasy
95	Dangerous Interlude	/86	Dell Candlelight Ecstasy
182	Delicate Balance	/83	Dell Candlelight Ecstasy
200	Midnight Memories	/83	Dell Candlelight Ecstasy
403	More Than Skin Deep	/86	Dell Ecstasy Romance

457

AUTHOR/TITLE INDEX

Ellis, Louise

1225	Nurse Camden's Cavalier	/68	Harlequin
1345	Three Nurses	/69	Harlequin
1369	Rona Came To Rothmere	/70	Harlequin
1394	Nurse Sandra's Second Summer	/70	Harlequin
1473	Silent Heart	/71	Harlequin

Ellis, Lyn

488	Dear John...	04/94	Harlequin	Temptation
532	In Praise Of Younger Men	03/95	Harlequin	Temptation
575	Michael's Angel	02/96	Harlequin	Temptation

Ellis, Monique

A Mother's Delight	03/95	Zebra	Anthology
The Fortescue Diamond	09/94	Zebra	Regency
Delacey's Angel	05/95	Zebra	Regency

Ellis, Patricia

684	Sweet Protector	11/89	Silhouette	Romance
799	Champagne And Wildflowers	06/91	Silhouette	Romance
820	Pillow Talk	10/91	Silhouette	Romance
846	Keeping Up With The Joneses	02/92	Silhouette	Romance
931	Sorry, Wrong Number	04/93	Silhouette	Romance

Ellison, Marjorie

741	Journey Into Yesterday (Nurse At Hand)	/63	Harlequin

Ellison, Suzanne

46	Nowhere To Run	07/86	Harlequin	Intrigue
165	Wings Of Gold		Harlequin	Superromance
258	Pinecones And Orchids		Harlequin	Superromance
283	For All The Right Reasons		Harlequin	Superromance
308	Words Unspoken		Harlequin	Superromance
315	Fair Play		Harlequin	Superromance
369	Candle In The Window		Harlequin	Superromance
393	With Open Arms		Harlequin	Superromance
420	Heart Of The West		Harlequin	Superromance
423	Soul Of The West		Harlequin	Superromance
427	Spirit Of The West		Harlequin	Superromance
452	A Dangerous Loyalty		Harlequin	Superromance
488	Shifting Sands	02/92	Harlequin	Superromance
5	Blazing Star	07/92	Harlequin	Tyler
7	Arrowpoint	09/92	Harlequin	Tyler
	Soul Of The West	06/95	Harlequin	Western Lovers
	Eagle Knight	05/91	Harper	
	Hannah	07/92	Harper	
	Sunburst	09/93	Harper	
	Sycamore Settlement	/86	Zondervan	Saga
	Sycamore Steeple	/87	Zondervan	Saga
	One More River	/85	Zondervan	Serenata

Elmblad, Mary

Erickson, Lynn

347	Shadow On The Sun		Harlequin	Superromance
370	In From The Cold		Harlequin	Superromance
404	West Of The Sun		Harlequin	Superromance
439	The Northern Light		Harlequin	Superromance
482	Silver Lady	01/92	Harlequin	Superromance
520	A Wing And A Prayer	10/92	Harlequin	Superromance
549	Paradox	06/93	Harlequin	Superromance
564	Wildfire	09/93	Harlequin	Superromance
578	The Last Buccaneer	01/94	Harlequin	Superromance
596	Dancing In The Dark	06/94	Harlequin	Superromance
614	Laurel And The Lawman (Grapevine)	10/94	Harlequin	Superromance
626	Out Of The Darkness (Showcase)	01/95	Harlequin	Superromance
656	Apache Springs (Reunited)	08/95	Harlequin	Superromance
690	The Baby Contract	05/96	Harlequin	Superromance
	West Of The Sun	09/95	Harlequin	Western Lovers
	Aspen	08/95	Mira	
	High Country Pride		Pocket	
	Gentle Betrayer		Pocket	
	The Silver Kiss		Richard Gallen	
	This Raging Flower		Richard Gallen	
	Sweet Nemesis		Richard Gallen	

Erickson, Lyyn

	West Of The Sun	08/95	Harlequin	Western Lovers

Ernenwein, Leslie

88	Renegade Ramrod	/50	Harlequin
89	The Faro Kid	/50	Harlequin
143	Rebel Yell	/51	Harlequin
145	Rio Renegade	/51	Harlequin
171	Savage Justice	/52	Harlequin
204	Gun Hawk	/53	Harlequin
355	Savage Justice	/56	Harlequin
371	Renegade Ramrod	/56	Harlequin
386	The Faro Kid	/57	Harlequin

Erskine, Barbara

	Kingdom Of Shadows		
	Lady Of Hay		
	Midnight Is A Lonely Place	07/94	Dutton

Erskine, Helen

140	Fortunes Of Love	03/82	Silhouette	Romance

Erwin, Annabel

	Lilliane	/76	Warner

Esler, Anthony

	Blade Of Castlemayne	Historical
	For Love Of A Pirate	Sweet & Savage

Essex, Marianna

AUTHOR/TITLE INDEX

Essex, Marianna
   41   Torrent Of Love   Nal Rapture Romance

Essig, Terry

552	House Calls	01/88	Silhouette Romance
662	The Wedding March	07/89	Silhouette Romance
725	Fearless Father	06/90	Silhouette Romance
1015	Housemates (Celebration 1000!)	06/94	Silhouette Romance
1044	Hardheaded Woman	11/94	Silhouette Romance
1114	Daddy On Board	11/95	Silhouette Romance
796	Father Of The Brood	02/93	Silhouette Special Edition

Estrada, Rita Clay

	Summer Song			
	Temptation 10th Anniversary	06/94	Harlequin	Temptation
48	The Will And The Way	02/85	Harlequin	Temptation
72	A Woman's Choice	08/85	Harlequin	Temptation
100	Something To Treasure	03/86	Harlequin	Temptation
136	The Best Things In Life	12/86	Harlequin	Temptation
166	The Ivory Key	08/87	Harlequin	Temptation
188	A Little Magic	01/88	Harlequin	Temptation
220	Trust	09/88	Harlequin	Temptation
265	Second To None	09/89	Harlequin	Temptation
313	To Buy A Groom	09/90	Harlequin	Temptation
349	The Lady Says No	06/91	Harlequin	Temptation
361	Twice Loved	09/91	Harlequin	Temptation
450	One More Time	07/93	Harlequin	Temptation
474	The Colonel's Daughter	01/94	Harlequin	Temptation
500	Forms Of Love (Lost Loves)	07/94	Harlequin	Temptation
518	The Twelve Gifts Of Christmas	12/94	Harlequin	Temptation
573	The Stormchaser	02/96	Harlequin	Temptation
595	Love Me, Love My Bed	07/96	Harlequin	Temptation
	Bride On The Run	04/92	Harlequin	To Have And To Hold
	The Best Things In Life	08/95	Harlequin	Western Lovers
	Interlude In Time		Leisure	
	A Valentine Sampler	01/93	Leisure	Contemporary

Evan, Quinn Taylor

Daughter Of The Mist	07/96	Zebra

Evanick, Marcia

	My Special Angel	03/94	Bantam Loveswept
322	Perfect Morning	04/89	Bantam Loveswept
404	Indescribably Delicious	06/90	Bantam Loveswept
427	Satin Sheets And Strawberries	10/90	Bantam Loveswept
467	Guardian Spirit	04/91	Bantam Loveswept
487	Sizzle	08/91	Bantam Loveswept
513	Midnight Kiss	12/91	Bantam Loveswept
535	Gretchen And The Big Bad Wolf	04/92	Bantam Loveswept
570	Sweet Temptation	10/92	Bantam Loveswept

Evanick, Marcia

597	Over The Rainbow	02/93	Bantam Loveswept
629	In Daddy's Arms	07/93	Bantam Loveswept
674	More Than A Misteress	03/94	Bantam Loveswept
687	Playing For Keeps	05/94	Bantam Loveswept
715	Out Of A Dream	11/94	Bantam Loveswept
743	Emma And The Handsome Devil	05/95	Bantam Loveswept
770	My True Love Gave To Me	01/96	Bantam Loveswept
779	Family First	03/96	Bantam Loveswept
676	By The Light Of The Moon	11/95	Silhouette Intimate Moments
717	His Chose Bride	06/96	Silhouette Intimate Moments

Evanovich, Janet

	One For The Money	08/94	
254	The Grand Finale	05/88	Bantam Loveswept
289	Thanksgiving	11/88	Bantam Loveswept
303	Manhunt	01/89	Bantam Loveswept
343	Ivan Takes A Wife	08/89	Bantam Loveswept
362	Back To The Bedroom	11/89	Bantam Loveswept
392	Smitten	04/90	Bantam Loveswept
422	Wife For Hire	09/90	Bantam Loveswept
460	The Rocky Road To Romance	03/91	Bantam Loveswept
537	Naughty Neighbor	04/92	Bantam Loveswept

Evans, Ann

701	Hot & Bothered	07/96	Harlequin Superromance
415	Flamingo Moon	01/92	Silhouette Intimate Moments

Evans, Claire

22	Led Into Sunlight	/81	Berkley Second Chance At Love
64	Apollo's Dream	/82	Berkley Second Chance At Love

Evans, John

49	Weep Not Fair Lady	/50	Harlequin

Evans, Laurel

144	Business After Hours	06/84	Silhouette Desire
167	Timeless Rituals	10/84	Silhouette Desire
200	A Permanent Arrangement	04/85	Silhouette Desire
248	Moonlight Serenade	12/85	Silhouette Desire
278	Designing Heart	05/86	Silhouette Desire
401	Built To Last	01/88	Silhouette Desire

Evans, M.

	Time And Time Again	09/91	Pinnacle

Evans, Patricia Gardner

	Mistletoe Marriages	11/94	Harlequin Anthology
	Lover Come Back	01/94	Harlequin By Request
14	Silver Noose		Harlequin Historical
	Santa's Little Helpers - "Comfort And Joy"	11/95	Silhouette Anthology
151	Flashpoint	07/86	Silhouette Intimate Moments
228	Whatever It Takes	02/88	Silhouette Intimate Moments

AUTHOR/TITLE INDEX

Evans, Patricia Gardner

243	Summer Of The Wolf	06/88	Silhouette Intimate Moments
493	Quinn Eisley's War	05/93	Silhouette Intimate Moments
	Over The Rainbow	/91	Silhouette Summer Sizzlers

Evans, Patricia Garnder

559	Keeper	04/94	Silhouette Intimate Moments

Evererr, Gail

209	Teach Me To Love		Dell Candlelight

Everett, Gail

211	Love Is The Winner		Dell Candlelight

Everitt, Marjorie

	Country Blues	/92	Avalon
	Sweet Dreams, Serena	/91	Avalon
	River Of Stars		Avalon
	Somewhere Near Paradise	10/92	Avalon
	Small Details	07/93	Avalon
	A Touch Of Honey		Avalon Career Romance

Ewing, Jean

	Flowers For The Bride	04/95	Zebra Anthology
1	Scandal's Reward	08/94	Zebra Regency Series
2	Virtue's Reward	02/95	Zebra Regency Series

Ewing, Tess

48	Starburst	/82	Berkley Second Chance At Love

Fabian, Erika

116	Sky Riders		Harlequin Superromance

Fabian, Robert

306	Fabian Of The Yard	/54	Harlequin
321	London After Dark	/54	Harlequin

Fabio,

Pirate	11/93	Avon
Rogue	05/94	Avon
Viking	11/94	Avon
Comanche	05/95	Avon
Champion	11/95	Avon
Dangerous	01/96	Zebra

Fairchild, Elisabeth

The Silent Suitor	04/94	Nal
The Counterfeit Coachman	11/94	Nal Regency

Fairchilde, Sarah

Dance Of Desire	Zebra Regency

Faire, Zabrina

Pretender To Love	Regency
The Midnight Match	Warner
Lady Blue	Warner
Tiffany's True Love	Warner
Athen's Airs	Warner

AUTHOR/TITLE INDEX

Faire, Zabrina

	Bold Pursuit		Warner
	Enchanting Jenny		Warner
	The Romany Rebel		Warner
	The Wicked Cousin		Warner
	Pretty Kitty		Warner

Fairfax, Lynn

28	Aphrodite's Legend	/82	Berkley	Second Chance At Love
37	Heartland	/82	Berkley	Second Chance At Love

Fairman, Paul W.

139	The Glass Ladder	/51	Harlequin
202	Copper Town	/52	Harlequin

Faith, Barbara

	Enchanted Dawn			
13	A Silence Of Dreams	08/93	Harlequin	
155	Gamblin's Man	01/93	Harlequin	Historical
43	Dark, Dark My Lover's Eyes	11/94	Harlequin	Shadows
	The Sundancer's		Richard Gallen	
	The Moonkissed		Richard Gallen	
	Men Of Summer - "The Sheikh's Woman"	07/96	Silhouette	Anthology
670	Lion Of The Desert	10/91	Silhouette	Desire
16	The Promise Of Summer	08/83	Silhouette	Intimate Moments
47	Wind Whispers	04/84	Silhouette	Intimate Moments
63	Bedouin Bride	08/84	Silhouette	Intimate Moments
101	Awake To Splendor	07/85	Silhouette	Intimate Moments
124	Island In Turquoise	12/85	Silhouette	Intimate Moments
140	Tomorrow Is Forever	04/86	Silhouette	Intimate Moments
146	Sing Me A Love Song	06/86	Silhouette	Intimate Moments
173	Desert Song	01/87	Silhouette	Intimate Moments
193	Kiss Of The Dragon	06/87	Silhouette	Intimate Moments
208	Asking For Trouble	09/87	Silhouette	Intimate Moments
244	Beyond Forever	06/88	Silhouette	Intimate Moments
262	Flower Of The Desert	11/88	Silhouette	Intimate Moments
277	In A Rebel's Arms	03/89	Silhouette	Intimate Moments
306	Capricorn Moon	10/89	Silhouette	Intimate Moments
332	Danger In Paradise	04/90	Silhouette	Intimate Moments
361	Lord Of The Desert	12/90	Silhouette	Intimate Moments
432	The Matador	05/92	Silhouette	Intimate Moments
446	Queen Of Hearts	09/92	Silhouette	Intimate Moments
502	Cloud Man	06/93	Silhouette	Intimate Moments
544	Midnight Man	01/94	Silhouette	Intimate Moments
578	Desert Man (Romantic Traditions)	07/94	Silhouette	Intimate Moments
623	Moonlight Lady	02/95	Silhouette	Intimate Moments
730	Long-Lost Wife?	08/96	Silhouette	Intimate Moments
335	Return To Summer	09/86	Silhouette	Special Edition
436	Say Hello Again	02/88	Silhouette	Special Edition
533	Heather On The Hill	06/89	Silhouette	Special Edition

AUTHOR/TITLE INDEX

Faith, Barbara

615	Choices Of The Heart	08/90	Silhouette Special Edition
650	Echoes Of Summer	02/91	Silhouette Special Edition
715	Mr. Macho Meets His Match	01/92	Silhouette Special Edition
812	This Above All	05/93	Silhouette Special Edition
975	Scarlet Woman	08/95	Silhouette Special Edition
1033	Happy Father's Day	06/96	Silhouette Special Edition
	Fiesta!	/88	Silhouette Summer Sizzlers

Falcon, Debra

	Angel's Sin	11/94	Pinnacle

Falcon, Sally

3	Southern Hospitality	07/90	Meteor
30	Remember The Night	02/91	Meteor
55	A Forever Man	08/91	Meteor
107	Stolen Kisses	09/92	Meteor

Farnes, Eleanor

487	The Happy Enterprise	/59	Harlequin
722	Doctor's Orders	/63	Harlequin
753	Doctor Max	/63	Harlequin
806	The Golden Peaks	/64	Harlequin
912	The Dream And The Dancer	/65	Harlequin
942	The House By The Lake	/65	Harlequin
975	Sister Of The Housemaster	/65	Harlequin
998	Magic Symphony	/66	Harlequin
1064	Mistress Of The House	/66	Harlequin
1087	A Home For Jocelyn	/67	Harlequin
1109	The Fortunes Of Springfield	/67	Harlequin
1142	Secret Heiress	/67	Harlequin
1171	The Wings Of Memory	/68	Harlequin
1207	The Young Intruder	/68	Harlequin
1246	The Constant Heart	/68	Harlequin
1280	The Flight Of The Swan	/69	Harlequin
1335	The Red Cliffs	/69	Harlequin
1458	The Enchanted Island	/71	Harlequin
1497	The Doctor's Circle	/71	Harlequin
1584	A Castle In Spain	/72	Harlequin
1639	The Valley Of The Eagles	/72	Harlequin
1662	A Serpent In Eden	/73	Harlequin
1765	The Splendid Legacy	/74	Harlequin
1787	The Runaway Visitors	/74	Harlequin
10	The Rose And The Thorn		Mills & Boon

Farraday, Alicia

69	The Suitable Suitor	03/92	Harlequin Regency

Farrant, Sarah

	Sweet Joel		Playboy Press

Farrell, Majorie

Farrell, Majorie

Sweet Awakening 04/95 Topaz

Farrell, Marjorie

Lady Arden's Redemption 03/92 Nal Regency

Autumn Rose Nal Regency

Lord Ashton's Wager 05/94 Nal Regency

A Regency Christmas 4 11/92 Nal Super Regency

Miss Ware's Refusal /91 Nal Signet Regency

Heartless Lord Harry 09/93 Nal Signet Regency

Lady Barbara's Dilemma 03/93 Penguin Regency

Desert Hearts 05/96 Topaz

Farrington, Renee

No Secret So Close Dell Candlelight

Faulkner, Colleen

Forbidden Caress

Snowfire

Sweet Savage Lies

Love's Wicked Deceptions

Love's Sweet Bounty 02/91 Zebra

Passion's Savage Moon Zebra

Patriot's Passion 09/91 Zebra

Savage Surrender 03/92 Zebra

Temptation's Tender Kiss 06/90 Zebra

Sweet Deceptions 10/92 Zebra

O' Brian's Bride 04/95 Zebra

Destined To Be Mine 05/96 Zebra

To Love And To Honor 05/95 Zebra Anthology

Raging Desire Zebra Heartfire

Traitor's Caress Zebra Heartfire

Captive Zebra Historical

Favor, Erika

678 Mountain Home 10/89 Silhouette Romance

Faye, Alane

Mermaid's Dream 05/95 Pinnacle Time-Travel

Faye, Mandalyn

Beyond All Measure 02/96 Kensington Denise Little Presents

Faye, Shirley

16 Face To Face 10/90 Meteor

66 Back Of Beyond 11/91 Meteor

Fearn, John Russell

218 The Golden Amazon /53 Harlequin

320 The Deathless Amazon /54 Harlequin

421 The Golden Amazon's Triumph /58 Harlequin

Feather, Jane

Hearts Folly Avon

Chase The Dawn Avon

AUTHOR/TITLE INDEX

Feather, Jane

Reckless Angel		Avon
Bold Destiny		Avon
Brazen Whispers	12/90	Avon
Silver Nights		Avon
Eagle And The Dove	12/91	Avon Romance
Valentine	01/95	Bantam
Violet	06/95	Bantam
Virtue	/93	Bantam Fanfare
Vixen	01/94	Bantam Fanfare
Velvet		Bantam Fanfare
Love's Charade		Zebra
Beloved Enemy		Zebra Heartfire
Reckless Seduction	/87	Zebra Heartfire
Smuggler's Lady		Zebra Regency

Felldin, Jeanne

Boundless Love		
A Doctor's Heart		Zebra

Fellows, Catherine

Entanglement		Regency

Fenton, Julia

Black Tie Only	05/90	Contemporary
Blue Orchids	07/92	Jove

Fenwick, Patricia

841	Truant Heart (Doctor In Brazil)	/64	Harlequin
1133	Wish On A Star	/67	Harlequin
1253	Dream Come True	/68	Harlequin

Ferguson, Jo Ann

At The Rainbow's End		
Ride The Night Wind	02/95	Harper Monogram
Under The Outlaw Moon		Leisure
The Wolfe Wager	04/95	Zebra Anthology
The Lynx And The Lady	12/94	Zebra Heartfire
The Fortune Hunter	06/93	Zebra Regency
Mother's Day Regency	04/94	Zebra Regency
The Smithfield Bargain	04/94	Zebra Regency
An Undomesticated Wife	10/94	Zebra Regency

Ferguson, Maggie

284	Looks Are Deceiving	07/94	Harlequin Intrigue
347	Crime Of Passion	11/95	Harlequin Intrigue

Ferjutz, Kelly

Secret Shores	05/93	Berkley Great Lakes
Windsong	02/94	Jove Historical

Ferrarella, Marie

December 32nd -- And Always	06/83	Bantam Loveswept
Irresistible Forces	03/84	Bantam Loveswept

AUTHOR/TITLE INDEX

Ferrarella, Marie

	No Way To Treat A Lover	09/86	Bantam Loveswept
	Risking It All	03/87	Cloverdale
145	Pocketful Of Rainbows	04/86	Harlequin American
26	It Happened One Night	07/96	Harlequin Here Come The Grooms
	Thick As Thieves	07/85	Harlequin Intrigue
	Sapphire And Shadow	09/91	Harper
	Choices	10/93	Harper
	Flash And Fire	04/94	Harper
	Smoldering Embers	08/82	Scal
	Scenes From The Heart	03/83	Scal
	Claimed By Rapture	09/83	Scal
	Last Year's Hunk	04/86	Silhouette
	Maybe Baby	07/96	Silhouette
	The Night Santa Claus Returned	11/92	Silhouette Christmas Stories
	Tried And True	01/84	Silhouette Desire
	Buyer Beware	06/84	Silhouette Desire
	Through Laughter And Tears	09/84	Silhouette Desire
	Grand Theft	01/85	Silhouette Desire
	A Woman Of Integrity	03/85	Silhouette Desire
	Country Blue	08/85	Silhouette Desire
	Foxy Lady	11/86	Silhouette Desire
	Chocolate Dreams	04/87	Silhouette Desire
	No Laughing Matter	10/87	Silhouette Desire
988	Husband: Optional	03/96	Silhouette Desire
	Forgotten Honeymoon		Silhouette Fortune's Children
	The Amnesiac Bride		Silhouette Intimate Moments
496	Holding Out For A Hero	05/93	Silhouette Intimate Moments
501	Heroes Great And Small	06/93	Silhouette Intimate Moments
538	Christmas Every Day	12/93	Silhouette Intimate Moments
601	Callaghan's Way (American Hero)	11/94	Silhouette Intimate Moments
661	Caitlin's Guardian Angel	09/95	Silhouette Intimate Moments
686	Happy New Year---Baby!	01/96	Silhouette Intimate Moments
	My Phony Valentine	02/97	Silhouette Love And Laughter
	Man Under Cover	07/85	Silhouette Romance
	Please Stand By	11/85	Silhouette Romance
	Mine By Write	01/86	Silhouette Romance
	Getting Physical	06/86	Silhouette Romance
	The Man Who Would Be Daddy	/96	Silhouette Romance
	Your Baby Or Mine		Silhouette Romance
588	The Gift	07/88	Silhouette Romance
613	Five-Alarm Affair	11/88	Silhouette Romance
632	Heart To Heart	02/89	Silhouette Romance
686	Mother For Hire	11/89	Silhouette Romance
730	Borrowed Baby	07/90	Silhouette Romance
744	Her Special Angel	09/90	Silhouette Romance
766	The Undoing Of Justin Starbuck	01/91	Silhouette Romance

AUTHOR/TITLE INDEX

Field, Sandra

1280	Goodbye Forever		Harlequin	Presents
1336	Love At First Sight		Harlequin	Presents
1416	The Land Of Maybe	12/91	Harlequin	Presents
1448	Happy Ending	04/92	Harlequin	Presents
1506	Safety In Numbers	11/92	Harlequin	Presents
1557	Taken By Storm	06/93	Harlequin	Presents
1598	One-Night Stand	10/93	Harlequin	Presents
1646	Travelling Light	04/94	Harlequin	Presents
1709	Wildfire	12/94	Harlequin	Presents
1739	The Sun At Midnight	05/95	Harlequin	Presents
1806	Beyond Reach	04/96	Harlequin	Presents
1830	Second Honeymoon	08/96	Harlequin	Presents
1762	The Dating Game	09/95	Harlequin	Presents Plus
2398	The Winds Of Winter		Harlequin	Romance
2457	The Storms Of Spring		Harlequin	Romance
2480	Sight Of A Stranger		Harlequin	Romance
2577	The Tides Of Summer		Harlequin	Romance

Fielding, Liz

252	Bittersweet Deception	10/95	Harlequin	
277	Prisoner Of The Heart	04/96	Harlequin	
141	An Image Of You	06/93	Harlequin	Direct
166	A Point Of Pride	12/93	Harlequin	Direct
182	Instant Fire	04/94	Harlequin	Direct
217	A Stranger's Kiss	01/95	Harlequin	Direct
235	Old Desires	06/95	Harlequin	Direct
245	Dangerous Flirtation	08/95	Harlequin	Direct

Finch, Carol

	Beloved Betrayal		Zebra
	Captive Bride		Zebra
	Dawn's Desire		Zebra
	Ecstasy's Embrace		Zebra
	Lone Star Surrender		Zebra
	Love's Hidden Treasure	05/90	Zebra
	Montana Moonfire	12/90	Zebra
	Moonlight Enchantress		Zebra
	Wild Mountain Honey	08/91	Zebra
	Wildfire		Zebra
	Midnight Fires		Zebra
	Texas Angel		Zebra
	Storm Fire	05/89	Zebra
	Satin Surrender		Zebra
	Passion's Vixen		Zebra
	Endless Passion		Zebra
	Rapture's Dream		Zebra
	Thunder's Tender Touch		Zebra
	Apache Knight	10/94	Zebra

AUTHOR/TITLE INDEX

Finch, Carol

Canyon Moon	07/95	Zebra	
A Christmas Rendezvous	/91	Zebra	Anthology
Love's Treasure	05/90	Zebra	Hologram
A Bid For Love	05/94	Zebra	To Love Again

Findley, Ferguson

97	My Old Man's Badge	/51	Harlequin
129	Hire This Killer	/51	Harlequin
250	The Man In The Middle	/53	Harlequin

Finlay, Fiona

1175	Moon Over Madrid	/68	Harlequin

Finley, Glenna

Stowaway For Love	03/92	Nal
Island Rendezvous		Nal
The Marrying Kind		Nal
Journey To Love		Nal Penguin
Treasure Of The Heart		Nal Penguin
Love Lies North		Nal Penguin
Bridal Affair		Nal Penguin
Kiss A Stranger		Nal Penguin
Love In Danger		Nal Penguin
When Love Speaks		Nal Penguin
The Romantic Spirit		Nal Penguin
Surrender My Love		Nal Penguin
A Promising Affair		Nal Penguin
Love's Magic Spell		Nal Penguin
The Reluctant Maiden		Nal Penguin
The Captured Heart		Nal Penguin
Holiday For Love		Nal Penguin
Love For A Rogue		Nal Penguin
The Marriage Meyer		Nal Penguin
Wildfire Of Love		Nal Penguin
To Catch A Bride		Nal Penguin
Love's Hidden Fire	08/90	Penguin

Finnigan, Karen

Fires Of Midnight	Diamond

Firth, Susanne

624	Master Of Shadows	Harlequin Presents
2307	Dark Encounter	Harlequin Romance
2344	Prince Of Darkness	Harlequin Romance
2493	The Overlord	Harlequin Romance
2564	Lions Walk Alone	Harlequin Romance

Fitzcharles, Mara

156	Mac Laren's Memory	06/93	Meteor Kismet
161	Luke's Lady	07/93	Meteor Kismet

Fitzgerald, Catherine

AUTHOR/TITLE INDEX

Fitzgerald, Catherine
    Passion Song
Fitzgerald, Ellen

The Gambler's Bride			
Rogue's Bride	01/86	Nal	Regency
The Forgotten Marriage	04/86	Nal	Regency
Lessons In Love	07/86	Nal	Regency
Heirs Of Bellair	01/87	Nal	Regency
Venetian Masquerade	04/87	Nal	Regency
A Streak Of Luck	07/87	Nal	Regency
Romany Summer	10/87	Nal	Regency
Julia's Portion	04/88	Nal	Regency
Marriage By Decree	10/88	Nal	Regency
An Unwelcome Alliance	03/89	Nal	Regency
The Player Knight	07/89	Nal	Regency
Lord Calihan		Nal	Penguin Regency
A Navel Alliance		Nal	Penguin Regency
The Irish Heiress		Nal	Penguin Regency
Lesson In Love		Nal	Penguin Regency
Venetian Masquerade		Nal	Penguin Regency
The Dangerous Dr. Langhorn		Nal	Penguin Regency
Scandal's Daughter		Nal	Penguin Regency
The Forgotten Marriage		Nal	Penguin Regency
The Damsels From Derbyshire	/92	Walker	
Ardent Apparitions	08/92	Walker	Regency

Fitzgerald, Julia
    Beyond Ecstasy
    Royal Slave
    Taboo
Fitzgerald, Nancy
    Graver Square
    Mayfair

Chelsea		Ballantine Regency

Fitzgerald, Sara

166	Affairs Of State	10/84	Silhouette Desire
	Rumors	09/92	Warner

Fitzjames, Phoebe

Renegade's Angel		Zebra Heartfire
Silver Angel	08/94	Zebra Historical

Flanders, Rebecca

	Yesterday Comes Tomorrow	07/92	Harlequin
	Afterglow	07/85	Harlequin American
6	A Matter Of Trust		Harlequin American
24	Best Of Friends		Harlequin American
41	Suddenly Love		Harlequin American
51	Gilded Heart		Harlequin American

474

Flanders, Rebecca

58	Second Sight		Harlequin	American
66	Desert Fire		Harlequin	American
74	The Third Time		Harlequin	American
83	Daydreams		Harlequin	American
100	Open Hands		Harlequin	American
105	Rainbows And Unicorn		Harlequin	American
118	Uncertain Images		Harlequin	American
128	The Last Frontier		Harlequin	American
141	The Straight Game		Harlequin	American
155	Minor Miracles		Harlequin	American
167	After The Storm		Harlequin	American
183	Painted Sunsets		Harlequin	American
257	Search The Heavens		Harlequin	American
357	The Sensation		Harlequin	American
417	Under The Mistletoe	12/91	Harlequin	American
454	Once Upon A Time	09/92	Harlequin	American
477	The Last Real Man	03/93	Harlequin	American
490	Sunchasers	06/93	Harlequin	American
517	Forever Always	01/94	Harlequin	American
538	Kissed By The Sea	06/94	Harlequin	American
558	Quinn's Way	11/94	Harlequin	American
1	The Key		Harlequin	Intrigue
8	Silver Threads		Harlequin	Intrigue
13	Easy Access		Harlequin	Intrigue
24	After The Storm	09/94	Harlequin	Men Made In America
40	The Last Frontier	/95	Harlequin	Men Made In America
632	Morning Song		Harlequin	Presents
666	Falkone's Promise		Harlequin	Presents
2623	A Modern Girl		Harlequin	Romance
54	Secret Of The Wolf	07/95	Harlequin	Shadows
180	The Growing Season		Harlequin	Superromance
	Painted Sunsets	03/95	Harlequin	Western Lovers
57	Wolf In Waiting	10/95	Silhouette	Shadows
59	Shadow Of The Wolf	12/95	Silhouette	Shadows

Flannery, Constance O' Day

Timeless Passion		
Time-Swept Lovers		
Time-Kissed Destiny		
Time-Kept Promises		
This Time Forever		
A Time For Love		
Once In A Lifetime		Zebra

Fletcher, Aaron

Wallaby Track	06/94	Leisure

Fletcher, Donna

Playing Cupid	11/94	Diamond	A Town Called Harmony

475

AUTHOR/TITLE INDEX

Fletcher, Donna
 The Rebellious Bride   09/93 Diamond Wildflower
 The Buccaneer   07/95 Jove Historical
 Tame My Wild Touch   09/92 Zebra Heartfire
 San Francisco Surrender 11/90 Zebra Heartfire
 Untamed Fire   10/91 Zebra Heartfire

Fletcher, Ellen
 95 Pure Instinct   06/92 Meteor

Fletcher, Inglis
 Men Of Albemarle   /42 Bantam
 Toil Of The Brave   /46 Bantam
 Lusty Wind For Carolina /44 Bantam
 Queen's Gift   /52 Bantam
 Raleigh's Eden   /40 Bantam

Fletcher, Leigh
 Lilac Seduction   09/92 Zebra Historical

Fletcher, Verne
 303 Captain Gentleman /54 Harlequin

Fleury, Jacqueline
 The Cinderella Bride   /89 Warner Regency

Flindt, Dawn
 448 The Power Within 04/88 Silhouette Special Edition
 617 Prairie Cry   08/90 Silhouette Special Edition

Flixton, Katherine
 Glengarrick's Heir   Ballantine

Flores, Frances
 15 Desperate Longings Dell Candlelight Ecstasy

Flores, Janis
 High Dominion
 Siren Song   11/92 Fawcett Gold Medal
 654 Done Driftin' (The Dunleavy Leagacy) 08/95 Harlequin Superromance
 658 Done Cryin'   09/95 Harlequin Superromance
 662 Never Done Dreamin' 10/95 Harlequin Superromance
 The Reluctant Bride   05/96 Harlequin Weddings By Dewilde

Flournoy, Sheryl
 Flames Of Passion   Pocket
 Destiny's Embrace   Pocket
 371 Jason's Touch   08/87 Silhouette Desire

Flynn, Christine
 254 When Snow Meets Fire 01/86 Silhouette Desire
 296 The Myth And The Magic 08/86 Silhouette Desire
 352 A Place To Belong 05/87 Silhouette Desire
 377 Meet Me At Midnight 09/87 Silhouette Desire
 537 Daughter Of The Dawn 12/93 Silhouette Intimate Moments
 435 Stolen Promise   05/86 Silhouette Romance
 623 Courtney's Conspiracy 01/89 Silhouette Romance

Forrest, Chelsey
  272   An Artist's Touch   01/84 Silhouette Romance

Forrest, Pamela K.
      Desert Angel   07/94 Zebra
      Autumn Ecstasy   Zebra Heartfire
      Renegade   07/96 Zebra Lovegram

Forrest, Pamela Kae
      Sweet Silver Passion   Zebra Heartfire

Forrester, Helen
      The Lemon Tree   03/92 Harper

Forster, Gwynne
      Sealed With A Kiss   09/95 Pinnacle Arabesque

Forster, Rebecca
      Character Witness   01/96 Kensington
      Vanities   07/93 Pinnacle
      Vows   04/94 Zebra
      Dreams   05/95 Zebra
      Seasons   04/96 Zebra
      Rainbow's End   09/92 Zebra Lucky In Love
  14   Golden Threads   12/92 Zebra Lucky In Love

Forster, Suzanne
      Heroes   Bantam Loveswept
      Night Of The Panther   /92 Bantam Loveswept
  314 Wild Honey   03/89 Bantam Loveswept
  384 Wild Child   03/90 Bantam Loveswept
  414 The Devil And Ms. Moody 08/90 Bantam Loveswept
  449 Lord Of Lightning   01/91 Bantam Loveswept
  497 Private Dancer   09/91 Bantam Loveswept
  541 Child Bride   05/92 Bantam Loveswept
  581 Night Of The Panther 11/92 Bantam Loveswept
  604 Surrender, Baby   03/93 Bantam Loveswept
      Come Midnight   02/95 Berkley
      Blush   02/96 Berkley
      Shameless   02/94 Berkley Contemporary
      Moonlight, Madness & Magic 05/93 Doubleday Anthology
  215 Undercover Angel   06/85 Silhouette Desire
  273 Hot Properties   04/86 Silhouette Desire
  327 The Man At Ivy Bridge 01/87 Silhouette Desire
  446 Island Heat   09/88 Silhouette Desire
  519 Mr. Lonelyhearts   07/87 Silhouette Romance
  627 The Passions Of Kate Madigan 01/89 Silhouette Romance
      Naked Came The Ladies 02/94 Starlog Moonlight Anthology

Forstot, Marilyn
  22   Sunshine Riches   02/93 Zebra Lucky In Love

Forsythe, Cathy
      Love Between The Lines 07/95 Avalon

Forsythe, Cathy
1167　The Marriage Contract　　　07/96　Silhouette Romance
Forsythe, Melissa
2750　The Perfect Choice　　　　　　　Harlequin Romance
3035　Queen Of Hearts　　　　　　　　Harlequin Romance
Foster, Jeanne
1　Deborah Leigh　　　　　　　/81　Fawcett Frontier Women
2　Eden Richards　　　　　　　/82　Fawcett Frontier Women
3　Woman Of Three Worlds　　/84　Fawcett Frontier Women
Foster, John T.
Vicksburg　　　　　　　　　　　Zebra
Foster, Lori
572　Impetuous　　　　　　　　01/96　Harlequin Temptation
Fowlkes, Mary
2677　To Tame A Proud Lady　　　　Harlequin Romance
Fox, Alicia
151　Legal Tender　　　　　　04/87　Harlequin Temptation
Fox, Diana
The Man On The Romance Cover　06/93　Starlog Moonlight Contemporary
Fox, Elaine
Hand & Heart Of A Soldier　07/96　Dorchester
Traveler　　　　　　　　01/96　Leisure Time Travel
Fox, Lauren
177　Sparring Partners　　　/84　Berkley Second Chance At Love
197　Country Pleasures　　　/84　Berkley Second Chance At Love
266　Passion's Dance　　　　/85　Berkley Second Chance At Love
282　Storm And Starlight　　/85　Berkley Second Chance At Love
Fox, Natalie
18　Dreams Are For Living　10/95　Harlequin Presents
27　One Man, One Love　　03/96　Harlequin Presents
1473　Nights Of Desire　　　07/92　Harlequin Presents
1653　A Special Sort Of Man　05/94　Harlequin Presents
1718　Revenge　　　　　　01/95　Harlequin Presents
Fox, Norman A.
96　The Rider From Yonder　/51　Harlequin
Fox, Susan
Marry Me, Cowboy!　　04/95　Harlequin Promotion
2762　The Driftwood Dragon　05/86　Harlequin Romance
2763　Vows Of The Heart　　　　Harlequin Romance
2930　The Black Sheep　　　　　Harlequin Romance
2983　Not Part Of The Bargain　　Harlequin Romance
3268　The Bad Penny　　　06/93　Harlequin Romance
Not Part Of The Bargain　10/95　Harlequin Western Lovers
Foxe, Pamela
216　Your Cheating Heart　01/85　Silhouette Special Edition

AUTHOR/TITLE INDEX

Foxx, Rosalind
  Surrender By Moonlight | | Leisure Historical
Frances, Robin
  253   Taking A Chance | | Harlequin American
Francis, Emily
  2757   Aegean Enchantment | | Harlequin Romance
Francis, Mariana
  2887   Love's Perjury | 02/88 | Harlequin Romance
Francis, Robin
  38   Memories Of Love | | Harlequin American
  88   Season Of Dreams | | Harlequin American
  295   The Shocking Ms. Pilgrim | | Harlequin American
  301   Charmed Circle | | Harlequin American
  147   Button, Button | | Harlequin Intrigue
  159   Double Dare | | Harlequin Intrigue
  171   All Fall Down | 10/91 | Harlequin Intrigue
  197   When She Was Bad | 10/92 | Harlequin Intrigue
Francis, Sara
  2624   Kate's Way | | Harlequin Romance
  2673   California Dreaming | | Harlequin Romance
Francis, Sharon
  42   Garden Of Silvery Delights | /82 | Berkley Second Chance At Love
  161   Earthly Splendor | /84 | Berkley Second Chance At Love
  769   Hot Time | 01/91 | Silhouette Romance
  811   Irresistible Force | 08/91 | Silhouette Romance
Franklin, Edwina
  148   No Pain, No Gaine | | Harlequin Intrigue
Franklin, Janet
  585   Free To Dream | 08/90 | Silhouette Desire
  691   Makeshift Marriage | 12/89 | Silhouette Romance
  491   The Right Mistake | 11/88 | Silhouette Special Edition
Franz, Carol
  If Not For Love | | Tower Books
Fraser, Alison
  697   Princess | | Harlequin Presents
  721   The Price Of Freedom | | Harlequin Presents
  745   Coming Home | | Harlequin Presents
  865   A Man Worth Knowing | | Harlequin Presents
  1135   A Lifetime And Beyond | | Harlequin Presents
  1425   Time To Let Go | 01/92 | Harlequin Presents
  1675   Love Without Reason | 08/94 | Harlequin Presents
  1753   Tainted Love | 07/95 | Harlequin Presents
Fraser, Jane
  814   A Long Way From Home | /64 | Harlequin
  848   The Keeper's House | /64 | Harlequin
  958   Young Bar | /65 | Harlequin

Fraser, Jane
| 1232 | A Day Like Spring | /68 | Harlequin |

Fraser, Kathleen
	Love's Tender Promise		
	Passage To Paradise		Nal Penguin
	Love's Redemption		Nal Penguin
	Highland Flame		Nal Penguin

Frazier, Amy
1043	A Good Groom Is Hard To Find	07/96	Sihouette Special Edition
954	The Secret Baby	04/95	Silhouette Special Edition
1030	New Bride In Town	05/96	Silhouette Special Edition
1036	Waiting At The Altar	06/96	Silhouette Special Edition

Frazier, Pamela
	The Willful Widow		Berkley
	The Virtuous Mistress		Berkley
	A Delicate Dilemma		Berkley
	The Gallant Governess		Berkley
	The Benevolent Bride		Berkley

Fredd, Carla
| | Fire And Ice | 09/95 | Pinnacle Arabesque |

Frederick, Kate
	The Black Wind Of Penrose Island		Zebra Gothic
	The Periwinkle Brooch		Zebra Gothic
	The Secret Bride Of Crannoch Castle		Zebra Gothic

Frederick, Thea
| 204 | Beloved Adversary | /84 | Berkley Second Chance At Love |

Freed, Jan
| 645 | Too Many Bosses (Women Who Dare) | 05/95 | Harlequin Superromance |
| 676 | The Texas Way | 01/96 | Harlequin Superromance |

Freeman, Cynthia
	Always And Forever		Jove
	Illusions Of Love		Jove
	The Last Princess		Jove
	Seasons Of The Heart		Jove

Freeman, Joy
| | The Last Frost Fair | | St. Martin's |
| | A Suitable Match | | St. Martin's |

Freethy, Barbara
| | Daniel's Gift | 03/96 | Avon |

Freiman, Kate
93	No Limit To Love	06/92	Meteor
176	Spring Fever	10/93	Meteor
876	Jake's Angel	03/94	Silhouette Special Edition
971	Here To Stay	07/95	Silhouette Special Edition
1041	The Bachelor And The Baby Wish	07/96	Silhouette Special Edition

French, Emily

AUTHOR/TITLE INDEX

French, Emily
214	Capture (March Madness)	03/94	Harlequin	Historical
306	Illusion	02/96	Harlequin	Historical

French, Judith E.
	Starfire		Avon	
	Bold Surrender		Avon	
	Tender Fortune		Avon	
	By Love Alone		Avon	
	Lovestorm		Avon	
	Scarlet Ribbons		Avon	
	Windsong		Avon	
	To Love And To Honor	04/93	Avon	Anthology
	A Christmas Present	12/94	Avon	Anthology
	Under The Mistletoe	10/93	Avon	Christmas Anthology
1	Fortune's Mistress	03/93	Avon	Fortune Trilogy
2	Fortune's Flame	10/93	Avon	Fortune Trilogy
3	Fortune's Bride	04/94	Avon	Fortune Trilogy
	This Fierce Loving	10/94	Avon	Historical
1	Moonfeather	12/90	Avon	Indian Moon Trilogy
2	Highland Moon	07/91	Avon	Indian Moon Trilogy
3	Moondancer	03/92	Avon	Indian Moon Trilogy
	Warrior Dreams	12/88	Avon	Romance
	Shawnee Moon	06/95	Avon	Romantic Treasure
	Sundancer's Woman	02/96	Avon	Sequel/This Fierce Loving

French, Marilyn
	The Bleeding Heart		Ballantine
	Her Mother's Daughter		Ballantine
	The Women's Room		Ballantine

Friend, Oscar J.
94	The Range Doctor	/51	Harlequin

Friends, Jalynn
	Texas Rapture	04/83	Zebra

Frisbie, R.D.
37	Amaru	/50	Harlequin

Fritch, Elizabeth
	Sweet Silver Moon		
	Tides Of Rapture		Zebra
	California Book 1: Passion's Trail		Zebra
	California Book 2: Golden Fires		Zebra
	The Flame		Zebra The Richmond Series
	The Fire		Zebra The Richmond Series
	The Embers		Zebra The Richmond Series
	The Sparks		Zebra The Richmond Series

Frost, Eleanor
53	Elusive Paradise	/84	Nal Rapture Romance
68	A Public Affair		Nal Rapture Romance

AUTHOR/TITLE INDEX

Frost, Joan Van Emery
    Lisa | | Leisure
    This Fiery Promise | | Leisure

Fruchey, Deborah
    The Unwilling Heiress | /86 | Walker

Fulford, Paula
   54   If Ever You Need Me | 03/83 | Silhouette Desire
   20   Island Destiny | 07/80 | Silhouette Romance

Fulford, Stephanie James
   55   To Tame The Hunter | 04/83 | Silhouette Desire

Fullbrook, Gladys
  727   Nurses Of The Tourist Service | /63 | Harlequin
  771   Nurse Prue In Ceylong | /63 | Harlequin
  899   The Magic Moment | /65 | Harlequin
 1018   Hospital In The Tropics | /66 | Harlequin
 1082   Army Nurse In Cyprus | /67 | Harlequin
 1321   Thread Of Gold | /69 | Harlequin
 1346   A House Called Kangaroo | /69 | Harlequin
 1412   Journey Of Enchantment | /70 | Harlequin

Fuller, Samuel Michael
   9   The Dark Page | /49 | Harlequin

Fyfe, Sheila
    Appointment With Love | | Career Romance
    Rhapsody In Love | 10/92 | Avalon

Gabaldon, Diana
    Amber | |
    Outlander | 07/92 | Dell
    Dragonfly In Amber | 01/94 | Dell
    Voyager | 01/94 | Doubleday

Gabriel, Mary
 2703   Never Kiss A Stranger | | Harlequin Romance

Gacy, Linda M.
    Life Without Rhyme | 05/93 | Avalon

Gaddis, Peggy
  368   Meredith Blake, M.D. | /56 | Harlequin
  394   Lady Doctor | /57 | Harlequin
  405   City Nurse | /57 | Harlequin
  471   Nurse Hilary | /59 | Harlequin
  523   Doctor Reid | /60 | Harlequin
  544   Doctor Sara | /60 | Harlequin

Gaeddert, Lou Ann
    Roses After Rain | 03/92 | St. Martin's
    Perfect Strangers | 03/92 | St. Martin's
    Ever After | 03/92 | St. Martin's

Gaetlin, Kimberleigh
    Sky Of Ashes, Sea Of Flames | | Berkley

AUTHOR/TITLE INDEX

Gaffney, Patricia

Lily	10/91	Leisure
Another Eden	10/92	Leisure Historical
Fortune's Lady	10/89	Leisure Historical
Thief Of Hearts	07/90	Leisure Historical
Sweet Treason	01/89	Leisure Historical
A Victorian Christmas	11/92	Nal Super Signet Historical
To Love And To Cherish	02/95	Nal Topaz Wyckerley Trilogy #1
To Have And To Hold	09/95	Nal Topaz Wyckerley Trilogy #2
From This Day Forward	04/96	Nal Topaz Wyckerley Trilogy #3
Sweet Everlasting	07/93	Penguin Topaz
Crooked Hearts	04/94	Penguin Topaz
Forever And Ever	04/96	Topaz
Wild At Heart	01/97	Topaz

Gage, Elizabeth

Pandora's Box	09/91	Pocket

Gage, Elsie

Your Obedient Servant		Nal Penguin Regency
Regency Belles		Pocket Cotillion Regency

Gage, Jennifer

With All My Heart	03/94	Zebra To Love Again

Gaines, Diana

Nantucket Woman

Gair, Diana

2519	Highlands Rapture		Harlequin Romance
2530	Jungle Antagonist		Harlequin Romance

Gale, Roberta

Moorise	05/96	Pinnacle Arabesque

Gale, Shannon

702	Beneath Sierra Skies	02/90	Silhouette Romance

Gallagher, Patricia

	Mystic Rose	/81	Avon
	All For Love	/82	Avon
	Echoes And Embers	/83	Avon
	Shannon	/78	Avon
	Summer Of Sighs	/79	Avon
	Shadows Of Passion	/80	Avon
	The Thicket	/80	Avon
	The Fires Of Brimstone	/79	Avon
	Answer To The Heaven	/80	Avon
1	Castles In The Air	/76	Avon
2	No Greater Love	/79	Avon
	The Sons And The Daughters	/84	Bantam, Pocket, Simon & Schus.
3	On Wings Of Dreams	/85	Berkley
	A Perfect To Love	/87	Berkley/Jove

Gallant, Jennie

AUTHOR/TITLE INDEX

Gallant, Jennie

	Flowers Of Eden	/79	Fawcett
	Lady Hathaway's House Party	/80	Fawcett Regency
	Minuet	/80	Fawcett Regency
	The Moonless Night	/80	Fawcett Regency
	Olivia	/80	Fawcett Regency
	The Black Diamond	/81	Fawcett Victorian Gothic
	Thick As Thieves	01/93	Fawcett Crest Regency Romance
	Destiny's Dream	/88	Leisure
	Emerald Hazard	/88	Leisure

Gallant, Phoebe

	With Someone Like You	07/94	Zebra

Galloway, Kara

322	Sleight Of Heart	11/90	Harlequin Temptation
347	Love At Second Sight (Editor's Choice)	05/91	Harlequin Temptation

Galloway, Laura

	Dark Rendezvous Dungariff		Zebra
	Forbidden Delight	07/90	Zebra Heartfire

Galt, Serena

149	Double Game	07/84	Silhouette Desire

Gamble, M.L.

110	Stranger Than Fiction	03/89	Harlequin Intrigue
146	Diamond Of Deceit		Harlequin Intrigue
153	When Murder Calls	01/91	Harlequin Intrigue
172	If Looks Could Kill	10/91	Harlequin Intrigue
226	Dead Magnolias	06/93	Harlequin Intrigue
321	Trust With Your Life (Dangerous Man)	05/95	Harlequin Intrigue

Gardner, Hayley

10	Holiday Husband	12/95	Silhouette Yours Truly

Gardner, Joy

	Fortune's Bride		Pocket

Gardner, Kit

117	Arabesque	03/92	Harlequin Historical
138	The Dream	08/92	Harlequin Historical
160	The Stolen Heart	02/93	Harlequin Historical
193	The Gilded Lion	10/93	Harlequin Historical
217	Island Star	04/94	Harlequin Historical
274	Twilight	06/95	Harlequin Historical

Gardner, Toni

	Rapture's Rainbow		

Garfield, Patrice

1	River Pines		River Pines Saga
2	Rone Daniels		Northwest Publ. River Pines Saga

Garland, Kit

	Dance With A Stranger	08/95	Dell

Garland, Sherry

Garland, Sherry
    Where The Cherry Trees Bloom

Garlock, Dorothy

6	A Love For All Time		Bantam Loveswept
33	The Planting Season	02/84	Bantam Loveswept
	This Loving Land		Richard Gallen
	The Searching Hearts		Richard Gallen
	A Gentle Giving	01/93	Warner
	Annie Lash		Warner
	Dream River	/88	Warner
	Glorious Dawn		Warner
	Homeplace		Warner
	Lonesome River		Warner
	Midnight Blue		Warner
	Nightrose		Warner
	Restless Wind		Warner
	Ribbon In The Sky		Warner
	River Of Tomorrow		Warner
	Wayward Wind		Warner
	Wild Sweet Wilderness		Warner
	Wind Of Promise		Warner
	Sins Of Summer	06/94	Warner
	Yesteryear	01/95	Warner
	Tenderness	07/93	Warner
	Midnight Blue	07/89	Warner
	Almost Eden	10/95	Warner
	Love And Cherish	05/95	Warner
	This Loving Land	07/96	Warner
	Forever, Victoria	11/93	Warner Popular
	The Searching Hearts		Warner Popular
	This Loving Land		Warner Popular
	The Wabash River Trilogy		Warner Popular
	The Colorado Trilogy		Warner Popular

Garnar, Pauline

1325	No Sooner Loved	/69	Harlequin
1444	Fond Deceiver	/70	Harlequin

Garner, Faith E. W.

	Wake-Up To Love	11/95	Avalon

Garnett, Juliana

	The Magic	07/96	Bantam

Garrett, Sally

90	Until Forever		Harlequin Superromance
139	Mountain Skies		Harlequin Superromance
173	Northern Fires		Harlequin Superromance
201	Twin Bridges		Harlequin Superromance
225	Until Now		Harlequin Superromance

Garrett, Sally

243	Weaver Of Dreams		Harlequin Superromance
275	Visions		Harlequin Superromance
309	Promises To Keep		Harlequin Superromance
344	Desert Star		Harlequin Superromance
464	Children Of The Heart	08/91	Harlequin Superromance
524	String Of Miracles	02/93	Harlequin Superromance
554	Edge Of The Sky	07/93	Harlequin Superromance

Garrett, Sara

148	Anything You Can Do	05/93	Meteor Kismet

Garrett, Sibylle

476	Desperate Choices	02/93	Silhouette Initmate Moments
184	September Rainbow	03/87	Silhouette Intimate Moments
211	Surrender To A Stranger	10/87	Silhouette Intimate Moments
271	Rebel's Return	01/89	Silhouette Intimate Moments
301	Sullivan's Challenge	09/89	Silhouette Intimate Moments
366	The Twilight Prince	01/91	Silhouette Intimate Moments
573	Knight's Corner	06/94	Silhouette Intimate Moments

Garrett, Wendy

	Love's Magic Spell		Zebra
	Arizona Lovestorm		Zebra Heartfire
	Sweet Southern Caress	03/91	Zebra Heartfire
	Carolina Dawn	10/94	Zebra Historical
	Western Enchantress	04/93	Zebra Lovegram

Garrod, Rene

	The Wild Rose		Avon
	Montana Magic		Zebra
	Wild Irish Embrace		Zebra
	Wild Conquest		Zebra
1	Her Heart's Desire	/94	Zebra Carrigan Brothers
2	Her Heart's Delight	03/95	Zebra Carrigan Brothers
	Ecstasy's Bride		Zebra Heartfire
	Passion's Endless Tide		Zebra Heartfire
	Silken Caress		Zebra Heartfire
	Temptation's Wild Embrace		Zebra Heartfire
	Colorado Caress		Zebra Heartfire

Garth, Will

220	Masked Rider	/53	Harlequin

Garwood, Julie

	The Prize	08/91	Pocket
	The Secret	05/92	Pocket
	The Bride		Pocket
	Gentle Warrior		Pocket
	The Gift		Pocket
	Guardian Angel		Pocket
	Honor's Splendor		Pocket

Garwood, Julie
    The Lion's Lady   Pocket
    Rebellious Desire   Pocket
    Prince Charming   06/94   Pocket
    Castles   04/93   Pocket
    Saving Grace   02/94   Pocket
    For The Roses   09/95   Pocket

Gaskin, Catherine
    I Know My Love   Suspense

Gaston, Pat
    Love To Be Loved
    The Love Arena
    This Man Is Mine   10/93   Starlog Moonlight Contemporary

Gault, Cinda
  296   Past Convictions   Harlequin Superromance

Gauthier, La Florya
    Whispers In The Sand   /92   Marron

Gayle, Margaret
   52   Precious Interlude   Harlequin Superromance
  118   To Catch The Wind   Harlequin Superromance
  169   One In A Million   Harlequin Superromance
  260   What Comes Naturally   Harlequin Superromance

Gayle, Roberta
    Sunshine And Shadows   04/95   Pinnacle Arabesque

Gayle, Susan
  307   Temperature's Rising   07/90   Harlequin Temptation

Gear, Kathleen & Michael
    People Of The Lakes   10/94   Tor Historical

Gedney, Mona K.
    The Easter Charade   Zebra Regency
    A Scandalous Charade   08/94   Zebra Regency
    A Lady Of Fortune   Zebra Regency Romance

Gellis, Roberta
    The English Heiress
    Fortune's Bride
    Bond Of Blood
    The Cornish Heiress
    The Dragon And The Rose
    The Kent Heiress
    Knight's Honor
    The Sword And The Swan
    Siren Song
    Winter Song
    Tapestry Of Dreams
    Fire Song
    A Silver Mirror   01/94   Berkley Historical

George, Catherine

1065	Touch Me In The Morning		Harlequin	Presents
1152	Villain Of The Piece		Harlequin	Presents
1184	True Paradise		Harlequin	Presents
1225	Loveknot		Harlequin	Presents
1255	Ever Since Eden		Harlequin	Presents
1321	Come Back To Me		Harlequin	Presents
2535	Reluctant Paragon		Harlequin	Romance
2571	Dream Of Midsummer		Harlequin	Romance
2720	Desirable Property		Harlequin	Romance
2822	The Folly Of Loving		Harlequin	Romance
2924	Man Of Iron		Harlequin	Romance
2942	This Time Around		Harlequin	Romance
3081	Consolation Prize		Harlequin	Romance
3129	Arrogant Interloper		Harlequin	Romance
3147	A Civilized Arrangement	09/91	Harlequin	Romance
3177	Unlikely Cupid	02/92	Harlequin	Romance
3201	Brazilian Enchantment	06/92	Harlequin	Romance
3236	Leader Of The Pack	12/92	Harlequin	Romance
3261	Out Of The Storm	04/93	Harlequin	Romance
3310	Lawful Possession	04/94	Harlequin	Romance
3345	Summer Of The Storm	01/95	Harlequin	Romance
3353	Evidence Of Sin	03/95	Harlequin	Romance
3360	A Brief Encounter (Sealed With A Kiss)	05/95	Harlequin	Romance
3368	A Family Secret	07/95	Harlequin	Romance
3396	Fallen Hero	02/96	Harlequin	Romance
3420	Earthbound Angel	08/96	Harlequin	Romance

George, Elizabeth

	Playing For The Ashes	09/94	Bantam

George, Peter

249	Come Blonde, Came Murder	/53	Harlequin

George, Rebecca

	Daphane	
	Call Home The Heart	Nal
	Tender Longing	Pocket
	A Wild Desire	Pocket

George, Teresa

	Yesterday's Promise	02/95	Pinnacle	Time-Travel

Gerard, Cindy

484	Maverick	07/91	Bantam	Loveswept
514	Temptation From The Past	12/91	Bantam	Loveswept
547	Slow Burn	06/92	Bantam	Loveswept
628	Man Around The House	07/93	Bantam	Loveswept
637	Dream Tide	09/93	Bantam	Loveswept
660	Perfect Double	01/94	Bantam	Loveswept
708	Into The Night	09/94	Bantam	Loveswept

AUTHOR/TITLE INDEX

Gideon, Nancy
  Texas Bride   02/95   Zebra Lovegram
Gideon, Robin
  Royal Rapture   08/93   Zebra
  Passion's Bandit   05/94   Zebra
  Royal Ecstasy   08/92   Zebra Heartfire
  Ecstasy's Princess   Zebra Heartfire
  Outlaw Ecstasy   Zebra Heartfire
  Passion's Tender Embrace   Zebra Heartfire
  Pirate's Passionate Slave   Zebra Heartfire
  Wild Caress   Zebra Heartfire
  Shadow Passion   Zebra Heartfire
Giencke, Jill
  Fatal Facts   12/92   Avalon
  Secrets Of Echo Moon   Avalon Mystery Romance
Gilbert, Anna
  Look Of Innocence   Historical
  A Family Likeness   Dell
  Flowers For Lilian   Dell
  The Leavetaking   Dell
  A Walk In The Wood   Dell
Gilbert, Jacqueline
  2102 Every Wise Man   /77   Harlequin
  2214 Country Cousin   /78   Harlequin
   160 Dear Villain   /76   Harlequin Presents
   600 House Called Bellevigne   Harlequin Presents
   801 Capricorn Man   Harlequin Presents
   929 Poppy Girl   Harlequin Presents
  1073 Sweet Pretence   Harlequin Presents
  2308 Scorpio Summer   Harlequin Romance
  2492 The Trodden Paths   Harlequin Romance
  2631 The Chequered Silence   Harlequin Romance
Gilbert-Lewis, Jeane
   126 Common Ground   01/93   Meteor Kismet
Giles, Katherine
  A Share Of Earth And Glory   Berkley
Giles, Raymond
  Rebels Of Sabrehill   Ballantine
  Rogue Black   Ballantine
  Sabrehill   Ballantine
  Slaves Of Sabrehill   Ballantine
  Storm Over Sabrehill   Ballantine
  Daughter Of Deceit   Ballantine
  The Secret Woman   Ballantine
  The House Of A Thousand Lanterns   Ballantine
  Bride Of Pendorric   Ballantine

AUTHOR/TITLE INDEX

Giles, Raymond

| | The Night Of The Seventh Moon | | Ballantine | |
| | Dark Master | | Fawcett Gold Medal |

Gill, Judy

	Bad Billy Culver	09/91	Bantam Fanfare
228	Head Over Heels	01/88	Bantam Loveswept
270	Pockets Full Of Joy	08/88	Bantam Loveswept
282	Renegade	10/88	Bantam Loveswept
294	Hennessey's Heaven	12/88	Bantam Loveswept
307	Light Another Candle	02/89	Bantam Loveswept
335	Mermaid	06/89	Bantam Loveswept
339	A Scent Of Roses	07/89	Bantam Loveswept
377	Golden Swan	01/90	Bantam Loveswept
389	Stargazer	03/90	Bantam Loveswept
406	Desperado	06/90	Bantam Loveswept
424	Dream Man	09/90	Bantam Loveswept
436	Moonlight Man	11/90	Bantam Loveswept
485	Sharing Sunrise	07/91	Bantam Loveswept
509	Dangerous Proposition	11/91	Bantam Loveswept
524	Golden Warrior	02/92	Bantam Loveswept
549	Summer Lover	06/92	Bantam Loveswept
575	Forbidden Dreams	10/92	Bantam Loveswept
605	Healing Touch	03/93	Bantam Loveswept
645	Sheer Delight	10/93	Bantam Loveswept
678	Kiss And Make Up	04/94	Bantam Loveswept
698	Loving Voices	07/94	Bantam Loveswept
733	Siren Song	03/95	Bantam Loveswept
747	Twice The Trouble	05/95	Bantam Loveswept
	The Other Side Of The Hill	/76	Robert Hale
	Catherine's Image	/77	Robert Hale
	A Harvest Of Jewels	/77	Robert Hale
	Till Summer's End	/78	Robert Hale

Gill, Judy Griffith

| | There's Something About Nanny | 11/96 | Harlequin Love & Laughter |
| | Ali The Hun (Tentative Title) | /97 | Harlequin Love & Laughter |

Gillen, Lucy

1383	A Wife For Andrew	/70	Harlequin
1408	The Silver Fishes	/70	Harlequin
1425	Good Morning, Doctor Houston	/70	Harlequin
1450	Heir To Glen Ghyll	/70	Harlequin
1481	Nurse Helen	/71	Harlequin
1507	Marriage By Request	/71	Harlequin
1533	The Girl At Smuggler's Rest	/71	Harlequin
1553	Doctor Toby	/72	Harlequin
1579	Winter At Cray	/72	Harlequin
1604	That Man Next Door	/72	Harlequin
1627	My Beautiful Heathen	/72	Harlequin

Gillen, Lucy

1649	Sweet Kate	/73	Harlequin
1669	A Time Remembered	/73	Harlequin
1683	Dangerous Stranger	/73	Harlequin
1711	Summer Season	/73	Harlequin
1736	The Enchanted Ring	/73	Harlequin
1754	The Pretty Witch	/74	Harlequin
1782	Painted Wings	/74	Harlequin
1806	The Pengelly Jade	/74	Harlequin
1822	The Runaway Bride	/74	Harlequin
1847	The Changing Years	/75	Harlequin
1861	The Stairway To Enchantment	/75	Harlequin
1877	Means To An End	/75	Harlequin
1895	Glen Of Sighs	/75	Harlequin
1908	A Touch Of Honey	/75	Harlequin
1928	Gentle Tyrant	/75	Harlequin
1930	Web Of Silver	/75	Harlequin
1958	All The Long Summer	/76	Harlequin
1979	A Handful Of Stars	/76	Harlequin
1995	The Hungry Tide	/76	Harlequin
2012	Return To Deepwater	/76	Harlequin
2026	The House Of Kingdom	/76	Harlequin
2092	Master Of Ben Ross	/77	Harlequin
2134	Heron's Point	/78	Harlequin
2178	Back Of Beyond	/78	Harlequin
2319	Hepburn's Quay		Harlequin Romance

Gillenwater, Sharon

Unwilling Heart		
Heather Moon		
Secret Splendor	01/92	Diamond Regency
Highland Whispers	06/89	Leisure
Love Song	05/95	Questar Christian Romance

Gillespie, Jane

Ivory Temptress	St. Martin's
Ladysmeade	St. Martin's
Teverton Hall	St. Martin's
Bright Sea	St. Martin's

Gillette, Louisa

Glorious Treasure	Pocket
River To Rapture	Pocket
Pas De Deux	Tapestry

Gillgannon, Mary

Dragon Of The Island	11/94	Pinnacle Denise Little Presents
Leopards' Lady	07/95	Pinnacle Denise Little Presents
Dragon's Dream	03/95	Pinnacle Denise Little Presents

Gillis, Jacquelyn

Gillis, Jacquelyn
    A Perfect Mismatch   06/92 Jove Regency
    Otherwise Engaged   01/92 Jove Regency
Gillman, Olga
  734 Doctor Andrew, Guardian   /63 Harlequin
  857 The Quiet Spot (Island Doctor)   /64 Harlequin
Gilman, Dorothy
    Tightrope Walker   Suspense
Gilmer, Donna
    Eye Of The Wind
Gilmore, Cecile
  46 Fair Stranger   /50 Harlequin
Gilmore, Monique
    No Ordinary Love   11/94 Pinnacle Arabesque
Gilmour, Ann
  1121 Team Doctor   /67 Harlequin
Gilmour, Barbara
  1154 You Can't Stay Here   /67 Harlequin
Gilpin, Joanna
  163 First Mates   07/87 Harlequin Temptation
  239 A Simple "I Do"   02/89 Harlequin Temptation
  330 Chance It   01/91 Harlequin Temptation
Gilzean, Elizabeth
  443 Nurse On Call   /58 Harlequin
  458 Next Patient, Doctor Anne   /59 Harlequin
  462 Love From A Surgeon   /59 Harlequin
  490 Nurse Mac Lean Goes West   /59 Harlequin
  503 Nurse In Charge   /60 Harlequin
  548 The Healing Word   /60 Harlequin
  571 Children's Hospital   /61 Harlequin
  581 Yankee Surgeon   /61 Harlequin
  649 Kate Of Outpatients   /62 Harlequin
  685 Doctor Mark Temple   /62 Harlequin
  709 Senior Surgeon At St. David's   /63 Harlequin
  1001 No Place For Surgeons   /66 Harlequin
  1026 Doctor In Corsica   /66 Harlequin
Girard, Paula Tanner
    Lord Wakeford's Gold Watch   06/95 Zebra Regency
    Charade Of Hearts   03/96 Zebra Regency
Giusto, Layle
    Sweet Promise   12/94 Pinnacle Arabesque
Gladden, Theresa
  472 Romancing Susan   05/91 Bantam Loveswept
  515 Just Desserts   12/91 Bantam Loveswept
  545 P.S., I Love You   05/92 Bantam Loveswept
  579 Bad Company   11/92 Bantam Loveswept

Gladden, Theresa

603	Hart's Law	03/93	Bantam	Loveswept
644	Angie And The Ghostbuster	10/93	Bantam	Loveswept
704	Perfect Timing	08/94	Bantam	Loveswept

Gladstone, Eve

23	A Taste Of Deception	08/85	Harlequin	Intrigue
49	Checkpoint		Harlequin	Intrigue
75	Operation S.N.A.R.E.		Harlequin	Intrigue
111	Enigma		Harlequin	Intrigue
228	Ghostwriter	06/93	Harlequin	Intrigue
295	Time And Tide	10/94	Harlequin	Intrigue
297	All's Fair		Harlequin	Superromance
324	Merriman Co. 1: One Hot Summer	09/88	Harlequin	Superromance
349	Merriman Co. 2: After All These Years	03/89	Harlequin	Superromance
380	Merriman Co. 3: Wouldn't It Be Lovely	11/89	Harlequin	Superromance
414	Between Two Moons		Harlequin	Superromance
108	Ballinger's Rules	12/83	Silhouette	Desire
221	The Confidence Man	07/85	Silhouette	Desire
284	Night Talk	06/86	Silhouette	Desire
55	Power Play	06/84	Silhouette	Intimate Moments
138	Illusions	04/86	Silhouette	Intimate Moments
78	Fortune's Play	02/83	Silhouette	Special Edition

Gladstone, Maggie

	The Reluctant Debutante	Playboy Press
	The Scandalous Lady	Playboy Press
	The Fortunate Belle	Playboy Press
	The Love Duel	Playboy Press
	The Impudent Widow	Playboy Press
	The Lady's Masquerade	Playboy Press
	The Love Tangle	Playboy Press
	The Reluctant Protege	Playboy Press

Glass, Amanda

	Shield's Lady	Warner

Glay, George Albert

19	Gina	/49	Harlequin
112	Gina (Reprint)	/51	Harlequin
188	Beggars Might Ride	/52	Harlequin
287	Gina	/54	Harlequin

Glenn, Dorothy

45	The Hell Raiser		Harlequin	Historical
242	Sunshine Every Morning	06/85	Silhouette	Special Edition

Glenn, Elizabeth

14	Dark Star Of Love		Harlequin	American
36	Taste Of Love		Harlequin	American
67	What Love Endures		Harlequin	Superromance
124	The Homing Instinct	09/86	Harlequin	Temptation

AUTHOR/TITLE INDEX

Glenn, Elizabeth

175	Where Memories Begin	10/87	Harlequin	Temptation
195	More Than Words	03/88	Harlequin	Temptation
224	First A Friend	10/88	Harlequin	Temptation
238	Gone Fishin'	02/89	Harlequin	Temptation

Glenn, Victoria

321	Not Meant For Love	09/84	Silhouette	Romance
362	Heart Of Glass	05/85	Silhouette	Romance
386	Mermaid	09/85	Silhouette	Romance
396	The Matthews Affair	11/85	Silhouette	Romance
455	Man By The Fire	09/86	Silhouette	Romance
508	One Of The Family	06/87	Silhouette	Romance
534	The Winter Heart	10/87	Silhouette	Romance
585	Moon In The Water	06/88	Silhouette	Romance
628	The Tender Tyrant	02/89	Silhouette	Romance
652	The Enchanted Summer	06/89	Silhouette	Romance
718	Second Time Lucky	05/90	Silhouette	Romance
813	Life With Lindy	08/91	Silhouette	Romance
837	Too Good To Be True	12/91	Silhouette	Romance

Glick, Ruth

382	The Closer We Get		Harlequin	Superromance
499	Make Me A Miracle	05/92	Harlequin	Superromance

Glover, Judith

	Sisters And Brothers		St. Martin's
	The Stallion Man		St. Martin's
	The Imagination Of The Heart		St. Martin's

Gluyas, Constance

	The King's Brat		
	My Lady Benbrook		
	Lord Sin		
	Born To Be King		Historical
	Flame Of The South		Nal Penguin
	Woman Of Fury		Nal Penguin
	Madam Tudor		Nal Penguin
	The Passionate Savage		Nal Penguin
1	Savage Eden		Nal Penguin
2	Rogue's Mistress		Nal Penguin

Godwin, Elizabeth

	The Passion And The Rage		Ballantine Regency

Goforth, Ellen

5	Path Of Desire	05/80	Silhouette	Romance
144	A New Dawn	04/82	Silhouette	Romance

Goldenbaum, Sally

233	The Baron	01/88	Bantam	Loveswept
669	Moonlight On Monterey Bay	02/94	Bantam	Loveswept
692	For Men Only	06/94	Bantam	Loveswept

498

Goldenbaum, Sally

423	Honeymoon Hotel	05/88	Silhouette Desire
460	Chantilly Lace	11/88	Silhouette Desire
520	Once In Love With Jessie	09/89	Silhouette Desire
557	The Passionate Accountant	03/90	Silhouette Desire
603	A Fresh Start	11/90	Silhouette Desire
659	Mornings At Seven	08/91	Silhouette Desire

Goldie, Patricia

| | Under Southern Stars | | Berkley |

Goldman, James

| | Myself As Witness | | Historical |

Goldreich, Gloria

| | Mothers | 04/92 | Bantam Fanfare |

Goldrick, Emma

93	Ice Lady	09/91	Harlequin Direct
688	Blow Your House Down		Harlequin Presents
791	Miss Mary's Husband		Harlequin Presents
825	Night Bells Blooming		Harlequin Presents
841	Rent A Bride Ltd.		Harlequin Presents
866	Daughter Of The Sea		Harlequin Presents
890	The Over Mountain Man		Harlequin Presents
953	Hidden Treasures		Harlequin Presents
1035	If Love Be Blind		Harlequin Presents
1087	My Brother's Keeper		Harlequin Presents
1208	Madeleine's Marriage	10/89	Harlequin Presents
1281	A Heart As Big As Texas		Harlequin Presents
1360	Love Is In The C		Harlequin Presents
1465	Silence Speaks For Love	06/92	Harlequin Presents
1488	Smuggler's Love	09/92	Harlequin Presents
1520	Loveable Katie Lovewell	01/93	Harlequin Presents
1545	Spirit Of Love	04/93	Harlequin Presents
1546	A Dangerous Love	04/93	Harlequin Presents
1681	The Unmarried Bride	09/94	Harlequin Presents
1576	The Widow's Mite	08/93	Harlequin Presents Plus
1608	Summer Storms	12/93	Harlequin Presents Plus
2661	The Road	/85	Harlequin Romance
2739	Trouble With Bridges		Harlequin Romance
2846	Tempered By Fire		Harlequin Romance
2858	King Of The Hill		Harlequin Romance
2889	Temporary Paragon	02/88	Harlequin Romance
2943	To Tame A Tycoon		Harlequin Romance
2967	The Latimore Bride		Harlequin Romance
2984	Pilgrim's Promise	06/89	Harlequin Romance
3111	The Girl He Left Behind		Harlequin Romance
3134	Mississippi Miss	07/91	Harlequin Romance
3164	A Touch Of Forgiveness	12/91	Harlequin Romance

AUTHOR/TITLE INDEX

Goldrick, Emma

3188	Doubly Delicious	04/92	Harlequin Romance
3303	Baby Makes Three	03/94	Harlequin Romance
3335	The Balleymore Bride	11/94	Harlequin Romance
3351	Leonie's Luck (Kids & Kisses)	03/95	Harlequin Romance
3359	Faith, Hope And Marriage (Kids & Kisses)	05/95	Harlequin Romance
3375	The Baby Caper	09/95	Harlequin Romance
3392	Husband Material	01/96	Harlequin Romance

Golon, Sergeanne

| | Angelique | | Historical |

Good, Susanna

| | Burning Secrets | | Richard Gallen |

Goodchild, George

| 222 | Mad Mike | /53 | Harlequin |
| 403 | Next Of Kin | /57 | Harlequin |

Goodis, David

| 311 | Convicted | /54 | Harlequin |

Goodman, Jo

	Passion's Sweet Revenge		Zebra
	Sweet Fire		Zebra
	Tempting Torment		Zebra
	Violet Fire		Zebra
	Wild, Sweet Ecstasy		Zebra
	Midnight Princess		Zebra
	Crystal Passion		Zebra
	Seaswept Abandon		Zebra
	Velvet Night		Zebra
	Scarlet Lies		Zebra
	Passion's Bride		Zebra
	Forever In My Heart	07/94	Zebra
	Always In My Dreams	05/95	Zebra
	A Christmas Rendezvous	/91	Zebra Anthology
	Rogue's Mistress	04/93	Zebra Lovegram

Goodman, Liza

| 134 | Flight Of Swallows | 05/93 | Harlequin Direct |

Goodwin, Hope

| | Storm Over Edgecliff | | Avalon Mystery Romance |

Gordon, Anita

1	The Valiant Heart	08/91	Jove Heart Trilogy
2	The Defiant Heart	07/93	Jove Heart Trilogy
3	The Captive Heart	09/95	Jove Heart Trilogy

Gordon, Deborah

	Runaway Time	09/95	Avon
	Runaway Magic	08/96	Avon
	Runaway Bride	09/94	Avon Historical
	Beating The Odds	05/92	Harper

Gordon, Emma

Crossing Eden   Warner

Gordon, Laura

220	Double Black Diamond	03/93	Harlequin	Intrigue
255	Scarlet Season	12/93	Harlequin	Intrigue
282	Dominoes	07/94	Harlequin	Intrigue
316	Full Moon Rising	03/95	Harlequin	Intrigue
345	Lethal Lover	11/95	Harlequin	Intrigue

Gordon, Lucy

47	Once Upon A Time	10/96	Harlequin	Here Come The Grooms
119	Royal Harlot	06/94	Harlequin	Historical
3410	For The Love Of Emma	05/96	Harlequin	Romance
	1993 Christmas Stories	11/93	Silhouette	Anthology
164	Take All Myself	10/84	Silhouette	Desire
179	The Judgement Of Paris	12/84	Silhouette	Desire
245	A Coldhearted Man	11/85	Silhouette	Desire
317	My Only Love, My Only Hate	11/86	Silhouette	Desire
333	A Fragile Beauty	02/87	Silhouette	Desire
363	Just Good Friends	07/87	Silhouette	Desire
380	Eagle's Prey	10/87	Silhouette	Desire
416	For Love Alone	04/88	Silhouette	Desire
493	Vengeance Is Mine	05/89	Silhouette	Desire
544	Convicted Of Love	01/90	Silhouette	Desire
627	The Sicilian	03/91	Silhouette	Desire
669	On His Honor	10/91	Silhouette	Desire
777	Married In Haste	04/93	Silhouette	Desire
864	Uncaged	06/94	Silhouette	Desire
953	Two Faced Woman	09/95	Silhouette	Desire
982	This Is My Child	02/96	Silhouette	Desire
306	The Carrister Pride	07/84	Silhouette	Romance
353	Island Of Dreams	04/85	Silhouette	Romance
390	Virtue And Vice	10/85	Silhouette	Romance
420	Once Upon A Time	03/86	Silhouette	Romance
503	A Pearl Beyond Price	05/87	Silhouette	Romance
524	Golden Boy	08/87	Silhouette	Romance
596	A Night Of Passion	08/88	Silhouette	Romance
611	A Woman Of Spirit	11/88	Silhouette	Romance
639	A True Marriage	03/89	Silhouette	Romance
754	Song Of The Lorelei	11/90	Silhouette	Romance
904	Heaven And Earth	12/92	Silhouette	Romance
952	Instant Father	08/93	Silhouette	Romance
1079	This Man And This Woman	05/95	Silhouette	Romance
148	Legacy Of Fire	02/84	Silhouette	Special Edition
185	Enchantment In Venice	08/84	Silhouette	Special Edition
547	Bought Woman	09/89	Silhouette	Special Edition
749	Outcast Woman	06/92	Silhouette	Special Edition
902	Seduced By Innocence	08/94	Silhouette	Special Edition

AUTHOR/TITLE INDEX

Gordon, Susan
    Match Of The Season   Walker

Gordon, Victoria

251	A Magical Affair	10/95	Harlequin	
195	A Taxing Affair	08/94	Harlequin	Direct
689	Blind Man's Bluff		Harlequin	Presents
2427	The Sugar Dragon		Harlequin	Romance
2433	Wolf At The Door		Harlequin	Romance
2438	The Everywhere Man		Harlequin	Romance
2458	Dream House		Harlequin	Romance
2469	Always The Boss		Harlequin	Romance
2531	Dinner At Wyatt's		Harlequin	Romance
2540	Battle Of Wills		Harlequin	Romance
2690	Stag At Bay		Harlequin	Romance
2714	Bushranger's Mountain		Harlequin	Romance
2727	Cyclone Season		Harlequin	Romance
2775	Age Of Consent		Harlequin	Romance
2854	Forest Fever		Harlequin	Romance
3025	Arafura Pirate		Harlequin	Romance
3098	Love Thy Neighbor		Harlequin	Romance
3342	Gift-Wrapped (Christmas)	12/94	Harlequin	Romance

Gorton, Kaitlyn

307	Cloud Castles	10/89	Silhouette	Intimate Moments
942	Heart, Home And Hope	02/95	Silhouette	Special Edition

Goudge, Eileen
    Garden Of Lies   05/89   Viking

Gould, Judith
    Dazzle   Nal Onyx
    Never Too Rich   Nal Onyx
    Texas Born   Nal Onyx
    Love-Makers   Nal Signet
    Sins   Nal Signet

Gowland, J.S.
    455   Smoke Over Sikanaska   /59   Harlequin

Grabriel, Marius
    The Original Sin   04/93   Bantam

Grace, Carol

690	Make Room For Nanny	12/89	Silhouette	Romance
751	A Taste Of Heaven	10/90	Silhouette	Romance
882	Home Is Where The Heart Is	08/92	Silhouette	Romance
955	Mail-Order Mate	08/93	Silhouette	Romance
1010	The Lady Wore Spurs (Celebration 1000!)	05/94	Silhouette	Romance
1057	Lonely Millionaire	01/95	Silhouette	Romance
1105	Almost A Husband	09/95	Silhouette	Romance
1142	Almost Married	03/96	Silhouette	Romance
1153	The Rancher And The Lost Bride	05/96	Silhouette	Romance

AUTHOR/TITLE INDEX

Grace, Janet

71	A Most Unusual Lady	04/92	Harlequin Regency

Grace, Rosemary

| 544 | Honky Tonk Dreams | 07/94 | Harlequin American |
| 619 | Flyboy | 02/96 | Harlequin American |

Grady, Liz

| 198 | Too Close For Comfort | /84 | Berkley Second Chance At Love |
| 283 | Heart Of The Hunter | /85 | Berkley Second Chance At Love |

Graham, Elizabeth

	A Heart To Come Home To	/92	Avalon
2062	The Girl From Finlay's River	/77	Harlequin
2088	The Shores Of Eden	/77	Harlequin
2126	Fraser's Bride	/77	Harlequin
2170	Heart Of The Eagle	/78	Harlequin
2190	Mason's Ridge	/78	Harlequin
2223	New Man At Cedar Hills	/78	Harlequin
392	Dangerous Tide		Harlequin Presents
403	Thief Of Copper Canyon		Harlequin Presents
446	Madrona Island		Harlequin Presents
493	Passionate Imposter		Harlequin Presents
543	Stormy Vigil		Harlequin Presents
583	Vision Of Love		Harlequin Presents
617	Highland Gathering		Harlequin Presents
2237	Return To Silver Creek		Harlequin Romance
2263	Man From Down Under		Harlequin Romance
2320	Devil On Horseback		Harlequin Romance
2326	Come Next Spring		Harlequin Romance
2374	Jacintha Point		Harlequin Romance
2708	Passion's Vine		Harlequin Romance
2715	Big Sur		Harlequin Romance
	Courting Eden	07/96	Zebra Lovegram

Graham, Heather

	A Pirate's Love		
	To Love A Rebel		Bantam
	Runaway	08/95	Delacorte Press
	One Wore Blue	07/91	Dell
	And One Wore Gray	04/92	Dell
	And One Rode West	11/92	Dell
	Devil's Mistress		Dell
	Every Time I Love You		Dell
	Golden Surrender		Dell
	The Viking's Woman		Dell
94	An Angel's Share	/86	Dell Candlelight Ecstasy
154	A Season For Love	/83	Dell Candlelight Ecstasy
177	Quiet Walks The Tiger	/83	Dell Candlelight Ecstasy
1	Sweet Savage Eden		Dell North American Woman

AUTHOR/TITLE INDEX

Graham, Heather

2	A Priate's Pleasure		Dell North American Woman
3	Love Not A Rebel		Dell North American Woman
	A Season For Love/ Quiet Walks The Tiger	08/91	Leisure
	Tender Taming/ When Next We Love	02/94	Leisure
	Love's Legacy	11/95	Leisure Anthology
	Night, Sea And Stars	07/96	Zebra

Graham, Lewis

151	The Great I Am	/52	Harlequin

Graham, Lynne

1167	The Veranchetti Marriage		Harlequin Presents
1313	An Arabian Courtship		Harlequin Presents
1409	An Insatiable Passion	11/91	Harlequin Presents
1489	A Fiery Baptism	09/92	Harlequin Presents
1551	Tempestuous Reunion	06/93	Harlequin Presents
1740	Indecent Deception	05/95	Harlequin Presents
1758	Bond Of Hatred	08/95	Harlequin Presents
1792	Crime Of Passion	02/96	Harlequin Presents
1824	A Savage Betrayal	07/96	Harlequin Presents
1696	A Vengeful Passion	11/94	Harlequin Presents Plus
1712	Angel Of Darkness	01/95	Harlequin Presents Plus
1779	The Unfaithful Wife	12/95	Harlequin Presents Plus

Grahame, Lucia

	The Painted Lady	07/94	

Graihan, Deborah

	Fire Queen		Bantam

Gramm, Nancy

339	Then Came Love	03/87	Silhouette Desire
422	About Last Night	05/88	Silhouette Desire
479	High Jinx	02/89	Silhouette Desire

Granau, Mary Ellen

	Gentle Conquerer		Bantam
	Passionate Warriors		Bantam

Granbeck, Marilyn

	Winds Of Desire		Berkley
	Ceila		Berkley
	Elena		Berkley
	The Fifth Jade Of Heaven		Berkley

Granger, Katherine

206	Wanton Ways	/84	Berkley Second Chance At Love
301	Man Of Her Dreams	/85	Berkley Second Chance At Love
13	Moments To Share	/84	Berkley To Have And To Hold
392	Ruffled Feathers	12/87	Silhouette Desire
410	Unwedded Bliss	03/88	Silhouette Desire
428	He Loves Me, He Loves Me Not	06/88	Silhouette Desire
452	A Match Made In Heaven	10/88	Silhouette Desire

504

Granger, Katherine

536	Halfway To Heaven	12/89	Silhouette	Desire
573	Temporary Honeymoon	06/90	Silhouette	Desire
509	A Love For All Seasons	02/89	Silhouette	Special Edition

Grant, Anna

	Dark Angel	03/94	Zebra Lovegram

Grant, Jeanne

	Tender Loving Care		Berkley	
	No More Mr. Nice Guy		Berkley	
	Sweets To The Sweet		Berkley	
	Ain't Misbehaving		Berkley	
	Conquer The Memories		Berkley	
	Cupid's Confederates		Berkley	
	Trouble In Paradise		Berkley	
	Sunburst		Berkley	
119	Man From Tennessee		Berkley	Second Chance At Love
149	A Daring Proposition		Berkley	Second Chance At Love
167	Kisses From Heaven		Berkley	Second Chance At Love
184	Wintergreen		Berkley	Second Chance At Love
184	Wintergreen	/84	Berkley	Second Chance At Love
220	Silver And Spice		Berkley	Second Chance At Love
256	Ain't Misbehaving		Berkley	Second Chance At Love
270	Can't Say No		Berkley	Second Chance At Love
270	Can't Say No	/85	Berkley	Second Chance At Love
293	Pink Satin	/85	Berkley	Second Chance At Love
14	Sunburst	/84	Berkley	To Have And To Hold
28	Trouble In Paradise	/84	Berkley	To Have And To Hold

Grant, Laurie

300	Devil's Dare	01/96	Harelquin	Historical
170	Beloved Deceiver	04/93	Harlequin	Historical
205	The Raven And The Swan	01/94	Harlequin	Historical
257	Lord Liar	02/95	Harlequin	Historical
	Defiant Heart	/87	Leisure	
	Forever Love	/87	Leisure	
	Emerald Fire	11/90	Warner	
	Love's Own Crown	/89	Warner	

Grant, Natalie

454	In The Know		Harlequin Superromance

Grant, Sabrina

	Walk In Beauty		Ballantine Regency

Grant, Sara

581	The Scorpio Man	06/88	Silhouette	Romance
619	The Kerandraon Legacy	12/88	Silhouette	Romance
709	A Child Called Matthew	03/90	Silhouette	Romance

Grant, Vanessa

895	Storm		Harlequin Presents

AUTHOR/TITLE INDEX

Grant, Vanessa

1088	Jenny's Turn		Harlequin Presents
1112	Stray Lady		Harlequin Presents
1179	Takeover Man		Harlequin Presents
1209	Stranded Heart		Harlequin Presents
1234	Awakening Dreams		Harlequin Presents
1264	Wild Passage		Harlequin Presents
1289	Taking Chances		Harlequin Presents
1322	So Much For Dreams		Harlequin Presents
1386	One Secret To Many	08/91	Harlequin Presents
1426	The Touch Of Love	01/92	Harlequin Presents
1490	Angela's Affair	09/92	Harlequin Presents
1528	With Strings Attached	02/93	Harlequin Presents
1622	When Love Returns	01/94	Harlequin Presents
1670	Hidden Memories	07/94	Harlequin Presents
2888	The Chauvinist	02/88	Harlequin Romance
	Catalina's Lover	10/95	Worldwide Libr. Stolen Moments

Grasso, Patricia

	Highland Belle		
	Courting An Angel	11/95	Dell
	Emerald Enchantment	03/92	Dell Historical
	Love In A Mist	12/94	Dell Historical

Grasson, Patricia

	Desert Eden	04/93	Dell

Graves, Keller

	Lawman's Lady	Zebra Heartfire
	Velvet Vixen	Zebra Heartfire
	Brazen Embrace	Zebra Heartfire
	Desire's Fury	Zebra Heartfire
	Rapture's Gambler	Zebra Heartfire

Graves, Tricia

38	Heart On Trial	Nal Rapture Romance

Gray, Evelyn

1	Camberleigh	Berkley
2	Mayfair	Berkley

Gray, Georgina

	Fashion's Frown	Ballantine Regency

Gray, Ginna

	For The Love Of Grace	11/95	
	Soul Mates	/96	
	Bad Boys	09/93	Harlequin By Request: Anthology
	Where Angels Fear	04/95	Harlequin Western Lovers
	Fools Rush In	07/95	Harlequin Western Lovers
	Quiet Fires	05/91	Harper
	Coming Home	08/95	Pinnacle Denise Little Presents
	For The Love Of Grace	12/95	Pinnacle Denise Little Presents

506

Gray, Ginna

	No Truer Love	11/96	Pinnacle	Denise Little Presents
	Wanted: Mother - "Soul Mates"	05/96	Silhouette	Anthology
	Season Of Miracles	11/87	Silhouette	Christmas Stories
285	The Gentling	03/84	Silhouette	Romance
311	The Perfect Match	08/84	Silhouette	Romance
338	Heart Of The Hurricane	01/85	Silhouette	Romance
352	Images	04/85	Silhouette	Romance
374	First Love, Last Love	07/85	Silhouette	Romance
417	The Courtship Of Dani	02/86	Silhouette	Romance
826	Sting Of The Scorpion	11/91	Silhouette	Romance
171	Golden Illusion	06/84	Silhouette	Special Edition
265	The Heart's Yearning	10/85	Silhouette	Special Edition
320	Sweet Promise	07/86	Silhouette	Special Edition
373	Cristen's Choice	04/87	Silhouette	Special Edition
416	Fools Rush In	11/87	Silhouette	Special Edition
468	Where Angels Fear	07/88	Silhouette	Special Edition
528	If There Be Love	05/89	Silhouette	Special Edition
661	Once In A Lifetime	04/91	Silhouette	Special Edition
722	A Good Man Walks In	02/92	Silhouette	Special Edition
792	Building Dreams	01/93	Silhouette	Special Edition
854	Forever-Blaines & Mc Calls Of Crockett, Tx	12/93	Silhouette	Special Edition
891	Always-Blaines & Mc Calls Of Crockett, Tx	06/94	Silhouette	Special Edition
973	The Bride Price (That Special Woman!)	08/95	Silhouette	Special Edition

Gray, Janet

298	Hearts Are Wild	/85	Berkley	Second Chance At Love

Gray, Janice

1167	Dear Barbarian	/67	Harlequin	
1230	Crown Of Content	/68	Harlequin	
1275	Shake Out The Stars	/69	Harlequin	
1707	Garden Of The Sun	/73	Harlequin	
1744	Winter Loving	/73	Harlequin	
1852	Star Light, Star Bright	/75	Harlequin	
1886	Take All My Loves	/75	Harlequin	
1911	Stormy Harvest	/75	Harlequin	
1931	Lullaby Of Leaves	/75	Harlequin	
2014	Moonglade	/76	Harlequin	
2029	A Kiss For Apollo	/76	Harlequin	
2089	Green For A Season	/77	Harlequin	
2294	Heart Of The Scorpion		Harlequin	Romance

Gray, Kerrie

666	Love Is A Gypsy	08/89	Silhouette	Romance

Gray, Marcy

477	A Pirate At Heart	02/89	Silhouette	Desire
704	So Easy To Love	02/90	Silhouette	Romance
792	Be My Wife	05/91	Silhouette	Romance

Gray, Marcy
  967 Rainbow's Promise   10/93 Silhouette Romance
Gray, Samantha
  708 The Mark Of Zorro   03/90 Silhouette Romance
Gray, Suzanna
      Mountain Magic   12/93 Diamond Homespun Historical
Gray, Valerie
      A Spy At The Gate   Leisure
Gray, Vanessa
      The Errant Bridegroom   03/86 Nal Regency
      The Reckless Orphan   07/86 Nal Regency
      The Orphan's Disguise   11/86 Nal Regency
      The Lonely Earl   11/87 Nal Regency
      The Lost Legacy   12/87 Nal Regency
      Best Laid Plans   Nal Penguin
      The Lady's Revenge   Nal Penguin
      The Unruly Bride   Nal Penguin
      The Duke's Messenger   Nal Penguin
      The Duke's Daughter   Nal Penguin
      The Reckless Gambler   Nal Penguin
      The Dutiful Daughter   Nal Penguin
      The Wicked Guardian   Nal Penguin
      The Accessible Aunt   Nal Penguin
      The Innocent Deceiver   Nal Penguin
      The Masked Heiress   Nal Penguin
      The Wayward Governess   Nal Penguin
      A Lady Of Property   Nal Penguin
      The Heart Remembers   Nal Penguin
Grayson, Elizabeth
      A Place Called Home   12/95 Avon Historical
      Bride Of The Wilderness   01/95 Berkley Historical
Grayson, Leanne
      Rebel Wind   10/93 Penguin Topaz
Grazia, Theresa
      Capital Watch   Warner
      The English Bride   Warner
Greco, Margaret
      Jenny's Choice   /68 Valentine Books
Green, Anne
      Bright River Trilogy
Green, Billie
    7 A Tryst With Mr. Lincoln   06/83 Bantam Loveswept
  16 A Very Reluctant Knight   09/83 Bantam Loveswept
  26 Once In A Blue Moon   12/83 Bantam Loveswept
  38 Temporary Angel   03/84 Bantam Loveswept
  43 To See The Daisies...First 05/84 Bantam Loveswept

AUTHOR/TITLE INDEX

Green, Billie

65	The Last Hero	10/84	Bantam	Loveswept
75	The Count From Wisconsin	01/85	Bantam	Loveswept
87	Dreams Of Joe	04/85	Bantam	Loveswept
108	A Tough Act To Follow	09/85	Bantam	Loveswept
129	Mrs. Gallagher And The Ne'er Well	02/86	Bantam	Loveswept
155	Glory Round	09/86	Bantam	Loveswept
182	Makin' Whoopee	03/87	Bantam	Loveswept
215	Loving Jenny	10/87	Bantam	Loveswept
329	Waiting For Lila	05/89	Bantam	Loveswept
372	Bad For Each Other	01/90	Bantam	Loveswept
431	Sweet And Wilde	10/90	Bantam	Loveswept
456	Starbright	03/91	Bantam	Loveswept
504	In Annie's Eyes	11/91	Bantam	Loveswept
564	Man From The Mist	09/92	Bantam	Loveswept
618	Wildfire	06/93	Bantam	Loveswept
661	Baby, Come Back	01/94	Bantam	Loveswept
711	Starwalker	10/94	Bantam	Loveswept
297	Jesse's Girl	03/86	Silhouette	Special Edition
346	A Special Man	11/86	Silhouette	Special Edition
379	Voyage Of The Nightingale	05/87	Silhouette	Special Edition
415	Time After Time	11/87	Silhouette	Special Edition
763	That Boy From Trash Town	09/92	Silhouette	Special Edition
	The Image Of A Girl	/88	Silhouette	Summer Sizzlers

Green, Grace

260	A Bittersweet Promise	12/95	Harlequin	
215	Love's Dark Shadow	01/95	Harlequin	Direct
223	Island Of Shells	03/95	Harlequin	Direct
233	A Woman's Love	05/95	Harlequin	Direct
1323	Tender Betrayal		Harlequin	Presents
1475	Risk Of The Heart	07/92	Harlequin	Presents
1539	Winter Destiny	03/93	Harlequin	Presents
1694	Snowdrops For A Bride	10/94	Harlequin	Presents

Green, Iris

27	The Bronzed Hawk	12/83	Bantam	Loveswept

Green, Judith

Unsuitable Company	12/92	Bantam	Fanfare

Green, Lois

Naked Came The Ladies	02/94	Starlog	Moonlight Anthology

Green, Maria

Winter's Flame		Avon
Daring Gamble	05/92	Berkley Diamond
Lady In Disgrace	10/93	Jove
The Raven And The Dove	05/94	Zebra

Green, Sharon

Flame Of Fury	11/93	Avon Historical

Green, Sharon

	Silken Dreams	12/94	Avon Historical
152	Haunted House		Harlequin Intrigue
224	Werewolf Moon	04/93	Harlequin Intrigue
244	Fantasy Man	09/93	Harlequin Intrigue

Greene, Jennifer

	Riley's Baby	/90	Sil. Birds, Bees & Babies
	Santa's Little Helpers - "Twelfth Night"	11/95	Silhouette Anthology
263	Body And Soul	02/86	Silhouette Desire
293	Foolish Pleasure	07/86	Silhouette Desire
326	Madam's Room	01/87	Silhouette Desire
350	Dear Reader	05/87	Silhouette Desire
366	Minx	07/87	Silhouette Desire
385	Lady Be Good	11/87	Silhouette Desire
421	Love Potion	05/88	Silhouette Desire
439	The Castle Keep	08/88	Silhouette Desire
463	Lady Of The Island	12/88	Silhouette Desire
481	Night Of The Hunter	03/89	Silhouette Desire
498	Dancing In The Dark	05/89	Silhouette Desire
553	Heat Wave	03/90	Silhouette Desire
600	Slow Dance	10/90	Silhouette Desire
619	Night Light	02/91	Silhouette Desire
671	Falconer	10/91	Silhouette Desire
728	Just Like Old Times	08/92	Silhouette Desire
756	It Had To Be You	12/92	Silhouette Desire
786	Quicksand	05/93	Silhouette Desire
847	Bewitched	04/94	Silhouette Desire
855	Bothered (Jock's Boys)	05/94	Silhouette Desire
861	Bewildered (Jock's Boys)	06/94	Silhouette Desire
893	A Groom For Red Riding Hood (Jilted!)	11/94	Silhouette Desire
931	Single Dad (Man Of The Month)	06/95	Silhouette Desire
966	Arizona Heat	11/95	Silhouette Desire
998	The Unwilling Bride	05/96	Silhouette Desire
221	Secrets	01/88	Silhouette Intimate Moments
305	Devil's Night	10/89	Silhouette Intimate Moments
345	Broken Blossom	08/90	Silhouette Intimate Moments
418	Pink Topaz	02/92	Silhouette Intimate Moments

Greene, Juli

| 499 | Beneath A Summer Moon | 04/87 | Silhouette Romance |

Greene, Maria

	Lady Midnight		Avon
	Desperate Deception		Avon
	Reckless Splendor		Avon
	Forever Love		Avon
	Winter's Flame	06/90	Avon Romance
	Gentleman Butler	04/93	Diamond
	Daring Gamble	05/92	Diamond Regency

Greene, Maria

	Lover's Knot		Jove Regency
	Lady In Disgrace	10/93	Jove Regency
	An Inconvenient Marriage	03/94	Jove Regency
	The Blackhurst Rubies	03/95	Jove Regency
	The Fox Hunt	04/95	Jove Regency
	Mine Forevermore	07/93	Zebra Heartfire

Greenleaf, Jeanne

| | Above All, Love | | Walker |

Greenleigh, Denice

	Birchwood Hall		Ballantine Regency
	Distant Relations		Ballantine Regency
	A Friend Of The Family		Ballantine Regency

Greenwood, Leigh

	An Old-Fashioned Southern Christmas	11/94	Leisure Anthology
	Their First Noel	11/95	Leisure Anthology
	Laurel	03/95	Leisure Seven Brides
	Iris		Leisure Seven Brides
	Fern		Leisure Seven Brides
	Rose		Leisure Seven Brides
	Daisy	/95	Leisure Seven Brides
	Rebel Enchantress	11/92	Zebra
	Prisoner Of Lies	05/93	Zebra
	The Captain's Caress		Zebra Heartfire
	Colorado Bride		Zebra Heartfire
	Scarlet Sunset, Silver Nights		Zebra Heartfire
	Seductive Wager		Zebra Heartfire
	Sweet Temptation		Zebra Heartfire
	Wicked Wyoming Nights		Zebra Heartfire
	Wyoming Wildfire		Zebra Heartfire
	Arizona Embrace	04/93	Zebra Heartfire

Gregg, Elizabeth

| | Goldspun Promises | 10/94 | Topaz |

Gregg, Margo

| 9 | Prodigal Lover | 09/90 | Meteor |

Gregg, Meredith

| | Love From Elizabeth | /88 | Walker |

Gregor, Carol

1074	Marry In Haste		Harlequin Presents
1129	The Trusting Heart		Harlequin Presents
1338	Bitter Secret		Harlequin Presents
1512	African Assignment	12/92	Harlequin Presents
2732	Lord Of The Air		Harlequin Romance
3124	Pretence Of Love		Harlequin Romance

Gregory, Jeri

| | The Legacy Of Hunter House | | Berkley |

Greiman, Lois

Surrender My Heart	03/93	Avon
Highland Flame	03/96	Avon
Highland Jewel	03/94	Avon Historical
My Desperado	10/94	Diamond Wildflower
To Tame An Outlaw	10/94	Diamond Wildflower
The Gambler	01/96	Jove Historical

Grey, Belinda

20	The Passionate Puritan		Mills & Boon
29	Loom Of Love		Mills & Boon
35	Sweet Wind Of Morning		Mills & Boon

Grey, Gillian

The Unmatchable Miss Mirabella	11/93	Avon

Grey, Jillian

Sins	12/94	Zebra

Grey, Kitty

A Regency Valentine	02/92	Fawcett Crest Regency
Current Confusion	/89	Walker
A Regency Valentine	/91	Walker

Grey, Millie

104	Suspicion	08/85	Bantam Loveswept
144	Wild Blue Yonder	06/86	Bantam Loveswept

Grey, Nicole

1	Draw The Line	08/93	Zebra Girlfriends
2	Do The Right Thing	08/93	Zebra Girlfriends
3	Deal Me Out	08/93	Zebra Girlfriends
4	Don't Be Cruel	10/93	Zebra Girlfriends

Grey, Shirley

21	The Crescent Moon		Mills & Boon

Grice, Julia

Satin Embraces		
Enchanted Nights		Nal Penguin
Season Of Desire		Nal Penguin
Kimberly Flame		Nal Penguin
Fiery Hearts		Tapestry

Grieg, Maysie

Girl In Jeopardy		Dell Candlelight

Grierson, Linden

1791	The Trees Of Tarrentall	/74	Harlequin
1820	Rising River	/74	Harlequin

Griffin, Jocelyn

2543	The White Wave		Harlequin Romance
8	Beloved Intruder		Harlequin Superromance
69	Battle With Desire		Harlequin Superromance
195	Hostages To Fortune	10/84	Silhouette Special Edition

Griffith, Kathryn Meyer

Griffith, Kathryn Meyer
    The Heart Of The Rose   Leisure

Griffith, Roslynn
    Princess Royale   Harper
    Shadows In The Mirror   09/95   Harper
    Pretty Birds Of Passage   09/93   Harper Historical
    The Wind Casts No Shadows   08/94   Harper Historical
    Heart Of The Jaguar   12/94   Harper Monogram

Grijalva, Lucy
    Undercover Love   09/94   Lion Hearted

Grimstead, Hettie
  1403   Whisper To The Stars   /70   Harlequin

Grinstead, J.E.
    75   Maverick Guns   /50   Harlequin
  119   When Texans Ride   /51   Harlequin
  411   Range King   /58   Harlequin
  417   Maverick Guns   /58   Harlequin

Gronau, Mary E.
    Gentle Conqueror

Gross, Martha
    Merry Christmas My Love   11/93   Zebra Anthology
    Hurricane Hero   08/94   Zebra To Love Again
    Something Wonderful   04/95   Zebra To Love Again

Grove, Donna
    A Touch Of Camelot   09/94   Harper Monogram
    Broken Vows   03/95   Harper Monogram
    Return To Camelot   09/95   Harper Monogram
    Broken Vows   03/95   Harper Monogram

Grove, Jo Ann A.
    An Honest Love   04/95   Barbour & Co.
    The Rekindled Flame   07/95   Barbour & Co.

Grundman, Donna
    A Distant Eden   Bantam

Guccione, Leslie Davis
  279   Before The Wind   05/86   Silhouette Desire
  523   Branigan's Touch   10/89   Silhouette Desire
  554   Private Practice   03/90   Silhouette Desire
  674   A Gallant Gentleman   11/91   Silhouette Desire
  713   Rough And Ready   05/92   Silhouette Desire
  748   A Rock And A Hard Place 11/92   Silhouette Desire
  795   Derek   07/93   Silhouette Desire
  870   Major Distractions   07/94   Silhouette Desire
  311   Bittersweet Harvest   10/86   Silhouette Desire - Branigan Brothers
  353   Still Waters   05/87   Silhouette Desire - Branigan Brothers
  376   Something In Common   09/87   Silhouette Desire - Branigan Brothers
  902   Branigan's Break   01/95   Silhouette Desire - Branigan Brothers

Guhrke, Laura Lee
    Prelude To Heaven   01/94   Harper Historical
    Conor's Way   04/96   Harper Historical
Gunn, Tom
  24   Painted Post Outlaws   /49   Harlequin
Guntrum, Suzanne Simmons
  353   The Golden Raintree   Harlequin American
  416   Home In His Arms   11/91   Harlequin American
  133   Christmas In April   12/86   Harlequin Temptation
  169   The Genuine Article   09/87   Harlequin Temptation
  202   Made In Heaven   05/88   Harlequin Temptation
Guss, Linda
  15   Hot Spell   12/92   Zebra Lucky In Love
Gwyn, Marion
    Love Comes Unbidden   04/94   Lovespell
Haaf, Beverly T.
    The Crystal Pawns   Popular Lib.
    The Chanting   Popular Lib.
Hadary, Simone
  59   Embraced By Destiny   /82   Berkley Second Chance At Love
Haddrill, Marilyn
    Night Of Shadows   /92   Avalon
Hadley, Liza
  186   Willing Or Not   05/94   Harlequin Direct
Haeger, Diane
    Angel Bride   09/94   Pocket Historical
Hagan, Lorinda
    Bold Blades Flashing   Leisure
Hagan, Patricia
    This Savage Heart
    Love's Wine
    Dark Journey Home   Contemporary Gothic
    Winds Of Terror   Contemporary Gothic
    Invitation To The Wedding   Contemporary Romance
    Boy Meets Girl   Contemporary Romance
    A Marriage Made In Heaven   Contemporary Romance
    Golden Roses   Avon
    Passion's Fury   Avon
    Dark Journey Home   Avon
    Winds Of Terror   Avon
    Souls Aflame   Avon
    Love And Triumph   Avon Coltrane Saga
    The Raging Hearts   Avon Coltrane Saga
    Love & Glory   Avon Coltrane Saga
    Love & Honor   Avon Coltrane Saga
    Loves & Dreams   Avon Coltrane Saga

Hagan, Patricia

	Love & Fury		Avon Coltrane Saga
	Love & Splendor		Avon Coltrane Saga
	Love And War		Avon Coltrane Saga
84	The Daring	07/91	Harlequin Historical
143	The Desire	10/92	Harlequin Historical
	Midnight Rose		Harper
	Heaven In A Wildflower	03/92	Harper
	Starlight	07/94	Harper
	Orchids In Moonlight	11/93	Harper Historical
	A Forever Kind Of Love	12/92	Harper Monogram
	Daisies Are Forever	12/92	Harper Monogram
	Love & War	08/94	Harper Monogram
	Simply Heaven	12/95	Harper Monogram
	Say You Love Me	04/95	Harper Monogram
	Souls Aflame	07/96	Harper Monogram
33	A Touch Of Love	03/91	Meteor
69	Ocean Of Dreams	12/91	Meteor

Hailstock, Shirley

	Whispers Of Love	09/94	Pinnacle Arabesque
	Clara's Promise	06/95	Pinnacle Arabesque
	Holiday Cheer: "Invitation To Love"	12/95	Pinnacle Arabesque Anthology

Haines, Pamela

	The Diamond Waterfall		Nal Penguin

Hale, Antoinette

93	Island Of Desire	/86	Dell Candlelight Ecstasy

Hale, Arlene

	The Reunion		Dell Candlelight
169	Midnight Nightmare		Dell Candlelight
170	The Divided Heart		Dell Candlelight
171	Dangerous Yesterdays		Dell Candlelight
172	Perilous Weekend		Dell Candlelight
181	Wait For Love		Dell Candlelight
200	Dr. Myra Comes Home		Dell Candlelight
203	A Happy Ending		Dell Candlelight
207	Share Your Heart		Dell Candlelight

Hale, Dorothea

29	A Woman's Prerogative		Harlequin American
50	Flight Of Fancy		Harlequin American

Haley, Jocelyn

11	Love Wild And Free		Harlequin Superromance
31	Winds Of Desire		Harlequin Superromance
54	Serenade For A Lost Love		Harlequin Superromance
88	Cry Of The Falcon		Harlequin Superromance
122	Shadows In The Sun		Harlequin Superromance
217	A Time To Love		Harlequin Superromance

AUTHOR/TITLE INDEX

Haley, Jocelyn
  218 Wildcat Summer   Harlequin Superromance
  254 Drive The Night Away   Harlequin Superromance

Haley, Wendy
      Dead Heat   02/94   Suspense
      This Dark Paradise   04/94   Berkley
      Secret Loves   03/94   Berkley Contemporary

Halford, Laura
      Seaswept   10/90   Avon

Hall, Diana
  309 Warrior's Deception   03/96   Harlequin Historical

Hall, Gimane
      Ecstasy's Empire   Nal Penguin

Hall, Libby
  373 Hearts At Risk   Harlequin American
  189 The Perfect Woman   02/88   Harlequin Temptation

Hall, Olivia M.
  103 Wanton City   /51   Harlequin

Halldorson, Phyllis
   43 To Choose A Wife   10/96   Harlequin Here Come The Grooms
      A Memorable Noel   /91   Silhouette Christmas Stories
   31 Temporary Bride   09/80   Silhouette Romance
   79 To Start Again   05/81   Silhouette Romance
  247 Mountain Melody   09/83   Silhouette Romance
  282 If Ever I Loved You   03/84   Silhouette Romance
  367 Design For Two Hearts   06/85   Silhouette Romance
  395 Forgotten Love   11/85   Silhouette Romance
  456 An Honest Lover   09/86   Silhouette Romance
  515 To Choose A Wife   07/87   Silhouette Romance
  566 Return To Raindance   03/88   Silhouette Romance
  584 Raindance Autumn   06/88   Silhouette Romance
  653 Ageless Passion, Timeless Love 06/89   Silhouette Romance
  689 Dream Again Of Love   12/89   Silhouette Romance
  760 Only The Nanny Knows For Sure 12/90   Silhouette Romance
  791 Lady Diamond   05/91   Silhouette Romance
  948 More Than You Know   07/93   Silhouette Romance
 1060 Father In The Middle (Fabulous Fathers) 02/95   Silhouette Romance
 1133 Mail Order Wife   02/96   Silhouette Romance
  290 My Heart's Undoing   02/86   Silhouette Special Edition
  368 The Showgirl And The Professor 03/87   Silhouette Special Edition
  430 Cross My Heart   01/88   Silhouette Special Edition
  510 Ask Not Of Me, Love   02/89   Silhouette Special Edition
  621 All We Know Of Heaven   09/90   Silhouette Special Edition
  734 You Could Love Me   04/92   Silhouette Special Edition
  764 Luscious Lady   09/92   Silhouette Special Edition
  863 A Haven In His Arms   01/94   Silhouette Special Edition

AUTHOR/TITLE INDEX

Halldorson, Phyllis
958	Truly Married	05/95	Silhouette Special Edition
999	The Bride And The Baby	12/95	Silhouette Special Edition

Halleran, E.E.
58	Outposts Of Vengeance	/50	Harlequin
61	Shadow Of The Badlands	/50	Harlequin

Halliday, Ena
2	Marielle	/82	Pocket Tapestry
10	Lysette	/83	Pocket Tapestry
19	Delphine	/83	Pocket Tapestry

Halliday, Sylvia
	Summer Darkness, Winter Light	05/95	Kensington

Hallquist, F. Jacquelyn
	The House On Whiffen Cove	01/93	Dell
	Shadows Of Black Briar Hall	11/91	Diamond Gothic

Halston, Carole
	To Mother With Love: "Neighborly Affair"	05/92	Silhouette Anthology
62	Stand-In Bride	02/81	Silhouette Romance
83	Love Legacy	06/81	Silhouette Romance
152	Undercover Girl	05/82	Silhouette Romance
208	Sunset In Paradise	03/83	Silhouette Romance
8	The Keys To Daniel's House	03/82	Silhouette Special Edition
41	Collision Course	08/82	Silhouette Special Edition
86	The Marriage Bonus	04/83	Silhouette Special Edition
115	Summer Course In Love	09/83	Silhouette Special Edition
139	A Hard Bargain	01/84	Silhouette Special Edition
163	Something Lost, Something Gained	05/84	Silhouette Special Edition
211	A Common Heritage	01/85	Silhouette Special Edition
223	The Black Night	02/85	Silhouette Special Edition
253	Almost Heaven	08/85	Silhouette Special Edition
291	Surprise Offense	02/86	Silhouette Special Edition
328	Matched Pair	08/86	Silhouette Special Edition
356	Honeymoon For One	01/87	Silhouette Special Edition
388	The Baby Trap	06/87	Silhouette Special Edition
423	High Bid	12/87	Silhouette Special Edition
461	Intensive Care	06/88	Silhouette Special Edition
500	Compromising Positions	01/89	Silhouette Special Edition
543	Ben's Touch	08/89	Silhouette Special Edition
567	Unfinished Business	12/89	Silhouette Special Edition
642	Courage To Love	12/90	Silhouette Special Edition
682	Yours, Mine And ... Ours	07/91	Silhouette Special Edition
800	The Pride Of St. Charles Avenue	03/93	Silhouette Special Edition
829	More Than He Bargained For	08/93	Silhouette Special Edition
915	Bachelor Dad	10/94	Silhouette Special Edition
950	A Self-Made Man	04/95	Silhouette Special Edition

Halter, Caroline

AUTHOR/TITLE INDEX

Hampson, Anne

1467	Beyond The Sweet Waters	/71	Harlequin
1491	When The Bough Breaks	/71	Harlequin
1522	Love Hath An Island	/71	Harlequin
1551	Stars Of Spring	/71	Harlequin
1570	Heaven Is High	/72	Harlequin
1595	Gold Is The Sunrise	/72	Harlequin
1622	There Came A Tyrant	/72	Harlequin
1646	Isle Of The Rainbows	/72	Harlequin
1672	The Rebel Bride	/73	Harlequin
1678	The Plantation Boss	/73	Harlequin
2082	Call Of The Outback	/77	Harlequin
2099	Boss Of Bali Creek	/77	Harlequin
2119	Moon Without Stars	/77	Harlequin
2130	Isle Of Desire	/78	Harlequin
2138	Sweet Is The Web	/78	Harlequin
2160	The Shadow Between	/78	Harlequin
2163	Fly Beyond The Sunset	/78	Harlequin
2182	Under Moonglow	/78	Harlequin
2186	Call Of The Veld	/78	Harlequin
2215	Leaf In The Storm	/78	Harlequin
1	Gates Of Steel	/73	Harlequin Presents
2	Master Of Moonrock	/73	Harlequin Presents
7	Dear Stranger	/73	Harlequin Presents
10	Waves Of Fire	/73	Harlequin Presents
13	A Kiss From Satan	/73	Harlequin Presents
16	Wings Of Night	/73	Harlequin Presents
19	South Of Mandraki	/73	Harlequin Presents
22	The Hawk And The Dove	/73	Harlequin Presents
25	By Fountains Wild	/73	Harlequin Presents
28	Dark Avenger	/73	Harlequin Presents
31	Blue Hills Of Sintra	/74	Harlequin Presents
34	Stormy The Way	/74	Harlequin Presents
37	An Eagle Swooped	/74	Harlequin Presents
40	Wife For A Penny	/74	Harlequin Presents
44	Petals Drifting	/74	Harlequin Presents
47	When The Clouds Part	/74	Harlequin Presents
51	Hunter Of The East	/74	Harlequin Presents
56	After Sundown	/74	Harlequin Presents
59	Beloved Rake	/74	Harlequin Presents
63	Stars Over Sarawak	/74	Harlequin Presents
72	The Way Of A Tyrant	/74	Harlequin Presents
79	The Black Eagle	/75	Harlequin Presents
87	Fetters Of Hate	/75	Harlequin Presents
95	Dark Hills Rising	/75	Harlequin Presents
108	Pride And Power	/75	Harlequin Presents
115	The Fair Island	/75	Harlequin Presents

Hampson, Anne

125	Dear Plutocrat	/76	Harlequin	Presents
132	Enchanted Dawn	/76	Harlequin	Presents
143	A Man To Be Feared	/76	Harlequin	Presents
152	Autumn Twilight	/76	Harlequin	Presents
168	Dangerous Friendship	/76	Harlequin	Presents
181	Isle At The Rainbow's End	/77	Harlequin	Presents
187	Hills Of Kalamata	/77	Harlequin	Presents
196	Follow A Shadow	/77	Harlequin	Presents
209	Song Of The Waves	/77	Harlequin	Presents
293	Moon Dragon		Harlequin	Presents
463	Bride For A Night		Harlequin	Presents
470	Beloved Vagabond		Harlequin	Presents
476	Bitter Harvest		Harlequin	Presents
483	A Rose From Lucifer		Harlequin	Presents
494	Windward Crest		Harlequin	Presents
507	South Of Capricorn		Harlequin	Presents
515	Unwanted Bride		Harlequin	Presents
535	Chateau In The Palms		Harlequin	Presents
2230	Harbour Of Love		Harlequin	Romance
2233	To Tame A Vixen		Harlequin	Romance
2246	For Love Of A Pagan		Harlequin	Romance
2266	South Of The Moon		Harlequin	Romance
2272	Where South Wind Blows		Harlequin	Romance
2353	Temple Of The Dawn		Harlequin	Romance
1	Payment In Full	05/80	Silhouette	Romance
4	Stormy Masquerade	05/80	Silhouette	Romance
16	Second Tomorrow	07/80	Silhouette	Romance
27	The Dawn Steals Softly	08/80	Silhouette	Romance
28	Man Of The Outback	09/80	Silhouette	Romance
40	Where Eagles Nest	11/80	Silhouette	Romance
52	Man Without A Heart	01/81	Silhouette	Romance
64	Shadow Of Apollo	03/81	Silhouette	Romance
94	Enchantment	08/81	Silhouette	Romance
108	Fascination	10/81	Silhouette	Romance
119	Desire	12/81	Silhouette	Romance
128	Realm Of The Pagans	01/82	Silhouette	Romance
136	Man Without Honor	03/82	Silhouette	Romance
147	Stardust	04/82	Silhouette	Romance
151	A Kiss And A Promise	05/82	Silhouette	Romance
155	Devotion	06/82	Silhouette	Romance
160	Strangers May Marry	07/82	Silhouette	Romance
178	The Tender Years	10/82	Silhouette	Romance
185	To Buy A Memory	11/82	Silhouette	Romance
190	Another Eden	12/82	Silhouette	Romance
196	When Love Comes	01/83	Silhouette	Romance
202	Dreamtime	02/83	Silhouette	Romance

Hanson, Rick

    Spare Parts   10/94 Kensington

Hara, Monique

    The Mists Of Milwood   Zebra Gothic

    The Ruby Tears Of Edgecliff Manor   Zebra Gothic

Haran, Maeve

    Having It All   10/92 Bantam Fanfare

Harbaugh, Karen

    The Devil's Bargain   04/95 Signet Regency

    The Vampire Viscount   09/95 Signet Regency

Harding, Allison

    Also Georgianna   St. Martin's

Harding, Rhonda

    Legal Tender   /93 Harlequin Intrigue

Hardwick, Mollie

    I Remember Love   St. Martin's

    Lover's Meeting   St. Martin's

    Malice Domestic   St. Martin's

    The Merrymaid   St. Martin's

    Uneaseful Death   St. Martin's

    Willowwood   St. Martin's

    Monday's Child   St. Martin's

    The Duchess Of Duke Street   St. Martin's

    Thomas And Sarah   St. Martin's

    The Crystal Dove   St. Martin's

    Blood Royal   St. Martin's

    The Shakespeare Girl   St. Martin's Historical

Hardy, Antoinette

   191 Fit To Be Loved   09/84 Silhouette Special Edition

Hardy, Laura

    76 Burning Memories   05/81 Silhouette Romance

   101 Playing With Fire   09/81 Silhouette Romance

   130 Dream Master   02/82 Silhouette Romance

   184 Dark Fantasy   11/82 Silhouette Romance

   309 Men Are Dangerous   07/84 Silhouette Romance

    25 Tears And Red Roses   06/82 Silhouette Special Edition

Hardy, W.G.

   201 The Unfulfilled   /52 Harlequin

   215 Run Back The River   /53 Harlequin

Hargis, Barbara

    Heart Song   Avon

Harkness, Judith

    The Determined Bachelor   05/86 Nal Regency

    Lady Charlotte's Ruse   06/86 Nal Regency

    The Admiral's Daughter   Nal Penguin Regency

    The Montague Scandal   Nal Penguin Regency

Harkness, Judith
    Contrary Cousins   Nal Penguin Regency

Harland, Christina
    Waiting Wives   02/91   Bantam Fanfare

Harlow, Sharon
    Yours Truly   04/94   Diamond Homespun
    Country Kiss   02/93   Diamond Homespun
    Harvest Hearts   11/93   Jove Historical Anthology

Harmon, Anne
    Wyoming Wildfire   04/93   Diamond Wildflower
    Desert Flame   12/92   Diamond Wildflower
    Golden Promise   03/94   Zebra Wildflower

Harmon, Danelle
    My Lady Pirate   08/94   Avon Historical
    Master Of My Dreams   09/93   Avon Historical
    Pirate In My Arms   06/91   Avon Romance
    Captain Of My Heart   10/92   Avon Romance

Harmse, Deborah
  585   A Man To Believe In   12/92   Bantam Loveswept
  691   In The Arms Of The Law   06/94   Bantam Loveswept

Harper, Karen
    Almost Forever   08/91   Berkley
    Eden's Gate   12/90   Berkley
    Tame The Wind   01/89   Berkley
    One Fervent Fire   04/87   Berkley
    The Firelands   Charter
    River Of The Sky   08/94   Dutton Historical
    Country Christmas   11/93   Nal Anthology
    Dark Road Home   03/96   Penguin Signet
    The Wings Of Morning   08/94   Signet
    Promises To Keep   12/94   Signet
    Blossoms: "Violets Are Blue"   03/95   Signet Anthology
    Circle Of Gold   04/93   Signet Historical
    Rapture's Crown   /85   Zebra
    Sweet Passion's Pain   /84   Zebra
    Passion's Reign   /83   Zebra
    Island Ecstasy   /82   Zebra
    Midnight Mirage   /85   Zebra

Harper, Madeline
  133   Dangerous Charade   07/92   Harlequin Historical
        Christmas Baby   12/96   Harlequin Intrigue
  325   Tall, Dark And Deadly (Dangerous Man)   06/95   Harlequin Intrigue
        The Highwayman   09/96   Harlequin Temptation
   32   Every Intimate Detail   10/84   Harlequin Temptation
  106   After The Rain   05/86   Harlequin Temptation
  165   The Ultimate Seduction   08/87   Harlequin Temptation

Hart, Jessica
  3382 Legally Binding   10/95 Harlequin Romance
  3406 The Right Kind Of Man   04/96 Harlequin Romance
Hart, Joan Mary
  631 Stranger At The Wedding   02/89 Silhouette Romance
Hart, Mallory Dorn
    Defy The Sun   Pocket
    Sparklers   Pocket
    Jasmin On The Wind   Pocket
Hart, Neesa
    Restless   05/96 Pinnacle Denise Little Present
Hart, Pam
  123 Lies And Shadows   01/93 Meteor Kismet
Hart, Shirley
  161 A Dangerous Haven   /83 Dell Candlelight Ecstasy
  183 A Night To Remember   /83 Dell Candlelight Ecstasy
Hart, Susannah
  72 Nobody's Baby   06/83 Silhouette Desire
  186 A Legend In His Own Time 01/85 Silhouette Desire
Hart, Teresa
    Hearts Are Wild   04/93 Jove Brides Of The West
Hart, Virginia
  2811 Sweet Pretender   Harlequin Romance
  2882 Night Of The Spring   01/88 Harlequin Romance
  2980 Without Rainbows   Harlequin Romance
  3135 Love Or Money   07/91 Harlequin Romance
  3272 Pet Peeves   07/93 Harlequin Romance
  3305 The Perfect Scoundrel   03/94 Harlequin Romance
Harte, Amanda
    Silver Thorns   09/96 Pinnacle Denise Little Presents
Harte, Samantha
    Kiss Of Gold
    Sweet Whispers
    Summer Sea
    Autumn Blaze   02/93 Diamond Wildflower
    Sunflower Sky   09/94 Harper Monogram
Hartwig, Daphne
    Big Sky Burning   02/92 Harper
Harvey, Judy
  23 In Loving Regret   Harlequin American
Harvey, Kathryn
    Butterfly
    Stars
Harvey, Marianne
    The Proud Hunter   Dell

AUTHOR/TITLE INDEX

Harvey, Marianne

The Dark Horseman /86 Dell

The Wild One Dell

Harvey, Samantha

2481 The Driftwood Beach Harlequin Romance

2522 The Distance Man Harlequin Romance

2541 Boy With Kite Harlequin Romance

2764 Amaryllis Dreaming 05/86 Harlequin Romance

Harwell, Connie

Texas Woman Leisure

Ryan's Enchantress 04/93 Leisure Historical

Haskell, Leigh

The Vengeful Viscount 11/90 Nal Penguin

The Paragon Bride /89 Nal Signet

Haskell, Mary

203 Heaven On Earth /84 Berkley Second Chance At Love

272 A Bit Of Daring /85 Berkley Second Chance At Love

8 Hold Fast ' Til Dawn /84 Berkley To Have And To Hold

17 All That Glitters /84 Berkley To Have And To Hold

Hastings, Brooke

25 So Sweet A Sin 07/89 Harlequin Historical

Eight Nights 11/88 Silhouette Christmas Stories

37 Interested Parties 02/84 Silhouette Intimate Moments

64 Reasonable Doubts 08/84 Silhouette Intimate Moments

13 Playing For Keeps 06/80 Silhouette Romance

26 Innocent Fire 08/80 Silhouette Romance

44 Desert Fire 11/80 Silhouette Romance

67 Island Conquest 03/81 Silhouette Romance

102 Winner Take All 09/81 Silhouette Romance

528 Too Close For Comfort 09/87 Silhouette Romance

2 Intimate Strangers 02/82 Silhouette Special Edition

21 Rough Diamond 05/82 Silhouette Special Edition

49 A Matter Of Time 10/82 Silhouette Special Edition

79 An Act Of Love 03/83 Silhouette Special Edition

156 Tell Me No Lies 03/84 Silhouette Special Edition

250 Hard To Handle 07/85 Silhouette Special Edition

294 As Time Goes By 02/86 Silhouette Special Edition

312 Forward Pass 05/86 Silhouette Special Edition

349 Double Jeopardy 12/86 Silhouette Special Edition

385 Forbidden Fruit 06/87 Silhouette Special Edition

439 Catch A Falling Star 03/88 Silhouette Special Edition

486 Both Sides Now 10/88 Silhouette Special Edition

571 Reluctant Mistress 01/90 Silhouette Special Edition

630 Seduction 10/90 Silhouette Special Edition

Hastings, Julia

Island Ecstasy

AUTHOR/TITLE INDEX

Haviland, Diana

	The Moreland Legacy		Fawcett
	The Passionate Pretenders		Fawcett
	Love's Promised Land		Fawcett
	Defy The Storm		Fawcett
	Proud Surrender		Fawcett
	Fortune's Daughter		Fawcett
	Embrace The Flame		Zebra
	Stolen Splendor	/94	Zebra
	Pirate's Kiss		Zebra Historical

Hawkes, Sarah

| 264 | An Unmarried Man | 08/89 | Harlequin Temptation |

Hawley, S. R.

	Lethal Legacy	/91	Avalon
	Formula For Murder	08/92	Avalon
	Desert Secrets		Avalon Mystery Romance
	Desert Gold		Avalon Mystery Romance

Hawthorne, Alaina

672	Out Of The Blue	09/89	Silhouette Romance
1029	The Bridal Path	08/94	Silhouette Romance
1069	My Dearly Beloved	03/95	Silhouette Romance
1164	Make-Believe Bride	07/96	Silhouette Romance
1180	Introducing Daddy	10/96	Silhouette Romance

Hayden, Laura

	A Margin In Time	03/95	Pinnacle Denise Little Presents
	Chance Of A Lifetime	07/96	Pinnacle Denise Little Presents
	Ghost Of A Chance	07/96	Pinnacle Denise Little Presents

Haye, Jan

758	Helping Doctor Medway	/63	Harlequin
897	Nurse Hilary's Holiday Task	/65	Harlequin
977	The Doctor's Difficult Daughter	/66	Harlequin

Hayes, Allison

	Spellbound	10/90	Avon Romance
	Storm Dancers	12/91	Avon Romance
1032	Marry Me, Now!	05/96	Silhouette Special Edition

Hayes, Karen

| | Summer Poem | | |

Hayes, M.R.

| | The Winter Women | | Nal |

Hayes, Morgan

| 591 | Twilight Whispers | 04/94 | Harlequin Superromance |
| 632 | Premonitions (Women Who Dare) | 02/95 | Harlequin Superromance |

Hayes, Sally Tyler

439	Whose Child Is This?	07/92	Silhouette Intimate Moments
485	Dixon's Bluff	03/93	Silhouette Intimate Moments
549	Days Gone By	02/94	Silhouette Intimate Moments

AUTHOR/TITLE INDEX

Hayes, Sally Tyler
611	Not His Wife	12/94	Silhouette Intimate Moments
671	Our Child?	10/95	Silhouette Intimate Moments
700	Homecoming	03/96	Silhouette Intimate Moments

Hayle, Felicity
995	Nurse Ronnie's Vocation	/66	Harlequin
1217	A Promise Is For Keeping	/68	Harlequin
1337	The Campbells Are Coming	/69	Harlequin

Haynesworth, Susan
606	O' Daniel's Pride	10/88	Silhouette Romance

Hayward, Lee
Bluegrass And Roses	12/95	Zebra

Hayworth, Evelyne
534	The Ghost Of Ludlow Fair	Dell Candlelight

Hazard, Barbara
The Tangled Web	04/81	Ballantine Historical
Caroline	11/81	Ballantine Historical
The Covington Inheritance	02/82	Ballantine Historical
Beth	05/80	Ballantine Historical
Dangerous Deceits	05/82	Ballantine Historical
Dangerous Lady	12/80	Ballantine Historical
Kathleen	03/80	Ballantine Historical
Monday's Child	08/93	Fawcett Crest Regency
Wednesday's Child	07/94	Fawcett Crest Regency
Thursday's Child	02/95	Fawcett Crest Regency
Friday's Child	10/95	Fawcett Crest Regency
Tuesday's Child	12/93	Fawcett Crest Regency
Mad Masquerade	04/85	Nal
A Handful Of Dreams	08/92	Nal Onyx
Call Back The Dream	01/90	Nal Onyx
The Heart Remembers	07/90	Nal Onyx
Midnight Magic	06/91	Nal Onyx
The Cloisonne Locket	11/86	Nal Regency
The Royal Snuff Box	03/87	Nal Regency
The Calico Countess	06/87	Nal Regency
A Surfeit Of Suitors	09/87	Nal Regency
Lady Lochinvar	11/87	Nal Regency
The Queen Bee	08/88	Nal Regency
An Enchanting Stranger	10/84	Nal Regency
The Turnabout Twins	05/86	Nal Penguin Regency
The Dreadful Duke	11/85	Nal Penguin Regency
The Disobedient Daughter	06/82	Nal Penguin Regency
The Singular Miss Carrington		Nal Penguin Regency
The Emerald Duchess	01/85	Nal Signet
The Rake's Protege	06/85	Nal Signet
The Singular Miss Carrington	08/84	Nal Signet Regency

Heath, Sandra

Title	Date	Publisher	Genre
The Makeshift Marriage	02/83	Nal Signet	Regency
The Absent Wife	08/87	Nal Signet	Regency
Rakehell's Widow	08/84	Nal Signet	Regency
A Commercial Enterprise	10/84	Nal Signet	Regency
A Matter Of Duty	03/88	Nal Signet	Regency
An Impossible Confession	09/88	Nal Signet	Regency
The Pilfered Plume	10/89	Nal Signet	Regency
A Christmas Courtship	12/90	Nal Signet	Regency
Smuggler's Daughter	/79	Nal Signet	Regency
A Change Of Fortune	/85	Nal Signet	Regency
Opera Dancer	/80	Nal Signet	Regency
My Lady Domino	/83	Nal Signet	Regency
Mally	/80	Nal Signet	Regency
The Sherbourne Sapphires	/82	Nal Signet	Regency
Lady Sabrina's Secret	05/93	Nal Signet	Regency
Cruel Lord Cranham	07/94	Nal Signet	Regency
A Highland Conquest	02/94	Nal Signet	Regency
The Halloween Husband	09/94	Nal Signet	Regency
Magic At Midnight	05/95	Nal Signet	Regency
The Courting Of Jenny Bright	/80	Nal Signet	Regency
Shades Of The Past	06/96	Nal Signet	Time-Travel Regency
Summer's Secret	01/97	Nal Signet	Time-Travel Regency
Halloween Magic	09/96	Nal Signet	Witchcraft Regency
Tokens Of Love: 5 Regency Love Stories	01/93	Penguin	Anthology

Heaven, Constance

The House Of Kuragin			
The Astrov Inheritance			
The Place Of Stones			
The Fires Of Glenlochy			
The Queen And The Gypsy			
Lord Of Ravensley			
The Wildcliffe Bird			
The Ravensley Touch			
Daughter Of Marignac			
Castle Of Doves			
The Craven Legacy			
Castle Of Eagles		Period Romance	

Hecht, Ben

	Title	Date	Publisher
32	Hollywood Mystery	/50	Harlequin

Hecklemann, Charles N.

	Title	Date	Publisher
198	Rawhider	/52	Harlequin

Heggan, Christiane

Title	Date	Publisher
Gloss	12/91	Nal Onyx
Cannes	06/90	Nal Onyx
Passions	02/93	Nal Onyx

Heggan, Christiane
    Betrayals   09/94 Nal Onyx
    Silver Lining   05/95 Nal Onyx
    Never Say Never   08/96 Nal Onyx
Hehl, Eileen
    Lucky In Love   08/92 Bantam Sweet Dreams
    Earth Angel   10/93 Zebra To Love Again
    Garden Of Love   02/95 Zebra To Love Again
Heland, Victoria
    Mayfair Wager   Berkley
    The Artful Cousin   Berkley
Held, G. N.
    Burning Secrets   /91 Avalon
Heley, Veronica
    The Tarrant Rose   Ballantine Historical
Heller, Jane
    Cha Cha Cha   07/94 Kensington
    The Club   06/95 Kensington
Helm, Georgia
  112   Mad Hatter   10/92 Meteor
Helton, Venita
    Pirate's Prize   08/94 Harper Monogram
    Sapphire   05/93 Harper Monogram
Henaghan, Rosalie
  253   Love, Desire And You   10/95 Harlequin
  1422 The Sophisticated Urchin /70 Harlequin
  2462 Coppers Girl   Harlequin Romance
  2572 Man Form Ti Kouka   Harlequin Romance
  2621 For Ever And A Day   Harlequin Romance
  2751 Safe Harbour   Harlequin Romance
  3027 Spell Of The Mountain   Harlequin Romance
  3170 Windswept   01/92 Harlequin Romance
Henchman, Jane
    To London, To London   Ballantine Historical
    Rendezvous With Love   Ballantine Historical
Henderson, Beth
  935   New Year's Eve   01/95 Silhouette Special Edition
  1002 Mr. Angel   12/95 Silhouette Special Edition
  11   Fortune And Folly   11/92 Zebra Lucky In Love
Henderson, George C.
  134   The Killers   /51 Harlequin
Henderson, Lorraine
    Heavenly Persuasion   12/95 Leisure Love Spell
Hendrickson, Emily
    A Scandalous Suggestion 07/91 Nal Regency

Hendrickson, Emily

A Perfect Performance	10/91	Nal	Regency
The Dashing Miss Fairchild	01/92	Nal	Regency
The Wicked Proposal	05/92	Nal	Regency
The Fashionable Spy	10/92	Nal	Regency
Mrs. Mc Vinnie's London Session		Nal	Regency
Miss Cheney's Charade	03/94	Nal	Regency
Althea's Grand Tour	10/94	Nal	Regency
Miss Wyndham's Escapade	09/90	Nal Penguin	Regency
The Colonial Upstart	04/90	Nal Penguin	Regency
Lady Sara's Scheme	06/89	Nal Penguin	Regency
Elizabeth's Rake	01/93	Penguin	Regency
Lord Dancy's Delight	06/93	Penguin	Regency
The Rake And The Redhead	01/94	Signet	
A Regency Christmas: "Christmas Mouse"	11/93	Signet	Anthology
A Regency Christmas: "Christmas Knight"	11/94	Signet	Anthology
A Country Miss	11/88	Signet	Regency
Double Deceit	12/90	Signet	Regency
The Gallant Lord Ives	11/89	Signet	Regency
Queen Of The May	12/89	Signet	Regency
Hidden Inheritance	03/89	Signet	Regency
A Perfect Performance	10/91	Signet	Regency
The Scoundrel's Bride	07/94	Signet	Regency
Lord Dancy's Delight	07/94	Signet	Regency
Julia's Spirit	10/93	Signet	Regency
The Abandoned Rake	05/95	Signet	Regency
The Contrary Corinthian	01/95	Signet	Regency
Lord Barry's Dream House	02/96	Signet	Regency
The Debonair Duke	07/96	Signet	Regency
Harriet's Beau	05/97	Signet	Regency

Hendrickson, Margaret

Four In Hand	01/93	Penguin	Regency

Hendrix, Lisa

Drifter's Moon	01/95	Diamond	Historical
Hostage Heart	01/94	Diamond	Wildflower

Hendryx, James B.

156	Blood Of The North	/52	Harlequin

Heneghan, Rosalie

185	Colours Of Love	05/94	Harlequin Direct
3194	For Love Or Power	05/92	Harlequin Romance

Henke, Courtney

340	Chameleon	07/89	Bantam Loveswept
368	The Dragon's Revenge	12/89	Bantam Loveswept
394	Jinx	04/90	Bantam Loveswept
476	In A Golden Web	06/91	Bantam Loveswept

Henke, Shirl

Henke, Shirl

A Fire In The Blood	04/94	Leisure
Love A Rebel, Love A Rogue	10/94	Leisure
Mc Cory's Lady	/95	Leisure
Terms Of Love	10/92	Leisure Historical
Night Wind's Woman	08/93	Leisure Historical
Paradise And More	11/91	Leisure Historical
An Old-Fashioned Valentine	02/93	Leisure Historical
Terms Of Surrender	05/93	Leisure Historical
White Apache's Woman	10/93	Leisure Historical
Broken Vows	10/95	Leisure Historical
Bouquet	07/94	Onyx
A Dream Come True	03/94	Penguin Topaz Man Anthology
Bride Of Fortune	05/96	St. Martin's
Secrets Of The Heart	/94	Topaz Anthology
Cactus Flower		Warner
Moon Flower		Warner
Night Flower	05/90	Warner
Love Unwilling		Warner
Capture The Sun		Warner
Golden Lady		Warner

Henley, Liz

876	Just Her Type	07/92	Silhouette Romance

Henley, Virginia

Wild Hearts		
Tempted		
Desired	12/94	
The Pirate And The Pagan		
Irish Gypsy		Avon
Bold Conquest	10/93	Avon
Seduced	01/94	Bantam
The Dragon And The Jewel	12/91	Dell
The Falcon And The Flower		Dell
The Hawk And The Dove		Dell
The Priate And The Pagan		Dell
The Raven And The Rose		Dell
Enticed	08/94	Dell
Love's Legacy	11/95	Leisure Anthology

Henricks, Betty

102	Fire In Paradise	/86	Dell Candlelight Ecstasy

Henry, Anne

76	Cherokee Summer		Harlequin American
90	The Glory Run		Harlequin American
114	The Storm Within		Harlequin American
135	Tough Act To Follow		Harlequin American
171	I Love You, Jonathan	10/86	Harlequin American

AUTHOR/TITLE INDEX

Herter, Lori

	Confession	09/92	Berkley
	Obsession	01/93	Berkley
	Eternity	12/93	Berkley
574	No Time For Love		Dell Candlelight
	Possession	02/92	Diamond
	Shadows Short Story Collection	10/93	Harlequin Anthology
28	The Willow File	03/94	Harlequin Shadows
344	Loving Deception	02/85	Silhouette Romance
	Listen Up, Lover	08/95	Silhouette Yours Truly
14	How Much Is That Couple In The Window?	02/96	Silhouette Yours Truly
25	Blind-Date Bride	08/96	Silhouette Yours Truly
	Naked Came The Ladies	02/94	Starlog Moonlight Anthology

Hess, Norah

	Forever The Flame		
	Hunter's Moon		
	Wildfire	07/89	Berkley
	Kentucky Bride	07/96	Dorchester
	Storm	08/94	Leisure
	Sage	04/94	Leisure
	Kentucky Woman		Leisure
	Fancy	/95	Leisure
	A Wilderness Christmas	11/95	Leisure Anthology
	A Frontier Christmas	11/92	Leisure Historical
	Devil In Spurs		Leisure Historical
	Hawke's Pride		Leisure Historical
	Mountain Rose	03/93	Leisure Historical

Hewitt, Elizabeth

	Airs And Graces		Nal
	Captain Black		Nal
	Marriage By Consent		Nal
	A Sporting Proposition		Nal
	False Of Heart	08/92	Nal Super Regency
	An Innocent Deception	09/87	Nal Penguin Regency
	A Private Understanding	01/90	Nal Penguin Regency
	The Ice Maiden	06/88	Nal Penguin Regency
	A Lasting Attachment	04/89	Nal Penguin Regency
	The Worth Inheritance	07/86	Nal Penguin Regency
	The Fortune Hunter	07/86	Nal Penguin Regency
	Broken Vows	07/87	Nal Penguin Regency
	Lady China		Nal Penguin Regency
	True Colors	05/93	Penguin Super Regency

Heyer, Georgette

	Black Sheep
	Beauvallet
	Powder And Patch
	A Convenient Marriage

Heyer, Georgette

Devil's Club				
The Masqueraders				
Regency Buck				
The Conquerer				
An Infamous Army				
Royal Escape				
The Spanish Bride				
False Colors				
Pistols For Two				
The Corinthian				
Penhallow				
Envious Casca				
The Unfinished Clue				
The Foundling				
The Nonesuch				
Fredericka				
Lady Of Quality				
The Black Moth				
The Cotillion	07/94			
Cousin Kate		Gothic		
Simon The Coldheart		Historical		
April Lady	10/91	Harper		
Bath Tangle	08/91	Harper		
Civil Contract	05/91	Harper		
Cotillion	06/91	Harper		
Friday's Child		Harper		
The Reluctant Widow		Harper		
The Toll-Gate	07/91	Harper		
Sylvester (Or The Wicked Uncle)	12/91	Harper		
Sprig Muslin	02/92	Harper		
Venetia	04/92	Harper		
The Foundling	07/92	Harper		
The Grand Sophy	09/92	Harper		
The Unknown Ajax	10/92	Harper		
Arabella	11/92	Harper		
The Quiet Gentleman	05/92	Harper	Regency	
Faro's Daughter	10/92	Nal	Regency	
These Old Shades	01/88	Nal	Regency	
Charity Girl	03/88	Nal	Regency	

Heywood, Philippa

| 9 | The Cautious Heart | /81 | Berkley Second Chance At Love |

Heywood, Sally

1200	Fantasy Lover	Harlequin Presents
1235	Today, Tomorrow	Harlequin Presents
1256	Law Of Love	Harlequin Presents
1306	Love's Sweet Harvest	Harlequin Presents

Heywood, Sally

1344	Hazard Of Love		Harlequin Presents
1378	Bride Of Ravenscroft	07/91	Harlequin Presents
1417	Simply Forever	12/91	Harlequin Presents
1441	Jungle Lover	03/92	Harlequin Presents
1466	The Gemini Bride	06/92	Harlequin Presents
1521	Steps To Heaven	01/93	Harlequin Presents
2925	Impossible To Forget		Harlequin Romance
3072	A Summer Kind Of Love		Harlequin Romance

Hiatt, Brenda

70	Gabriella	03/92	Harlequin Regency
81	The Ugly Duckling	09/92	Harlequin Regency
91	Lord Dearborn's Destiny	02/93	Harlequin Regency
102	Daring Deception	07/93	Harlequin Regency
112	A Christmas Bride	12/93	Harlequin Regency
	Regency Diamonds: Azalea	08/94	Harlequin Regency Anthology
592	Bridge Over Time	04/94	Harlequin Superromance

Higdon, Lisa

	Take Heart	07/96	Jove Our Town

Higgins, Joyce

547	Dreams Are Forever	12/87	Silhouette Romance

High, Monique Raphael

Between Two Worlds		Leisure

Hill, Deborah

This Is The House		Nal Penguin
The House Of Kingsley Merrick		Nal Penguin

Hill, Donna

Deception	07/96	Kensington Arabesque
Rooms Of The Heart	07/90	Odyssey Books
Indiscretions	03/91	Odyssey Books
Temptation	09/95	Pinnacle
Scandalous	05/95	Pinnacle Arabesque
Spirit Of The Season	12/94	Zebra Anthology

Hill, Fiona

The Country Gentleman		St. Martin's
The Trellised Lane		St. Martin's
The Wedding Portrait		St. Martin's
The Practical Heart		St. Martin's
Love In A Major Key		St. Martin's
Sweet's Folly		St. Martin's
The Love Child		St. Martin's
The Stanhaoke Girls		St. Martin's
The Autumn Rose		St. Martin's Regency

Hill, Grace Livingston

65	An Unwilling Guest	09/93
66	Girl From Montana	10/93

Hill, Grace Livingston

67	A Daily Rate	10/93	
68	The Story Of A Whim	11/93	
69	According To The Pattern	11/93	
70	In The Way	01/94	
74	Lo, Michael	03/94	
75	The Witness	03/94	
76	City Of Fire	04/94	
	The Girl From Montana	/82	Revell Co.
	A Daily Rate	/82	Revell Co.
	Duskin	/89	Tyndale House
1	Where Two Ways Met	/88	Tyndale House
2	Bright Arrows	/88	Tyndale House
3	A Girl To Come Home To	/88	Tyndale House
4	Amorelle	/89	Tyndale House
5	Kerry	/89	Tyndale House
6	All Through The Night	/89	Tyndale House
7	The Best Man	07/89	Tyndale House
8	Ariel Custer	09/89	Tyndale House
9	The Girl In The Woods	11/89	Tyndale House
10	Crimson Rose	01/92	Tyndale House
11	More Than Conqueror	01/90	Tyndale House
12	Head Of The House	03/90	Tyndale House
13	In Tune With Wedding Bells	04/94	Tyndale House
14	Stranger Within The Gates	05/90	Tyndale House
15	Marigold	07/90	Tyndale House
16	Rainbow Cottage	09/90	Tyndale House
17	Maris	11/90	Tyndale House
18	Brentwood	01/91	Tyndale House
19	Daphne Deane	03/91	Tyndale House
20	The Substitute Guest	05/91	Tyndale House
21	The War Romance/Salvation Army	06/91	Tyndale House
22	Rose Galbraith	07/91	Tyndale House
23	Time Of The Singing Of Birds	09/91	Tyndale House
24	By Way Of The Silverthorns	11/91	Tyndale House
25	Sunrise	01/92	Tyndale House
26	The Seventh Hour	02/92	Tyndale House
27	April Gold	03/92	Tyndale House
28	White Orchids	/89	Tyndale House
29	Homing	04/92	Tyndale House
30	Matched Pearls	04/92	Tyndale House
31	Strange Proposal	05/94	Tyndale House
32	Coming Through The Rye	05/92	Tyndale House
33	Happiness Hill	05/92	Tyndale House
34	The Patch Of Blue	07/92	Tyndale House
35	Partners	05/94	Tyndale House
36	Patricia	07/92	Tyndale House

Hill, Grace Livingston

37	Silver Wings	08/92	Tyndale House
38	Spice Box	08/92	Tyndale House
39	The Search	09/92	Tyndale House
40	The Tryst	09/92	Tyndale House
41	Blue Ruin	10/92	Tyndale House
42	A New Name	10/92	Tyndale House
43	Dawn Of The Morning	11/92	Tyndale House
44	Beloved Stranger	11/92	Tyndale House
45	Gold Shoe	01/93	Tyndale House
46	Through These Fires	01/93	Tyndale House
47	Street Of The City	02/93	Tyndale House
48	Beauty For Ashes	02/93	Tyndale House
49	Enchanted Barn	03/93	Tyndale House
50	Finding Of Jasper Holt	03/93	Tyndale House
51	Red Signal	04/93	Tyndale House
52	Tomorrow About This Time	04/93	Tyndale House
53	Job's Niece	05/93	Tyndale House
54	Obsession Of Victoria Gracen	05/93	Tyndale House
55	Ladybird	07/93	Tyndale House
56	Prodigal Girl	07/93	Tyndale House
57	Honor Girl	08/93	Tyndale House
58	Chance Of A Lifetime	08/93	Tyndale House
59	Astra	09/93	Tyndale House
60	Miranda	09/91	Tyndale House
61	Mystery Flowers	07/91	Tyndale House
62	Christmas Bride	07/94	Tyndale House
63	The Man Of The Desert	05/91	Tyndale House
64	Miss Lavinia's Call	03/91	Tyndale House
71	Exit Betty	01/94	Tyndale House
72	White Lady	02/94	Tyndale House
73	Not Under The Law	02/94	Tyndale House
77	The Ransom	/88	Tyndale House
78	Found Treasure	/88	Tyndale House
79	The Big Blue Soldier	/88	Tyndale House
80	The Challengers	/89	Tyndale House
82	The White Flower	07/89	Tyndale House
83	Marcia Schuyler	09/89	Tyndale House
84	Cloudy Jewel	11/89	Tyndale House
85	Crimson Mountain	01/90	Tyndale House
86	The Mystery Of May	03/90	Tyndale House
87	Out Of The Storm	05/90	Tyndale House
88	Phoebe Deane	07/90	Tyndale House
89	Re-Creations	09/90	Tyndale House
90	Sound Of The Trumpet	11/90	Tyndale House
91	A Voice In The Wilderness	01/91	Tyndale House
92	The Honeymoon House	02/92	Tyndale House

AUTHOR/TITLE INDEX

Hill, Grace Livingston

93	Katharine's Yesterday	03/92	Tyndale House
94	The Angel Of His Presence	07/94	Tyndale House

Hill, Heather

60	Green Paradise	02/81	Silhouette Romance
171	Lady Moon	08/82	Silhouette Romance

Hill, Johanna

Daughter Of Liberty		Pocket
Gilded Hearts		Pocket
Song Of The Rose		Tapestry

Hill, Judith

Fires In The Night	02/91	Zebra Heartfire
A Knight Of Desire	09/92	Zebra Lovegram

Hill, Pamela

The Brocken	09/91	St. Martin's
The Heatherton Heritage		St. Martin's
The Sutbury		St. Martin's
Antemia		St. Martin's
My Lady Glamis		St. Martin's
Tsar's Woman		St. Martin's
The House Of Cray		St. Martin's
A Place Of Ravens		St. Martin's
Fire Opal		St. Martin's
Danclere		St. Martin's
Stranger's Forest		St. Martin's
Whitton's Folly		St. Martin's
The Malvie Inheritance		St. Martin's
The Woman In The Cloak		St. Martin's
Flaming Janet		St. Martin's
Shadow Of Palaces		St. Martin's
Marjorie Of Scotland		St. Martin's
Here Lies Margot		St. Martin's
Maddalene		St. Martin's
Forget Not Ariadne		St. Martin's
Julia		St. Martin's
The Brocken		St. Martin's
The Devil Of Aske		St. Martin's Gothic
The Green Salamander		St. Martin's Historical
Norah		St. Martin's Period Romance

Hill, Sandra

Frankly, My Dear	07/96	Dorchester
The Tarnished Lady	09/95	Leisure Historical
The Reluctant Viking	09/94	Leisure Time Travel
The Outlaw Viking	09/94	Leisure Time Travel

Hill, Susan

Mrs. De Winter	12/94	William Morrow Historical

547

Hillary, Anne

505	The Bartered Bride	Dell Candlelight Regency
578	The Mismatched Lovers	Dell Candlelight Regency
661	Compromised Love	Dell Candlelight Regency
	Hearts In Hiding	Zebra Pinnacle/Regency Romance

Hilliard, Nerina

557	The Time Is Short (Nurse Carol's Secret)	/60	Harlequin
840	The House Of Adriano	/64	Harlequin
927	The Scars Shall Fade	/65	Harlequin
1268	Dark Star	/69	Harlequin
1302	Teachers Must Learn	/69	Harlequin
2003	Land Of The Sun	/76	Harlequin
2040	Sister To Meryl	/77	Harlequin
116	Dark Intruder	/75	Harlequin Presents

Hills, Ida

34	Heartbreaker Mine	Harlequin American

Hilton, Linda

	Firefly	
	Legacy Of Honor	Leisure
	Moonsilver	03/95 Pocket
	Desire's Slave	Zebra Heartfire
	Secret Fires	Zebra Heartfire
	Shadows By Starlight	10/93 Zebra Heartfire
	Sweet Secret Surrender	04/92 Zebra Heartfire

Hilton, Margery

1022	Young Ellis	/66	Harlequin
1068	The Dutch Uncle	/66	Harlequin
1125	Darling Rhadamanthus	/67	Harlequin
1188	The Grotto Of Jade	/68	Harlequin
1367	Interlude In Arcady	/70	Harlequin
1438	Bitter Masquerade	/70	Harlequin
1501	The Whispering Grove	/71	Harlequin
1536	Trust In Tomorrow	/71	Harlequin
1581	The House Of The Amulet	/72	Harlequin
1610	Dear Conquistador	/72	Harlequin
1634	The Spell Of The Enchanter	/72	Harlequin
1670	Frail Sanctuary	/73	Harlequin
1710	The Inshine Girl	/73	Harlequin
1752	Miranda's Marriage	/74	Harlequin
1950	The Beach Of Sweet Returns	/76	Harlequin
2135	The House Of Strange Music	/78	Harlequin
2213	The Dark Side Of Marriage	/78	Harlequin
52	A Man Without Mercy	/74	Harlequin Presents
103	The Flower Of Eternity	/75	Harlequin Presents
163	Girl Crusoe	/76	Harlequin Presents
297	The Velvet Touch		Harlequin Presents

Hilton, Margery
- 357 Snow Bride — Harlequin Presents
- 2473 Way Of A Man — Harlequin Romance

Hinchman, Jane
- Dreamspinner /86 Walker

Hingle, Metsy
- 900 Seduced 12/94 Silhouette Desire
- 978 Surrender 01/96 Silhouette Desire

Hirsch, Richard
- 154 Rasputin And Crimes That Shook The Worl /52 Harlequin

Hirschfeld, Burt
- Aspen Affair — Harper

Hites, Dana Lynn
- 92 To Love Again 05/92 Meteor

Hix, Martha
- River Magic 03/95 Lovegram
- 779 Texas Tycoon 03/91 Silhouette Romance
- 344 Every Moment Counts 11/86 Silhouette Special Edition
- Caress Of Fire — Zebra
- Mexican Fire — Zebra
- Magnolia Nights — Zebra Heartfire
- Wild Texas Rose — Zebra Heartfire
- Wild Sierra Rogue 07/93 Zebra Lovegram
- Mail-Order Man 06/94 Zebra Lovegram
- 1 River Magic 04/95 Zebra Magic Lamp Trilogy

Hoag, Tami
- Cry Wolf 06/93 Bantam
- Dark Paradise 04/94 Bantam
- Night Sins 01/95 Bantam
- Guilty As Sin 03/96 Bantam
- Magic 06/91 Bantam Fanfare
- Lucky's Lady 04/92 Bantam Fanfare
- Still Waters 11/92 Bantam Fanfare
- 253 The Trouble With J. J. 05/88 Bantam Loveswept
- 276 Mc Knight In Shining Armor 09/88 Bantam Loveswept
- 304 Rumor Has It 01/89 Bantam Loveswept
- 315 Mismatch 03/89 Bantam Loveswept
- 331 Man Of Her Dreams 06/89 Bantam Loveswept
- 351 Straight From The Heart 09/89 Bantam Loveswept
- 434 Tempestuous 11/90 Bantam Loveswept
- 458 The Restless Heart 03/91 Bantam Loveswept
- 480 Sarah's Sin 07/91 Bantam Loveswept
- 493 Heart Of Dixie 09/91 Bantam Loveswept
- 532 Taken By Storm 03/92 Bantam Loveswept
- 561 The Last White Knight 08/92 Bantam Loveswept
- 393 Heart Of Gold 04/90 Bantam Loveswept:Rainbow Chasers

AUTHOR/TITLE INDEX

Hoag, Tami
| 405 | Keeping Company | 06/90 | Bantam Loveswept:Rainbow Chasers |
| 417 | Reilly's Return | 08/90 | Bantam Loveswept:Rainbow Chasers |

Hobbs, Margaret
| 172 | The Hitching Post | 09/87 | Harlequin Temptation |

Hocker, Karla
	The Incorrigible Sopia	08/92	Walker Regency
	The Impertinent Miss Bancroft	08/91	Walker Regency
	The Devilish Marquis		Warner
	An Honorable Affair		Warner
	A Bed For Independence		Warner
	A Madcap Scheme		Warner
	A Daring Alliance		Warner
	An Improper Companion	06/89	Zebra
	A Deceitful Heart	02/93	Zebra
	A Christmas Charade	11/91	Zebra Regency
	Lady Maryann's Dilemma		Zebra Regency
	Love Tangle		Zebra Regency
	A Scandalous Lady		Zebra Regency
	June Love	05/95	Zebra Regency

Hockett, Kathryn
	River Of Passion	07/94	
	Cherokee's Caress		Zebra
	Endless Ecstasy		Zebra
	Gentle Warrior		Zebra
	Seductive Surrender		Zebra
	Sweet Savage Surrender		Zebra
	Angel Of Passion		Zebra Heartfire
	River Of Passion	05/93	Zebra Lovegram

Hockett, Marica
	Rapture's Delight	/88	Zebra
	Renegade	/89	Zebra
	Surrender The Moonlight	/90	Zebra

Hodge, Jane Aiken
	Strangers In Company		Gothic
	Red Sky At Night		Historical
	Lover's Delight		Historical
	Runaway Bride		Regency
	One Way To Venice		Suspense

Hodges, Carl G.
| 182 | Crime On My Hands | /52 | Harlequin |

Hodgson, Anne
| | To Love And To Cherish | 12/93 | Harper Historical |

Hoffman, Alice
| | Second Nature | /95 | Berkley |
| | Turtle Moon | 04/93 | Berkley |

Hoffman, Kate

456	Indecent Exposure	08/93	Harlequin Temptation
475	Wanted: Wife	01/94	Harlequin Temptation
487	Love Potion #9	04/94	Harlequin Temptation
515	Lady Of The Night	11/94	Harlequin Temptation
525	Bachelor Husband (Bachelor Arms)	02/95	Harlequin Temptation
529	The Strong, Silent Type (Bachelor Arms)	03/95	Harlequin Temptation
533	A Happily Unmarried Man (Bachelor Arms)	04/95	Harlequin Temptation
546	Never Love A Cowboy (Secret Fantasies)	07/95	Harlequin Temptation

Hoffman, Louise

	House Of Intrigue		Dell Candlelight

Hoffmann, Kate

577	The Pirate	03/96	Harlequin Temptation
	Dressed To Thrill	06/96	Harlequin Weddings By Dewilde

Hohl, Joan

	Love Beyond Time	07/94	Avon Time Travel Anthology
	Silver Thunder	09/92	Dell
	Shadow's Kiss	02/94	Dell Ghost
30	Moments Harsh, Moments Gentle	12/94	Harlequin Men Made In America
	Someone Waiting	07/95	Harlequin Western Lovers
	Window On Tomorrow		Leisure Contemporary
	Window On Yesterday		Leisure Contemporary
	Window On Today		Leisure Contemporary
	Nevada Silver	10/94	Mira
	One Tough Hombre	06/95	Mira
	Thorne's Way	01/96	Mira
	Falcon's Flight	10/95	Mira
	Lady Ice	02/95	Mira
312	California Copper	10/86	Silhouette Desire - Trilogy 2
	1993 Christmas Stories	11/93	Silhouette Anthology
	Men Of Summer - "Gone Fishing"	07/96	Silhouette Anthology
247	A Much Needed Holiday	12/85	Silhouette Desire
354	Lady Ice	05/87	Silhouette Desire
372	One Touch Hombre	08/87	Silhouette Desire
390	Falcon's Flight	11/87	Silhouette Desire
475	The Gentleman Insists	02/89	Silhouette Desire
540	Christmas Stranger	12/89	Silhouette Desire
612	Handsome Devil	12/90	Silhouette Desire
732	Convenient Husband	08/92	Silhouette Desire
762	Lyon's Club	01/93	Silhouette Desire
806	Big, Bad Wolfe: Wolfe Waiting	09/93	Silhouette Desire
865	Wolfe Watching	07/94	Silhouette Desire
884	Wolfe Waiting	10/94	Silhouette Desire
973	Wolfe Wedding	01/96	Silhouette Desire
294	Texas Gold	07/86	Silhouette Desire - Trilogy 1
330	Nevada Silver	01/87	Silhouette Desire - Trilogy 3
35	Moments Harsh, Moments Gentle	01/84	Silhouette Intimate Moments

551

AUTHOR/TITLE INDEX

AUTHOR/TITLE INDEX

Holland, Sarah

29	Blue Fire	04/96	Harlequin	Presents
516	Too Hot To Handle		Harlequin	Presents
536	Tomorrow Began Yesterday		Harlequin	Presents
552	The Devil's Mistress		Harlequin	Presents
576	Deadly Angel		Harlequin	Presents
601	Fever Pitch		Harlequin	Presents
1192	The Heat Is On		Harlequin	Presents
1387	An Adult Love	08/91	Harlequin	Presents
2705	Bluebeard's Bride		Harlequin	Romance

Holland, Sheila

	Maiden Castle	Playboy Press
	Dancing Hell	Playboy Press
	Shadow Of Dawn	Playboy Press
	Love's Bright Flame	Playboy Press
	The Merchant's Daughter	Playboy Press
	The Notorious Gentleman	Playboy Press
	Miss Charlotte's Fancy	Playboy Press Period Romance
	Secrets	Worldwide Lib.

Holliday, Arlene

	Wild Texas Blossom	02/94	Zebra	Heartfire
	His Wildest Fantasy	11/94	Zebra	Lovegram
	Summer Wind	07/95	Zebra	Lovegram

Hollis, Erica

37	Passion's Triumph		Harlequin Superromance

Hollister, Raine

484	Exception To The Rule	03/93	Silhouette Intimate Moments

Holloway, Teresa

227	The Girl In Studio B	/67	Valentine Books

Holm, Stef Ann

	King Of The Pirates	07/94	
	Silver Desires		Leisure
	Firefly		Leisure Historical
	Seasons Of Gold	02/92	Pocket
	Snowbird	09/94	Pocket
	Weeping Angel	05/95	Pocket

Holmberg, Anne

	Far Star	03/95	Leisure Love Spell

Holmes, Dee

699	His Runaway Son	07/96	Harlequin Superromance
	The Farrell Marriage	02/92	Silhouette Intimate Moments
327	Black Horse Island	03/90	Silhouette Intimate Moments
395	Maybe This Time	08/91	Silhouette Intimate Moments
419	The Farrell Marriage	02/92	Silhouette Intimate Moments
465	Without Price	12/92	Silhouette Intimate Moments
495	Take Back The Night	05/93	Silhouette Intimate Moments

Holmes, Dee

541	Cuts Both Ways (American Heroes)	01/94	Silhouette	Intimate Moments
591	Watched	09/94	Silhouette	Intimate Moments
628	Dillon's Reckoning	03/95	Silhouette	Intimate Moments
660	The Return Of Slade	03/91	Silhouette	Special Edition

Holmes, Mary Mayer

The Wind Rose		Nal Penguin
The Irish Bride		Warner
Savage Tides		Warner
The White Raven		Warner

Holt, Tex

155	Canyon Of The Damned	/52	Harlequin

Holt, Victoria

The Demon Lover		Ballantine
The Devil On Horseback		Ballantine
The House Of A Thousand Lanterns		Ballantine
The India Fan		Ballantine
The Judas Kiss		Ballantine
The King Of The Castle		Ballantine
Kirkland Revels		Ballantine
The Landower Legacy		Ballantine
The Legend Of The Seventh Virgin		Ballantine
The Mask Of The Enchantress		Ballantine
Menfreya In The Morning		Ballantine
The Pride Of The Peacock		Ballantine
The Queen's Confession		Ballantine
The Road To Paradise Island		Ballantine
Secret For A Nightingale		Ballantine
The Shadow Of The Lynx		Ballantine
The Silk Vendetta		Ballantine
The Time Of The Hunter's Moon		Ballantine
Bride Of Pendorric		Ballantine
Daughter Of Deceit		Ballantine
Mistress Of Mellyn		Ballantine Gothic
My Enemy, The Queen		Ballantine Historical
Snare Of Serpents		Fawcett Crest
The Shivering Sands		Fawcett Crest
The Secret Woman		Fawcett Crest
The Spring Of The Tiger		Fawcett Crest
Bride Of Pendorric		Fawcett Crest
On The Night Of The Seventh Moon		Fawcett Crest
The Curse Of The Kings		Fawcett Crest
Lord Of The Far Island		Fawcett Crest
Seven For A Secret	11/93	Fawcett Crest

Hood, Ann

Something Blue	07/92	Bantam Fanfare

Hooper, Kay

	Summer Of The Unicorn			
	Velvet Lightning			
	Christmas Love Stories	/91	Avon	Anthology
	My Guardian Angel	02/95	Bantam	Anthology
	Adelaide, The Enchantress	/84	Bantam	Delaneys Of Killaroo
	Star-Crossed Lovers	03/91	Bantam	Fanfare
	The Matchmaker	08/91	Bantam	Fanfare
	The Delaney Christmas Carol	12/92	Bantam	Fanfare
	Finale		Bantam	Loveswept
32	C. J.'s Fate	02/84	Bantam	Loveswept
46	Something Different	05/84	Bantam	Loveswept
62	Pepper's Way	09/84	Bantam	Loveswept
71	If There Be Dragons	12/84	Bantam	Loveswept
83	Illegal Possession	03/85	Bantam	Loveswept
128	Rebel Waltz	02/86	Bantam	Loveswept
149	Time After Time	07/86	Bantam	Loveswept
189	In Serena's Web	04/87	Bantam	Loveswept
193	Raven On The Wing	05/87	Bantam	Loveswept
219	Rafferty's Wife	11/87	Bantam	Loveswept
225	Zach's Law	12/87	Bantam	Loveswept
231	The Fall Of Lucas Kendrick	01/88	Bantam	Loveswept
237	Unmasking Kelsey	02/88	Bantam	Loveswept
256	Outlaw Derek	05/88	Bantam	Loveswept
286	Shades Of Gray	10/88	Bantam	Loveswept
296	Captain's Paradise	12/88	Bantam	Loveswept
312	It Takes A Thief	03/89	Bantam	Loveswept
321	Aces High	04/89	Bantam	Loveswept
348	Golden Threads	09/89	Bantam	Loveswept
360	The Glass Shoe	10/89	Bantam	Loveswept
390	What Dreams May Come	04/90	Bantam	Loveswept
408	Through The Looking Glass	07/90	Bantam	Loveswept
426	The Lady And The Lion	10/90	Bantam	Loveswept
595	Men Of Mysteries Past: The Touch Of Max	02/93	Bantam	Loveswept
595	The Touch Of Max	02/93	Bantam	Loveswept
607	Men Of Mysteries Past: Hunting The Wolfe	04/93	Bantam	Loveswept
619	Men Of Mysteries Past: The Trouble With J	06/93	Bantam	Loveswept
631	All For Quinn	08/93	Bantam	Loveswept
682	Josie	04/94	Bantam	Loveswept
703	The Haunting Of Josie	08/94	Bantam	Loveswept
167	Rafe, The Maverick		Bantam	Loveswept:Shamrock Trinity
	Amanda	10/95	Bantam	Suspense
	Golden Flames	/84	Bantam	The Delaneys
	Eye Of The Beholder	03/94	Berkley	Contemporary
77	Mask Of Passion		Dell	Candlelight Ecstasy
90	Breathless Surrender		Dell	Candlelight Ecstasy
153	On Wings Of Magic	/83	Dell	Candlelight Ecstasy

Hooper, Kay

665	Lady Thief		Dell Candlelight Regency
	Once Upon A Time: Glass Shoe		Doubleday
	Once Upon A Time: Golden Threads		Doubleday
	Once Upon A Time: What Dreams May Co		Doubleday
	Kissed By Magic/ Belonging To Taylor	11/92	Jove
	Elusive Dawn	09/93	Jove
	On Her Doorstep	07/94	Jove
	Return Engagement	01/95	Jove
	The Wizard Of Seattle	05/93	Jove
	Hearts Of Gold	02/94	Jove Anthology
	Promo: Larger Than Life		Loveswept
297	Enemy Mine	08/89	Silhouette Intimate Moments
388	The Haviland Touch	06/91	Silhouette Intimate Moments

Hoos, Suzanne

	The Haunting Of Raven Manor	/91	Leisure
	Whispers In The Night	07/92	Leisure Gothic
	Mistress Of The Muse	05/93	Leisure Gothic

Hoover, Saranne

	Greenfire		Leisure

Hope, Jacqueline

145	Love Captive	04/82	Silhouette Romance

Hope, Margaret

16	The Queen's Captain		Mills & Boon
30	Hostage Most Royal		Mills & Boon

Hopson, William

110	Tombstone Stage	/51	Harlequin
158	Yucca City Outlaw	/52	Harlequin
236	Gunthrower	/53	Harlequin
275	Hell's Horseman	/54	Harlequin
304	High Saddle	/54	Harlequin
309	Notched Guns	/54	Harlequin
360	Yucca City Outlaw	/56	Harlequin

Horler, Sydney

307	The Cage	/54	Harlequin
322	The Webb	/54	Harlequin
400	The Cage	/57	Harlequin
410	Dark Journey	/58	Harlequin
425	The Return Of Nighthawk	/58	Harlequin
488	The Man Who Died Twice	/59	Harlequin

Horsman, Jennifer

	Cormion Rapture		
	Passion's Joy		
	Magic Embrace		
	With One Look	07/94	Avon
	Virgin Star	07/93	Avon

Horsman, Jennifer

	A Christmas Together	10/94	Avon	Anthology
	With One Look	07/94	Avon	Historical
	Awaken My Fire	07/92	Avon	Romantic Treasures
	Forever And A Lifetime		Zebra	

Horton, Naomi

15	Mc Connell's Bride	05/96	Harlequin	Here Come The Grooms
42	Strangers No More	09/96	Harlequin	Here Come The Grooms
	Dreaming Of Angels	11/91	Silhouette	Christmas Stories
162	Dream Builders	09/84	Silhouette	Desire
236	River Of Dreams	10/85	Silhouette	Desire
269	Split Images	03/86	Silhouette	Desire
302	Star Light, Star Bright	09/86	Silhouette	Desire
320	Lady Liberty	12/86	Silhouette	Desire
365	No Walls Between Us	07/87	Silhouette	Desire
385	Pure Chemistry	11/87	Silhouette	Desire
435	Crossfire	07/88	Silhouette	Desire
487	Dangerous Kind Of Man	04/89	Silhouette	Desire
518	The Ideal Man	09/89	Silhouette	Desire
596	Cat's Play	10/90	Silhouette	Desire
630	Mc Allister's Lady	03/91	Silhouette	Desire
656	No Lies Between Us	08/91	Silhouette	Desire
719	Mc Connell's Bride	06/92	Silhouette	Desire
769	Chastity's Pirate	03/93	Silhouette	Desire
873	What Are Friends For? (Centerfolds)	08/94	Silhouette	Desire
323	Strangers No More	02/90	Silhouette	Intimate Moments
343	In Safe Keeping	07/90	Silhouette	Intimate Moments
425	Dangerous Stranger	04/92	Silhouette	Intimate Moments
505	Hell On Wheels	07/93	Silhouette	Intimate Moments
543	Born To Be Bad	01/94	Silhouette	Intimate Moments
312	Risk Factor	02/85	Silhouette	Romance
	Wild Ways	04/97	Silhouette	Wild Hearts Trilogy
	Wild Breed	07/97	Silhouette	Wild Hearts Trilogy
721	Wild Blood	07/96	Silhouette	Wild Hearts Trilogy

Horton, Susan Naomi

	Bartered Bride	06/92	Silhouette	Desire
	Road Warrior (Tentative Title)	10/92	Silhouette	Intimate Moments

Houghton, Elizabeth

485	Island Hospital	/59	Harlequin	
556	Staff Nurse In The Tyrol	/60	Harlequin	
594	Doctor Sara Comes Home	/61	Harlequin	
664	Love For The Matron	/62	Harlequin	
726	Surgeon For Tonight	/63	Harlequin	
835	Part-Time Angel (Part-Time Nurse)	/64	Harlequin	
1010	Doctor Of Research	/66	Harlequin	
1074	New Surgeon At St. Lucian's	/67	Harlequin	
1153	The Return Of Sister Barnett	/67	Harlequin	

Houghton, Elizabeth
1209   The Stubborn Dr. Stephen   /68 . Harlequin
Houseman, Jennifer
      Passion's Joy   Zebra
Houseman, Phyllis
  65   To Catch A Lorelei   11/91   Meteor
  82   Call Back Our Yesterdays   03/92   Meteor
  96   There Is A Season   06/92   Meteor
      The Verdict Is Love   02/89   Pageant
Houston, Henrietta
  75   An Improper Betrothment   /83   Berkley Regency
Houston, James
      Ghost Fox   Avon
Howard, Alyssa
 100   Southern Persuasion   11/83   Silhouette Desire
 186   Love Is Elected   11/82   Silhouette Romance
Howard, Eleanor
      Cloak Of Fate   Pocket
      Fortune's Choice   Pocket Richard Gallen Books
Howard, Jessica
      Prairie Flame   Berkley
Howard, Joy
  60   Stormy Paradise   Harlequin Superromance
Howard, Julia
 165   A Passionate Venture   /83   Dell Candlelight Ecstasy
 194   A Lasting Image   /83   Dell Candlelight Ecstasy
Howard, Linda
      Heart Of Fire   /94
      Everlasting Love   05/95   Anthology
      Summer Sizzlers   06/93   Harlequin Anthology
      Almost Forever   12/94   Mira
      An Independent Wife   04/95   Mira
      The Cutting Edge   04/95   Mira
      Duncan's Bride   07/95   Mira
      Against The Rules   01/96   Mira
      Midnight Rainbow   05/96   Mira
      Angel Creek   11/91   Pocket
      Touch Of Fire   10/92   Pocket
      A Lady Of The West   Pocket
      Dream Man   06/95   Pocket
      After The Night   12/95   Pocket
      Bluebird Winter   /87   Silhouette Christmas Stories
  22   Against The Rules   10/83   Silhouette Intimate Moments
  92   Tears Of The Renegade   04/85   Silhouette Intimate Moments
 129   Midnight Rainbow   02/86   Silhouette Intimate Moments
 177   Diamond Bay   02/87   Silhouette Intimate Moments

AUTHOR/TITLE INDEX

Howard, Linda

201	Heartbreaker	08/87	Silhouette	Intimate Moments
281	Mac Kenzie's Mountain	04/89	Silhouette	Intimate Moments
349	Duncan's Bride	09/90	Silhouette	Intimate Moments
445	Mackenzie's Mission	09/92	Silhouette	Intimate Moments
607	Loving Evangeline (American Hero)	12/94	Silhouette	Intimate Moments
691	Mackenzie's Pleasure	02/96	Silhouette	Intimate Moments
22	All That Glitters	05/82	Silhouette	Special Edition
46	An Independent Wife	09/82	Silhouette	Special Edition
177	Come Lie With Me	07/84	Silhouette	Special Edition
230	Sarah's Child	04/85	Silhouette	Special Edition
260	The Cutting Edge	09/85	Silhouette	Special Edition
327	Almost Forever	08/86	Silhouette	Special Edition
440	Mirrors	03/88	Silhouette	Special Edition
452	White Lies	05/88	Silhouette	Special Edition
	The Way Home	/91	Silhouette	To Mother With Love
	Shades Of Twilight	07/96	Simon/Schuster	

Howard, Stephanie

261	Beware A Lover's Lie	12/95	Harlequin	
268	Dangerous Pretence	02/96	Harlequin	
283	Lord Of The Manor	06/96	Harlequin	
136	Kiss And Say Goodbye	05/93	Harlequin	Direct
143	Battle For Love	07/93	Harlequin	Direct
160	Unchain My Heart	11/93	Harlequin	Direct
171	Love's Vendetta	02/94	Harlequin	Direct
183	Dangerous Inheritance	05/94	Harlequin	Direct
196	No Going Back	08/94	Harlequin	Direct
204	The Pharaoh's Kiss	10/94	Harlequin	Direct
213	Counterfeit Love	12/94	Harlequin	Direct
225	Conspiracy Of Love	03/95	Harlequin	Direct
241	A Scandalous Affair	07/95	Harlequin	Direct
1098	Reluctant Prisoner		Harlequin	Presents
1130	Dark Lucifer		Harlequin	Presents
1273	Bride For A Price		Harlequin	Presents
1307	Kiss Of The Falcon		Harlequin	Presents
1450	A Bride For Strathallane	04/92	Harlequin	Presents
3093	Master Of Glen Crannach		Harlequin	Romance
3112	An Impossible Passion		Harlequin	Romance
3153	Wicked Deceiver	10/91	Harlequin	Romance
3195	Romantic Journey	05/92	Harlequin	Romance
3220	A Matter Of Honour	09/92	Harlequin	Romance
3237	Dangerous Infatuation	12/92	Harlequin	Romance
3247	A Roman Marriage	02/93	Harlequin	Romance
3269	Kiss And Say Goodbye	05/93	Harlequin	Romance
3373	The Best For Last (Sealed With A Kiss)	08/95	Harlequin	Romance

Howard, Teresa

	Sweet Georgia Peach	02/92	Zebra

Howard, Teresa

	Cherokee Embrace	01/92	Zebra Heartfire
	Confederate Vixen	10/93	Zebra Heartfire
	Velvet Thunder	03/94	Zebra Heartfire
	Desire's Bride	11/92	Zebra Heartfire

Howard, Veronica

657	Rebel In Love		Dell Candlelight Regency

Howatch, Susan

	Cashelmara		
	Penamrric		Gothic
	Call In The Night		Suspense

Howe, Susanna

	Masquerade		Berkley

Howell, Dorothy

	Anna's Treasure	01/95	Diamond Homespun
	Tea Time	09/95	Jove Homespun

Howell, Elizabeth

	Only His		Avon

Howell, Hannah

	Defiant Enchantress		
	Conqueror's Kiss	11/91	Avon
	Kentucky Bride	03/94	Avon Historical
	Wild Conquest	05/93	Avon Historical
	Silver Flame	09/92	Avon Romance
	Compromised Hearts	10/89	Leisure
	Beauty And The Beast	09/92	Leisure Historical
	Elfking's Lady		Leisure Historical
	Promised Passion		Leisure Historical
	Stolen Ecstasy		Leisure Historical
	Amber Flame	03/93	Leisure Historical
	Elfking's Lady	07/93	Leisure Historical
	Only You	06/95	Zebra

Howey, Carole

	Touched My Moonlight	08/95	Leisure
	Sweet Chance	02/95	Leisure
	Sheik's Promise	03/94	Love Spell

Hoy, Elizabeth

433	Because Of Doctor Danville	/58	Harlequin
449	Come Back, My Dream (Nurse In Training)	/59	Harlequin
472	Young Doctor Kirkdene	/59	Harlequin
483	My Heart Has Wings	/59	Harlequin
491	Nurse Tennant	/59	Harlequin
497	You Took My Heart (Doctor Garth)	/59	Harlequin
501	Do Something Dangerous	/59	Harlequin
507	It's Wise To Forget	/60	Harlequin
526	When You Have Found Me	/60	Harlequin

AUTHOR/TITLE INDEX

Hudson, Jan

397	Step Into My Parlor	05/90	Bantam	Loveswept
443	Deeper And Deeper	12/90	Bantam	Loveswept
464	Big And Bright	04/91	Bantam	Loveswept
529	Call Me Sin	03/92	Bantam	Loveswept
584	Sunny Says	12/92	Bantam	Loveswept
663	Fly With Me	01/94	Bantam	Loveswept
667	Slightly Shady	02/94	Bantam	Loveswept
700	One Tough Texan	07/94	Bantam	Loveswept
716	Hot Streak	11/94	Bantam	Loveswept
755	Rogue Fever	09/95	Bantam	Loveswept
	Dream Of Me	05/95	Pinnacle	Denise Little Presents
	Angel Hours	10/96	Pinnacle	Denise Little Presents

Hudson, Janis Reams

613	Truth Or Dare	05/93	Bantam	Loveswept
731	Caught In The Act	03/95	Bantam	Loveswept
744	Thick As Thieves	05/95	Bantam	Loveswept
775	Angel On A Harley	02/96	Bantam	Loveswept
	Worth The Effort	09/93	Meteor	
29	Foster Love	02/91	Meteor	
72	Coming Home	12/91	Meteor	
103	For The Thrill	08/92	Meteor	
	Remember My Heart	09/95	Pinnacle	
1037	Resist Me If You Can	06/96	Silhouette	Special Edition
	Apache Temptation	09/93	Zebra	
	Apache Legacy	06/94	Zebra	
	Apache Magic		Zebra	Heartfire
	Wild Texas Flame		Zebra	Heartfire
	Apache Heartsong	03/95	Zebra	Lovegram
	Apache Flame	04/96	Zebra	Lovegram
2	Sammi's Heart	09/92	Zebra	Lucky In Love

Hudson, Meg

25	To Love A Stranger		Harlequin American
9	Sweet Dawn Of Desire		Harlequin Superromance
36	Love's Sound In Silence		Harlequin Superromance
53	Return To Rapture		Harlequin Superromance
64	Though Hearts Resist		Harlequin Superromance
70	A Charm For Adonis		Harlequin Superromance
79	Two Worlds, One Love		Harlequin Superromance
94	Beloved Stranger		Harlequin Superromance
106	The Rising Road		Harlequin Superromance
126	Now, In September		Harlequin Superromance
141	Champagne Promises		Harlequin Superromance
174	A Gift From The Sea		Harlequin Superromance
188	More Than A Memory		Harlequin Superromance
234	The Forever Promise		Harlequin Superromance
250	A Way To Remember		Harlequin Superromance

Hudson, Meg

274	Chance Meeting		Harlequin Superromance
295	The Day Before Dawn		Harlequin Superromance
357	Until April		Harlequin Superromance
465	The Leftover Girl	08/91	Harlequin Superromance

Hughes, Cally

	A Lasting Treasure	/83	Berkley Second Chance At Love
	Innocent Seduction	/83	Berkley Second Chance At Love
	Cupid's Revenge	/83	Berkley Second Chance At Love
	Whatever It Takes	/84	Berkley To Have And To Hold
	Treasure To Share	/84	Berkley To Have And To Hold
	Never Too Late	/84	Berkley To Have And To Hold
15	Whatever It Takes	/84	Berkley To Have And To Hold
25	Treasure To Share	/84	Berkley To Have And To Hold

Hughes, Charlotte

159	Too Many Husbands	10/86	Bantam Loveswept
220	Straight Shootin' Lady	11/87	Bantam Loveswept
241	Travelin' Man	03/88	Bantam Loveswept
297	Sweet Misery	12/88	Bantam Loveswept
345	Tigress	08/89	Bantam Loveswept
365	Scoundrel	11/89	Bantam Loveswept
409	Private Eyes	07/90	Bantam Loveswept
433	Restless Nights	11/90	Bantam Loveswept
445	Louisiana Lovin'	01/91	Bantam Loveswept
475	Tough Guy, Savvy Lady	06/91	Bantam Loveswept
494	The Lady And The Cowboy	09/91	Bantam Loveswept
556	Rascal	07/92	Bantam Loveswept
578	Island Rogue	11/92	Bantam Loveswept
596	The Incredible Hunk	02/93	Bantam Loveswept
654	Kissed By A Rogue	12/93	Bantam Loveswept
684	The Devil And Miss Goody Two-Shoes	05/94	Bantam Loveswept
719	The Cop And The Mother-To-Be	12/94	Bantam Loveswept
734	Husband Wanted	03/95	Bantam Loveswept
764	Ready-Made Family	09/95	Bantam Loveswept
	Moonlight, Madness And Magic	05/93	Doubleday Anthology

Hughes, Dorothy B.

| 44 | The So Blue Marble | /50 | Harlequin |

Hughes, Faye

736	Can't Fight The Feeling	03/95	Bantam Loveswept
756	Gotta Have It	09/95	Bantam Loveswept
777	Wild At Heart	02/96	Bantam Loveswept

Hughes, Linda

| 144 | Outside The Rules | 04/93 | Meteor Kismet |

Hughes, Samantha

| 179 | Desert Splendor | /83 | Dell Candlelight Ecstasy |

Hughes, Tracy

AUTHOR/TITLE INDEX

Hughes, Tracy

381	Honorbound		Harlequin American
410	Second Chances	10/91	Harlequin American
438	Father Knows Best	05/92	Harlequin American
455	Sand Man	09/92	Harlequin American
502	Delta Dust	09/93	Harlequin American
542	Heaven Knows	07/94	Harlequin American
578	To Heaven And Back (Heartbeat)	04/95	Harlequin American
2744	Quiet Lightning		Harlequin Romance
2792	Impressions		Harlequin Romance
304	Above The Clouds		Harlequin Superromance
342	Calloway Corners: Jo	09/93	Harlequin Superromance
381	Emerald Windows		Harlequin Superromance
399	White Lies & Alibis		Harlequin Superromance
594	The Princess And The Pauper	06/94	Harlequin Superromance
623	Catch A Falling Star (Showcase)	12/94	Harlequin Superromance

Hughesdon, Beverly

	Song Of Songs		Warner

Hulme, Anne

8	The Unexpected American	08/89	Harlequin Regency
40	A Scandalous Bargain	12/90	Harlequin Regency
49	False Fortune	05/91	Harlequin Regency
26	A Poor Relation		Mills & Boon

Humphrey, Aileen

	The Golden Swan		Diamond
	Love Potion	02/95	Jove Anthology
	Sweet Iris	07/94	Jove Tea Rose Romance

Hungengerg, Kristin

	Unknown Dreams	03/93	Avalon

Hunt, Angela Elweel

1	Dreamers	01/96	Bethany House Trilogy
	Roanoke	01/96	Tyndale House Keepers Of The Rings
	Jamestown	01/96	Tyndale House Keepers Of The Rings
1	Afton Of Margate Castle	/93	Tyndale House Theyn Chronicles

Hunt, Howard

3	Maelstrom	/49	Harlequin

Hunt, Jena

55	Sweet Victory	/82	Berkley Second Chance At Love

Hunter, Elizabeth

654	Cherry-Blossom Clinic	/62	Harlequin
1071	Spiced With Cloves	/66	Harlequin
1758	The Crescent Moon	/74	Harlequin
1780	The Tower Of The Winds	/74	Harlequin
1807	The Tree Of Idleness	/74	Harlequin
1844	The Beads Of Nemesis	/75	Harlequin
1888	The Bonds Of Matrimony	/75	Harlequin

Hunter, Elizabeth

1912	The Spanish Inheritance	/75	Harlequin
1926	The Voice In The Thunder	/75	Harlequin
1940	The Sycamore Song	/76	Harlequin
2032	The Bride Price	/76	Harlequin
2048	The Realms Of Gold	/77	Harlequin
2120	Pride Of Madeira	/77	Harlequin
18	The Lion's Shadow	07/80	Silhouette Romance
51	Bride Of The Sun	12/80	Silhouette Romance
65	A Touch Of Magic	03/81	Silhouette Romance
91	Written In The Stars	07/81	Silhouette Romance
137	One More Time	03/82	Silhouette Romance
167	A Silver Nutmeg	08/82	Silhouette Romance
198	London Pride	01/83	Silhouette Romance
218	Fountains Of Paradise	04/83	Silhouette Romance
240	Shared Destiny	08/83	Silhouette Romance
257	A Tower Of Strength	11/83	Silhouette Romance
268	Kiss Of The Rising Sun	01/84	Silhouette Romance
278	A Time To Wed	02/84	Silhouette Romance
290	Rain On The Wind	04/84	Silhouette Romance
298	Song Of Surrender	06/84	Silhouette Romance
310	Loving Relations	08/84	Silhouette Romance
322	Pathway To Heaven	10/84	Silhouette Romance
360	Legend Of The Sun	05/85	Silhouette Romance
385	Eye Of The Wind	09/85	Silhouette Romance
438	The Painted Veil	06/86	Silhouette Romance
577	The Tides Of Love	05/88	Silhouette Romance

Hunter, Hillary

496	Cooper's Last Stand	06/94	Harlequin Temptation

Hunter, Jillian

	Tiger Dance	09/91	Avon
	Shadows Of Splendor		Avon
	A Deeper Magic	08/94	Pinnacle Denise Little Presents
	Glenlyon's Bride	09/95	Pinnacle Denise Little Presents

Hunter, Joan

	Roxanna
	Under The Raging Moon
	Cavalier's Woman
	Lord Of Kestle Mount

Hunton, Mary

611	Nurse Blade's First Week	/61	Harlequin
729	One With The Wind (Surgeons At Arms)	/63	Harlequin
·1041	Nurse Averil's Ward	/66	Harlequin

Hurley, Ann

181	Chasing The Rainbow	01/85	Silhouette Desire
233	Year Of The Poet	09/85	Silhouette Desire

AUTHOR/TITLE INDEX

Hyatt, Betty Hale

196	Portrait Of Errin		Dell Candlelight
208	The Brigand's Bride		Dell Candlelight
210	Villa San Gabriel		Dell Candlelight
257	The Chevalier's Lady		Dell Candlelight Regency
257	The Chevalier's Lady		Dell Candlelight Regency
	Fandora's Story		Playboy Press
	Anna's Story		Playboy Press
	Linnet's Story		Playboy Press
	The Vesper Bells	/67	Valentine

Hylton, Sara

	The Crimson Falcon		
	Desert Splendor		

Ibbotson, Eva

	Company Of Swans		Avon
	Countess Below Stairs		Avon
	Madensky Square	09/91	Avon
	Magic Flutes		Warner

Ihle, Sharon

	The Law And Miss Penny	11/94	Harper
	Marrying Miss Shylo	11/94	Harper
	Wild Cat	10/93	Harper Historical
	Wild Rose	04/93	Harper Historical
	The Marrying Kind	03/96	Harper Historical
	The Bride Wore Spurs	06/95	Harper Monogram

Ingrahm, Pamela

964	Cowboy Homecoming	11/95	Silhouette Desire

Inman, Elizabeth

	The Rake's Quarry	11/94	Zebra Regency

Innes, Jean

	Secret Touch		Zebra
	Blackmaddie	07/92	Zebra Gothic
	Buccaneer's Bride		Zebra Heartfire
	Dream Lover		Zebra Heartfire
	Golden Captive		Zebra Heartfire
	Love's Fortune	05/95	Zebra Lovegram

Ireland, Liz

639	Heaven-Sent Husband	07/96	Harlequin American
286	Cecilia And The Stranger	09/95	Harlequin Historical
330	Millie And The Fugitive	08/96	Harlequin Historical
963	Man Trap	09/93	Silhouette Romance
988	The Birds And The Bees (Fabulous Fathers)	02/94	Silhouette Romance
1058	Mom For A Week (Mr. Right, Inc.)	01/95	Silhouette Romance

Irwin, Margaret

	Gay Gailiard		Historical

Issacs, Susan

Issacs, Susan

| | Magic Hour | 02/92 | Harper |
| | Close Relations | 02/92 | Harper |

Ives, Averil

624	Nurse Linnet's Release	/61	Harlequin
632	Nurse For The Doctor	/61	Harlequin
683	Desire For The Star (Doctor's Desire)	/62	Harlequin
872	Haven Of The Heart	/64	Harlequin
984	Island In The Dawn	/66	Harlequin
1047	Master Of Hearts	/66	Harlequin

Jac, Cheryln

| | Hearts Deceived | 05/94 | Zebra |

Jack, Cherylyn

| | Night's Immortal Touch | 06/95 | Pinnacle |

Jackson, Eileen

	A Servant Of Quality	07/88	Nal Regency
	The Secret Bluestocking		Nal Penguin Regency
	Lord Revington's Lady		Nal Penguin Regency

Jackson, Elizabeth

| | Wicked Corinthian | | Nal |
| | A Brilliant Alliance | 03/93 | Penguin Regency |

Jackson, Helen Hunt

| | Ramona | | Avon |

Jackson, Lisa

	Lover, Come Back	02/94	Harlequin Anthology
	The Millionaire And The Cowgirl	08/96	Harlequin Fortune's Children
	Yesterday's Lies	10/95	Harlequin Western Lovers
	1993 Christmas Stories	11/93	Silhouette Anthology
79	Gypsy Wind	01/85	Silhouette Intimate Moments
158	Mystic	09/86	Silhouette Intimate Moments
717	His Bride To Be	04/90	Silhouette Romance
118	A Twist Of Fate	09/83	Silhouette Special Edition
180	The Shadow Of Time	07/84	Silhouette Special Edition
194	Tears Of Pride	10/84	Silhouette Special Edition
215	Pirate's Gold	01/85	Silhouette Special Edition
233	A Dangerous Precedent	04/85	Silhouette Special Edition
244	Innocent By Association	06/85	Silhouette Special Edition
264	Midnight Sun	09/85	Silhouette Special Edition
282	Devil's Gambit	12/85	Silhouette Special Edition
296	Zachary's Law	03/86	Silhouette Special Edition
315	Yesterday's Lies	06/86	Silhouette Special Edition
358	One Man's Love	01/87	Silhouette Special Edition
376	Renegade Son	04/87	Silhouette Special Edition
394	Snowbound	07/87	Silhouette Special Edition
419	Summer Rain	11/87	Silhouette Special Edition
467	Prodigal Brother	07/88	Silhouette Special Edition

AUTHOR/TITLE INDEX

Jackson, Lisa

495	In Honor's Shadow	12/88	Silhouette	Special Edition
525	Aftermath	05/89	Silhouette	Special Edition
569	Tender Trap	12/89	Silhouette	Special Edition
611	With No Regrets	07/90	Silhouette	Special Edition
636	Double Exposure	11/90	Silhouette	Special Edition
653	Mystery Man	02/91	Silhouette	Special Edition
691	Obsession	09/91	Silhouette	Special Edition
720	Sail Away	01/92	Silhouette	Special Edition
743	Million Dollar Baby	05/92	Silhouette	Special Edition
787	He's A Bad Boy	01/93	Silhouette	Special Edition
799	He's Just A Cowboy	03/93	Silhouette	Special Edition
811	He's The Rich Boy	05/93	Silhouette	Special Edition
835	A Husband To Remember	09/93	Silhouette	Special Edition
866	He's My Soldier Boy (Mavericks)	02/94	Silhouette	Special Edition
914	A Is For Always (Love Letters)	10/94	Silhouette	Special Edition
920	B Is For Baby (Love Letters)	11/94	Silhouette	Special Edition
926	C Is For Cowboy (Love Letters)	12/94	Silhouette	Special Edition
985	D Is For Dani's Baby	10/95	Silhouette	Special Edition
1004	New Year's Daddy	01/96	Silhouette	Special Edition
	Treasures	02/94	Zebra	
	Wishes	12/95	Zebra	
	Intimacies	02/95	Zebra	
	Wishes	11/95	Zebra	

Jacobs, Lynn

101	Dangerous Engagement	01/92	Harlequin	Direct
117	Stars In Their Eyes	09/92	Harlequin	Direct
193	Risk To Love	07/94	Harlequin	Direct
3020	Folly To Love		Harlequin	Romance

Jade, Jacqueline

316	A Lucky Star	11/86	Silhouette	Desire

Jaffre, Susanne

Promises And Lies

Jagger, Brenda

An Independent Woman	Nal Penguin
The Barforth Women	Nal Penguin
A Song Twice Over	Nal Penguin

Jakes, John

California Gold	
The Bastard	Kent Family Chronicles
The Rebels	Kent Family Chronicles
The Seekers	Kent Family Chronicles
The Fairies	Kent Family Chronicles
The Titans	Kent Family Chronicles
The Warriors	Kent Family Chronicles
The Lawless	Kent Family Chronicles

AUTHOR/TITLE INDEX

Jakes, John

The Americans		Kent Family Chronicles
North And South		The North And South Trilogy
Love And War		The North And South Trilogy
Heaven And Hell		The North And South Trilogy

James, Amalia

Dream Images	/82	Bantam
Tangled Promises	/82	Bantam
Midsummer Dreams	/82	Bantam

James, Anna

	Day Beyond Destiny	/81	Jove	
	The Darker Side Of Love	/80	Jove	
	Sweet Love, Better Love	/79	Jove	
	A World Of Her Own		Richard Gallen	
13	Edge Of Love	08/83	Silhouette	Intimate Moments
42	Her Own Rules	03/84	Silhouette	Intimate Moments
65	Love On The Line	09/84	Silhouette	Intimate Moments
104	The Venetian Necklace	07/85	Silhouette	Intimate Moments
115	Nina's Songs	10/85	Silhouette	Intimate Moments
135	Images	03/86	Silhouette	Intimate Moments
147	The Reluctant Swan	06/86	Silhouette	Intimate Moments
167	The Dream Makers	11/86	Silhouette	Intimate Moments
207	Passage To Zaphir	09/87	Silhouette	Intimate Moments
255	Stairway To The Moon	09/88	Silhouette	Intimate Moments
286	The Treasure Of Kavos	05/89	Silhouette	Intimate Moments
371	Their Song Unending	03/87	Silhouette	Special Edition

James, Arlene

24	The Perfect Wedding	06/96	Harlequin	Here Come The Grooms
6	Married With Children	/96	Silhouette	Fortune's Children
2	Proud Spirit	/96	Silhouette	Inspirations
11	A Wish For Always	/96	Silhouette	Inspirations
16	Partners For Life	/96	Silhouette	Inspirations
27	No Stranger To Love	/96	Silhouette	Inspirations
	Desperately Seeking Daddy	/96	Silhouette	Romance
141	City Girl	03/82	Silhouette	Romance
235	No Easy Conquest	07/83	Silhouette	Romance
253	Two Of A Kind	10/83	Silhouette	Romance
327	A Meeting Of Hearts	10/84	Silhouette	Romance
384	An Obvious Virtue	09/85	Silhouette	Romance
404	Now Or Never	12/85	Silhouette	Romance
421	Reason Enough	03/86	Silhouette	Romance
446	The Right Moves	07/86	Silhouette	Romance
471	Strange Bedfellows	11/86	Silhouette	Romance
495	The Private Garden	03/87	Silhouette	Romance
518	The Boy Next Door	07/87	Silhouette	Romance
559	Under A Desert Sky	02/88	Silhouette	Romance
578	A Delicate Balance	05/88	Silhouette	Romance

AUTHOR/TITLE INDEX

James, Arlene

614	The Discerning Heart	11/88	Silhouette	Romance
661	Dream Of A Lifetime	07/89	Silhouette	Romance
687	Finally Home	11/89	Silhouette	Romance
705	A Perfect Gentleman	02/90	Silhouette	Romance
728	Family Man	06/90	Silhouette	Romance
770	A Man Of His Word	01/91	Silhouette	Romance
806	Tough Guy	07/91	Silhouette	Romance
830	Gold Digger	11/91	Silhouette	Romance
866	Palace City Prince	05/92	Silhouette	Romance
962	The Perfect Wedding	09/93	Silhouette	Romance
968	An Old-Fashioned Lover	10/93	Silhouette	Romance
974	A Wife Worth Waiting For	11/93	Silhouette	Romance
1024	Mail-Order Brood (Fabulous Fathers)	08/94	Silhouette	Romance
1061	The Rogue Who Came To Stay	02/95	Silhouette	Romance
1144	Most Wanted Dad	04/96	Silhouette	Romance
664	A Rumor Of Love	04/91	Silhouette	Special Edition
776	Husband In The Making	11/92	Silhouette	Special Edition
869	With Baby In Mind	02/94	Silhouette	Special Edition
964	Child Of Her Heart	06/95	Silhouette	Special Edition

James, B. J.

	More Than Friends	11/92	Bantam	Fanfare
60	When You Speak Love	09/84	Bantam	Loveswept
73	More Than Friends	12/84	Bantam	Loveswept
84	A Stranger Called Adam	03/85	Bantam	Loveswept
332	The Sound Of Goodbye	02/87	Silhouette	Desire
396	Twice In A Lifetime	12/87	Silhouette	Desire
529	Shiloh's Promise	11/89	Silhouette	Desire
595	Winter Morning	10/90	Silhouette	Desire
672	Slade's Woman	10/91	Silhouette	Desire
692	A Step Away	02/92	Silhouette	Desire
709	Tears Of The Rose	05/92	Silhouette	Desire
751	The Man With The Midnight Eyes	12/92	Silhouette	Desire
789	Pride And Promises	06/93	Silhouette	Desire
823	Another Time, Another Place	12/93	Silhouette	Desire
844	The Hand Of An Angel	03/94	Silhouette	Desire
945	Heart Of The Hunter	08/95	Silhouette	Desire
951	The Saint Of Bourbon Street	09/95	Silhouette	Desire
956	A Wolf In The Desert	10/95	Silhouette	Desire
	Broken Spurs	09/96	Silhouette	Intimate Moments

James, Dana

125	A Tempting Shore	01/93	Harlequin	Direct
162	Bay Of Rainbows	11/93	Harlequin	Direct
2632	Desert Flower		Harlequin	Romance
2841	The Marati Legacy		Harlequin	Romance
2872	The Eagle And The Sun		Harlequin	Romance
2926	Tarik's Mountain		Harlequin	Romance

AUTHOR/TITLE INDEX

James, Dana

2973	Snowfire	Harlequin Romance
2992	Pool Of Dreaming	Harlequin Romance
3068	Love's Ransom	Harlequin Romance

James, Deana

	Love Fire	
	Texas Storm	
	Texas Torment	
	Seek Only Passion	07/94
	Acts Of Passion	Zebra
	Captive Angel	Zebra
	Crimson Obsession	Zebra
	Masque Of Sapphire	Zebra
	Speak Only Love	Zebra
	Texas Star	Zebra
	Wild Texas Heart	Zebra
	Love Stone	Zebra
	Love Spell	Zebra
	Texas Tempest	Zebra
	Angel's Caress	07/89 Zebra
	Beloved Rogue	08/94 Zebra
	Duchess	09/95 Zebra

James, Deborah

	Warrior's Touch	07/94
	Beloved Warrior	06/93 Berkley Historical
	Amazing Grace	03/95 Diamond A Town Called Harmony
	Golden Fury	11/92 Diamond Wildflower
	Tender Outlaw	09/94 Diamond Wildflower

James, Ellen

3052	Home For Love	Harlequin Romance
3069	The Turquoise Heart	Harlequin Romance
3118	Two Against Love	Harlequin Romance
3154	Love's Harbor	10/91 Harlequin Romance
3202	Love Your Enemy	06/92 Harlequin Romance
3254	Growing Attraction	03/93 Harlequin Romance
3291	Home For Christmas	12/93 Harlequin Romance
3329	The Confirmed Bachelor	09/94 Harlequin Romance
613	Tempting Eve	09/94 Harlequin Superromance
641	Forbidden (Women Who Dare)	04/95 Harlequin Superromance
651	A Kiss Too Late (Reunited)	07/95 Harlequin Superromance
685	Mother In The Making	03/96 Harlequin Superromance

James, Kristen

	The Golden Sky	Richard Gallen
	Summer Sky	Richard Gallen
	The Sapphire Sky	Richard Gallen

James, Kristin

AUTHOR/TITLE INDEX

James, Kristin

	Promised Brides - "Jesse's Wife"	04/96	Harlequin Anthology
1	Satan's Angel	07/88	Harlequin Historical
43	The Gentleman		Harlequin Historical
57	The Yankee		Harlequin Historical
62	A Wedding Gift	06/85	Harlequin Temptation
	Tumbleweed Christmas	/89	Sil. Hist. Christmas Stories
962	Once In A Blue Moon	11/95	Silhouette Desire
986	The Last Groom On Earth	03/96	Silhouette Desire
1	Dreams Of Evening	05/83	Silhouette Intimate Moments
17	The Amber Sky	09/83	Silhouette Intimate Moments
45	Morning Star	04/84	Silhouette Intimate Moments
69	Secret Fires	10/84	Silhouette Intimate Moments
89	Worlds Apart	04/85	Silhouette Intimate Moments
125	Cutter's Lady	01/86	Silhouette Intimate Moments
136	A Very Special Flavor	03/86	Silhouette Intimate Moments
385	Salt Of The Earth	06/91	Silhouette Intimate Moments
393	The Letter Of The Law	08/91	Silhouette Intimate Moments

James, Margaret

545	Ring The Bell Softly		Dell Candlelight

James, Nicola

	Love's Silent Promise	/91	Avalon

James, Robin

58	The Golden Touch	/82	Berkley Second Chance At Love
1	The Testimony	/84	Berkley To Have And To Hold

James, Sally

	Heir To Rowanlea		Ballantine Historical

James, Samantha

	Outlaw Heart	11/93	Avon
	My Cherished Heart		Avon
	My Rebellious Heart	04/93	Avon
	Gabriel's Bride	05/94	Avon Historical
	My Lord Conqueror	03/95	Avon Historical
	My Cherished Enemy	05/92	Avon Romance

James, Sandra

44	To Tame The Hunter	/95	Harlequin Men Made In America
205	A Family Affair		Harlequin Superromance
249	Belonging		Harlequin Superromance
277	Stronger By Far		Harlequin Superromance
306	Guardian Angel	03/88	Harlequin Superromance
335	Spring Thunder		Harlequin Superromance
352	Summer Lightning		Harlequin Superromance
386	North Of Eden		Harlequin Superromance
435	Almost Heaven		Harlequin Superromance
456	Gun Shy		Harlequin Superromance
514	Nothing But Trouble	09/92	Harlequin Superromance

573

AUTHOR/TITLE INDEX

AUTHOR/TITLE INDEX

Jenkins, Kate
227 Suddenly, Sunshine 11/88 Harlequin Temptation
269 The Reluctant Bachelor 10/89 Harlequin Temptation
343 Terminally Single 04/91 Harlequin Temptation

Jenkins, Linda
498 Too Far To Fall 10/91 Bantam Loveswept
548 Mr. Wonderful 06/92 Bantam Loveswept
612 Tall Order 05/93 Bantam Loveswept
639 Secret Admirer 09/93 Bantam Loveswept
677 Wicked Ways 03/94 Bantam Loveswept
86 Maverick's Lady 04/92 Meteor

Jenkins, Vivian Knight
36 By Love Possessed 07/94 Harlequin Shadows

Jennet, Anna
Timeless 05/94 Berkley Anthology
Reckless 03/93 Diamond Historical
Fire 11/95 Jove Historical
My Lady Captor 05/96 Jove Historical

Jensen, Kathryn
685 Time And Again 01/96 Silhouette Intimate Moments

Jensen, Muriel
73 Winter's Bounty Harlequin American
119 Lovers Never Lose Harlequin American
176 The Mallory Touch Harlequin American
200 Fantasies And Memories Harlequin American
219 Love And Lavender Harlequin American
244 The Duck Shack Agreement Harlequin American
267 Stings Harlequin American
283 Side By Side Harlequin American
321 A Carol Christmas Harlequin American
339 Everything Harlequin American
358 A Wild Iris Harlequin American
392 The Miracle Harlequin American
414 Racing With The Moon 11/91 Harlequin American
425 Valentine Heart And Flowers 02/92 Harlequin American
464 Middle Of The Rainbow 02/93 Harlequin American
478 One And One Makes Three 03/93 Harlequin American
507 The Unexpected Groom 10/93 Harlequin American
522 Night Prince 02/94 Harlequin American
534 Make-Believe Mom 06/94 Harlequin American
549 The Wedding Gamble (Weddings, Inc.) 09/94 Harlequin American
569 The Courtship Of Dusty's Daddy 02/95 Harlequin American
603 Mommy On Board 10/95 Harlequin American
606 Make Way For Mommy 11/95 Harlequin American
610 Merry Christmas, Mommy 12/95 Harlequin American
My Comic Valentine 1994 02/94 Harlequin Anthology

Johansen, Iris

	Satin Ice	/84	Bantam	
	This Fierce Splendor	/84	Bantam	
	Midnight Warrior	08/94	Bantam	
	Dark Rider	04/95	Bantam	
	Lion's Bride	/95	Bantam	
	The Ugly Duckling	05/96	Bantam	
	Matilda, The Adventuress	/84	Bantam	Delaneys Of Killaroo
	The Golden Barbarian	02/91	Bantam	Fanfare
	Storm Winds	06/91	Bantam	Fanfare
	Reap The Wind	10/91	Bantam	Fanfare
	Last Bridge Home	09/92	Bantam	Fanfare
	The Wind Dancer	02/90	Bantam	Fanfare
	The Magnificent Rogue	08/93	Bantam	Historical
	The Beloved Scoundrel	01/94	Bantam	Historical
14	Stormy Vows	08/83	Bantam	Loveswept
17	Tempest At Sea	09/83	Bantam	Loveswept
29	The Lady And The Unicorn	01/84	Bantam	Loveswept
31	The Golden Valkyrif	01/84	Bantam	Loveswept
35	The Trustworthy Redhead	03/84	Bantam	Loveswept
40	Return To Santa Flores	04/84	Bantam	Loveswept
44	No Red Roses	05/84	Bantam	Loveswept
55	Capture The Rainbow	08/84	Bantam	Loveswept
59	Touch The Horizon	09/84	Bantam	Loveswept
82	White Satin	02/85	Bantam	Loveswept
86	Blue Velvet	03/85	Bantam	Loveswept
122	A Summer Smile	12/85	Bantam	Loveswept
126	And The Desert Blooms	01/86	Bantam	Loveswept
148	Always	07/86	Bantam	Loveswept
152	Everlasting	08/86	Bantam	Loveswept
176	' Til The End Of Time	01/87	Bantam	Loveswept
187	Last Bridge Home	04/87	Bantam	Loveswept
191	Across The River Of Yesterday	05/87	Bantam	Loveswept
221	The Spellbinder	11/87	Bantam	Loveswept
232	Star Light, Star Bright	01/88	Bantam	Loveswept
257	Man From Half Moon Bay	05/88	Bantam	Loveswept
274	Blue Skies And Shining Promises	08/88	Bantam	Loveswept
280	Strong, Hot Winds	09/88	Bantam	Loveswept
342	Magnificent Folly	08/89	Bantam	Loveswept
364	Wicked Jake Darcy	11/89	Bantam	Loveswept
378	Notorious	02/90	Bantam	Loveswept
420	Tender Savage	09/90	Bantam	Loveswept
438	An Unexpected Song	12/90	Bantam	Loveswept
481	A Tough Man To Tame	07/91	Bantam	Loveswept
522	Winter Bride	02/92	Bantam	Loveswept
622	Star-Spangled Bride	06/93	Bantam	Loveswept
168	York, The Renegade		Bantam	Loveswept: Shamrock Trinity

Johansen, Iris

| | Wild Silver | /84 | Bantam The Delaneys |
| | Golden Barbarian | | Doubleday |

John, Nancy

119	Night With A Stranger	02/84	Silhouette Desire
292	Secret Love	07/86	Silhouette Desire
17	Tormenting Flame	07/80	Silhouette Romance
34	The Spanish House	10/80	Silhouette Romance
57	To Trust Tomorrow	01/81	Silhouette Romance
85	Outback Summer	06/81	Silhouette Romance
115	A Man For Always	11/81	Silhouette Romance
192	Make-Believe Bride	12/82	Silhouette Romance
262	Window To Happiness	12/83	Silhouette Romance
431	Lookalike Love	05/86	Silhouette Romance
17	So Many Tomorrows	04/82	Silhouette Special Edition
38	Web Of Passion	08/82	Silhouette Special Edition
75	Summer Rhapsody	02/83	Silhouette Special Edition
106	Never Too Late	07/83	Silhouette Special Edition
166	Dream Of Yesterday	05/84	Silhouette Special Edition
193	Champagne Nights	10/84	Silhouette Special Edition
219	Rendezvous	02/85	Silhouette Special Edition
238	The Moongate Wish	05/85	Silhouette Special Edition

Johns, Karen

| | Proud Surrender | | Avon |

Johns, Michele

| | Heart Sounds | 04/93 | Harper |

Johnson, Barbara Ferry

	The Heirs Of Love		Avon
	Delta Blood		Avon
	Homeward Winds The River		Avon
	Lioness		Avon
	Tara's Song		Avon

Johnson, Betsy

21	Wedding Eve	06/96	Harlequin Here Come The Grooms
585	Private Wagers	03/90	Silhouette Special Edition
766	Wedding Eve	09/92	Silhouette Special Edition

Johnson, Claire

| 760 | Dragon's Point | | Harlequin Presents |

Johnson, Janice Kay

483	Seize The Day	01/92	Harlequin Superromance
561	Home Again	08/93	Harlequin Superromance
627	Her Sister's Baby (9 Months)	01/95	Harlequin Superromance
648	In The Dark Of The Night	06/95	Harlequin Superromance
677	His Friend's Wife	01/96	Harlequin Superromance
149	Night And Day	04/87	Harlequin Temptation

Johnson, Katrina

Johnson, Katrina
  183   Evening Street   /52   Harlequin

Johnson, Linda O.
      A Glimpse Of Forever   12/95   Leisure

Johnson, Martha
      Legacy Of Dreams   06/95   Harper Ghost Suspense
      Deadly Secret   02/94   Zebra Suspense

Johnson, Maud B.
      Tomorrow And Forever   Richard Gallen

Johnson, Susan
      The Play
      Hot Streak
      Love Storm   06/95   Bantam
      Pure Sin   11/94   Bantam
      Brazen   11/95   Bantam
      Breathless   11/96   Bantam
    1   Blaze   09/92   Bantam Braddock-Black Series
    2   Silver Flame   06/93   Bantam Braddock-Black Series
    3   Forbidden   09/91   Bantam Braddock-Black Series
      Sweet Love Survive   06/96   Bantam Fanfare
      Outlaw   11/93   Bantam Fanfare
      Sinful   02/93   Doubleday
      Seized By Love   10/93   Doubleday
  51   Golden Paradise   Harlequin Historical

Johnson, Velda
      Presence In An Empty Room   Gothic
      Silver Dolphin   Suspense

Johnston, Coleen L.
      King's Flower   01/93   St. Martin's American Coverlett

Johnston, Joan
      Coulter's Wife
      To Have And To Hold   06/94   Avon Anthology
      A Christmas Together   10/94   Avon Anthology
      The Barefoot Bride   01/92   Dell
      Sweetwater Seduction   Dell
      Outlaw's Bride   11/93   Dell
      Captive   04/96   Dell
      Maverick Heart   12/95   Dell
      Kid Calhoun   03/93   Dell Historical
      "One Simple Wish"   07/93   Harlequin Anthology
      Outlaws & Heroes - "Taming The Lone Wol 09/95   Harlequin Anthology
      Loving Defiance   Pocket
      Comanche Woman   Pocket Texas Trilogy
      Frontier Woman   Pocket Texas Trilogy
      Texas Woman   Pocket Texas Trilogy
      Abduction And Seduction 03/95   Silhouette Anthology

Johnston, Joan

424	Fit To Be Tied	05/88	Silhouette Desire
489	Marriage By The Book	04/89	Silhouette Desire
652	Never Tease A Wolf	07/91	Silhouette Desire
658	A Wolf In Sheep's Clothing	08/91	Silhouette Desire
710	A Little Time In Texas	05/92	Silhouette Desire
746	Honey And The Hired Hand	11/92	Silhouette Desire
779	The Rancher And The Runaway Bride	04/93	Silhouette Desire
785	The Cowboy And The Princess	05/93	Silhouette Desire
791	The Wrangler And The Rich Girl	06/93	Silhouette Desire
842	The Cowboy Takes A Wife (Hawk's Way)	03/94	Silhouette Desire
878	The Unforgiving Bride (Hawk's Way)	09/94	Silhouette Desire
896	The Headstrong Bride (Hawk's Way)	12/94	Silhouette Desire
937	The Disobedient Bride	07/95	Silhouette Desire
1004	The Temporary Groom	06/96	Silhouette Desire

Johnston, Linda O.

A Glimpse Of Forever	12/95	Leisure Time-Travel
The Glass Slipper	07/96	Love Spell

Jones, H. Bedford

228	Drums Of Dambala	/53	Harlequin
232	Malay Gold	/53	Harlequin

Jones, Jenna

A Delicate Deception	07/96	Kensington Regency
A Merry Escapade	08/95	Zebra Regency

Jones, Jill

Emily's Secret	07/95	St. Martin's

Jones, Kathy

Rebel's Mistress	11/91	Zebra
Sweet Obsession		Zebra
Counterfeit Caress		Zebra
Defiant Captive		Zebra Heartfire
Golden Fire		Zebra Heartfire

Jones, Marian

68	Bonds Of Enchantment	Harlequin Superromance

Jones, Marti

A Love Through Time		Leisure
Stardust Time	/95	Leisure
Blind Fortune	/95	Leisure
Dreamweaver	08/94	Leisure Historical
Time's Healing Heart	06/94	Leisure Lovespell

Jones, Melissa Lynn

An Alluring Deceit		
Out Of The Common Way	09/93	Fawcett Crest Regency

Jones, Paula

To Spite The Devil	07/94	Pinnacle Denise Little Presents
Beloved Enemy	07/94	Simon/Schuster

Jordan, Penny

Jordan, Penny

1057	A Savage Adoration		Harlequin	Presents
1075	Loving		Harlequin	Presents
1089	Fight For Love		Harlequin	Presents
1105	Substitute Lover		Harlequin	Presents
1113	Levelling The Score		Harlequin	Presents
1137	For One Night		Harlequin	Presents
1153	An Expert Teacher		Harlequin	Presents
1169	Force Of Feeling		Harlequin	Presents
1180	A Reason For Being	06/89	Harlequin	Presents
1193	Potential Danger		Harlequin	Presents
1201	Without Trust		Harlequin	Presents
1216	Lovers Touch		Harlequin	Presents
1243	Valentine's Night		Harlequin	Presents
1265	Equal Opportunity		Harlequin	Presents
1282	Beyond Compare		Harlequin	Presents
1297	Free Spirit		Harlequin	Presents
1314	Payment In Love		Harlequin	Presents
1324	A Rekindled Pass		Harlequin	Presents
1339	Time For Trust		Harlequin	Presents
1353	So Close And No Closer		Harlequin	Presents
1369	Bitter Betrayal		Harlequin	Presents
1388	Breaking Away	08/91	Harlequin	Presents
1404	Unspoken Desire	10/91	Harlequin	Presents
1418	Rival Attractions	12/91	Harlequin	Presents
1427	Out Of The Night	01/92	Harlequin	Presents
1442	Game Of Love	03/92	Harlequin	Presents
1456	A Kind Of Madness	05/92	Harlequin	Presents
1476	Second Time Loving	07/92	Harlequin	Presents
1491	Payment Due	09/92	Harlequin	Presents
1508	A Forbidden Loving	11/92	Harlequin	Presents
1529	A Time To Dream	02/93	Harlequin	Presents
1544	Dangerous Interloper	04/93	Harlequin	Presents
1552	Second-Best Husband	06/93	Harlequin	Presents
1559	A Cure For Love	06/93	Harlequin	Presents
1625	Mistaken Adversary	02/94	Harlequin	Presents
1673	Lesson To Learn	08/94	Harlequin	Presents
1705	Law Of Attraction	12/94	Harlequin	Presents
1734	Tug Of Love	04/95	Harlequin	Presents
1746	Passionate Possession	06/95	Harlequin	Presents
1805	An Unforgettable Man	04/96	Harlequin	Presents
1821	Unwanted Wedding	07/96	Harlequin	Presents
1575	A Cure For Love	08/93	Harlequin	Presents Plus
1599	Stranger From The Past	11/93	Harlequin	Presents Plus
1655	Past Passion	06/94	Harlequin	Presents Plus
1719	A Matter Of Trust	02/95	Harlequin	Presents Plus
1756	Past Loving	08/95	Harlequin	Presents Plus

Kalpakian, Laura
    The Lattie Days
Kandel, Aben
  23 City For Conquest   /49   Harlequin
Kane, Andrea
    My Heart's Desire   10/91   Pocket
    Dream Castle   07/92   Pocket
    Masque Of Betrayal   06/93   Pocket
    Samantha   12/94   Pocket
    Echoes In The Mist   07/94   Pocket
    The Last Duke   06/95   Pocket
    A Gift Of Love   11/95   Pocket Anthology
Kane, Carol
    Diva   Harper
Kane, Elaine
    Desert Flame   06/93   Zebra Heartfire
    Tempted   05/94   Zebra Heartfire
    Desert Flame   05/93   Zebra Heartfire
Kane, Frank
  126 Death About Face   /51   Harlequin
Kane, Kathleen
    Keeping Faith   07/94   Diamond A Town Called Harmony
    Coming Home   12/94   Diamond A Town Called Harmony
    Sweet Hearts   02/93   Diamond Anthology
    Charms   01/95   Diamond Historical
    Mountain Dawn   09/92   Diamond Homespun
    Hearts Of Gold   02/94   Jove Anthology
    Wishes   08/95   Jove Historical
Kane, Valerie
  19 Sunday Driver   11/90   Meteor
Karr, Jillian
    Something Borrowed, Something Blue   12/93   Doubleday
Karr, Lee
  15 Footsteps In The Night   09/93   Harlequin
    Lovers Dark And Dangerous   10/94   Silhouette Anthology
 662 A Twist In Time   09/95   Silhouette Intimate Moments
 712 Child Of The Night   05/96   Silhouette Intimate Moments
   3 Stranger In The Mist   03/93   Silhouette Shadows
    Beyond The Texas Rainbows   11/89   Warner
    Forbidden Dreams   04/90   Warner
    The Dark Secret Of Hunter's Hall 04/93   Ze Gothic
    Castle Of Crushed Shamrocks   Zebra Gothic
    Dark Cries Of Gray Oaks   Zebra Gothic
    Mistress Of Moontide Manor   Zebra Gothic
    The Red Stones Of Ravengate   Zebra Gothic
    The Whispering Winds Of Blackbriar Bay   Zebra Gothic

Kauffman, Donna
  801 Bayou Heat   08/96 Bantam Loveswept
  760 1: Surrender The Dark   09/96 Bantam Three Musketeers Trilogy
  771 2: Born To Be Wild   12/95 Bantam Three Musketeers Trilogy
  776 3: Midnight Heat   01/96 Bantam Three Musketeers Trilogy

Kay, Catherine
  45 Dawn Of Passion   Harlequin Superromance
  80 Interlude   Harlequin Superromance
  127 Critic's Choice   06/84 Harlequin Superromance

Kay, Karen
  Lakota Surrender   11/94 Avon
  Proud Wolf's Woman   07/96 Avon
  Lakota Princess   08/95 Avon Historical

Kaye, Amber
  Endless Surrender   09/92 Zebra Heartfire
  Haunted By Love   06/93 Zebra Heartfire

Kaye, Barbara
  19 Call Of Eden   Harlequin American
  Deep In The Heart   06/94 Harlequin Crystal Creek
  After The Lights Go Out 08/93 Harlequin Crystal Creek
  Let's Turn Back The Years 08/94 Harlequin Crystal Creek
  6 After The Lights Go Out 08/93 Harlequin Crystal Creek
  12 Everybody's Talkin'   02/94 Harlequin Crystal Creek
  529 Let's Turn Back The Years 08/94 Harlequin Crystal Creek
  46 A Heart Divided   Harlequin Superromance
  124 Come Spring   Harlequin Superromance
  161 Home At Last   10/92 Harlequin Superromance
  206 Southern Nights   Harlequin Superromance
  219 Just One Look   Harlequin Superromance
  257 A Season For Roses   Harlequin Superromance
  270 By Special Request   Harlequin Superromance
  316 The Right Place To Be   Harlequin Superromance
  332 Traditions   Harlequin Superromance
  379 Ramblin' Man   Harlequin Superromance
  411 Choice Of A Lifetime   Harlequin Superromance
  433 Challenge Of A Lifetime   Harlequin Superromance
  449 Chance Of A Lifetime   Harlequin Superromance
  495 Love Me Tender   04/92 Harlequin Superromance
  540 For The Love Of Ivy   03/93 Harlequin Superromance
  Ramblin' Man   05/95 Harlequin Western Lovers

Kaye, Gayle
  925 Hard Hat And Lace   03/93 Silhouette Romance
  961 His Delicate Condition 09/93 Silhouette Romance
  1014 Daddy Trouble   06/94 Silhouette Romance

Kaye, Judy
  3021 Letters Of Love   Harlequin Romance

Kaye, Judy
3182 Ariana's Magic   03/92 Harlequin Romance
Kaye, M. M.
     The Far Pavilions   Historical
     Shadow Of The Moon   Historical
Kaye, Mandalyn
     The Promise   01/95 Pinnacle Denise Little Presents
     A Matter Of Honor   12/96 Pinnacle Denise Little Presents
Keane, Lucy
282 Dance To The Devil's Tune   05/96 Harlequin
3136 False Impressions   07/91 Harlequin Romance
3178 Magic Carpets   02/92 Harlequin Romance
Kearney, Susan
340 Tara's Child   09/95 Harlequin Intrigue
378 A Baby To Love   07/96 Harlequin Intrigue
Kearny, Jillian
     Agent Of Love   Warner
Kearsley, Susanna
     Undertow   03/93 Avalon
Keast, Karen
     The Silence Of The Angels
294 Forbidden Dream   /85   Berkley Second Chance At Love
13 China Star   Harlequin Historical
     Taylor's Ladies   /90   Silhouette Birds, Bees & Babies
752 The Silence Of Angels   12/92 Silhouette Desire
435 Once Burned...   02/88 Silhouette Special Edition
536 A Tender Silence   07/89 Silhouette Special Edition
614 Night Spice   08/90 Silhouette Special Edition
688 The Surprise Of His   08/91 Silhouette Special Edition
Keaton, Corey
194 The Nesting Instinct   03/88 Harlequin Temptation
Keelyn, Patricia
590 Keeping Katie   04/94 Harlequin Superromance
631 Where The Heart Is (9 Months)   02/95 Harlequin Superromance
682 Once A Wife   03/96 Harlequin Superromance
582 Nobody's Hero   04/96 Harlequin Temptation
Keene, Day
167 Love Me And Die   /52   Harlequin
168 Hunt The Killer   /52   Harlequin
180 If The Coffin Fits   /52   Harlequin
185 Naked Fury   /52   Harlequin
229 Framed In Guildt   /53   Harlequin
253 Wake Up To Murder   /53   Harlequin
Keene, Sarah
2698 A Tender Season   Harlequin Romance
2740 Air Of Enchantment   Harlequin Romance

AUTHOR/TITLE INDEX

AUTHOR/TITLE INDEX

Kent, Katherine

28	Precious Possession		Nal Rapture Romance
52	Silk And Steel	02/84	Nal Rapture Romance
63	Reluctant Surrender		Nal Rapture Romance
	Dreamtide		Richard Gallen
	Tawny Rose		Walker

Kent, Lynnette

138	No Illusion	03/93	Meteor Kismet

Kent, Pamela

604	Flight To The Stars	/61	Harlequin
791	City Of Palms	/64	Harlequin
804	Bladon's Rock (Doctor Gaston)	/64	Harlequin
829	Sweet Barbary	/64	Harlequin
909	Desert Doorway	/65	Harlequin
943	Enemy Lover	/65	Harlequin
983	Moon Over Africa	/66	Harlequin
1005	Gideon Faber's Chance	/66	Harlequin
1035	Star Creek	/66	Harlequin
1061	Meet Me In Istanbul	/66	Harlequin
1091	Cuckoo In The Night	/67	Harlequin
1134	The Man Who Came Back	/67	Harlequin
1234	Desert Gold	/68	Harlequin
1274	Man From The Sea	/69	Harlequin
1384	Beloved Enemies	/70	Harlequin
1798	Nile Dusk	/74	Harlequin

Kenyon, Cory

407	Sheer Delight	/86	Dell Ecstasy Romance

Kenyon, Joanna

32	Dangerous Paradise	12/83	Silhouette Intimate Moments

Kenyon, Sherrilyn

	Daemon's Angel	04/95	Leisure Love Spell
	Paradise City	08/94	Love Spell Futuristic

Kenyon, Theda

31	The Golden Feather	/50	Harlequin

Keppel, Charlotte

My Name Is Clary Brown

Ker, Madeleine

642	Aquamarine		Harlequin Presents
656	Virtuous Lady		Harlequin Presents
672	Pacific Aphrodite		Harlequin Presents
699	The Winged Lion		Harlequin Presents
778	Out Of This Darkness		Harlequin Presents
795	Fire Of The Gods		Harlequin Presents
884	Danger Zone		Harlequin Presents
947	Impact		Harlequin Presents
1090	Frazer's Law		Harlequin Presents

AUTHOR/TITLE INDEX

Kidd, Flora

1058	Nurse At Rowanbank	/66	Harlequin
1122	Whistle And I'll Come	/67	Harlequin
1191	Love Alters Not	/68	Harlequin
1265	Stange As A Dream	/69	Harlequin
1471	When Birds Do Sing	/71	Harlequin
1503	My Heart Remembers	/71	Harlequin
1540	The Dazzle On The Sea	/71	Harlequin
1573	Love Is Fire	/72	Harlequin
1602	Remedy For Love	/72	Harlequin
1640	If Love Be Love	/72	Harlequin
1663	The Cave Of The White Rose	/73	Harlequin
1684	The Taming Of Lisa	/73	Harlequin
1732	Beyond The Sunset	/73	Harlequin
1774	The Legend Of The Swans	/74	Harlequin
1796	Gallant's Fancy	/74	Harlequin
1833	The Paper Marriage	/74	Harlequin
1865	Stranger In The Glen	/75	Harlequin
1907	Enchantment In Blue	/75	Harlequin
1977	The Dance Of Courtship	/76	Harlequin
1999	The Summer Wife	/76	Harlequin
2056	The Black Knight	/77	Harlequin
2146	To Play With Fire	/78	Harlequin
212	Dangerous Pretence	/77	Harlequin Presents
216	Jungle Of Desire	/77	Harlequin Presents
240	Night Of The Yellow Moon	/78	Harlequin Presents
261	Sweet Torment	/78	Harlequin Presents
276	Castle Of Temptation		Harlequin Presents
304	Marriage In Mexico		Harlequin Presents
309	Passionate Encounter		Harlequin Presents
327	Together Again		Harlequin Presents
333	Tangled Shadows		Harlequin Presents
344	Stay Through The Night		Harlequin Presents
370	Arranged Marriage		Harlequin Presents
379	The Silken Bond		Harlequin Presents
400	Wife By Contract		Harlequin Presents
434	Beyond Control		Harlequin Presents
447	Personal Affair		Harlequin Presents
464	Passionate Stranger		Harlequin Presents
485	Bride For A Captain		Harlequin Presents
495	Meeting At Midnight		Harlequin Presents
520	Makebelieve Marriage		Harlequin Presents
554	Between Pride And Pa		Harlequin Presents
577	Tempted To Love		Harlequin Presents
592	Dark Seduction		Harlequin Presents
643	Tropical Tempest		Harlequin Presents
657	Dangerous Encounter		Harlequin Presents

AUTHOR/TITLE INDEX

Kilgore, Katherine
    Tame The Wind   10/93   Harper Monogram
Kilgore, Kay
    On Wings Of Love   10/93   Zebra To Love Again
Kilpatrick, Nancy
    Near Death   10/94   Pocket
Kimbrough, Colleen
  30   Swept Off Her Feet   10/84   Harlequin Temptation
Kincaid, Katharine
    Beloved Bondage   07/94
    Nebraska Embrace   Zebra
    Stormswept   Zebra
    Tropical Captive   Zebra
    Wildly My Love   06/90   Zebra
    Ruby Orchid   Zebra
    Crimson Desire   Zebra
    Crimson Embrace   Zebra
    Defiant Vixen   Zebra
    Violet Smoke   Zebra
    Sea Flame   Zebra Heartfire
    Midnight Treasure   08/92   Zebra Lovegram Romance
Kincaid, Nell
  149   With Every Loving Touch   /83   Dell Candlelight Ecstasy
  185   Turn Back The Dawn   /83   Dell Candlelight Ecstasy
Kincaid, Stephanie
  522   Stolen Dreams   Dell Candlelight
King, Barrie
    Contessa   07/93   Ballantine Historical
    Julia   05/94   Fawcett
King, Carol
    Loving Challenge   Zebra
    Emerald Enchantress   Zebra Heartfire
    Sweet Velvet Passion   Zebra Heartfire
    Wanton Secrets   Zebra Heartfire
King, Dianne
  101   When Dreams Come True   Harlequin Superromance
  182   Believe In Magic   Harlequin Superromance
  10   Friend Of The Heart   05/84   Harlequin Temptation
  68   Essence Of Summer   07/85   Harlequin Temptation
King, Josie
  228   Dance At Your Wedding   06/83   Silhouette Romance
King, Lauren
    Tender Temptation   Zebra Heartfire
King, Rebecca
  234   Heart Of The Jaguar   05/95   Harlequin Direct
  1477   Dark Guardian   07/92   Harlequin Presents

Kingsley, Katherine

| | No Sweeter Heaven | 08/93 | Penguin Topaz |
| | No Brighter Dream | 10/94 | Topaz |

Kingsley, Mary

	A Gentleman's Desire		Zebra Regency
	A Maddening Minx	03/92	Zebra Regency
	The Rake's Reward	08/91	Zebra Regency
	Sabrina		Zebra Regency
	A Summer Folly		Zebra Regency
	Maddening Minx	03/92	Zebra Regency
	An Intriquing Affair	08/93	Zebra Regency
	Scandal's Lady	02/94	Zebra Regency

Kingston, Kate

170	A Warning Of Magic	01/94	Harlequin Direct
1428	Wild Champagne	01/92	Harlequin Presents
2981	Alien Moonlight		Harlequin Romance

Kingston, Meredith

2	Winter Love Song	/81	Berkley Second Chance At Love
10	Aloha Yesterday	/81	Berkley Second Chance At Love
24	Passion's Games	/81	Berkley Second Chance At Love
72	Mixed Doubles	/83	Berkley Second Chance At Love

Kinsale, Laura

	Hidden Heart		Avon
	Midsummer Moon	/87	Avon
	Prince Of Midnight	/90	Avon
	Seize The Fire	/89	Avon
	Uncertain Magic		Avon
	Flowers From The Storm	10/92	Avon
	The Shadow And The Star	10/91	Avon
	For My Lady's Heart	12/93	Berkley Historical
	The Dream Hunter	12/94	Berkley Historical

Kirby, Rowan

	Leah's Love Song		
2675	Silent Stream		Harlequin Romance
2758	Hunger		Harlequin Romance
2776	Power Point		Harlequin Romance
2829	Contrasts		Harlequin Romance
2847	Fusion		Harlequin Romance
2873	Shadow Fall		Harlequin Romance
2907	Harmonies		Harlequin Romance
2960	Only My Dreams		Harlequin Romance

Kirk, Alexandra

	Jamaican Midnight	/84	Avon
	Sand Castles	/82	Bantam
	Images Of Love	/82	Bantam
326	A Kiss Away	/86	Berkley Second Chance At Love

AUTHOR/TITLE INDEX

Kirk, Alexandra

342	A Prince Among Men	/86	Berkley	Second Chance At Love
375	All For Love	/86	Berkley	Second Chance At Love
398	Best Intentions	/87	Berkley	Second Chance At Love
412	Two's Company	/87	Berkley	Second Chance At Love
430	Prince Charming Replies	/88	Berkley	Second Chance At Love
	Shadow On The Hill	/85	Golden Apple	
	Thrown For A Loss	/84	Nal - Signet	

Kirk, Margaret P.

	Gypsy	Zebra Historical & Family Sagas

Kirk, Mariel

2786	Prisoner Of Shadow Mountain	Harlequin Romance

Kirk, Mary Alice

387	In Your Wildest Dreams	11/87	Silhouette Desire
462	Promises	06/88	Silhouette Special Edition
524	Phoenix Rising	05/89	Silhouette Special Edition
628	Miracles	10/90	Silhouette Special Edition
714	Embers	12/91	Silhouette Special Edition

Kirk, Risa

200	Beyond Compare		Harlequin Superromance
238	Tempting Fate		Harlequin Superromance
273	Dreams To Mend		Harlequin Superromance
300	Without A Doubt		Harlequin Superromance
361	Playing With Fire		Harlequin Superromance
408	Undercover Affair		Harlequin Superromance
441	Send No Regrets		Harlequin Superromance
476	Made To Order	11/91	Harlequin Superromance
542	Worth The Wait	04/93	Harlequin Superromance
579	The Dog From Rodeo Drive	01/94	Harlequin Superromance
607	Days Of Thunder	08/94	Harlequin Superromance

Kirkland, Martha

The Message	03/93	Avalon
The Marrying Season	07/95	Signet Regency
The Secret Nabob	12/95	Signet Regency

Kirkland, Rainy

Bewitching Kisses	05/91	Zebra Heartfire
Passion's Golden Bounty	06/90	Zebra Heartfire
Ecstasy's Flame	11/92	Zebra Heartfire

Kistler, Julie

158	The Van Renn Legacy	07/86	Harlequin American
207	Christmas In July		Harlequin American
266	Always A Bridesmaid		Harlequin American
329	Best Wishes		Harlequin American
418	Christmas In Toyland	12/91	Harlequin American
429	Flannery's Rainbow	03/92	Harlequin American
471	Finn's Angel	01/93	Harlequin American

602

AUTHOR/TITLE INDEX

AUTHOR/TITLE INDEX

Koen, Karleen
  Now Face To Face   05/96 Random
Kohake, Rosanne
  Ambrosia   Avon
  For Honor's Glory   Avon
Kohl, Candice
  Destiny's Disguise   Lion Hearted Historical
Kohman, Catherine
  The Beckoning Ghost   07/95 Leisure Love Spell
Kolaczyk, Anne
   89 Captain Wonder   04/85 Bantam Loveswept
  125 Oranges In The Snow   01/86 Bantam Loveswept
  131 The Butler And His Lady   03/86 Bantam Loveswept
  184 Sultry Nights   03/87 Bantam Loveswept
Koontz, Dean
  Dark Rivers Of The Heart   11/94 Knopf
  The Door To December   10/94 Signet
Kopp, Nancy
  Acts & Omissions   09/94 Onyx
Korbel, Kathleen
  Shadows Short Story Collection   10/93 Harlequin Anthology
  Undercover Lovers   06/94 Harlequin Anthology
  Intimate Moments 10th Anniversary   05/93 Silhouette Anthology
  286 Playing The Game   06/86 Silhouette Desire
  389 A Prince Of A Guy   11/87 Silhouette Desire
  455 The Princess And The Pea   10/88 Silhouette Desire
  582 Hotshot   07/90 Silhouette Desire
  668 A Fine Madness   10/91 Silhouette Desire
  703 Isn't It Romantic?   04/92 Silhouette Desire
 1015 Don't Fence Me In   08/96 Silhouette Desire
  163 A Stranger's Smile   10/86 Silhouette Intimate Moments
  191 Worth Any Risk   05/87 Silhouette Intimate Moments
  222 Edge Of The World   01/88 Silhouette Intimate Moments
  276 Perchance To Dream   02/89 Silhouette Intimate Moments
  309 The Ice Cream Man   11/89 Silhouette Intimate Moments
  351 Lightning Strikes   09/90 Silhouette Intimate Moments
  396 A Rose For Maggie   08/91 Silhouette Intimate Moments
  413 Jake's Way   01/92 Silhouette Intimate Moments
  571 Simple Gifts (American Hero)   06/94 Silhouette Intimate Moments
  602 A Soldier's Heart   11/94 Silhouette Intimate Moments
  The Road To Mandalay   /89   Silhouette Summer Sizzlers
Koskinen, Sue
  Witches Brew   01/95 Northwest
Kotselas, Janet
  Clarke   02/90 Ballantine
Kovats, Nancy

605

Kovats, Nancy
    Passion's Gold   Zebra

Krahn, Betina
    Rapture's Ransom
    Passion's Storm
    Rebel Passion
    Hidden Fires   02/95
    Caught In The Act   Avon
    My Warrior's Heart   08/92   Avon
    Behind Closed Doors   09/91   Avon
    The Princess And The Barbarian   08/93   Avon
    Stardust   09/94   Avon Anthology
    Christmas Romance   /91   Avon Anthology
    The Last Bachelor   09/94   Bantam
    The Perfect Mistress   10/95   Bantam
    A Victorian Christmas   11/92   Nal Super Signet Historical
    Caught In The Act   Warner
    Midnight Magic   07/95   Zebra
    Passion's Treasure   Zebra
    Love's Brazen Fire   07/95   Zebra
    Passion's Ransom   05/89   Zebra

Kramer, Amanda
  1002   Baby Bonus   05/96   Silhouette Desire

Kramer, Kathryn
    Lady Rogue
    Midsummer Of Night's Desire
    Siren Song
    Flame From The Sea   /87   Berkley
    Destiny And Desire   /88   Berkley
    Desire's Deceptions   /89   Berkley
    Love's Blazing Ecstasy   Berkley
    Lady Rogue   07/91   Dell
    Desire's Masquerade   /87   Dell
    Under Gypsy Skies   /88   Dell
    Treasure Of The Heart   /90   Dell
    Highland Bride   Jove
    Midsummer Night's Desire   07/92   Leisure Historical
    An Old-Fashioned Valentine   02/93   Leisure Historical
    Love's Blazing Ecstasy   /85   Nal Signet

Krause, Kathleen
    Mellona   /95   Leisure
    Harvest Sheet   Leisure
    The Blue Sky   Leisure
    Bright Dreams, Dark Desires   Leisure

Kreisel, Linda
    Harbor Lights   07/96   Jove Our Town

Krentz, Jayne Ann

	Endless Love	05/95	Anthology
	Mystique	06/95	Bantam
10	Legacy		Harlequin Intrigue
17	The Waiting Game		Harlequin Intrigue
3	Call It Destiny	07/93	Harlequin Men Made In America
37	Uneasy Alliance	03/95	Harlequin Men Made In America
47	The Waiting Game	06/95	Harlequin Men Made In America
11	Uneasy Alliance	05/84	Harlequin Temptation
21	Call It Destiny	08/84	Harlequin Temptation
34	Ghost Of A Chance	11/84	Harlequin Temptation
45	Man With A Past	02/85	Harlequin Temptation
74	Witchcraft	09/85	Harlequin Temptation
91	True Colors	01/86	Harlequin Temptation
109	The Ties That Bind	06/86	Harlequin Temptation
125	Between The Lines	10/86	Harlequin Temptation
146	The Family Way	03/87	Harlequin Temptation
157	The Main Attraction	06/87	Harlequin Temptation
168	Chance Of A Lifetime	08/87	Harlequin Temptation
177	Test Of Time	11/87	Harlequin Temptation
191	Full Bloom	02/88	Harlequin Temptation
219	Joy	09/88	Harlequin Temptation
229	Dreams, Part 1	12/88	Harlequin Temptation
230	Dreams, Part 2	12/88	Harlequin Temptation
241	A Woman's Touch	03/89	Harlequin Temptation
270	Lady's Choice	10/89	Harlequin Temptation
287	Ladies & Legends 1: The Pirate	02/90	Harlequin Temptation
293	Ladies & Legends 2: The Adventurer	04/90	Harlequin Temptation
302	Ladies & Legends 3: The Cowboy	06/90	Harlequin Temptation
341	Too Wild To Wed?	04/91	Harlequin Temptation
365	The Wedding Night	10/91	Harlequin Temptation
377	The Private Eye (Rebels & Rogues)	01/92	Harlequin Temptation
	Sweet Fortune	10/91	Pocket
	Perfect Partners	04/92	Pocket
	Family Man	10/92	Pocket
	The Golden Chance	/90	Pocket
	Silver Linings	/91	Pocket
	Hidden Talents	11/93	Pocket
	Wildest Hearts	03/93	Pocket
	Grand Passion	08/94	Pocket
	Trust Me	08/95	Pocket
	Midnight Jewels	/87	Popular Lib.
	Whirlwind Courtship	/87	Tiara
	Midnight Jewels	08/92	Warner
	Crystal Flame		Warner
	A Coral Kiss		Warner
	Gift Of Fire		Warner

Krentz, Jayne Ann
    Gift Of Gold   04/93   Warner
    Sweet Starfire   01/94   Warner
    Crystal Flame   08/94   Warner
    Twist Of Fate   /86   Worldwide Lib

Krentz, Joan
    California Copper   07/95   Mira

Kreps, Penelope
    Shadow Over Windsong   /91   Avalon

Krinard, Susan
    Star Crossed   08/95   Bantam
    My Guardian Angel   02/95   Bantam Anthology
    Prince Of Wolves   08/94   Bantam Fanfare

Kriske, Anne
    A Haven In Winter   12/91   Berkley

Kroeger, Kelly
    Backstage Romance   05/92   Bantam Sweet Dreams

Krueger, Elizabeth
    774   A Saving Grace   02/91   Silhouette Romance
    798   And The Walls Came Tumbling Down   06/91   Silhouette Romance
    872   His Father's House   06/92   Silhouette Romance
    960   Dark Prince   09/93   Silhouette Romance
    1155   Family Mine   05/96   Silhouette Romance
    723   For The Children   02/92   Silhouette Special Edition

Kurland, Lynn
    Stardust Of Yesterday   04/96   Jove Haunting Hearts

Kurr, Maureen
    Deceptive Heart
    Sword Of The Heart   Leisure

Kwock, Laureen
    One Touch Of Paradise   /91   Avalon
    680   Miss Claringdon's Condition   Dell Candlelight Regency

Kyle, Susan
    The Morcai Batallion   03/80   Manor Books
    Escapade   12/92   Warner
    Fire Brand   02/89   Warner
    Night Fever   02/90   Warner
    True Colors   05/91   Warner
    After Midnight   11/93   Warner
    All That Glitters   10/95   Warner
    Diamond Spur   01/88   Warner

La Barre, Harriet
    Stranger In Vienna   Warner

La Dame, Cathryn
    55   Winter's Start   01/81   Silhouette Romance

AUTHOR/TITLE INDEX

La Danne, Cathryn
   209   Trail Of The Unicorn   03/83   Silhouette Romance
La Foy, Leslie Marie
         Thread Through Time   Lion Hearted Time Travel
La Velle, Linn
         Before Summer Ends   /92   Avalon
Lab, Olivia Kennedy
         Under The Portico   04/96 Book World
Lacey, Anne
    93   Love Feud   05/83 Silhouette Special Edition
   155   Softly At Sunset   03/84 Silhouette Special Edition
   188   A Song In The Night   09/84 Silhouette Special Edition
   317   Magic Season   06/86 Silhouette Special Edition
   365   Golden Firestorm   02/87 Silhouette Special Edition
   395   Treasures Of The Heart   07/87 Silhouette Special Edition
   422   Intrepid Heart   12/87 Silhouette Special Edition
   449   Rapture Deep   04/88 Silhouette Special Edition
   498   A Charmed Life   12/88 Silhouette Special Edition
   538   Light For Another Night   07/89 Silhouette Special Edition
Ladd, Linda
         Dragon Fire   Avon
         Dreamsong   Avon
         Fireglow   Avon
         Frostfire   Avon
         Midnight Fire   Avon
         Moon Spell   Avon
         Silverswept   Avon
         Wildstar   Avon
         Christmas Romance   /91   Avon Anthology
         White Rose   06/94 Penguin Topaz
         White Lily   08/93 Penguin Topaz
         White Orchid   04/95 Penguin Topaz
Laden, Janis
         Scottish Rose   Zebra
         Fires In The Snow   07/92 Zebra Regency
         Bewitching Minx   Zebra Regency
         Moonlight Veil   Zebra Regency
         A Noble Mistress   Zebra Regency
         Sapphire Temptation   Zebra Regency
         Scottish Rose   Zebra Regency
         A Whisper Of Scandal   Zebra Regency
Ladley, Anne
         The Runaway Heart   Avalon
         Moriah's Magic   10/92 Avalon
         Prescription For Love   Avalon Career Romance
         Programmed For Danger   Avalon Career Romance

609

AUTHOR/TITLE INDEX

Ladley, Anne
    Where The Heart Seeks Shelter   Avalon Career Romance

Laiman, Leah
    For Richer, For Poorer   07/94   Pocket
    Another Summer Of Love   08/95   Pocket

Laity, Sally
    Second Spring   /92   Barbour Publs.
    The Kiss Goodbye   /92   Barbour Publs.

Lake, Patricia
  465   Untamed Witch   Harlequin Presents
  501   Perfect Passion   Harlequin Presents
  521   Wipe Away The Tears   Harlequin Presents
  538   Heartless Love   Harlequin Presents
  570   A Step Backwards   Harlequin Presents
  578   The Silver Casket   Harlequin Presents
  593   Moment Of Madness   Harlequin Presents
  634   Fated Affair   Harlequin Presents
  707   Illusion Of Love   Harlequin Presents
  730   Fidelity   Harlequin Presents
  907   Dark Betrayal   Harlequin Presents
  986   Fascination   Harlequin Presents

Lake, Rozella
 1862   Chateau In Provence   /75   Harlequin
 1893   If Dreams Came True   /75   Harlequin

Laker, Rosalind
    Ride The Blue Riband   Historical
    Circle Of Pearls   11/91   Bantam Fanfare

Lakso, Elaine
  713   High Spirits   10/94   Bantam Loveswept
  592   Forever Young   04/90   Silhouette Special Edition

Lamb, Arnette
    Border Bride   07/94
    Border Lord   07/94
    Betrothal   06/92   Pocket
    Chieftain   03/94   Pocket
    Maiden Of Inverness   03/95   Pocket
    Betrayed   /95   Pocket
    A Holiday Of Love   12/94   Pocket Anthology
   1   Highland Rogue   07/91   Pocket Mac Kenzie Trilogy
   2   Beguiled   05/96   Pocket Mac Kenzie Trilogy
   3   True Heart   09/97   Pocket Mac Kenzie Trilogy
    Cherished Moments   04/95   St. Martin's Anthology
    Threads Of Destiny   08/90   Warner

Lamb, Charlotte
 1722   Follow A Stranger   /73   Harlequin
 1751   Carnival Coast   /74   Harlequin

Lamb, Charlotte

Lamb, Charlotte

644	Haunted		Harlequin Presents
658	A Secret Intimacy		Harlequin Presents
668	Darkness Of The Heart		Harlequin Presents
700	Infatuation		Harlequin Presents
731	Scandalous		Harlequin Presents
747	A Naked Plan		Harlequin Presents
762	For Adults Only		Harlequin Presents
772	Love Games		Harlequin Presents
827	Man Hunt		Harlequin Presents
842	Who's Been Sleeping In My Bed?		Harlequin Presents
851	Sleeping Desire		Harlequin Presents
874	The Bride Said No		Harlequin Presents
898	Explosive Meeting		Harlequin Presents
971	Heat Of The Night		Harlequin Presents
987	Love In The Dark		Harlequin Presents
1001	Hide And Seek		Harlequin Presents
1025	Circle Of Fate		Harlequin Presents
1042	Kiss Of Fire		Harlequin Presents
1059	Whirlwind		Harlequin Presents
1081	Echo Of Passion		Harlequin Presents
1106	Out Of Control		Harlequin Presents
1170	No More Lonely		Harlequin Presents
1202	Desperation		Harlequin Presents
1236	Seductive Stranger		Harlequin Presents
1290	Runaway Wife		Harlequin Presents
1345	Rites Of Possession		Harlequin Presents
1370	Dark Pursuit		Harlequin Presents
1393	Spellbinding	09/91	Harlequin Presents
1410	Dark Music	11/91	Harlequin Presents
1435	The Threat Of Love	02/92	Harlequin Presents
1467	Heart On Fire	06/92	Harlequin Presents
1480	Shotgun Wedding	08/92	Harlequin Presents
1498	Besieged	10/92	Harlequin Presents
1509	Battle For Possession	11/92	Harlequin Presents
1513	Too Close For Comfort	12/92	Harlequin Presents
1522	Playing Hard To Get	01/93	Harlequin Presents
1530	A Sweet Addiction	02/93	Harlequin Presents
1540	Surrender	03/93	Harlequin Presents
1560	Sleeping Partners	06/93	Harlequin Presents
1560	Sleeping Partners	06/93	Harlequin Presents
1618	Dreaming	01/94	Harlequin Presents
1658	Fire In The Blood	06/94	Harlequin Presents
1706	Guilty Love	12/94	Harlequin Presents
1733	Body And Soul	04/95	Harlequin Presents
1763	Dark Fate	09/95	Harlequin Presents
1816	Secret Obsession	06/96	Harlequin Presents

Lamb, Charlotte
1822	Deadly Rivals	07/96	Harlequin Presents
1828	Haunted Dreams	08/96	Harlequin Presents
1584	Forbidden Fruit	09/93	Harlequin Presents Plus
1672	Falling In Love	08/94	Harlequin Presents Plus
1687	Wounds Of Passion	10/94	Harlequin Presents Plus
1720	Vampire Lover	02/95	Harlequin Presents Plus
1743	Dying For You	06/95	Harlequin Presents Plus
2696	Kingfisher Morning		Harlequin Romance
2804	The Heron Quest		Harlequin Romance
2950	You Can Love A Stranger		Harlequin Romance
	A Violation		Worldwide Lib.

Lambert, Elizabeth
Wings Of Desire	Avon

Lambert, Willa
23	From This Beloved Hour		Harlequin Superromance
59	Love's Golden Spell		Harlequin Superromance

Lammert, Charlotte
Mistress Of Falcon Court	Zebra Gothic

Lampman, Carolyn
	Meadowlark	01/95	Harper
2	Shadows In The Wind	02/94	Harper Cheyenne Trilogy
1	Murphy's Rainbow		Harper Cheyenne Triology
	Willow Creek	08/94	Harper Monogram

Lancaster, Bruce
Roll, Shenandoah	Historical

Lancaster, Joan
Summer Eyes

Lancaster, Lisa
Capture The Wind

Lancaster, Lydia
Heaven's Horizon	
The Arms Of A Stranger	Tapestry
False Paradise	Tapestry
Passion And Proud Hearts	Warner

Lancour, Jeanne
The Storm And The Sword	Bantam

Landers, Dawn
Naked Came The Ladies	02/94	Starlog Moonlight Anthology

Landers, Lynda Stowe
Savanna Sunset	/92	Avalon
Angel In Blue Jeans	12/92	Avalon
A Season To Remember		Avalon Career Romance

Landis, Jill Marie
Loving Hearts	02/92	Diamond Anthology
Sweet Hearts	02/93	Diamond Anthology

AUTHOR/TITLE INDEX

Langan, Ruth Ryan

	Captive Of Desire	04/90	Pocket
	The Heart's Secrets	02/89	Pocket
	Passage West	07/88	Pocket
	Destiny's Daughter	11/87	Pocket
	September's Dream	01/86	Pocket
	Nevada Nights	01/85	Pocket
	Christmas At Bitter Creek	12/90	Silhouette Hist. Christmas Stories
121	Just Like Yesterday	12/81	Silhouette Romance
224	Hidden Isle	05/83	Silhouette Romance
303	No Gentle Love	06/84	Silhouette Romance
317	Eden Of Temptation	09/84	Silhouette Romance
371	This Time Forever	07/85	Silhouette Romance
407	Family Secrets	01/86	Silhouette Romance
458	Mysteries Of The Heart	09/86	Silhouette Romance
492	The Proper Miss Porter	03/87	Silhouette Romance
119	Beloved Gambler	09/83	Silhouette Special Edition
218	To Love A Dreamer	02/85	Silhouette Special Edition
266	Star-Crossed	10/85	Silhouette Special Edition
354	Whims Of Fate	12/86	Silhouette Special Edition

Lange, Emma

	Regency Valentine		Nal
	The False Fiancee'		Nal
	The Scottish Rebel		Nal
	A Second Match	11/93	Nal
	A Heart In Peril	06/94	Nal
	The Unmanageable Miss Marlowe	09/91	Nal Regency
	Irish Earl's Ruse	06/92	Nal Regency
	The Cost Of Honor	02/88	Nal Regency
	Brighton Intrigue	01/89	Nal Regency
	The Unwavering Miss Winslow	09/89	Nal Regency
	Miss Marlowe's Revenge	09/91	Nal Regency
	A Regency Christmas 4	11/92	Nal Super Regency
	The Reforming Of Lord Roth	12/90	Nal Penguin
	The Cast Of Honor		Nal Penguin Regency
	The Earl's Return	04/93	Penguin Regency
	Exeter's Daugher	08/95	Signet Regency
	The Irish Rake	05/96	Signet Regency

Langtry, Ellen

67	The Fierce Gentleness	06/83	Silhouette Desire

Lanham, Cheryl

| | Secret Loves | 03/94 | Berkley Contemporary |

Lanigan, Catherine

	Promise Made		Avon
	At Long Last Love	02/94	Avon
	Dangerous Love	08/96	Mira

616

Lansdowne, Judith
    Amelia's Intrigue — 07/95   Zebra Regency
Larkin, Elinor
  618   The Twice Bought Bride — Dell Candlelight Regency
  655   Love's Tempest — Dell Candlelight Regency
Larkin, Kara
  1047   Home Ties — 11/94   Silhouette Romance
Larkin, Rochelle
  1   Harvest Of Desire — Leisure
  2   Mistress Of Desire — Leisure
  3   Torches Of Desire — Leisure
Larson, Shirley
    A Fatal Attraction — Dell Candlelight Ecstasy
    Brand Of Passion — Dell Candlelight Ecstasy
    Caught In The Rain — Dell Candlelight Ecstasy
    Wild Rhapsody — Dell Candlelight Ecstasy
    Surrender To The Night — Dell Candlelight Ecstasy
    A Dangerous Haven — Dell Candlelight Ecstasy
    A Night To Remember — Dell Candlelight Ecstasy
    Play To Win — Dell Candlelight Ecstasy
    Balance Of Power — Dell Candlelight Ecstasy
    Suspicion And Seduction — Dell Candlelight Ecstasy
    On Any Terms — Dell Candlelight Ecstasy
  232   See Only Me — Harlequin Superromance
  368   Honor Bound — Harlequin Superromance
  64   Where The Heart Is — 06/85   Harlequin Temptation
  99   A Face In The Crowd — 03/86   Harlequin Temptation
  145   Laughter In The Rain — 03/87   Harlequin Temptation
  178   Wit And Wisdom — 11/87   Harlequin Temptation
  214   Building On Dreams — 08/88   Harlequin Temptation
  314   Just Jake — 09/90   Harlequin Temptation
    Laughter In The Rain — 07/95   Harlequin Western Lovers
    Out Of The Fire — 08/92   Leisure Historical
  131   To Touch The Fire — 04/84   Silhouette Desire
  369   A Slice Of Paradise — 06/85   Silhouette Romance
    Season Of Loving — 03/88   Worldwide Libr.
Lasko, Elaine
  713   High Spirits — 09/95   Bantam Loveswept
  739   Tasting Trouble — 04/95   Bantam Loveswept
Laurel, Lisa Kaye
  1107   The Groom Maker — 09/95   Silhouette Romance
  1173   Mommy For The Moment — 08/96   Silhouette Romance
Laurence, Anne
  394   Always Say Yes — Harlequin Superromance
  539   Remember When — 03/93   Harlequin Superromance
  573   No Turning Back — 11/93   Harlequin Superromance

Lawrence, Terry

288	Where There's Smoke There's Fire	11/88	Bantam Loveswept
399	The Outsider	05/90	Bantam Loveswept
416	Wanted: The Perfect Man	08/90	Bantam Loveswept
441	Unfinished Passion	12/90	Bantam Loveswept
457	Passion's Flight	03/91	Bantam Loveswept
482	In The Still Of The Night	07/91	Bantam Loveswept
517	Ever Since Adam	01/92	Bantam Loveswept
536	For Lovers Only	04/92	Bantam Loveswept
568	Dangerous In The Dark	09/92	Bantam Loveswept
590	Renegade Ways	01/93	Bantam Loveswept
640	Dancing On The Edge	09/93	Bantam Loveswept
662	The Shadow Lover	01/94	Bantam Loveswept
685	Close Encounters	05/94	Bantam Loveswept
718	A Man's Man	12/94	Bantam Loveswept
768	Driven To Distraction	12/95	Bantam Loveswept
788	Fugitive Father	05/96	Bantam Loveswept
465	Cabin Fever	12/88	Silhouette Desire
526	Before Dawn	10/89	Silhouette Desire

Lawton, Lynna

Under Crimson Sails		Belmont Tower
Glory's Mistress		Leisure Historical

Laye, Patricia

The Taming Of Lord Whitfield	04/92	Jove Regency
A Novel Affair	06/91	Jove Regency
Touch Of Venus		Zebra Regency

Layle, Emmey

Cousin Caroline	Mills & Boon

Layton, Andrea

Love's Gentle Fugitive	Playboy Press

Layton, Edith

The Gilded Cage	/90	Berkley
Regency Christmas		Nal
The Crimson Crown	/91	Nal
False Angel		Nal
Lord Of Dishonor		Nal
The Mysterious Heir		Nal
The False Fiancee		Nal
The Silvery Moon	01/92	Nal Onyx
A Regency Valentine 2	01/92	Nal Super Regency
A Victorian Christmas	11/92	Nal Super Signet Historical
The Disdainful Marquis		Nal Penguin Regency
The Indian Maiden	06/86	Nal Penguin Regency
Red Jack's Daughter	09/86	Nal Penguin Regency
Lady Of Spirit	10/86	Nal Penguin Regency
The Duke's Wager	11/86	Nal Penguin Regency

Layton, Edith

Lord Of Dishonor		Nal Penguin Regency
The Fire Flower	07/89	Nal Penguin Regency
The Wedding	04/95	Pocket
The Mysterious Heir	01/84	Signet
The Duke's Progression	11/89	Signet A Regency Christmas
Dashing & Dangerous	05/95	Signet Anthology
Surrender To Love	03/89	Signet Love Trilogy
The Game Of Love	07/88	Signet Love Trilogy
Love In Disguise	08/87	Signet Love Trilogy
The Disdainful Marquis	05/95	Signet Regency
A Dreamspun Christmas	11/94	Topaz Anthology

Lazana, Windy

Sweet Abandon

Le Butt, Paul

227	We Too Can Die	/53	Harlequin

Le Clair, Laurie

3	Cherokee Caress	09/93	Starlog Rhapsody Historical

Le Claire, Day

3028	Jinxed		Harlequin Romance
3139	Where There's A Will	08/91	Harlequin Romance
3183	In The Market	03/92	Harlequin Romance
3238	A Wholesale Arrangement	12/92	Harlequin Romance
3285	To Catch A Ghost	10/93	Harlequin Romance
3301	Once A Cowboy... (Back To The Ranch)	02/94	Harlequin Romance
3338	Who's Holding The Baby? (Kids & Kisses)	11/94	Harlequin Romance
3361	Mail-Order Bridegroom	05/95	Harlequin Romance
3376	One-Night Wife	09/95	Harlequin Romance
3404	Make Believe Engagement	04/96	Harlequin Romance

Le Mon, Lynn

This Rebel Hunger		Richard Gallen

Le Roy, Irene

235	Nothing To Hide	04/88	Silhouette Intimate Moments

Le Varre, Deborah

Captive Mistress

Leabo, Karen

	The Bounty Hunter	/96	
783	Hell On Wheels	04/96	Bantam Loveswept
37	Runaway Bride	09/96	Harlequin Here Come The Grooms
629	Close Quarters	03/91	Silhouette Desire
676	Lindy And The Law	11/91	Silhouette Desire
704	Unearthly Delights	04/92	Silhouette Desire
767	The Cop	02/93	Silhouette Desire
794	Ben	07/93	Silhouette Desire
824	Feathers And Lace	12/93	Silhouette Desire
838	Twilight Man	02/94	Silhouette Desire

AUTHOR/TITLE INDEX

AUTHOR/TITLE INDEX

Lee, Doris
  383   Reluctant Bride   09/85 Silhouette Romance
  131   A Fire In The Soul   11/83 Silhouette Special Edition

Lee, Joyce
  671   Oh, What A Tangled Web   Dell Candlelight Regency

Lee, Linda
       Desert Rose   08/91 Diamond

Lee, Linda Francis
       Texas Angel   05/94 Diamond Wildflower
       Wild Hearts   12/94 Diamond Wildflower
       Blue Waltz   01/96 Jove Historical
       The Wallflower   08/95 Jove Sons And Daughters

Lee, Lucy
   10   Heart's Fury   Harlequin Superromance
   44   The Rite Of Love   Harlequin Superromance
   93   Heart's Paradise   Harlequin Superromance

Lee, Lydia
       The Impetuous Pandora   10/90 Jove Regency
       The Magnificent Mirabelle   08/88 Pageant
  642   Valentino's Pleasure   04/89 Silhouette Romance
  784   Thank Your Lucky Stars   04/91 Silhouette Romance
  844   The Kat's Meow   02/92 Silhouette Romance

Lee, Miranda
       Outback Man   06/93 Harlequin Presents
 1362 After The Affair   Harlequin Presents
 1419 An Obsessive Desire   12/91 Harlequin Presents
 1481 The Reluctant Lover   08/92 Harlequin Presents
 1562 Outback, Man   06/93 Harlequin Presents
 1589 Scandalous Seduction   09/93 Harlequin Presents
 1614 Asking For Trouble   12/93 Harlequin Presents
 1651 A Date With Destiny   06/94 Harlequin Presents
 1702 Knight To The Rescue   11/94 Harlequin Presents
 1728 Marriage In Jeopardy   03/95 Harlequin Presents
 1737 An Outrageous Proposal   05/95 Harlequin Presents
 1754 Seduction & Sacrifice (Hearts Of Fire) 07/95 Harlequin Presents
 1760 Desire & Deception (Hearts Of Fire) 08/95 Harlequin Presents
 1766 Passion & The Past   09/95 Harlequin Presents
 1772 Fantasies & The Future   10/95 Harlequin Presents
 1778 Scandals & Secrets   11/95 Harlequin Presents
 1784 Marriage & Miracles   12/95 Harlequin Presents
 1791 Mistress Of Deception   02/96 Harlequin Presents
 1811 The Bride In Blue   05/96 Harlequin Presents
 1664 A Daring Proposition   07/94 Harlequin Presents Plus
 1711 Beth And Barbarian   01/95 Harlequin Presents Plus

Lee, Rachel
   10   Imminent Thunder   06/93 Harlequin

Lee, Rachel

	Cowboy Cop	07/95	Harlequin	Montana Mavericks
37	Thunder Mountain	08/94	Harlequin	Shadows
	Lovers Dark And Dangerous	10/94	Silhouette	Anthology
	A Conard County Reckoning	03/96	Silhouette	Anthology
370	An Officer And A Gentleman	02/91	Silhouette	Intimate Moments
394	Serious Risks	08/91	Silhouette	Intimate Moments
430	Defying Gravity	05/92	Silhouette	Intimate Moments
449	Exile's End	09/92	Silhouette	Intimate Moments
463	A Cherokee Thunder	12/92	Silhouette	Intimate Moments
482	Miss Emmaline And The Archangel	03/93	Silhouette	Intimate Moments
494	Ironheart	05/93	Silhouette	Intimate Moments
535	Lost Warriors	12/93	Silhouette	Intimate Moments
566	Point Of No Return	05/94	Silhouette	Intimate Moments
613	A Question Of Justice	01/95	Silhouette	Intimate Moments

Lee, Rebecca Hagan

	Liar's Moon	07/93		
	Taking Chances	08/94	Diamond	A Town Called Harmony
	Golden Chances	08/92	Diamond	Homespun
	Harvest Moon	07/93	Diamond	Homespun
	A Homespun Mother's Day	05/94	Diamond	Homespun
	Something Borrowed	02/95	Diamond	Homespun

Lee, Sandra

196	Over The Rainbow	03/88	Harlequin	Temptation
387	Love Lessons	03/92	Harlequin	Temptation

Lee, Sharon

	Shooting Star	/89	Ivy Books	Fortunes Series

Lees, Marguerite

505	Meet Doctor Kettering	/60	Harlequin
510	Doctor Halcott	/60	Harlequin
515	A Case For Nurse Clair	/60	Harlequin
536	Hospital At Night	/60	Harlequin
540	Village Nurse	/60	Harlequin
561	The Girl Who Kept Faith	/60	Harlequin
688	Stevie, Student Nurse	/62	Harlequin
704	Private Case	/62	Harlequin
720	General Hospital	/63	Harlequin
733	Stevie, Staff Nurse	/63	Harlequin
756	Ward Hostess	/63	Harlequin
769	Nursing Auxiliary	/63	Harlequin
795	Back Room Girl (Hospital Technician)	/64	Harlequin
881	Don't Marry A Doctor	/65	Harlequin
1205	The Sun And The Sea	/68	Harlequin
1235	Love As It Flies	/68	Harlequin
1264	Secret Star	/68	Harlequin
1303	Still Waters	/69	Harlequin

Lees, Marguerite

2034	Green Folly	/77	Harlequin	

Leffers, Laura Lynn

	Dance On The Water	03/96	Blue Star	

Lehman, Paul Evan

81	Idaho	/50	Harlequin	
82	The Cold Trail	/50	Harlequin	
105	Vengeance Valley	/51	Harlequin	
118	Range Justice	/51	Harlequin	
128	Law Of The '45	/51	Harlequin	
172	Gun Law	/52	Harlequin	
270	Fighting Buckaroo	/54	Harlequin	
353	Gun Law	/56	Harlequin	
358	Redrock Gold	/56	Harlequin	
404	Law In The Saddle	/57	Harlequin	

Lehr, Helene

	Capture The Dream		Avon	
	A Gallant Passion		Avon	
	The Passionate Rebel	07/94	Love Spell	Historical
	White Heather	/95	Love Spell	Historical

Leiber, Vivian

576	Baby Makes Nine	03/95	Harlequin	American
640	Blue-Jeaned Prince	07/96	Harlequin	American
822	Casey's Flyboy	10/91	Silhouette	Romance
871	Goody Two-Shoes	06/92	Silhouette	Romance
896	Her Own Prince Charming	10/92	Silhouette	Romance
1070	Safety Of His Arms	03/95	Silhouette	Romance

Leigh, Ana

	A Question Of Honor			
	Tender Is The Touch	02/94	Avon	
	The Tide Of Fortune	02/94	Avon	
	The Mackenzies: Luke	05/96	Avon	
	Forever My Love	02/95	Avon	Historical
	Proud Pillars Rising		Leisure	
	Love's Long Journey		Leisure	
	The Golden Spike	06/94	Leisure	
	Angel Hunter	12/92	Leisure	Historical
	These Hallowed Hills	08/91	Leisure	Historical
	A Kindled Flame		Leisure	Historical
	Oh, Promised Destiny		Leisure	Historical
	Paradise Redeemed		Leisure	Historical
	Sweet Enemy Mine		Leisure	Historical

Leigh, Barbara

98	To Touch The Sun	10/91	Harlequin	Historical
177	Web Of Loving Lies	06/93	Harlequin	Historical
254	For Love Alone	01/95	Harlequin	Historical

AUTHOR/TITLE INDEX

Leigh, Barbara
297   For Love Of Rory   12/95   Harlequin Historical
Leigh, Catherine
3075   Place For The Heart   Harlequin Romance
Leigh, Cynthia
   Silken Tiger   Diamond
Leigh, Elizabeth
   Creole Caress   Zebra
   Louisiana Passion   09/92   Zebra Heartfire
   Counterfeit Caress   11/91   Zebra Heartfire
   Fiery Virginia Jewel   Zebra Heartfire
   Prairie Ecstasy   04/93   Zebra Heartfire
   Dulcimer   09/95   Zebra Lovegram
Leigh, Helena
   Green Vineyards   Berkley
Leigh, Janet
   House Of Destiny   07/96   Mira
Leigh, Jo
   94   Special Effects   06/92   Meteor
   177   Wild Beauty   09/93   Meteor
   569   Suspect   05/94   Silhouette Intimate Moments
   659   Hunted   08/95   Silhouette Intimate Moments
Leigh, Lori
   On Winds Of Love
Leigh, Meredith
   An Elegant Education   /88   Walker
Leigh, Petra
   Rosewood   Pocket Richard Gallen Books
Leigh, Roberta
  1196   Dark Inheritance   /68   Harlequin
  1269   Pretence   /69   Harlequin
  1424   The Vengeful Heart   /70   Harlequin
  1696   My Heart's A Dancer   /73   Harlequin
  1715   In Name Only   /73   Harlequin
  1783   Cinderella In Mink   /74   Harlequin
  1800   Shade Of The Palms   /74   Harlequin
   64   Beloved Ballerina   /74   Harlequin Presents
   68   And Then Came Love   /74   Harlequin Presents
   76   Heart Of The Lion   /75   Harlequin Presents
  109   Temporary Wife   /75   Harlequin Presents
  127   Man In A Million   /76   Harlequin Presents
  161   To Buy A Bride   /76   Harlequin Presents
  169   Cupboard Love   /76   Harlequin Presents
  175   Man Without A Heart   /77   Harlequin Presents
  182   Unwilling Bridegroom   /77   Harlequin Presents
  193   Too Young To Love   /77   Harlequin Presents

AUTHOR/TITLE INDEX

Leigh, Victoria

554	Where There's A Will ...	07/92	Bantam	Loveswept
601	Flyboy	03/93	Bantam	Loveswept
625	Raising Harry	07/93	Bantam	Loveswept
646	Take A Chance On Love	10/93	Bantam	Loveswept
680	Gentle Learning	04/94	Bantam	Loveswept
680	Dangerous Love	04/94	Bantam	Loveswept
712	Blackthorne's Woman	10/94	Bantam	Loveswept
729	Stalking The Giant	02/95	Bantam	Loveswept
751	Catch Me If You Can	08/95	Bantam	Loveswept
766	Night Of The Hawk	11/95	Bantam	Loveswept

Leinster, Murray

281	Outlaw Deputy	/54	Harlequin

Leitfred, Robert H.

174	Murder Is My Rackey	/52	Harlequin

Lemery, Alysse

46	Twilight Dawn		Harlequin American
98	Wishing Star		Harlequin American
199	Winter's End		Harlequin American

Lenke, Gail

	The Wolf's Embrace	Leisure

Lennox, Jacqueline

429	Force Of Habit	06/88	Silhouette	Desire

Lennox, Marion

285	Storm Haven	06/96	Harlequin	
219	A Loving Legacy	02/95	Harlequin	Direct
227	Legacy Of Shadows	04/95	Harlequin	Direct

Lenore, Lisa

18	Dance Of Desire		Harlequin Superromance
39	Love's Hour Of Danger		Harlequin Superromance

Leonard, Phyllis G.

	Prey Of The Eagle	Gothic

Leone, Laura

478	One Sultry Summer	02/89	Silhouette	Desire
501	Wildflower	06/89	Silhouette	Desire
507	A Wilder Name	07/89	Silhouette	Desire
531	Ulterior Motives	11/89	Silhouette	Desire
560	Guilty Secrets	04/90	Silhouette	Desire
610	Upon A Midnight Clear	12/90	Silhouette	Desire
632	Celestial Bodies	04/91	Silhouette	Desire
696	The Black Sheep	02/92	Silhouette	Desire
737	Untouched By Man	09/92	Silhouette	Desire
834	Under The Voodoo Moon	01/94	Silhouette	Desire
608	A Woman's Work	07/90	Silhouette	Special Edition
681	The Bandit King	07/91	Silhouette	Special Edition

Leosing, Jan

AUTHOR/TITLE INDEX

Leosing, Jan
    Destiny Interlude
    A Moment In Time
Leslie, Doris
    Prime Minister's Wife   Historical
Leslie, Lynn

551	Cruisin' Mr. Diamond	09/94	Harlequin American
129	Street Of Dreams		Harlequin Intrigue
192	The Last Good-Night	08/92	Harlequin Intrigue
287	Night Of The Nile	08/94	Harlequin Intrigue
485	Defy The Night	01/92	Harlequin Superromance
566	Courage, My Love (Women Who Dare)	10/93	Harlequin Superromance
604	Singapore Fling	07/94	Harlequin Superromance

Lesoing, Jan
    Forever Yesterday   Pageant
Lester, Samantha

521	Love's Captive		Dell Candlelight
250	The Lady Rothschild		Dell Candlelight Regency
612	The Duke's Ward		Dell Candlelight Regency
637	The Brash American		Dell Candlelight Regency

Letts, Billie
    Where The Heart Is   07/96   Warner
Levitt, Dianne
    Grayson's Daughter
    Greenwill
    Private Sins   07/93   Zebra Pinnacle
Lewellyn, Caroline
    The Masks Of Rome   Ballantine
Lewis, Hilda
    Wife To The Bastard   Historical
Lewis, Kim
    Loving Becky   08/96   Dell Regency
Lewis, Linda

1113	Honeymoon Suite	10/95	Silhouette Romance
1135	The Husband Hunt	02/96	Silhouette Romance

Lewis, Mary
    7   Midsummer Bride   05/80   Silhouette Romance
Lewis, Sherry

628	Call Me Mom (Women Who Dare)	01/95	Harlequin Superromance
692	This Montana Home	05/96	Harlequin Superromance

Lewis, Susan
    Dance While You Can   12/91   Harper
    Class Apart   Harper
Lewty, Marjorie
    953   Alex Rayner, Dental Nurse   /65   Harlequin

Lewty, Marjorie

Ley, Alice Chetwynd

Lide, Mary

Liggett, Walter W.

AUTHOR/TITLE INDEX

Lindsay, Perry

16	No Nice Girl	/49	Harlequin

Lindsay, Phillip

225	Sir Rusty Sword	/53	Harlequin
280	The Nut Brown Maid	/54	Harlequin

Lindsay, Rachel

888	Heart Of A Rose	/65	Harlequin
1014	House Of Lorraine	/66	Harlequin
1039	The Taming Of Laura	/66	Harlequin
1614	Love And Lucy Granger	/72	Harlequin
1648	Moonlight And Magic	/72	Harlequin
1667	A Question Of Marriage	/73	Harlequin
1742	Alien Corn	/73	Harlequin
1763	Cage Of Gold	/74	Harlequin
45	The Price Of Love	/74	Harlequin Presents
48	Business Affair	/74	Harlequin Presents
53	Mask Of Gold	/74	Harlequin Presents
60	Castle In The Trees	/74	Harlequin Presents
73	Food For Love	/74	Harlequin Presents
80	Innocent Deception	/75	Harlequin Presents
85	Love In Disguise	/75	Harlequin Presents
104	Affair In Venice	/75	Harlequin Presents
117	Prince For Sale	/75	Harlequin Presents
164	Secretary Wife	/76	Harlequin Presents
172	Roman Affair	/77	Harlequin Presents
176	Tinsel Star	/77	Harlequin Presents
184	A Man To Tame	/77	Harlequin Presents
188	The Marquis Takes A Wife	/77	Harlequin Presents
201	Forbidden Love	/77	Harlequin Presents
217	Prescription For Love	/77	Harlequin Presents
220	Brazilian Affair	/78	Harlequin Presents
228	Forgotten Marriage	/78	Harlequin Presents
241	Love And Dr. Forrest	/78	Harlequin Presents
249	Unwanted Wife	/78	Harlequin Presents
257	Rough Diamond Lover	/78	Harlequin Presents
265	An Affair To Forget	/78	Harlequin Presents
274	Man Out Of Reach		Harlequin Presents
280	Designing Man		Harlequin Presents
315	My Sister's Keeper		Harlequin Presents
346	The Widening Stream		Harlequin Presents
359	Man Of Ice		Harlequin Presents
375	Rent A Wife		Harlequin Presents
381	Love And No Marriage		Harlequin Presents
413	Wife For A Year		Harlequin Presents
467	Untouched Wife		Harlequin Presents
555	Substitute Wife		Harlequin Presents

Lindsey, Betina

631

Lindsey, Betina

Swan Witch		
The Serpent Beguiled	12/92	Pocket
Waltz With A Lady		Pocket
Swan Bride		Pocket

Lindsey, Dana

398	Second Thoughts	06/92	Harlequin Temptation
1071	Julie's Garden	03/95	Silhouette Romance
1172	The Honeymoon Quest	08/96	Silhouette Romance

Lindsey, Dawn

Devil's Lady		Nal
Dunraven's Folly		Nal
Proper Proposal		Nal
The Talisman Ring		Nal
The Barbarous Scot	12/91	Nal Regency
Rebel Lady	08/92	Nal Regency
The Nonpareil	02/86	Nal Regency
Notorious Lady	06/87	Nal Regency
The Great Lady Tony	06/91	Nal Regency
An Independent Woman	02/94	Nal Regency
The Reluctant Heroine	07/93	Penguin Regency

Lindsey, Devon

Crimson Intrigue	

Lindsey, Johanna

Brave The Wild Wind		Avon
Captive Bride		Avon
Defy Not The Heart		Avon
A Gentle Feuding		Avon
Gentle Rogue	11/90	Avon
Glorious Angel		Avon
Heart Of Thunder		Avon
A Heart So Wild		Avon
Love Only Once		Avon
Man Of My Dreams	06/92	Avon
Once A Princess		Avon
Paradise Wild		Avon
Pirate's Love		Avon
Prisoner Of My Desire	11/91	Avon
Savage Thunder		Avon
Secret Fire		Avon
Silver Angel		Avon
So Speaks The Heart		Avon
Tender Is The Storm		Avon
Tender Rebel		Avon
Warrior's Woman		Avon
When Love Awaits		Avon

Lindsey, Johanna

	Angel		Avon	
	Keeper Of The Heart	11/93	Avon	
	The Magic Of You	05/93	Avon	
	You Belong To Me	11/94	Avon	
	Until Forever	09/95	Avon	
1	Fires Of Winter		Avon	Viking Trilogy
2	Hearts Aflame		Avon	Viking Trilogy
3	Surrender My Love	04/94	Avon	Viking Trilogy
	Love Me Forever	10/95	William Morrow	

Lindsey, Patrice

53	Golden Gamble	08/91	Meteor

Lindsey, Terri

865	Going My Way	05/92	Silhouette Romance
1106	Dream Bride	09/95	Silhouette Romance

Link, Gail

	There Never Was A Time	/95	Leisure	
1	Enchantadora	11/91	Leisure	
2	All I Ask Of You	09/94	Leisure	
	Wolf's Embrace	11/92	Leisure	Historical
	Never Call It Loving	10/93	Leisure	Historical
1035	Marriage-To-Be?	06/96	Silhouette	Special Edition

Linton, Isobel

	A Mother's Delight	03/95	Zebra Anthology
	A Gentleman's Daughter	04/95	Zebra Regency

Linz, Cathie

52	Remembrance Of Love	04/82	Dell Candlelight Ecstasy
157	Wildfire	07/83	Dell Candlelight Ecstasy
178	A Summer's Embrace	10/83	Dell Candlelight Ecstasy
203	A Charming Strategy	01/84	Dell Candlelight Ecstasy
242	A Private Account	06/84	Dell Candlelight Ecstasy
266	Winner Takes All	09/84	Dell Candlelight Ecstasy
313	Pride And Joy	02/85	Dell Candlelight Ecstasy
330	A Glimpse Of Paradise	02/85	Dell Candlelight Ecstasy
364	Tender Guardian	09/85	Dell Candlelight Ecstasy
394	Lover And Deceiver	01/86	Dell Candlelight Ecstasy
482	A Handful Of Trouble	01/87	Dell Candlelight Ecstasy
130	Continental Lover	07/86	Dell Supreme
10	Baby Wanted	05/95	Harlequin Montana Mav.
1023	Michael's Baby #1	09/96	Silhouette 3 Weddings & Gift Trilogy
1029	Hunter's Seduction #2	10/96	Silhouette 3 Weddings & Gift Trilogy
1035	Abbie And The Cowboy #3	11/96	Silhouette 3 Weddings & Gift Trilogy
	Husband Needed (Tentative Title)	/97	Silhouette Desire
408	Change Of Heart	02/88	Silhouette Desire
443	A Friend In Need	08/88	Silhouette Desire
484	As Good As Gold	03/89	Silhouette Desire

Linz, Cathie

519	Adam's Way	09/89	Silhouette Desire
575	Smiles	06/90	Silhouette Desire
616	Handyman	01/91	Silhouette Desire
665	Smooth Sailing	09/91	Silhouette Desire
722	Flirting With Trouble	07/92	Silhouette Desire
761	Male Ordered Bride	01/93	Silhouette Desire
804	Escapades	08/93	Silhouette Desire
846	Midnight Ice	03/94	Silhouette Desire
894	Bridal Blues (Jilted!)	11/94	Silhouette Desire
958	A Wife In Time	10/95	Silhouette Desire
1032	One Of A Kind Marriage (Hasty Weddings)	09/94	Silhouette Romance
	Time Flies	/95	Silhouette Time Travel

Litton, Pamela

69	Stardust And Whirlwinds	03/91	Harlequin Historical
122	Dance With The Devil	04/92	Harlequin Historical
	Scoundrel	01/94	Jove Historical

Livingston, Georgette

| 92 | Serengeti Sunrise | | Harlequin Superromance |

Lloyd, Frances

200	Savage Moon	01/83	Silhouette Romance
319	Desert Rose	09/84	Silhouette Romance
425	Wild Horizon's	04/86	Silhouette Romance
473	The Castaways	12/86	Silhouette Romance
497	Tomorrow's Dawn	04/87	Silhouette Romance
549	Touched By Magic	12/87	Silhouette Romance
569	The Takeover Man	04/88	Silhouette Romance
624	Lord Of The Glen	01/89	Silhouette Romance
804	Let Me Call You Sweetheart	07/91	Silhouette Romance

Lock, Diane E.

| | True Love | 02/94 | Zebra Over 45 |

Lockhart, Lynn

| 498 | Date With An Outlaw | 08/93 | Harlequin American |
| 527 | Nickie's Ghost | 03/94 | Harlequin American |

Lockwood, Ethel

| | Witness To The Wedding | | Bantam Red Rose Romance |

Lockwood, Karen

	Harvest Song	01/93	Diamond Homespun
	Country Kiss	02/93	Diamond Homespun
	Winter Song	11/93	Diamond Homespun
	Seasons Of Love: "Summer Storm"	08/95	Harper Anthology
	Summer Magic	07/93	Jove Anthology
	Hearts Of Gold	02/94	Jove Anthology
	Lilac Circle	12/95	Jove Homespun
	Stolen Kisses	11/94	Jove Tea Rose Romance

Loeser, Pamela

AUTHOR/TITLE INDEX

Loeser, Pamela

  186   Secret Harmony   11/93   Meteor

Lofts, Norah

         A Wayside Tavern
         Madsen
         The Judas Kiss
         The Town House
         Bless This House
         Here Was A Man
         The Concubine
         Pargeters
         Lovers All Untrue
         Knight's Acre
         Nethergate   Historical
         House At Sunset   Suspense
         Jassy   Ballantine

Logan, Anne

  507   Gulf Breezes   07/92   Harlequin Superromance
  550   Twin Oaks   06/93   Harlequin Superromance
  585   Dial "D" For Destiny   02/94   Harlequin Superromance
  688   That Old Devil Moon   04/96   Harlequin Superromance

Logan, Cait

         Rugged Glory   09/91   Berkley Second Chance At Love
  325   Lady On The Line   03/86   Berkley Second Chance At Love
  432   A Lady's Choice   02/88   Berkley Second Chance At Love
  442   A Lady's Desire   07/88   Berkley Second Chance At Love
         Wild Dawn   06/92   Diamond
         Gambler's Lady   07/92   Diamond
         Tame The Fury   Diamond
         Night Fire   03/94   Diamond Historical
         Delilah   03/95   Jove Historical
  726   Midnight Rider   07/92   Silhouette Desire

Logan, Daisy

   50   Reckless Longing   /82   Berkley Second Chance At Love
 138   Southern Pleasure   /83   Berkley Second Chance At Love
 163   Sweet Bliss   /83   Berkley Second Chance At Love

Logan, Jessica

   20   Journey Into Love   Harlequin Superromance
   27   Promise To Possess   Harlequin Superromance
   41   Dark Promise Of Delight   Harlequin Superromance
   99   The Awakening Touch   Harlequin Superromance

Logan, Kate

 402   Blue Skies And Promises   08/91   Harlequin American

Logan, Kristina

         Afternoon Delight   /94   Silhouette Romance
 738   Promise Of Marriage   08/90   Silhouette Romance

AUTHOR/TITLE INDEX

Logan, Kristina

817	Hometown Hero	09/91	Silhouette	Romance
852	Two To Tango	03/92	Silhouette	Romance
870	The Right Man For Loving	06/92	Silhouette	Romance
918	To The Rescue	02/93	Silhouette	Romance
950	The Man Behind The Magic	07/93	Silhouette	Romance
998	A Man Like Jake	03/94	Silhouette	Romance

Logan, Leandra

	I'm Your Baby Tonight	09/94	Harlequin	American
559	Secret Agent Dad	11/94	Harlequin	American
601	The Last Bridesmaid	10/95	Harlequin	American
	Cand Cane Kisses	12/96	Harlequin	Love And Laughter
	Heavensent Husband	10/96	Harlequin	Temptation
320	The Cupid Connection	10/90	Harlequin	Temptation
362	Dilllon After Dark	09/91	Harlequin	Temptation
393	The Last Honest Man (Rebels & Rogues)	05/92	Harlequin	Temptation
433	The Missing Heir	03/93	Harlequin	Temptation
472	Joyride	12/93	Harlequin	Temptation
491	Her Favorite Husband	05/94	Harlequin	Temptation
519	Happy Birthday, Baby	12/94	Harlequin	Temptation
535	Bargain Basement Baby	04/95	Harlequin	Temptation
564	Angel Baby	11/95	Harlequin	Temptation
5	A Bride For Daddy	08/96	Harlequin	Weddings By Dewilde
	The Education Of Jake Flynn	09/96	Harlequin	Yours Truly

Logan, Sara

135	Game Of Hearts	02/82	Silhouette	Romance

Loghry, Lizabeth

61	Shadow Of Deceit		Harlequin	Intrigue

London, Cait

	The Wedding: Gamble	08/96	Dell	
	Spring Fancy - "Lightfoot & Loving"	02/94	Harlequin	Anthology
	Silhouette Spring Fancy Collection	03/94	Silhouette	Anthology
502	The Loving Season	06/89	Silhouette	Desire
593	Angel Vs. Maclean	09/90	Silhouette	Desire
611	The Pendragon Virus	12/90	Silhouette	Desire
641	The Daddy Candidate	05/91	Silhouette	Desire
726	Midnight Rider	07/92	Silhouette	Desire
763	The Cowboy	02/93	Silhouette	Desire
782	Maybe No, Maybe Yes	05/93	Silhouette	Desire
811	The Seduction Of Jake Tallman	10/93	Silhouette	Desire
871	Fusion	08/94	Silhouette	Desire
891	The Bride Says No	11/94	Silhouette	Desire
919	Mr. Easy	04/95	Silhouette	Desire
968	Miracles And Mistletoe	12/95	Silhouette	Desire
1006	The Cowboy And The Cradle	06/96	Silhouette	Desire
	Tallchief's Bride	09/96	Silhouette	Tallchiefs

Lorraine, Marian

589	The Ardent Suitor		Dell Candlelight Regency
639	The Enterprising Minx		Dell Candlelight Regency
	The Mischievous Spinster		Walker

Lorrimer, Claire

	Tamarisk		
	The Chatelaine		Ballantine

Lough, Loree

	Follow The Leader	11/95	Barbour & Co.
	Pocketful Of Promises	12/95	Barbour & Co.
	Montana Sky	03/96	Barbour & Co.
	Priscilla Hires A Husband	04/96	Barbour & Co.

Louis, Jacqueline

84	Love's Stormy Height		Harlequin Superromance

Louis, Pat

14	Treasure Of The Year		Harlequin Superromance

Lovan, Thea

28	Passionate Journey	11/82	Silhouette Desire
281	A Tender Passion	03/84	Silhouette Romance
326	A Story Well Told	10/84	Silhouette Romance
361	The Blue Sea Of August	05/85	Silhouette Romance

Lovelace, Jane

	Rolissa		Walker
	Eccentric Lady		Walker

Lovelace, Merline

	Renegades (Promotion)	08/95	Harlequin Anthology
220	Alena	05/94	Harlequin Historical
230	Sweet Song Of Love (Destiny's Women)	07/94	Harlequin Historical
236	Siren's Call (Destiny's Women)	09/94	Harlequin Historical
275	His Lady's Ransom	07/95	Harlequin Historical
320	Lady Of The Upper Kingdom	06/96	Harlequin Historical
3	Maggie And Her Colonel	03/94	Harlequin Stolen Moments
125	Bits And Pieces	01/93	Meteor
872	Dreams And Schemes (Centerfolds)	08/94	Silhouette Desire
593	Somewhere In Time (Spellbound)	09/94	Silhouette Intimate Moments
637	Night Of The Jaguar	05/95	Silhouette Intimate Moments
657	The Cowboy And The Cossack	08/95	Silhouette Intimate Moments
669	Undercover Man	10/95	Silhouette Intimate Moments
692	Perfect Double	02/96	Silhouette Intimate Moments

Lowell, Anne Hunter

	Risking It All	03/87	Cloverdale

Lowell, Elizabeth

	Only His		Avon
	Only Mine		Avon
	Only You	07/92	Avon
	Forbidden	10/93	Avon

Lowell, Elizabeth

	Lover In The Rough	01/94	Avon
	Forget Me Not	12/94	Avon
	Untamed	/94	Avon
	Only Love	06/95	Avon
	A Woman Without Lies	12/95	Avon
	Enchanted	08/94	Avon Historical
199	Reckless Love	01/94	Harlequin Historical
	Outlaw	10/94	Mira
	Granite Man	01/95	Mira
	Warrior	04/95	Mira
	Tell Me No Lies	08/95	Mira
77	Summer Thunder	07/83	Silhouette Desire
265	The Fire Of Spring	03/86	Silhouette Desire
319	To Hot To Handle	12/86	Silhouette Desire
355	Love Song For A Raven	06/87	Silhouette Desire
415	Fever	04/88	Silhouette Desire
462	Dark Fire	11/88	Silhouette Desire
546	Fire And Rain	01/90	Silhouette Desire
624	Outlaw	02/91	Silhouette Desire
625	Granite Man	03/91	Silhouette Desire
631	Warrior	04/91	Silhouette Desire
18	The Danver's Touch	09/83	Silhouette Intimate Moments
34	Lover In The Rough	01/84	Silhouette Intimate Moments
56	An Old Fashioned Love	06/84	Silhouette Intimate Moments
57	Summer Games	07/84	Silhouette Intimate Moments
72	Forget Me Not	10/84	Silhouette Intimate Moments
81	A Woman Without Lies	02/85	Silhouette Intimate Moments
97	Traveling Man	06/85	Silhouette Intimate Moments
109	Valley Of The Sun	09/85	Silhouette Intimate Moments
128	Sequel	01/86	Silhouette Intimate Moments
141	Fires Of Eden	05/86	Silhouette Intimate Moments
178	Sweet Wind, Wild Wind	02/87	Silhouette Intimate Moments
256	Chain Lightning	09/88	Silhouette Intimate Moments

Lowery, Lynn

	Starflower		
	Sweet Rush Of Passion		Bantam

Lucas, Mayo

	Camelot Jones	06/89	Avon
	Matters Of The Heart		Avon

Luellen, Valentina

	The Passionate Pirate	08/86	Harlequin Historical
6	Francesca		Mills & Boon
9	Madelon		Mills & Boon
17	Gambler's Prize		Mills & Boon
31	A Pride Of Mac Donalds		Mills & Boon
34	The Countess		Mills & Boon

Lynch, Miriam

| | Regency Ball | | Ballantine Regency |
| 201 | Winter In A Dark Land | | Dell Candlelight |

Lyndell, Catherine

	Arianne		
	Border Fires		
	Midsummer Rose	05/92	Pocket
	Stolen Dreams		Pocket
	Tapestry Of Pride		Pocket
	Masquerade		Pocket
	Alliance Of Love		Pocket
	Captive Hearts		Pocket
	Vows Of Desire		Pocket
	Journey To Desire		Pocket

Lyndon, Diana

	My Lord, My Love		Pocket Cotillion Regency
	The Country Rose		Pocket Cotillion Regency
	Her Heart's Desire		Pocket Cotillion Regency

Lynley, Elinor

| | Song Of The Bayou | | Nal Penguin |

Lynn, Anita

| | For The Love Of Hollie | 04/95 | Lion Hearted |

Lynn, Ann

234	Beautiful Dreamer	08/94	Harlequin Historical
	Slave Of My Heart	01/90	Zebra
	Flame Of My Heart		Zebra
	Passion's Chase	08/92	Zebra Heartfire
	Midnight Safari		Zebra Heartfire

Lynn, Leslie

	Scandal's Child		Ballantine
	The Rake's Redemption		Ballantine Regency
	The Duke's Deceit	04/93	Fawcett Crest
	A Soldier's Heart	01/92	Fawcett Crest Regency
	Autumn Love	10/93	Fawcett Crest Regency

Lynn, Patricia

| 191 | Everything About Him | 12/93 | Meteor |

Lynn, Sheryl

190	Double Vision	07/92	Harlequin Intrigue
258	Simon Says	01/94	Harlequin Intrigue
306	Ladykiller	01/95	Harlequin Intrigue
331	Dark Knight (Mirror Images)	07/95	Harlequin Intrigue
336	Dark Star (Mirror Images)	08/95	Harlequin Intrigue
367	The Other Laura	04/96	Harlequin Intrigue
	Honeymoon Suite	05/95	St. Martin's Anthology

Lynn, Terri

| | Rightful Place | | Harlequin Superromance |

641

AUTHOR/TITLE INDEX

Lynn, Terri

534	Uncommon Stock	02/93	Harlequin Superromance
555	Valentine's Summer	07/93	Harlequin Superromance

Lynn, Virginia

River's Dream	04/91	Bantam Fanfare
Cutter's Woman	10/91	Bantam Fanfare
Summer's Knight	03/92	Bantam Fanfare
Lyon's Prize	10/92	Bantam Fanfare
The New Moon River	07/94	Bantam Fanfare

Lynne, Suzanna

2007	Beloved Viking	/76	Harlequin
88	Red Feather Love	/75	Harlequin Presents

Lynne, Victoria

Captured	07/95	Avon

Lynnford, Janet

Pirate's Rose	06/95	Topaz

Lynson, Jane

Captain Rakehell	Ballantine Regency
The Duke's Downfall	Fawcett

Lyon, Mary

779	Love's Tangled Web	Harlequin Presents

Lyons, Leila

Pillars Of Heaven	Richard Gallen

Lyons, Maggie

Bayou Passions	Berkley

Lyons, Mary

625	Passionate Escape		Harlequin Presents
673	Caribbean Confusion		Harlequin Presents
701	Desire In The Desert		Harlequin Presents
714	Spanish Serenade		Harlequin Presents
763	Dangerous Stunt		Harlequin Presents
796	Mended Engagement		Harlequin Presents
828	Eclipse Of The Heart		Harlequin Presents
908	Passionate Deception		Harlequin Presents
938	Escape From The Hare		Harlequin Presents
1002	Hay Fever		Harlequin Presents
1144	Stranger At Winterfl		Harlequin Presents
1171	Hurricane		Harlequin Presents
1276	Love In A Spin		Harlequin Presents
1346	No Surrender		Harlequin Presents
1499	Dark And Dangerous	10/92	Harlequin Presents
1610	Silver Lady	12/93	Harlequin Presents
1633	Love Is The Key	03/94	Harlequin Presents
1781	The Yuletide Bride	12/95	Harlequin Presents
1801	It Started With A Kiss	03/96	Harlequin Presents

Mac Donald, Elisabeth

Mac Donald, Elisabeth
    Voices On The Wind   12/94 Avon Historical
  90 Estero Bay   08/91 Harlequin Historical
  18 Love Me Again   07/84 Harlequin Temptation
Mac Donald, Elizabeth
    Falling Stars   Pocket
    Wyoming Star   Pocket
Mac Donald, Roslyn
 583 An Independent Lady   06/88 Silhouette Romance
 261 Second Generation   09/85 Silhouette Special Edition
 293 Transfer Of Loyalties   02/86 Silhouette Special Edition
Mac Donald, Ruby
    Smooth Sailing   05/95 Zebra To Love Again
Mac Gowen, Wynema
    Catching The Rainbows 07/96 Kensington Denise Little Presents
Mac Gregor, D.J.
    Naked In Death   07/95 Berkley Romantic Suspense
Mac Gregor, Miriam
 273 Man Of His Word   03/96 Harlequin
 148 His Cousin's Keeper   08/93 Harlequin Direct
 172 Wilder's Wilderness   02/94 Harlequin Direct
 210 Heir To Glengyle   11/94 Harlequin Direct
2710 Boss Of Brightlands   Harlequin Romance
2733 Spring At Sevenoaks   Harlequin Romance
2794 Call Of The Mountain   Harlequin Romance
2823 Winter At Whitecliff   Harlequin Romance
2849 Stairway To Destiny   Harlequin Romance
2890 Autumn At Aubrey's   02/88 Harlequin Romance
2931 Rider Of The Hills   Harlequin Romance
2996 Lord Of The Lodge   Harlequin Romance
3022 Riddell Of Rivermoon   Harlequin Romance
3060 Man Of The House   Harlequin Romance
3083 Carville's Castle   Harlequin Romance
3140 Master Of Marshlands 08/91 Harlequin Romance
3225 The Intruder   10/92 Harlequin Romance
3255 The Orchard King   03/93 Harlequin Romance
Mac Iver, Sharon
    River Song   10/91 Berkley
    Dakota Dream   01/91 Berkley
Mac Keever, Maggie
    Our Tabby   Ballantine Regency
    Lady Sherry & The Highwayman   Ballantine Regency
    Lady Sweetbriar   Ballantine Regency
    Strange Bedfellows   Ballantine Regency
    Fair Fatality   Ballantine Regency
    Jessabelle   Ballantine Regency

Mac Keever, Maggie

	Lady In The Straw		Ballantine Regency
	The Misses Milliken		Ballantine Regency
	An Eligible Connection		Ballantine Regency
	A Banbury Tale		Ballantine Regency
	Lady Bliss		Ballantine Regency
	A Notorious Lady		Ballantine Regency
	Lord Fairchild's Daughter		Ballantine Regency
	Sweet Vixen		Ballantine Regency

Mac Kenzie, Maura

	The Daddy List	07/95	
6	Sweet Seduction		Harlequin Superromance
76	Mirror Of The Heart		Harlequin Superromance

Mac Lean, Jan

2210	To Begin Again	/78	Harlequin
2287	Bitter Homecoming		Harlequin Romance
2295	Early Summer		Harlequin Romance
2348	White Fire		Harlequin Romance
2547	All Our Tomorrows		Harlequin Romance

Mac Leod, Charlotte

	Rest You Merry	11/93	Avon

Mac Leod, Jean S.

431	The Silent Valley	/58	Harlequin
434	Dear Doctor Everett	/58	Harlequin
451	Air Ambulance	/59	Harlequin
516	Prisoner Of Love	/60	Harlequin
517	Journey In The Sun (Doctors Together)	/60	Harlequin
541	The Way In The Dark	/60	Harlequin
543	The Little Doctor	/60	Harlequin
545	Nurse Lange	/60	Harlequin
547	The Gated Road	/60	Harlequin
586	Cameron Of Gare	/61	Harlequin
597	This Much To Give (Special Nurse)	/61	Harlequin
599	Run Away From Love (Nurse Companion)	/61	Harlequin
606	Silent Bondage (Doctor In Bondage)	/61	Harlequin
607	Silent Bondage (Doctor In Bondage)	/61	Harlequin
630	Stranger In Their Midst	/61	Harlequin
638	Mountain Clinic	/62	Harlequin
651	Dangerous Obsession	/62	Harlequin
674	The Silver Dragon	/62	Harlequin
711	My Heart's In The Highlands	/63	Harlequin
748	The Valley Of Palms	/63	Harlequin
797	The Black Cameron	/64	Harlequin
853	Sugar Island	/64	Harlequin
939	Doctor's Daughter	/65	Harlequin
966	Crane Castle	/65	Harlequin

AUTHOR/TITLE INDEX

Macaluso, Pamela

182	Rose Among Thornes	11/93	Meteor
897	Hometown Wedding	12/94	Silhouette Desire
928	Dream Wedding (Just Married)	05/95	Silhouette Desire
970	Christmas Wedding	12/95	Silhouette Desire

Mace, Merlda

25	Blondes Don't Cry	/49	Harlequin

Macias, Stacie

	The Rains Of Hamakua	/92	Avalon

Macias, Susan

	Frontier Flame	01/92	Diamond Historical
	Tender Victory	02/93	Diamond Historical
	Sweet Escape	08/94	Diamond Historical
	Fire In The Dark	08/95	Harper Monogram
	Honeysuckle Devine	02/96	Harper Monogram
91	First Mate	05/92	Meteor
159	Master Of The Chase	07/93	Meteor Kismet

Mack, Amanda

631	Makeshift Mistress		Dell Candlelight Regency

Mack, Dorothy

221	The Raven Sisters		Dell Candlelight Regency
225	The Substitute Bride		Dell Candlelight Regency
253	The Impossible Ward		Dell Candlelight Regency
602	A Companion In Joy		Dell Candlelight Regency
666	The Belle Of Bath		Dell Candlelight Regency
	The Chaperone Unlikely		Nal
	The Luckless Elopement		Nal
	The Mock Marriage		Nal
	A Prior Attachment		Nal
	The Reluctant Heart		Nal
	The Courtship Of Chloe	08/92	Nal Regency
	The Last Waltz	03/86	Nal Regency
	An Unconventional Courtship	08/87	Nal Regency
	The Steadfast Heart	12/88	Nal Regency
	The Blackmailed Bridegroom		Nal Regency
	The General's Granddaughter		Nal Regency
	The Lost Heir	07/93	Penguin Regency
	A Temporary Betrothal	04/95	Signet Regency

Mackenzie, Myrna

1046	The Baby Wish	11/94	Silhouette Romance
1090	The Daddy List (Fabulous Fathers)	07/95	Silhouette Romance
1182	Babies And A Blue-Eyed Man	10/96	Silhouette Romance

Mackey, Mary

	Season Of Shadows	05/92	Bantam Fanfare

Maclay, Charlotte

474	The Villain's Lady	02/93	Harlequin American

AUTHOR/TITLE INDEX

647

Macomber, Debbie

	Morning Comes Softly	04/93	Harper	
	One Night	08/94	Harper	
	Touched By Angels	11/95	Harper	
	Purrfect Love		Harper	Anthology
	Someday Soon	06/95	Harper	Monogram
	Sooner Or Later	06/96	Harper	Monogram
	Mrs. Miracle	10/96	Harper	Monogram
	Starlight	02/95	Mira	
	Reflections Of Yesterday	07/95	Mira	
	Fallen Angel	10/96	Mira	
	For All My Tomorrows	07/96	Mira	
	The Playboy And The Widow	03/96	Mira	
	Promise Me Forever	10/95	Mira	
	Christmas Stories - "Let It Snow"	11/86	Silhouette	Anthology
	Christmas Masquerade	11/91	Silhouette	Anthology
	Three Mothers & A Cradle	05/95	Silhouette	Anthology
	Silver Bells	12/96	Silhouette	Anthology
	Yesterday Once More	06/96	Silhouette	Anthology
	Christmas Treasures	11/92	Silhouette	Anthology
	To Mother With Love	/93	Silhouette	Anthology
1	Heartsong	/96	Silhouette	Inspirations
9	Undercover Dreamer	/96	Silhouette	Inspirations
15	A Girl Like Janet	/96	Silhouette	Inspirations
21	Thanksgiving Prayer	/96	Silhouette	Inspirations
23	The Gift Of Christmas	/96	Silhouette	Inspirations
29	Love Thy Neighbor	/29	Silhouette	Inspirations
316	That Wintry Feeling	09/84	Silhouette	Romance
341	Promise Me Forever	02/85	Silhouette	Romance
349	Adam's Image	03/85	Silhouette	Romance
379	The Trouble With Cassi	08/85	Silhouette	Romance
392	A Friend Or Two	10/85	Silhouette	Romance
405	Christmas Masquerade	12/85	Silhouette	Romance
415	Shadow Chasing	02/86	Silhouette	Romance
426	Yesterday's Hero	04/86	Silhouette	Romance
437	Laughter In The Rain	06/86	Silhouette	Romance
449	Jury Of His Peers	08/86	Silhouette	Romance
461	Yesterday Once More	10/86	Silhouette	Romance
474	Friends--- And Then Some	12/86	Silhouette	Romance
494	Sugar And Spice	03/87	Silhouette	Romance
512	No Competition	06/87	Silhouette	Romance
522	Love 'n' Marriage	08/87	Silhouette	Romance
539	Mail-Order Bride	11/87	Silhouette	Romance
555	Legendary Lovers 1: Cindy And The Prince	01/88	Silhouette	Romance
567	Legendary Lovers 2: Some Kind Of Wonder	03/88	Silhouette	Romance
579	Legendary Lovers 3: Almost Paradise	05/88	Silhouette	Romance
603	Any Sunday	09/88	Silhouette	Romance

AUTHOR/TITLE INDEX

Macomber, Debbie

629	Almost An Angel	02/89	Silhouette	Romance
671	The Way To A Man's Heart	09/89	Silhouette	Romance
1012	The Bachelor Prince (Celebration 1000!)	06/94	Silhouette	Romance
128	Starlight	11/83	Silhouette	Special Edition
241	Borrowed Dreams	06/85	Silhouette	Special Edition
284	Reflections Of Yesterday	01/86	Silhouette	Special Edition
322	White Lace And Promises	07/86	Silhouette	Special Edition
392	All Things Considered	07/87	Silhouette	Special Edition
482	The Playboy And The Widow	10/88	Silhouette	Special Edition
494	Navy Wife	12/88	Silhouette	Special Edition
518	Navy Blues	04/89	Silhouette	Special Edition
530	For All My Tomorrows	06/89	Silhouette	Special Edition
570	Denim And Diamonds	12/89	Silhouette	Special Edition
577	Fallen Angel	02/90	Silhouette	Special Edition
606	The Courtship Of Carol Sommars	06/90	Silhouette	Special Edition
626	The Cowboy's Lady	10/90	Silhouette	Special Edition
637	The Sheriff Takes A Wife	12/90	Silhouette	Special Edition
662	Navy Brat	04/91	Silhouette	Special Edition
683	Navy Woman	07/91	Silhouette	Special Edition
697	Navy Baby	10/91	Silhouette	Special Edition
732	Marriage Of Inconvenience	03/92	Silhouette	Special Edition
744	Stand-In Wife	05/92	Silhouette	Special Edition
756	Bride On The Loose	07/92	Silhouette	Special Edition
798	Hasty Wedding	02/93	Silhouette	Special Edition
831	Groom Wanted	08/93	Silhouette	Special Edition
836	Bride Wanted (From This Day Forward)	09/93	Silhouette	Special Edition
842	Marriage Wanted (From This Day Forward)	10/93	Silhouette	Special Edition
895	Baby Blessed	07/94	Silhouette	Special Edition
937	Same Time, Next Year	02/95	Silhouette	Special Edition
1003	Just Married	01/96	Silhouette	Special Edition
	Wanted: Perfect Partner	08/95	Silhouette	Yours Truly
	The Marrying Kind	05/96	Zebra	Anthology
	A Spring Bouquet	05/96	Zebra	Anthology

Madden, Mickee

Everlastin'	01/95	Pinnacle	

Maderich, Robin

Faith And Honor		Warner

Madl, Linda

Speak Of Love	12/91	Pocket
Sweet Ransom		Pocket
Sunny	09/90	Pocket

Magner, Lee

Beguiling Pretender	/87	Dell	Candlelight Ecstasy
Night Of The Matador	/87	Dell	Candlelight Ecstasy
Hidden Charms	/85	Dell	Candlelight Ecstasy

Magner, Lee

	The Gambler's Game	/86	Dell Candlelight Ecstasy
	The Torch Song	/86	Dell Candlelight Ecstasy
	Tender Refuge	/85	Dell Candlelight Ecstasy
86	Hidden Charms	/86	Dell Candlelight Ecstasy
246	Mustang Man	07/88	Silhouette Intimate Moments
274	Master Of The Hunt	02/89	Silhouette Intimate Moments
312	Mistress Of Foxgrove	11/89	Silhouette Intimate Moments
326	Sutter's Wife	03/90	Silhouette Intimate Moments
356	The Dragon's Lair	10/90	Silhouette Intimate Moments
382	Stolen Dreams	05/91	Silhouette Intimate Moments
420	Song Of The Mourning Dove	02/92	Silhouette Intimate Moments
507	Standoff	07/93	Silhouette Intimate Moments
556	Banished	03/94	Silhouette Intimate Moments
699	Dangerous	03/96	Silhouette Intimate Moments

Mahon, Annette

	Lei Of Love	04/96	Avalon

Mahon, Kay

	Defy The Thunder		

Major, Ann

	Bad Boys	09/93	Harlequin By Request: Anthology
9	Dream Come True	01/94	Harlequin Men Made In America
38	The Wrong Man	/95	Harlequin Men Made In America
	Wild Lady	08/95	Harlequin Western Lovers
	The Fairy Tale Girl	10/95	Harlequin Western Lovers
	Destiny's Child	12/95	Harlequin Western Lovers
	Birds, Bees & Babies - 1994	05/94	Silhouette Anthology
	Too Hot To Handle	07/95	Silhouette Anthology
	Silhouette Summer Sizzlers - "Fancy's Man"	06/95	Silhouette Anthology
	Santa's Special Miracle	/90	Silhouette Christmas Stories
	Cheyenne's Child		Silhouette Desire
16	Dream Come True	09/82	Silhouette Desire
35	Meant To Be	12/82	Silhouette Desire
99	Love Me Again	11/83	Silhouette Desire
151	The Wrong Man	08/84	Silhouette Desire
198	Golden Man	03/85	Silhouette Desire
229	Beyond Love	09/85	Silhouette Desire
301	In Every Stranger's Face	09/86	Silhouette Desire
331	What This Passion Means	02/87	Silhouette Desire
445	Passion's Child	09/88	Silhouette Desire
451	Destiny's Child	10/88	Silhouette Desire
457	Night Child	11/88	Silhouette Desire
535	Wilderness Child	12/89	Silhouette Desire
564	Scandal's Child	04/90	Silhouette Desire
648	The Goodbye Child	06/91	Silhouette Desire
690	A Knight In Tarnished Armor	01/92	Silhouette Desire
716	Married To The Enemy	06/92	Silhouette Desire

AUTHOR/TITLE INDEX

Major, Ann

805	Wild Honey	09/93	Silhouette	Desire
819	Wild Midnight (Something Wild)	11/93	Silhouette	Desire
835	Wild Innocence	02/94	Silhouette	Desire
889	The Accidental Bridegroom	11/94	Silhouette	Desire
967	A Cowboy Christmas	12/95	Silhouette	Desire
1003	The Accidental Bodyguard	06/96	Silhouette	Desire
54	Seize The Moment	06/84	Silhouette	Intimate Moments
90	Wild Lady	07/81	Silhouette	Romance
150	A Touch Of Fire	05/82	Silhouette	Romance
83	Brand Of Diamonds	03/83	Silhouette	Special Edition
229	Dazzle	04/85	Silhouette	Special Edition
390	The Fairytale Girl	06/87	Silhouette	Special Edition
	The Barefooted Enchantress	/92	Silhouette	Summer Sizzlers 1992

Makewell, Kathleen

Winter Masquerade		Nal Penguin
The Devil's Heart		Nal Penguin

Malcolm, Aleen

Devlyn Tremayne		
The Daughters Of Cameron		Bantam
Kenlaren		Bantam
Ride Out The Storm		Bantam
The Taming		Bantam

Malcolm, Anthea

A Sensible Match	04/93	Zebra	
A Christmas Delight	/91	Zebra	Anthology
The Counterfeit Heart		Zebra	Regency
The Courting Of Philippa		Zebra	Regency
Frivolous Pretence		Zebra	Regency
An Improper Proposal		Zebra	Regency
A Touch Of Scandal		Zebra	Regency
The Widow's Gambit		Zebra	Regency

Malcolm, Margaret

584	The Healing Touch (Village Hospital)	/61	Harlequin
592	Marriage Compromise	/61	Harlequin
596	Hope For The Doctor	/61	Harlequin
600	Jean Marlowe, Hospital Librarian	/61	Harlequin
613	Nurse In The House	/61	Harlequin
634	Love Without Wings (Surgeon's Wife)	/61	Harlequin
723	Fortune Goes Begging	/63	Harlequin
777	Scatterbrains - Student Nurse	/63	Harlequin
809	Send For Nurse Vincent	/64	Harlequin
923	Kit Cavendish - Private Nurse	/65	Harlequin
945	Doctor Sandy	/65	Harlequin
978	Dr. Gregory Misunderstands	/66	Harlequin
1002	A Doctor For Diana	/66	Harlequin

Malek, Doreen Owens

290	Firestorm	07/86	Silhouette Desire
343	Bright River	04/87	Silhouette Desire
450	Roughneck	09/88	Silhouette Desire
747	Arrow In The Snow	11/92	Silhouette Desire
778	The Harder They Fall	04/93	Silhouette Desire
869	Above The Law	07/94	Silhouette Desire
983	Daddy's Choice	02/96	Silhouette Desire
88	The Eden Tree	03/85	Silhouette Intimate Moments
105	Devil's Deception	08/85	Silhouette Intimate Moments
169	Montega's Mistress	12/86	Silhouette Intimate Moments
204	Danger Zone	08/87	Silhouette Intimate Moments
282	A Marriage Of Convenience	04/89	Silhouette Intimate Moments
620	Marriage In Name Only	02/95	Silhouette Intimate Moments
363	The Crystal Unicorn	05/85	Silhouette Romance
154	A Ruling Passion	03/84	Silhouette Special Edition
	Fair Game	/89	Warner

Malina, Fred

36	Murder Over Broadway	/50	Harlequin

Malkind, Margaret

295	Late Night Rendezvous	12/88	Bantam Loveswept
104	A Lust For Danger	/86	Dell Candlelight Ecstasy
227	Winds Of Fear	02/88	Silhouette Intimate Moments

Mallery, Susan

270	Justin's Bride	05/95	Harlequin Historical
554	Tempting Faith	03/94	Silhouette Intimate Moments
646	The Only Way Out	06/95	Silhouette Intimate Moments
717	Tender Loving Care	01/92	Silhouette Special Edition
802	More Than Friends	03/93	Silhouette Special Edition
834	A Dad For Billie	08/93	Silhouette Special Edition
898	Cowboy Daddy	07/94	Silhouette Special Edition
933	The Best Bride (Hometown Heartbreakers)	01/95	Silhouette Special Edition
939	Marriage On Demand	02/95	Silhouette Special Edition
969	Father In Training	07/95	Silhouette Special Edition
1008	The Bodygurad & Mrs. Jones	01/96	Silhouette Special Edition
1027	Part-Time Wife	05/96	Silhouette Special Edition
1042	Full-Time Father	07/96	Silhouette Special Edition

Mallin, Gail

60	A Most Unsuitable Duchess	10/91	Harlequin Regency

Mallory, Kathryn

6	A Frenchman's Kiss	06/82	Silhouette Desire
40	Gentle Conquest	01/83	Silhouette Desire
58	One Night's Deception	04/83	Silhouette Desire

Mallory, Tess

	Jewels Of Time	09/94	Lovespell

Malmont, Valerie S.

AUTHOR/TITLE INDEX

Mansfield, Elizabeth

A Marriage Of Inconvenience		Berkley
A Splendid Indiscretion		Berkley
The Magnificent Masquerade		Berkley
The Grand Passion		Berkley
A Grand Deception		Berkley
The Accidental Romance		Berkley
The Bartered Bride		Berkley
The Lady Disguised		Berkley
A Christmas Treasure	11/92	Berkley Regency
Passing Fancies	12/93	Berkley Regency
My Lord Murderer	09/92	Jove Regency
A Christmas Kiss (Unexpected Holiday)	11/91	Jove Regency
A Very Dutiful Daughter	11/92	Jove Regency
Regency Sting	12/92	Jove Regency
A Regency Match	01/93	Jove Regency
A Brilliant Mismatch	06/95	Jove Regency
A Prior Engagement		Jove Regency
A Regency Holiday	11/91	Jove Regency
A Regency Charade	04/93	Jove Regency
Duel Of Hearts	03/93	Jove Regency
Her Man Of Affairs	02/93	Jove Regency
The Phantom Lover	10/92	Jove Regency
The Counterfeit Husband	08/93	Jove Regency
The Fifth Kiss	05/93	Jove Regency
The Reluctant Flirt	06/93	Jove Regency
The Frost Fair	07/93	Jove Regency
Love Lessons	10/93	Jove Regency
Winter Wonderland	11/93	Jove Regency
Passing Fancies	12/93	Jove Regency
Her Heart's Captain	09/93	Jove Regency
Mother's Choice	05/94	Jove Regency
The Magnificent Masquerade	06/94	Jove Regency
An Accidental Romance	09/94	Jove Regency
The Bartered Bride	12/94	Jove Regency
A Prior Engagement	03/95	Jove Regency
A Brilliant Mismatch	06/95	Jove Regency
Poor Caroline	07/95	Jove Regency
My Lord Murderer	09/95	Jove Regency
The Phantom Lover	12/95	Jove Regency
Matched Pairs	01/96	Jove Regency
A Very Dutiful Daughter	03/96	Jove Regency
Regency Sting	06/96	Jove Regency
My Lord Murderer	08/95	Jove Regency

Manz, Elizabeth

Wasted Space	09/96	St. Martin's
Scare Tactics	04/96	St. Martin's

AUTHOR/TITLE INDEX

AUTHOR/TITLE INDEX

Marnay, Jane
  1006 The Courageous Heart   /66 Harlequin

Mars, Diana
      Sweet Surrender
  182 Sweet Trespass   /84 Berkley Second Chance At Love
  279 Sweet Enchantment   /85 Berkley Second Chance At Love
  906 Peril In Paradise   01/95 Silhouette Desire
  942 Mixed-Up Matrimony   07/95 Silhouette Desire

Mars, Kasey
      The Silent Rose   11/94 Pinnacle Denise Little Presents
      The Dream   09/95 Pinnacle Denise Little Presents

Marsh, Ellen Tanner
      Silk And Splendor   Avon
      Tame The Wild Heart   Avon
      Sable   Berkley
      Wrap Me In Splendor   Berkley
      Scarlet And Gold   Berkley
      Reap The Savage Wind   Berkley
      The Enchanted Prince   /95 Leisure
  978 Bed And Breakfast   08/95 Silhouette Special Edition
      A Christmas Embrace   11/94 St. Martin's
      If This Be Magic   Warner
      In My Wildest Dreams   Warner

Marsh, Joan
      Prince Of Hearts   Dell Candlelight

Marsh, Lillian
  51 Love's Masquerade   /82 Berkley Second Chance At Love

Marsh, Valerie
  820 Dark Obsession   Harlequin Presents
  2676 Echo Of Betrayal   Harlequin Romance

Marshall, Bevlyn
  407 Lonely At The Top   09/87 Silhouette Special Edition
  441 The Pride Of His Life   03/88 Silhouette Special Edition
  506 Grady's Lady   02/89 Silhouette Special Edition
  544 Radio Daze   08/89 Silhouette Special Edition
  562 Goddess Of Joy   11/89 Silhouette Special Edition
  598 Treasure Deep   05/90 Silhouette Special Edition
  665 Thunderbolt   04/91 Silhouette Special Edition
  704 Above The Clouds   11/91 Silhouette Special Edition
  753 Swiss Bliss   07/92 Silhouette Special Edition

Marshall, Edison
      Cortez And Mariana   Historical
  200 Doctor Of Lonesome River   /52 Harlequin
  239 Mission Of Revenge   /53 Harlequin

Marshall, Jacqueline
  54 Drastic Measures   Harlequin Intrigue

AUTHOR/TITLE INDEX

Marshall, Joanne

  569   The Peacock Bed   Dell Candlelight

Marshall, Paula

	Reluctant Bridegrooms	05/95	Harlequin Promotion
96	Cousin Harry	04/93	Harlequin Regency
107	An Improper Duenna	10/93	Harlequin Regency
	Regency Diamonds: The Cyprian's Sister	08/94	Harlequin Regency Anthology

Marshall, Raymond

255	Lady --Here's Your Wreath	/53	Harlequin
265	The Paw In The Bottle	/54	Harlequin
300	Mallory	/54	Harlequin
310	Why Pick On Me?	/54	Harlequin
317	Blondes' Requiem	/54	Harlequin
340	The Pick-Up	/55	Harlequin
341	Ruthless	/55	Harlequin
382	Never Trust A Woman	/57	Harlequin

Martel, Aimee

136	The Fires Within	05/84	Silhouette Desire
249	Hero At Large	12/85	Silhouette Desire

Marten, Jacqueline

	Moonshine And Glory	09/95	Pinnacle Denise Little Presents
	Just A Kiss Away	08/95	Pinnacle Denise Little Presents
	Darcy's Kiss	04/96	Pinnacle Denise Little Presents
	Glory In The Flower		Pocket
	Dream Walker		Pocket
	Forever More		Pocket
	English Rose		Pocket
	Irish Rose		Pocket
	French Rose		Pocket
	Loving Longest		Pocket
	An Unforgotten Love		Pocket
	Kiss Me Catronia		Pocket
	To Pluck A Rose		Pocket
	In The Long Green Glass		Pocket
	Bryarly		Pocket

Martin, Chuck

389	Circle F Cowboy	/57	Harlequin
390	Adopted Derelicts	/57	Harlequin

Martin, Deborah

	Creole Nights	12/92	Leisure Historical
	Moonlight Enchantment		Leisure Historical
	By Love Unveiled	05/93	Penguin Topaz
	Silver Deceptions	01/94	Penguin Topaz
	Midnight Rider	03/96	St. Martin's
	Dangerous Angel	09/94	Topaz
	Stormswept	08/95	Topaz

658

Martin, Nancy

305	Sable And Secrets		Harlequin Superromance
1	A Whirlwind	03/92	Harlequin Tyler
4	Monkey Wrench	06/92	Harlequin Tyler
461	Hit Man	11/88	Silhouette Desire
522	A Living Legend	09/89	Silhouette Desire
576	Showdown	06/90	Silhouette Desire
590	Ready, Willing And Abel	09/90	Silhouette Desire
608	Looking For Trouble	12/90	Silhouette Desire
776	Good Golly, Miss Molly	04/93	Silhouette Desire
826	Fortune's Cookie	12/93	Silhouette Desire
858	Wish Upon A Star	05/94	Silhouette Desire
916	Pauper & The Pregnant Princess	03/95	Silhouette Desire
927	The Cop And The Chorus Girl	05/95	Silhouette Desire
60	Black Diamonds	07/84	Silhouette Intimate Moments

Martin, Prudence

148	Moonlight Rapture	/83	Dell Candlelight Ecstasy
168	Champagne Flight	/83	Dell Candlelight Ecstasy
	Passion's Persuasion		Zebra Regency
	Wager On Love		Zebra Regency

Martin, Rhona

	Gallows Wedding		Berkley

Martin, Sally

	Fair Schemer	10/93	Avon
	Sweet Fancy	05/94	Avon Regency
	Numbered Kisses	12/92	Jove Regency
	The Reluctant Bridegroom	10/91	Jove Regency

Martin, W.

	Island Magic		Avalon
	Love On Trial		Avalon Career Romance

Marton, Sandra

	The Second Mrs. Adams	/97	Harlequin Presents
	A Proper Wife	/97	Harlequin Presents
	Master Of El Corazon	/97	Harlequin Presents
	No Need For Love	/97	Harlequin Presents
988	A Game Of Deceit		Harlequin Presents
1027	Out Of Shadows		Harlequin Presents
1067	Intimate Strangers		Harlequin Presents
1082	Lovescenes		Harlequin Presents
1121	Heart Of The Hank		Harlequin Presents
1155	A Flood Of Sweet Fire		Harlequin Presents
1194	Deal With The Devil		Harlequin Presents
1219	Cherish The Flame		Harlequin Presents
1244	Eye Of The Storm		Harlequin Presents
1277	Fly Like An Eagle		Harlequin Presents
1308	From This Day Forward		Harlequin Presents

Marton, Sandra

1347	Night Fires		Harlequin Presents
1379	Consenting Adults	07/91	Harlequin Presents
1411	Garden Of Eden	11/91	Harlequin Presents
1443	By Dreams Betrayed	03/92	Harlequin Presents
1457	Lost In A Dream	05/92	Harlequin Presents
1524	That Long-Ago Summer	01/93	Harlequin Presents
1574	Roarke's Kingdom	07/93	Harlequin Presents
1637	The Corsican Gambit	06/94	Harlequin Presents
1660	Roman Spring (Postcards From Europe)	06/94	Harlequin Presents
1736	A Woman Accused	04/95	Harlequin Presents
1751	A Bride For The Taking (Wedlocked!)	07/95	Harlequin Presents
1808	An Indecent Proposal	04/96	Harlequin Presents
1813	Guardian Groom	05/96	Harlequin Presents
1819	Hollywood Wedding	06/96	Harlequin Presents
1825	Spring Bride	07/96	Harlequin Presents
1780	Hostage Of The Hawk	12/95	Harlequin Presents Plus
	' Til Tomorrow	02/96	Pinnacle Denise Little Presents
	Until You	/97	Pinnacle Denise Little Presents

Marton, Suzanne

1348	Trial By Love		Harlequin Presents

Martyn, Norma

	The Dreamtime Legacy	11/92	Bantam Fanfare

Mason, A.E.W.

460	At The Villa Rose	/59	Harlequin

Mason, Connie

Taken By Youn	02/96	Avon
Pure Temptation	07/96	Dorchester
Tender Fury		Leisure
Bold Land, Bold Love		Leisure
Desert Ecstasy		Leisure
Brave Land, Brave Love	/92	Leisure
Wild Land, Wild Love	/92	Leisure
Tears Like Rain	07/94	Leisure
Beyond The Horizon	/95	Leisure
Treasures Of The Heart		Leisure
Tempt The Devil	/95	Leisure
Sierra	07/95	Leisure
The Lion's Bride	12/95	Leisure
Wilderness Christmas	11/93	Leisure Anthology
An Old-Fashioned Southern Christmas	11/94	Leisure Anthology
Their First Noel	11/95	Leisure Anthology
A Wilderness Christmas	11/95	Leisure Anthology
A Frontier Christmas	11/92	Leisure Historical
My Lady Vixen	12/92	Leisure Historical
Ice And Rapture	01/93	Leisure Historical

Mason, Connie

Caress And Conquer		Leisure Historical
For Honor's Sake	09/91	Leisure Historical
Tempt The Devil		Leisure Historical
These Hallowed Hills		Leisure Historical
Ice & Rapture	01/93	Leisure Historical
Wild Is My Heart	02/93	Leisure Historical
Promised Splendor	04/93	Leisure Historical
A Promise Of Thunder	06/93	Leisure Historical
Wind Rider	12/94	Leisure Historical

Mason, F. Van Wyke

Golden Admiral		Historical

Mason, Felicia

For The Love Of You	10/94	Pinnacle
Body And Soul	06/95	Pinnacle

Mason, Van Wyck

74	Spider House	/50	Harlequin

Massey, Ellen Gray

Too Many Secrets	/91	Avalon
Moon Silver	/91	Avalon
The Bequest	03/93	Avalon

Massey, Jessica

Stormy Surrender		Dell

Massie, Sonia

A Spring Bouquet	05/96	Zebra Anthology

Massie, Sonja

	Carousel		
	Dream Carver		
	Far And Away	06/92	Berkley
348	Legacy Of The Wolf	11/86	Silhouette Special Edition

Masterton, Graham

Lady Of Fortune		Warner

Mather, Anne

1451	The Arrogant Duke	/70	Harlequin
1487	Charlotte's Hurricane	/71	Harlequin
1574	Lord Of Zaracus	/72	Harlequin
1600	The Reluctant Governess	/72	Harlequin
1631	Masquerade	/72	Harlequin
1656	Autumn Of The Witch	/73	Harlequin
3	Sweet Revenge	/73	Harlequin Presents
4	The Pleasure And The Pain	/73	Harlequin Presents
8	The Sanchez Tradition	/73	Harlequin Presents
11	Who Rides The Tiger	/73	Harlequin Presents
14	Storm In A Rain Barrel	/73	Harlequin Presents
17	Living With Adam	/73	Harlequin Presents
20	A Distant Sound Of Thunder	/73	Harlequin Presents

Mather, Anne

23	Legend Of Lexandros	/73	Harlequin Presents
26	Dark Enemy	/73	Harlequin Presents
29	Monkshood	/73	Harlequin Presents
32	Jake Howard's Wife	/74	Harlequin Presents
35	Seen By Candlelight	/74	Harlequin Presents
38	Moon Witch	/74	Harlequin Presents
41	Dangerous Enchantment	/74	Harlequin Presents
46	Prelude To Enchantment	/74	Harlequin Presents
49	A Savage Beauty	/74	Harlequin Presents
54	The Night Of The Bulls	/74	Harlequin Presents
57	Legacy Of The Past	/74	Harlequin Presents
61	Chase A Green Shadow	/74	Harlequin Presents
65	White Rose Of Winter	/74	Harlequin Presents
69	Master Of Falcon's Head	/74	Harlequin Presents
74	Leopard In The Snow	/74	Harlequin Presents
77	The Japanese Screen	/75	Harlequin Presents
86	Rachel Trevellyan	/75	Harlequin Presents
92	Mask Of Scars	/75	Harlequin Presents
96	Silver Fruit Upon Silver Trees	/75	Harlequin Presents
100	Dark Moonless Night	/75	Harlequin Presents
105	No Gentle Possession	/75	Harlequin Presents
110	Witchstone	/75	Harlequin Presents
112	The Waterfalls Of The Moon	/75	Harlequin Presents
119	Pale Dawn, Dark Sunset	/75	Harlequin Presents
126	Take What You Want	/76	Harlequin Presents
133	Come The Vintage	/76	Harlequin Presents
135	Dark Castle	/76	Harlequin Presents
141	All The Fire	/76	Harlequin Presents
144	Country Of The Falcon	/76	Harlequin Presents
148	For The Love Of Sara	/76	Harlequin Presents
153	Dark Venetian	/76	Harlequin Presents
156	The Shrouded Web	/76	Harlequin Presents
165	The Arrogance Of Love	/76	Harlequin Presents
170	The High Valley	/76	Harlequin Presents
173	Valley Deep, Mountain High	/77	Harlequin Presents
177	Smouldering Flame	/77	Harlequin Presents
185	Wild Enchantress	/77	Harlequin Presents
189	Beware The Beast	/77	Harlequin Presents
194	Alien Wife	/77	Harlequin Presents
197	The Medici Lover	/77	Harlequin Presents
202	Dangerous Rhapsody	/77	Harlequin Presents
205	Devil's Mount	/77	Harlequin Presents
210	Born Out Of Love	/77	Harlequin Presents
218	A Trial Marriage	/77	Harlequin Presents
221	Forbidden	/78	Harlequin Presents
224	Come Running	/78	Harlequin Presents

663

Mather, Anne

234	Devil In Velvet	/78	Harlequin	Presents
250	Loren's Baby	/78	Harlequin	Presents
254	Rooted In Dishonour	/78	Harlequin	Presents
262	Proud Harvest	/78	Harlequin	Presents
266	Scorpion's Dance	/78	Harlequin	Presents
269	Follow Thy Desire		Harlequin	Presents
278	Captive Destiny		Harlequin	Presents
281	Charade In Winter		Harlequin	Presents
287	Fallen Angel		Harlequin	Presents
306	Melting Fire		Harlequin	Presents
322	The Judas Trap		Harlequin	Presents
329	Lure Of Eagles		Harlequin	Presents
335	Appollo's Seed		Harlequin	Presents
347	Hell Or High Water		Harlequin	Presents
351	Spirit Of Alantis		Harlequin	Presents
376	Whisper Of Darkness		Harlequin	Presents
382	Sandstorm		Harlequin	Presents
402	Images Of Love		Harlequin	Presents
405	Edge Of Temptation		Harlequin	Presents
429	A Haunting Compulsion		Harlequin	Presents
436	Forbidden Flame		Harlequin	Presents
449	Castles Of Sand		Harlequin	Presents
468	Innocent Obsession		Harlequin	Presents
490	Duelling Fire		Harlequin	Presents
509	Smokescreen		Harlequin	Presents
530	Impetuous Masquerade		Harlequin	Presents
546	Season Of Mists		Harlequin	Presents
563	A Passionate Affair		Harlequin	Presents
586	An Elusive Desire		Harlequin	Presents
610	Cage Of Shadows		Harlequin	Presents
683	Sirocco		Harlequin	Presents
715	Moondrift		Harlequin	Presents
810	Act Of Possession		Harlequin	Presents
843	Stolen Summer		Harlequin	Presents
869	Pale Orchid		Harlequin	Presents
899	All Consuming Passion		Harlequin	Presents
1003	Night Heat		Harlequin	Presents
1044	Burning Inheritance		Harlequin	Presents
1122	Trial Of Innocence		Harlequin	Presents
1210	Dark Mosaic		Harlequin	Presents
1251	A Fever In The Blood		Harlequin	Presents
1315	A Relative Betrayal		Harlequin	Presents
1354	Indiscretion		Harlequin	Presents
1444	Blind Passion	03/92	Harlequin	Presents
1445	Seed Of Vengeance	03/92	Harlequin	Presents
1458	Such Sweet Poison	05/92	Harlequin	Presents

Mather, Anne

1492	Betrayed	09/92	Harlequin	Presents
1514	Diamond Fire	02/93	Harlequin	Presents
1542	Guilty	03/93	Harlequin	Presents
1553	Dangerous Sanctuary	06/93	Harlequin	Presents
1561	Rich As Skin	06/93	Harlequin	Presents
1567	Rich As Sin	07/93	Harlequin	Presents
1617	Snowfire	01/94	Harlequin	Presents
1649	Tender Assault	06/94	Harlequin	Presents
1697	Strange Intimacy	11/94	Harlequin	Presents
1722	Brittle Bondage	02/95	Harlequin	Presents
1731	Raw Silk	04/95	Harlequin	Presents
1759	Treacherous Longings (Dangerous Liasons)	08/95	Harlequin	Presents
1797	A Woman Of Passion	03/96	Harlequin	Presents
1591	Tidewater Seduction	10/93	Harlequin	Presents Plus
1663	A Secret Rebellion	07/94	Harlequin	Presents Plus
	Wild Concerto		Worldwide Lib.	
	Stormspell		Worldwide Lib.	
	Hidden In The Flame	07/85	Worldwide Lib.	

Mather, Carole

| 383 | Yesterday's Scars | | Harlequin | Presents |

Mathews, Jan

70	A Flame Too Fierce	/83	Berkley	Second Chance At Love
185	No Easy Surrender	/84	Berkley	Second Chance At Love
273	Thief Of Hearts	/85	Berkley	Second Chance At Love

Mathews, Laura

| | Miss Ryder's Memoirs | 09/88 | Nal | Regency |

Mathhews, Laura

| | Holiday In Bath | | Warner | Regency |

Matlock, Curtiss Ann

	The Loves Of Ruby Dee	02/96	Avon	
31	Annie In The Morning	08/96	Harlequin	Here Come The Grooms
37	The Forever Rose	01/90	Harlequin	Historical
251	White Gold	01/95	Harlequin	Historical
16	A Time To Keep	05/94	Harlequin	Men Made In America
36	A Time And A Season	05/95	Harlequin	Men Made In America
	Wellspring	07/95	Harlequin	Western Lovers
	To Mother With Love: "More Than A Moth	04/91	Silhouette	Anthology
	1993 Keepsake Christmas Stories	11/93	Silhouette	Anthology
	Miracle On I-40	11/88	Silhouette	Christmas Stories
422	Crosswinds	03/86	Silhouette	Romance
482	For Each Tomorrow	01/87	Silhouette	Romance
605	Good Vibrations	10/88	Silhouette	Romance
275	A Time And A Season	11/85	Silhouette	Special Edition
333	Lindsey's Rainbow	09/86	Silhouette	Special Edition
384	A Time To Keep	05/87	Silhouette	Special Edition

AUTHOR/TITLE INDEX

Matlock, Curtiss Ann

426	Last Chance Cafe	12/87	Silhouette Special Edition
454	Wellspring	05/88	Silhouette Special Edition
589	Intimate Circle	04/90	Silhouette Special Edition
601	Love Finds Yancy Cordell	06/90	Silhouette Special Edition
668	Heaven In Texas	05/91	Silhouette Special Edition
695	Annie In The Morning	09/91	Silhouette Special Edition
757	Last Of The Good Guys	08/92	Silhouette Special Edition
805	True Blue Hearts	04/93	Silhouette Special Edition
860	Summertime (The Breen Men)	01/94	Silhouette Special Edition

Matranga, Frances Carfi

| 526 | Destiny In Rome | | Dell Candlelight |

Matthewman, Phyllis

| 825 | Make Up Your Mind, Nurse | /64 | Harlequin |
| 1231 | Imitation Marriage | /68 | Harlequin |

Matthews, Bay

109	Rambler's Rest	01/92	Harlequin Historical
	A Christmas For Carole	/89	Silhouette Christmas Stories
298	Bittersweet Sacrifice	03/86	Silhouette Special Edition
347	Roses And Regrets	11/86	Silhouette Special Edition
391	Some Warm Hunger	07/87	Silhouette Special Edition
420	Lessons In Loving	11/87	Silhouette Special Edition
464	Amarillo By Morning	07/88	Silhouette Special Edition
505	Summer's Promise	02/89	Silhouette Special Edition
613	Laughter On The Wind	08/90	Silhouette Special Edition
648	Sweet Lies, Satin Sins	01/91	Silhouette Special Edition
825	Worth Waiting For	07/93	Silhouette Special Edition
859	Hardhearted (That Special Woman!)	01/94	Silhouette Special Edition

Matthews, Brenda

| | Naked Came The Ladies | 02/94 | Starlog Moonlight Anthology |

Matthews, Laura

	Alicia		
	A Baronet's Wife		
	Holiday In Bath		
	Lord Greywell's Dilemma		
	Miss Ryder's Memoirs		
	The Aim Of A Lady		Nal
	The Ardent Lady Amelia		Nal
	The Seventh Suitor	08/91	Nal Regency
	Lord Clayborne's Fancy	10/91	Nal Regency
	The Proud Viscount	05/87	Nal Regency
	A Very Proper Widow	05/87	Nal Regency
	A Curious Courting	01/93	Penguin Regency
	The Village Spinster	02/93	Penguin Regency
	The Nomad Harp	05/93	Penguin Regency
	In My Lady's Chamber	07/93	Penguin Regency

666

Matthews, Laura

    The Lady Next Door   09/93   Signet

Matthews, Patricia

    Love's Sweet Agony

    Tides Of Love

    Embers Of Dawn

    Flames Of Glory

    Dancer Of Dreams

    Gambler In Love

    Tame The Reckless Heart

    Oasis

    Love's Tender Fury

    Dark Fires

    Sapphire

    Empire

    The Death Of Love

    Midnight Whispers

    Midnight Lavender

    The Enchanted   Harlequin Historical

    Thursday And The Lady   11/87   Harlequin Historical

    The Dreaming Tree   06/89   Worldwide Lib.

    Mirrors   05/88   Worldwide Libr.

    Love's Bold Journey   Zebra Pinnacle

    Love's Daring Dream   Zebra Pinnacle

    Love, Forever More   Zebra Pinnacle

    Love's Avenging Heart   Zebra Pinnacle

    Love's Raging Tide   Zebra Pinnacle

    Love's Golden Destiny   Zebra Pinnacle

    Love's Magic Moment   Zebra Pinnacle

    Love's Pagan Heart   Zebra Pinnacle

    Love's Wildest Promise   Zebra Pinnacle

Matthews, Phoebe

  682   The Unsuitable Lovers   Dell Candlelight Regency

Maugham, W. Somerset

  266   Catalina   /54   Harlequin

Maxam, Mia

  205   Race The Tide   02/83   Silhouette Romance

  236   Lost In Love   07/83   Silhouette Romance

  324   Loyal Opposition   10/84   Silhouette Romance

  450   Something Sentimental 08/86   Silhouette Romance

  513   On Restless Wings   06/87   Silhouette Romance

Maxwell, A.E.

  267   Redwood Empire   05/95   Harlequin Historical

Maxwell, Ann

    The Diamond Tiger   06/92   Harper

    The King Of Nothing   07/92   Harper

Mayhar, Ardath
    People Of The Mesa   03/92   Diamond

Mayhew, Margaret
    Regency Charade   /86   Walker

Mayne, Elizabeth
259	All That Matters (March Madness)	03/95	Harlequin Historical
291	Heart Of The Hawk	11/95	Harlequin Historical
313	Man Of The Mist	04/96	Harlequin Historical

Mayne, Sharon
390	Heart Trouble	04/92	Harlequin Temptation
419	The Right Moves	11/92	Harlequin Temptation
435	Winner Takes All	03/93	Harlequin Temptation

Maynell, Laurence
    The Fortunate Miss East   Nal Penguin Regency

Mayo, Margaret
1980	Destiny Paradise	/76	Harlequin
1996	Shades Of Autumn	/76	Harlequin
2028	Perilous Waters	/76	Harlequin
2051	Land Of Ice And Fire	/77	Harlequin
2086	Rainbow Magic	/77	Harlequin
2118	Seq Gypsy	/77	Harlequin
194	Ruthless Stranger	07/94	Harlequin Direct
216	Intrigue	01/95	Harlequin Direct
224	Yesterday's Dreams	03/95	Harlequin Direct
31	Reluctant Hostage	05/96	Harlequin Presents
963	Passionate Vengeance		Harlequin Presents
1045	Savage Affair		Harlequin Presents
1108	A Painful Loving		Harlequin Presents
1187	Prisoner Of The Mind		Harlequin Presents
1525	A Fiery Encounter	01/93	Harlequin Presents
1652	Stormy Relationship	06/94	Harlequin Presents
2280	Afraid To Love		Harlequin Romance
2327	Stormy Affair		Harlequin Romance
2360	Valley Of The Hawk		Harlequin Romance
2385	Burning Desire		Harlequin Romance
2386	The Silver Thaw		Harlequin Romance
2439	A Taste Of Paradise		Harlequin Romance
2557	Dangerous Journey		Harlequin Romance
2602	Return A Stranger		Harlequin Romance
2795	Impulsive Challenge		Harlequin Romance
2805	At Dagger's Drawn		Harlequin Romance
2937	Feelings		Harlequin Romance
2955	Unexpected Inheritance		Harlequin Romance
3003	Bittersweet Pursuit		Harlequin Romance
3029	Conflict		Harlequin Romance
3155	Trapped	10/91	Harlequin Romance

AUTHOR/TITLE INDEX

Mayo, Margaret

3190	An Impossible Situation	04/92	Harlequin	Romance

Mc Allister, Anne

89	Starstruck		Harlequin	American
108	Quicksilver Season		Harlequin	American
132	A Chance Of Rainbows		Harlequin	American
186	Body And Soul	02/87	Harlequin	American
202	Dream Chases		Harlequin	American
234	Marry Sunshine		Harlequin	American
275	Gifts Of The Spirit		Harlequin	American
309	Saving Grace	07/89	Harlequin	American
341	Imagine		Harlequin	American
387	I Thee Wed		Harlequin	American
459	Mackenzie's Baby	10/92	Harlequin	American
466	A Cowboy For Christmas	12/92	Harlequin	American
533	The Eight Second Wedding	06/94	Harlequin	American
	Christmas Celebration	09/93	Harlequin	Anthology
22	To Tame A Wolf	08/94	Harlequin	Men Made In America
49	Starstruck	10/95	Harlequin	Men Made In America
	A Baby For Christmas	12/95	Harlequin	Presents
844	Lightning Storm		Harlequin	Presents
1060	To Tame A Wolf		Harlequin	Presents
1099	The Marriage Trap		Harlequin	Presents
1257	Once A Hero		Harlequin	Presents
1371	Out Of Bounds		Harlequin	Presents
1459	Island Interlude	05/92	Harlequin	Presents
1620	Call Up The Wind	01/94	Harlequin	Presents
1769	The Alexakis Bride	10/95	Harlequin	Presents
1680	Catch Me If You Can	09/94	Harlequin	Presents Plus
	Marry Me, Cowboy!	04/95	Harlequin	Promotion
2721	Dare To Trust		Harlequin	Romance
	Tanner's Temptation	/94	Silhouette	Desire
	Cowboy Pride	11/95	Silhouette	Desire
907	Cowboys Don't Cry	02/95	Silhouette	Desire
944	Cowboys Don't Quit (Code Of The West)	08/95	Silhouette	Desire
969	Cowboys Don't Stay	12/95	Silhouette	Desire
1009	The Cowboy And The Kid	07/97	Silhouette	Desire

Mc Allister, Heather

543	Jilt Trip (Grooms On The Run)	06/95	Harlequin	Temptation
583	Bedded Bliss	04/96	Harlequin	Temptation

Mc Allister, Patricia

	Gypsy Jewel	09/93	Zebra	Heartfire
	Mountain Angel	01/95	Zebra	Lovegram
	Sea Raven	02/96	Zebra	Lovegram

Mc Aneny, Marjorie

	Summer Love Match	11/88	Crown	Pageant

AUTHOR/TITLE INDEX

Mc Arthur, A.
216 No Mean City   /53   Harlequin
Mc Bain, Laurie
     Devil's Desire   Avon
     Tears Of Gold   Avon
     When Splendor Falls   Avon
     Wild Bells To The Wild Sky   Avon
  1 Moonstruck Madness   Avon
  2 Chance The Winds Of Fortune   Avon
  3 Dark Before The Rising Sun   Avon
Mc Bride, Caitlin
     Journey Of The Heart   04/94 Diamond Historical
     Highland Fling   12/93 Jove Historical Anthology
Mc Bride, Harper
 10 Gentleman In Paradise   Dell Candlelight Ecstasy
175 Tender Torment   /83   Dell Candlelight Ecstasy
Mc Bride, Jule
500 Wild Card Wedding   08/93 Harlequin American
519 Baby Trap   01/94 Harlequin American
546 The Wrong Wife?   08/94 Harlequin American
562 The Baby & The Bodyguard   12/94 Harlequin American
577 Bride Of The Badlands   04/95 Harlequin American
599 The Baby Maker   09/95 Harlequin American
617 The Bounty Hunter's Baby   02/96 Harlequin American
636 Baby Romeo: P.I.   06/96 Harlequin American
Mc Bride, Mary
     Outlaw Brides - "The Ballad Of Josie Dove" 06/96 Harlequin Anthology
121 The Fourth Of Forever   06/94 Harlequin Historical
164 Riverbend   03/93 Harlequin Historical
189 Fly Away Home   09/93 Harlequin Historical
221 The Fourth Of Forever   05/94 Harlequin Historical
237 The Sugarman   09/94 Harlequin Historical
256 The Gunslinger   02/95 Harlequin Historical
294 Forever And A Day   11/95 Harlequin Historical
323 Darling Jack   07/96 Harlequin Historical
Mc Cafferty, Jeanne
     Star Gazer   07/94 St. Martin's
Mc Caffree, Sharon
  4 Now And Forever   Harlequin American
 87 Misplaced Destiny   Harlequin American
110 Secret Longings   Harlequin American
 85 Passport To Passion   Harlequin Superromance
 36 One Bright Morning   11/84 Harlequin Temptation
Mc Caffrey, Anne
     The Year Of The Lucy
     Restoree

671

AUTHOR/TITLE INDEX

Mc Caffrey, Anne
    Ring Of Fear
    The Lady   /88   Ballantine

Mc Call, Dinah
    Jackson Rule   07/96   Harper Monogram

Mc Call, Eva
    Edge Of Heaven   /96   Bright Mountain

Mc Call, Kathleen
    Ivory Rose   /88   Zebra
    Windswept Heart   /88   Zebra

Mc Callum, Kristy
  1500   Tiger Moon   10/92   Harlequin Presents

Mc Cann, Heather
  207   The Master Detective   02/93   Harlequin Intrigue
  236   Whispers In The Dark   07/93   Harlequin Intrigue

Mc Carry, Charles
    The Bride Of The Wilderness   Nal Penguin

Mc Carthy, Betsy
  332   The Golden Rose   11/84   Silhouette Romance

Mc Carthy, Candace
    Embrace Me Sweet Stranger
    Rapture's Betrayal
  409   Together In The Night   /86   Dell Ecstasy Romance
    Heaven's Fire   03/95   Zebra
    Warrior's Caress   09/92   Zebra Heartfire
    Smuggler's Woman   08/91   Zebra Heartfire
    Sea Mistress   09/93   Zebra Heartfire
    Heaven's Fire   04/95   Zebra Lovegram

Mc Carthy, Jane
    Carlotta's Castle   Dell Candlelight

Mc Carthy, Susanne
  17   Practised Deceiver   10/95   Harlequin Presents
  36   Master Of Deceit   07/96   Harlequin Presents
  979   A Long Way From Heaven   Harlequin Presents
  1036   Don't Ask For Tomorrow   Harlequin Presents
  1123   Too Much To Lose   Harlequin Presents
  1146   Caught In A Dream   Harlequin Presents
  1299   Love Is For The Luck   Harlequin Presents
  1372   Tangled Threads   Harlequin Presents
  1412   A Casual Affair   11/91   Harlequin Presents
  1493   Dance For A Stranger   09/92   Harlequin Presents
  1717   Satan's Contract   01/95   Harlequin Presents
  1748   A Candle For The Devil (Secrets...) 06/95   Harlequin Presents

Mc Cartney, Brenna
    Passion's Blossom

Mc Cary, Reed

Mc Cary, Reed

297	The Vice Merchants	/54	Harlequin

Mc Cauley, Barbara

621	Woman Tamer	02/91	Silhouette Desire
698	Man From Cougar Pass	03/92	Silhouette Desire
771	Her Kind Of Man	03/93	Silhouette Desire
803	Whitehorn's Woman	08/93	Silhouette Desire
832	A Man Like Cade	01/94	Silhouette Desire
875	Nightfire (Centerfolds)	08/94	Silhouette Desire
917	Texas Heat (Hearts Of Stone)	03/95	Silhouette Desire
948	Texas Temptation (Hearts Of Stone)	08/95	Silhouette Desire
971	Texas Pride	12/95	Silhouette Desire

Mc Clure, Holly S.

	To Tame A Heart	/91	Avalon
	Dreams Of Joy		Avalon
	Snow-Kissed Magic		Avalon
	Island Magic	07/93	Avalon

Mc Comas, Mary Kay

	The Ditz	10/90	Bantam Loveswept
260	Divine Design	06/88	Bantam Loveswept
287	Obsessions	10/88	Bantam Loveswept
325	Bound To Happen	05/89	Bantam Loveswept
358	Familiar Words	10/89	Bantam Loveswept
370	Poor Emily	12/89	Bantam Loveswept
401	Lovin' A Good Ol' Boy	05/90	Bantam Loveswept
430	Favors	10/90	Bantam Loveswept
462	Kiss Me, Kelly	04/91	Bantam Loveswept
491	Asking For Trouble	08/91	Bantam Loveswept
506	To Give A Heart Wings	11/91	Bantam Loveswept
542	Sweet Dreamin' Baby	05/92	Bantam Loveswept
611	The Trouble With Magic	04/93	Bantam Loveswept
686	The One For Me	05/94	Bantam Loveswept
702	Wait For Me	08/94	Bantam Loveswept
722	Passing Through Midnight	01/95	Bantam Loveswept
738	Talk Of The Town	04/95	Bantam Loveswept
	Someday, Somewhere	11/88	Crown Pagent

Mc Conachie, Audrey

	No Blueprint For Love	08/92	Avalon

Mc Connell, Margaret S.

1643	The Glory Of The Love	/72	Harlequin

Mc Cord, Joseph

13	His Wife The Doctor	/49	Harlequin
50	One Way Street	/50	Harlequin

Mc Cormack, Cara

	Drury's Bluff	10/95	Barbaour & Co.

Mc Cormick, Claudia

Mc Cormick, Claudia
    Raven At Sunrise   Diamond
Mc Courtney, Lorena
  546 Legacy Of The Heart   Dell Candlelight
   73 No Strings Attached   09/85 Harlequin Temptation
  120 By Invitation Only   08/86 Harlequin Temptation
  158 With Flying Colors   06/87 Harlequin Temptation
  251 Free-Fall   05/89 Harlequin Temptation
       Betrayed   02/96 Questar
Mc Coy, Cathryn
  132 On Love's Own Terms   04/84 Silhouette Desire
Mc Cray, Judy
  841 Lake Of Dreams   01/92 Silhouette Romance
Mc Cue, Noelle Berry
    3 The Joining Stone   05/83 Bantam Loveswept
   11 Beloved Intruder   07/83 Bantam Loveswept
   50 In Search Of Joy   06/84 Bantam Loveswept
    5 Only The Present   Dell Candlelight Ecstasy
    8 Ocean Of Regret   Dell Candlelight Ecstasy
       Forever Eden/ Only The Present   Leisure Contemporary
       Ocean Of Regrets/ Once More With Passion   Leisure Contemporary
  510 Magic Touch   07/89 Silhouette Desire
  572 Look Beyond The Dream 06/90 Silhouette Desire
  694 Moonlight Miracle   02/92 Silhouette Desire
  707 Moonlight Promise   04/92 Silhouette Desire
  815 Moonlight Dream   10/93 Silhouette Desire
Mc Culley, Johnson
  260 The Outlaw Trail   /53 Harlequin
Mc Culloch, Sara
       Not Quite A Lady   Ballantine Regency
Mc Cullough, Helen
       Time To Love
Mc Cullough, Karen G.
       Stormtide   /92 Avalon
       Blue December   /91 Avalon
       The Night Prowlers   Avalon Mystery Romance
Mc Cune, Evelyn
       Empress   11/94 Ballantine
Mc Cutcheon, Pam
  614 A Little Something Extra 01/96 Harlequin American
       Golden Prophecies   02/95 Leisure Love Spell
Mc Daniel, Jan
       Angels In The Sand
       A Distant Dream
       The Gifts Of Spring
       October's Magic

AUTHOR/TITLE INDEX

Mc Gauran, Jan
    By My Lady's Honor   08/94   Dell   Historical
Mc Gauran, Joanna
    A Love So Fierce   05/93   Dell   Historical
Mc Gill, Joyce
  441   Unforgivable   08/92   Silhouette   Initmate Moments
  347   Through The Looking Glass   08/90   Silhouette   Intimate Moments
  368   A Loving Touch   01/91   Silhouette   Intimate Moments
Mc Giveny, Maura
  674   A Grand Illusion   Harlequin   Presents
  723   Promises To Keep   Harlequin   Presents
  803   Almost A Bride   Harlequin   Presents
  2511   Duquesa By Default   Harlequin   Romance
  2679   Megan's Folly   Harlequin   Romance
  2781   The Right Time   Harlequin   Romance
Mc Goldrick, May
    The Thistle And The Rose   08/95   Topaz
    Angel Of Skye   /96   Topaz
Mc Gorian, Gladys
    The Prince Regent's Silver Bell   /87   Walker
Mc Gowan, Jan
    Flame In The Night
    Heart Of The Storm
    Silversea   Pocket
    The Golden Lady   Pocket
    Winds Of Enchantment   Pocket
Mc Gowan, Wynema
    The Irishman   03/95   Pinnacle   Denise Little Presents
    Catching Rainbows   07/96   Pinnacle   Denise Little Presents
Mc Grath, Laura
  2588   Mayan Magic   Harlequin   Romance
Mc Grath, Lieut. Tom
  299   Copper   /54   Harlequin
Mc Graw, Terry
  439   Hero In Blue   06/86   Silhouette   Romance
  476   The Eyes Of A Stranger   12/86   Silhouette   Romance
Mc Guire, Jenny
  232   Christmas Wishes   12/88   Harlequin   Temptation
Mc Guire, Molly
  436   Forever Yours   04/92   Harlequin   American
  484   My Prince Charming   04/93   Harlequin   American
Mc Intyre, Hope
  160   Moon On East Mountain   09/84   Silhouette   Desire
Mc Kay, Rena
  36   Bridal Tap   10/80   Silhouette   Romance

Mc Kay, Rena

92	Desert Devil	07/81	Silhouette Romance
239	Valley Of Broken Hearts	08/83	Silhouette Romance
291	The Singing Stone	04/84	Silhouette Romance
347	Golden Echo	03/85	Silhouette Romance
713	Just You And Me	04/90	Silhouette Romance
853	Honey I'm Home	03/92	Silhouette Romance
1004	Romancing Cody	04/94	Silhouette Romance

Mc Kay, Simon

| | The Seas Of Fortune | | Berkley |

Mc Kean, Margarett

| 32 | Heartthrob | /82 | Berkley Second Chance At Love |

Mc Kee, Jan

	Montana Skies		
68	Sweet Justice	03/91	Harlequin Historical
	Hearts Echo		Tapestry

Mc Kee, Lynn Armistead

	Walks In Stardust	07/94	Diamond
	Woman Of The Mists	/94	Diamond
	Touches The Stars	/94	Diamond

Mc Kenna, Lindsay

	Men In Uniform	04/94	Harlequin Anthology
71	Sun Woman	04/91	Harlequin Historical
108	Lord Of Shadowhawk	01/92	Harlequin Historical
125	King Of Swords	05/92	Harlequin Historical
171	Brave Heart	06/93	Harlequin Historical
35	Too Near The Fire	03/95	Harlequin Men Made In America
27	Hangar 13	03/94	Harlequin Shadows
	Chase The Clouds	03/95	Harlequin Western Lovers
	Texas Wildcat	10/95	Harlequin Western Lovers
	Heart Of The Eagle	11/95	Harlequin Western Lovers
	Lovers Dark And Dangerous	10/94	Silhouette Anthology
	Always And Forever	/90	Silhouette Christmas Stories
75	Chase The Clouds	07/83	Silhouette Desire
134	Wilderness Passion	05/84	Silhouette Desire
165	Too Near The Fire	10/84	Silhouette Desire
184	Texas Wildcat	01/85	Silhouette Desire
208	Red Tail	05/85	Silhouette Desire
44	Love Me Before Dawn	03/84	Silhouette Intimate Moments
82	Captive Of Fate	03/83	Silhouette Special Edition
338	Heart Of The Eagle	10/86	Silhouette Special Edition
377	A Measure Of Love	04/87	Silhouette Special Edition
397	Solitaire	08/87	Silhouette Special Edition
434	Heart Of The Tiger	02/88	Silhouette Special Edition
529	A Question Of Honor	06/89	Silhouette Special Edition
535	No Surrender	07/89	Silhouette Special Edition

AUTHOR/TITLE INDEX

Mc Kenna, Lindsay

541	Return Of A Hero	08/89	Silhouette Special Edition
649	Dawn Of Valor	02/91	Silhouette Special Edition
667	No Quarter Given	05/91	Silhouette Special Edition
673	The Gauntlet	06/91	Silhouette Special Edition
679	Under Fire	07/91	Silhouette Special Edition
721	Ride The Tiger	02/92	Silhouette Special Edition
727	One Man's War	03/92	Silhouette Special Edition
733	Off Limits	04/92	Silhouette Special Edition
818	Heart Of The Wolf	06/93	Silhouette Special Edition
824	The Rogue	07/93	Silhouette Special Edition
830	Commando	08/93	Silhouette Special Edition
853	Point Of Departure	12/93	Silhouette Special Edition
878	Shadows And Light (Men Of Courage)	04/94	Silhouette Special Edition
884	Dangerous Alliance (Men Of Courage)	05/94	Silhouette Special Edition
890	Countdown (Men Of Courage)	06/94	Silhouette Special Edition
986	Morgan's Wife (Morgan's Mercenaries)	10/95	Silhouette Special Edition
992	Morgan's Son (Morgan's Mercenaries)	11/95	Silhouette Special Edition
998	Morgan's Rescue (Morgan's Mercenaries)	12/95	Silhouette Special Edition
1005	Morgan's Marriage (Morgan's Mercenaries)	01/96	Silhouette Special Edition

Mc Kenna, Tate

90	Man Of The Hour	/86	Dell Candlelight Ecstasy
172	Enduring Love	/83	Dell Candlelight Ecstasy
201	Daring Proposal	/83	Dell Candlelight Ecstasy
112	Partners In Peril	/86	Dell Ecstasy Supreme
	Legacy Of Love/Captive Desire	09/92	Leisure Contemporary Romance

Mc Kenzie, Kate

143	Bed And Breakfast	02/87	Harlequin Temptation

Mc Kenzie, Melinda

48	Beyond All Stars		Nal Rapture Romance
62	Blue Ribbon Dawn		Nal Rapture Romance

Mc Keone, Dixie

9	Sweet Doro	09/89	Harlequin Regency
2642	Connoisseur's Choice		Harlequin Romance
2722	Matchmaking Department		Harlequin Romance
2838	The Harlequin Hero		Harlequin Romance
2867	Exclusive Contract		Harlequin Romance

Mc Kinney, Meagan

Lions And Lace	05/92	Dell
My Wicked Enchantress	/88	Dell
No Choice But Surrender		Dell
Till Dawn Tames The Night	/91	Dell
When Angels Fall	04/90	Dell
A Man To Slay Dragons	07/96	Zebra

Mc Kinney, Megan

Fair Is The Rose	11/93	Bantam

AUTHOR/TITLE INDEX

Mc Kinney, Megan
    The Ground She Walks Upon   04/94 Delacorte
Mc Knight, Carolyn
  539 Gravetide   Dell Candlelight
Mc Knight, Jenna
  426 Eleven Year Match   02/92 Harlequin American
  512 Alligator Alley   11/93 Harlequin American
  539 The Bride, The Bachelor & The Baby   06/94 Harlequin American
  605 The Cowboy Hires A Wife   11/95 Harlequin American
  628 Two Weddings And A Feud   04/96 Harlequin American
Mc Lean, Cara
  131 The Perfect Mix   11/86 Harlequin Temptation
Mc Lean, Joyce
    Scatter The Tempest
    Shower Of The Stars
Mc Leay, Alison
    Passage Home   10/91 Avon
Mc Leod, Ken
  283 A Body For A Blonde   /54 Harlequin
Mc Linn, Patricia
  587 Hoops   03/90 Silhouette Special Edition
  641 A New World   12/90 Silhouette Special Edition
  712 Prelude To A Wedding   12/91 Silhouette Special Edition
  718 Wedding Party   01/92 Silhouette Special Edition
  813 Grady's Wedding   05/93 Silhouette Special Edition
  864 Not A Family Man   01/94 Silhouette Special Edition
  904 Rodeo Nights   08/94 Silhouette Special Edition
  959 A Stranger In The Family   05/95 Silhouette Special Edition
Mc Mahon, Barbara
  263 Living For Love   01/96 Harlequin
  287 Shining Through   07/96 Harlequin
  151 Miss Prim And Proper   09/93 Harlequin Direct
  178 Love's Unexpected Turn   03/94 Harlequin Direct
  198 Love's Fantasy   08/94 Harlequin Direct
  208 A Bride To Love   11/94 Harlequin Direct
  2643 Come Into The Sun   Harlequin Romance
  2777 Bluebells On The Hill   Harlequin Romance
  2895 Winter Stranger, Summer Lover   Harlequin Romance
  3221 Island Paradise   09/92 Harlequin Romance
  3263 One Love Forever   04/93 Harlequin Romance
  3369 Wanted: Wife And Mother   07/95 Harlequin Romance
  915 One Stubborn Cowboy   03/95 Silhouette Desire
  977 Cowboy's Bride   01/96 Silhouette Desire
  1017 Bride Of A Thousand Days   08/96 Silhouette Desire
  1132 Sheik Daddy   02/96 Silhouette Romance
Mc Mahon, Kay

Mc Mahon, Kay

	Ecstasy's Conquest		
	Dara's Desire		
	River Rapture		
	Betray The Night	11/91	Jove
	Defy The Thunder		Jove
	Chase The Dawn	09/92	Jove
	Bandit's Brazen Kiss		Zebra
	Love's Desperate Deceit		Zebra
	Passion's Slave		Zebra
	Tender Lies		Zebra
	Yankee's Lady		Zebra
	Wild Rapture		Zebra
	Defiant Sptifire		Zebra
	The Pirate's Lady		Zebra
	Virginia Vixen		Zebra

Mc Millan, Maxine

378	Race For The Roses	08/85	Silhouette Romance

Mc Millan, Terry

	Disappearing Acts	09/93	Pocket

Mc Minn, Suzanne

150	Never Say Goodbye	05/93	Meteor Kismet

Mc Naught, Judith

86	Tender Triumph		Harlequin Superromance
16	Double Standards	06/84	Harlequin Temptation
	Paradise	06/92	Pocket
	Once And Always		Pocket
	Something Wonderful		Pocket
	A Kingdom Of Dreams	/90	Pocket
	Almost Heaven		Pocket
	Whitney, My Love	/85	Pocket
	Until You	/94	Pocket
	Perfect	08/94	Pocket
	A Gift Of Love	11/95	Pocket Anthology
	A Holiday Of Love	12/94	Pocket Anthology

Mc Neil, Anne

	A Mind Of Her Own		Nal Penguin Regency

Mc Nicholas, Betty

	An Obsession With Honor		

Mc Pherren, Charlotte

	Song Of The Willow	07/93	Leisure Historical
	Love And Fortune	01/94	Leisure Historical

Mc Rae, Melinda

	An Unlikely Attraction	09/91	Nal Regency
	A Highly Respectable Widow	01/92	Nal Regency
	Married By Mistake	05/92	Nal Regency

Mc Rae, Melinda

The Highland Lord	12/92	Nal Regency
A Regency Christmas 3	11/91	Nal Super Regency
A Love For All Seasons	05/92	Nal Super Regency
A Regency Summer	06/92	Nal Super Regency
The Duke's Daughter	10/91	Nal Penguin
From The Heart	01/94	Nal Signet Anthology
Lady Leprechaun	05/93	Penguin Regency
Rakes And Rogues	06/93	Penguin Super Signet Historical
Prince Of Thieves	05/94	Penguin Topaz
Dashing & Dangerous	05/95	Signet Anthology
Stolen Hearts	09/95	Topaz

Mc Reynolds, Glenna

198	Scout's Honor	07/87	Bantam Loveswept
223	Thieves In The Night	12/87	Bantam Loveswept
323	Stevie Lee	04/89	Bantam Loveswept
382	Dateline: Kydd And Rios	02/90	Bantam Loveswept
413	Blue Dalton	07/90	Bantam Loveswept
478	Outlaw Carson	06/91	Bantam Loveswept
500	Moonlight And Shadows	10/91	Bantam Loveswept
562	A Piece Of Heaven	08/92	Bantam Loveswept
577	Shameless	11/92	Bantam Loveswept
626	The Courting Cowboy	07/93	Bantam Loveswept
653	Avenging Angel	11/93	Bantam Loveswept
693	The Dragon & The Dove	06/94	Bantam Loveswept
726	Dragon's Eden	02/95	Bantam Loveswept

Mc Williams, Judith

215	Suspicion	04/94	Harlequin Historical
249	Betrayed (Northpoint)	12/94	Harlequin Historical
32	In Good Faith	01/95	Harlequin Men Made In America
78	Polished With Love	10/85	Harlequin Temptation
103	In Good Faith	04/86	Harlequin Temptation
119	Serendipity	08/86	Harlequin Temptation
160	No Reservations	06/87	Harlequin Temptation
184	Honorable Intentions	12/87	Harlequin Temptation
253	The Royal Treatment	06/89	Harlequin Temptation
301	Satisfaction Guaranteed	06/90	Harlequin Temptation
372	Looking Good	11/91	Harlequin Temptation
404	Sweet Stuff	07/92	Harlequin Temptation
440	Not My Baby!	04/93	Harlequin Temptation
441	Reluctant Partner	08/88	Silhouette Desire
545	A Perfect Season	01/90	Silhouette Desire
597	That's My Baby	10/90	Silhouette Desire
911	Anything's Possible! (Spellbound)	02/95	Silhouette Desire
954	The Man From Atlantis	09/95	Silhouette Desire
1001	Instant Husband	05/96	Silhouette Desire
479	Gift Of The Gods	01/87	Silhouette Romance

AUTHOR/TITLE INDEX

Merritt, Emma

386	Silver Sea		Harlequin American
523	Make-Believe	11/92	Harlequin Superromance
	Emerald Enchantment	02/95	St. Martin's Anthology
	A Dreamspun Christmas	11/94	Topaz Anthology
	Beneath A Texas Star		Zebra
	Comanche Bride		Zebra
	Masque Of Jade		Zebra
	Sweet, Wild Love		Zebra
	Viking Captive		Zebra
	Satin Secret		Zebra
	Emerald Ecstasy		Zebra
	Restless Flames		Zebra
	A Christmas Rendezvous	/91	Zebra Anthology
	Texas Touch	08/92	Zebra Lovegram Romance

Merritt, Jackie

114	Wyoming Territory	02/92	Harlequin Historical
2	The Widow And The Rodeo Man	09/94	Harlequin Montana Mavericks
169	The Rancher Takes A Wife	12/94	Harlequin Montana Mavericks
	Big Ski Country	10/95	Harlequin Western Lovers
	Silhouette Summer Sizzlers	06/94	Silhouette Anthology
466	Big Sky Country	12/88	Silhouette Desire
551	Heartbreak Hotel	02/90	Silhouette Desire
566	Babe In The Woods	05/90	Silhouette Desire
587	Maggie's Man	08/90	Silhouette Desire
605	Ramblin' Man	11/90	Silhouette Desire
622	Maverick Heat	02/91	Silhouette Desire
642	Sweet On Jessie	05/91	Silhouette Desire
664	Mustange Valley	09/91	Silhouette Desire
683	The Lady And The Lumberjack	12/91	Silhouette Desire
705	Boss Lady	04/92	Silhouette Desire
721	Shipwrecked!	07/92	Silhouette Desire
740	Black Creek Ranch	10/92	Silhouette Desire
757	A Man Like Michael	01/93	Silhouette Desire
774	Tennessee Waltz	03/93	Silhouette Desire
790	Montana Sky	06/93	Silhouette Desire
813	Imitation Love	10/93	Silhouette Desire
841	Wrangler's Lady	03/94	Silhouette Desire
849	Myster Lady (Saxon Brothers)	04/94	Silhouette Desire
854	Persistent Lady (Saxon Brothers)	05/94	Silhouette Desire
866	Nevada Drifter	07/94	Silhouette Desire
914	Accidental Bride	03/95	Silhouette Desire
935	Hesitant Husband	06/95	Silhouette Desire
965	Rebel Love	11/95	Silhouette Desire
980	Assignment: Marriage	02/96	Silhouette Desire
1014	Montana Fever	07/96	Silhouette Desire
2	The Widow & The Rodeo Man	09/94	Silhouette Montana Maverick

Merritt, Jackie
   988   A Man And A Million   10/95   Silhouette Special Edition

Merwin, Sam Jr.
   62   Message From A Corpse   /50   Harlequin
   70   Knife In My Back   /50   Harlequin
   87   Murder In Miniatures   /50   Harlequin
  122   A Matter Of Policy   /51   Harlequin

Mesta, Emily
   34   Fugitive Heart   Harlequin Superromance
   73   Forbidden Destiny   Harlequin Superromance

Metcalf, Jill
        Spring Blossom   08/92   Diamond Homespun
        Autumn Leaves   05/93   Diamond Homespun
        Lila's Dance   10/93   Diamond Homespun
        A Homespun Mother's Day   05/94   Diamond Homespun
        Family Reunion   06/94   Diamond Homespun

Metzger, Barbara
        Minor Indiscretions   Ballantine
        My Lady Innkeeper   Ballantine
        Lady In Green   04/93   Ballantine
        A Loyal Companion   Ballantine
        Cupboard Kisses   Ballantine Regency
        An Early Engagement   Ballantine Regency
        The Earl And The Heiress   Ballantine Regency
        Betking's Folly   Ballantine Regency
        Lady Whilton's Wedding   04/95   Ballantine Regency
        A Loyal Companion   /94   Fawcett
        An Angel For The Earl   03/94   Fawcett Regency
        A Suspicious Affair   07/94   Fawcett Regency
        The Luck Of The Devil   08/91   Fawcett Crest Regency Romance
        An Affair Of Interest   01/92   Fawcett Crest Regency Romance
        Christmas Wishes   11/92   Fawcett Crest Regency Romance
        Autumn Loves   10/93   Fawcett Crest Regency Romance
        Rake's Ransom   /86   Walker
        The Earl And The Heiress   Walker

Meyer, Anita
  581   Chandler's Child   07/94   Silhouette Intimate Moments

Meyer, Suzanne
  139   In For Life   Harlequin Intrigue

Meyers, Helen R.
  172   The Law Is No Lady   03/95   Harlequin Montana Mavericks

Meyers, Julie
  396   In The Cards   Harlequin Superromance
  258   Face To Face   07/89   Harlequin Temptation

Meyrick, Polly
   18   The Damask Rose   Mills & Boon

AUTHOR/TITLE INDEX

Michael, Judith
  Post Of Gold
  Deceptions
  Inheritance
  A Tangled Web   09/95
  A Ruling Passion   03/93
  Sleeping Beauty
Michael, Marie
   9 December 32nd...And Always   06/83   Bantam Loveswept
 37 Irresistible Forces   03/84   Bantam Loveswept
156 No Way To Treat A Lover   09/86   Bantam Loveswept
Michaels, Barbara
  The Wizard's Daughter
  The Master Of Blacktower
  Houses Of Stone
  Patriot's Dream
  Vanish With The Rose
  The Walker In Shadows
  Into The Darkness
  Black Rainbow
  Smoke And Mirrors
  Sons Of Wolf
  Someone In The House
  The Crying Child
  The Sea King's Daughter
  Search The Shadows
  Wings Of The Falcon
  Prince Of Darkness
  Shattered Silk
  Ammie, Come Home
  Be Buried In The Rain
  The Dark On The Other Side
  Scattered Blossoms
  Witch   Gothic
  Wait For What Will Come   Suspense
  House Of Many Shadows   /74   Berkley
  Greygallows   /87   Berkley Gothic
Michaels, Carol
  Charade Of Hearts   04/92   Diamond Regency
Michaels, Elizabeth
 17 Tollin's Daughter   01/90   Harlequin Regency
 58 The Fabric Of Love   09/91   Harlequin Regency
 83 The Cynic   10/92   Harlequin Regency
101 Lord Barton's Honour   07/93   Harlequin Regency
Michaels, Elizabeth Ann
  A Jewel So Rare   04/92   Pocket

685

Michaels, Elizabeth Ann

	Destiny's Will	01/91	Pocket
	From A Silver Heart	07/93	Pocket
	Illicit	12/95	Zebra
	Sweet Madness Mine	12/94	Zebra Historical

Michaels, Fern

	For All Their Lives	11/91	Ballantine
	Texas Sunrise	01/93	Ballantine
	All She Can Be		Ballantine
	Captive Embraces		Ballantine
	Captive Innocence		Ballantine
	Captive Passions		Ballantine
	Captive Secrets		Ballantine
	Captive Splendours		Ballantine
	Cinders To Satin		Ballantine
	Free Spirit		Ballantine
	Sins Of Omission		Ballantine
	Sins Of The Flesh		Ballantine
	Tender Warrior		Ballantine
	Texas Fury		Ballantine
	Texas Heat		Ballantine
	Texas Rich		Ballantine
	To Taste The Wine		Ballantine
	Valentina		Ballantine
	For All Their Lives		Ballantine
	Texas Sunrise		Ballantine
	The Seasons Of Her Life	04/94	Ballantine
	Heartbreak Ranch	04/97	Harlequin Anthology
	Paint Me Rainbows	10/94	Mira
	Wild Honey		Pocket
	The Delta Ladies	02/95	Pocket
15	Sea Gypsy	06/80	Silhouette Romance
32	Golden Lasso	09/80	Silhouette Romance
61	Whisper My Name	02/81	Silhouette Romance
87	Beyond Tomorrow	06/81	Silhouette Romance
114	Paint Me Rainbows	11/81	Silhouette Romance
146	Nightstar	04/82	Silhouette Romance
	Dear Emily	04/95	Zebra To Love Again

Michaels, Irene

	Frenchman's Mistress		Bantam

Michaels, Jan

32	Pursuit In The Wilderness	12/85	Harlequin Intrigue
71	The Only Witness		Harlequin Intrigue
89	Red Dog Run		Harlequin Intrigue
96	Into The Night		Harlequin Intrigue

Michaels, Jenevy

Michaels, Kristin

	To Begin With Love	/75	Nal Signet
	A Special Kind Of Love	/76	Nal Signet
	Enchanted Twilight	/76	Nal Signet
	Enchanted Journey	/77	Nal Signet
	Make Believe Love	/77	Nal Signet
	Song Of The Heart	/77	Nal Signet
	Voyage Of Love	/77	Nal Signet
	Magic Side Of The Moon	/79	Nal Signet

Michaels, Laura

81	Tune In Tomorrow	03/92	Meteor

Michaels, Leigh

702	Kiss Yesterday Goodbye	06/84	Harlequin Presents
811	Deadline For Love	08/85	Harlequin Presents
835	Dreams To Keep	11/85	Harlequin Presents
876	Touch Not My Heart	04/86	Harlequin Presents
900	Leaving Home	07/86	Harlequin Presents
1004	The Grand Hotel	08/87	Harlequin Presents
1028	Brittany's Castle	11/87	Harlequin Presents
1049	Carlisle Pride	02/88	Harlequin Presents
1068	Rebel With A Cause	04/88	Harlequin Presents
1107	Close Collaboration	09/88	Harlequin Presents
1147	A New Desire	02/89	Harlequin Presents
1162	Exclusively Yours	04/89	Harlequin Presents
1245	Once And For Always	02/90	Harlequin Presents
1266	With No Reservations	05/90	Harlequin Presents
	Marrying The Boss	09/96	Harlequin Romance
	Baby, You're Mine	07/97	Harlequin Romance
	The Perfect Divorce	02/97	Harlequin Romance
2657	On September Hill	11/84	Harlequin Romance
2734	Wednesday's Child	12/85	Harlequin Romance
2748	Come Next Summer	02/86	Harlequin Romance
2806	Capture A Shadow	12/86	Harlequin Romance
2830	O' Hara's Legacy	04/87	Harlequin Romance
2879	Sell Me A Dream	12/87	Harlequin Romance
2951	Strictly Business	12/88	Harlequin Romance
2987	Just A Normal Marriage	06/89	Harlequin Romance
2997	Shades Of Yesterday	08/89	Harlequin Romance
3010	No Place Like Home	10/89	Harlequin Romance
3023	Let Me Count The Ways	12/89	Harlequin Romance
3070	A Matter Of Principal	08/90	Harlequin Romance
3086	An Imperfect Love	11/90	Harlequin Romance
3119	An Uncommon Affair	04/91	Harlequin Romance
3141	Promise Me Tomorrow	08/91	Harlequin Romance
3160	Temporary Measures	11/91	Harlequin Romance
3171	Garrett's Back In Town	01/92	Harlequin Romance
3184	Old School Ties	03/92	Harlequin Romance

AUTHOR/TITLE INDEX

Michaels, Leigh

3214	The Best-Made Plans	08/92	Harlequin	Romance
3233	The Unexpected Landlord	11/92	Harlequin	Romance
3248	Safe In My Heart	02/93	Harlequin	Romance
3263	Ties That Blind	06/93	Harlequin	Romance
3275	The Lake Effect	08/93	Harlequin	Romance
3290	Dating Games	11/93	Harlequin	Romance
3300	A Singular Honeymoon	02/94	Harlequin	Romance
3311	Traveling Man	05/94	Harlequin	Romance
3326	Family Secrets (Kids & Kisses)	08/94	Harlequin	Romance
3337	The Only Solution	11/94	Harlequin	Romance
3343	House Of Dreams	01/95	Harlequin	Romance
3352	Invitation To Love (Sealed With A Kiss)	03/95	Harlequin	Romance
3367	Taming A Tycoon	07/95	Harlequin	Romance
3388	The Unlikely Santa	12/95	Harlequin	Romance
3401	The Only Man For Maggie	03/96	Harlequin	Romance
3411	The Daddy Trap	06/96	Harlequin	Romance
	Some Kind Of Hero	02/91	Harlequin	Valentine

Michaels, Lorna

412	Blessing In Disguise	07/90	Harlequin	Superromance
503	A Matter Of Privilege	06/92	Harlequin	Superromance
528	Season Of Light	12/92	Harlequin	Superromance
633	The Reluctant Bodyguard	02/95	Harlequin	Superromance
523	The Reluctant Hunk	01/95	Harlequin	Temptation
584	The Great Chili Caper	04/96	Harlequin	Temptation

Michaels, Lynn

304	Remembrance (Editor's Choice)	06/90	Harlequin	Temptation
405	The Patriot (Rebels & Rogues)	08/92	Harlequin	Temptation
449	Second Sight	07/93	Harlequin	Temptation
481	Aftershock (Passion's Quest)	03/94	Harlequin	Temptation
511	Molly And The Phantom	10/94	Harlequin	Temptation
542	Nightwing (Secret Fantasies)	06/95	Harlequin	Temptation

Michaels, Margie

15	Beloved Pirate	/81	Berkley	Second Chance At Love
61	Mirage	/82	Berkley	Second Chance At Love
12	Untamed Desire	05/84	Harlequin	Temptation

Michaels, Marilyn

16	Passion's Flight	/81	Berkley	Second Chance At Love

Michaels, Susan

	An Infamous Fiasco		Warner	Regency

Michaels, Theresa

	Renegades (Promotion)	08/95	Harlequin	Anthology
	Renegades Anthology	06/95	Harlequin	Historical
104	A Corner Of Heaven	12/91	Harlequin	Historical
145	Gifts Of Love	10/92	Harlequin	Historical
243	Fire And Sword	11/94	Harlequin	Historical

AUTHOR/TITLE INDEX

Michaels, Theresa
276	Once A Maverick	07/95	Harlequin Historical
296	Once An Outlaw	12/95	Harlequin Historical
316	Once A Lawman	05/96	Harlequin Historical

Michel, Freda
Requiem For A Rake — Ballantine Regency

Michel, M. Scott
| 42 | House In Harlem | /50 | Harlequin |
| 64 | Sinister Warning | /50 | Harlequin |

Michelle, Suzanne
29	Enchanted Desert	11/82	Silhouette Desire
47	Silver Promises	02/83	Silhouette Desire
57	No Place For A Woman	04/83	Silhouette Desire
76	Stormy Surrender	07/83	Silhouette Desire
87	Recipe For Love	09/83	Silhouette Desire
106	Fancy Free	12/83	Silhouette Desire
128	Political Passions	04/84	Silhouette Desire
152	Sweetheart Of A Deal	08/84	Silhouette Desire
170	Forbidden Melody	11/84	Silhouette Desire
189	Starstruck Lovers	02/85	Silhouette Desire

Michels, Christine
| | Danger's Kiss | 12/94 | Leisure |
| | In Fugitive Arms | /95 | Leisure |

Mickle, Casey
| | The Devil's Darling | 11/94 | Berkley Jove |
| | My Lucky Lady | 12/94 | Berkley Jove |

Mikels, Jennifer
462	Lady Of The West	10/86	Silhouette Romance
487	Maverick	02/87	Silhouette Romance
511	Perfect Partners	06/87	Silhouette Romance
551	The Bewitching Hour	01/88	Silhouette Romance
66	A Sporting Affair	12/82	Silhouette Special Edition
124	Whirlwind	10/83	Silhouette Special Edition
478	Remember The Daffodils	09/88	Silhouette Special Edition
521	Double Identity	04/89	Silhouette Special Edition
574	Stargazer	01/90	Silhouette Special Edition
623	Freedom's Just Another Word	09/90	Silhouette Special Edition
694	A Real Charmer	09/91	Silhouette Special Edition
735	A Job For Jack	04/92	Silhouette Special Edition
807	Your Child, My Child	04/93	Silhouette Special Edition
870	Denver's Lady	02/94	Silhouette Special Edition
929	Jake Ryker's Back In Town	12/94	Silhouette Special Edition
947	Sara's Father	03/95	Silhouette Special Edition
993	Child Of Mine	11/95	Silhouette Special Edition
1023	Expecting: Baby	04/96	Silhouette Special Edition

Milan, Angel

AUTHOR/TITLE INDEX

Milan, Angel

34	Snow Spirit	12/82	Silhouette	Desire
64	Sonatina	05/83	Silhouette	Desire
96	Summer Son	10/83	Silhouette	Desire
118	Out Of Bounds	02/84	Silhouette	Desire
153	Danielle's Doll	08/84	Silhouette	Desire
214	Sugarfire	06/85	Silhouette	Desire
226	Anna's Child	08/85	Silhouette	Desire
285	Knock Any Time	06/86	Silhouette	Desire
39	Autumn Harvest	08/82	Silhouette	Special Edition
200	Sea Of Dreams	11/84	Silhouette	Special Edition

Milella, Jan

175	Night Heat	01/87	Silhouette	Intimate Moments
269	Once Forgotten	01/89	Silhouette	Intimate Moments

Miles, Cara

	Lord Of The Night	08/93	Avon	
	Beyond The Horizon		Avon	
	Love Me With Fury	09/91	Avon	Romance
	Promise Me Forever	03/92	Avon	Romance
	Surrender To The Fury	11/92	Avon	Romance

Miles, Cassie

	Magic Slippers	07/96	Avon	Anthology
567	Buffalo Mc Cloud	01/95	Harlequin	American
574	Borrowed Time	03/95	Harlequin	American
122	Hide And Seek		Harlequin	Intrigue
150	Handle With Care		Harlequin	Intrigue
237	Heartbreak Hotel	08/93	Harlequin	Intrigue
269	Are You Lonesome Tonight?	04/94	Harlequin	Intrigue
285	Don't Be Cruel	08/94	Harlequin	Intrigue
320	Mysterious Vows (Mail Order Bride)	04/95	Harlequin	Intrigue
332	The Suspect Groom (Mail Order Bride)	07/95	Harlequin	Intrigue
363	The Imposter	03/96	Harlequin	Intrigue
381	Rule Breaker	08/96	Harlequin	Intrigue
26	Tongue-Tied	09/84	Harlequin	Temptation
61	Acts Of Magic	06/85	Harlequin	Temptation
104	It's Only Natural	04/86	Harlequin	Temptation
170	Seems Like Old Times	09/87	Harlequin	Temptation
235	Monkey Business	01/89	Harlequin	Temptation
305	Under Lock And Key	07/90	Harlequin	Temptation
394	A Risky Proposition	05/92	Harlequin	Temptation
10	Full Steam	09/90	Meteor	

Miley, Meg

	Trail Of Diamonds	/95	Suspense
	Eyes Of Emerald	/95	Suspense
	Precious Pearls	/96	Suspense

Miller, Ann

Miller, Linda Lael

	Knights	05/96	Pocket Time-Travel
438	Used-To-Be Lovers	07/88	Silhouette Desire
480	Only Forever	02/89	Silhouette Desire
516	Just Kate	08/89	Silhouette Desire
547	Daring Moves	02/90	Silhouette Desire
568	Mixed Messages	05/90	Silhouette Desire
589	Escape From Cabriz	09/90	Silhouette Desire
607	Glory, Glory	12/90	Silhouette Desire
667	Wild About Harry	10/91	Silhouette Desire
59	Snowflakes On The Sea	07/84	Silhouette Intimate Moments
87	Part Of The Bargain	03/85	Silhouette Intimate Moments
277	State Secrets	12/85	Silhouette Special Edition
324	Ragged Rainbows	07/86	Silhouette Special Edition
754	There And Now	07/92	Silhouette Special Edition
762	Here And Then	08/92	Silhouette Special Edition

Miller, Nadine

115	Iron And Lace	11/92	Meteor

Miller, Sue

	Family Pictures	05/91	Harper
	For Love	04/93	Harper

Mills, Anita

	Christmas Rogues:"The Christmas Stranger"	11/95	Harlequin Anthology
	Regency Christmas		Nal
	The Devil's Match		Nal
	Newmarket Match		Nal
	Scandal Bound		Nal
	The Fire And The Fury	07/91	Nal Onyx
	Winter Roses	02/92	Nal Onyx
	The Rogue's Return	06/92	Nal Regency
	The Duke's Double	07/88	Nal Regency
	Duel Of Hearts	12/88	Nal Regency
	Full-Moon Magic	09/92	Nal Super Signet Historical
1	Lady Of Fire	08/94	Nal Penguin Medieval Trilogy
2	Fire And Steel		Nal Penguin Medieval Trilogy
3	Hearts Of Fire		Nal Penguin Medieval Triology
	Miss Gordon's Mistake		Nal Penguin Regency
	Follow The Heart		Nal Penguin Regency
	From The Heart	01/94	Nal Signet Anthology
	Rakes And Rogues	06/93	Penguin Super Signet Historical
	Secret Nights	07/94	Penguin Topaz
	Falling Stars	09/94	Penguin Topaz
	A Dream Come True	03/94	Penguin Topaz Man Presents: Anthology
	Moonlight Lovers	09/93	Signet Anthology
	Dashing & Dangerous	05/95	Signet Anthology
	The Last Wish	/90	Signet Regency Christmas Coll.
	Cherished Moments	04/95	St. Martin's Anthology

AUTHOR/TITLE INDEX

Mills, Catherine
  34 Lured Into Dawn   /82   Berkley Second Chance At Love
Mills, Deanie Francis
      Losers Weepers   09/94 Jove
Milne, Rosaleen
      Borrowed Plumes   Nal Penguin Regency
      The Major's Lady   Pocket Cotillion Regency
Minger, Elda

95	Another Chance At Heaven		Harlequin American
106	Touched By Love		Harlequin American
117	Seize The Fire		Harlequin American
133	Bachelor Mother		Harlequin American
162	Billion Dollar Baby	08/86	Harlequin American
229	Nothing In Common		Harlequin American
314	Wedding Of The Year		Harlequin American
338	Spike Is Missing		Harlequin American
469	Bride For A Night	01/93	Harlequin American
489	Daddy's Little Dividend	06/93	Harlequin American
510	Wed Again	11/93	Harlequin American
531	Teddy Bear Heir	04/94	Harlequin American
584	Baby By Chance	05/95	Harlequin American
20	Wedding Of The Year	06/96	Harlequin Here Come The Grooms
590	The Last Seduction	06/96	Harlequin Temptation
	Timeswept Brides	07/96	Jove Anthology
	Embrace The Night	05/94	Jove Tea Rose Romance
	Velvet Fire		Zebra Heartfire

Minger, Miriam

A Hint Of Rapture		Avon
Stolen Splendor		Avon
Captive Rose	03/91	Avon Romance
Defiant Imposter	02/92	Avon Romance
My Runaway Heart	11/95	Avon Sequel To Secrets Of Mid.
The Pagan's Prize	01/93	Jove Historical
Wild Angel	01/94	Jove Historical
Secrets Of Midnight	10/95	Jove Historical

Mitchell, Erica
      Bright Desire   Pocket
      Jade Moon   Pocket
Mitchell, Joseph
 210 Mc Sorley's Wonderful Saloon   /53   Harlequin
Mitchell, Margaret
      Gone With The Wind   /37   Mac Millan
Mittermeyer, Helen
      No Gentle Possession
      Rendezvous
      Stolen Scenes

AUTHOR/TITLE INDEX

Mittermeyer, Helen

	Desert Princess		
	Summer Heat		Anthology
	Southern Nights	07/92	Bantam Fanfare
	Princess Of The Veil		Bantam Loveswept
2	Surrender	05/83	Bantam Loveswept
15	Brief Delight	08/83	Bantam Loveswept
57	Unexpected Sunrise	08/84	Bantam Loveswept
67	Vortex	11/84	Bantam Loveswept
121	Tempest	12/85	Bantam Loveswept
210	Kismet	10/87	Bantam Loveswept
269	Ablaze	07/88	Bantam Loveswept
310	Blue Flame	02/89	Bantam Loveswept
341	White Heat	07/89	Bantam Loveswept
455	The Mask	02/91	Bantam Loveswept
489	A Moment In Time	08/91	Bantam Loveswept
516	Krystal	01/92	Bantam Loveswept
552	Her Very Own Butler	07/92	Bantam Loveswept
588	' Twas The Night	01/93	Bantam Loveswept
621	' Til We Meet Again	06/93	Bantam Loveswept
690	Magic In Pastel	06/94	Bantam Loveswept
754	Dynasty Jones	09/95	Bantam Loveswept
782	Divinity Brown	04/96	Bantam Loveswept
371	Quicksilver	12/89	Bantam Loveswept: Men Of Ice
396	Black Forest	05/90	Bantam Loveswept: Men Of Ice
425	Frozen Idol	09/90	Bantam Loveswept: Men Of Ice
	Golden Touch	11/88	Crown/Pageant
	Diamond Fire	04/89	Dell
	Brief Encounter	10/88	Dell
	Under The Sign Of Venus	07/93	Smithmark
	The Veil	/96	Warner

Mittman, Stephanie

	The Marriage Bed	05/96	Dell
	A Taste Of Honey	11/95	Harper Monogram

Moffett, Julie

	A Touch Of Fire	07/94	Leisure
	Fleeting Splendor	04/93	Leisure Historical
	The Double-Edged Blad	06/96	Leisure Love Spell

Molay, Mollie

560	From Drifter To Daddy	11/94	Harlequin American
597	Her Two Husbands	09/95	Harlequin American
616	Marriage By Mistake	01/96	Harlequin American
638	Like Father, Like Son	07/96	Harlequin American

Monet, Nicole

2	Love's Silver Web	06/82	Silhouette Desire
39	Shadow Of Betrayal	01/83	Silhouette Desire

Monet, Nicole

62	Passionate Silence	05/83	Silhouette Desire
133	Love And Old Lace	05/84	Silhouette Desire
177	Casey's Shadow	12/84	Silhouette Desire
228	Rand Emory's Woman	08/85	Silhouette Desire
266	The Sandcastle Man	03/86	Silhouette Desire
405	Stand By Me	02/88	Silhouette Desire
473	Twilight Over Eden	01/89	Silhouette Desire
615	Guardian Angel	11/88	Silhouette Romance

Monk, Karyn

	Surrender To A Stranger	/ 96	Bantam
	The Rebel And The Redcoat	05/96	Bantam
	My Guardian Angel	02/95	Bantam Anthology

Monroe, Carolyn

847	Kiss Of Bliss	02/92	Silhouette Romance
912	A Lovin' Spoonful	01/93	Silhouette Romance
970	Help Wanted: Daddy (Fabulous Father)	11/93	Silhouette Romance

Monroe, Mary Alice

| | The Long Road Home | 03/95 | Harper |

Monson, Christine

	A Flame Run Wild		
	Rangoon		
	Surrender The Night		
	Golden Nights		Warner
	The Fiery Splendor		Warner

Montague, Jeanne

	Passion Flame		Ace
	Diamond Heart	04/90	Pocket
	The Clock Tower		St. Martin's Gothic
	Midnight Moon		St. Martin's Gothic
	The Castle Of The Winds		St. Martin's Gothic

Montague, Lisa

| 14 | Lady Of Darkness | | Mills & Boon |
| 37 | The Emperor's Jewel | | Mills & Boon |

Montana, Pat

993	One Unbelievable Man	02/94	Silhouette Romance
1076	Babies, Inc. (Bundles Of Joy)	04/95	Silhouette Romance
1111	Storybook Cowboy	10/95	Silhouette Romance

Monteith, Hayton

	To Love A Stranger		
	Relentless Love		
	Jinx Lady		
	Lover's Knot		
	Pilgrim Soul		
	Lotus Blossom		
	Endless Obsession		

Montgomery, Marianne
    A Passionate Pretender   Nal Penguin

Montrose, David
  262 The Body On Mount Royal   /53 Harlequin

Montrose, Sarah
    The Golden Heiress   Berkley Regency

Moon, Arthur
    The Passions   Zebra
    The Pagans   Zebra
    The Proud   Zebra

Moon, Modean
   77 Dare To Dream   09/84 Harlequin American
 113 Hiding Places   Harlequin American
 146 An Uncommon Hero   Harlequin American
 271 Simple Words   Harlequin American
    The Covenant   09/95 Harper
 868 The Giving   07/94 Silhouette Desire
 904 Interrupted Honeymoon   01/95 Silhouette Desire
 995 Forgotten Vows   04/96 Silhouette Desire
    Evermore   02/93 Warner

Mooney, Martin
  28 One Year With Grace   /50 Harlequin

Moore, Amos
  66 Royce Of The Royal Mounted /50 Harlequin
 399 Royce Of The Royal Mounted /57 Harlequin

Moore, Anne
    Tangled Vows   Pocket

Moore, Brian
 102 Wreath For A Redhead   /51 Harlequin
 117 The Executioners   /51 Harlequin

Moore, Charlotte
 975 Not The Marrying Kind   11/93 Silhouette Romance
1088 Belated Bride   06/95 Silhouette Romance
1129 The Maverick Takes A Wife 01/96 Silhouette Romance
  62 Trust Me   03/96 Silhouette Shadows

Moore, Diana
    Blossoms In The Wind

Moore, Ellen
  85 One Snowy Night   04/92 Meteor

Moore, Frances Sarah
    Hidden Boundary   Bantam Red Rose Romance

Moore, Gwyneth
  16 Men Were Deceivers Ever 12/89 Harlequin Regency
  27 The Dirty Frog   06/90 Harlequin Regency
  57 Love's Lady Lost   09/91 Harlequin Regency

AUTHOR/TITLE INDEX

Moore, Kate

	To Kiss A Thief	01/92	Avon	Regency Romance
	Mercenary Major	06/94	Avon	Regency Romance
	An Improper Widow	02/95	Avon	Regency Romance
	Sweet Bargain	03/93	Avon	Regency Romance

Moore, Lisa

45	September Song		Nal	Rapture Romance

Moore, Margaret

	Mistletoe Marriages	11/94	Harlequin	Anthology
118	A Warrior's Heart	03/92	Harlequin	Historical
149	China Blossom	11/92	Harlequin	Historical
175	A Warrior's Quest	06/93	Harlequin	Historical
200	The Viking	01/94	Harlequin	Historical
224	A Warrior's Way	06/94	Harlequin	Historical
248	Vows (Weddings, Inc.)	12/94	Harlequin	Historical
268	The Saxon	05/95	Harlequin	Historical
295	The Welshman's Way	12/95	Harlequin	Historical
311	The Norman's Heart	04/96	Harlequin	Historical
328	The Baron's Quest	08/96	Harlequin	Historical

Moore, Marjorie

446	To Please The Doctor	/58	Harlequin	
459	Second Love (Ring For The Nurse)	/59	Harlequin	
492	Follow A Dream (Hospital Pro)	/59	Harlequin	
500	Unsteady Flame (Honorary Surgeon)	/59	Harlequin	
504	Peter Raynal, Surgeon	/60	Harlequin	
508	Senior Surgeon	/60	Harlequin	
509	A Year To Remember (Nurse Secretary)	/60	Harlequin	
520	Doctor Derrington	/60	Harlequin	
589	The Doctor's Challenge	/61	Harlequin	
609	Copper Beeches (Doctor's Secretary)	/61	Harlequin	
659	Gone Away	/62	Harlequin	
1103	Heart Of Gold	/67	Harlequin	

Moore, Mary

1315	Where The Kowhai Blooms	/69	Harlequin	
1557	Along The Ribbonwood Track	/72	Harlequin	
1578	Rata Flowers Are Red	/72	Harlequin	
1712	Matai Valley Magic	/73	Harlequin	
2349	Man Of High Country		Harlequin	Romance
2512	Run Before The Wind		Harlequin	Romance
2606	Springs Of Love		Harlequin	Romance
2686	Lake Haupiri Moon		Harlequin	Romance
2927	A Golden Touch		Harlequin	Romance

Moore, Patti

25	Gift Of Orchids	/81	Berkley	Second Chance At Love

Moore, Paula

	The Perfect Couple	Richard Gallen

Moore, Paula
  This Golden Rapture   Richard Gallen
  Nothing But Roses   Richard Gallen
Moore, Rayanne
 8 Thin White Line   Harlequin American
 65 Images On Silver   Harlequin American
Moore, Sandra
 918 High Country Cowboy (Premiere)   10/94 Silhouette Special Edition
Moore, Susan
  Paths Of Fortune   St. Martin's
  A World Too Wide   St. Martin's
Moorhouse, Catherine
  Dorothea   Bantam
  Adriana   Bantam
  Louisa   Bantam
Moreland, Peggy
 515 A Little Bit Country   08/89 Silhouette Desire
 598 Run For The Roses   10/90 Silhouette Desire
 682 Miss Prim   12/91 Silhouette Desire
 767 The Rescuer   02/93 Silhouette Desire
 837 Seven Year Itch   02/94 Silhouette Desire
 867 The Baby Doctor   07/94 Silhouette Desire
 · 921 Miss Lizzy's Legacy   04/95 Silhouette Desire
Morgan, Alice
 35 Branded Heart   Harlequin American
 68 Deception For Desire   Harlequin American
Morgan, Diana
 286 Anything Goes   /85 Berkley Second Chance At Love
 20 Emerald Dreams   Nal Rapture Romance
 43 Amber Dreams   Nal Rapture Romance
 72 Lady In Flight   06/84 Nal Rapture Romance
 293 Behind Closed Doors   05/84 Silhouette Romance
  Chapel Hill   Warner
Morgan, Elizabeth
  A Christmas Delight   /91 Zebra Anthology
  Amanda's Folly   Zebra Regency
Morgan, Jane
  Lord Courtney's Lady   Berkley
Morgan, Kathleen
 1 The Knowing Crystal   03/91 Leisure Futuristic Trilogy
 2 Heart's Lair   09/91 Leisure Futuristic Trilogy
 3 Crystal Fire   08/92 Leisure Futuristic Trilogy
  Child Of The Mist   01/93 Leisure Historical
  Firestar   10/93 Leisure Lovespell
  Demon Prince   04/94 Leisure Lovespell
  Heart's Surrender   11/94 Pinnacle

AUTHOR/TITLE INDEX

Morgan, Raye
  892 Sorry, The Bride Has Escaped (Jilted!)   11/94 Silhouette Desire
  997 Baby Dreams   05/96 Silhouette Desire
1010 A Gift For Baby   07/96 Silhouette Desire
  427 Roses Never Fade   04/86 Silhouette Romance

Morgan, Tracy
  430 Michael's Wife   02/93 Harlequin Temptation

Moritmer, Carole
  522 Red Rose For Love   Harlequin Presents
  659 Pagan Enchantment   Harlequin Presents

Morland, Lynette
  339 Occupational Hazard   01/85 Silhouette Romance
  432 Irish Eyes   05/86 Silhouette Romance
  443 Magic City   07/86 Silhouette Romance
  483 No Questions Asked   01/87 Silhouette Romance
  548 Mid-Air   12/87 Silhouette Romance

Morrell, Karen
  For The Love Of Laura   08/92 Avalon
  Wish Upon A Star   10/92 Avalon
  Twice In A Blue Moon   10/93 Avalon

Morris, Elizabeth
  178 This Day Forward   Harlequin American
  221 A Touch Of Moonshine   Harlequin American
  23 This Day Forward   06/96 Harlequin Here Come The Grooms
  125 Teaspoon Of Murder   Harlequin Intrigue
  208 The First Horseman   02/93 Harlequin Intrigue

Morris, Gilbert
  1 Covenant Of Love   Tyndale House Appomattox Saga
  2 Gate Of His Enemies   Tyndale House Appomattox Saga
  3 Where Honor Dwells   Tyndale House Appomattox Saga
  4 Land Of The Shadow   /93 Tyndale House Appomattox Saga

Morris, Julianna
1097 Baby Talk (Bundles Of Joy)   08/95 Silhouette Romance

Morris, Suzanne
  Galveston

Morrison, Jo
  312 Always   08/90 Harlequin Temptation
  370 An Imperfect Hero   11/91 Harlequin Temptation

Morrow, Victoria
  Angel In My Arms   06/92 Pocket
  Beneath A Pale Moon   Pocket
  Jenny's Dream   Pocket

Morse, Nancy
  83 Echoes   03/92 Meteor
  Silver Lady   Richard Gallen

Mortimer, Carole

579	Golden Fever		Harlequin Presents
587	Hidden Love		Harlequin Presents
594	Love's Only Deception		Harlequin Presents
603	Captive Loving		Harlequin Presents
611	Fantasy Girl		Harlequin Presents
619	Heaven Here On Earth		Harlequin Presents
627	Lifelong Affair		Harlequin Presents
636	Love Unspoken		Harlequin Presents
645	Undying Love		Harlequin Presents
651	Subtle Revenge		Harlequin Presents
669	Trust Summer Madness		Harlequin Presents
675	The Failed Marriage		Harlequin Presents
684	Sensual Encounter		Harlequin Presents
716	Everlasting Love		Harlequin Presents
724	Hard To Get		Harlequin Presents
740	A Lost Love		Harlequin Presents
757	Untamed		Harlequin Presents
773	An Unwilling Desire		Harlequin Presents
780	A Past Revenge		Harlequin Presents
786	The Passionate Lover		Harlequin Presents
797	Tempestuous Affair		Harlequin Presents
804	Cherish Tomorrow		Harlequin Presents
812	A No Rish Affair		Harlequin Presents
829	Lovers In The Aftermath		Harlequin Presents
852	The Devil's Price		Harlequin Presents
860	Lady Surrender		Harlequin Presents
877	Knight's Possession		Harlequin Presents
892	Darkness Into Light		Harlequin Presents
909	No Longer A Dream		Harlequin Presents
923	The Wade Dynasty		Harlequin Presents
939	Glass Slippers And Unicorns		Harlequin Presents
955	Hawk's Prey		Harlequin Presents
989	Velvet Promise		Harlequin Presents
1005	A Rogue And A Prirate		Harlequin Presents
1019	After The Loving		Harlequin Presents
1037	Tangled Hearts		Harlequin Presents
1050	Taggart's Woman		Harlequin Presents
1069	Secret Passion		Harlequin Presents
1083	Wish For The Moon		Harlequin Presents
1100	Uncertain Destiny		Harlequin Presents
1117	One Chance At Love		Harlequin Presents
1131	To Love Again		Harlequin Presents
1227	The Loving Gift		Harlequin Presents
1258	Elusive As The Unicorn	04/90	Harlequin Presents
1325	A Christmas Affair		Harlequin Presents
1451	Memories Of The Past	04/92	Harlequin Presents

AUTHOR/TITLE INDEX

Mortimer, Carole

1468	Romance Of A Lifetime	06/92	Harlequin	Presents
1543	Saving Grace	06/93	Harlequin	Presents
1551	The Jilted Bridegroom	05/93	Harlequin	Presents
1657	Gracious Lady	06/94	Harlequin	Presents
1689	Fated Attraction	10/94	Harlequin	Presents
1727	War Of Love	03/95	Harlequin	Presents
1793	The One And Only	02/96	Harlequin	Presents
1823	Two's Company	07/96	Harlequin	Presents
1583	Private Lives	09/93	Harlequin	Presents Plus
1607	Mother Of The Bride	12/93	Harlequin	Presents Plus
1631	Elusive Obsession	03/94	Harlequin	Presents Plus
1671	Return Engagement	08/94	Harlequin	Presents Plus
1703	Hunter's Moon	12/94	Harlequin	Presents Plus
	Just One Night	03/88	Harlequin	Signature Romance
	Gypsy	/86	Harlequin	Signature Romance
	Merlyn's Magic		Harlequin	Signature Romance

Mosco, Maise

Almonds And Raisins	Harper
Children's Children	Harper
Scattered Seed	Harper
Out Of Ashes	Harper

Moss, W. Stanley

165	Rats With Baby Faces	/52	Harlequin

Motley, Annette

The Quickenberry Tree	
Green Dragon, White Tiger	Nal Penguin

Moulton, Nancy

Crosswinds	/85	Avon	Romance
Dark Desires	/88	Avon	Romance
Defiant Destiny	/82	Avon	Romance
Defiant Heart	/89	Avon	Romance
Tempest Of The Heart	/87	Avon	Romance
Savage Heat	05/91	Zebra	Heartfire

Moyer, Florence

Changing Winds

Muir, Lucy

18	The Imprudent Wager	01/90	Harlequin	Regency
33	Sussex Summer	09/90	Harlequin	Regency
43	Highland Rivalry	02/91	Harlequin	Regency

Muir, Rae

308	The Pearl Stallion	03/96	Harlequin	Historical

Mulford, Clarence E.

107	The Man From Bar-20	/51	Harlequin
131	Tex	/51	Harlequin

Munchmore, Pat

AUTHOR/TITLE INDEX

Murray, Annabel

1228	Don't Ask Why		Harlequin Presents
1259	Black Lion Of Skiape		Harlequin Presents
1283	Island Turmoil		Harlequin Presents
1340	Let Fate Decide		Harlequin Presents
1613	A Man For Christmas	12/93	Harlequin Presents
2549	Roots Of Heaven		Harlequin Romance
2558	Keegan's Kingdom		Harlequin Romance
2596	Chrysanthemum & Sword		Harlequin Romance
2612	Villa Of Vengeance		Harlequin Romance
2625	Dear Green Isle		Harlequin Romance
2717	The Cotswold Lion		Harlequin Romance
2782	The Plumed Serpent		Harlequin Romance
2819	Wild For To Hold		Harlequin Romance
2843	Ring Of Claddagh		Harlequin Romance
2932	Heart's Treasure		Harlequin Romance
2952	Colour The Sky Red		Harlequin Romance
2974	Sympathetic Stranger		Harlequin Romance

Murray, E. P.

	Savage River	

Murray, Julia

11	The Notorious Lady May	Mills & Boon
32	Wed For A Wager	Mills & Boon

Murrey, Jeneth

748	Double Doubting	Harlequin Presents
781	Had We Never Loved	Harlequin Presents
787	The Daughter Of Night	Harlequin Presents
990	Bittersweet Marriage	Harlequin Presents
2470	The Bright Side Of Day	Harlequin Romance
2483	Hell Is My Heaven	Harlequin Romance
2559	Tame A Proud Heart	Harlequin Romance
2567	Forsaking All Others	Harlequin Romance
2637	The Road To Forever	Harlequin Romance
2697	The Gabrielli Man	Harlequin Romance
2728	Return To Arkady	Harlequin Romance
2807	The Waiting Man	Harlequin Romance
3039	Impulsive Proposal	Harlequin Romance

Murry, Susan

	Love Birds	01/95 Avalon

Musgrave, Jacqueline

20	Northern Lights	05/82 Silhouette Special Edition

Mutch, Karin

1478	Eve's Own Eden	/71	Harlequin
66	Cindy, Tread Lightly	/74	Harlequin Presents
149	The Story Of Jody	/76	Harlequin Presents

Myers, Beth

AUTHOR/TITLE INDEX

Myers, Beth
189   The Steady Flame   Dell Candlelight

Myers, Helen R.

370	Partners For Life	08/87	Silhouette Desire
454	Smooth Operator	10/88	Silhouette Desire
471	That Fontaine Woman!	01/89	Silhouette Desire
506	The Pirate O' Keefe	07/89	Silhouette Desire
570	Kiss Me Kate	05/90	Silhouette Desire
599	After You	10/90	Silhouette Desire
650	When Gabriel Called	07/91	Silhouette Desire
738	Navarrone	09/92	Silhouette Desire
797	Jake	07/93	Silhouette Desire
857	Once Upon A Full Moon	05/94	Silhouette Desire
941	The Rebel And The Hero	07/95	Silhouette Desire
990	Just A Memory Away	03/96	Silhouette Desire
	The Law Is No Lady	03/95	Silhouette Montana Mavericks
557	Donovan's Mermaid	02/88	Silhouette Romance
643	Someone To Watch Over Me	04/89	Silhouette Romance
677	Confidentially Yours	10/89	Silhouette Romance
737	Invitation To A Wedding	08/90	Silhouette Romance
776	A Fine Arrangement	02/91	Silhouette Romance
814	Through My Eyes	09/91	Silhouette Romance
861	Three Little Chaperones	04/92	Silhouette Romance
908	Forbidden Passion	02/93	Silhouette Romance
1002	A Father's Promise (Fabulous Father)	04/94	Silhouette Romance
1049	To Wed At Christmas	12/94	Silhouette Romance
1121	The Merry Matchmakers	12/95	Silhouette Romance
1169	Baby In A Basket	08/96	Silhouette Romance
6	Night Mist	04/93	Silhouette Shadows
23	Whispers In The Woods	01/94	Silhouette Shadows
49	Watching For Willa	02/95	Silhouette Shadows
	Seawitch		Silhouette Shadows Anthology
	After That Night		Silhouette Special Edtion

Myers, Judy
535   Dream Builder   02/93 Harlequin Superromance

Myers, Virginia
105   Sunlight On Sand   Harlequin Superromance

Myrus, Joyce

	Beyond Surrender		
	Angel's Ecstasy		Zebra
	Desperado's Kiss		Zebra
	Island Enchantress		Zebra
	Master Of Moonlight	04/95	Zebra Lovegram

Napier, Susan
885   Sweet As My Revenge   Harlequin Presents
924   Counterfeit Secretary   Harlequin Presents

AUTHOR/TITLE INDEX

Napier, Susan

940	The Lonely Season		Harlequin	Presents
1051	True Enchanter		Harlequin	Presents
1093	Reasons Of The Heart		Harlequin	Presents
1211	Another Time		Harlequin	Presents
1252	The Love Conspiracy		Harlequin	Presents
1284	A Bewitching Compulsion		Harlequin	Presents
1332	Fortune's Mistress		Harlequin	Presents
1380	No Reprieve	07/91	Harlequin	Presents
1460	Deal Of A Lifetime	05/92	Harlequin	Presents
1483	Devil To Pay	08/92	Harlequin	Presents
1531	Tempt Me Not	02/93	Harlequin	Presents
1554	Secret Admirer	06/93	Harlequin	Presents
1595	Winter Of Dreams (Year Down Under)	10/93	Harlequin	Presents
1674	The Cruellest Lie	08/94	Harlequin	Presents
1707	Phantom Lover	12/94	Harlequin	Presents
1788	The Sister Swap	01/96	Harlequin	Presents
1616	The Hawk And The Lamb	01/94	Harlequin	Presents Plus
1744	Dying For You	06/95	Harlequin	Presents Plus
2711	Love In The Valley		Harlequin	Romance
2723	Sweet Vixen		Harlequin	Romance

Nash, Jean

Forever, My Love		Avon	
Surrender The Heart		Avon	
Golden Reckoning		Avon	
The Last Of The Lattimers		Leisure	
Vol 1: The Silver Web		Leisure	
Vol 2: The Golden Thread		Leisure	
Sand Castles	/88	Pageant	
Surrender The Heart		Pageant	

Nash, Petra

	Mischief & Mayhem	03/95	Harlequin	Promotion
36	Lady Harriet's Harvest	10/90	Harlequin	Regency
93	Mr. Ravenworth's Ward	03/93	Harlequin	Regency

Naughton, Lee

2236	Sand Thru My Fingers		Harlequin Romance

Nauman, Eileen

	Hostage Heart		Avon	
385	My Only One		Harlequin	American
51	Touch The Heavens	03/85	Harlequin	Temptation
76	Dare To Love	09/85	Harlequin	Temptation
101	The Right Touch	04/86	Harlequin	Temptation
568	Come Gentle The Dawn	12/89	Silhouette	Special Edition
	Night Flight		Warner	

Nazworth, Lenora H.

River's Call	05/93	Avalon	

708

AUTHOR/TITLE INDEX

Nazworth, Lenora H.

	Dance Of The Butterfly	10/95	Avalon
	Carly' Song	03/96	Leisure An Angel's Touch

Neal, Hilary

662	Tread Softly, Nurse	/62	Harlequin
812	Factory Nurse	/64	Harlequin
931	Charge Nurse	/65	Harlequin
1034	Nurse Meg's Decision	/66	Harlequin

Neels, Betty

1361	Sister Peters In Amsterdam	/70	Harlequin
1385	Nurse In Holland	/70	Harlequin
1409	Blow Hot, Blow Cold	/70	Harlequin
1441	Nurse Harriet Goes To Holland	/70	Harlequin
1465	Damsel In Green	/71	Harlequin
1498	Fate Is Remarkable	/71	Harlequin
1529	Tulips For Augusta	/71	Harlequin
1569	Tangle Autumn	/72	Harlequin
1593	Wish With The Candles	/72	Harlequin
1625	Victory For Victoria	/72	Harlequin
1641	The Fifth Day Of Christmas	/72	Harlequin
1666	Saturday's Child	/73	Harlequin
1689	Cassandra By Chance	/73	Harlequin
1705	Three For A Wedding	/73	Harlequin
1737	Winter Of Change	/73	Harlequin
1761	Stars Through The Mist	/74	Harlequin
1775	Master Of Saramanca	/74	Harlequin
1777	Enchanting Samantha	/74	Harlequin
1801	Uncertain Summer	/74	Harlequin
1817	The Gemel Ring	/74	Harlequin
1841	The Magic Of Living	/75	Harlequin
1857	Cruise To A Wedding	/75	Harlequin
1881	The End Of The Rainbow	/75	Harlequin
1905	Tabitha In Moonlight	/75	Harlequin
1921	Heaven Is Gentle	/75	Harlequin
1937	Henrietta's Own Castle	/76	Harlequin
1954	A Star Looks Down	/76	Harlequin
1970	Cobweb Morning	/76	Harlequin
1987	The Moon For Lavinia	/76	Harlequin
2009	Esmeralda	/76	Harlequin
2025	Roses For Christmas	/76	Harlequin
2041	The Edge Of Winter	/77	Harlequin
2063	A Gem Of A Girl	/77	Harlequin
2080	A Small Slice Of Summer	/77	Harlequin
2095	A Matter Of Chance	/77	Harlequin
2110	The Hasty Marriage	/77	Harlequin
2127	Grasp A Nettle	/77	Harlequin
2137	Pineapple Girl	/78	Harlequin

AUTHOR/TITLE INDEX

Neels, Betty

2153	The Little Dragon	/78	Harlequin
2169	Britannia All At Sea	/78	Harlequin
2202	Philomena's Miracle	/78	Harlequin
2226	Never While Grass Grows		Harlequin Romance
2250	Ring In A Teacup		Harlequin Romance
2275	Sun And Candlelight		Harlequin Romance
2301	Promise Of Happiness		Harlequin Romance
2314	Midnight Sun's Magic		Harlequin Romance
2338	Winter Wedding		Harlequin Romance
2367	Last April Fair		Harlequin Romance
2393	Caroline's Waterloo		Harlequin Romance
2403	Hannah		Harlequin Romance
2415	When May Follows		Harlequin Romance
2440	Not Once But Twice		Harlequin Romance
2463	An Apple From Eve		Harlequin Romance
2500	Judith		Harlequin Romance
2520	A Girl To Love		Harlequin Romance
2542	All Else Confusion		Harlequin Romance
2550	A Dream Come True		Harlequin Romance
2566	Midsummer Star		Harlequin Romance
2597	Roses And Champagne		Harlequin Romance
2626	Never Too Late		Harlequin Romance
2656	Polly		Harlequin Romance
2666	Once For All Time		Harlequin Romance
2680	Heidelberg Wedding		Harlequin Romance
2692	Year's Happy Ending		Harlequin Romance
2712	A Summer Idyll		Harlequin Romance
2729	At The End Of The Day		Harlequin Romance
2741	Magic In Vienna		Harlequin Romance
2752	Never The Time Or Place		Harlequin Romance
2787	A Girl Named Rose		Harlequin Romance
2808	Two Weeks To Remember		Harlequin Romance
2824	The Secret Pool		Harlequin Romance
2855	Stormy Springtime		Harlequin Romance
2874	Off With The Old Love		Harlequin Romance
2891	The Doubtful Marriage	02/88	Harlequin Romance
2914	A Gentle Awakening		Harlequin Romance
2933	The Course Of True Love		Harlequin Romance
2956	When Two Paths Meet		Harlequin Romance
3004	Paradise For Two		Harlequin Romance
3024	The Fateful Bargain		Harlequin Romance
3036	No Need To Say Good Bye		Harlequin Romance
3053	The Chain Of Destiny		Harlequin Romance
3071	Hilltop Tryst		Harlequin Romance
3084	The Convenient Wife		Harlequin Romance
3105	The Girl With Green Eyes		Harlequin Romance

Neels, Betty

3131	A Suitable Match		Harlequin Romance
3149	Roses Have Thorns	09/91	Harlequin Romance
3161	A Little Moonlight	11/91	Harlequin Romance
3185	The Most Marvellous Summer	03/92	Harlequin Romance
3197	The Final Touch	05/92	Harlequin Romance
3208	A Kind Of Magic	07/92	Harlequin Romance
3222	An Unlikely Romance	09/92	Harlequin Romance
3249	Romantic Encounter	02/93	Harlequin Romance
3267	A Happy Meeting	06/93	Harlequin Romance
3279	The Quiet Professor	09/93	Harlequin Romance
3287	An Old-Fashioned Girl	11/93	Harlequin Romance
3299	Two For The Heart	02/94	Harlequin Romance
3315	A Girl In A Million	06/94	Harlequin Romance
3323	At Odds With Love	08/94	Harlequin Romance
3339	The Awakened Heart	12/94	Harlequin Romance
3347	A Valentine For Daisy (Kids & Kisses)	02/95	Harlequin Romance
3355	Dearest Love (Sealed With A Kiss)	04/95	Harlequin Romance
3363	A Secret Infatuation	06/95	Harlequin Romance
3371	Wedding Bells For Beatrice	08/95	Harlequin Romance
3389	A Christmas Wish	12/95	Harlequin Romance
3400	Waiting For Deborah	03/96	Harlequin Romance
3415	The Bachelor's Wedding	07/96	Harlequin Romance

Neff, Mindy

644	A Family Man	08/96	Harlequin American

Neggers, Carla

	Everlasting Love	05/95	Anthology
	Dancing Season	/84	Avon Finding Mr. Right
	The Uneven Score	/85	Avon Velvet Glove
	The Knotted Skein	/84	Avon Velvet Glove
	The Venus Shoe	/84	Avon Velvet Glove
5	Matching Wits	05/83	Bantam Loveswept
20	Heart On A String	10/83	Bantam Loveswept
36	A Touch Of Magic	03/84	Bantam Loveswept
	Tempting Fate	03/93	Berkley
	Southern Comfort	/84	Dell Candlelight Ecstasy
	Interior Designs	/85	Dell Candlelight Ecstasy
	Apple Of My Eye	/85	Dell Candlelight Ecstasy
	Outrageous Desire	/83	Dell Richard Gallen
	Claim The Crown	/87	Harlequin
	New Year's Resolution: Husband For Hire	01/96	Harlequin Anthology
45	Finders Keepers	/95	Harlequin Men Made In America
108	Captivated	05/86	Harlequin Temptation
162	Trade Secrets	07/87	Harlequin Temptation
190	Family Matters	02/88	Harlequin Temptation
208	All In A Name	06/88	Harlequin Temptation
236	A Winning Battle	01/89	Harlequin Temptation

Nelson, Louella
96	Sentinel At Dawn		Harlequin Superromance
128	Freedom's Fortune		Harlequin Superromance
	Naked Came The Ladies	02/94	Starlog Moonlight Anthology

Nelson, Rachelle
	Cherished Reward	07/96	Jove
	The Flirt	12/95	Jove Sons And Daughters

Nelson, Valerie K.
714	Conduct Unbecoming	/63	Harlequin
744	Verena Fayre, Probationer	/63	Harlequin
764	Nurse Ann Wood	/63	Harlequin
793	The Starched Cap	/64	Harlequin
818	The Second Year (Second Year Nurse)	/64	Harlequin
834	Nurse Annabel	/64	Harlequin
852	The Fair Stranger	/64	Harlequin
890	Two Sisters	/65	Harlequin
940	Substitute Nurse	/65	Harlequin
961	Nurse Jane And Cousin Paul	/65	Harlequin
1590	The Girl From Over The Sea	/72	Harlequin

Neri, Penelope
Passion's Rapture		
Love's Legacy	11/95	Leisure Anthology
Beloved Scoundrel		Zebra
Cherish The Night		Zebra
Crimson Angel		Zebra
Desert Captive		Zebra
Forever And Beyond		Zebra
Forever In His Arms		Zebra
Jasmine Paradise		Zebra
Loving Lies		Zebra
Midnight Captive		Zebra
Passion's Betrayal		Zebra
Sea Jewel		Zebra
Silver Rose		Zebra
Hearts Enchanted		Zebra
Bold Breathless Nights		Zebra
A Stolen Moment	06/94	Zebra
Master Of Midnight	12/95	Zebra

Nevins, Kate
191	Spellbound	/84	Berkley Second Chance At Love
267	Venetian Sunrise	/85	Berkley Second Chance At Love

Newman, Holly
A Heart In Jeopardy		Berkley
The Waylaid Heart	/90	Berkley
A Christmas Treasure	11/92	Berkley Regency
The Heart's Companion	11/90	Charter/Diamond

Newman, Holly

Honor's Players		Warner
Gentlemen's Trade		Warner
A Grand Gesture		Warner Regency

Newsome, Muriel

Curse Of The Moors	11/92	Diamond Gothic
The Secrets Of Montroth House		Diamond Gothic
Watchful Eyes	02/93	Diamond Gothic

Nicholas, Deborah

Night Vision		Dell
Silent Sonata	05/94	Dell Suspense

Nicholas, Robin

1017	The Cowboy And His Lady	06/94	Silhouette Romance
1149	Wrangler's Wedding	04/96	Silhouette Romance

Nichols, Charlotte

403	Eye Of The Beholder	12/85	Silhouette Romance

Nichols, Margaret

5	Close To My Heart	/49	Harlequin
30	Portrait Of Love	/50	Harlequin

Nichols, Suzanne

392	Rings Of Gold		Harlequin Superromance
458	Satin Whispers	07/91	Harlequin Superromance

Nicholson, Peggy

732	The Darling Jade		Harlequin Presents
741	Run So Far		Harlequin Presents
764	Dolphins For Luck		Harlequin Presents
3009	Tender Offer		Harlequin Romance
3100	Burning Dreams		Harlequin Romance
3172	Checkmate	01/92	Harlequin Romance
3250	Pure And Simple	02/93	Harlequin Romance
3322	The Truth About George	07/94	Harlequin Romance
193	Soft Lies, Summer Light		Harlequin Superromance
237	Child's Play		Harlequin Superromance
290	The Light Fantastic		Harlequin Superromance
698	You Again	07/96	Harlequin Superromance

Nickels, Meryl

Love's Lying Eyes		Zebra Heartfire
Love's Wild Frontier		Zebra Heartfire

Nickson, Hilda

555	Love The Physician	/60	Harlequin
670	Operation Love	/62	Harlequin
702	Surgeons In Love	/62	Harlequin
735	Quayside Hospital	/63	Harlequin
745	Tender Nurse	/63	Harlequin
776	Nurse Foster's Foolish Heart	/63	Harlequin
794	Surgeon's Return	/64	Harlequin

AUTHOR/TITLE INDEX

Nickson, Hilda

820	The World Of Nurse Mitchell	/64	Harlequin
836	He Whom I Love (Doctor Phillip)	/64	Harlequin
882	For Love Of A Surgeon	/65	Harlequin
986	Surgeon At Witteringham	/66	Harlequin
1050	Nurse Adele	/66	Harlequin
1210	A Friend Of The Family	/68	Harlequin
1279	Gather Then The Rose	/69	Harlequin
1323	Moonlight On The Water	/69	Harlequin
1360	This Desirable Residence	/69	Harlequin
1437	To My Dear Niece	/70	Harlequin
1484	On A May Morning	/71	Harlequin
1556	No Enemy	/72	Harlequin
1647	The Sweet Spring	/72	Harlequin
1718	Lord Of The Forest	/73	Harlequin
2859	Voyage Of Discovery		Harlequin Romance

Nickson, Jeanne

	Tears Of The Moon	09/92	Leisure Historical
	Shadow Of The Condor	09/94	Love Spell Historical

Nicole, Marie

21	Thick As Thieves	07/85	Harlequin Intrigue
30	Code Name: Love		Harlequin Intrigue
112	Tried And True	01/84	Silhouette Desire
142	Buyer Beware	06/84	Silhouette Desire
161	Through Laughter And Tears	09/84	Silhouette Desire
182	Grand Theft: Heart	01/85	Silhouette Desire
197	A Woman Of Integrity	03/85	Silhouette Desire
224	Country Blue	08/85	Silhouette Desire
274	Last Year's Hunk	04/86	Silhouette Desire
315	Foxy Lady	11/86	Silhouette Desire
346	Chocolate Dreams	04/87	Silhouette Desire
382	No Laughing Matter	10/87	Silhouette Desire
373	Man Undercover	07/85	Silhouette Romance
394	Please Stand By	11/85	Silhouette Romance
411	Mine By Write	01/86	Silhouette Romance
440	Getting Physical	06/86	Silhouette Romance

Nielsen, Virginia

110	Trusting		Harlequin Superromance
159	Moonlight On Snow		Harlequin Superromance
226	Crimson Rivers		Harlequin Superromance
279	Room For One More		Harlequin Superromance
397	Jessica's Song		Harlequin Superromance
506	Of Dolls And Angels	07/92	Harlequin Superromance

Nielson, Virginia

	The Secrets Of Bellefleur	03/95	Ballantine Historical

Nolan, Frederick

AUTHOR/TITLE INDEX

Nolan, Frederick
  White Nights, Red Dawn   Zebra
Nolan, Jenny
  31   Summer Lace   /82   Berkley Second Chance At Love
Norman, Colleen
  894   A Family To Cherish   06/94   Silhouette Special Edition
Norman, Dee
  417   White Nights   11/87   Silhouette Special Edition
Norman, Hilary
  Laura   10/94   Dutton
  Fascination   04/93   Onyx
Norman, Nicole
  Heather Song   Richard Gallen
Norrell, Marjorie
  665   A Problem For Doctor Brett   /62   Harlequin
  759   No Regrets (Young Doctor Ashley)   /63   Harlequin
  819   Nurse Saxon's Patient   /64   Harlequin
  883   Nurse Trudie Is Engaged   /65   Harlequin
  906   Nurse Molly   /65   Harlequin
  930   There's Always Someone (Staff Nurse Sally)   /65   Harlequin
  946   Phantom Rival (Nurse Judith's Engagement)   /65   Harlequin
  962   Nurse Madeline Of Eden Grove   /65   Harlequin
  993   Send For Nurse Alison   /66   Harlequin
  1009   Nurse At Fairchilds   /66   Harlequin
  1042   Promise The Doctor   /66   Harlequin
  1057   Lesley Bowen, M.D.   /66   Harlequin
  1073   The Torpington Annexe   /67   Harlequin
  1097   Thank You, Nurse Conway   /67   Harlequin
  1129   My Friend, Doctor John   /67   Harlequin
  1177   The Marriage Of Doctor Royle   /68   Harlequin
  1241   Nurse Barlow's Jinx   /68   Harlequin
  1273   If They Could Only Forget   /69   Harlequin
  1305   The Project And The Lady   /69   Harlequin
  1329   The Unexpected Millstone   /69   Harlequin
  1353   Nurse Lavinia's Mistake   /69   Harlequin
  1377   Sister Darling   /70   Harlequin
  1410   More Than Kind (Nurse Deborah)   /70   Harlequin
  1433   The Pursuit Of Doctor Lloyd   /70   Harlequin
  1457   Nurse Kelsey Abroad   /71   Harlequin
  1513   Change Of Duty   /71   Harlequin
  1545   Pride's Banner   /71   Harlequin
  1577   Dr. Maitland's Secretary   /72   Harlequin
Norris, Carol
  A Feast On Passions   Richard Gallen
Norris, Maureen
  165   Starry Eyed   /84   Berkley Second Chance At Love

AUTHOR/TITLE INDEX

Norris, Maureen
   205   Seaswept   /84   Berkley Second Chance At Love

North, Miranda
       Sweet Lies   Zebra
       Desert Slave   Zebra Heartfire
       Forever Paradise   Zebra Heartfire
       Desert Slave   05/89 Zebra Heartfire

North, Rebecca
       A June Betrothal   04/93 Zebra Anthology
       Chloe's Elopement 06/93 Zebra Regency Anthology

Northan, Irene
   42   The Marriage Brokers 01/91 Harlequin Regency
   55   Love's Parole   08/91 Harlequin Regency

Norton, Andre
       Opal-Eyed Fan   Gothic

Norton, Bess
  514   The Quiet One (Twin Nurse) /60 Harlequin
  653   The Waiting Room /62 Harlequin
  710   A Nurse Is Born /63 Harlequin

Norway, Kate
  427   Nurse Brookes /58 Harlequin
  463   The Morning Star (Nurse Brodie) /59 Harlequin
  499   Junior Pro /59 Harlequin
  525   Nurse Elliot's Diary /60 Harlequin
  642   The White Jacket /62 Harlequin
 1449   Dedication Jones /70 Harlequin
 1505   Paper Halo /71 Harlequin

Nowasky, Jan
       Tender Embrace   04/94 Berkley Homespun

Nuelle, Helen
  540   The Long Enchantment Dell Candlelight
  605   The Danger In Loving Dell Candlelight Regency

Nuelle, Helen S.
  194   Shadows Of Amanda Dell Candlelight

Nusser, Lynda
       Naked Came The Ladies 02/94 Starlog Moonlight Anthology

Nuys, Joan Van
       Forever Beloved   05/96 Avon

Nye, Nelson C.
   29   Gunfighter Breed   /50 Harlequin

Nye, Valerie
   23   Crystal Fire   /81 Berkley Second Chance At Love

O' Banyon, Constance
       Forever My Love   05/92 Harper
       Song Of The Nightingale 08/92 Harper

AUTHOR/TITLE INDEX

O' Banyon, Constance

La Flamme	08/95	Harper
Desert Song	06/94	Harper Monogram
The Flamme		Jove
Timeswept Brides	07/96	Jove Anthology
Cheyenne Sunrise		Zebra
Dakota Dreams		Zebra
Ecstasy's Promise		Zebra
Golden Paradise		Zebra
Lavender Lies		Zebra
Moontide Embrace		Zebra
Pirate's Princess		Zebra
Rebel Temptress		Zebra
September Moon		Zebra
Velvet Chains		Zebra
Enchanted Ecstasy		Zebra
Savage Desire		Zebra
Savage Splendor		Zebra
Enchantress		Zebra Historical
Love's Stolen Promises		Zebra Historical
Savage Autumn		Zebra Savage Seasons
Savage Spring		Zebra Savage Seasons
Savage Summer		Zebra Savage Seasons
Savage Winter		Zebra Savage Seasons

O' Brian, Soliee

So Wild The Dream	Bantam
Farewell, The Stranger	Bantam
Bayou	Bantam
Too Swift The Tide	Bantam
Heiress To Evil	Bantam

O' Brien, Judith

Rhapsody In Time	06/94	Pocket
Ashton's Bride	04/95	Pocket
Long Time Coming	11/95	Pocket
A Gift Of Love	11/95	Pocket Anthology
Once Upon A Rose	05/96	Pocket Time-Travel

O' Brien, Kathleen

1011	Sunswept Summer		Harlequin Presents
1189	White Midnight		Harlequin Presents
1267	Dreams On Fire		Harlequin Presents
1355	Bargain With The Winner	/92	Harlequin Presents
1515	Between Mist And Midnight	02/93	Harlequin Presents
1642	A Forgotten Magic	04/94	Harlequin Presents
1698	Michael's Silence	11/94	Harlequin Presents
1600	When Dragons Dream	11/93	Harlequin Presents Plus
526	Memory Lapse (Secret Fantasies)	02/95	Harlequin Temptation

O' Brien, Maryann
  Night Train   11/94   Diamond Wildflower
  Gambler's Desire   07/95   Jove Wildflower
O' Brien, Me
  I'll Love You Til I Die   07/95   St. Martin's
O' Bryan, Sofi
  180   The Secret Of The Priory   Dell Candlelight
O' Caragh, Mary
  445   Mirage   07/86   Silhouette Romance
O' Connell, June
  His And Hers   04/93   Bantam
  Love On The Upbeat   07/92   Bantam Sweet Dreams
O' Connell, Shannon
  859   That Darn Cat!   04/92   Silhouette Romance
O' Connor, Megan
  563   Pippa   Dell Candlelight Regency
O' Day-Flannery, Constance
  Secret Loves   03/94   Berkley Contemporary
  Once In A Lifetime   11/91   Zebra
  This Time, Forever   /91   Zebra
  A Time For Love   03/90   Zebra
  Time-Kept Promises   Zebra
  Time-Kissed Destiny   Zebra
  Timeless Passion   Zebra
  Timeswept Lovers   Zebra
O' Dell, Amanda
  Kentucky Fire   Zebra Heartfire
O' Donnell, Bernard
  327   The World's Worst Women   /55   Harlequin
O' Donnell, Jodi
  Last Chance City Limits   /96
  969   Still Sweet On Him (Premiere)   10/93   Silhouette Romance
  992   The Farmer Takes A Wife   02/94   Silhouette Romance
  1021 A Man To Remember (Celebration 1000!)   07/94   Silhouette Romance
  1080 Daddy Was A Cowboy (Stetsons & Lace)   05/95   Silhouette Romance
  1045 Of Texas Ladies, Cowboys And Babies   08/96   Silhouette Special Edition
O' Donnell, Kate
  Defy The Wind   Avon
  Frontier Enchantress   Zebra Heartfire
O' Donnell, Laurel
  The Angel And The Prince   03/96   Zebra Historical
O' Grady, Leslie
  So Wild A Dream   Nal Penguin
  Passion's Fortune   Nal Penguin
  Seek The Wild Shore   Nal Penguin

AUTHOR/TITLE INDEX

O' Grady, Leslie

    Lord Raven's Widow · · · · · · · · · · · St. Martin's

    The Artist's Daughter · · · · · · · · · St. Martin's

    Lady Jade · · · · · · · · · · · · · · · · St. Martin's

    The Second Sister · · · · · · · · · · · St. Martin's

    Sapphire And Silk · · · · · · · · · · · St. Martin's

    Wildwinds · · · · · · · · · · · · · · · · St. Martin's

O' Greene, Jennifer

    Royal Capture · · · · · · · · · · · · · · Bantam

O' Hallion, Sheila

    Masquerade Of Hearts

    Kathleen

    The Captured Heart · · · · · · · · · · Harper Collins

    The Ravished Bride · · · · · 09/92 · Pocket

    Fire And Innocence · · · · · · · · · · Pocket

    American Princess · · · · · · · · · · Pocket

    The Captured Heart · · · · · · · · · · Pocket

O' Hara, Gerri

    Race Against Love · · · · · · 08/92 · Avalon

O' Hara, Kate

 2560 · Summerhaze · · · · · · · · · · Harlequin Romance

O' Meill, Suzannah

    Return To Innismere · · · · · 11/91 · Harper

O' More, Peggy

    Pixie · · · · · · · · · · · · · · /60 · Valentine Books

O' Neal, Katherine

    Master Of Paradise · · · · · · 12/95 · Bantam

    The Last Highwayman · · · · 02/93 · Bantam Fanfare

O' Neil, Olivia

    Imperial Nights · · · · · · · · · · · · Berkley

    Indigo Nights · · · · · · · · · · · · · Berkley

    Dragon Star · · · · · · · · · · · · · · Berkley

O' Neill, Dorothy P.

    Change Of Heart · · · · · · · 03/93 · Avalon

O' Neill, Jude

  464 · Just One Look · · · · · 10/86 · Silhouette Romance

  387 · The Midnight Hour · · 06/87 · Silhouette Special Edition

  408 · A Family Of Two · · · 09/87 · Silhouette Special Edition

  477 · Summer Light · · · · · 09/88 · Silhouette Special Edition

O' Neill, Suzannah

    A Victorian Romance · · · · · 01/93 · Harper

    Innismere · · · · · · · · · · · 07/91 · Harper

    Return To Innismere · · · · · 11/91 · Harper

O' Rourke, Frank

  402 · The Football Gravy Train · · · /57 · Harlequin

  424 · Flashing Spikes · · · · · · · · /58 · Harlequin

AUTHOR/TITLE INDEX

Oaks, Marian
To Love Again   02/92   Zebra
My Kind Of Love   10/94   Zebra   To Love Again
Offord, Lenore Glen
159   The Smiling Tiger   /52   Harlequin
Ogan, Margaret Nettles
560   Ruthana   Dell   Candlelight
Ogilvie, Charlot
Love Song On A Chinese Flute   Zebra   Historical & Family Sagas
Oldfield, Elizabeth
604   Dream Hero   Harlequin   Presents
608   Second Time Around   Harlequin   Presents
637   Florida Fever   Harlequin   Presents
652   Beloved Stranger   Harlequin   Presents
676   Take It Or Leave It   Harlequin   Presents
685   Fighting Lady   Harlequin   Presents
691   Submission   Harlequin   Presents
742   Rough And Ready   Harlequin   Presents
758   Too Far, Too Fast   Harlequin   Presents
765   The Ego Trap   Harlequin   Presents
805   Dragon Man   Harlequin   Presents
901   Sunstroke   Harlequin   Presents
948   Bodycheck   Harlequin   Presents
964   Bachelor In Paradise   Harlequin   Presents
1012   Beware Of Married Men   Harlequin   Presents
1030   Touch And Go   Harlequin   Presents
1077   Quicksands   Harlequin   Presents
1101   Living Dangerously   Harlequin   Presents
1132   Close Proximity   Harlequin   Presents
1212   Sparring Partners   Harlequin   Presents
1300   Rendezvous In Rio   Harlequin   Presents
1328   In Spite Of Themselves   Harlequin   Presents
1333   The Price Of Passion   Harlequin   Presents
1365   Love Gamble   Harlequin   Presents
1395   Flawed Hero   09/91   Harlequin   Presents
1429   An Accidental Affair   01/92   Harlequin   Presents
1484   Stay Until Dawn   08/92   Harlequin   Presents
1636   Designed To Annoy   03/94   Harlequin   Presents
1676   Sudden Fire (Postcards From Europe)   08/94   Harlequin   Presents
1747   Final Surrender (Too Hot To Handle)   06/95   Harlequin   Presents
1800   Dark Victory   03/96   Harlequin   Presents
1831   Fast And Loose   08/96   Harlequin   Presents
1773   Love's Prisoner   01/96   Harlequin   Presents Plus
Oliver, Patricia
Lord Gresham's Lady   11/94   Nal Regency
Blossoms: "Hyacinths For Victoria"   04/95   Signet Anthology

Oliver, Patricia

	Lord Harry's Angel	04/93	Signet Regency
	Miss Drayton's Downfall	03/94	Signet Regency
	The Runaway Duchess	09/93	Signet Regency
	Roses For Harriet	04/95	Signet Regency
	An Immodest Proposal	09/95	Signet Regency
	The Colonel's Lady	05/96	Signet Regency

Oliver, Tess

14	Red, Red Rose	06/80	Silhouette Romance
78	Double Or Nothing	05/81	Silhouette Romance

Olney, Patricia

789	Still Mr. & Mrs.	05/96	Bantam Loveswept

Olshaker, Thelma

	Intimate Strangers

Oppenheim, E. Phillips

221	The Great Impersonation	/53	Harlequin

Oppenheimer, Joan

	Trouble At The Gaboury's	/88	Walker

Ormsby, Patricia

19	Joanna	Mills & Boon
28	Set To Partners	Mills & Boon
36	Heir Presumptive	Mills & Boon

Orr, Alice Harron

56	Sabotage		Harlequin Intrigue
169	Past Sins	09/91	Harlequin Intrigue
216	Cold Summer	02/93	Harlequin Intrigue
266	Camp Fear	03/94	Harlequin Intrigue
324	Key West Heat	03/95	Harlequin Intrigue
369	Manhattan Heat	05/96	Harlequin Intrigue

Orr, Zelma

7	Miracles Take Longer	Harlequin American
18	In The Eyes Of Love	Harlequin American
55	Love Is A Fairy Tale	Harlequin American
82	Measure Of Love	Harlequin American
94	Someone Else's Heart	Harlequin American
111	From This Day	Harlequin American
124	Where Fires Once Burned	Harlequin American
12	Night Shadows	Harlequin Intrigue

Orvis, Kenneth

367	Hickory House	/56	Harlequin

Orwig, Sara

	Sweet Desire		
	Memphis	07/94	
1	New Orleans		Southern Trilogy
2	Memphis		Southern Trilogy
3	Atlanta	03/95	Southern Trilogy

AUTHOR/TITLE INDEX

AUTHOR/TITLE INDEX

Osborn, Elane
	Desire's Moon	11/91	Diamond
	Skylark		Diamond
642	Shelter In His Arms	05/95	Silhouette Intimate Moments
	Silken Roses		St. Martin's

Osborne, Betsy
268	The Steele Trap	/85	Berkley Second Chance At Love
288	The Phoenix Heart	/85	Berkley Second Chance At Love

Osborne, Liz
	Promises To Keep	04/95	Harper

Osborne, Maggie
66	Flight Of Fancy		Nal Rapture Romance
	Rage To Love		Nal Penguin
	Lady Reluctant		St. Martin's
	Emerald Rain	06/91	St. Martin's
	The Wives Of Bowie Stone	12/94	Warner
	The Seduction Of Samantha Kincade	08/95	Warner
	The Wives Of Bowie Stone	12/94	Warner

Osler, E.B.
261	Light In The Wilderness	/53	Harlequin

Overfield, Joan
	Belle Of The Ball	04/93	Avon Regency
	The Dutiful Duke	02/94	Avon Regency
	The Viscount's Vixen	11/92	Avon Regency Romance
	A Proper Taming	08/94	Avon Regency Romance
	Her Ladyships Man		Ballantine Regency
	The Prodigal Spinster	/88	Ballantine Regency
	Bride's Leap	07/91	Fawcett Crest Regency Romance
	Charleston Tangle		Warner
	The Cabinetmaker's Daughter		Warner Regency
	A Heart's Disguise		Zebra Regency
	A Spirited Bluestocking		Zebra Regency
	A Christmas Affair		Zebra Regency
	The Traitor's Daughter	07/94	Zebra Regency

Owen, Ann
41	The Sands Of Time	11/80	Silhouette Romance

Owen, Ruth
558	Meltdown	08/92	Bantam Loveswept
632	Smooth Operator	08/93	Bantam Loveswept
676	The Last American Hero	03/94	Bantam Loveswept
705	Taming The Pirate	08/94	Bantam Loveswept
714	Sorcerer	11/94	Bantam Loveswept
763	Body Heat	09/95	Bantam Loveswept
786	And Babies Make Four	05/96	Bantam Loveswept

Owen, Wanda
	Rapture's Bounty		

Owen, Wanda

	Deceptive Desires		Zebra
	Kiss Of Fire		Zebra
	Savage Fury		Zebra
	Tempting Texas Treasure		Zebra
	Wild Magnolia		Zebra
	Golden Ecstasy		Zebra
	Summer Splendor		Zebra
	Moonlight Splendor		Zebra
	Texas Captive		Zebra
	The Captain's Vixen		Zebra
	Ecstasy's Fancy		Zebra
	Golden Gypsy		Zebra
	Texas Wildfire		Zebra
	Louisiana Lovesong	09/93	Zebra
	Texas Magic	09/92	Zebra Lovegram Romance

Owens, Marissa

95	Dangerous Charade	05/85	Silhouette Intimate Moments

Pace, A.

	Sweet Deception		Avalon
	That Touch Of Magic		Avalon Career Romance
	A Time To Dance		Avalon Career Romance

Pace, De Wanna

Surrender, Sweet Stranger

Pace, Laurel

192	On Wings Of Love	03/87	Harlequin American
172	Destiny's Promise	06/93	Harlequin Historical
242	Winds Of Destiny	10/94	Harlequin Historical
112	Deception By Design		Harlequin Intrigue
174	Ghostwalk	11/91	Harlequin Intrigue
191	Broken Lullaby	08/92	Harlequin Intrigue
247	Blood Ties	01/94	Harlequin Intrigue

Pace, Miriam

	That Winning Touch	/92	Avalon
	Warm Creature Comforts		Avalon Career Romance
	New Orleans		Zebra

Pacheco, Christine

960	The Rogue And The Rich Girl	10/95	Silhouette Desire

Pacotti, Pamela

Legacy Of Secrets
Winds Of Desire

Pacter, Trudi

	Kiss And Tell		Harper Collins
	Screen Kisses		Harper Collins
	The Sleeping Partner	07/92	Harper Collins

Pade, Victoria

Pade, Victoria

Page, Betsy

Page, Laurel

Paige, Laurie

Paige, Laurie

727	A Season For Homecoming	06/90	Silhouette Romance
733	Home Fires Burning Bright	07/90	Silhouette Romance
772	Man From The North Country	02/91	Silhouette Romance
917	Cara's Beloved	02/93	Silhouette Romance
923	Sally's Beau	03/93	Silhouette Romance
933	Victoria's Conquest	04/93	Silhouette Romance
994	Caleb's Son (Fabulous Fathers)	03/94	Silhouette Romance
1013	A Rogue's Heart	06/94	Silhouette Romance
1151	An Unexpected Delivery	05/96	Silhouette Romance
	A Place For Eagles	/94	Silhouette Special Edition
	Rogue's Domain	/94	Silhouette Special Edition
	The Way Of A Man	/94	Silhouette Special Edition
170	Lover's Choice	06/84	Silhouette Special Edition
755	Man Without A Past	07/92	Silhouette Special Edition
828	Home For A Wild Heart	07/93	Silhouette Special Edition
839	A Place For Eagles (A Wild River Trilogy)	09/93	Silhouette Special Edition
849	The Way Of A Man (Wild River Trilogy)	11/93	Silhouette Special Edition
887	Wild Is The Wind (Wild River)	05/94	Silhouette Special Edition
910	A River To Cross (Wild River)	09/94	Silhouette Special Edition
1021	Molly Darling	04/96	Silhouette Special Edition
9	Christmas Kisses For A Dollar	12/95	Silhouette Yours Truly

Paige, Natalie

840	A Love Like Romeo And Juliet	09/93	Silhouette Special Edition

Paisley, Rebecca

	Midnight And Magnolias	12/92	Avon
	Under The Mistletoe	10/93	Avon Christmas Anthology
	Diamonds And Dreams	10/91	Avon Romance
	Moonlight And Magic	11/90	Avon Romance
	The Barefoot Bride		Avon Romance
	Rainbows And Rapture	06/92	Avon Romantic Treasures
	Heartstrings	08/94	Dell
	A Basket Of Wishes	07/95	Dell
	Love Potion	02/95	Jove Anthology
	Harvest Hearts	11/93	Jove Historical Anthology

Palmer, Catherine

	The Burning Plains		
	Secret Loves	03/94	Berkley Contemporary
	Falcon Moon	10/94	Diamond Historical
	Outlaw Heart	07/92	Diamond Wildflower
	Gunman's Lady	05/93	Diamond Wildflower
	Renegade Flame	10/93	Diamond Wildflower
	Sometimes Forever	08/96	Jove Historical
367	Land Of Enchantment	01/91	Silhouette Intimate Moments
403	Forbidden	10/91	Silhouette Intimate Moments
426	Weeping Grass	04/92	Silhouette Intimate Moments
461	Red Hot	11/92	Silhouette Intimate Moments

AUTHOR/TITLE INDEX

Palmer, Catherine

551	For The Love Of A Child	02/94	Silhouette Intimate Moments
627	His Best Friend's Wife	03/95	Silhouette Intimate Moments

Palmer, Diana

	The Wild Winds		Doubleday
	Lacy	12/91	Fawcett Ivy Books
	Amelia	08/93	Fawcett Ivy Books
	Trilby	01/93	Fawcett Ivy Books
	Nora	08/94	Fawcett Ivy Books
	Noelle	09/95	Fawcett Ivy Books
	Heart Of Ice	03/96	Harlequin
	Soldier Of Fortune	01/94	Harlequin
	Christmas Memories	12/94	Harlequin Anthology
	Lover, Come Back	02/94	Harlequin Anthology
	"Paper Husband"	10/96	Harlequin Duet
12	September Morning	04/96	Harlequin Here Come The Grooms
13	Love By Proxy	04/94	Harlequin Men Made In America
1	Rogue Stallion	08/94	Harlequin Montana Mavericks
	Betrayed By Love	06/95	Harlequin Western Lovers
	Nora	08/94	Ivy
	Noelle	08/95	Ivy
	Love's Legacy: "Annabelle's Legacy"	01/96	Leisure
127	Now And Forever	03/79	Macfadden
139	Storm Over The Lake	04/79	Macfadden
150	To Have And To Hold	05/79	Macfadden
179	Sweet Enemy	08/79	Macfadden
218	Love On Trial	10/80	Macfadden
223	Dream's End	12/80	Macfadden
250	Bound By A Promise	09/80	Macfadden
256	To Love And Cherish	11/80	Macfadden
268	If Winter Comes	01/81	Macfadden
278	At Winter's End	02/81	Macfadden
	Christmas Stories: "The Humbug Man"	11/87	Silhouette Anthology
	Summer Sizzlers: "Miss Greenhorn"	06/90	Silhouette Anthology
	To Mother With Love	06/93	Silhouette Anthology
	Abduction And Seduction: "Redbird"	03/95	Silhouette Anthology
	Long, Tall Texans	07/94	Silhouette Collection
12	The Cowboy And The Lady	08/82	Silhouette Desire
26	September Morning	11/82	Silhouette Desire
50	Friends And Lovers	03/83	Silhouette Desire
80	Fire And Ice	08/83	Silhouette Desire
102	Snow Kisses	11/83	Silhouette Desire
110	Diamond Girl	01/84	Silhouette Desire
157	The Rawhide Man	09/84	Silhouette Desire
175	Lady Love	12/84	Silhouette Desire
193	Cattleman's Choice	03/85	Silhouette Desire
230	The Tender Stranger	09/85	Silhouette Desire

AUTHOR/TITLE INDEX

Palmer, Diana

AUTHOR/TITLE INDEX

Palmer, Diana

991   Maggie's Dad   11/95   Silhouette Special Edition

Palmer, Rachel

4   Love Beyond Desire   Harlequin Superromance

58   No Sweeter Song   Harlequin Superromance

Palmieri, Marilyn

Campaign Promises   Meteor

Palmieri, Marina

54   Daydreams   08/91   Meteor

Pape, Sharon

33   The Portal   06/94   Harlequin Shadows

Pappano, Marilyn

	Christmas Memories	12/94	Harlequin	Anthology
31	Within Reach	01/95	Harlequin	Men Made In America
	Cody Daniels Returns	08/95	Harlequin	Western Lovers
	The Greatest Gift	11/89	Silhouette	Christmas Stories
483	Room At The Inn	03/89	Silhouette	Desire
	Daddy: Discovered	11/96	Silhouette	Intimate Moments
182	Within Reach	03/87	Silhouette	Intimate Moments
214	The Lights Of Home	11/87	Silhouette	Intimate Moments
233	Guilt By Association	04/88	Silhouette	Intimate Moments
258	Cody Daniel's Return	10/88	Silhouette	Intimate Moments
268	Room At The Inn	12/88	Silhouette	Intimate Moments
294	Something Of Heaven	07/89	Silhouette	Intimate Moments
310	Somebody's Baby	11/89	Silhouette	Intimate Moments
338	Not Without Honor	06/90	Silhouette	Intimate Moments
363	Safe Haven	12/90	Silhouette	Intimate Moments
381	A Dangerous Man	05/91	Silhouette	Intimate Moments
405	Probable Cause	11/91	Silhouette	Intimate Moments
424	Operation Homefront	03/92	Silhouette	Intimate Moments
437	Somebody's Lady	07/92	Silhouette	Intimate Moments
469	No Retreat	01/93	Silhouette	Intimate Moments
486	Memories Of Laura	03/93	Silhouette	Intimate Moments
512	Sweet Annie's Pass	08/93	Silhouette	Intimate Moments
542	Finally A Father (Romantic Traditions)	01/94	Silhouette	Intimate Moments
583	Michael's Gift	08/94	Silhouette	Intimate Moments
609	Regarding Remy (Southern Knights)	12/94	Silhouette	Intimate Moments
626	A Man Like Smith (Southern Knights)	03/95	Silhouette	Intimate Moments
703	Survive The Night	04/96	Silhouette	Intimate Moments
	Jamey	/97	Silhouette	Serenity Street Knights
	Reid	/97	Silhouette	Serenity Street Knights
	Nicholas	/97	Silhouette	Serenity Street Knights
	Loving Abby	06/91	Silhouette	Summer Sizzlers
	In Sinful Harmony	06/95	Warner	
	Passion	04/96	Warner	
	Suspicion	02/97	Warner	

AUTHOR/TITLE INDEX

Paquin, Ethel
44   Summer Wine   01/85   Harlequin   Temptation

Paradise, Mary
     Marriage Chest   Historical

Parenteau, Shirley
34   Hemlock Feathers   Harlequin   Historical
88   Golden Prospect   08/91   Harlequin   Historical
137   The Naked Huntress   08/92   Harlequin   Historical

Pargeter, Margaret
1899   Winds From The Sea   /75   Harlequin
1951   Ride A Black Horse   /76   Harlequin
1973   The Kilted Stranger   /76   Harlequin
2022   Hold Me Captive   /76   Harlequin
2058   Blue Skies, Dark Waters   /77   Harlequin
2112   Never Go Back   /77   Harlequin
2140   Flamingo Moon   /78   Harlequin
2168   Wild Inheritance   /78   Harlequin
2183   Better To Forget   /78   Harlequin
2193   Midnight Magic   /78   Harlequin
2211   The Jewelled Caftan   /78   Harlequin
145   Stormy Rapture   /76   Harlequin   Presents
366   Savage Possession   Harlequin   Presents
431   The Dark Oasis   Harlequin   Presents
453   Boomerang Bride   Harlequin   Presents
503   Collision   Harlequin   Presents
523   The Loving Slave   Harlequin   Presents
540   Not Far Enough   Harlequin   Presents
548   Storm Cycle   Harlequin   Presents
572   Prelude To A Song   Harlequin   Presents
580   Substitute Bride   Harlequin   Presents
588   Clouded Rapture   Harlequin   Presents
595   Man From Kimberley's   Harlequin   Presents
620   The Demetrious Line   Harlequin   Presents
638   Caribbean Gold   Harlequin   Presents
653   Chains Of Regret   Harlequin   Presents
660   Storm In The Night   Harlequin   Presents
788   Total Surrender   Harlequin   Presents
813   Captive Of Fate   Harlequin   Presents
821   Born Of The Wind   Harlequin   Presents
845   Impasse   Harlequin   Presents
861   Model Of Deception   Harlequin   Presents
2227   The Wild Rowan   Harlequin   Romance
2241   A Man Called Cameron   Harlequin   Romance
2284   Only You   Harlequin   Romance
2296   The Devil's Bride   Harlequin   Romance
2350   Autumn Song   Harlequin   Romance
2375   Kiss Of A Tyrant   Harlequin   Romance

AUTHOR/TITLE INDEX

Pargeter, Margaret

Parker, Laura

	Rebellious Angels		Warner
	A Wilder Love		Warner
1	Rose Of The Mists		Warner
2	A Rose In Splendor		Warner
3	The Secret Rose		Warner
	Risque	02/96	Zebra

Parker, Norah

	Gypsy Lover		Zebra Heartfire

Parker, Una-Mary

	Veil Of Secrets	04/91	Signet

Parmett, Doris

234	Stiff Competition	02/88	Bantam Loveswept
267	Made For Each Other	07/88	Bantam Loveswept
316	Diamond In The Rough	03/89	Bantam Loveswept
349	Sassy	09/89	Bantam Loveswept
388	Heartthrob	03/90	Bantam Loveswept
412	Off Limits	07/90	Bantam Loveswept
446	Sweet Mischief	01/91	Bantam Loveswept
530	Mr. Perfect	03/92	Bantam Loveswept
540	Unfinished Business	05/92	Bantam Loveswept
563	Fiery Angel	08/92	Bantam Loveswept
649	Bad Attitude	11/93	Bantam Loveswept
	Lies	02/93	Berkley Jove
	Risk	03/94	Jove

Parnell, Andrea

	Lovespell		
	Whispers At Midnight		
186	Aurelia	08/93	Harlequin Historical
	Delilah's Flame		Nal Penguin
	Dark Splendor		Nal Penguin Regency
251	The Silver Swan	08/88	Silhouette Intimate Moments
	Wild Glory		Warner
	My Only Desire	11/93	Zebra Heartfire
	Devil Moon	11/94	Zebra Lovegram

Parr, Delia

	Evergreen	02/95	St. Martin's
	The Fire In Autumn	01/96	St. Martin's
	The Fire In Winter	11/95	St. Martin's

Parris, Laura

60	High Valley Of The S		Harlequin American

Parrish, Mardi

	A Find For All Time	09/95	Avalon

Parrish, Mary

	Love's Gentle Season		
	Love's Quiet Corner		

AUTHOR/TITLE INDEX

Parrish, Patt

85	Lifetime Affair	12/85	Harlequin Temptation

Parther, Marilyn

	A Certain Enchantment	/96	Avalon

Parv, Valerie

272	Outback Temptation	03/96	Harlequin
290	Island Of Dreams	07/96	Harlequin
107	A Fair Exchange	04/92	Harlequin Direct
1229	Man Without A Past		Harlequin Presents
1260	Tasmanian Devil		Harlequin Presents
1510	That Midas Man	11/92	Harlequin Presents
2589	Tall Dark Stranger		Harlequin Romance
2628	Remember Me, My Love		Harlequin Romance
2644	The Dreaming Dunes		Harlequin Romance
2693	Man And Wife		Harlequin Romance
2765	Ask Me No Questions	05/86	Harlequin Romance
2778	Reutrn To Faraway		Harlequin Romance
2788	Heartbreak Plains		Harlequin Romance
2797	Boss Of Yarrakina		Harlequin Romance
2860	The Love Artist		Harlequin Romance
2896	Man Shy		Harlequin Romance
2909	Sapphire Nights		Harlequin Romance
2934	Snowy River Man		Harlequin Romance
2969	Centrefold		Harlequin Romance
3005	Crocodile Creek		Harlequin Romance
3125	Lightning's Lady		Harlequin Romance
3209	Far From Over	07/92	Harlequin Romance
3366	P.S. I Love You (Sealed With A Kiss)	06/95	Harlequin Romance
507	The Leopard Tree	05/87	Silhouette Romance

Pascoe, Irene M.

	Dark Tides	10/92	Diamond Gothic
	The Curse Of Belle Haven	09/91	Diamond Gothic

Patrick, Ann

17	Opening Act	11/90	Meteor
38	Hearts Collide	04/91	Meteor
62	For Services Rendered	10/91	Meteor
190	Comfort And Joy	12/93	Meteor
	Home For Christmas	12/93	Meteor Kismet
166	Betting On Love	08/93	Meteor Kismet
	Say You Love Me	03/94	Silhouette Special Edition

Patrick, De Ann

	Kindred Spirits		Pocket
	Montana Bride		Tapestry

Patrick, Lynn

87	Double Or Nothing	/86	Dell Candlelight Ecstasy
25	The Marriage Project	07/96	Harlequin Here Come The Grooms

734

AUTHOR/TITLE INDEX

Patrick, Lynn

343	Good Vibrations		Harlequin Superromance
421	The Marriage Project		Harlequin Superromance
461	Cheek To Cheek	07/91	Harlequin Superromance
396	Wild Thing	05/92	Harlequin Temptation

Patrick, Natalie

1095	Wedding Bells And Diaper Pins	07/95	Silhouette Romance
1130	The Marriage Chase	01/96	Silhouette Romance

Patrick, Roslynn

	Princess Royale	Harper

Patten, Darlene

570	A Half-Dozen Reasons	04/88	Silhouette Romance
800	A Place Called Home	06/91	Silhouette Romance

Patterson, Morgan

1366	Wild Flowers Wind	Harlequin Presents
2667	Darker Fire	Harlequin Romance

Paul, Danielle

13	Chameleon	06/84	Harlequin Temptation

Paul, Paula

	Lady Of The Shadows	07/92	Berkley Gothic
	The Mistress At Blackwater	08/93	Berkley Gothic
47	Silent Partner		Harlequin Intrigue
67	Night Of The Jaguar		Harlequin Intrigue
	Sweet Ivy's Gold	01/93	Harper

Paul, Sandra

883	Last Chance For Marriage	08/92	Silhouette Romance
1016	The Reluctant Hero	06/94	Silhouette Romance
1087	His Accidental Angel (Spellbound)	06/95	Silhouette Romance

Paul, Susan

266	The Bride's Portion	04/95	Harlequin Historical
301	The Heiress Bride	01/96	Harlequin Historical

Paxton, Diane

The White Raven	Avon

Paxton, Jean

Divided Loyalty	Warner

Payes, Rachel

O Charitable Death	Historical

Payes, Rachel Cosgrove

Devil's Court	
Forbidden Island	
Emeralds And Jade	
Love's Charade	Playboy Press
Love's Promenade	Playboy Press
Love's Renegade	Playboy Press
Love's Escapade	Playboy Press
Love's Serenade	Playboy Press

AUTHOR/TITLE INDEX

Payes, Rachel Cosgrove
    The Dark Tower Of Trelochen   Zebra

Payne, Tiffany
  283 Stirrings Of The Heart   03/84 Silhouette Romance

Peacock, Max
  286 Colonel Blood   /54 Harlequin

Peak, Caroline
  960 A Perfect Surprise   05/95 Silhouette Special Edition

Peake, Kay
  1779 The Man At Kambala   /74 Harlequin

Peake, Lillian

1572	This Moment In Time	/72	Harlequin	
1594	Mist Across The Moors	/72	Harlequin	
1628	The Library Tree	/72	Harlequin	
1650	The Real Thing	/73	Harlequin	
1674	Man Out Of Reach	/73	Harlequin	
1700	Gone Before Morning	/73	Harlequin	
1726	Man In Charge	/73	Harlequin	
1778	A Sense Of Belonging	/74	Harlequin	
1831	Master Of The House	/74	Harlequin	
1855	The Impossible Marriage	/75	Harlequin	
1868	The Dream On The Hill	/75	Harlequin	
1900	Moonrise Over The Mountains	/75	Harlequin	
1944	Heart In The Sunlight	/76	Harlequin	
2220	Rebel In Love	/78	Harlequin	
113	Man Of Granite	/75	Harlequin	Presents
120	Till The End Of Time	/75	Harlequin	Presents
136	The Sun Of Summer	/76	Harlequin	Presents
150	The Tender Night	/76	Harlequin	Presents
157	The Distant Dream	/76	Harlequin	Presents
166	Familiar Stranger	/76	Harlequin	Presents
186	A Bitter Loving	/77	Harlequin	Presents
190	This Man Her Enemy	/77	Harlequin	Presents
198	No Friend Of Mine	/77	Harlequin	Presents
206	The Little Imposter	/77	Harlequin	Presents
213	Somewhere To Lay My Head	/77	Harlequin	Presents
225	A Girl Alone	/78	Harlequin	Presents
229	Passionate Involvement	/78	Harlequin	Presents
316	No Second Parting		Harlequin	Presents
330	Enemy From The Past		Harlequin	Presents
341	Run For Your Love		Harlequin	Presents
353	Dangerous Deception		Harlequin	Presents
384	A Ring For A Fortune		Harlequin	Presents
407	A Secret Affair		Harlequin	Presents
424	Barratt's Woman		Harlequin	Presents
454	Strangers Into Lovers		Harlequin	Presents

Peake, Lillian

474	Across A Crowded Room		Harlequin Presents
496	Day Of Possession		Harlequin Presents
524	Bitter Revenge		Harlequin Presents
612	Passionate Intruder		Harlequin Presents
886	Ice Into Fire		Harlequin Presents
949	Elusive Paradise		Harlequin Presents
966	Love In The Moonlight		Harlequin Presents
1124	Take This Woman		Harlequin Presents
1157	The Bitter Taste Of Love		Harlequin Presents
1268	Dance To My Tune		Harlequin Presents
1316	Climb Every Mountain		Harlequin Presents
1485	Irresistible Enemy	08/92	Harlequin Presents
1532	Undercover Affair	02/93	Harlequin Presents
1580	Gold Ring Of Revenge	08/93	Harlequin Presents
1629	Stranger Passing By	02/94	Harlequin Presents
1700	No Promise Of Love	11/94	Harlequin Presents
2279	Stranger On The Beach		Harlequin Romance
2404	Promise At Midnight		Harlequin Romance
2603	Night Of Possession		Harlequin Romance
2614	Come Love Me		Harlequin Romance
2651	A Woman In Love		Harlequin Romance

Peale, Constance F.

19	Give Us Forever		Harlequin Superromance

Peart, Jane

568	Spanish Masquerade		Dell Candlelight
	The House Of Haunted Dreams	02/92	Diamond Gothic
	The Secret At Octagon House		Diamond Gothic

Pedersen, Gloria

	Nighthawk's Embrace

Pega, Bonnie

557	Only You	07/92	Bantam Loveswept
627	Then Comes Marriage	07/93	Bantam Loveswept
647	Wild Thing	10/93	Bantam Loveswept
665	Animal Magnetism	01/94	Bantam Loveswept
773	The Rebel And His Bride	01/96	Bantam Loveswept
	Emerald Enchantment	02/95	St. Martin's Anthology

Peil, Stobie

Rebel Wind	02/95	Pinnacle Denise Little Presents

Pelham, Howard

The Law Of San Luis Wash	/91	Avalon

Pellicane, Patricia

Desire's Rebel	
Ecstasy's Treasure	
Sweet Seduction	
Embers Of Desire	Leisure

Pellicane, Patricia

	Charity's Pride		Pocket	
	Whispers In The Wind		Pocket	
	Creole Captive		Zebra	
	Desperado Passion		Zebra	
	This Wild Heart		Zebra	
	Deceptions Of The Heart		Zebra	
	Fire's Tender Kiss		Zebra	
	Frontier Temptress		Zebra	
	Nights Of Passion	04/94	Zebra	
5	Summer Heat	10/92	Zebra	Lucky In Love

Pelton, Sonya T.

	Awake Savage Heart		Zebra	
	Captive Dove		Zebra	
	Ecstasy's Magic		Zebra	
	Forbidden Dawn		Zebra	
	Love, Hear My Heart		Zebra	
	Texas Tigress		Zebra	
	Tiger Rose		Zebra	
	Wild Island Sands		Zebra	
	Phantom Love		Zebra	
	Captive Caress		Zebra	
	Passion's Paradise		Zebra	
	Captive Chains		Zebra	
	Twilight Temptress		Zebra	
	Windswept Passion		Zebra	
	Bittersweet Bondage		Zebra	
	Awake Savage Heart		Zebra	
	Love Hear My Heart		Zebra	
	Dakota Flame	06/89	Zebra	
	Secret Jewel	04/94	Zebra	
	Heavensent	10/95	Zebra	Historical

Pemberton, Margaret

	Some Distant Shore		Richard Gallen	

Pemberton, Nan

	Love's Illusion		Pocket	Cotillion Regency

Pence, Joanne

	Too Many Cooks	09/94	Harper	Suspense
	Something's Cooking	04/93	Harper	Suspense
	Cooking Up Trouble	05/95	Harper	Suspense
	Cooking Most Deadly	09/96	Harper	Suspense
219	Armed And Dangerous	12/87	Silhouette	Intimate Moments

Pender, Laura

	Intrigue 10th Anniversary	09/94	Harlequin	Intrigue
62	Taste Of Treason		Harlequin	Intrigue
70	Hit And Run		Harlequin	Intrigue

AUTHOR/TITLE INDEX

AUTHOR/TITLE INDEX

Pershing, Diane

	Up Close And Personal	08/95	Bantam Loveswept
525	Sultry Whispers	02/92	Bantam Loveswept
551	Intimate View	06/92	Bantam Loveswept
608	Breathless	04/93	Bantam Loveswept
615	Satisfaction	05/93	Bantam Loveswept
659	Heartquake	12/93	Bantam Loveswept

Pershing, Karen

168	Opposites Attract		Harlequin American

Pershing, Marie

531	First A Dream		Dell Candlelight
553	Maybe Tomorrow		Dell Candlelight

Peters, Anne

497	Like Wildfire	05/89	Silhouette Desire
739	Through Thick And Thin	08/90	Silhouette Romance
803	Next Stop: Marriage	07/91	Silhouette Romance
821	And Daddy Makes Three	10/91	Silhouette Romance
850	Storky Jones Is Back In Town	03/92	Silhouette Romance
875	Nobody's Perfect	07/92	Silhouette Romance
899	The Real Malloy	11/92	Silhouette Romance
927	The Pursuit Of Happiness	03/93	Silhouette Romance
946	Accidental Dad	07/93	Silhouette Romance
995	His Only Deception	03/94	Silhouette Romance
1031	Mc Cullough's Bride (Hasty Weddings)	09/94	Silhouette Romance
1104	Green Card Wife	09/95	Silhouette Romance
1110	Stand-In Husband	10/95	Silhouette Romance
1116	Along Comes Baby	11/95	Silhouette Romance

Peters, Clarice

	Roxanne		Ballantine Regency
	The False Betrothal		Ballantine Regency
	Rosalind		Ballantine Regency
	Samantha		Ballantine Regency
	Thea		Ballantine Regency
	The London Tangle	04/95	Ballantine Regency
2	The Marquis And The Miss	05/89	Harlequin Regency
11	Vanessa	10/89	Harlequin Regency
23	Prescott's Lady	04/90	Harlequin Regency
53	Heart's Wager	07/91	Harlequin Regency
65	Belle Of Portman Square	01/92	Harlequin Regency
82	The Absentee Earl	09/92	Harlequin Regency

Peters, Elizabeth

	Street Of The Five Moons		Suspense
	Die For Love	/84	Tor Suspense
	Night Train To Memphis	10/94	Warner

Peters, Natasha

	Savage Surrender		Berkley

AUTHOR/TITLE INDEX

Peters, Sue

1850	The Storm Within	/75	Harlequin
1874	Design For Destiny	/75	Harlequin
1916	Wheels Of Conflict	/75	Harlequin
1959	Deep Furrows	/76	Harlequin
1975	Clouded Waters	/76	Harlequin
2030	One Special Rose	/76	Harlequin
2104	Portrait Of Paradise	/77	Harlequin
2156	Lure Of The Falcon	/78	Harlequin
2204	Entrance To The Harbour	/78	Harlequin
159	Maid For Marriage	11/93	Harlequin Direct
181	Tomorrow's Man	04/94	Harlequin Direct
2351	Shadow Of An Eagle		Harlequin Romance
2368	Claws Of A Wildcat		Harlequin Romance
2410	Marriage In Haste		Harlequin Romance
2423	Tug Of War		Harlequin Romance
2471	Dangerous Rapture		Harlequin Romance
2501	Man Of Teak		Harlequin Romance
2583	Lightning Strikes Twice		Harlequin Romance
2812	Never Touch A Tiger		Harlequin Romance
2892	Entrance To Eden	02/88	Harlequin Romance
2915	Capture A Nightingale		Harlequin Romance
2938	One Woman Man		Harlequin Romance
3018	Unwilling Woman		Harlequin Romance
3226	Weekend Wife	10/92	Harlequin Romance

Petersen, Herman

17	The D.A.'s Daughter	/49	Harlequin

Peterson, Carrie

22	The Secrets Of Sebastian Beaumont	12/93	Harlequin Shadows

Peterson, Tracie

A Kingdom Divided	02/95	Barbour & Co.
The Heart's Calling	03/95	Barbour & Co.
Alas My Love	03/96	Barbour & Co. Sequel To A Kingdom Divided

Petit, Diane

Heart Of Gold	06/95	Avalon

Petkus, Peggy Murphy

Millionaire's Hill	Zebra Historical & Family Sagas
Millionaire's Row	Zebra Historical & Family Sagas

Petrie, Glen

Hand Of Glory	St. Martin's
Marianna	St. Martin's
Branch Bearers	St. Martin's

Petty, Mary Eileen

Lady Of The Moors	Diamond Gothic

Phelps, Lauren

The News Is Love	12/92	Bantam Sweet Dreams

AUTHOR/TITLE INDEX

Phelps, Lauren M.

	The Unsettled Heart	/92	Avalon
	Dangerous Reckoning	/91	Avalon
	After Harvest Comes	/91	Avalon
	The Love Gamble	12/92	Avalon

Phillips, Alan

| 522 | The Living Legend | /60 | Harlequin |

Phillips, Dorothy

71	Marriage To A Stranger		Dell Candlelight Ecstasy
411	Sing Together Softly		Dell Candlelight Ecstasy
458	She Wanted Red Velvet		Dell Candlelight Ecstasy

Phillips, Johanna

20	Gentle Torment		Berkley Second Chance At Love
20	Gentle Torment	/81	Berkley Second Chance At Love
30	Amber-Eyed Man		Berkley Second Chance At Love
30	Amber-Eyed Man	/82	Berkley Second Chance At Love
43	Strange Possessions		Berkley Second Chance At Love
43	Strange Possession	/82	Berkley Second Chance At Love
88	Passion's Song		Berkley Second Chance At Love
125	Hidden Dreams		Berkley Second Chance At Love

Phillips, Laura

22	Never Let Go	12/90	Meteor
40	Catch A Rising Star	04/91	Meteor
78	To Love A Cowboy	02/92	Meteor
99	Moon Showers	07/92	Meteor
110	Beginnings	10/92	Meteor

Phillips, Michael

| | The Eleventh Hour | 07/93 | Tyndale House Secret Of The Rose |

Phillips, Paige

| 372 | The Tender Hours | 05/96 | Harlequin Intrigue |

Phillips, Patricia

	Flame Of Love		
	The Rose And The Flame	08/92	Leisure Historical
	Nightingale		Leisure Historical
	The Constant Flame	06/93	Leisure Historical

Phillips, Susan

| 470 | Sheer Honesty | 11/86 | Silhouette Romance |

Phillips, Susan Elizabeth

	Rapture's Legacy		
	It Had To Be You	08/94	Avon
	Glitter Baby	02/86	Avon
	Heaven, Texas	04/95	Avon
	Kiss An Angel	02/96	Avon
	The Copeland Bride	/83	Bantam
	Risen Glory	/84	Bantam
	Fancy Pants	10/89	Pocket

AUTHOR/TITLE INDEX

Phillips, Susan Elizabeth
    Hot Shot   06/91   Pocket
    Honey Moon   06/93   Pocket
Phillips, Tori
  307   Fool's Paradise   03/96   Harlequin Historical
Pianka, Phyllis
    The Thackery Jewels   12/94   Harlequin Regency
Pianka, Phyllis Taylor
  543   The Sleeping Heiress   Dell
  627   The Paisley Butterfly   Dell Candlelight Regency
   16   Midsummer Madness   Harlequin Intrigue
    3   The Tart Shoppe   06/89   Harlequin Regency
   34   The Calico Countess   09/90   Harlequin Regency
   48   The Lark's Nest   04/91   Harlequin Regency
   80   A Coventry Courtship   08/92   Harlequin Regency
Pickart, Joan Elliott
    To First Be Friends
    Irresistible   01/92   Bantam Loveswept
    Night Magic   04/92   Bantam Loveswept
    Preston Harper, M.D.   08/90   Bantam Loveswept
    Storming The Castle   10/90   Bantam Loveswept
    To Love And To Cherish 11/90   Bantam Loveswept
   61   Breaking All The Rules   09/84   Bantam Loveswept
   74   Charade   12/84   Bantam Loveswept
   80   The Finishing Touch   02/85   Bantam Loveswept
   85   All The Tomorrows   03/85   Bantam Loveswept
   90   Look For The Sea Gulls 04/85   Bantam Loveswept
   94   Waiting For Prince Charming 05/85   Bantam Loveswept
   99   Fascination   07/85   Bantam Loveswept
  105   The Shadowless Day   08/85   Bantam Loveswept
  110   Sunlight's Promise   09/85   Bantam Loveswept
  114   Rainbow's Angel   10/85   Bantam Loveswept
  116   Midnight Ryder   11/85   Bantam Loveswept
  138   The Eagle Catcher   04/86   Bantam Loveswept
  146   Journey's End   06/86   Bantam Loveswept
  153   Mister Lonelyhearts   08/86   Bantam Loveswept
  162   Secrets Of Autumn   10/86   Bantam Loveswept
  166   Listen For The Drummer 11/86   Bantam Loveswept
  179   Kaleidoscope   02/87   Bantam Loveswept
  190   Wild Poppies   05/87   Bantam Loveswept
  204   Reforming Freddy   08/87   Bantam Loveswept
  213   Leprechaun   10/87   Bantam Loveswept
  218   Lucky Penny   11/87   Bantam Loveswept
  230   Illusions   01/88   Bantam Loveswept
  238   Midsummer Sorcery   02/88   Bantam Loveswept
  243   Kiss Me Again, Sam   03/88   Bantam Loveswept

AUTHOR/TITLE INDEX

Pickart, Joan Elliott

249	January In July	04/88	Bantam Loveswept
259	Warm Fuzzies	06/88	Bantam Loveswept
265	The Enchanting Miss Annabella	07/88	Bantam Loveswept
271	Tattered Wings	08/88	Bantam Loveswept
285	Tucker Boone	10/88	Bantam Loveswept
291	Man Of The Night	11/88	Bantam Loveswept
305	Serenity Cove	01/89	Bantam Loveswept
317	Riddles And Rhymes	03/89	Bantam Loveswept
324	To First Be Friends	05/89	Bantam Loveswept
332	Holly's Hope	06/89	Bantam Loveswept
346	Sweet Bliss	08/89	Bantam Loveswept
369	The Magic Of The Moon	12/89	Bantam Loveswept
386	Mixed Signals	03/90	Bantam Loveswept
398	Whispered Wishes	05/90	Bantam Loveswept
418	Preston Harper, M. D.	08/90	Bantam Loveswept
429	Storming The Castle	10/90	Bantam Loveswept
435	To Love And To Cherish	11/90	Bantam Loveswept
453	From This Day Forward	02/91	Bantam Loveswept
470	Memories	05/91	Bantam Loveswept
492	The Devil In Stone	09/91	Bantam Loveswept
521	Irresistible	01/92	Bantam Loveswept
534	Night Magic	04/92	Bantam Loveswept
594	Angels Singing	02/93	Bantam Loveswept
	The Bonnie Blue	08/90	Doubleday
	Amber, Sing Softly	08/94	Pinnacle Denise Little Presents
961	Angels And Elves	11/95	Silhouette Desire
999	Apache Dream Bride	05/96	Silhouette Desire
1011	Friends, Lovers ... And Babies!	02/96	Silhouette Special Edition
1025	The Father Of Her Child	04/96	Silhouette Special Edition
	Family Secrets	02/89	Warner

Piel, Stobie

	Rebel Wind	03/95	Kensington Denise Little Presents
	Flights Of Angels	12/96	Kensington Denise Little Presents

Pinnell, Bill

	Terror On The Border	/91	Avalon

Pizzey, Erin

	First Lady	12/91	Harper
	Snow Leopard Of Shanghai		Harper
	Consul General's Daughter		Harper
	The Watershed	05/92	Harper
	In The Shadow Of The Castle	12/92	Harper

Plaidy, Jean

	Lilith
	Murder Most Royal
	The Wandering Prince

Plaidy, Jean

The Three Crowns			
The Vow On The Heron			
The Queen Of Lord M			
The Captive Of Kensington Palace			
The Goldsmith's Wife			
Caroline, The Queen		Ballantine	
The Courts Of Love		Ballantine	
The Prince And The Quakeress		Ballantine	
The Regent's Daughter		Ballantine	
The Third George		Ballantine	
The Prince And The Quakeress		Ballantine	
The Reluctant Queen		Ballantine	
The Rose Without A Thorn	09/95	Ballantine	Historical
The Plantagenet Prelude		Ballantine	Plantagenet Saga
Prince Of Darkness		Ballantine	Plantagenet Saga
The Lady In The Tower		Ballantine	Queens Of England
The Princess Of Celle		Ballantine	Queens Of England
Queen In Waiting		Ballantine	Queens Of England
Victoria Victorious		Ballantine	Queens Of England
The Queen's Secret		Ballantine	Queens Of England
Indiscretions Of The Queen		Ballantine	The Georgian Saga
Queen Of This Realm		Ballantine	The Georgian Saga
Melisande	10/93	Fawcett Crest	
Goddess Of The Green Room	02/92	Fawcett Crest	Historical
Victoria In The Wings	10/92	Fawcett Crest	Historical

113	Beyond The Blue Mountains	/51	Harlequin
178	The Goldsmith's Wife	/52	Harlequin
179	Madame Serpent	/52	Harlequin
203	Daughter Of Satan	/52	Harlequin
268	The Unholy Woman	/54	Harlequin
269	Queen Jezebel	/54	Harlequin

Plain, Belva

Evergreem		
Whispers	05/93	Delacorte
Treasures	03/93	Dell

Plante, Edmund

Garden Of Evil	07/91	Leisure

Playfair, Helen

Flying High	05/94	Zebra
Merry Christmas My Love	11/93	Zebra Anthology

Plowman, Mary Sharon

This Time	04/94	Goodfellow

Poenbeck, Pat

Golden Temptress		Leisure

Pollock, Rosemary

AUTHOR/TITLE INDEX

Potter, Patricia

	Rainbow	08/91	Bantam	Fanfare
	Lawless	02/92	Bantam	Fanfare
	Lightning	08/92	Bantam	Fanfare
	Relentless	05/94	Bantam	Fanfare
	Notorious	11/93	Bantam	Fanfare
	Renegade	05/93	Bantam	Fanfare
	Southern Nights	07/92	Bantam	Fanfare
	Defiant	08/95	Bantam	Fanfare
518	The Greatest Gift	01/92	Bantam	Loveswept
602	Troubadour	03/93	Bantam	Loveswept
746	Impetuous	05/95	Bantam	Loveswept
	"Against The Wind"	07/93	Harlequin	Anthology
	Christmas Rogues - "The Homecoming"	11/95	Harlequin	Anthology
6	Swampfire		Harlequin	Historical
15	Between The Thunder		Harlequin	Historical
20	Samara		Harlequin	Historical
26	Seize The Fire		Harlequin	Historical
35	Chase The Thunder		Harlequin	Historical
48	Dragonfire		Harlequin	Historical
63	The Silver Link	02/91	Harlequin	Historical
78	The Abduction	05/91	Harlequin	Historical
	Island Of Dreams	11/93	Harper	
	Miracle Of The Heart	/90	Sil. Hist. Christmas Stories	

Powell, Cynthia

| 785 | Untamed | 04/96 | Bantam | Loveswept |

Power, Elizabeth

164	Host Of Riches	12/93	Harlequin	Direct
191	Close Captivity	07/94	Harlequin	Direct
1078	Shadow In The Sun		Harlequin	Presents
1341	The Devil's Eden		Harlequin	Presents
1768	Straw On The Wind	10/95	Harlequin	Presents Plus
2825	Rude Awakening		Harlequin	Romance

Power, Jo Ann

	You And No Other	12/94	Pocket	
	Treasures	04/96	Pocket	
	Gifts	09/96	Pocket	
	Angel Of Midnight	09/95	Pocket	
	From This Day Forward	01/95	Zebra	
	Remembrance	02/95	Zebra	
	The Mark Of The Chadwicks	02/93	Zebra	Gothic
	The Last Duchess Of Wolffs Lair	07/93	Zebra	Gothic

Powers, Martha Jean

	Proxy Bride		Ballantine	Regency
	Gazebo Rendezvous		Ballantine	Regency
	The Gray Fox Wagers		Ballantine	Regency

AUTHOR/TITLE INDEX

Powers, Martha Jean

	Double Masquerade	Berkley Regency
	The Runaway Heart	Berkley Regency
	False Pretenses	Jove Regency
	A Regency Holiday	Jove Regency

Powers, Nora

48	Of The West	02/83	Silhouette Desire
59	Time Stands Still	04/83	Silhouette Desire
84	In A Moment's Time	08/83	Silhouette Desire
117	The Brief Interlude	02/84	Silhouette Desire
148	In A Stranger's Arms	07/84	Silhouette Desire
196	A Different Reality	03/85	Silhouette Desire
256	No Man's Kisses	01/86	Silhouette Desire
3	Affairs Of The Heart	05/80	Silhouette Romance
42	Design For Love	11/80	Silhouette Romance
391	A Woman's Wiles	10/85	Silhouette Romance
637	Woman Of The West	03/89	Silhouette Romance

Powers, Tom

15	Virgin With Butterflies	/49	Harlequin

Pozzessere, Heather Graham

1	The Last Cavalier	03/93	Harlequin
	"Lonesome Rider"	07/93	Harlequin Anthology
	Renegades (Promotion)	08/95	Harlequin Anthology
9	Dark Stranger		Harlequin Historical
19	Rides A Hero		Harlequin Historical
33	Apache Summer		Harlequin Historical
66	Forbidden Fire	02/91	Harlequin Historical
	An Angel's Touch	10/95	Kensington
	Slow Burn	10/94	Mira
	Eyes Of Fire	10/95	Mira
	Bride Of The Tiger	04/96	Mira
	Home For Christmas	/89	Sil. Hist. Christmas Stories
	Intimate Moments 10th Anniversary	05/93	Silhouette Anthology
	The Christmas Bride	/91	Silhouette Christmas Stories
118	Night Moves	11/85	Silhouette Intimate Moments
132	The Di Medici Bride	02/86	Silhouette Intimate Moments
145	Double Entendre	06/86	Silhouette Intimate Moments
165	The Games Of Love	11/86	Silhouette Intimate Moments
174	A Matter Of Circumstances	01/87	Silhouette Intimate Moments
192	Bride Of The Tiger	05/87	Silhouette Intimate Moments
205	All In The Family	09/87	Silhouette Intimate Moments
220	King Of The Castle	12/87	Silhouette Intimate Moments
225	Strangers In Paradise	02/88	Silhouette Intimate Moments
248	Angel Of Mercy	07/88	Silhouette Intimate Moments
260	This Rough Magic	10/88	Silhouette Intimate Moments
265	Lucia In Love	12/88	Silhouette Intimate Moments
293	Borrowed Angel	07/89	Silhouette Intimate Moments

AUTHOR/TITLE INDEX

Pozzessere, Heather Graham

328	A Perilous Eden	03/90	Silhouette Intimate Moments
340	Forever My Love	06/90	Silhouette Intimate Moments
352	Wedding Bell Blues	09/90	Silhouette Intimate Moments
386	Snowfire	06/91	Silhouette Intimate Moments
416	Hatfield And Mc Coy	01/92	Silhouette Intimate Moments
450	Mistress Of Magic	09/92	Silhouette Intimate Moments
499	Between Roc And A Hard Place	06/93	Silhouette Intimate Moments
525	The Trouble With Andrew	10/93	Silhouette Intimate Moments
1	The Last Cavalier	03/93	Silhouette Shadows
	For All Of Her Life	04/95	Zebra
	Down In New Orleans	05/96	Zebrza Romantic Suspense

Prather, Marilyn

	A Light In The Darkness	02/95	Avalon
	A Deadly Reunion	07/95	Avalon
	A Certain Enchantment		Avalon

Pratt, Rosina

	An Unquestionable Lady		Zebra Regency

Prentice, Wendy

1342	Conditional Surrender		Harlequin Presents

Presley, Victoria

	Traded Secrets	05/96	Leisure Time-Travel

Pressley, Hilda

529	Theatre Nurse	/60	Harlequin
570	Night Nurse	/61	Harlequin
619	Staff Nurse On Gynae	/61	Harlequin
666	Love, The Surgeon	/62	Harlequin
696	Staff Nurses In Love	/62	Harlequin
751	Night Superintendent	/63	Harlequin
788	The Gentle Surgeon	/64	Harlequin
900	There Came A Surgeon	/65	Harlequin
932	Nurse's Dilemma	/65	Harlequin
987	Senior Staff Nurse	/66	Harlequin
1233	A Love Of Her Own	/68	Harlequin
1295	Suddenly, It Was Spring	/69	Harlequin
1327	More Than Gold	/69	Harlequin
1389	Man Of The Forest	/70	Harlequin
1429	The Man In Possession	/70	Harlequin
1469	To The Highest Bidder	/71	Harlequin
1509	A Summer To Remember	/71	Harlequin
1565	Harbinger Of Spring	/72	Harlequin
1601	The Newcomer	/72	Harlequin
1821	When Winter Has Gone	/74	Harlequin

Preston, Fayrene

	Silken Thunder		Bantam
	Sydney, The Temptress	/84	Bantam Delaneys Of Killaroo

Price, Ashland
    Captive Conquest
    Autumn Angel   Zebra Heartfire
    Cajun Caress   Zebra Heartfire
    Wild Irish Heather   Zebra Heartfire
    Viking Tempest   10/94   Zebra Lovegram
Price, Dianne
    Proud Captive   Zebra
    The Savage Spirits Of Seahedger Manor   Zebra
Price, Eugenia
    The Beloved Invader
    New Moon Rising
    Maria
    Lighthouse
    Margaret's Story
    Bright Captivity
    Stranger In Savannah   Jove
    Before The Darkness Falls   Jove
    Don Juan Mc Queen   Jove
    Savannah   01/93   Jove
    To See Your Face Again   Jove
Price, Laurel
   370   May Wine, September   Harlequin American
Price, Marjorie
    Renegade Heart   Zebra
    Desire's Dawning   Zebra Heartfire
    Emerald Embrace   Zebra Heartfire
Price, Melinda
    A Rose For Lady Edwina   Zebra Pinnacle/Regency Romance
Prine, Linda
    Naked Came The Ladies   02/94   Starlog Moonlight Anthology
Pritchard, Pat
   187   The Candy Dad   12/93   Meteor
   154   Rough Edges   06/93   Meteor Kismet
Procter, Kate
   1253   Wild Enchantment   Harlequin Presents
   1292   Reckless Heart   Harlequin Presents
Proctor, Carol
    The Drawing Master's Dilemma   Nal
    An Unlikely Guardian   Nal
    A Dashing Widow   09/91   Nal Regency
    Theodora's Dreadful Mistake   10/92   Nal Regency
    A Regency Valentine 2   01/92   Nal Super Regency
    The Dangerous Dandy   03/93   Penguin Regency
    Tokens Of Love: Five Regency Love Stories   01/93   Penguin Super Regency
Proctor, Kate

AUTHOR/TITLE INDEX

Proctor, Kate
38	No Mistress But Love	08/96	Harlequin Presents
1195	Sweet Captivity		Harlequin Presents
1389	Lawfully Wedded Stranger	08/91	Harlequin Presents
1526	The Price Of Desire	01/93	Harlequin Presents
1661	Contract To Love	06/94	Harlequin Presents
1710	Bittersweet Yesterdays	12/94	Harlequin Presents
1767	Prince Of Darkness	10/95	Harlequin Presents Plus

Prole, Lozania
138	Emma Hart	/51	Harlequin
272	The Fabulous Nell Gwynne	/54	Harlequin
373	Tonight, Josephine!	/56	Harlequin

Provost, Gary
| | Mermaids And Magic Words | | Avalon Career Romance |

Pryce, Melinda
	Tides Of Love	07/92	Berkley
	Thief Of Hearts		Diamond Regency
	Suddenly A Lady	07/92	Diamond Regency
	The Last Lord	01/93	Diamond Regency
	A Love To Treasure	03/92	Diamond Regency
	Loving Spirits	10/94	Jove Regency
	Summertime Splendor	07/92	Jove Regency Collection
	A Rose For Lady Edwina	06/90	Pinnacle Press

Pryor, Pauline
| 667 | The Faint-Hearted Felon | | Dell Candlelight Regency |

Pryor, Vanessa
| | A Taste Of Wine | | Richard Gallen |

Purcell, Dierdre
| | Roses After Rain | 05/96 | Signet |

Putnam, Alice
| | Murder In The Morning | /91 | Avalon |
| | Love's Sweet Refuge | /91 | Avalon |

Putnam, Eileen
| | Noble Deception | 03/92 | Berkley Regency |
| | So Reckless A Love | 03/95 | Diamond Historical |

Putney, Mary Jo
	Promised Brides:"Wedding Of The Century"	04/96	Harlequin Anthology
	Sunshine For Christmas	11/90	Nal A Regency Christmas 2
	The Christmas Cuckoo	11/91	Nal A Regency Christmas 3
	The Christmas Tart	11/92	Nal A Regency Christmas 4
	The Black Beast Of Belleterre	11/92	Nal A Victorian Christmas
	A Victorian Christmas	11/92	Nal Onyx
	Uncommon Vows	04/91	Nal Onyx
	Dearly Beloved	03/90	Nal Onyx
	The Would-Be Widow	07/88	Nal Signet Regency
	The Controversial Countess	01/89	Nal Signet Regency

AUTHOR/TITLE INDEX

Putney, Mary Jo

The Rogue And The Runaway	07/90	Nal	Signet Regency
Carousel Of Hearts	11/89	Nal	Signet Regency
Lady Of Fortune	09/88	Nal	Signet Regency
The Diabolical Baron	11/87	Nal	Signet Regency
The Rake And The Reformer	09/89	Nal	Signet Super Regency
Silk And Shadows	12/91	Nal	Onyx Silk Trilogy
Silk And Secrets	07/92	Nal	Onyx Silk Trilogy
Veils Of Silk	12/92	Nal	Onyx Silk Trilogy
A Regency Christmas 3	11/91	Nal	Signet Anthology
A Regency Christmas 4	11/92	Nal	Signet Anthology
Rakes And Rogues	06/93	Nal	Signet Anthology
A Regency Christmas 2:"Sunshine For Chris	11/90	Nal	Signet Anthology
River Of Fire	11/96	Signet	
Dashing & Dangerous	05/95	Signet	Anthology
Thunder And Roses	05/93	Topaz	Fallen Angels
Petals In The Storm	12/93	Topaz	Fallen Angels
Dancing On The Wind	09/95	Topaz	Fallen Angels
Shattered Vows	02/96	Topaz	Fallen Angels
Angel Rogue	04/95	Topaz	Fallen Angels

Pyatt, Rosina

Unquestionable Lady		Zebra

Pykare, Nina

501	The Scandalous Season	Dell	Candlelight Regency
548	Love In Disguise	Dell	Candlelight Regency
554	A Man Of Her Choosing	Dell	Candlelight Regency
581	The Dazzled Heart	Dell	Candlelight Regency
594	Lady Incognita	Dell	Candlelight Regency
610	Love's Folly	Dell	Candlelight Regency
645	The Innocent Heart	Dell	Candlelight Regency
675	Love Plays A Part	Dell	Candlelight Regency

Pykare, Nina Coombs

Montana Sunrise		
The Perfect Match		
A Touch Of Heaven	/91	Avalon
No Time For Kisses	12/92	Avalon
The Haunting Of Grey Cliffs	12/92	Diamond Gothic
The Lost Duchess Of Greyden Castle		Zebra Gothic

Quentin, Dorothy

1596	The Inn By The Lake	/72	Harlequin
1724	Wedding At Blue River	/73	Harlequin

Quick, Amanda

Dangerous		Bantam
Desire	01/94	Bantam
Deception	06/93	Bantam
Mistress	07/94	Bantam

Quick, Amanda

Mystique	09/95	Bantam
Scandal	03/91	Bantam Fanfare
Rendezvous	11/91	Bantam Fanfare
Ravished	07/92	Bantam Fanfare
Reckless	12/92	Bantam Fanfare
Seduction	/90	Bantam Fanfare
Surrender	/90	Bantam Fanfare

Quin-Harkin, Janet

Fool's Gold	06/91	Harper

Quinn, Colleen

Defiant Rose	03/92	Diamond
Wild Is The Night	06/91	Diamond
Loving Hearts	02/92	Diamond
Married For Love	05/93	Diamond
Sweet Hearts	02/93	Diamond Anthology
Unveiled	05/93	Diamond Historical
Golden Splendor		Zebra
Daring Desire		Zebra
Colorado Flame		Zebra Heartfire
Outlaw's Angel		Zebra Heartfire
Twilight Ecstasy		Zebra Heartfire

Quinn, Julia

	Splendid	04/95	Avon
	Dancing At Midnight	12/95	Avon
460	Wade Conner's Revenge	11/92	Silhouette Initmate Moments
540	Birthright	12/93	Silhouette Intimate Moments

Quinn, Samantha

551	A Promise Made	09/89	Silhouette Special Edition

Quinn, Tara Taylor

	Lost And Found (Tentative)	/95	Harlequin Superromance
	Jacob's Girls	/95	Harlequin Superromance
567	Yesterday's Secrets	10/93	Harlequin Superromance
584	Mcgillus V. Wright	02/94	Harlequin Superromance
600	Dare To Love	06/94	Harlequin Superromance
624	No Cure For Love	12/94	Harlequin Superromance
661	Jacob's Girls	09/95	Harlequin Superromance
696	The Birth Mother	06/96	Harlequin Superromance

Rabe, Sheila

A Christmas Treasure	11/92	Berkley Regency
The Lost Heir	08/92	Diamond Regency
Faint Heart		Diamond Regency
The Improper Miss Prym		Diamond Regency
Lady Luck	12/92	Diamond Regency
Beauty And The Beastly Duke (Tent. Title)	05/93	Diamond Regency
The Wedding Deception	05/93	Diamond Regency

AUTHOR/TITLE INDEX

Rabe, Sheila
    Miss Plympton's Peril   09/94   Jove Regency
    The Accidental Bride   06/94   Zebra
    A Mother's Delight   03/95   Zebra Anthology
    The Ghostly Charade   Zebra Regency
    Bringing Out Betsy   12/94   Zebra Regency
    An Innocent Imposter   04/95   Zebra Regency

Rabl, S.S.
   34   Mobtown Clipper   /50   Harlequin

Radcliffe, Janette
    American Baroness   Bantam
    Stormy Surrender   Bantam
    Hidden Fires   Bantam
    Lovers And Liars   Bantam
   174   The Moonlight Gondola   Dell Candlelight
   185   The Gentleman Pirate   Dell Candlelight
   190   White Jasmine   Dell Candlelight
   198   Lord Stephen's Lady   Dell Candlelight
   204   The Azure Castle   Dell Candlelight
   206   The Topaz Charm   Dell Candlelight
   216   A Gift Of Violets   Dell Candlelight Regency

Raddall, Thomas H.
   141   Roger Sudden   /51   Harlequin
   189   The Nymph And The Lamp   /52   Harlequin
   196   His Majesty's Yankees   /52   Harlequin
   298   Pride's Fancy   /54   Harlequin

Raddon's, Charlene
    Taming Jenna   06/94   Zebra Heartfire
    Brianna   12/94   Zebra Heartfire
    Passious Honor   06/95   Zebra Heartfire

Radke, Nancy
    Turn Again Love   Lion Hearted Contemporary

Radko, Karren
   155   Dreams And Wishes   06/93   Meteor Kismet

Rae, Patricia
    Ways Of The Wind
    Storm Tide   Zebra

Raeschild, Sheila
    Earth Songs   Nal Penguin

Raffel, Elizabeth
   180   Lost Without Love   /83   Dell Candlelight Ecstasy

Rafferty, Carin
   320   Full Circle   Harlequin American
   359   A Change Of Seasons   Harlequin American
   281   I Do, Again   01/90   Harlequin Temptation
   319   My Fair Baby   10/90   Harlequin Temptation

AUTHOR/TITLE INDEX

Rafferty, Carin

363	Sherlock And Watson	09/91	Harlequin	Temptation
373	Christmas Knight	12/91	Harlequin	Temptation
381	The Hood (Rebels & Rogues)	02/92	Harlequin	Temptation
446	Expose	06/93	Harlequin	Temptation
505	Even Cowboys Get The Blues (Lost Loves)	09/94	Harlequin	Temptation
1	Touch Of The Night	02/94	Topaz	Touch Trilogy
2	Touch Of Magic	02/95	Topaz	Touch Trilogy
3	Touch Of Lightning	10/95	Topaz	Touch Trilogy

Raftery, Miriam

	Apollo's Fault	03/96	Leisure Time Travel

Ragosta, Millie Baker

	If Winter Comes		Lion Hearted Paranormal

Ragsdale, Clyde B.

166	The Big Fist	/52	Harlequin

Raines, Jocelyn

	Romance Inc.	02/96	Pocket

Rainville, Rita

8	Mc Cade's Woman	04/96	Harlequin	Here Come The Grooms
	Lights Out	/90	Silhouette	Christmas
495	A Touch Of Class	05/89	Silhouette	Desire
639	Paid In Full	05/91	Silhouette	Desire
792	High Spirits	06/93	Silhouette	Desire
828	Tumbleweed And Gibraltar	12/93	Silhouette	Desire
874	Hot Property (Centerfolds)	08/94	Silhouette	Desire
918	Bedazzled	03/95	Silhouette	Desire
984	Husband Material	02/96	Silhouette	Desire
313	Challenge The Devil	08/84	Silhouette	Romance
346	Mc Cade's Woman	03/85	Silhouette	Romance
370	Lady Moonlight	07/85	Silhouette	Romance
400	Written On The Wind	12/85	Silhouette	Romance
418	The Perfect Touch	03/86	Silhouette	Romance
448	The Glorious Quest	08/86	Silhouette	Romance
478	Family Affair	01/87	Silhouette	Romance
502	It Takes A Thief	05/87	Silhouette	Romance
535	Gentle Persuasion	10/87	Silhouette	Romance
556	Never Love A Cowboy	02/88	Silhouette	Romance
598	Valley Of Rainbows	09/88	Silhouette	Romance
663	No Way To Treat A Lady	07/89	Silhouette	Romance
706	Never On Sundae	03/90	Silhouette	Romance
746	One Moment Of Magic	09/90	Silhouette	Romance
832	Arc Of The Arrow	12/91	Silhouette	Romance
873	Alone At Last	06/92	Silhouette	Romance

Ramey, J.J.R.

	Once Again, My Love	/91	Marron

Ramin, Terese

AUTHOR/TITLE INDEX

Ramin, Terese
  477 Winter Beach   02/93 Silhouette Initmate Moments
  279 Water From The Moon   03/89 Silhouette Intimate Moments
  634 A Certain Slant Of Light   04/95 Silhouette Intimate Moments
  680 Five Kids, One Christmas   12/95 Silhouette Intimate Moments
  656 Accompanying Alice   03/91 Silhouette Special Edition
Ramirez, Jeanette
       Lady Of Lochabar   Harper
       Yankee Duchess   10/93 Harper Historical
Ramsay, Eileen
       The Mysterious Marquis   /86   Walker
Rand, Erika
  259 Lying Eyes   01/94 Harlequin Intrigue
Randal, Jude
  889 Just One Of The Guys   09/92 Silhouette Romance
  914 Northern Manhunt   01/93 Silhouette Romance
  986 A Miracle For Bryan   01/94 Silhouette Romance
Randall, Caitlin
   37 Roses   04/91 Meteor
Randall, Linda
  220 A World Of Their Own   02/85 Silhouette Special Edition
Randall, Lindsay
       Desire's Storm
       Silver Sword
       Two Hearts Too Wild
       Jade Temptation   Zebra Heartfire
       Fortune's Desire   Zebra Heartfire
Randall, Rona
       Dragonmede   Gothic
       Mating Dance   Historical
  219 Girls In White   /53   Harlequin
Randolph, Ellen
       The Rushden Legacy   /86   Walker
Randolph, Melanie
    9 Heart Full Of Rainbows   /84   Berkley To Have And To Hold
Rangel, Doris
  878 Legacy   Harlequin Presents
Ranney, Karen
       Tapestry   04/95 Zebra Lovegram
Ransom, Dana
       Dakota Dawn   11/91 Zebra
       Dakota Desire   Zebra
       Wild Scottish Embrace   Zebra
       Dakota Promises   07/94 Zebra
    1 Midnight Kiss   /94   Zebra

Ransom, Dana

2	Midnight Temptation	11/94	Zebra
3	Midnight Surrender	11/94	Zebra
	A Bride's Passion	05/93	Zebra Anthology
	Alexandra's Ecstasy		Zebra Heartfire
	Liar's Promise		Zebra Heartfire
	Love's Glorious Gamble		Zebra Heartfire
	Wild Savage Love		Zebra Heartfire
	Wild Wyoming Love		Zebra Heartfire
	The Pirate's Captive	/87	Zebra Heartfire
	Rebel Vixen		Zebra Heartfire
	Texas Destiny	08/94	Zebra Historical
3	Love's Own Reward	09/92	Zebra Lucky In Love
18	Totally Yours	01/93	Zebra Lucky In Love
27	Lifetime Investment	03/93	Zebra Lucky In Love
40	From This Day Forward	05/93	Zebra Lucky In Love

Ransom, Katherine

408	Come Fly With Me	09/91	Harlequin American
440	Marriage-Go-Round	05/92	Harlequin American
450	Out Of Her League	08/92	Harlequin American
37	O'Hara's Woman		Nal Rapture Romance
65	Wish On A Star		Nal Rapture Romance

Rasky, Frank

450	Gay Canadian Rogues	/59	Harlequin

Rasley, Alicia

	A Midsummer's Delight	/94	Kinsington
	Bosom-Bows		Lion Hearted Regency
	Poetic Justice	06/94	Zebra
	Knight Errant	10/92	Zebra Regency
	Lessons In Love	08/94	Zebra Regency
	Gwen's Christmas Ghost	11/95	Zebra Regency

Ravenlock, Constance

676	Rendezvous At Gramercy		Dell Candlelight Regency

Rawlings, Ellen

	A Christmas Treasure	11/92	Berkley Regency
	A Perfect Arrangement	09/92	Diamond Regency
	A Larcenous Affair	10/91	Diamond Regency
	A Serious Pursuit		Diamond Regency
	A Convenient Marriage	07/93	Diamond Regency

Rawlings, Louisa

60	Stranger In My Arms	12/90	Harlequin Historical
86	Autumn Rose	07/91	Harlequin Historical
157	Wicked Stranger	01/93	Harlequin Historical
194	Scarlet Woman	10/93	Harlequin Historical
	Dreams So Fleeting	/85	Warner
	Promise Of Summer	/89	Warner Popular

Rawlings, Louisa
    Stolen Spring   /88   Warner Popular
    Forever Wild   /86   Warner Popular

Rawlins, Debbi
  580   Marriage Incorporated (In Name Only)   04/95   Harlequin American
  618   The Cowboy And The Centerfold   02/96   Harlequin American
  622   The Outlaw And The City Slicker   03/96   Harlequin American

Ray, Angie
    Ghostly Enchantment   03/94   Harper Monogram
    Sweet Deceiver   04/95   Harper Monogram
    A Delicate Condition   11/95   Harper Monogram

Ray, Francis
    Fallen Angel   09/92   Odyssey Books
    Forever Yours   07/94   Pinnacle
    Undeniable   03/95   Pinnacle
    The Bargain   11/95   Pinnacle Denise Little Presents
    Spirit Of The Season   12/94   Zebra Anthology

Ray, Jane
  1013   Mary Into Mair   /66   Harlequin

Raye, Kimberly
  60   ' Til We Meet Again   01/96   Silhouette Shadows
  65   Now And Forever   06/96   Silhouette Shadows

Raymer, Kimberly
    Winner Take All   Zebra Pinnacle

Raynes, Jean
    Legacy Of The Wolf   Playboy Press

Raynor, Claire
    So Ho Square   Nal Penguin
    Bedford Row   Nal Penguin
    Gower Street   Nal Penguin
    The Haymarket   Nal Penguin
    Paddington Green   Nal Penguin

Reavis, Cheryl
    Promise Me A Rainbow   /90   Berkley
    Yesterday's Waltz   /90   Berkley
    This Side Of Paradise   /84   Berkley Second Chance At Love
    Such Rough Splendor   /85   Berkley Second Chance At Love
    Dillon's Promise   /86   Berkley Second Chance At Love
    One From The Heart   /87   Berkley Second Chance At Love
    Fire Under Heaven   /88   Berkley Second Chance At Love
  126   The Prisoner   05/92   Harlequin Historical
  319   The Bartered Bride   06/96   Harlequin Historical
    So This Is Love   /91   Silhouette Mother's Day Anth.
    To Mother With Love   /91   Silhouette Mother's Day Anth.
  487   A Crime Of The Heart   11/88   Silhouette Special Edition
  627   Patrick Gallagher's Widow   10/90   Silhouette Special Edition

Reavis, Cheryl
  901 One Of Our Own (That Special Woman!) 08/94 Silhouette Special Edition
 1039 Meggi's Baby 07/96 Silhouette Special Edition
Receveur, Betty Layman
      Molly Gallagher
      Oh, Kentucky! 07/92 Ballantine Historical Fiction
Redd, Joanne
      Border Bride Bantam
      To Love An Eagle Bantam
      Chasing A Dream Bantam
      Everytime I Love You Bantam
      Dance With Fire 04/92 Dell
      Apache Bride Dell
      Chasing A Dream Dell
      Desert Bride 06/89 Dell
      Steal The Flame Dell
      To Love An Eagle Dell
Reddin, Joan
   16 Secret Promise 12/92 Zebra Lucky In Love
Reding, Jaclyn
      Deception's Bride 12/93 Diamond Historical
      Tempting Fate 01/95 Topaz
      Chasing Dreams 09/95 Topaz
Redmond, Shirley-Raye
      Stone Of The Sun Avalon Mystery Romance
Reece, Colleen
      Belated Follower 12/95 Barbour & Co. Biblical Novel
      Flower Of The West 10/95 Barbour & Co. Flowers Chronicles #2
      Flower Of The North 02/96 Barbour & Co. Flowers Chronicles #3
      Captives Of The Canyon 02/95 Barbour & Co. Inspirational Western
      Flickering Flames 04/95 Barbour & Co. Shepherd Of Love Hospital
Reece, Jean
   10 The Devil's Dare 09/89 Harlequin Regency
Reed, Blair
   40 Pass Key To Murder /50 Harlequin
Reed, Leslie
      Letter Of Intent Warner
Reeger, Jacki
  658 The Lady Casts Her Lures 12/93 Bantam Loveswept
Reep, Diana
  601 The Blakemore Touch 09/88 Silhouette Romance
Rees, Eleanor
 1285 The Seal Wife Harlequin Presents
 1452 Pirate's Hostage 04/92 Harlequin Presents
 1645 Hijacked Honeymoon 04/94 Harlequin Presents

AUTHOR/TITLE INDEX

Reeves, Barbara

	The Dangerous Marquis	09/94	Avon Regency
	The Much Maligned Lord	09/93	Avon Regency
	A Scandalous Courtship	03/94	Avon Regency Romance
	Lacy's Dilemma	03/95	Avon Regency Romance
	The Carriage Trade	02/92	Walker Regency
	Georgina's Campaign	/91	Walker Regency

Reeves, Joan

162	Summer's Fortune	07/93	Meteor Kismet

Reid, Henrietta

1094	My Dark Rapparee	/67	Harlequin
1126	Man Of The Islands	/67	Harlequin
1206	Substitute For Love	/68	Harlequin
1247	Laird Of Storr	/68	Harlequin
1292	Falcon's Keep	/69	Harlequin
1317	Beloved Sparrow	/69	Harlequin
1380	Reluctant Masquerade	/70	Harlequin
1430	Hunter's Moon	/70	Harlequin
1460	The Black Delaney	/71	Harlequin
1495	Rival Sisters	/71	Harlequin
1528	The Made Marriage	/71	Harlequin
1575	Sister Of The Bride	/72	Harlequin
1621	Garth Of Tregillis	/72	Harlequin
1720	Intruder At Windgates	/73	Harlequin
1764	Bird Of Prey	/74	Harlequin
1851	Dragon Island	/75	Harlequin
1902	The Man At The Helm	/75	Harlequin
1953	Love's Puppet	/76	Harlequin
2001	Greek Bridal	/76	Harlequin
2049	The Tartan Ribbon	/77	Harlequin
2113	Push The Past Behind	/77	Harlequin
2345	Paradise Plantation		Harlequin Romance
2442	Lord Of The Isles		Harlequin Romance
2524	New Boss At Birchfield		Harlequin Romance

Reid, Michelle

1140	A Question Of Pride		Harlequin Presents
1478	No Way To Begin	07/92	Harlequin Presents
1533	The Dark Side Of Desire	02/93	Harlequin Presents
1597	Coercion To Love	10/93	Harlequin Presents
1665	Lost In Love	07/94	Harlequin Presents
1752	Passion Becomes You	07/95	Harlequin Presents
1776	Slave To Love	01/96	Harlequin Presents
1799	The Ultimate Betrayal	03/96	Harlequin Presents
1615	House Of Glass	01/94	Harlequin Presents Plus
1695	Passionate Scandal	11/94	Harlequin Presents Plus
2994	Eye Of Heaven		Harlequin Romance

AUTHOR/TITLE INDEX

Reid, Sally Helen
    Close Call   07/94 Zebra

Reisser, Anne N.
    28 Love, Catch A Wild Bird   01/84 Bantam Loveswept
    20 The Face Of Love   Dell Candlelight Ecstasy
          The Captive Love/ Face Of Love   Leisure Contemporary Romance
          Deceptive Love/ By Love Betrayed Leisure Contemporary Romance

Rellas, Dorothy
    44 Hidden Motives   Harlequin Intrigue

Renick, Jeane
    Trust Me   09/92 Harper Monogram
    Always   04/93 Harper Monogram
    Loving Mollie   08/95 Harper Monogram

Rennie, George Murdock
    257 One Man Front   /53 Harlequin

Resnick, Laura
    160 Sleight Of Hand   07/93 Meteor Kismet

Rettke, Marian Pope
    Georgiana   Berkley
    Highland Rapture   Berkley

Reynolds, Catherine
    47 A Thoroughly Compromised Bride   04/91 Harlequin Regency
    109 The Highwayman   11/93 Harlequin Regency

Reynolds, Elizabeth
    158 An Ocean Of Love   06/82 Silhouette Romance

Reynolds, Maureen
    Wild Nights, Silver Dreams
    Tempting Eden   09/93 Bantam
    Smoke Eyes   12/92 Bantam Fanfare
    One Golden Hour   Pageant

Rhoades, Knight
    85 She Died On The Stairway   /50 Harlequin

Rhoades, Sandra K.
    917 A Risky Business   Harlequin Presents
    956 Bitter Legacy   Harlequin Presents
    1021 Shadows In The Limelight   Harlequin Presents
    1214 Yesterday's Embers   Harlequin Presents
    1381 Stormy Reunion   07/91 Harlequin Presents
    3030 Foolish Deceiver   Harlequin Romance

Rhodes, Karen
    6 Shining Tide   10/92 Zebra Lucky In Love
    25 Strings Of Fortune   03/93 Zebra Lucky In Love
    38 Home Fires   05/93 Zebra Lucky In Love

Rhys, Jean
    Wide Sargasso Sea

Rice, Darcy

25	Love With Interest	01/91	Meteor
71	Island Secrets	12/91	Meteor

Rice, Luanne

	Blue Moon	09/94	Bantam

Rice, Molly

315	Silent Masquerade	03/95	Harlequin Intrigue
348	Unforgettable	11/95	Harlequin Intrigue
440	Where The River Runs		Harlequin Superromance
490	Chance Encounter	03/92	Harlequin Superromance

Rice, Patricia

Faith And The Highwayman	09/92	Nal
Rebel Dreams	09/91	Nal Onyx
Touched By Magic	03/92	Nal Onyx
Devil's Lady	09/92	Nal Onyx
Love Forever After	05/90	Nal Onyx
Lacy Scorceress	06/85	Nal Onyx
Love Betrayed	02/87	Nal Onyx
Silver Enchantress	07/88	Nal Onyx
Lord Rogue	01/89	Nal Onyx
Cheyenne's Lady	12/89	Nal Onyx
Moon Dreams	01/91	Nal Onyx
Shelter From The Storm	03/93	Nal Onyx
Mad Maria's Daughter	04/92	Nal Regency
Artful Deceptions	08/92	Nal Regency
The Genuine Article	10/94	Nal Regency
Blossoms: "A Golden Crocus"	03/95	Onyx Anthology
Texas Lily	07/94	Penguin Topaz
Moonlight And Memories	10/93	Penguin Topaz
Paper Tiger	10/95	Penguin Topaz
Indigo Moon	02/88	Signet
Lady Sorceress	06/85	Signet
Full-Moon Magic	09/92	Signet Anthology
A Victorian Christmas	11/92	Signet Anthology
A Regency Christmas: "The Kissing Bough"	11/89	Signet Anthology
Regency Valentine	02/91	Signet Anthology
Moonlight Lovers	09/93	Signet Anthology
A Country Christmas: "Friends Are Forever"	11/93	Signet Anthology
Denim & Lace	07/96	Topaz
Secrets Of The Heart:"Keeping The Fire Hot	12/94	Topaz Anthology
Paper Roses	02/95	Topaz Historical
Paper Moon	03/96	Topaz Historical
Love's First Surrender	02/84	Zebra
Moonlight Mistress	07/85	Zebra

Rich, Harriet

179	Bride Of Belvale		Dell Candlelight

Rich, Mary Lou

	Colorado Tempest	10/92	Diamond Wildflower
	Bandit's Kiss	01/93	Diamond Wildflower
	Heart's Folly	05/96	Jove Homespun
	The Tomboy	02/96	Jove Sons And Daughters

Rich, Sue

	Rawhide And Roses	08/93	Pocket
	The Silver Witch	01/95	Pocket
	Mistress Of Sin	04/94	Pocket
	Aim For The Heart	02/96	Pocket
1	The Scarlett Temptress	09/91	Pocket
2	Shadowed Vows	08/92	Pocket
3	Wayward Angel	09/95	Pocket

Richards, Cinda

237	This Side Of Paradise		Berkley Second Chance At Love
280	Such Rough Splendor		Berkley Second Chance At Love
330	Dillon's Promise		Berkley Second Chance At Love
382	Fire Under Heaven		Berkley Second Chance At Love
426	One From The Heart		Berkley Second Chance At Love

Richards, Claire

202	Renaissance Summer	04/85	Silhouette Desire

Richards, Denise

44	Deadly Coincidence	05/91	Meteor
119	A Family Affair	12/92	Meteor
147	Hannah's Hero	05/93	Meteor Kismet

Richards, Emilie

	Once More With Feeling	08/96	Avon
18	Angel And The Saint	05/96	Harlequin Here Come The Grooms
29	Outback Nights	07/96	Harlequin Here Come The Grooms
18	Bayou Midnight	06/94	Harlequin Men Made In America
172	The Unmasking		Harlequin Superromance
204	Something So Right		Harlequin Superromance
240	Season Of Miracles		Harlequin Superromance
1	Iron Lace	06/96	Mira
2	Rising Tides	/97	Mira
	Christmas Classics - "Season Of Miracles"	/89	Silhouette Anthology
	Birds, Bees & Babies - " Labor Dispute"	05/90	Silhouette Anthology
	Christmas Magic - "Sweet Sea Spirit"	/91	Silhouette Anthology
	Intimate Moments 10th Anniversary	05/93	Silhouette Anthology
	1993 Christmas Stories	11/93	Silhouette Anthology
	Christmas Classics - "Naughty Or Nice"	12/93	Silhouette Anthology
	Woman Without A Name	12/96	Silhouette Intimate Moments
152	Lady Of The Night	07/86	Silhouette Intimate Moments
188	Bayou Midnight	04/87	Silhouette Intimate Moments
249	From Glowing Embers	08/88	Silhouette Intimate Moments
261	Smoke Screen	11/88	Silhouette Intimate Moments

AUTHOR/TITLE INDEX

Richards, Emilie

273	Rainbow Fire	02/89	Silhouette Intimate Moments
285	Out Of Ashes	05/89	Silhouette Intimate Moments
337	Runaway	06/90	Silhouette Intimate Moments
341	The Way Back Home	07/90	Silhouette Intimate Moments
357	Fugitive	11/90	Silhouette Intimate Moments
401	Desert Shadows	10/91	Silhouette Intimate Moments
409	Twilight Shadows	12/91	Silhouette Intimate Moments
456	From A Distance	10/92	Silhouette Intimate Moments
498	Somewhere Out There	05/93	Silhouette Intimate Moments
511	Dragonslayer	08/93	Silhouette Intimate Moments
625	Duncan's Lady	03/95	Silhouette Intimate Moments
644	Iain Ross's Woman	06/95	Silhouette Intimate Moments
655	Macdougall's Darling	08/95	Silhouette Intimate Moments
372	Brendan's Song	07/85	Silhouette Romance
393	Sweet Georgia Gal	10/85	Silhouette Romance
401	Gilding The Lily	12/85	Silhouette Romance
413	Sweet Sea Spirit	02/86	Silhouette Romance
429	Angel And The Saint	04/86	Silhouette Romance
441	Sweet Mockingbird's Call	06/86	Silhouette Romance
453	Good Time Man	08/86	Silhouette Romance
466	Sweet Mountain Magic	11/86	Silhouette Romance
489	Sweet Homecoming	02/87	Silhouette Romance
520	Aloha Always	08/87	Silhouette Romance
536	Outback Nights	10/87	Silhouette Romance
675	Island Glory	09/89	Silhouette Romance
433	All The Right Reasons	02/88	Silhouette Special Edition
456	A Classic Encounter	05/88	Silhouette Special Edition
684	All Those Years Ago	07/91	Silhouette Special Edition
750	One Perfect Rose	06/92	Silhouette Special Edition
873	The Trouble With Joe	03/94	Silhouette Special Edition

Richards, Leigh

21	Spring Fires	07/80	Silhouette Romance

Richards, Penny

526	Passionate Kisses	04/94	Harlequin Crystal Creek
532	Unanswered Prayers	11/94	Harlequin Crystal Creek
323	Unforgettable		Harlequin Superromance
350	Calloway Corners: Eden	09/93	Harlequin Superromance
	Dreamers And Deceivers	10/91	Harper
921	The Greatest Gift Of All	11/94	Silhouette Special Edition
949	Where Dreams Have Been...	04/95	Silhouette Special Edition
1015	Sisters	03/96	Silhouette Special Edition

Richards, Serena

	Masquerade		
	Escapade		Berkley
	Rendezvous		Berkley

Richards-Akers, Nancy

The Heart And The Heather	08/94	Avon Medieval Trilogy
The Heart And The Holly	05/96	Avon Medieval Trilogy
The Heart And The Rose	08/95	Avon Medieval Trilogy
Lady Sarah's Charade		Avon Regency
Miss Wickham's Betrothal	09/92	Avon Regency
Lord Fortune's Prize	06/93	Avon Regency
The Devil's Wager	05/92	Fawcett Crest Regency
The Lilac Garland		Warner
The Mayfair Season		Warner
Philadelphia Folly		Warner
A Season Abroad		Warner

Richardson, Evelyn

The Reluctant Heiress	/96	
The Nabob's Ward	11/91	Nal Regency
The Bluestocking's Dilemma	11/92	Nal Regency
The Education Of Lady Francis	11/89	Nal Regency
The Willful Widow	/94	Nal Regency
Ms. Cresswell's London Triumph	10/90	Nal Penguin

Richardson, Susan

186	Fiddlin' Fool	04/87	Bantam Loveswept
205	A Slow Simmer	08/87	Bantam Loveswept
240	Cajun Nights	03/88	Bantam Loveswept

Richey, Cynthia

Love's Masquerade	07/90	Walker
A June Betrothal	04/93	Zebra Anthology
The Secret Scribbler	05/94	Zebra Regency
The Fashionable Miss Fonteyne	11/94	Zebra Regency

Richmond, Clare

174	The Runaway Heart		Harlequin American
215	Bride's Inn		Harlequin American
352	Pirate's Legacy		Harlequin American
476	Hawaiian Heat	02/93	Harlequin American

Richmond, Emma

279	A Wayward Love	05/96	Harlequin
291	Fate Of Happiness	08/96	Harlequin
	Christmas Journeys: "A Man To Live For"	09/95	Harlequin Anthology
1203	Take Away The Pride		Harlequin Presents
1230	Unwilling Heart		Harlequin Presents
1317	Heart In Hiding		Harlequin Presents
1373	A Taste Of Heaven		Harlequin Presents
1421	Law Of Possession	12/91	Harlequin Presents
1461	A Foolish Dream	05/92	Harlequin Presents
1516	Unfair Assumptions	12/92	Harlequin Presents
1582	A Stranger's Trust	08/93	Harlequin Presents
1669	More Than A Dream	07/94	Harlequin Presents

Richmond, Emma
1624	Deliberate Provocation	02/94	Harlequin	Presents Plus
3349	Love Of My Heart	02/95	Harlequin	Romance
3374	A Family Closeness (Family Ties)	08/95	Harlequin	Romance

Ridgway, Christie
12	The Wedding Date	01/96	Silhouette	Yours Truly

Ridley, Sheila
655	Outpost Hospital	/62	Harlequin

Riefe, Barbara
	Wicked Fire	Berkley
	Black Fire	Berkley
	Wild Fire	Berkley
	The Shackelford Legacy	Berkley
	Olivia	Berkley
	Julia	Berkley
	Lucretia	Berkley

Rieger, Catherine
Waltz At Devil's House	05/93	Diamond
The Shadow Of The Raven	06/92	Diamond Gothic
Waltz In The Shadows	11/93	Jove Gothic Romance

Riggs, Paula Detmer
633	Rough Passage	04/91	Silhouette	Desire
744	A Man Of Honor	10/92	Silhouette	Desire
898	Murdock's Family	12/94	Silhouette	Desire
440	Paroled!	07/92	Silhouette	Initmate Moments
481	Firebrand	03/93	Silhouette	Initmate Moments
183	Beautiful Dreamer	03/87	Silhouette	Intimate Moments
226	Fantasy Man	02/88	Silhouette	Intimate Moments
250	Suspicious Minds	08/88	Silhouette	Intimate Moments
283	Desperate Measures	04/89	Silhouette	Intimate Moments
303	Full Circle	09/89	Silhouette	Intimate Moments
314	Tender Offer	12/89	Silhouette	Intimate Moments
344	A Lasting Promise	07/90	Silhouette	Intimate Moments
364	Forgotten Dreams	12/90	Silhouette	Intimate Moments
398	Silent Impact	09/91	Silhouette	Intimate Moments
524	Once Upon A Wedding	10/93	Silhouette	Intimate Moments
548	No Easy Way Out	02/94	Silhouette	Intimate Moments
656	The Bachelor Party (Always A Bridesmaid)	08/95	Silhouette	Intimate Moments
667	Her Secret, His Child	10/95	Silhouette	Intimate Moments
	Island Magic	/92	Silhouette	Summer Sizzlers

Riker, Leigh
Morning Rain	08/91	Harper
Unforgettable	04/93	Harper
Tears Of Jade	12/93	Harper Monogram
Just One Of Those Things	09/94	Harper Monogram
Unforgettable		Harper Monogram

AUTHOR/TITLE INDEX

Riker, Leigh

	Oh, Susannah	01/95	Harper Monogram
	Danny Boy	07/95	Harper Monogram
	Acts Of Passion	/85	Popular Lib.

Riley, Eugenia

	Rogue's Mistress	11/91	Avon
	Phantom In Time	07/96	Avon
	Taming Kate	09/92	Avon Romance
	Timeswept Bride	08/95	Avon Romantic Treasure
	Phantom In Time	07/96	Avon Romantic Treasure
102	Remember Me, Love	07/85	Bantam Loveswept
135	Stubborn Cinderella	04/86	Bantam Loveswept
174	Where The Heart Is	01/87	Bantam Loveswept
292	Love Nest	03/90	Harlequin Temptation
324	The Perfect Mate	11/90	Harlequin Temptation
391	Stellar Attraction	04/92	Harlequin Temptation
	Old-Fashioned Valentine:"Two Hearts In Ti	02/93	Leisure Anthology
	Christmas Angels	11/95	Leisure Anthology
	A Tryst In Time	01/92	Leisure Time Travel
	Tempest In Time	01/93	Leisure Time-Travel
	Christmas Angels:"Tryst With An Angel"	11/95	Love Spell Anthology
	The Night It Rained	/89	Pageant
	Angel Flame	/90	Warner
	Laurel's Love	/86	Warner
	Sweet Reckoning	/87	Warner
	Mississippi Madness	/89	Warner
	Ecstasy's Triumph	/83	Zebra

Riley, Judith Merkle

	A Vision Of Light		Bantam

Riley, Mildred E.

	Yamilla	06/90	Odyssey Books
	Akayna, Sachem's Daughter	11/92	Odyssey Books
	Journey's End	02/95	Pinnacle Arabesque

Rimmer, Christine

40	Temporary Temptress	09/96	Harlequin Here Come The Grooms
154	The Road Home	05/87	Harlequin Temptation
418	No Turning Back	04/88	Silhouette Desire
458	Call It Fate	11/88	Silhouette Desire
602	Temporary Temptress	11/90	Silhouette Desire
640	Hard Luck Lady	05/91	Silhouette Desire
729	Midsummer Madness	08/92	Silhouette Desire
812	Counterfeit Bride	10/93	Silhouette Desire
940	Cat's Cradle (Opposites Attract)	07/95	Silhouette Desire
646	Double Dare	01/91	Silhouette Special Edition
698	Slow Larkin's Revenge	10/91	Silhouette Special Edition
719	Earth Angel	01/92	Silhouette Special Edition

Rimmer, Christine

794	Wagered Woman	02/93	Silhouette Special Edition
833	Born Innocent	08/93	Silhouette Special Edition
886	Man Of The Mountain (The Jones Gang)	05/94	Silhouette Special Edition
896	Sweetbriar Summit (The Jones Gang)	07/94	Silhouette Special Edition
908	A Home For The Hunter (That Jones Gang)	09/94	Silhouette Special Edition
925	For The Baby's Sake (That Special Woman!)	12/94	Silhouette Special Edition
979	Sunshine And The Shadowmaster	09/95	Silhouette Special Edition
1010	The Man, The Moon & The Marriage Vow	02/96	Silhouette Special Edition
1040	No Less Than A Lifetime	07/96	Silhouette Special Edition

Rinehold, Connie

	The Liberation Of Katie Mc Call		Dell
	Twilight Cameo	03/92	Dell
	Letters From A Stranger	04/93	Dell Contemporary
	More Than Just A Night	02/92	Dell Historical
	Madam's Daughter	05/94	Dell Historical
380	Veil Of Tears		Harlequin American
374	Silken Threads		Harlequin Superromance

Ring, Thomasina

	Dream Catcher	06/92	Leisure
	Time-Spun Rapture	07/90	Leisure
	Time-Spun Treasure	07/90	Leisure Time Travel

Ripley, Alexandra

	Who's The Lady In The President's Bed		
	The Time Returns		
	American Royal		
	Summerblood		
	On Leaving Charleston		Warner
	Charleston		Warner
	New Orleans Legacy		Warner
	Scarlett (Sequel To Gone With The Wind)	10/92	Warner

Ripy, Margaret

71	A Second Chance On Love	04/81	Silhouette Romance
170	A Treasure Of Love	08/82	Silhouette Romance
28	The Flaming Tree	06/82	Silhouette Special Edition
76	Tomorrow's Memory	02/83	Silhouette Special Edition
114	Rainy Day Dreams	08/83	Silhouette Special Edition
134	A Matter Of Pride	12/83	Silhouette Special Edition
164	Firebird	05/84	Silhouette Special Edition
189	Feathers In The Wind	09/84	Silhouette Special Edition
209	Promise Her Tomorrow	12/84	Silhouette Special Edition
351	Wildcatter's Promise	12/86	Silhouette Special Edition

Ritter, Margaret

	Burning Woman		

Rivers, Dorothy

567	Spring Comes To Harley Street	/61	Harlequin

Rivers, Dorothy

631	Doctor's House	/61	Harlequin
1088	Spanish Moonlight	/67	Harlequin
1110	Labour Of Love	/67	Harlequin
1135	There Will Come A Stranger	/67	Harlequin
1163	Love In The Wilderness	/67	Harlequin
1198	Happy Ever After	/68	Harlequin
1260	We Live In Secret	/68	Harlequin
1304	Sharlie For Short	/69	Harlequin

Rivers, Francine

	Rebel In His Arms	/81	Ace
	Redeeming Love	12/91	Bantam Fanfare
	Outlaw's Embrace	/86	Charter
	A Fire In The Heart	/87	Charter
	Not So Wild A Dream	/85	Jove
	Kathleen	/79	Jove
	This Golden Valley		Jove
	Sarina		Jove
	Sycamore Hill		Jove
1	A Voice In The Wind	/93	Tyndale House Mark Of The Lion
2	An Echo In The Darkness	07/94	Tyndale House Mark Of The Lion
3	As Sure As The Dawn	06/95	Tyndale House Mark Of The Lion

Rivers, Nikki

550	Seducing Spencer	09/94	Harlequin American
592	Daddy's Little Matchmaker	07/95	Harlequin American

Robards, Karen

Island Desire		
This Side Of Heaven	07/94	
Walking After Midnight	/95	
Green Eyes		Avon
Morning Song		Avon
Tiger's Eye		Avon
Dark Of The Moon	01/95	Avon Historical
Desire In The Sun	03/95	Avon Historical
Green Eyes	08/95	Avon Historical
Nobody's Angel	12/92	Dell
Maggy's Child	12/94	Dell
One Summer	/93	Dell
Sea Fire	09/92	Leisure Historical
Forbidden Love	03/94	Leisure Historical
Island Flame	05/93	Leisure Historical
Loving Julia	/86	Warner
Night Magic	/88	Warner
To Love A Child	/88	Warner
Wild Orchid	/86	Warner
To Love A Man	03/94	Warner
Amanda Rose	05/95	Warner

Robb, Christine
   Twilight's Key
Robb, J.D.
      Immortal In Death   07/96   Berkley Romantic Suspense
   1   Naked In Death   07/95   Berkley Romantic Suspense
   2   Glory In Death   11/95   Berkley Romantic Suspense
Robb, JoAnn
   29   Stardust And Diamonds   Nal Rapture Romance
   49   Dreamlover   Nal Rapture Romance
   61   Sterling Deceptions   Nal Rapture Romance
   70   A Secure Arrangement   06/84   Nal Rapture Romance
Robb, John
   231   Legionnaire   /53   Harlequin
Robb, Sandra
   43   Surrender In Paradise   11/80   Silhouette Romance
Robbins, Denise
   Fauna   Avon
Robbins, Gina
   Whispers Of Love   09/94   Pinnacle Press Historical
Robbins, Joann
   94   Winning Season   10/83   Silhouette Desire
Robbins, Kay
   On Her Doorstep   Berkley
   73   Return Engagement   /83   Berkley Second Chance At Love
   110   Taken By Storm   Berkley Second Chance At Love
   130   Elusive Dawn   Berkley Second Chance At Love
   155   Kissed By Magic   Berkley Second Chance At Love
   190   Moonlight Rhapsody   /84   Berkley Second Chance At Love
   262   Eye Of The Beholder   Berkley Second Chance At Love
   322   Belonging To Taylor   Berkley Second Chance At Love
Robbins, Rebecca
   The Mischievous Maid   Avon Regency
   Lucky In Love   04/94   Avon Regency
   An Unusual Inheritance   10/94   Avon Regency Romance
Robbins, Serena
   35   Isel Of Rapture   Harlequin Superromance
Roberts, Alina
   4   Prairie Summer (Great Escapes)   03/94   Harlequin Stolen Moments
Roberts, Ann Victoria
   Louisa Elliott   08/90   Avon
Roberts, Annie Sims
   5   The Sugar Cup (Great Escapes)   03/94   Harlequin Stolen Moments
Roberts, Casey
   429   Homecoming   Harlequin Superromance
   493   Walking On Air   03/92   Harlequin Superromance

AUTHOR/TITLE INDEX

Roberts, Casey

547	Shenanigans	06/93	Harlequin	Superromance

Roberts, Doreen

28	In The Line Of Duty	07/96	Harlequin	Here Come The Grooms
442	Road To Freedom	08/92	Silhouette	Initmate Moments
475	In A Stranger's Eyes	02/93	Silhouette	Initmate Moments
215	Gambler's Gold	11/87	Silhouette	Intimate Moments
239	Willing Accomplice	05/88	Silhouette	Intimate Moments
266	Forbidden Jade	12/88	Silhouette	Intimate Moments
295	Threat Of Exposure	07/89	Silhouette	Intimate Moments
319	Desert Heat	01/90	Silhouette	Intimate Moments
379	In The Line Of Duty	04/91	Silhouette	Intimate Moments
422	Broken Wings	03/92	Silhouette	Intimate Moments
513	Only A Dream Away	08/93	Silhouette	Intimate Moments
567	Where There's Smoke	05/94	Silhouette	Intimate Moments
653	So Little Time	07/95	Silhouette	Intimate Moments
705	A Cowboy's Heart	04/96	Silhouette	Intimate Moments
765	Home For The Holidays	12/90	Silhouette	Romance

Roberts, Janet Louise

	Weeping Lady		Historical
	A Marriage Of Inconvenience		Dell Candlelight
239	The Dancing Doll		Dell Candlelight Regency
240	My Lady Mischief		Dell Candlelight Regency
245	La Casa Dorada		Dell Candlelight Regency
246	The Golden Thistle		Dell Candlelight Regency
247	The First Waltz		Dell Candlelight Regency
248	The Cardross Luck		Dell Candlelight Regency

Roberts, Kelsey

248	Legal Tender	01/94	Harlequin	Intrigue
276	Stolen Memories	05/94	Harlequin	Intrigue
294	Things Remembered	10/94	Harlequin	Intrigue
326	Unspoken Confessions (The Rose Tattoo)	06/95	Harlequin	Intrigue
330	Unlawfully Wedded (The Rose Tattoo)	07/95	Harlequin	Intrigue
334	Undying Laughter (The Rose Tattoo)	08/95	Harlequin	Intrigue
349	Handsome As Sin	12/95	Harlequin	Intrigue
374	The Baby Exchange	06/96	Harlequin	Intrigue

Roberts, Kenneth

	Lydia Bailey		Historical

Roberts, Leigh

81	Moonlight Splendor		Harlequin	Superromance
390	A Piece Of Cake		Harlequin	Superromance
543	Built To Last	04/93	Harlequin	Superromance
20	Love Circuits	07/84	Harlequin	Temptation
55	Siren Song	04/85	Harlequin	Temptation
97	Head Over Heels	03/86	Harlequin	Temptation
147	Birds Of A Feather	03/87	Harlequin	Temptation

772

AUTHOR/TITLE INDEX

Roberts, Leigh

| 186 | The Wishing Poll | 01/88 | Harlequin Temptation |

Roberts, Meg-Lynn

	A Perfect Match	04/93	Zebra
	Lover's Vows	02/95	Zebra Anthology
	A Midnight Masquerade	10/93	Zebra Holiday Regency
	An Alluring Lady	05/92	Zebra Regency
	Christmas Escapade	12/94	Zebra Regency

Roberts, Nora

	Genuine Lies	09/91	Bantam Fanfare
	Carnal Innocence	01/92	Bantam Fanfare
	Divine Evil	10/92	Bantam Fanfare
	Public Secrets	/90	Bantam Fanfare
	Sacred Sins	/87	Bantam Fanfare
	Sweet Revenge	/89	Bantam Fanfare
	Brazen Virtues	/88	Bantam Fanfare
	Hot Ice	/87	Bantam Fanfare
	Montana Sky	03/96	G. P. Putnam
4	Rebellion		Harlequin Historical
21	Lawless	/89	Harlequin Historical
19	Night Moves	/85	Harlequin Intrigue
	The Name Of The Game	06/93	Harlequin Lang. Of Love
	Dual Image	04/93	Harlequin Lang. Of Love
	Second Nature	04/93	Harlequin Lang. Of Love
	Command Performance	12/93	Harlequin Lang. Of Love
	Blithe Images	12/93	Harlequin Lang. Of Love
	Affaire Royale	10/93	Harlequin Lang. Of Love
	Less Of A Stranger	10/93	Harlequin Lang. Of Love
	The Playboy Prince	02/94	Harlequin Lang. Of Love
	Treasures Lost, Treasures Found	02/94	Harlequin Lang. Of Love
	Risky Business	04/94	Harlequin Lang. Of Love
	Loving Jack	04/94	Harlequin Lang. Of Love
	Temptation	06/94	Harlequin Lang. Of Love
	Best Laid Plans	06/94	Harlequin Lang. Of Love
	Mind Over Matter	08/94	Harlequin Lang. Of Love
	The Welcoming	08/94	Harlequin Lang. Of Love
	Honest Illusions	08/93	Jove
	Hidden Riches	05/95	Jove
1	Born In Fire	10/94	Jove Irish Trilogy
2	Born In Ice	10/95	Jove Irish Trilogy
3	Born In Shame	01/96	Jove Irish Trilogy
	Daring To Dream	08/96	Jove Sisters Trilogy #1
	Waiting To Dream	01/97	Jove Sisters Trilogy #2
	Finding The Dream	/98	Jove Sisters Trilogy #3
	Dance To The Piper	11/94	Mira
	The Last Honest Woman	02/95	Mira
	Skin Deep	10/95	Mira

Roberts, Nora

	Without A Trace	02/96	Mira 4th O'Hurleys
	Promise Me Tomorrow	/84	Pocket
	Private Scandals	08/93	Putnam
	True Betrayals	06/95	Putnam Romantic Suspense
	Birds, Bees & Babies - 1994	05/94	Silhouette Anthology
	Jingle Bells, Wedding Bells	11/94	Silhouette Anthology
	"All I Want For Christmas"	/94	Silhouette Anthology
	Home For Christmas	/86	Silhouette Christmas Stories
33	Promise Me Tomorrow	12/82	Silhouette Desire
649	A Man For Amanda	07/91	Silhouette Desire
	In From The Cold	/90	Silhouette Hist. Christ. Stories
433	Unfinished Business	06/92	Silhouette Initmate Moments
	Megan's Mate	/96	Silhouette Intimate Moments
2	Once More With Feeling	05/83	Silhouette Intimate Moments
12	Tonight And Always	07/83	Silhouette Intimate Moments
25	This Magic Moment	11/83	Silhouette Intimate Moments
33	Endings And Beginnings	01/84	Silhouette Intimate Moments
49	A Matter Of Choice	05/84	Silhouette Intimate Moments
70	Rules Of The Game	10/84	Silhouette Intimate Moments
85	The Right Path	03/85	Silhouette Intimate Moments
94	Partners	05/85	Silhouette Intimate Moments
114	Boundary Lines	10/85	Silhouette Intimate Moments
123	Dual Image	12/85	Silhouette Intimate Moments
131	The Art Of Deception	02/86	Silhouette Intimate Moments
142	Affair Royale	05/86	Silhouette Intimate Moments
150	Treasures Lost, Treasures Found	07/86	Silhouette Intimate Moments
160	Risky Business	09/86	Silhouette Intimate Moments
185	Mind Over Matter	04/87	Silhouette Intimate Moments
198	Command Performance	07/87	Silhouette Intimate Moments
212	The Playboy Prince	10/87	Silhouette Intimate Moments
232	Irish Rose	03/88	Silhouette Intimate Moments
264	The Name Of The Game	11/88	Silhouette Intimate Moments
300	Gabriel's Angel	08/89	Silhouette Intimate Moments
313	Time Was	12/89	Silhouette Intimate Moments
317	Times Change	01/90	Silhouette Intimate Moments
365	Night Shift	01/91	Silhouette Intimate Moments
373	Night Shadow	03/91	Silhouette Intimate Moments
397	Suzanna's Surrender	09/91	Silhouette Intimate Moments
529	Nightshade (American Hero, Night Tales)	11/93	Silhouette Intimate Moments
595	Night Smoke	10/94	Silhouette Intimate Moments
631	The Return Of Rafe Mackade (Heartbreaker	04/95	Silhouette Intimate Moments
81	Irish Thoroughbred	05/81	Silhouette Romance
127	Blithe Images	01/82	Silhouette Romance
143	Song Of The West	04/82	Silhouette Romance
163	Search For Love	07/82	Silhouette Romance
180	Island Of Flowers	10/82	Silhouette Romance

AUTHOR/TITLE INDEX

Roberts, Nora

199	From This Day	01/83	Silhouette	Romance
215	Her Mother's Keeper	04/83	Silhouette	Romance
252	Untamed	10/83	Silhouette	Romance
274	Storm Warning	02/84	Silhouette	Romance
280	Sullivan's Woman	03/84	Silhouette	Romance
299	Less Of A Stranger	06/84	Silhouette	Romance
529	Temptation	09/87	Silhouette	Romance
801	Courting Catherine	06/91	Silhouette	Romance
	Waiting For Nick	/96	Silhouette	Special Edition
59	The Heart's Victory	11/82	Silhouette	Special Edition
100	Reflections	06/83	Silhouette	Special Edition
116	Dance Of Dreams	09/83	Silhouette	Special Edition
162	First Impressions	04/84	Silhouette	Special Edition
175	The Law Is A Lady	07/84	Silhouette	Special Edition
199	Opposites Attract	11/84	Silhouette	Special Edition
225	MacGregor 1: Playing The Odds	03/85	Silhouette	Special Edition
235	MacGregor 2: Tempting Fate	05/85	Silhouette	Special Edition
247	MacGregor 3: All The Possibilities	07/85	Silhouette	Special Edition
259	MacGregor 4: One Man's Art	09/85	Silhouette	Special Edition
271	Summer Desserts	11/85	Silhouette	Special Edition
288	Second Nature	01/86	Silhouette	Special Edition
306	One Summer	04/86	Silhouette	Special Edition
318	Lessons Learned	06/86	Silhouette	Special Edition
345	A Will And A Way	11/86	Silhouette	Special Edition
361	MacGregor 5: For Now, Forever	02/87	Silhouette	Special Edition
427	Local Hero	01/88	Silhouette	Special Edition
451	The Last Honest Woman	05/88	Silhouette	Special Edition
463	Dance To The Piper	07/88	Silhouette	Special Edition
475	Skin Deep	09/88	Silhouette	Special Edition
499	Loving Jack	01/89	Silhouette	Special Edition
511	Best Laid Plans	03/89	Silhouette	Special Edition
553	The Welcoming	10/89	Silhouette	Special Edition
583	Taming Natasha	03/90	Silhouette	Special Edition
625	Without A Trace	10/90	Silhouette	Special Edition
685	For The Love Of Lila	08/91	Silhouette	Special Edition
697	The Heart Of Devin Mackade	03/96	Silhouette	Special Edition
709	Luring A Lady	12/91	Silhouette	Special Edition
768	Captivated	09/92	Silhouette	Special Edition
774	Entranced	10/92	Silhouette	Special Edition
780	Charmed	11/92	Silhouette	Special Edition
810	Falling For Rachel	04/93	Silhouette	Special Edition
872	Convincing Alex (Those Wilde Ukranians)	03/94	Silhouette	Special Edition
1000	The Pride Of Jared Mackade	12/95	Silhouette	Special Edition
1022	The Fall Of Shane Mackade	04/96	Silhouette	Special Edition
	Impulse	/89	Silhouette	Summer Sizzlers

Roberts, Peggy

775

Roberts, Peggy
    Mrs. Perfect
    Heart's Desire   12/94
    The Gilded Dove   Ballantine
    Desire's Dream   Ballantine
    Renegade Heart   Ballantine
    Creole Angel   Ballantine
    Golden Promises   Ballantine
    Tender Betrayal   Ballantine
    Tomorrow's Dream   Ballantine
    Where Eagles Soar   Fawcett Gold Medal
    Cheyenne Dreams   Fawcett Gold Medal
    Merry Christmas My Love   11/93   Zebra Anthology
    Whispers At Midnight   04/94   Zebra Pinnacle
    Just In Time   06/93   Zebra To Love Again

Roberts, Phyllis
    213   A Man Like David   08/88   Harlequin Temptation

Roberts, Suzanne
    525   Love's Sweet Illusion   Dell Candlelight
    547   Farewell To Alexandria   Dell Candlelight

Roberts, Willo Davis
    231   To Share A Dream   08/94   Harlequin Historical
    My Rebel, My Love   Tapestry

Robertson, Denise
    None To Make You Cry   12/91   Harper

Robins, Denise
    629   To Love Again   /61   Harlequin

Robins, Gina
    Love's Sweetest Secret   Zebra
    Mississippi Mistress   Zebra
    Diamond Fire   Zebra
    Always, Forever   Zebra
    Secret Splendor   Zebra
    Love's Reckless Rebel   Zebra
    Texas Temptation   Zebra
    Mississippi Masquerade   09/90   Zebra
    Forbidden Kiss   12/95   Zebra
    Deception's Sweet Kiss   04/90   Zebra Hologram
    Captive Enchantress   06/89   Zebra Hologram

Robins, Madeline
    The Heiress Companion   Ballantine Regency
    Lady John   Ballantine Regency
    My Dear Jenny   Ballantine Regency

Robinson, Diane Gates
    The Falcon And The Swan   Zebra
    Delta Desire   Zebra Heartfire

Robinson, Diane Gates

    Revenge So Sweet   Zebra Heartfire

Robinson, Irene

  15 Cherished Destiny   Harlequin Superromance

Robinson, Suzanne

	Lord Of Enchantment	12/94	Bantam
	Lord Of The Dragon	08/95	Bantam
	Lady Gallant	01/92	Bantam Fanfare
	Lady Hellfire	06/92	Bantam Fanfare
	Lady Dangerous	02/94	Bantam Fanfare
	Lady Defiant	01/93	Bantam Fanfare
	Lady Valiant		Bantam Fanfare
	Heart Of The Falcon		Doubleday

Robson, Lucia St. Clair

	Light A Distant Fire	01/92	Ballantine Historical
	Ride The Wind	01/92	Ballantine Historical
	Walk In My Soul	01/92	Ballantine Historical
	The Tokaido Road	05/92	Ballantine Historical

Roby, Mary Linn

	White Peacock		Regency
	The Treasure Chest		Berkley
555	Passing Fancy		Dell Candlelight Romance
	My Lady's Mask		Warner
	Fortune's Smile		Warner

Roby, Mary Lynn

555	Passing Fancy		Dell Candlelight Regency

Rock, Pam

	Love's Changing Moon	07/94	Love Spell Futuristic
	Moon Of Desire	/95	Love Spell Futuristic
	A World Away	08/95	Love Spell Futuristic

Rodgers, M.J.

492	Fire Magic	06/93	Harlequin American
520	The Adventuress	01/94	Harlequin American
563	The Gift-Wrapped Groom	12/94	Harlequin American
	Intrigue 10th Anniversary	09/94	Harlequin Intrigue
	All The Evidence	02/94	Harlequin Intrigue
102	For Love Or Money		Harlequin Intrigue
128	A Taste Of Death		Harlequin Intrigue
140	Bloodstone		Harlequin Intrigue
157	Dead Ringer		Harlequin Intrigue
214	To Die For	02/93	Harlequin Intrigue
254	Santa Claus Is Coming	12/93	Harlequin Intrigue
271	On The Scent	04/94	Harlequin Intrigue
290	Who Is Jane Williams?	09/94	Harlequin Intrigue
335	Beauty Vs. The Beast (Justice, Inc.)	08/95	Harlequin Intrigue
342	Baby Vs. The Bar	10/95	Harlequin Intrigue

Rodgers, M.J.
350 Heart Vs. Humbug — 12/95 Harlequin Intrigue
375 Love Vs. Illusion — 06/96 Harlequin Intrigue
Roding, Frances
1052 Open To Influence — Harlequin Presents
1163 Man Of Stone — Harlequin Presents
·1190 A Different Dream — Harlequin Presents
1213 A Law Unto Himself — Harlequin Presents
1293 Gentle Deception — Harlequin Presents
2901 Some Sort Of Spell — Harlequin Romance
Roeburt, John
98 Jigger Moran — /51 Harlequin
104 Tough Cop — /51 Harlequin
109 Corpse On The Town — /51 Harlequin
115 Manhatten Underworld — /51 Harlequin
Roenbuck, Patricia
Golden Temptress — 10/92 Leisure Futuristic Romance
The Golden Conquest — 10/92 Leisure Futuristic Romance
Roesch, E. P.
Ashana — 11/91 Ballantine Historical Fiction
Rofheart, Martha
Fortune Made His Sword — Historical
Rogers, Evelyn
Brazen Embrace
Rapture's Gamble
Desire's Fury
Velvet Vixon
Lawman's Lady
Love Beyond Time — 07/94 Avon Time Travel Anthology
Wicked — 03/96 Leisure Love Spell
A Love So Wild — Zebra
Surrender To The Night — Zebra
Sweet Texas Magic — Zebra
Wanton Slave — Zebra
Desert Fire — 12/92 Zebra
Angels — 12/95 Zebra
A Christmas Rendezvous — /91 Zebra Anthology
2 Raven — 02/95 Zebra Chadwick Trilogy
Midnight Sins — 06/89 Zebra Heartfire
Texas Kiss — Zebra Heartfire
Rogers, Gayle
Nakoa's Woman — Bantam
Rogers, M. J.
176 Bones Of Contention — 12/91 Harlequin Intrigue
185 Risky Business — 05/92 Harlequin Intrigue
202 All This Evidence — 11/92 Harlequin Intrigue

Rogers, Marylyle

Dark Whispers	02/92	Pocket
Eagle's Song	12/92	Pocket
Enchanted Desire	/85	Pocket
A Minstrel's Song	/86	Pocket
The Dragon's Fire	/88	Pocket
Wary Hearts	/88	Pocket
Hidden Hearts	/89	Pocket
Proud Hearts	/90	Pocket
Chanting The Morning Star	11/93	Pocket
Chanting The Dawn		Pocket
Twilight Secrets	12/94	Pocket Historical
Emerald Enchantment	02/95	St. Martin's Anthology

Rogers, Rosemary

Bound By Desire		Avon
Crowd Pleasers		Avon
Insiders		Avon
Love Play		Avon
Surrender To Love		Avon
Wicked Loving Lies		Avon
Wildest Heart		Avon
The Tea Planter's Bride	04/95	Avon
The Wanton	07/96	Avon
Sweet Savage Love		Avon Steve & Ginny Book 1
Dark Fires		Avon Steve & Ginny Book 2
Lost Love, Last Love		Avon Steve & Ginny Book 3

Roland, Michelle

54	Venus Rising	/82	Berkley Second Chance At Love

Roland, Paula

Faro's Lady		Zebra
The Rogue's Bride		Zebra Regency

Rolofson, Kristine

179	One Of The Family	11/87	Harlequin Temptation
259	Stuck On You	07/89	Harlequin Temptation
290	Bound For Bliss	03/90	Harlequin Temptation
323	Somebody's Hero	11/90	Harlequin Temptation
348	The Last Great Affair	05/91	Harlequin Temptation
415	All That Glitters	10/92	Harlequin Temptation
425	The Perfect Husband	01/93	Harlequin Temptation
469	I'll Be Seeing You (Lovers & Legends)	12/93	Harlequin Temptation
478	Madeleine's Cowboy	02/94	Harlequin Temptation
494	Baby Blues	06/94	Harlequin Temptation
507	Plain Jane's Man	09/94	Harlequin Temptation
548	Jessie's Lawman	07/95	Harlequin Temptation
560	Make-Believe Honeymoon	10/95	Harlequin Temptation
569	The Cowboy	01/96	Harlequin Temptation

Rome, Elaine
85	Stark Lightning	07/91	Harlequin Historical

Rome, Margaret
1307	A Chance To Win	/69	Harlequin
1611	Chateau Of Flowers	/72	Harlequin
1645	Bride Of The Rif	/72	Harlequin
1676	The Girl At Eagles' Mount	/73	Harlequin
1701	Bird Of Paradise	/73	Harlequin
1776	The Island Of Pearls	/74	Harlequin
1939	The Girl At Danes' Dyke	/76	Harlequin
1957	Valley Of Paradise	/76	Harlequin
2052	Bride Of Zarco	/77	Harlequin
2096	The Thistle And The Rose	/77	Harlequin
2152	Lion In Venice	/78	Harlequin
58	Man Of Fire	/74	Harlequin Presents
62	The Marriage Of Caroline Lindsay	/74	Harlequin Presents
101	Palace Of The Hawk	/75	Harlequin Presents
118	The Bartered Bride	/75	Harlequin Presents
128	Cove Of Promises	/76	Harlequin Presents
158	Adam's Rib	/76	Harlequin Presents
438	Second Best Bride		Harlequin Presents
532	Castle Of The Fountain		Harlequin Presents
2235	Son Of Adam		Harlequin Romance
2264	Isle Of Calyspso		Harlequin Romance
2332	Champagne Spring		Harlequin Romance
2369	Marriage By Capture		Harlequin Romance
2445	Miss High And Mighty		Harlequin Romance
2464	Castle In Spain		Harlequin Romance
2487	King Of Kielder		Harlequin Romance
2513	Valley Of Gentians		Harlequin Romance
2553	Rapture Of The Deep		Harlequin Romance
2561	Lord Of The Land		Harlequin Romance
2584	Bay Of Angels		Harlequin Romance
2615	Castle Of The Lion		Harlequin Romance
2694	Bride By Contract		Harlequin Romance
2759	Pagan Gold		Harlequin Romance
25	Maid Of The Border		Mills & Boon

Ronns, Edward
127	Dark Memory	/51	Harlequin

Rose, Jeanne
26	The Prince Of Air And Darkness	02/94	Harlequin Shadows
55	Heart Of Dreams	08/95	Harlequin Shadows
913	Believing In Angels	01/93	Silhouette Romance
1027	Love On The Run	08/94	Silhouette Romance
64	Good Night, My Love	05/96	Silhouette Shadows

Rose, Jennifer

AUTHOR/TITLE INDEX

Rose, Jennifer

4	Out Of A Dream	/81	Berkley	Second Chance At Love
35	Shamrock Season	/82	Berkley	Second Chance At Love
278	Suddenly That Summer	/85	Berkley	Second Chance At Love
2	A Taste Of Heaven	/84	Berkley	To Have And To Hold
11	Keys To The Heart	/84	Berkley	To Have And To Hold
27	Kisses Sweeter Than Wine	/84	Berkley	To Have And To Hold

Rose, Kathryn

1294	Designed With Love		Harlequin Presents

Roseberry, Sherry

	Tender Deceptions	06/91	Berkley
	Love Only Once	08/93	Diamond Historical

Rosemoor, Patricia

	Intrigue 10th Anniversary	09/94	Harlequin Intrigue
38	Double Images		Harlequin Intrigue
55	Dangerous Illusions		Harlequin Intrigue
74	Death Spiral		Harlequin Intrigue
81	Crimson Holiday		Harlequin Intrigue
95	Ambushed		Harlequin Intrigue
113	Do Unto Others		Harlequin Intrigue
121	Ticket To Nowhere		Harlequin Intrigue
161	Pushed To The Limit		Harlequin Intrigue
163	Squaring Accounts		Harlequin Intrigue
165	No Holds Barred	07/91	Harlequin Intrigue
199	The Kiss Of Death	10/92	Harlequin Intrigue
219	Torch Job	03/93	Harlequin Intrigue
243	Dead Heat	09/93	Harlequin Intrigue
250	Haunted	11/93	Harlequin Intrigue
283	Silent Sea	07/94	Harlequin Intrigue
291	Crimson Nightmare	09/94	Harlequin Intrigue
317	Drop Dead Gorgeous	04/95	Harlequin Intrigue
346	The Desperado	11/95	Harlequin Intrigue
361	Lucky Devil	03/96	Harlequin Intrigue
382	See Me In Your Dreams	08/96	Harlequin Intrigue
301	Against All Odds		Harlequin Superromance
334	Working It Out		Harlequin Superromance
	Ambushed	09/95	Harlequin Western Lovers

Ross, Berelee

178	Annabelle	06/93	Harlequin Historical

Ross, Clarissa

Whispers In The Night		Bantam Red Rose Romance
Fan The Wanton Flame		Richard Gallen
Denver's Lady		Warner

Ross, Erin

18	Second Harvest	09/82	Silhouette Desire
89	Time For Tomorrow	09/83	Silhouette Desire

Ross, Erin

114	Fragrant Harbor	01/84	Silhouette	Desire
137	Tide's End	05/84	Silhouette	Desire
155	Odds Against	08/84	Silhouette	Desire
171	Child Of My Heart	11/84	Silhouette	Desire
217	Roses For Remembering	07/85	Silhouette	Desire
280	Willing Spirit	05/86	Silhouette	Desire
383	Carnival Madness	10/87	Silhouette	Desire
107	Flower Of The Orient	07/83	Silhouette	Special Edition

Ross, Jo Ann

	Secret Sins			
	Temperature Rising	03/94	Harlequin	Anthology
27	Risky Pleasure		Harlequin	Intrigue
36	Bait And Switch		Harlequin	Intrigue
	I Do, I Do ... For Now	08/96	Harlequin	Love & Laughter
42	Stormy Courtship	01/85	Harlequin	Temptation
67	Love Thy Neighbor	07/85	Harlequin	Temptation
77	Duskfire	10/85	Harlequin	Temptation
96	Without Precedent	02/86	Harlequin	Temptation
115	A Hero At Heart	07/86	Harlequin	Temptation
126	Magic In The Night	10/86	Harlequin	Temptation
137	Playing For Keeps	01/87	Harlequin	Temptation
153	Tempting Fate	05/87	Harlequin	Temptation
171	Hot On The Trail	09/87	Harlequin	Temptation
187	Worth Waiting For	01/88	Harlequin	Temptation
193	Spirit Of Love	03/88	Harlequin	Temptation
201	In A Class By Himself	05/88	Harlequin	Temptation
209	Wilde 'n' Wonderful	07/88	Harlequin	Temptation
221	Eve's Choice	10/88	Harlequin	Temptation
233	Murphy's Law	01/89	Harlequin	Temptation
296	Guarded Moments	04/90	Harlequin	Temptation
333	Tangled Hearts	02/91	Harlequin	Temptation
345	Tangled Lives (Spin-Off To #333)	05/91	Harlequin	Temptation
382	Dark Desires	02/92	Harlequin	Temptation
409	The Knight In Shining Armor	09/92	Harlequin	Temptation
432	Star-Crossed Lovers	02/93	Harlequin	Temptation
436	Moonstruck Lovers	03/93	Harlequin	Temptation
453	The Prince & The Showgirl	08/93	Harlequin	Temptation
471	Lovestorm	12/93	Harlequin	Temptation
482	Angel Of Desire	03/94	Harlequin	Temptation
489	The Return Of Caine O' Halloran	05/94	Harlequin	Temptation
506	Scandals	09/94	Harlequin	Temptation
537	Never A Bride (Bachelor Arms)	05/95	Harlequin	Temptation
541	For Richer Or Poorer (Bachelor Arms)	06/95	Harlequin	Temptation
545	Three Grooms And A Wedding	07/95	Harlequin	Temptation
562	Private Passions	11/95	Harlequin	Temptation
585	The Outlaw	05/96	Harlequin	Temptation

Ross, Jo Ann

	Legacy Of Lies	02/95	Mira	
	Stormy Courtship	08/95	Mira	
	Confessions	01/96	Mira	
	Tempting Fate	05/96	Mira	
15	It Happened One Week	03/96	Silhouette	Yours Truly

Ross, Kathryn

109	Playing By The Rules	05/92	Harlequin	Direct
199	By Love Alone	09/94	Harlequin	Direct
214	Total Possession	12/94	Harlequin	Direct
1405	No Regrets	10/91	Harlequin	Presents
1807	Ruthless Contract	04/96	Harlequin	Presents

Ross, Marilyn

| | Delta Flame | | Warner | |

Rossiter, Claire

	Three Seasons Of Askrigg		Ace	
	Ann Of Summer Ho		Ace	
	The White Rose		Ace	
	On The Scent Of Danger		Avalon	Career Romance

Roszel, Renee

	Sex, Lies And Leprechauns	/93	Harlequin	
10	Hostage Heart		Harlequin	American
129	Another Man's Treasure		Harlequin	American
	Getting Over Harry	04/97	Harlequin	Romance
3198	Prince Of Delights	05/92	Harlequin	Romance
3251	A Bride For Ransom	02/93	Harlequin	Romance
3317	Dare To Kiss A Cowboy	06/94	Harlequin	Romance
3370	Make-Believe Marriage	07/95	Harlequin	Romance
3370	To Lasso A Lady	/96	Harlequin	Romance
246	Another Heaven	04/89	Harlequin	Temptation
279	Legendary Lover (Award Of Excellence)	12/89	Harlequin	Temptation
334	Valentine's Knight	02/91	Harlequin	Temptation
378	Unwilling Wife	01/92	Harlequin	Temptation
422	Devil To Pay	02/93	Harlequin	Temptation
468	No More Mr. Nice	11/93	Harlequin	Temptation
483	Sex, Lies And Leprechauns	03/94	Harlequin	Temptation
512	Ghost Whispers	10/94	Harlequin	Temptation
90	Wild Flight	09/83	Silhouette	Desire
207	Wind Shadow	12/84	Silhouette	Special Edition
313	Nobody's Fool	06/86	Silhouette	Special Edition
26	Brides For Brazen Gulch	08/96	Silhouette	Yours Truly

Roth, Jillian

| 55 | Bittersweet Temptation | /84 | Nal | Rapture Romance |
| 71 | On Wings Of Desire | 06/84 | Nal | Rapture Romance |

Roth, Pamela

| 254 | Too Many Weddings | 06/89 | Harlequin | Temptation |

Roth, Pamela
   359   Easy Does It   08/91   Harlequin Temptation
Rothman, Marcy Elias
       The Divided Heart   09/94   Nal Signet Regency
       The Kinder Heart   /94   Signet Regency
       The Lonely Heart   /95   Signet Regency
       The Willing Heart   /95   Signet Regency
Rothwell, Una
  2165   A Long Way To Go   /78   Harlequin
Rowan, Barbara
   663   In Care Of The Doctor   /62   Harlequin
   799   Love Is For Ever   /64   Harlequin
   845   Flower For A Bride   /64   Harlequin
   902   Mountain Of Dreams   /65   Harlequin
  1554   The Keys Of The Castle   /72   Harlequin
Rowan, Deidre
       Silver Wood   /72   Fawcett
       Dragon's Mount   /73   Fawcett
       Shadow Of The Volcano   /75   Fawcett
       Time Of The Burning Mask /76   Fawcett
       Ravensgate   /77   Fawcett
Rowe, Margaret
  2428   The Wild Man   Harlequin Romance
Rowe, Melanie
   133   Sands Of Xanadu   02/82   Silhouette Romance
   129   Sea Of Gold   11/83   Silhouette Special Edition
Rowe, Myra
       Treasure's Golden Dream   Warner
       Cajun Rose   Warner
       Creole Moon   Warner
       Cypress Moon   Warner
       Pair Of Hearts   Warner
       A Splendid Yearning   Warner
       Tender Torment   Zebra
       River Temptress   Zebra Hologram
       Louisiana Lady   Zebra Hologram
       Wild Embrace   Zebra Hologram
Rowe, Patricia
       Keepers Of The Misty Time 04/94   Warner
Royall, Vanessa
       Fires Of Delight   Bantam
       Flames Of Desire   Bantam
       Firebrand's Woman   Bantam
       The Passionate And The Proud Bantam
       Seize The Dawn   Bantam
       Come Faith, Come Fire   /83   Dell

AUTHOR/TITLE INDEX

Rudick, Marilynne
128	Fixing To Stay	10/86	Harlequin Temptation
308	Glory Days	07/90	Harlequin Temptation

Rufe, Barbara
Tempt Not This Flesh		Playboy Press
Barringer House		Playboy Press
Rowleston		Playboy Press
Auldern House		Playboy Press
This Ravaged Heart		Playboy Press
Far Beyond Desire		Playboy Press
Fire And Flesh		Playboy Press

Rupprecht, Olivia
	Letter To My Lover	09/94	Bantam Loveswept
428	Bad Boy Of New Orleans	10/90	Bantam Loveswept
461	Taboo	03/91	Bantam Loveswept
496	Behind Closed Doors	09/91	Bantam Loveswept
507	Date With The Devil	11/91	Bantam Loveswept
550	I Do!	06/92	Bantam Loveswept
569	Saints And Sinners	09/92	Bantam Loveswept
580	Hurts So Good	11/92	Bantam Loveswept
683	Honeymoon	04/94	Bantam Loveswept
683	Shotgun Wedding	04/94	Bantam Loveswept
730	Pistol In His Pocket	03/95	Bantam Loveswept
	Moonlight, Madness & Magic	05/93	Doubleday Anthology

Rush, Mallory
	Outlaws And Heroes - "Danger & Desire"	09/95	Harlequin Anthology
	Love Game	07/95	Harlequin Promotion
448	Love Slave	06/93	Harlequin Temptation
558	Kiss Of The Beast	10/95	Harlequin Temptation

Rush, Phillip
301	Mary Read, Buccaneer	/54	Harlequin

Russell, Ray'
Princess Pamela		Historical

Russell, Victor
329	People Of The Night	/55	Harlequin

Rutland, Eva
1	Matched Pair	05/89	Harlequin Regency
20	The Vicar's Daughter	02/90	Harlequin Regency
28	Enterprising Lady	06/90	Harlequin Regency
45	The Willful Lady	03/91	Harlequin Regency
89	Gretna Bride	01/93	Harlequin Regency
2897	To Love Them All		Harlequin Romance
2944	At First Sight		Harlequin Romance
3064	No Accounting For Love		Harlequin Romance
3240	Always Christmas	12/92	Harlequin Romance
3283	Foreign Affair	10/93	Harlequin Romance

Rutland, Eva

3412 Private Dancer   06/96 Harlequin Romance

Ryan, Allyson

471 Secrets Of Magnolia House   01/93 Silhouette Intimate Moments

398 Love Can Make It Better   08/87 Silhouette Special Edition

460 Moon And Sun   06/88 Silhouette Special Edition

Ryan, Jenna

88 Cast In Wax   Harlequin Intrigue

99 Suspended Animation   Harlequin Intrigue

118 Cloak And Dagger   Harlequin Intrigue

138 Carnival   Harlequin Intrigue

145 Southern Cross   Harlequin Intrigue

173 Masquerade   11/91 Harlequin Intrigue

189 Illusions   07/92 Harlequin Intrigue

205 Puppets #2   02/93 Harlequin Intrigue

221 Bittersweet Legacy   04/93 Harlequin Intrigue

239 The Visitor   08/93 Harlequin Intrigue

251 Midnight Masque   11/93 Harlequin Intrigue

265 When Night Falls   03/94 Harlequin Intrigue

364 Belladonna   03/96 Harlequin Intrigue

Ryan, Kristal

152 Persistence Pays   06/93 Meteor Kismet

Ryan, Nan

Desert Storm

Kathleen's Surrender

Mile High

Outlaw's Kiss   Bantam

Stardust   Bantam

The Legend Of Love   09/91 Dell

Written In The Stars   01/93 Dell

Cloudcastle   Dell

Savage Heat   Dell

Silken Boundage   Dell

Sun God   Dell

A Lifetime Of Heaven   02/94 Dell

The Legend Of Love   09/91 Dell

Because Your Mine   05/95 Nal Topaz

351 Love In The Air   05/87 Silhouette Desire

Love Me Tonight   08/94 Topaz Historical

Ryan, Patricia

A Sense Of Things   05/95 Harlequin Temptation

Flash Point   03/96 Harlequin Temptation

540 The Return Of The Black Sheep   05/95 Harlequin Temptation

571 A Burning Touch   01/96 Harlequin Temptation

A Golden Ribbon   01/96 Nal

Promised Heaven   06/96 Nal

AUTHOR/TITLE INDEX

Ryan, Patricia
    Falcon's Fire   12/95   Nal

Ryan, Rachel
   21   Love's Encore   Dell Candlelight Ecstasy
  151   Prime Time   /83   Dell Candlelight Ecstasy

Ryan, Taylor
  262   Love's Wild Wager (March Madness)   03/95   Harlequin Historical
  312   Birdie   04/96   Harlequin Historical

Ryberg, Dr. Percy E.
  161   Health, Sex And Birth Control   /52   Harlequin

Rydell, Sierra
  772   On Middle Ground   10/92   Silhouette Special Edition
  900   Homeward Bound   07/94   Silhouette Special Edition
 1044   The Road Back Home   07/96   Silhouette Special Edition

Ryder, Alex
  35   The Barbarian's Bride   07/96   Harlequin Presents

Sabatini, Rafael
    Scaramouche   Historical
  217   The Sea Hawk   /53   Harlequin

Saber, Robert O.
  305   Out Of The Night   /54   Harlequin

Sackett, Susan
    Passion's Gold   Avon
    Seaswept   Zebra
    A Taste Of Passion   Zebra
    A Stranger's Caress   04/94   Zebra
    Desire's Chains   Zebra Heartfire
    Emerald Angel   Zebra Heartfire
    Lawless Ecstasy   /90   Zebra Heartfire
    Moonlight Caress   Zebra Heartfire
    Passion's Golden Fire   Zebra Heartfire
    Island Captive   Zebra Heartfire
    A Taste Of Passion   07/92   Zebra Lovegram
    Reckless   05/93   Zebra Lovegram

Sadler, Barry
    Casca #12: The African Mercenary   07/92   Jove

Sage, Kathleen
    Many Fires   12/95   Jove Historical
    Out Of Eden   06/96   Jove Historical

Sage, Sheryl
    Passionate Surrender   09/93   Avon

Sala, Sharon
    Dreamcatcher   /96
    Second Chances   /96
    Chance Mc Call   08/93   Harper
  1   Diamond   02/94   Harper Gambler's Trilogy

Sala, Sharon

2	Queen		Harper Gambler's Trilogy
3	Lucky		Harper Gambler's Trilogy
60	Sara's Angel	09/91	Meteor
73	King's Ransom	01/92	Meteor
109	Honor's Promise	10/92	Meteor
158	Gentle Persuasion	07/93	Meteor
130	Always A Lady	02/93	Meteor Kismet
597	Annie And The Outlaw (The Wild West)	10/94	Silhouette Intimate Moments
650	The Miracle Man (Romantic Traditions)	07/95	Silhouette Intimate Moments
687	When You Call My Name	01/96	Silhouette Intimate Moments

Sale, Richard

59	Cardinal Rock	/50	Harlequin
79	Lazarus 7	/50	Harlequin

Salerno, Ann

195	Rain Of Flowers		Harlequin Superromance

Salisbury, Carola

Dark Inheritance		Historical

Salvato, Sharon

Donovan's Daughter		Bantam
Better Eden		Bantam

Samuel, Barbara

Lucien's Fall	08/95	Harper
A Bed Of Spices	09/93	Harper Historical
A Winter Ballad	11/94	Harper Monogram

Sanders, Betty Jane

1131	His Secret Son	01/96	Silhouette Romance

Sanders, Glenda

	Stardust	09/94	Avon Anthology
	More Than Kisses	12/94	Avon Historical
	Marriage By Design	04/94	Harlequin Anthology
	Temptation 10th Anniversary	06/94	Harlequin Temptation
234	Gypsy	01/89	Harlequin Temptation
257	Daddy, Darling	07/89	Harlequin Temptation
277	The All-American Male	12/89	Harlequin Temptation
300	Island Nights	05/90	Harlequin Temptation
316	Dark Secrets (Editor's Choice)	09/90	Harlequin Temptation
329	Doctor, Darling	01/91	Harlequin Temptation
356	A Human Touch	07/91	Harlequin Temptation
383	Babycakes	02/92	Harlequin Temptation
402	Haunting Secrets (Editor's Choice)	07/92	Harlequin Temptation
437	Dr. Hunk	04/93	Harlequin Temptation
454	Lovers' Secrets	08/93	Harlequin Temptation
493	What Might Have Been (Lost Loves)	06/94	Harlequin Temptation
510	Playboy Mc Coy	10/94	Harlequin Temptation
547	Not This Guy! (Grooms On The Run)	07/95	Harlequin Temptation

AUTHOR/TITLE INDEX

Sanders, Glenda
566	Look Into My Eyes	12/95	Harlequin Temptation
599	Midnight Train From Georgia	08/96	Harlequin Temptation

Sanders, L.
Lady Lucinde's Locket	11/90	Nal

Sanders, Madelyn
158	Under Venice		Harlequin Intrigue
187	Sarabande	06/92	Harlequin Intrigue
218	Darkness At Cottonwood Hall	03/93	Harlequin Intrigue
234	Laird's Mount	07/93	Harlequin Intrigue

Sanderson, Nora
752	The Ordeal Of Nurse Thompson	/63	Harlequin
761	The House In New Zealand	/63	Harlequin
762	Hospital In New Zealand	/63	Harlequin
787	The Two Faces Of Nurse Roberts	/64	Harlequin
865	A Partner For Doctor Philip	/64	Harlequin
922	The Taming Of Nurse Conway	/65	Harlequin
937	The Case For Nurse Sheridan	/65	Harlequin

Sandifer, Linda
Came A Stranger	07/94	
Embrace The Wind		
Heart Of The Hunter		Zebra
Pride's Passion		Zebra
Mountain Ecstasy		Zebra Heartfire
Midnight Hearts		Zebra Heartfire
Desire's Treasure	05/95	Zebra Lovegram

Sands, Glenda
337	The Mockingbird Suite	01/85	Silhouette Romance
389	A Taste Of Romance	10/85	Silhouette Romance
409	Heart Shift	01/86	Silhouette Romance
434	Tall, Dark And Handsome	05/86	Silhouette Romance
447	Amended Dreams	07/86	Silhouette Romance
477	Hero On Hold	12/86	Silhouette Romance
496	Logan's Woman	04/87	Silhouette Romance
514	The Things We Do For Love	07/87	Silhouette Romance
538	Treadmills And Pinwheels	11/87	Silhouette Romance
565	The Man Of Her Dreams	03/88	Silhouette Romance
602	Home Again	09/88	Silhouette Romance

Santore, Sue
480	A Man For Sylvia	01/87	Silhouette Romance

Sargent, Katherine
Cajun Lover		Ballantine Historical
Outcasts From Eden		Ballantine Historical

Sark, Sylvia
7	Sophie And The Prince	Mills & Boon

Satinwood, Deborah

AUTHOR/TITLE INDEX

Saunders, Jean
    Scarlet Rebel
149 The Kissing Time   05/82 Silhouette Romance
216 Love's Sweet Music   04/83 Silhouette Romance
243 The Language Of Love 08/83 Silhouette Romance
261 Taste The Wine   11/83 Silhouette Romance
289 Partners In Love   04/84 Silhouette Romance
    Golden Destiny   Tapestry
Saunders, Jeraldine
    Spanish Seranade   02/92 Harper
Saunders, Kate
    Night Shall Overtake Us   07/94 Dutton
Saunders, Laura
    Never To Be Alone   Dell Candlelight
Savage, Christina
    Tempest
    Love's Wildest Fires   Bantam
Savery, Jeanne
    Cupid Laughs Last
    The Late Lord Crawmere
    A Reformed Rake   07/94
    A Handful Of Promises   04/92 Walker Regency
    The Last Of The Winter Roses 07/91 Walker Regency
    An Acceptable Arrangement 11/92 Walker Regency
    Lady Stephanie   06/96 Zebra
    A Mother's Delight   03/95 Zebra Anthology
    A June Betrothal   04/93 Zebra Anthology
    A Christmas Treasury   11/94 Zebra Regency
    The Widow And The Rake 10/93 Zebra Regency
    A Lady's Deception   05/95 Zebra Regency
Sawyer, Lee
156 Time Remembered   06/82 Silhouette Romance
Sawyer, Meryl
    Never Kiss A Stranger   06/92 Dell
    Blind Chance   Dell
    Midnight In Marrakesh   Dell
    Promise Me Anything   12/94 Dell
Sawyer, Susan
    Courting Rebecca   12/95 Avon
    Loving Tyler   01/95 Avon Historical
Saxe, Coral Smith
    Silver And Sapphire   12/88 Bantam
169 Captured Moment   04/93 Harlequin Historical
    Enchantment   08/94 Love Spell
    A Stolen Rose   10/95 Love Spell
Saxon, Antonia

Saxon, Antonia

88	Paradiso	04/83	Silhouette	Special Edition
141	Above The Moon	01/84	Silhouette	Special Edition

Scanlan, Patricia

	Finishing Touches	11/94	Dell

Scheidies, Carolyn R.

	To Keep Faith	02/96	Barbour & Co.	Bonds Of Love #1
	To Be Strong	10/94	Barbour & Co.	Heartsong Presents

Schmidt, Anna

381	Give And Take	10/87	Silhouette	Desire

Schneider, Rosemary

925	Best Laid Plans		Harlequin Presents

Schofield, William G.

69	Payoff In Black	/50	Harlequin	
470	The Cat In The Convoy	/59	Harlequin	

Schone, Robin

	Awaken, My Love	07/95	Avon Time-Travel

Schoonover, Lawrence

	Key Of Gold		Historical

Schroeder, Martha

16	What Engagement Ring?!	03/96	Silhouette	Yours Truly

Schuler, Candace

	Father Knows Last!	05/94	Harlequin	Anthology
	There's Something About A Cowboy	06/95	Harlequin	By Request: Anthology
38	Easy Lovin'	09/96	Harlequin	Here Come The Grooms
43	For The Love Of Mike	/95	Harlequin	Men Made In America
	Just Another Pretty Face	09/93	Harlequin	Temptation
	No Man's Wife	12/96	Harlequin	Temptation
	Luck Of The Draw	06/96	Harlequin	Temptation
28	Desire's Child	09/84	Harlequin	Temptation
102	Designing Woman	04/86	Harlequin	Temptation
129	For The Love Of Mike	11/86	Harlequin	Temptation
183	Home Fires	12/87	Harlequin	Temptation
205	Soul Mates	06/88	Harlequin	Temptation
250	Almost Paradise	05/89	Harlequin	Temptation
261	Sophisticated Lady	08/89	Harlequin	Temptation
284	Wildcat	01/90	Harlequin	Temptation
331	Easy Lovin'	01/91	Harlequin	Temptation
375	A Dangerous Game	12/91	Harlequin	Temptation
397	The Mighty Quinn (Rebels & Rogues)	06/92	Harlequin	Temptation
451	The Other Woman	07/93	Harlequin	Temptation
467	The Right Direction (Hollywood Dynasty)	11/93	Harlequin	Temptation
497	The Personal Touch	07/94	Harlequin	Temptation
549	Lovers And Strangers (Bachelor Arms)	08/95	Harlequin	Temptation
553	Seduced And Betrayed	09/95	Harlequin	Temptation
557	Passion And Scandal	10/95	Harlequin	Temptation

AUTHOR/TITLE INDEX

Schulze, Dallas

	The Way Home	01/95	Dell	
154	Mackenzie's Lady		Harlequin	American
185	Stormwalker	02/87	Harlequin	American
235	Tell Me A Story		Harlequin	American
263	Lost And Found	10/88	Harlequin	American
291	Together Always		Harlequin	American
302	The Morning After		Harlequin	American
317	Of Dreams And Magic		Harlequin	American
349	Saturday's Child		Harlequin	American
368	A Summer To Come Home		Harlequin	American
394	Rafferty's Choice		Harlequin	American
409	A Practical Marriage	10/91	Harlequin	American
430	Charity's Angel	03/92	Harlequin	American
458	Angel And The Bad Man	10/92	Harlequin	American
465	A Christmas Marriage	12/92	Harlequin	American
486	Strong Arms Of The Law	06/93	Harlequin	American
	Outlaws And Heroes - "Gabriel's Angel"	09/95	Harlequin	Anthology
16	A Practical Marriage	05/96	Harlequin	Here Come The Grooms
134	Temptation's Price	07/92	Harlequin	Historical
6	Stormwalker	09/93	Harlequin	Men Made In America
	Birds, Bees & Babies - 1994	05/94	Silhouette	Anthology
462	The Hell-Raiser	11/92	Silhouette	Initmate Moments
170	Moment To Moment	12/86	Silhouette	Intimate Moments
247	Donovan's Promise	07/88	Silhouette	Intimate Moments
318	The Vow	01/90	Silhouette	Intimate Moments
377	The Baby Bargain	04/91	Silhouette	Intimate Moments
414	Everything But Marriage	01/92	Silhouette	Intimate Moments
500	Secondhand Husband	06/93	Silhouette	Intimate Moments
565	Michael's Father (American Hero)	05/94	Silhouette	Intimate Moments
584	Snow Bride	08/94	Silhouette	Intimate Moments
608	A Very Convenient Marriage	12/94	Silhouette	Intimate Moments
643	Another Man's Wife	06/95	Silhouette	Intimate Moments
727	Addie And The Renegade	08/96	Silhouette	Intimate Moments

Schulze, Hertha

120	Before And After	12/85	Bantam	Loveswept
196	Solid Gold Prospect	06/87	Bantam	Loveswept
222	Twice A Miracle	10/88	Harlequin	Temptation

Schulze, Julie

| 236 | Wildflower | | Harlequin | American |

Schwab, John Edison

| | 1968 - A Love Story | 11/94 | Pinnacle |

Scofield, Carin

| 122 | Winterfire | 12/81 | Silhouette | Romance |
| 249 | Silverwood | 09/83 | Silhouette | Romance |

Scofield, Lee

793

AUTHOR/TITLE INDEX

Scott, Amanda

	Lord Lyford's Secret		Nal
	The Bath Eccentric's Son	02/92	Nal Regency
	The Forthright Lady Gillian	11/92	Nal Regency
	Lady Escapade	01/86	Nal Regency
	Mistress Of The Hunt	02/87	Nal Regency
	Lady Meriel's Duty	09/87	Nal Regency
	Lady Brittany's Choice	05/88	Nal Regency
	Ravenwood's Lady	05/88	Nal Regency
	The Fugitive Heiress	09/88	Nal Regency
	The Kidnapped Bride	10/88	Nal Regency
	Greyfalcon's Reward	12/88	Nal Regency
	The Madcap Marchioness	05/89	Nal Regency
	Lady Hawk's Folly		Nal Regency
	An Affair Of Honor		Nal Regency
	The Indomitable Miss Harris		Nal Regency
	Lord Greyfalcon's Revenge		Nal Regency
	Lord Abberley's Nemesis		Nal Regency
	The Bath Charade	07/91	Nal Signet Regency
	The Bath Quadrille	01/91	Nal Signet Regency
	Dangerous Illusions	06/94	Pinnacle Denise Little Presents
	Highland Fling	02/95	Pinnacle Denise Little Presents
	The Bawdy Bride	09/95	Pinnacle Denise Little Presents
	Dangerous Games	06/96	Pinnacle Denise Little Presents
	The Fickle Fortune Hunter	09/93	Signet

Scott, Barbara

	Haunts Of The Heart	12/95	Southwest Publ.

Scott, Barbara A.

	Tug Of War	/93	May Davenport

Scott, Bradford

133	Frontier Doctor	/51	Harlequin
259	Silver City	/53	Harlequin

Scott, Celia

2568	Seeds Of April		Harlequin Romance
2638	Starfire		Harlequin Romance
2735	Where The Gods Dwell		Harlequin Romance
2831	A Talent For Loving		Harlequin Romance
2945	Catch A Dream		Harlequin Romance
2998	Love On A String		Harlequin Romance
3040	Rumor Has It		Harlequin Romance
3087	Give Me Your Answer		Harlequin Romance
3306	Relative Attraction	03/94	Harlequin Romance

Scott, Christine

1077	Hazardous Husband (Bundles Of Joy)	04/95	Silhouette Romance
1099	Imitation Bride	08/95	Silhouette Romance
1134	Cinderella Bride	02/96	Silhouette Romance

AUTHOR/TITLE INDEX

Scott, De Loras

	Fool For Love	05/91	Avon Historical
	Devil's Delight	07/92	Avon Romance
	Fortune's Gift	/91	Harlequin Hist. Christmas Stories
12	Bittersweet		Harlequin Historical
40	Fire And Ice		Harlequin Historical
52	The Miss And The Maverick		Harlequin Historical
123	Rogue's Honor	05/92	Harlequin Historical
151	Springtown	02/93	Harlequin Historical
179	Garters And Spurs	07/93	Harlequin Historical
204	Spitfire	01/94	Harlequin Historical
225	Timeless	06/94	Harlequin Historical
277	Addie's Lament	07/95	Harlequin Historical

Scott, Fela Dawson

	Black Wolf		Leisure
	Ghost Dancer	/91	Leisure Historical
	Spirit Of The Mountain	07/95	Leisure Historical

Scott, Joanna

86	In All Honesty	03/85	Silhouette Intimate Moments
50	Dusky Rose	12/80	Silhouette Romance
68	The Marriage Bargain	03/81	Silhouette Romance
117	Manhattan Masquerade	11/81	Silhouette Romance
169	Lover Come Back	08/82	Silhouette Romance
187	Moonlit Magic	11/82	Silhouette Romance
26	A Flight Of Swallows	06/82	Silhouette Special Edition
136	Exclusively Yours	12/83	Silhouette Special Edition
186	Corporate Policy	08/84	Silhouette Special Edition

Scott, Kristal Leigh

	Spring Will Come	/87	Worldwide Lib.
	Santa Fe Surrender	10/92	Zebra
	Bound By Ecstasy		Zebra Heartfire
	Lone Star Seduction		Zebra Heartfire

Scott, Lisa

	Fool For Love	05/91	Avon

Scott, Melissa

147	Territorial Rights	07/84	Silhouette Desire

Scott, Theresa

	Savage Revenge		Leisure
	Captive Legacy	01/96	Leisure
	Their First Noel: "The Treasure"	11/95	Leisure Anthology
	Bride Of Desire		Leisure Historical
	Savage Betrayal	/95	Leisure Historical
	Apache Conquest	07/93	Leisure Historical
	Broken Promise	/95	Leisure Hunters Of The Ice Age
	Yesterday's Dawn		Leisure Hunters Of The Ice Age
	Dark Renegade	06/94	Love Spell Hunters Of The Ice Age

Scott, Virginia Campbell
    Different Drummer   Cora Verlag

Scottalinie, Lisa
    Final Appeal   12/94   Dell

Seabaugh, Carolyn

468	Butterfly Autumn	11/86	Silhouette Romance
580	Lean On Me	02/90	Silhouette Special Edition
634	Cicada Summer	11/90	Silhouette Special Edition
1050	Just A Family Man	08/96	Silhouette Special Edition

Seale, Sara

469	Maggy	/59	Harlequin
560	Wintersbride	/60	Harlequin
583	This Merry Bond	/61	Harlequin
645	The Gentle Prisoner	/62	Harlequin
657	Orphan Bride	/62	Harlequin
661	Doctor's Ward	/62	Harlequin
692	The Only Charity	/62	Harlequin
719	Forbidden Island	/63	Harlequin
747	Lucy Lamb, Doctor's Wife	/63	Harlequin
781	Then She Fled Me	/63	Harlequin
816	The Youngest Bridesmaid	/64	Harlequin
838	Dear Dragon	/64	Harlequin
870	The Dark Stranger	/64	Harlequin
896	Child Friday	/65	Harlequin
918	These Delights	/65	Harlequin
949	The Third Uncle	/65	Harlequin
973	Time Of Grace	/65	Harlequin
991	Charity Child	/66	Harlequin
1021	Folly To Be Wise	/66	Harlequin
1045	Green Girl	/66	Harlequin
1072	The Young Amanda	/66	Harlequin
1096	Cloud Castle	/67	Harlequin
1114	Trevallion	/67	Harlequin
1144	The Truant Bride	/67	Harlequin
1174	The English Tutor	/68	Harlequin
1197	Penny Plain	/68	Harlequin
1218	Beggara May Sing	/68	Harlequin
1263	The Lordly One	/68	Harlequin
1293	I Know My Love	/69	Harlequin
1324	The Queen Of Hearts	/69	Harlequin
1347	The Truant Spirit	/69	Harlequin
1392	That Young Person	/70	Harlequin
1524	Dear Professor	/71	Harlequin
1597	The Unknown Mr. Brown	/72	Harlequin
1988	My Heart's Desire	/76	Harlequin
97	To Catch A Unicorn	/75	Harlequin Presents
137	The Silver Sty	/76	Harlequin Presents

Searight, Ellen
566   Golden Interlude   Dell Candlelight
Sears, Ruth Mc Carthy
    Jolie Benoit, R.N.   Dell Candlelight
175   The Encounter   Dell Candlelight
Segal, Harriet
    Susquehanna
    Catch The Wind
    Shady Mountain
Seger, Maura
    Elizabeth
    Sarah
    Perchance To Dream   Avon
    Fortune's Tide   05/90   Avon
107   Light On The Mountain   01/92   Harlequin Historical
127   The Lady And The Laird   06/92   Harlequin Historical
159   The Taming Of Amelia   02/93   Harlequin Historical
183   The Seduction Of Deanna   08/93   Harlequin Historical
244   The Tempting Of Julia   11/94   Harlequin Historical
181   Spring Frost, Summer Fire   Harlequin Superromance
69   Undercover   08/85   Harlequin Temptation
    Beloved Enemy   01/92   Harper
    Forevermore   05/94   Harper Monogram
    Rakes And Rogues   06/93   Penguin Super Signet Historical
    Rebellious Love   Pocket
    Forbidden Love   Pocket
    Flame On The Sun   Pocket
    Defiant Love   Pocket
    Moonlight And Memories   09/93   Signet
    Starbright   /86   Sil. Christmas Stories
    A Gift Beyond Price   /90   Sil. Christmas Treasures
282   Cajun Summer   05/86   Silhouette Desire
295   Treasure Hunt   08/86   Silhouette Desire
723   Princess Mc Gee   07/92   Silhouette Desire
61   Silver Zephyr   08/84   Silhouette Intimate Moments
96   Golden Chimera   05/85   Silhouette Intimate Moments
108   Comes A Stranger   08/85   Silhouette Intimate Moments
137   Shadows Of The Heart   04/86   Silhouette Intimate Moments
149   Quest Of The Eagle   07/86   Silhouette Intimate Moments
162   Dark Of The Moon   10/86   Silhouette Intimate Moments
176   Happily Ever After   01/87   Silhouette Intimate Moments
194   Legacy   06/87   Silhouette Intimate Moments
209   Sea Gate   10/87   Silhouette Intimate Moments
224   Day And Night   01/88   Silhouette Intimate Moments
236   Conflict Of Interest   04/88   Silhouette Intimate Moments
253   Unforgettable   09/88   Silhouette Intimate Moments
280   Change Of Plans   03/89   Silhouette Intimate Moments

Seger, Maura

342	Painted Lady	07/90	Silhouette	Intimate Moments
389	Caught In The Act	07/91	Silhouette	Intimate Moments
404	Sir Flynn And Lady Constance	10/91	Silhouette	Intimate Moments
464	Castle Of Dreams	12/92	Silhouette	Intimate Moments
520	Prince Conor	09/93	Silhouette	Intimate Moments
561	Full Of Surprises	04/94	Silhouette	Intimate Moments
617	The Surrender Of Nora (Belle Haven Saga)	01/95	Silhouette	Intimate Moments
675	Man Without A Memory	11/95	Silhouette	Intimate Moments
135	A Gift Beyond Price	12/83	Silhouette	Special Edition
492	Man Of The Hour	04/93	Silhouette	Special Edition
	Into The Storm		Warner	
	Before The Wind		Warner	
	Into The Storm		Warner	
	Edge Of Dawn	02/86	Worldwide Libr.	
	Eye Of The Storm		Worldwide Libr.	
	Echo Of Thunder	09/85	Worldwide Libr.	

Seidel, Kathleen Gilles

2	After All These Years		Harlequin	
2	The Same Last Name		Harlequin	American
17	A Risk Worth Taking		Harlequin	American
57	Mirrors And Mistakes		Harlequin	American
80	When Love Isn't Enough	09/84	Harlequin	American
	Till Stars Fall Down	03/94	Nal Signet	
	Again	09/94	Onyx	
	Maybe This Time		Pocket	

Seifert, Elizabeth

326	Girl Intern	/55	Harlequin	
364	Surgeon In Charge	/56	Harlequin	
369	Three Doctors	/56	Harlequin	
375	Miss Doctor	/56	Harlequin	
379	The Doctor Takes A Wife	/57	Harlequin	
392	Doctor Of Mercy	/57	Harlequin	
401	The Doctor Disagrees	/57	Harlequin	

Sellers, Alexandra

13	Captive Of Desire		Harlequin	Superromance
42	Fire In The Wind		Harlequin	Superromance
87	Season Of Storm		Harlequin	Superromance
6	The Forever Kind	04/84	Harlequin	Temptation
73	The Real Man	11/84	Silhouette	Intimate Moments
110	The Male Chauvinist	09/85	Silhouette	Intimate Moments
154	The Old Flame	08/86	Silhouette	Intimate Moments
348	The Best Of Friends	08/90	Silhouette	Intimate Moments
406	The Man Next Door	11/91	Silhouette	Intimate Moments
539	A Gentleman And A Scholar	12/93	Silhouette	Intimate Moments
579	The Vagabond	07/94	Silhouette	Intimate Moments
635	Dearest Enemy	04/95	Silhouette	Intimate Moments

AUTHOR/TITLE INDEX

Sellers, Alexandra
  689 Roughneck   01/96 Silhouette Intimate Moments

Sellers, Catherine
    1 Always   07/90 Meteor
   75 Rainbows & Love Songs   01/92 Meteor
  139 Fair Warning   04/93 Meteor Kismet

Sellers, Lorraine
   15 Shadow Dance   08/83 Silhouette Intimate Moments

Seton, Anya
       Green Darkness
       Smouldering Fires
       Katherine
       Winthrop Woman   Historical
       Devil Water   /62 Avon
       The Turquoise   /49 Avon
       The Mistletoe And The Sword /55 Avon
       Dragonwyck   /43 Pocket
       Foxfire   /50 Pyramid Books
       The Hearth And The Eagle   /48 Pyramid Books

Seymour, Ana
       Gabriel's Lady   10/96 Harlequin Historical
       Lucky Bride   01/97 Harlequin Historical
  116 The Bandit's Bride   03/92 Harlequin Historical
  173 Angel Of The Lake   06/93 Harlequin Historical
  238 Brides For Sale   09/94 Harlequin Historical
  290 Moonrise   10/95 Harlequin Historical
  318 Frontier Bride   05/96 Harlequin Historical

Shane, Sandi
   91 No Perfect Season   04/85 Silhouette Intimate Moments
  257 Sweet Burning   08/85 Silhouette Special Edition

Shannon, Bess
  298 Going, Going, Gone!   05/90 Harlequin Temptation

Shannon, Carl
   91 Lady, That's My Skull   /51 Harlequin

Shannon, Colleen
       The Hawk's Lady
       The Tender Devil
       Wild Heart Tamed
       Surrender The Night   07/92 Jove
       Midnight Rider   Jove
       Golden Fires   11/93 Jove Historical

Shannon, Evelyn
   84 Two For The Road   11/85 Harlequin Temptation

Shapiro, Joan
  151 Daniel Albatross   06/93 Meteor Kismet
       For Emmy's Sake   03/93 Zebra

AUTHOR/TITLE INDEX

Shapiro, Joan

Mac & Mike	04/93	Zebra
Dori's Miracle	12/94	Zebra
Merry Christmas My Love	11/93	Zebra Anthology
Hello Love	03/93	Zebra To Love Again
Sweets For The Sweet	07/94	Zebra To Love Again

Sharpe, Alice

Paradise Betrayed	/92	Avalon
A Time For Joy	/92	Avalon
Desert Magic	/92	Avalon
Sail Away!	/91	Avalon
Yesterday's Dreams	/91	Avalon
Deadly Inheritance	/91	Avalon
Annabelle's Secret	/91	Avalon
A Garland Of Love		Avalon
Just One More Secret		Avalon
Wedding Bell Blues	08/92	Avalon
China Moon	07/93	Avalon
A Storybook Love		Avalon Career Romance
Murder At The Marina		Avalon Mystery Romance
The Vanishing Bridegroom		Avalon Mystery Romance
1137 Going To The Chapel	02/96	Silhouette Romance

Shaw, Catherine

2465 Chateau Of Dreams		Harlequin Romance

Shaw, Linda

Ballad In Blue	/79	Ballantine
80 Odessa Gold	06/91	Harlequin Historical
10 Way Of The Willow	01/94	Harlequin Men Made In America
17 One Pale, Fawn Glove	06/94	Harlequin Men Made In America
Songbird		Pocket
The Innocent Deception		Richard Gallen
The Satin Vixen		Richard Gallen
78 The Sweet Rush Of April	01/85	Silhouette Intimate Moments
324 Case Dismissed	02/90	Silhouette Intimate Moments
360 One Sweet Sin	11/90	Silhouette Intimate Moments
458 Indian Summer	11/92	Silhouette Intimate Moments
19 December's Wine	05/82	Silhouette Special Edition
43 All She Ever Wanted	09/82	Silhouette Special Edition
67 After The Rain	01/83	Silhouette Special Edition
97 Way Of The Willow	06/83	Silhouette Special Edition
121 A Thistle In The Spring	10/83	Silhouette Special Edition
151 A Love Song And You	03/84	Silhouette Special Edition
224 One Pale, Fawn Glove	03/85	Silhouette Special Edition
276 Kisses Don't Count	11/85	Silhouette Special Edition
325 Something About Summer	08/86	Silhouette Special Edition
367 Fire At Dawn	02/87	Silhouette Special Edition
403 Santiago Heat	09/87	Silhouette Special Edition

Shaw, Linda

450	Disarray	04/88	Silhouette	Special Edition
492	Thunder High	11/88	Silhouette	Special Edition
540	Love This Stranger	07/89	Silhouette	Special Edition
	Jillie's Secret	/92	Silhouette	To Mother With Love

Shay, Kathryn

659	The Father Factor	09/95	Harlequin	Superromance

Shayne, Maggie

	Fairytale	05/96	Avon	
18	Twilight Phantasies	10/93	Harlequin	Shadows
30	Twilight Memories (Wings In The Night)	04/94	Harlequin	Shadows
38	Kiss Of The Shadow Man	08/94	Harlequin	Shadows
47	Twilight Illusions (Wings In The Night)	01/95	Harlequin	Shadows
	Strangers In The Night: "Beyond Twilight"	10/95	Silhouette	Anthology
522	Reckless Angel	09/93	Silhouette	Intimate Moments
568	Miranda's Viking (Spellbound)	05/94	Silhouette	Intimate Moments
598	Forgotten Vows...?	10/94	Silhouette	Intimate Moments
633	Out-Of-This-World Marriage (Spellbound)	04/95	Silhouette	Intimate Moments
694	Forever, Dad	02/96	Silhouette	Intimate Moments
716	The Littlest Cowboy	06/96	Silhouette	Intimate Moments

Sheehan, Michael

	The Cry Of The Jackal	/91	Avalon
	Harvest Of Love		Avalon Career Romance

Sheehan, Nancy

	The Heart's Journey	08/92	Avalon

Sheldon, Sidney

	The Stars Shine Down	09/93	Warner

Shellabarger, Samuel

	Lord Vanity	Historical

Shelley, Elizabeth

	The Caravan Of Desire	Richard Gallen

Shelley, Lauren

582	A Man Called Regret	07/94	Silhouette	Intimate Moments

Shepherd, Perdita

	A Promise In The Wind

Sheridan, Jane

	Damaris	St. Martin's
	My Lady Hayden	St. Martin's
	The Counsellor Heart	St. Martin's
	The Death Of An Angel	St. Martin's
	Gallow's Child	St. Martin's
	Love At Sunset	St. Martin's
	I, Martha Adams	St. Martin's
	Judgement Day	St. Martin's
	The Rockefeller Gift	St. Martin's
	The Windsor Plot	St. Martin's

Sheridan, Jane
    The Witch Hill Murders   St. Martin's
    The Brandenberg Hotel   St. Martin's
    Copper Gold   St. Martin's
Sherman, Jory
    Horne's Law   11/90   Tor
    The Medicine Horn   /91   Tor
    Grass Kingdom   /91   Warner
  1 Eagles Of Destiny   04/90   Zebra   Santa Fe Trail Trilogy
  2 The Rose And The Flame   /91   Zebra   Santa Fe Trail Trilogy
Sherrill, Suzanne
    Restoring Love   /82   Dell   Candlelight Ecstasy
    Desirable Compromise   /84   Dell   Candlelight Ecstasy
Sherrod, Barbara
    Gamester's Lady   09/94   Nal Signet   Regency
    Mary Ashe   Warner
    Lady Devine   Warner
    The Players   Warner   Regency
Sherrod, Velda
    A Leaf In The Wind   05/96   Leisure
Shertzer, Linda
    The Quilting Circle   /96   Berkley   Anthology
    Chasing Rainbows   09/94   Diamond   A Town Called Harmony
    Home Fires   12/92   Diamond   Homespun
    Pickett's Fence   07/94   Diamond   Homespun
    Home Again   06/96   Jove   Historical
    Highland Fling   12/93   Jove   Historical Anthology
    Homeward Bound   06/95   Jove   Homespun
Sherwood, Elizabeth
    Now And Forever   12/95   Pinnacle   Regency
    Louisiana Rose   09/94   Zebra   Lovegram
Sherwood, Valerie
    This Loving Torment
    These Golden Pleasures
    This Towering Passion
    Bold Breathless Love
    Rash Reckless Love
    Wild, Willful Love
    Rich Radiant Love
    Lonely, Lying Lips
    Born To Love
    Her Shining Splendor
    Her Crowning Glory
    Lisbon   Nal
    To Love A Rogue   Nal Onyx
    Love Song   Pocket

Sherwood, Valerie

	Wind Song		Pocket
	Night Song		Pocket
	Her Shining Splendor		Warner

Shields, Dinah

29	Just Before Dawn		Harlequin Intrigue

Shiplett, June Lund

	Lady Wildcat		
	Hold Back The Sun		Sweet & Savage
110	Sweet Vengeance	01/92	Harlequin Historical
139	Boston Renegade	09/92	Harlequin Historical
	Defy The Savage		Nal
	Gathering Of The Winds		Nal
	Journey To Yesterday		Nal
	The Raging Winds Of Heaven		Nal
	Reap The Bitter Winds		Nal
	Return To Yesterday		Nal
	The Wild Storms Of Heaven		Nal
	Winds Of Betrayal		Nal
	Wild Winds Calling	11/91	Nal

Shock, Marianne

69	The Queen's Defense	11/84	Bantam Loveswept
101	Worthy Opponents	07/85	Bantam Loveswept
127	Storm's Thunder	02/86	Bantam Loveswept
172	Inherited	12/86	Bantam Loveswept
412	Run Away Home	10/87	Silhouette Special Edition
952	What Price Glory	04/95	Silhouette Special Edition

Shoebridge, Marjorie

	Bride Of The Saracen Stone		
	Destiny's Desires		
	Reluctant Rapture		Leisure
	Ranleigh Court		Playboy Press
	A Wreath Of Orchids		Playboy Press
	To Love A Stranger		Warner
	Ranleigh Court		Warner

Shore, Anne

558	Tender Is The Touch		Dell Candlelight

Shore, Edwina

1172	Just Another Married Man		Harlequin Presents
1437	Not His Property	02/92	Harlequin Presents
2753	A Will To Love		Harlequin Romance
2798	The Last Barrier		Harlequin Romance
2946	A Not So Perfect Marriage		Harlequin Romance
2962	Storm Clouds Gathering		Harlequin Romance

Shore, Francine

	Lover's Run	07/84	Nal Rapture Romance

Silverwood, Jane

375	Handle With Care		Harlequin Superromance
434	High Stakes		Harlequin Superromance
438	Dark Waters		Harlequin Superromance
442	Bright Secrets		Harlequin Superromance
552	Eye Of The Jaguar	06/93	Harlequin Superromance
46	Voyage Of The Heart	02/85	Harlequin Temptation
93	Slow Melt	02/86	Harlequin Temptation
117	A Permanent Arrangement	08/86	Harlequin Temptation

Simmons, Deborah

	Heart's Masquerade	10/89	Avon
132	The Fortune Hunter	07/92	Harlequin Historical
185	Silent Heart	08/93	Harlequin Historical
208	The Squire's Daughter	02/94	Harlequin Historical
241	The Devil's Lady	10/94	Harlequin Historical
258	The Vicar's Daughter	02/95	Harlequin Historical
284	Taming The Wolf	09/95	Harlequin Historical
317	The Devil Earl	05/96	Harlequin Historical

Simmons, Mary Kay

With Rapture Bound

Simmons, Suzanne

	Desert Rogue	06/92	Avon Romance
12	The Tempestuous Lovers		Dell Candlelight Ecstasy
	Never As Strangers	/82	Dell Ecstasy
	As Night Follows Day	/82	Dell Ecstasy
	Summer Storm	/79	Mac Fadden Romance
	Winter Wine	/80	Mac Fadden Romance
	From This Day Forward	/80	Mac Fadden Romance
	Velvet Morning	/80	Mac Fadden Romance
	Touch The Wind	/80	Mac Fadden Romance
	Diamond In The Rough	01/94	Penguin Topaz
	Bed Of Roses	07/95	Topaz Historical

Simmons, Trana Mae

	Christmas Angels	11/95	Leisure Anthology
	Montana Surrender	08/93	Leisure Historical
	Forever Angels	/95	Leisure Historical
	Bittersweet Promises	/95	Leisure Historical
	Mountain Magic	09/95	Leisure Historical

Simms, Charlotte

	Silver Caress	08/90	Avon

Simms, Suzanne

6	Not His Wedding!	03/96	Harlequin Here Come The Grooms
9	Moment In Time	07/82	Silhouette Desire
17	Of Passion Born	09/82	Silhouette Desire
43	A Wild, Sweet Magic	02/83	Silhouette Desire
61	All Night Long	05/83	Silhouette Desire

Simms, Suzanne

79	So Sweet A Madness	08/83	Silhouette Desire
109	Only This Night	01/84	Silhouette Desire
150	Dream Within A Dream	07/84	Silhouette Desire
258	Nothing Ventured	01/86	Silhouette Desire
299	Moment Of Truth	08/86	Silhouette Desire
718	Not His Wedding!	06/92	Silhouette Desire
754	Not Her Wedding!	12/92	Silhouette Desire
850	The Brainy Beauty (Hazards, Inc.)	04/94	Silhouette Desire
862	The Pirate Princess (Hazards, Inc.)	06/94	Silhouette Desire
923	The Maddening Model (Hazards, Inc.)	04/95	Silhouette Desire

Simon, Joann

Love Once In Passing
Love Once Again
Hold Fast To Love
Beloved Captain

Simon, Laura

A Taste Of Heaven		Berkley
Garden Of Dreams	12/92	Berkley Historical
Until I Return		Worldwide Lib.

Simone, Sonia

Scandalous	01/94	Avon Historical
Brimstone	09/95	Harper
Midsummer Night's Madness	06/95	St. Martin's Anthology

Simons, Renee

187	Colton's Folly	04/87	Silhouette Intimate Moments

Simonson, Sheila

Bar Sinister	/86	Walker
Love And Folly	/89	Walker
Lady Elizabeth's Comet		Walker
A Cousinly Connection		Warner
The Bar Sinister		Zebra Regency
Love And Folly		Zebra Regency

Simpson, Carla

Silken Surrender		
Silver Mistress		
Deceived	05/94	Pinnacle Private Detective
Seduced	05/93	Pinnacle Private Detective
Ravished	12/94	Pinnacle Private Detective
Desperado's Caress		Zebra
Passion's Splendor		Zebra
Seductive Caress		Zebra
Memory And Desire		Zebra
Always, My Love	07/92	Zebra Historical

Simpson, Maggie

577	Baby Bonus	12/93	Harlequin Superromance

AUTHOR/TITLE INDEX

Sinclair, Olga

	The Man At The Manor		Dell Candlelight

Sinclair, Rebecca

	Wild Scottish Embrace		Zebra	
	California Caress		Zebra Heartfire	
	Passion's Wild Delight	05/90	Zebra Heartfire	
	Prairie Angel		Zebra Heartfire	
	Forbidden Desires	07/92	Zebra Lovegram	
	Montana Wildfire	12/91	Zebra Lovegram	
	Dangerous Desires	07/92	Zebra Lovegram	
	Sweet Texas Kiss	03/94	Zebra Lovegram	
	Scottish Ecstasy	04/93	Zebra Lovegram	

Sinclair, Tracy

	Under The Mistletoe	11/86	Silhouette Christmas Stories
39	Paradise Island	10/80	Silhouette Romance
123	Holiday In Jamaica	12/81	Silhouette Romance
174	Flight To Romance	09/82	Silhouette Romance
244	Stars In Her Eyes	09/83	Silhouette Romance
345	Catch A Rising Star	02/85	Silhouette Romance
459	Love Is Forever	09/86	Silhouette Romance
892	Anything But Marriage	10/92	Silhouette Romance
1006	The Best Is Yet To Be (Celebration 1000!)	05/94	Silhouette Romance
12	Never Give Your Heart	03/82	Silhouette Special Edition
34	Mixed Blessings	07/82	Silhouette Special Edition
52	Designed For Love	10/82	Silhouette Special Edition
68	Castles In The Air	01/83	Silhouette Special Edition
105	Fair Exchange	07/83	Silhouette Special Edition
140	Winter Of Love	01/84	Silhouette Special Edition
153	The Tangled Web	03/84	Silhouette Special Edition
183	The Harvest Is Love	08/84	Silhouette Special Edition
208	Pride's Folly	12/84	Silhouette Special Edition
232	Intrigue In Venice	04/85	Silhouette Special Edition
249	A Love So Tender	07/85	Silhouette Special Edition
287	Dream Girl	01/86	Silhouette Special Edition
309	Preview Of Paradise	05/86	Silhouette Special Edition
355	Forgive And Forget	01/87	Silhouette Special Edition
386	Mandrego	06/87	Silhouette Special Edition
421	No Room For Doubt	12/87	Silhouette Special Edition
453	More Precious Than Jewels	05/88	Silhouette Special Edition
481	Champagne For Breakfast	10/88	Silhouette Special Edition
493	Proof Positive	12/88	Silhouette Special Edition
512	Sky High	03/89	Silhouette Special Edition
531	King Of Hearts	06/89	Silhouette Special Edition
565	Miss Robinson Crusoe	12/89	Silhouette Special Edition
584	Willing Partners	03/90	Silhouette Special Edition
605	Golden Adventure	06/90	Silhouette Special Edition
619	The Girl Most Likely To	09/90	Silhouette Special Edition

Sinclair, Tracy

672	A Change Of Place	05/91	Silhouette Special Edition
701	The Man She Married	10/91	Silhouette Special Edition
725	If The Truth Be Told	02/92	Silhouette Special Edition
746	Dreamboat Of The Western World	06/92	Silhouette Special Edition
791	The Cat That Lived On Park Avenue	01/93	Silhouette Special Edition
821	Romance On The Menu	06/93	Silhouette Special Edition
847	Grand Prize Winner! (That Special Woman!)	11/93	Silhouette Special Edition
868	Marry Me Kate	02/94	Silhouette Special Edition
943	The Sultan's Wives (That Special Woman!)	03/95	Silhouette Special Edition
957	Does Anybody Know Who Allison Is?	05/95	Silhouette Special Edition
976	What She Did On Her Summer	08/95	Silhouette Special Edition
1018	For Love Of Her Child	03/96	Silhouette Special Edition

Singer, Kurt

230	Women Spies	/53	Harlequin
426	The World's Greatest Spy Stories	/58	Harlequin
465	My Greatest Crime Story	/59	Harlequin

Singleton, Linda Joy

Love To Spare	03/93	Bantam
Almost Perfect	04/92	Bantam Sweet Dreams
Opposites Attract	06/91	Bantam Sweet Dreams

Sites, Elizabeth

1059	The Man Who Changed Everything	01/95	Silhouette Romance
1094	Stranger In Her Arms	07/95	Silhouette Romance
1136	Make-Believe Mom	02/96	Silhouette Romance

Sizemore, Susan

The Autumn Lord	12/96	Harper
"One Riot, One Ranger"	05/94	Harper Anthology
Tall, Dark & Dangerous	08/95	Harper Anthology
Wings Of The Storm	11/92	Harper Monogram
My First Duchess	12/93	Harper Monogram
My Own True Love	02/94	Harper Monogram
St. Bartholomew's Fair	04/94	Harper Monogram
In My Dreams	10/94	Harper Monogram
Nothing Else Matters	07/95	Harper Monogram
After The Storm	02/96	Harper Monogram
Enchained Heart	11/93	Harper Monogram

Skillern, Christine

71	Moonstruck	01/83	Silhouette Special Edition

Skinner, Gloria Dale

Passion's Choice		Warner
Georgia Fever	07/92	Zebra Heartfire
Midnight Fire	08/94	Zebra Heartfire

Skye, Christina

Hour Of The Rose	04/94	Avon
Bridge Of Dreams	04/95	Avon

Small, Lass

	The Voice Of The Turtles	12/89	Silhouette	Christmas Stories
	Texas Blue Norther	10/96	Silhouette	Desire
241	Tangled Web	11/85	Silhouette	Desire
322	To Meet Again	12/86	Silhouette	Desire
341	Stolen Day	03/87	Silhouette	Desire
356	Possibles	06/87	Silhouette	Desire
373	Intrusive Man	09/87	Silhouette	Desire
397	To Love Again	01/88	Silhouette	Desire
413	Blindman's Bluff	03/88	Silhouette	Desire
437	Goldilocks And The Behr	07/88	Silhouette	Desire
453	Hide And Seek	10/88	Silhouette	Desire
491	Red Rover	04/89	Silhouette	Desire
505	Odd Man Out	07/89	Silhouette	Desire
534	Tagged	11/89	Silhouette	Desire
548	Contact	02/90	Silhouette	Desire
569	Wrong Address, Right Place	05/90	Silhouette	Desire
578	Not Easy	07/90	Silhouette	Desire
594	The Loner	09/90	Silhouette	Desire
613	Four Dollars And Fifty-One Cents	01/91	Silhouette	Desire
638	No Trespassing Allowed	05/91	Silhouette	Desire
655	The Molly Q	08/91	Silhouette	Desire
684	' Twas The Night	12/91	Silhouette	Desire
697	Dominic	03/92	Silhouette	Desire
731	A Restless Man	08/92	Silhouette	Desire
743	Two Halves	10/92	Silhouette	Desire
755	Beware Of Widows	12/92	Silhouette	Desire
775	A Disruptive Influence	04/93	Silhouette	Desire
800	Balanced	08/93	Silhouette	Desire
817	Tweed (Man Of Month)	11/93	Silhouette	Desire
830	A New Year	01/94	Silhouette	Desire
848	I'm Gonna Get You	04/94	Silhouette	Desire
860	Salty And Felicia	06/94	Silhouette	Desire
879	Lemon (Fabulous Brown Brothers)	09/94	Silhouette	Desire
895	An Obsolete Man (Man Of The Month)	12/94	Silhouette	Desire
901	A Nuisance (Man Of The Month)	01/95	Silhouette	Desire
926	Impulse	05/95	Silhouette	Desire
963	Whatever Comes	11/95	Silhouette	Desire
974	My House Or Yours?	01/96	Silhouette	Desire
994	A Stranger In Texas	04/96	Silhouette	Desire
444	An Irritating Man	07/86	Silhouette	Romance
521	Snow Bird	08/87	Silhouette	Romance
4	Not Looking For A Texas Man	09/95	Silhouette	Yours Truly
23	The Case Of The Lady In Apartment 308	07/96	Silhouette	Yours Truly
	Small Treasures	07/93	Smithmark	

Smart, Alexa

	Touch Of Paradise	06/96	Kensington Denise Little Presents

Smart, Alexa
    Masquerade   12/94 Pinnacle Denise Little Presents
    Shadows Of The Heart   10/95 Pinnacle Denise Little Presents
Smiley, Virginia Kester
    High Country Nurse   Dell Candlelight
    Guest At Gladehaven   Dell Candlelight
    Mansion Of Mystery   Dell Candlelight
Smith, Alana
  10 Whenever I Love You   07/82 Silhouette Desire
Smith, Arnold
  246 The Law's Outlaw   /53 Harlequin
Smith, Barbara Dawson
    Christmas Romance   /91 Avon Anthology
    Dreamspinner   05/90 Avon Romance
    Silver Splendor   08/89 Avon Romance
    Stolen Heart   11/88 Avon Romance
    Fire At Midnight   09/92 Avon Romantic Treasures
    Fire On The Wind   03/92 Avon Romantic Treasures
  246 No Regrets   06/85 Silhouette Special Edition
    A Glimpse Of Heaven   11/95 St. Martin
    Defiant Embrace   /85 Zebra
    Defiant Surrender   /87 Zebra
Smith, Bobbi
    Island Fire
    Love Beyond Time   07/94 Avon Time Travel Anthology
    Lady Deception   05/96 Leisure
    Arizona Caress   Zebra
    Bayou Bride   Zebra
    Desert Heart   Zebra
    Kiss Me Forever   Zebra
    Rapture's Rage   Zebra
    Sweet Silken Bondage   Zebra
    Forbidden Fires   Zebra
    Wanton Splendor   Zebra
    Rapture's Tempest   Zebra
    Arizona Temptress   Zebra
    Captive Pride   Zebra
    Texas Splendor   Zebra
    Pirate's Promise   Zebra
    Heaven   05/94 Zebra
    Dream Warrior   Zebra
    Lady Deception   05/96 Zebra
    The Lady's Hand   12/96 Zebra
    Capture My Heart   08/92 Zebra Special Release
Smith, Christine
  72 Murder Most Strange   Harlequin Intrigue

Smith, Dana Warren
  563 High Stakes   11/89   Silhouette Special Edition

Smith, Deborah

	Fall From Grace	04/95	Bantam	
	Silk And Stone	02/94	Bantam	
	The Beloved Woman	04/91	Bantam	Fanfare
	Follow The Sun	08/91	Bantam	Fanfare
	Miracle	11/91	Bantam	Fanfare
	Blue Willow	02/92	Bantam	Fanfare
245	Jed's Sweet Revenge	03/88	Bantam	Loveswept
255	Hold On Tight	05/88	Bantam	Loveswept
278	California Royale	09/88	Bantam	Loveswept
290	Caught By Surprise	11/88	Bantam	Loveswept
308	Never Let Go	02/89	Bantam	Loveswept
354	Hot Touch	10/89	Bantam	Loveswept
376	Sara's Surprise	01/90	Bantam	Loveswept
395	Legends	04/90	Bantam	Loveswept
411	Honey And Smoke	07/90	Bantam	Loveswept
450	The Silver Fox And The Red-Hot Dove	02/91	Bantam	Loveswept
468	Stranger In Camelot	05/91	Bantam	Loveswept
503	Heart Of The Dragon	10/91	Bantam	Loveswept
326	Sundance And The Princess	05/89	Bantam	Loveswept: Cherokee Tril.
338	Tempting The Wolf	07/89	Bantam	Loveswept: Cherokee Tril.
350	Kat's Tale	09/89	Bantam	Loveswept: Cherokee Tril.
	Hot Touch		Doubleday	

Smith, Doris E.

1341	Fire Is For Sharing	/69	Harlequin
1427	To Sing Me Home	/70	Harlequin
1454	Seven Of Magpies	/70	Harlequin
1599	Dear Deceiver	/72	Harlequin
1690	The One And Only	/73	Harlequin
1922	Cotswold Honey	/75	Harlequin
1992	Smuggled Love	/76	Harlequin
2071	Wild Heart	/77	Harlequin

Smith, Fela Dawson
        Black Wolf   04/94   Leisure

Smith, Harvey
  195 Nine To Five   /52   Harlequin

Smith, Haywood
        Shadows In Velvet   07/96   St. Martin's

Smith, Jeri

Witch Tree Inn	04/92	Diamond Gothic
The Haunting Of Victoria	03/93	Diamond Gothic

Smith, Joan

Romantic Rebel	/91	Ballantine
The Waltzing Widow	/91	Ballantine

AUTHOR/TITLE INDEX

Smith, Joan

Winter Wedding	/90	Ballantine
The Virgin & The Unicorn	08/95	Ballantine Regency
Strictly Business	/83	Bantam Dawnstar Romance
A Brush With Death	/90	Bantam Romantic Suspense
Follow That Blonde	/90	Bantam Romantic Suspense
The Polka Dot Nude	/89	Berkley Jove Romantic Suspense
Capriccio	/89	Berkley Jove Romantic Suspense
Memoirs Of A Hayden	/88	Fawcett
Strange Capers	/86	Fawcett
A Country Wooing	/87	Fawcett
Love's Harbinger	/87	Fawcett
Letters To A Lady	/87	Fawcett
Country Flirt	/87	Fawcett
Larcenous Lady	/87	Fawcett
Lover's Quarrels	/89	Fawcett
Silken Secrets	/88	Fawcett
Drury Lane Darling	/88	Fawcett
The Hermit's Daughter	/88	Fawcett
Royal Scamp	/89	Fawcett
Babe	/80	Fawcett
Valerie	/81	Fawcett
The Blue Diamond	/81	Fawcett
Reprise	/82	Fawcett
Wiles Of A Stranger	/82	Fawcett
Lover's Vows	/82	Fawcett
Reluctant Bride	/82	Fawcett
Lady Madeline's Folly	/83	Fawcett
Midnight Masquerade	/83	Fawcett
Royal Revels	/83	Fawcett
The Devious Duchess	/83	Fawcett
True Lady	/86	Fawcett
Bath Belles	/86	Fawcett
Cousin Cecelia	/90	Fawcett
Madcap Miss	/89	Fawcett
The Merry Month Of May	/90	Fawcett
Delsie	/81	Fawcett
Rose Tulawney		Fawcett
No Place For A Lady	07/94	Fawcett
Love Bade Me Welcome	/83	Fawcett Gothic
The Notorious Lord Havergal	07/91	Fawcett Regency
Bath Scandal	10/91	Fawcett Regency
Jennie Kissed Me	12/91	Fawcett Regency
Barefoot Baroness	03/92	Fawcett Regency
Dangerous Dalliance	05/92	Fawcett Regency
Francesca	08/92	Fawcett Regency
Wife Errant	10/92	Fawcett Regency

815

Smith, Joan

	The Spanish Lady	01/93	Fawcett Regency
	Perdita	/81	Fawcett Regency
	Gather Ye Rosebuds	06/93	Fawcett Regency
	Savage Lord Griffin	09/93	Fawcett Regency
	Autumn Loves	10/93	Fawcett Regency
	The Great Christmas Ball	11/93	Fawcett Regency
	Old Lover's Ghost	05/94	Fawcett Regency
	Regency Masquerade	08/94	Fawcett Regency
	Never Let Me Go	10/94	Fawcett Regency
	The Kissing Bough	11/94	Fawcett Regency
	Sweet And Twenty	/79	Fawcett Regency
	Endure My Heart	/80	Fawcett Regency
	Friends And Lovers	/81	Fawcett Regency
	Prelude	/82	Fawcett Regency
	The Notorious Lord Havergal	/91	Fawcett Regency
	A Kiss In The Dark	/95	Fawcett Regency
	The Virgin And The Unicorn	/95	Fawcett Regency
	Kissing Cousins	/95	Fawcett Regency
	A Tall, Dark Stranger	/96	Fawcett Regency
	Tea And Scandal	/96	Fawcett Regency
	A Whisper On The Wind	/90	Leisure Gothic
	Silver Water, Golden Sand	/89	Leisure Regency
	The Sipan Jaguar		Lion Hearted Suspense
234	Next Year's Blonde	07/83	Silhouette Romance
255	Caprice	10/83	Silhouette Romance
269	From Now On	01/84	Silhouette Romance
288	Chance Of A Lifetime	04/84	Silhouette Romance
302	Best Of Enemies	06/84	Silhouette Romance
315	Trouble In Paradise	08/84	Silhouette Romance
325	Future Perfect	10/84	Silhouette Romance
343	Tender Takeover	02/85	Silhouette Romance
354	The Yielding Art	04/85	Silhouette Romance
430	The Infamous Madame X	05/86	Silhouette Romance
452	Where There's A Will	08/86	Silhouette Romance
546	Dear Corrie	12/87	Silhouette Romance
562	If You Love Me	03/88	Silhouette Romance
591	By Hook Or By Crook	07/88	Silhouette Romance
617	After The Storm	12/88	Silhouette Romance
635	Maybe Next Time	03/89	Silhouette Romance
656	It Takes Two	06/89	Silhouette Romance
669	Thrill Of The Castle	08/89	Silhouette Romance
711	Sealed With A Kiss	03/90	Silhouette Romance
755	Her Nest Egg	11/90	Silhouette Romance
795	Her Lucky Break	05/91	Silhouette Romance
838	For Richer, For Poorer	01/92	Silhouette Romance
879	Getting To Know You	07/92	Silhouette Romance

Smith, Joan

919	Headed For Trouble	02/93	Silhouette	Romance
935	Can't Buy Me Love	06/93	Silhouette	Romance
956	John Loves Sally	08/93	Silhouette	Romance
972	Poor Little Rich Girl	11/93	Silhouette	Romance
	Behold A Mystery	/94	St. Martin's	
	Murder Will Speak	/96	St. Martin's	
	Lace For Milady	/80	Walker	
	Love's Way	/82	Walker	
	Aurora	/80	Walker	
	Dame Durden's Daughter	/78	Walker	
	Talk Of The Town	/79	Walker	
	Affair Of The Heart	/77	Walker	
	Escapde	/77	Walker	
	Aunt Sophie's Diamonds	/77	Walker	
	La Comtesse	/78	Walker	
	Imprudent Lady	/78	Walker	Regency

Smith, Karen Rose

	Wildflowers (Tentative)		Meteor	Kismet
	Shadows And Light	/94	Meteor	Kismet
74	A Man Worth Loving	01/92	Meteor	Kismet
100	Garden Of Fantasy	07/92	Meteor	Kismet
140	Love In Bloom	04/93	Meteor	Kismet
171	Because Of Francie		Meteor	Kismet
1075	Adam's Vow (Bundles Of Joy)	04/95	Silhouette	Romance
1102	Always Daddy	09/95	Silhouette	Romance
1128	Shane's Bride	01/96	Silhouette	Romance
1171	Cowboy At The Wedding	08/96	Silhouette	Romance
1181	A Groom And A Promise	10/96	Silhouette	Romance
930	Abigail And Mistletoe	12/94	Silhouette	Special Edition

Smith, Marcine

364	Never A Stranger	07/87	Silhouette	Desire
589	Murphy's Law	07/88	Silhouette	Romance
659	Waltz With The Flowers	07/89	Silhouette	Romance
683	The Perfect Wife	11/89	Silhouette	Romance
716	Just Neighbors	04/90	Silhouette	Romance
767	The Two Of Us	01/91	Silhouette	Romance
827	Love Shy	11/91	Silhouette	Romance

Smith, Marion

2598	The Beachcomber		Harlequin	Romance

Smith, Ruth Alana

158	The Wild Rose		Harlequin	Superromance
208	For Richer Or Poorer		Harlequin	Superromance
265	After Midnight		Harlequin	Superromance
311	The Second Time Around	06/88	Harlequin	Superromance
356	Spellbound		Harlequin	Superromance

AUTHOR/TITLE INDEX

Sommerfield, Sylvie F.

Wild Wyoming Heart		Zebra
Bittersweet		Zebra
Erin's Ecstasy		Zebra
Tazia's Torment		Zebra
Rebel Pride		Zebra
Rapture's Angel		Zebra
Deanna's Desire		Zebra
Tamara's Ecstasy		Zebra
Savage Rapture		Zebra
Kristen's Passion		Zebra
Cherish Me, Embrace Me		Zebra
Tame My Wild Heart		Zebra
Betray Not My Passion		Zebra
Savage Kiss		Zebra
Moonlit Magic		Zebra
Passion's Raging Storm	09/89	Zebra
Fires Of Surrender		Zebra
A Bride's Passion	05/93	Zebra Anthology
Love's Stolen Promises	08/92	Zebra Historical
Night Star		Zebra Historical

Sommerfield, Syvlie F,

Moon-Kissed Promises	04/93	Pinnacle Historical

Sommers, Beverly

169	Interlude Of Love	/83	Dell Candlelight Ecstasy
3	Ride A Painted Pony	11/84	Harlequin American
11	City Life, City Love		Harlequin American
26	Unscheduled Love		Harlequin American
62	Verdict Of Love		Harlequin American
69	The Last Key		Harlequin American
85	Mix And Match		Harlequin American
125	Changing Places		Harlequin American
137	Convictions		Harlequin American
152	Snowbird		Harlequin American
165	Le Club	07/86	Harlequin American
179	Silent Night		Harlequin American
191	Phoebe's Deputy	03/87	Harlequin American
216	Of Cats And Kings		Harlequin American
242	Teacher's Pet		Harlequin American
258	Reach For The Sky	06/88	Harlequin American
278	Losing It		Harlequin American
298	A Little Rebellion		Harlequin American
313	Getting Even		Harlequin American
331	Outside In		Harlequin American
3	Mistaken Identity		Harlequin Intrigue
87	Hold Back The Night	04/88	Harlequin Intrigue
164	Minor Adjustments	08/93	Meteor Kismet

AUTHOR/TITLE INDEX

AUTHOR/TITLE INDEX

Speer, Flora

	By Honor Bound	09/88	Leisure Historical
	Much Ado About Love		Leisure Historical
	Viking Passion	03/92	Leisure Historical
	Lady Lure	01/96	Leisure Love Spell
	Love Just In Time	02/95	Leisure Love Spell
	A Love Beyond Time	05/94	Lovespell
	A Time-Travel Christmas	12/93	Lovespell Anthology
	No Other Love	12/93	Lovespell Futuristic
	A Time To Love Again	08/93	Lovespell Time-Travel
	Castle Of The Heart	11/90	Pinnacle Historical
	Castle Of Dreams	04/90	Pinnacle Historical

Spellman, Cathy Cash

Paint The Wind		

Spencer, Candace

581	Between Friends	07/90	Silhouette Desire

Spencer, Catherine

296	Fires Of Summer		Harlequin American
	Once Bitten, Twice Shy - "Love's Sting"	03/96	Harlequin Anthology
910	Lasting Kind Of Love		Harlequin Presents
1406	The Loving Touch	10/91	Harlequin Presents
1587	Naturally Loving	09/93	Harlequin Presents
1682	Elegant Barbarian	09/94	Harlequin Presents
1812	That Man Callahan!	05/96	Harlequin Presents
1623	Dear Miss Jones	02/94	Harlequin Presents Plus
3138	Winter Roses	07/91	Harlequin Romance
3348	Lady Be Mine	02/95	Harlequin Romance
3365	Simply The Best (Family Ties)	06/95	Harlequin Romance

Spencer, Cheryl

Fortune's Bride		Avon

Spencer, La Vyrle

	Fulfillment	/79	Avon
	Forsaking All Others	/82	Berkley Second Chance At Love
	Family Blessings	02/94	G.P. Putnam
130	The Hellion		Harlequin Superromance
1	Spring Fancy	03/84	Harlequin Temptation
	Forgiving	02/92	Jove
	Bittersweet	04/94	Jove
	The Endearment		Jove
	The Gamble		Jove
	Morning Glory		Jove
	Separate Beds		Jove
	Twice Loved	09/95	Jove
	Vows		Jove
	Years	05/95	Jove
	Hummingbird	04/93	Jove

AUTHOR/TITLE INDEX

Spencer, La Vyrle

The Hellion	/89	Jove
Bygones	03/93	Jove
November Of The Heart	01/94	Jove
Separate Beds	01/94	Jove
Spring Fancy	/93	Jove
Home Song	01/96	Jove
A Promise To Cherish		Jove
A Heart Speaks (Promise To.../Forsaking...)	08/93	Jove 2 Novels
Sweet Memories	08/95	Mira
That Camden Summer	01/96	Putnam

Spencer, Mary

The Vow	03/94	Harper
Fire And Water	03/95	Harper
The Coming Home Place	07/94	Harper Monogram

Spenser, Emily

2668	Chateau Villon	Harlequin Romance
2681	Where The Wind Blows	Harlequin Romance
2813	Unlikely Lovers	Harlequin Romance
2898	Where Eagles Soar	Harlequin Romance

Spenser, Emma Jane

248	A Novel Approach	04/89	Harlequin Temptation
273	That Holiday Feeling	11/89	Harlequin Temptation
327	Two Can Play	12/90	Harlequin Temptation
336	Detente (Lovers Apart)	02/91	Harlequin Temptation

Spindler, Erica

423	Rhyme Or Reason	09/90	Bantam Loveswept
466	Wishing Moon	04/91	Bantam Loveswept
599	Tempting Chance	02/93	Bantam Loveswept
740	Slow Heat	04/95	Bantam Loveswept
	Red	07/95	Mira
	Forbidden Fruit	04/96	Mira
	A Winter's Rose	06/93	Silhouette
	Night Jasmine	/93	Silhouette
	Magnolia Dawn	/93	Silhouette
442	Heaven Sent	08/88	Silhouette Desire
482	Chances Are	03/89	Silhouette Desire
538	Read Between The Lines	12/89	Silhouette Desire
696	Longer Than	09/91	Silhouette Special Edition
728	Baby Mine	03/92	Silhouette Special Edition
817	A Winter's Rose	06/93	Silhouette Special Edition
838	Night Jasmine (Blossoms Of The South)	09/93	Silhouette Special Edition
857	Magnolia Dawn (Blossoms Of The South)	12/93	Silhouette Special Edition
903	Baby, Come Back	08/94	Silhouette Special Edition

Spitfire, Rosemary

337	My Darling Spitfire	Harlequin Presents

AUTHOR/TITLE INDEX

Sprenger, Terri
    Nighthawk's Woman   01/94   Zebra Heartfire

Springer, Lacey
  402   Kindred Hearts   12/85   Silhouette Romance
  419   A Silent Song   03/86   Silhouette Romance

St. Bastian, Margaret
    Miss Keating's Temptation   Ballantine Regency
    Dilemma In Duet   Ballantine Regency
    A Keeper For Lord Linford   Ballantine Regency
    The Plight Of Pamela Pollworth   Ballantine Regency
    By Way To Love   Ballantine Regency
    Her Knight On A Baye   Ballantine Regency
    The Honorable Miss Clarendon   Ballantine Regency
    Lord Dedringham's Divorce   Ballantine Regency
    My Lord Rakehell   Ballantine Regency
    Bow St. Gentlemen   Ballantine Regency
    Bow St. Brangle   Ballantine Regency
    The Young Lady From Alton St. Pancras   Ballantine Regency
    The Savage Yankee Squire   Ballantine Regency
    The Poor Relation   Ballantine Regency
    Miss Letty   Ballantine Regency
    The Courtship Of Col. Crowne   Ballantine Regency
    The Awakening Of Lord Dalby   Ballantine Regency
    Lord Orlando's Protege   Berkley
    Meg Miller   Berkley

St. Clair, Jessica
    Winter Roses
    Rapture's Fury   Zebra Heartfire

St. Clair, Joy
 2472   Heart Under Siege   Harlequin Romance

St. Claire, Erin
    7   Not Even For Love   07/82   Silhouette Desire
  41   Seduction By Design   01/83   Silhouette Desire
  73   A Kiss Remembered   07/83   Silhouette Desire
 139   Words Of Silk   05/84   Silhouette Desire
 488   The Thrill Of Victory   04/89   Silhouette Desire
  29   A Secret Splendor   12/83   Silhouette Intimate Moments
  76   Bittersweet Rain   11/84   Silhouette Intimate Moments
  93   Sweet Anger   04/85   Silhouette Intimate Moments
 112   Tiger Prince   09/85   Silhouette Intimate Moments
 120   Led Astray   11/85   Silhouette Intimate Moments
 133   Above And Beyond   03/86   Silhouette Intimate Moments
 144   Honor Bound   05/86   Silhouette Intimate Moments
 180   The Devil's Own   02/87   Silhouette Intimate Moments
 213   Two Alone   11/87   Silhouette Intimate Moments

St. Claire, Madeline

AUTHOR/TITLE INDEX

St. Claire, Madeline

299	Private Eyes	11/94	Harlequin Intrigue

St. George, Edith

124	Color My Dreams	03/84	Silhouette Desire
159	Velvet Is For Lovers	09/84	Silhouette Desire
69	West Of The Moon	03/81	Silhouette Romance
98	Midnight Wine	08/81	Silhouette Romance
126	Dream Once More	01/82	Silhouette Romance
225	Delta River Magic	05/83	Silhouette Romance
248	Rose-Colored Glass	09/83	Silhouette Romance

St. George, La Verne

	A Private Proposal	11/90	Avalon Career Romance

St. George, Margaret

142	Winter Magic		Harlequin American
159	Castles & Fairy Tales	05/86	Harlequin American
203	The Heart Club		Harlequin American
231	Where There's Smoke		Harlequin American
272	Heart's Desire		Harlequin American
323	Dear Santa		Harlequin American
345	American Pie		Harlequin American
421	Happy New Year, Darling	01/92	Harlequin American
462	The Pirate And His Lady	02/93	Harlequin American
501	A Wish...And A Kiss	09/93	Harlequin American
518	The Accidental Princess	01/94	Harlequin American
545	The Drop-In Bride	08/94	Harlequin American
582	Love Bites	05/95	Harlequin American
133	Jigsaw	03/90	Harlequin Intrigue
198	Murder By The Book	10/92	Harlequin Intrigue
230	Cache Poor	06/93	Harlequin Intrigue
358	The Renegade	02/96	Harlequin Intrigue
	Alexa		Nal-Signet
	Portrait In Passion		Nal/Signet
	Yankee Princess		Nal/Signet
	Chase The Heart	04/90	William Morrow

St. James, Jessica

561	The Perfect Lover	11/89	Silhouette Special Edition
603	Showdown At Sin Creek	06/90	Silhouette Special Edition
631	A Country Christmas	11/90	Silhouette Special Edition

St. James, Scotney

	Northern Fire, Northern Star		Zebra
	By Honor Bound		Zebra
	Outlaw's Lady	05/96	Zebra
	Warrior's Ecstasy		Zebra Heartfire
	Defiant Bride		Zebra Heartfire
	Rogue's Lady	10/94	Zebra Historical
21	Heather Mist	02/93	Zebra Lucky In Love

824

AUTHOR/TITLE INDEX

St. John, Cheryl
212	Rain Shadow (March Madness)	03/94	Harlequin Historical
240	Heaven Can Wait	10/94	Harlequin Historical
265	Land Of Dreams	04/95	Harlequin Historical
288	Saint Or Sinner	10/95	Harlequin Historical
327	Badlands Bride	08/96	Harlequin Historical

St. John, Lisa
60	Starfire		Nal Rapture Romance

St. John, Nicole
Wychwood	/77	Warner

St. Pierre, Lisann
Defiant Angel	03/88	Avon

St. Thomas, Robin
A Lady's Man (Tentative Title)	06/96	Zebra

Stables, Mira
Lissa	Regency
Miss Mouse	Ballantine Regency

Staff, Adrienne
97	What's A Nice Girl...?	06/85	Bantam Loveswept
124	Banjo Man	01/86	Bantam Loveswept
141	Crescendo	05/86	Bantam Loveswept
165	Kevin's Story	11/86	Bantam Loveswept
281	Paradise Cafe	09/88	Bantam Loveswept
356	The Great American Bachelor	10/89	Bantam Loveswept
617	Pleasure In The Sand	05/93	Bantam Loveswept
724	Spellbound	01/95	Bantam Loveswept
748	Dream Lover	05/95	Bantam Loveswept

Stafford, Caroline
Honor Of Ravensholme	Gothic

Stafford, Judith
32	The Lemon Cake	08/90	Harlequin Regency
51	A Hero's Welcome	06/91	Harlequin Regency
62	Cupid And The Vicar	11/91	Harlequin Regency
97	Becca's Independence	05/93	Harlequin Regency
111	Sarah's Angel	12/93	Harlequin Regency

Stafford, Lee
90	Love Takes Over	07/91	Harlequin Direct
110	Shadow In The Wings	05/92	Harlequin Direct
144	A Heart Divided	07/93	Harlequin Direct
184	The Willing Captive	05/94	Harlequin Direct
2963	Yesterday's Enemy		Harlequin Romance
3048	A Song In The Wilder		Harlequin Romance
3088	A Perfect Marriage		Harlequin Romance
3234	Summer's Echo	11/92	Harlequin Romance
40	Fountains Of Paradise		Mills & Boon

Stamford, Sarah

Stamford, Sarah
  619   The Magnificent Duchess   Dell Candlelight Regency
Standard, Patti
  636   Pretty As A Picture   03/89   Silhouette Romance
  829   For Brian's Sake   11/91   Silhouette Romance
  902   Under One Roof   11/92   Silhouette Romance
Stanford, Sondra
  2208 A Stranger's Kiss   /78   Harlequin
  2354 Bellefleur   Harlequin Romance
    6   Golden Tide   05/80   Silhouette Romance
   25   Shadow Of Love   08/80   Silhouette Romance
   35   Storm's End   10/80   Silhouette Romance
   46   No Trespassing   12/80   Silhouette Romance
   58   Long Winter's Night   02/81   Silhouette Romance
   77   Secret Marriage   05/81   Silhouette Romance
   88   And Then Came Dawn   07/81   Silhouette Romance
  100   Yesterday's Shadow   09/81   Silhouette Romance
  112   Whisper Wind   11/81   Silhouette Romance
  131   Tarnished Vows   02/82   Silhouette Romance
  530   Stolen Trust   09/87   Silhouette Romance
  586   Heart Of Gold   07/88   Silhouette Romance
  646   Proud Beloved   05/89   Silhouette Romance
    7   Silver Mist   03/82   Silhouette Special Edition
   37   Magnolia Moon   08/82   Silhouette Special Edition
   55   Sun Lover   11/82   Silhouette Special Edition
   91   Love's Gentle Chains   05/83   Silhouette Special Edition
  161   The Heart Knows Best   04/84   Silhouette Special Edition
  187   For All Time   09/84   Silhouette Special Edition
  210   A Corner Of Heaven   12/84   Silhouette Special Edition
  248   Cupid's Task   07/85   Silhouette Special Edition
  292   Bird In Flight   02/86   Silhouette Special Edition
  326   Equal Shares   08/86   Silhouette Special Edition
  445   Through All Eternity   04/88   Silhouette Special Edition
  560   A Man With Secrets   11/89   Silhouette Special Edition
  686   Secret Marriage   08/91   Silhouette Special Edition
Stanley, Beth
  486   Count On Me   02/92   Harlequin Superromance
Stanley, Edward
  209   The Rock Cried Out   /53   Harlequin
Stanley, Mary Lee
  183   No Trifling With Love   10/82   Silhouette Romance
Stanton, Elinor
   68   Surprise Ending   /82   Berkley Second Chance At Love
Stark, Francie
        Partners In Love   06/94   Zebra To Love Again
Stark, Michael

AUTHOR/TITLE INDEX

Stark, Michael
   121   Run For Your Life   /51   Harlequin

Starr, Cynthia
   201   Tears Of Gold   01/83   Silhouette Romance

Starr, Kate
   679   The Nurse Most Likely   /62   Harlequin
   828   Ship's Doctor   /64   Harlequin
   951   The Enchanted Trap   /65   Harlequin
  1076   Bells In The Wind   /67   Harlequin
  1105   Wrong Doctor John   /67   Harlequin
  1130   Dalton's Daughter   /67   Harlequin
  1166   Dolan Of Sugar Hills   /67   Harlequin
  1200   Satin For The Bride   /68   Harlequin

Starr, Leonora
  1147   Fantails   /67   Harlequin
  1236   Jemima   /68   Harlequin

Starr, Martha
    84   From Twilight To Sunrise   Harlequin American
    11   Bitter Fruit   Harlequin Intrigue

Statham, Frances Patton
       The Roswell Legacy   Ballantine
       Call The River Home   10/91   Fawcett

Staub, Molly Arost
       Pirate's Passion   06/90   Pocket

Steel, Danielle
       Message From Nam
       Zoya
       Family Album
       Full Circle
       Changes
       Thurston House
       Once In A Lifetime
       A Perfect Stranger
       Remembrance
       The Ring
       Loving
       To Love Again
       Summer's End
       Season Of Passion
       The Promise
       Now And Forever
       Passion's Promise
       No Greater Love   11/91   Delacorte Press
       Heartbeat   12/91   Delacorte Press
       Kaleidoscope   /87   Delacorte Press
       Secrets   /85   Delacorte Press

AUTHOR/TITLE INDEX

Steel, Danielle

Vanished	09/93	Delacorte Press
Daddy	/89	Dell
Star	/89	Dell
Fine Things	/87	Dell
Wanderlust	/86	Dell
Crossings	/82	Dell
Jewels	04/93	Dell
Palomino	/81	Dell
Mixed Blessings	/93	Dell
Five Days In Paris		Dell
Lightning		Dell
Wings		Dell
Accident		Dell
The Gift	/94	Dell
Going Home	/73	Doubleday

Steel, Judith

Apache Fire	/91	Zebra
Apache Heartbeat		Zebra Heartfire
Santa Fe Fantasy		Zebra Heartfire
Seduction's Raging Flames		Zebra Heartfire
Wild Colorado Passion		Zebra Heartfire
Lawman's Loving		Zebra Heartfire

Steele, Jessica

533	The Other Brother	Harlequin Presents
596	Price To Be Met	Harlequin Presents
605	Intimate Enemies	Harlequin Presents
621	No Quiet Refuge	Harlequin Presents
661	Reluctant Relative	Harlequin Presents
709	Imprudent Challenge	Harlequin Presents
717	Ruthless In All	Harlequin Presents
725	Gallant Antagonist	Harlequin Presents
749	Bond Of Vengeance	Harlequin Presents
766	No Holds Barred	Harlequin Presents
767	Facade	Harlequin Presents
836	Promise To Dishonour	Harlequin Presents
2289	Spring Girl	Harlequin Romance
2297	The Icicle Heart	Harlequin Romance
2304	Bitter Enchantment	Harlequin Romance
2309	Pride's Master	Harlequin Romance
2352	Hostage To Dishonour	Harlequin Romance
2355	Turbulent Convenant	Harlequin Romance
2370	The Other Woman	Harlequin Romance
2394	Magic Of His Kiss	Harlequin Romance
2424	Devil In Disguise	Harlequin Romance
2446	Innocent Abroad	Harlequin Romance
2451	Bachelor's Wife	Harlequin Romance

Steele, Jessica

2494	But Know Not Why		Harlequin Romance
2502	Dishonest Woman		Harlequin Romance
2504	Not To Be Trusted		Harlequin Romance
2555	Distrust Her Shadow		Harlequin Romance
2580	Tethered Liberty		Harlequin Romance
2607	Tomorrow Come Soon		Harlequin Romance
2687	No Honourable Compromise		Harlequin Romance
2789	Misleading Encounter		Harlequin Romance
2800	So Near So Far		Harlequin Romance
2850	Beyond Her Control		Harlequin Romance
2861	Relative Strangers		Harlequin Romance
2916	Unfriendly Alliance		Harlequin Romance
2928	Fortunes Of Love		Harlequin Romance
2964	Without Love		Harlequin Romance
2982	When The Loving Stops		Harlequin Romance
3011	To Stay Forever		Harlequin Romance
3041	Farewell To Love		Harlequin Romance
3065	Frozen Enchantment		Harlequin Romance
3077	Passport To Happiness		Harlequin Romance
3095	Unfriendly Proposition	12/90	Harlequin Romance
3114	Hidden Heart		Harlequin Romance
3126	A First Time For		Harlequin Romance
3156	Flight Of Discovery	10/91	Harlequin Romance
3173	Without Knowing Why	01/92	Harlequin Romance
3203	Runaway From Love	06/92	Harlequin Romance
3215	His Woman	08/92	Harlequin Romance
3227	Bad Neighbors	10/92	Harlequin Romance
3256	Destined To Meet	03/93	Harlequin Romance
3294	Hungarian Rhapsody	12/93	Harlequin Romance
3308	Relative Values	04/94	Harlequin Romance
3327	Italian Invader	09/94	Harlequin Romance
3356	Bachelor's Family	04/95	Harlequin Romance
3385	The Sister Secret	11/95	Harlequin Romance
3407	The Marriage Business	05/96	Harlequin Romance
3416	A Wife In Waiting	07/96	Harlequin Romance

Steen, Sandy

528	Shameless	07/94	Harlequin Crystal Creek
534	Somewhere Other Than The Night	12/94	Harlequin Crystal Creek
593	The Knight	07/96	Harlequin Temptation
155	Sweet Reason	08/86	Silhouette Intimate Moments
202	Past Perfect	08/87	Silhouette Intimate Moments
375	The Simple Truth	03/91	Silhouette Intimate Moments
459	Run To The Moon	11/92	Silhouette Intimate Moments
545	Sterling Advice	01/94	Silhouette Intimate Moments
710	Hunting Houston	05/96	Silhouette Intimate Moments
638	Vanquish The Night	12/90	Silhouette Special Edition

Steffen, Sandra

	Lucas: The Loner	/96	Meteor
90	Hold Back The Night	05/92	Meteor
145	Until Tomorrow	05/93	Meteor Kismet
972	Gift Wrapped Dad	12/95	Silhouette Desire
1005	Child Of Her Dreams	04/94	Silhouette Romance
1028	Bachelor Daddy	08/94	Silhouette Romance
1045	Bachelor At The Wedding (Wedding Wager)	11/94	Silhouette Romance
1056	Expectant Bachelor (Wedding Wager)	01/95	Silhouette Romance
1074	Lullaby And Goodnight (Bundles Of Joy)	04/95	Silhouette Romance
1138	A Father For Always	03/96	Silhouette Romance
1163	For Better, For Baby	07/96	Silhouette Romance

Stegman, Michele

	Fortune's Mistress		
	Fortune's Son	11/92	Leisure Historical

Stegner, Wallace

| 149 | Remembering Laughter | /52 | Harlequin |

Steinberg, Linda

| | September Spring | 02/94 | Zebra Over 45 |

Steinfeld, Ann

	The Doxy Masque		Ballantine Historical
	The Golden Marguerite		Ballantine Historical
	Royal Summer		Ballantine Historical

Stephens, Barbara

| | Midnight Waltz | 02/91 | Odyssey Books |

Stephens, Blythe

434	Wake To Darkness	06/92	Silhouette Intimate Moments
786	Gift Of Mischief	04/91	Silhouette Romance
554	Rainbow Days	10/89	Silhouette Special Edition

Stephens, Donna

	Wind Across Texas	08/93	Avon
	Wildfire	04/95	Avon
	Wild Flower	09/94	Avon Historical
	Heart Of The Wild	09/94	Avon Historical

Stephens, Jeanne

358	A Wild Iris		Harlequin American
18	Wild Horizons		Harlequin Historical
504	Sharing California	06/89	Silhouette Desire
14	Reckless Surrender	08/83	Silhouette Intimate Moments
38	Memories	02/84	Silhouette Intimate Moments
127	Whispers On The Wind	01/86	Silhouette Intimate Moments
161	The Haunted Season	10/86	Silhouette Intimate Moments
200	Mistress Of Cliff House	07/87	Silhouette Intimate Moments
259	Dangerous Choices	10/88	Silhouette Intimate Moments
308	At Risk	10/89	Silhouette Intimate Moments
353	Hiding Places	10/90	Silhouette Intimate Moments

AUTHOR/TITLE INDEX

Stephens, Jeanne

380	Summer Heat	04/91	Silhouette	Intimate Moments
22	Mexican Nights	08/80	Silhouette	Romance
80	Wonder And Wild Desire	05/81	Silhouette	Romance
189	Sweet Jasmine	11/82	Silhouette	Romance
531	Broken Dreams	09/87	Silhouette	Romance
30	Bride In Barbados	06/82	Silhouette	Special Edition
47	Pride's Possession	09/82	Silhouette	Special Edition
84	The Splendored Sky	03/83	Silhouette	Special Edition
108	No Other Love	07/83	Silhouette	Special Edition
217	Mandy's Song	01/85	Silhouette	Special Edition
252	Coming Home	07/85	Silhouette	Special Edition
295	This Long Winter Past	03/86	Silhouette	Special Edition
308	A Few Shining Hours	05/86	Silhouette	Special Edition
372	Return To Eden	03/87	Silhouette	Special Edition
431	Neptune Summer	01/88	Silhouette	Special Edition

Stephens, Kay

300	The Felsted Collection	06/84	Silhouette	Romance

Stephens, Sharon

	The Black Earl	Pocket	

Sterling, Donna

586	Something Old, Something New	05/96	Harlequin	Temptation

Sterling, Elaine K.

345	More Than A Feeling		Harlequin	Superromance

Sterling, Jessica

	The Welcome Light	09/91	St. Martin's

Stern, Susan

	Desert Nights	Diamond	

Stern, Tracy

	This I Promise You	Harper	

Stevens, Amanda

373	Stranger In Paradise	06/96	Harlequin	Intrigue
647	Love Is A Stranger	06/91	Silhouette	Desire
758	Angels Don't Cry	01/93	Silhouette	Desire
159	Killing Moon	09/86	Silhouette	Intimate Moments
199	The Dreaming	07/87	Silhouette	Intimate Moments
592	Fade To Black	09/94	Silhouette	Intimate Moments
14	The Seventh Night	08/93	Silhouette	Shadows
24	The Perfect Kiss	01/94	Silhouette	Shadows
48	Dark Obsession	01/95	Silhouette	Shadows
488	Obsessed!	04/93	Silhouette	Special Edition

Stevens, Jennifer

	Carolina Moon	02/94	Zebra Pinnacle
	Louisiana Heat		Zebra Pinnacle/ Magnolia Road

Stevens, Kelly R.

	Ragdoll	/94	Barbour & Co. Heartsong Presents

Stevens, Linda

130	Shadowplay		Harlequin	Intrigue
156	One Step Ahead		Harlequin	Intrigue
201	Perilous Pastime	11/92	Harlequin	Intrigue
225	Triplecross	06/93	Harlequin	Intrigue
252	Fright Night	11/93	Harlequin	Intrigue
303	The Kid Who Stole Christmas	12/94	Harlequin	Intrigue

Stevens, Lynsey

	Christmas Journeys - "Mistletoe Kisses"	09/94	Harlequin	Anthology
497	Ryan's Return		Harlequin	Presents
606	Man Of Vengeance		Harlequin	Presents
654	Forbidden Wine		Harlequin	Presents
692	Starting Over		Harlequin	Presents
774	Lingering Embers		Harlequin	Presents
996	Leave Yesterday Behind		Harlequin	Presents
1396	A Rising Passion	09/91	Harlequin	Presents
1643	Touched By Desire	04/94	Harlequin	Presents
2488	Play Our Song Again		Harlequin	Romance
2495	Race For Revenge		Harlequin	Romance
2507	Tropical Knight		Harlequin	Romance
2574	Closest Place Heaven		Harlequin	Romance
2608	The Ashby Affair		Harlequin	Romance
2706	Terebobi's Gold		Harlequin	Romance
2988	But Never Love		Harlequin	Romance

Stevens, R. J.

	A Woman Of Texas			

Stevens, Rosemary

1	A Crime Of Manners	05/96	Fawcett	Cats Of Mayfair
2	Miss Pymbroke's Rules	/97	Fawcett	Cats Of Mayfair

Stevens, Serita

	Daughter Of Desire		
	Tame The Wild Heart	Tapestry	

Stevens, Shira

	Deceptive Desire

Stevens, Susan

230	Ivory Innocence	06/83	Silhouette	Romance

Stevenson, Florence

	Curse Of The Concullons	Gothic	

Stevenson, Kate

576	A Piece Of Tomorrow	06/94	Silhouette	Intimate Moments

Steward, Ada

619	The Cowboy's Lover	11/94	Harlequin	Superromance
227	This Cherished Land	03/85	Silhouette	Special Edition
289	Love's Haunting Refrain	02/86	Silhouette	Special Edition
319	Misty Mornings, Magic Nights	07/86	Silhouette	Special Edition
343	A Walk In Paradise	11/86	Silhouette	Special Edition

AUTHOR/TITLE INDEX

Steward, Ada

604	Galahad's Bride	06/90	Silhouette Special Edition
680	Even Better Than Before	07/91	Silhouette Special Edition
759	Hot Wind In Eden	08/92	Silhouette Special Edition
808	Live, Laugh, Love	04/93	Silhouette Special Edition

Stewardson, Dawn

80	Peril In Paradise		Harlequin Intrigue
90	No Rhyme Or Reason		Harlequin Intrigue
222	Cat And Mouse	04/93	Harlequin Intrigue
257	The Mummy Case	01/94	Harlequin Intrigue
261	The Mummy Beads	02/94	Harlequin Intrigue
281	Hunter's Moon	07/94	Harlequin Intrigue
302	I'll Be Home For Christmas	12/94	Harlequin Intrigue
362	Love And Lies	03/96	Harlequin Intrigue
329	Vanishing Act		Harlequin Superromance
355	Deep Secrets		Harlequin Superromance
383	Blue Moon		Harlequin Superromance
405	Prize Passage		Harlequin Superromance
409	Heartbeat		Harlequin Superromance
432	Three's Company		Harlequin Superromance
477	Moon Shadow	11/91	Harlequin Superromance
498	Across The Misty	05/92	Harlequin Superromance
521	Cold Noses, Warm Kisses	10/92	Harlequin Superromance
551	Once Upon A Crime	06/93	Harlequin Superromance
571	The Yankee's Bride (Paranormal)	11/93	Harlequin Superromance
615	Gone With The West	10/94	Harlequin Superromance
653	Big Luke, Little Luke (4 Strong Men)	07/95	Harlequin Superromance
691	Sully's Kids	05/96	Harlequin Superromance

Stewart, Barbara

6	Love Me Not (Great Escapes)	03/94	Harlequin Stolen Moments

Stewart, Fred Mustard

Rage Against Heaven

Stewart, Judith

13	The Laird's French Bride		Mills & Boon

Stewart, Kathryn

372	Dangerous Bargain	02/91	Silhouette Intimate Moments

Stewart, Lois

Romantic Masquerade	11/90	Zebra
A Christmas Delight	/91	Zebra Anthology
A Mother's Delight	03/95	Zebra Anthology
Lost Love, New Love: "Mother's Delight"	04/95	Zebra Anthology
Dark Rendezvous At Dungariff	09/89	Zebra Gothic
The Lost Bride Of Kildrummond	09/91	Zebra Gothic
An Independent Lady		Zebra Regency
An Unscrupulous Bride	01/92	Zebra Regency
An Uncommon Affair		Zebra Regency

Stewart, Lois

	The Duke's Mistress	08/93	Zebra Regency
	A Reluctant Heart	09/94	Zebra Regency
	The Bartered Bride	08/95	Zebra Regency

Stewart, Lucy Phillips

232	The Captive Bride		Dell Candlelight Regency
251	Bride Of Chance		Dell Candlelight Regency
512	Bride Of Torquay		Dell Candlelight Regency
530	Bride Of A Stranger		Dell Candlelight Regency

Stewart, Marcy

	Darby's Angel	07/96	Kensington Regency
	Flowers For The Bride	04/95	Zebra Anthology
	Charity's Gambit	04/94	Zebra Regency
	Lord Merlyn's Magic	09/95	Zebra Regency

Stewart, Mariah

	Moments In Time	02/95	Pocket

Stewart, Mary

	Moon Spinners		Suspense
	The Stormy Petrel	07/94	Fawcett

Stewart, Nary

	Nine Coaches Waiting		Gothic

Stewart, Ruth

42	Ask Me No Secrets	01/83	Silhouette Desire

Stewart, Sally

2862	Love Upon The Wind		Harlequin Romance

Stirling, Elaine K.

28	Unsuspected Conduct		Harlequin Intrigue
35	Midnight Obsession		Harlequin Intrigue
53	Foul Play		Harlequin Intrigue
85	Chain Letter	03/88	Harlequin Intrigue
126	Sleepwalker		Harlequin Intrigue
261	This Time For Us		Harlequin Superromance
385	Cross Tides		Harlequin Superromance
139	Almost Heaven	01/87	Harlequin Temptation
332	Different Worlds (Lovers Apart)	01/91	Harlequin Temptation

Stirling, Jessica

	Treasures On Earth

Stirling, Jocelyn

	Promises To Keep

Stockenberg, Antoinette

	Emily's Ghost	05/92	Dell
	Time After Time	07/95	Dell
	Embers	08/94	Dell Supernatural

Stoddard, Charles

414	Devil's Portage	/58	Harlequin

AUTHOR/TITLE INDEX

Stokes, Manning Lee
432   The Lady Lost Her Head   /58   Harlequin

Stoks, Peggy
    Love's Bluff   06/94   Berkley Diamond Wildflower
    Wild Winds   12/93   Diamond Wildflower
    Frontier Heat   06/94   Diamond Wildflower

Stone, Elisa
31   A Shared Love   Nal Rapture Romance

Stone, Jean
    Sins Of Innocence   04/94   Bantam

Stone, Katherine
    Pearl Moon   03/95   Fawcett
    Illusions   02/94   Kensington Suspense
    Promises   09/93   Zebra
    Roomates   Zebra
    Twins To Bel Air   Zebra
    Rainbows   Zebra
    Happy Endings   02/95   Zebra

Stone, Natalie
198   Double Play   /83   Dell Candlelight Ecstasy

Stone, Sally
    Silver Fire   12/93   Zebra Heartfire

Stone, Thomas
142   Doctor By Day   /51   Harlequin

Storm, Elizabeth
93   Firing Line   Harlequin Intrigue

Stover, Deb
    A Willing Spirit   06/97   Pinnacle Denise Little Presents
    Shades Of Rose   05/95   Pinnacle Denise Little Presents

Stowe, Tanya
    Time's Embrace   11/93   Starlog Rhapsody Historical

Stoyenoff,
    One Night To Remember
    Where Love Waits

Strasser, Heidi
    Love's Memories   11/88   Crown Pageant

Stratford, Karen
    Fires Of Midnight   /90   Avon
    Lavender Flame   05/91   Avon Romance

Strather, Patricia
    Silvermore   Nal Penguin
    The Constant Star   Nal Penguin
    Grand Design   Nal Penguin
    Golden Windows   Nal Penguin

Stratton, Rebecca

Stratton, Rebecca

1748	The Golden Madonna	/74	Harlequin
1770	Fairwinds	/74	Harlequin
1799	The Bride Of Romano	/74	Harlequin
1816	Castles In Spain	/74	Harlequin
1839	Run From The Wind	/74	Harlequin
1858	Island Of Darkness	/75	Harlequin
1883	Autumn Concerto	/75	Harlequin
1898	Firebird	/75	Harlequin
1913	The Flight Of The Hawk	/75	Harlequin
1942	The Fire And The Fury	/76	Harlequin
1955	Moon Tide	/76	Harlequin
1976	The Goddess Of Mavisu	/76	Harlequin
1991	Isle Of The Golden Drum	/76	Harlequin
2006	Proud Stranger	/76	Harlequin
2018	Chateau D' Amour	/76	Harlequin
2036	The Road To Gafsa	/77	Harlequin
2050	Gemini Child	/77	Harlequin
2078	Girl In A White Hat	/77	Harlequin
2091	Inherit The Sun	/77	Harlequin
2106	More Than A Dream	/77	Harlequin
2131	The Sign Of The Ram	/78	Harlequin
2141	The Velvet Glove	/78	Harlequin
2154	Dream Of Winter	/78	Harlequin
2173	Spindrift	/78	Harlequin
2180	Image Of Love	/78	Harlequin
2201	Bargain For Paradise	/78	Harlequin
2222	Corsican Bandit	/78	Harlequin
106	Yellow Moon	/75	Harlequin Presents
121	The Warm Wind Of Farik	/75	Harlequin Presents
2261	Lost Heritage		Harlequin Romance
2268	The Eagle Of Vincela		Harlequin Romance
2274	Lark In Alien Sky		Harlequin Romance
2303	Close To The Heart		Harlequin Romance
2339	Tears Of Venus		Harlequin Romance
2356	Apollo's Daughter		Harlequin Romance
2376	Trader's Cay		Harlequin Romance
2399	The Inherited Bride		Harlequin Romance
2405	The Leo Man		Harlequin Romance
2434	The Silken Cage		Harlequin Romance
2452	The Black Invader		Harlequin Romance
2466	Dark Enigma		Harlequin Romance
2489	The Golden Spaniard		Harlequin Romance
2508	Charade		Harlequin Romance

Street, Kelly

294	Only Human	04/90	Harlequin Temptation
388	Under Her Influence	03/92	Harlequin Temptation

AUTHOR/TITLE INDEX

Stuart, Anne

557	The Demon Count		Dell Candlelight Romance
	My Valentine (Sampler)	02/93	Harlequin
9	Break The Night	06/93	Harlequin
30	Chain Of Love		Harlequin American
39	Heart's Ease		Harlequin American
52	Museum Piece		Harlequin American
93	Housebound		Harlequin American
126	Rocky Road		Harlequin American
177	Bewitching Hour		Harlequin American
213	Blue Sage		Harlequin American
246	Partners In Crime		Harlequin American
260	Cry For The Moon		Harlequin American
311	Glass Houses		Harlequin American
326	Crazy Like A Fox		Harlequin American
346	Rancho Diablo		Harlequin American
361	Angels Wings		Harlequin American
374	Lazarus Rising		Harlequin American
398	Night Of The Phantom	07/91	Harlequin American
413	Chasing Trouble	11/91	Harlequin American
434	Heat Lightning	04/92	Harlequin American
453	Rafe's Revenge	09/92	Harlequin American
473	One More Valentine	02/93	Harlequin American
513	Falling Angel	12/93	Harlequin American
525	Cinderman	03/94	Harlequin American
573	The Soldier & The Baby	03/95	Harlequin American
	American Romance 10th Anniversary	08/93	Harlequin Anthology
	New Year's Resolution: Kissing Frosty	01/96	Harlequin Anthology
1	Lazarus Rising	03/96	Harlequin Here Come The Grooms
5	Tangled Lies		Harlequin Intrigue
9	Catspaw		Harlequin Intrigue
59	Hand In Glove		Harlequin Intrigue
103	Catspaw I I		Harlequin Intrigue
329	Winter's Edge	07/95	Harlequin Intrigue
11	Tangled Lies	03/94	Harlequin Men Made In America
19	Rocky Road	07/94	Harlequin Men Made In America
	Blue Sage	08/95	Harlequin Western Lovers
	Rancho Diablo	01/96	Harlequin Western Lovers
	Highland Fling	12/93	Jove Historical Anthology
	The Prince Of Swords	09/96	Kensington
	Nightfall	02/95	Onyx Romantic Suspense
	Strangers In The Night - "Dark Journey"	10/95	Silhouette Anthology
321	Special Gifts	02/90	Silhouette Intimate Moments
429	Now You See Him ...	05/92	Silhouette Intimate Moments
	The Monster In The Closet	10/92	Silhouette Shadows Promotional

Stuart, Casey

	Highland Rogue		Zebra

838

Stuart, Casey

	Passion's Dream	/82	Zebra
	Waves Of Passion	/84	Zebra
	Moonlight Angel	/85	Zebra
	Passion's Flame	/85	Zebra
	Midnight Thunder	/86	Zebra
	Velvet Deception	/87	Zebra
	Beloved Pirate	/88	Zebra
	Passion's Prisoner	02/89	Zebra
	No Dragons To Slay	/90	Zebra

Stuart, Dee

	Wings Of The Morning		Richard Gallen

Stuart, Diana

	Destiny's Bride	/78	Berkley Historical
	Cry For Paradise	/81	Pocket Historical
172	Prime Specimen	11/84	Silhouette Desire
238	Leader Of The Pack	10/85	Silhouette Desire
257	The Shadow Between	01/86	Silhouette Desire
353	Out Of A Dream	12/86	Silhouette Special Edition
671	The Moon Pool	05/91	Silhouette Special Edition

Stuart, Elizabeth

	Reckless Angel	12/88	Pageant
	Heartstorm	05/89	St. Martin's
	Without Honor	/93	St. Martin's
	Bride Of The Lion	08/95	St. Martin's
	Where Love Dwells	/91	St. Martin's Historical

Stuart, Jan

255	A Risk Worth Taking		Dell Candlelight Ecstasy
324	Encore Of Desire		Dell Candlelight Ecstasy
453	No Greater Love		Dell Candlelight Ecstasy

Stuart, Vivian

558	Nurse In Malaya	/60	Harlequin
566	Jungle Doctor	/61	Harlequin
574	Along Came Doctor Ann	/61	Harlequin
678	Doctor In The Tropics	/62	Harlequin

Stubbs, Jean

	Dear Laura		Historical
1	By Our Beginnings		Nal Penguin
2	The Imperfect Jay		Nal Penguin
	Summer Secrets	02/92	St. Martin's
	Like We Used To Be	02/92	St. Martin's

Sturdy, Carl

47	Registered Nurse	/50	Harlequin

Suanders, Irene

	The Impetuous Twin	04/87	Nal Regency

Sullivan, Jo

Sullivan, Jo
  2544 Suspicion   Harlequin Romance

Sullivan, Joyce
   352 The Night Before Christmas   12/95 Harlequin Intrigue

Summers, Annette
    84 The Surprising Lady Rochdale   10/92 Harlequin Regency

Summers, Ashley
    36 Fires Of Memory   12/82 Silhouette Desire
    95 The Marring Kind   10/83 Silhouette Desire
   291 Juliet   07/86 Silhouette Desire
   374 Heart's Delight   09/87 Silhouette Desire
   509 Eternally Eve   07/89 Silhouette Desire
   675 Heart's Ease   11/91 Silhouette Desire
   197 Season Of Enchantment   01/83 Silhouette Romance
   223 A Private Eden   05/83 Silhouette Romance

Summers, Chloe
    34 No Easy Task   03/91 Meteor

Summers, Diana
        Louisiana
        A Rebel's Pleasure
        Fallen Angel   Playboy Press
        Love's Wicked Ways   Playboy Press
        Wild Is The Heart   Playboy Press

Summers, Essie
   625 Nurse Abroad   /61   Harlequin
   668 No Roses In June   /62   Harlequin
   724 House Of The Shining Tide   /63   Harlequin
   742 Come Blossom Time, My Love   /63   Harlequin
   774 Heatherleigh   /63   Harlequin
   784 Where No Roads Go   /63   Harlequin
   802 South To Forget   /64   Harlequin
   822 The Time And The Place   /64   Harlequin
   847 The Smoke And The Fire   /64   Harlequin
   862 Moon Over The Alps   /64   Harlequin
   886 Bachelors Galore   /65   Harlequin
   910 The Master Of Tawhai   /65   Harlequin
   933 Bride In Flight   /65   Harlequin
   957 No Legacy For Lindsay   /65   Harlequin
   982 No Orchids By Request   /66   Harlequin
 1015 Sweet Are The Ways   /66   Harlequin
 1055 Heir To Windrush Hill   /66   Harlequin
 1093 His Serene Miss Smith   /67   Harlequin
 1119 Postscript To Yesterday   /67   Harlequin
 1156 A Place Called Paradise   /67   Harlequin
 1283 Rosalind Comes Home   /69   Harlequin
 1326 Meet On My Ground   /69   Harlequin

Summers, Essie

1348	Revolt-- And Virginia	/69	Harlequin
1375	The Kindled Fire	/70	Harlequin
1416	Summer In December	/70	Harlequin
1445	The Bay Of The Nightingale	/70	Harlequin
1502	Return To Dragonshill	/71	Harlequin
1535	The House On Gregor's Brae	/71	Harlequin
1564	South Island Stowaway	/72	Harlequin
1702	A Touch Of Magic	/73	Harlequin
1731	The Forbidden Valley	/73	Harlequin
1854	Through All The Years	/75	Harlequin
1884	The Gold Of Noo	/75	Harlequin
1917	Anna Of Strathallan	/75	Harlequin
2000	Not By Appointment	/76	Harlequin
2021	Beyond The Foothills	/76	Harlequin
2068	Goblin Hill	/77	Harlequin
2133	Adair Of Starlight Peaks	/78	Harlequin
2148	Spring In September	/78	Harlequin
2239	The Luck Of Kingfisher		Harlequin Romance
2281	My Lady Of Fuchsias		Harlequin Romance
2322	One More River To Cross		Harlequin Romance
2453	The Tender Leaves		Harlequin Romance
2525	Daughter Of The Mist		Harlequin Romance
2590	Mountain For Luenda		Harlequin Romance
2622	A Lamp For Jonathan		Harlequin Romance
2645	Season Of Forgetfullness		Harlequin Romance
2688	Winter In July		Harlequin Romance
2766	To Bring You Joy	05/86	Harlequin Romance
2801	Autumn In April		Harlequin Romance
2883	High Country Governor		Harlequin Romance

Summers, Faye

	Stormspell		Leisure Historical
	Winterhall		Leisure Historical

Summers, Jackie

260	Embrace The Dawn (March Madness)	03/95	Harlequin Historical

Summerskill, Shirley

763	A Surgical Affair	/63	Harlequin

Summerville, Margaret

	Fortune's Folly	07/94	
	Rogue's Masquerade		Avon
571	Sensible Cecily		Dell Candlelight Regency
580	Infamous Isabelle		Dell Candlelight Regency
	A Wife For Warminster		Nal
	The Improper Playwright	03/92	Nal Regency
	Town Tangle	04/86	Nal Regency
	Knave's Gambit	09/86	Nal Regency

Summerville, Margaret

The Wicked Wager	02/87	Nal Regency
The Cotton Caliph	01/88	Nal Regency
Highland Lady		Nal Penguin Regency
Scandal's Daughter		Nal Penguin Regency
The Duke's Disappearance		Nal Penguin Regency
My Lord Tyrant	06/93	Penguin Regency

Sumner, Olivia

A Beguiling Intrigue	07/94	
An Improper Alliance	12/92	Zebra
The Golden Mountain		Zebra
Winter Enchantment	12/92	Zebra A Christmas To Cherish
The Mischievous Matchmaker	05/92	Zebra A Mother's Heart
A Daring Masquerade	11/91	Zebra Regency
A Most Unsuitable Bride	06/93	Zebra Regency

Sumners, Jeanne

Rose Of Passion, Rose Of Love		Bantam

Sunshine, Linda

23	Constant Stranger	10/82	Silhouette Desire

Suson, Marlene

	Devil's Angel	09/94	Avon Historical
1	Midnight Bride	04/95	Avon Midnight Trilogy
2	Midnight Lord	10/95	Avon Midnight Trilogy
3	Midnight Bandit	07/96	Avon Midnight Trilogy
	Devil's Bargain	/92	Avon Regency Romance
	Fair Imposter	08/92	Avon Regency Romance
	The Lily And The Hawk	06/93	Avon Regency Romance
	The Errant Earl	/89	Fawcett
	The Notorious Marquess	/88	Fawcett
	Lady Caro	/88	Fawcett
	The Duke's Revenge	/87	Fawcett
	The Infamous Bargain	/86	Fawcett
	The Reluctant Heiress	/85	Fawcett
	Desire's Command	/81	Richard Gallen

Sutcliffe, Katherine

Desire And Surrender		Avon
Fire In The Heart		Avon
Renegade Love		Avon
Shadow Play		Avon
Windstorm		Avon
Dream Fever	11/91	Avon
Christmas Romance	/91	Avon Anthology
My Only Love	04/93	Jove
Once A Hero	06/94	Jove
Miracle	02/95	Jove Historical
Devotion	02/96	Jove Historical

Taylor, Abra
73	Season Of Seduction	02/83	Silhouette Special Edition
103	Wild Is The Heart	07/83	Silhouette Special Edition
127	A Woman Of Daring	11/83	Silhouette Special Edition
157	Forbidden Summer	04/84	Silhouette Special Edition
192	Sea Spell	09/84	Silhouette Special Edition

Taylor, Angeline
| 184 | Black Jade | /52 | Harlequin |

Taylor, Day
	The Black Swan		Dell
	Moss Rose		Dell
	The Magnificent Dream		Dell
	Sands Of Gold	/86	Dell

Taylor, Dorothy E.
| | Fleur De Lis | | Avon |

Taylor, Janelle
	Moondust And Madness	05/86	Bantam
	Wild Is My Love	11/87	Bantam
	Wild Sweet Promise	04/89	Bantam
	Sharing Christmas	12/92	Dove
54	Valley Of Fire		Harlequin American
	Defiant Hearts	05/96	Kensington
	Destiny Mine	02/95	Kensington Western Romance
	Love's Legacy	11/95	Leisure Anthology
	Valley Of Fire	05/96	Mira
	Starlight And Splendor	09/95	Pinnacle
	Moonbeams And Magic	09/95	Pinnacle #4 Moondust Series
	Fortune's Flames	07/92	Zebra
	Promise Me Forever		Zebra
	Bittersweet Ecstasy		Zebra
	Brazen Ecstasy		Zebra
	Defiant Ecstasy		Zebra
	Destiny's Temptress		Zebra
	First Love, Wild Love		Zebra
	Follow The Wind		Zebra
	Forbidden Ecstasy		Zebra
	Forever Ecstasy		Zebra
	Love Me With A Fury		Zebra
	Passions Wild And Free		Zebra
	Savage Ecstasy		Zebra
	Stolen Ecstasy		Zebra
	Sweet Savage Heart		Zebra
	Tender Ecstasy		Zebra
	Whispered Kisses		Zebra
	The Other Side Of Love		Zebra
	Kiss Of The Night Wind		Zebra

Taylor, Janelle

Savage Conquest	04/92	Zebra
Chase The Wind	05/94	Zebra
A Christmas Rendezvous	/91	Zebra Anthology
The Last Viking Queen	02/94	Zebra Fantasy
Stardust And Shadows	09/92	Zebra Pinnacle
Golden Torment	08/92	Zebra Regency Romance

Taylor, Jayne

Whirlwind Courtship	/79	Tiara
Midnight Secrets	04/93	Zebra Historical
Anything For Love	07/95	Zebra To Love Again

Taylor, Jennifer

248	Spanish Nights	09/95	Harlequin
266	Jungle Fever	01/96	Harlequin
270	Desert Moon	02/96	Harlequin
274	Tides Of Love	03/96	Harlequin
169	Old Love, New Love	01/94	Harlequin Direct
189	Promise Me Love	06/94	Harlequin Direct
205	Love Is The Answer	10/94	Harlequin Direct
230	Lovestorm	04/95	Harlequin Direct
1173	Final Score		Harlequin Presents
1326	A Magical Touch		Harlequin Presents
1349	Tender Pursuit		Harlequin Presents
3142	Lovespell	08/91	Harlequin Romance
3252	Guilty Of Love	02/93	Harlequin Romance
3264	Love Is A Risk	04/93	Harlequin Romance

Taylor, Laura

502	Starfire	10/91	Bantam Loveswept
527	Promises	02/92	Bantam Loveswept
555	Desert Rose	07/92	Bantam Loveswept
576	Midnight Storm	11/92	Bantam Loveswept
600	Just Friends	03/93	Bantam Loveswept
634	Heartbreaker	08/93	Bantam Loveswept
652	Wilder's Woman	11/93	Bantam Loveswept
681	Winter Heart	04/94	Bantam Loveswept
765	Lonesome Tonight	09/95	Bantam Loveswept
772	Seduced	01/96	Bantam Loveswept
784	Dangerous Surrender	04/96	Bantam Loveswept
799	Fallen Angel	08/96	Bantam Loveswept
407	Troubled Waters	02/88	Silhouette Desire
586	Jade's Passion	08/90	Silhouette Desire

Taylor, Lucy

Avenue Of Dreams	07/90	Nal Signet
The Restless Years	07/92	Nal Signet

Taylor, Mary Ann

My Enemy, My Love	11/88	Crown Pageant

Tegler, Leta

    Wild Splendor   Avon

    Gabrielle   08/90 Avon

Tekilts, Susan P.

    Surrender The Night   10/94 Harper Monogram

Tempest, Jan

  775 That Nice Nurse Nevin   /63 Harlequin

  963 Nurse Willow's Ward   /65 Harlequin

  994 Jubilee Hospital   /66 Harlequin

Temple, Sara

  593 Kindred Spirits   04/90 Silhouette Special Edition

  674 Lifeline   06/91 Silhouette Special Edition

  736 The Liberation Of Layla 04/92 Silhouette Special Edition

Templeton, Janet

    Virtuous Vixen   Bantam

    Lady Fortune   Bantam

    The Scapegrace   Bantam

    Love Is A Scandal   Bantam

    A Suitor To Spare   Bantam

Temte, Myrna

   35 Silent Sam's Salvation   08/96 Harlequin Here Come The Grooms

    3 Sleeping With The Enemy 10/94 Harlequin Montana Mavericks

      Jingle Bells, Wedding Bells 11/94 Silhouette Anthology

  483 Wendy Wyoming   10/88 Silhouette Special Edition

  572 Powder River Reunion   01/90 Silhouette Special Edition

  643 The Last Good Man Alive 01/91 Silhouette Special Edition

  739 For Pete's Sake   05/92 Silhouette Special Edition

  745 Silent Sam's Salvation   06/92 Silhouette Special Edition

  751 Heartbreak Hank   07/92 Silhouette Special Edition

  816 The Forever Night   05/93 Silhouette Special Edition

  861 Room For Annie   01/94 Silhouette Special Edition

Terrell, Bob

    The Reluctant Lawman   /91 Avalon

Terrill, Dana

  181 Man Of Velvet   10/82 Silhouette Romance

Territo, Mary Jo

  190 Two To Tango   Harlequin Superromance

   52 Just Friends   03/85 Harlequin Temptation

  111 Catch A Rising Star   06/86 Harlequin Temptation

  121 The Vital Ingredient   09/86 Harlequin Temptation

  142 No Passing Fancy   02/87 Harlequin Temptation

  180 Before And After   11/87 Harlequin Temptation

Terry, Beverly

  414 Before The Loving   02/86 Silhouette Romance

  607 The Love Bandit   10/88 Silhouette Romance

  685 Thief Of Hearts   11/89 Silhouette Romance

AUTHOR/TITLE INDEX

Terry, Beverly
877   No More Mr. Nice Guy   07/92 Silhouette Romance

Tetel, Julie
       The Viking's Bride
       Promised Brides - "The Handfast"   04/96 Harlequin Anthology
128   Sweet Suspicions   06/92 Harlequin Historical
167   Sweet Seduction   04/93 Harlequin Historical
182   Sweet Sensations   07/93 Harlequin Historical
229   Simon's Lady   07/94 Harlequin Historical
255   Sweet Surrender   02/95 Harlequin Historical
287   Maclaurin's Lady   10/95 Harlequin Historical
105   The Temporary Bride   09/93 Harlequin Regency
       And Heaven, Too   Warner
       For Love Of Lord Roland   Warner
       Tangled Dreams   Warner
       And Heaven Too   Warner
       Swept Away   Warner
       The Viking's Bride   /87 Warner

Thacker, Cathy Gillen
37   Touch Of Fire   Harlequin American
75   Promise Me Today   Harlequin American
102   Heart's Journey   Harlequin American
134   Reach For The Stars   Harlequin American
143   A Family To Cherish   Harlequin American
156   Heaven Shared   Harlequin American
166   The Devlin Dare   Harlequin American
187   Rogue's Bargain   02/87 Harlequin American
233   Guardian Angel   Harlequin American
247   Family Affair   Harlequin American
262   Natural Touch   10/88 Harlequin American
277   Perfect Match   Harlequin American
307   One Man's Folly   Harlequin American
318   Lifetime Guarantee   Harlequin American
334   Meant To Be   Harlequin American
388   Father Of The Bride   Harlequin American
407   An Unexpected Family   09/91 Harlequin American
423   Tangled Web   01/92 Harlequin American
445   Home Free   07/92 Harlequin American
452   Anything's Possible   08/92 Harlequin American
456   The Cowboy's Mistress 09/92 Harlequin American
472   Honeymoon For Hire   01/93 Harlequin American
483   Beguiled Again   04/93 Harlequin American
494   Fiance For Sale   07/93 Harlequin American
506   Kidnapping Nick   10/93 Harlequin American
521   Baby On The Doorstep 02/94 Harlequin American
526   Daddy To The Rescue   03/94 Harlequin American
529   Too Many Moms   04/94 Harlequin American

AUTHOR/TITLE INDEX

Thacker, Cathy Gillen

540	Jenny And The Fortune Hunter	06/94	Harlequin	American
556	Love Potion #5	10/94	Harlequin	American
568	Miss Charlotte Surrenders	01/95	Harlequin	American
587	A Shotgun Wedding (In Name Only)	06/95	Harlequin	American
607	Daddy Christmas	11/95	Harlequin	American
613	Matchmaking Baby	01/96	Harlequin	American
625	The Cowboy's Bride	04/96	Harlequin	American
629	The Ranch Stud	05/96	Harlequin	American
633	The Maverick Marriage	06/96	Harlequin	American
	Marriage By Design	04/94	Harlequin	Anthology
19	Father Of The Bride	06/96	Harlequin	Here Come The Grooms
94	Fatal Amusement		Harlequin	Intrigue
104	Dream Spinners		Harlequin	Intrigue
137	Slalon To Terror		Harlequin	Intrigue
300	Guilty As Sin	11/94	Harlequin	Intrigue
46	The Devlin Dare	04/95	Harlequin	Men Made In America
47	Embrace Me, Love	02/85	Harlequin	Temptation
82	A Private Passion	11/85	Harlequin	Temptation

Thacker, Shelly

	Midnight Raider	02/92	Avon
	Stolen Glory		Avon
	Falcon On The Wind	01/91	Avon
	Silver And Sapphires	02/93	Avon
	Forever His	12/93	Avon
	A Stranger's Kiss	11/94	Avon
	Heaven And Earth	/96	Avon
	Hearts Run Wild	04/96	Avon

Thayer, Patricia

895	Just Maggie	10/92	Silhouette	Romance
1009	Race To The Altar (Celebration 1000!)	05/94	Silhouette	Romance
1064	The Cowboy's Courtship	02/95	Silhouette	Romance
1086	Wildcat Wedding (Stetsons & Lace)	06/95	Silhouette	Romance
1146	Reilly's Bride	04/96	Silhouette	Romance

Thayne, RaeAnne

800	The Mating Game	08/96	Bantam Loveswept

Thelen, Linda

	Magic Moments	10/94	Avalon

Thian, Valerie

1515	O Kiss Me, Kate	/71	Harlequin

Thiels, Kathryn

51	Alternate Arrangement	05/84	Silhouette	Intimate Moments
10	Texas Rose	03/82	Silhouette	Special Edition
234	An Acquired Taste	04/85	Silhouette	Special Edition

Thiels, Kathryn Gorsha

	Savage Fancy	Richard Gallen

Thies, Joyce

	Mountain Man	04/95	Harlequin Western Lovers
348	Spellbound	04/87	Silhouette Desire
359	False Pretenses	06/87	Silhouette Desire
378	The Primrose Path	09/87	Silhouette Desire
511	Mountain Man	08/89	Silhouette Desire
563	King Of The Mountain	04/90	Silhouette Desire
636	The Drifter	04/91	Silhouette Desire
661	Pride And Joy	09/91	Silhouette Desire
432	Moon Of The Raven	06/88	Silhouette Desire - Rising Moon Tril. 1
444	Reach For The Moon	08/88	Silhouette Desire - Rising Moon Tril. 2
456	Gypsy Moon	10/88	Silhouette Desire - Rising Moon Tril. 3

Thomas, Bree

	Love's Journey Home		Nal Rapture Romance

Thomas, Jodi

	Stardust	09/94	Avon Anthology
	The Tender Texan	08/91	Berkley
	Prairie Song	02/92	Diamond
	Loving Hearts	02/92	Diamond
	Northern Star	03/93	Diamond
	Cherish The Dream	04/93	Diamond
	Sweet Hearts	02/93	Diamond Anthology
	The Texan And The Lady	01/94	Diamond Historical
	To Tame A Texan's Heart	12/94	Diamond Historical
	Forever In Texas	09/95	Jove Historical
	Country Christmas	11/93	Nal Anthology
	Beneath The Texas Sky		Zebra Historical & Family Sagas

Thomas, Kate

1023	The Texas Touch (Celebration 1000!)	07/94	Silhouette Romance
1123	Jingle Bell Bride	12/95	Silhouette Romance

Thomas, Leslie

53	Goddess Of The Moon	10/82	Silhouette Special Edition

Thomas, Martha Lou

	Waltz With A Stranger	/86	Walker
	Lady True's Gate	/90	Walker

Thomas, Michele Y.

	Crystal Shadows		Zebra Gothic
	The House At Thunder Cove		Zebra Gothic
	The Shifting Shadows Of Moongate		Zebra Gothic

Thomas, Nicola

	Champagne Gold	08/92	Harper

Thomas, Penelope

	Heaven Knows	07/94	
	Master Of Blackwood	10/91	Harper
	Passion's Child		Harper
	Thief Of Hearts		Harper

AUTHOR/TITLE INDEX

Thomas, Penelope
| | Indiscretions | 04/94 | Harper | |
| | The Secret | 10/93 | Harper | Historical |

Thomas, Rosie
| | Strangers | | Pocket | |

Thompson, Marcella
2802	Breaking Free		Harlequin	Romance
2975	Bed, Breakfast & Bed		Harlequin	Romance
3106	Of Rascals And Rainbows		Harlequin	Romance
3326	On Blueberry Hill	08/94	Harlequin	Romance

Thompson, Pamela
| 99 | The Wellspring | | Harlequin | American |
| 7 | Rainbow Ribbon | | Harlequin | Intrigue |

Thompson, Sydney
| 351 | Dr. Parrish, Resident | /56 | Harlequin | |

Thompson, Trudy
| | Prisoner Of Passion | 01/95 | Lovespell | Futuristic |

Thompson, Vicki Lewis
	My Valentine	02/92	Harlequin	Anthology
	Hero In Disguise	12/96	Harlequin	Hometown Reunion
	Stuck With You	10/96	Harlequin	Love And Laughter
211	Butterflies In The Sun		Harlequin	Superromance
269	Golden Girl		Harlequin	Superromance
326	Sparks		Harlequin	Superromance
389	Connections		Harlequin	Superromance
497	Critical Moves	04/92	Harlequin	Superromance
572	Only In The Moonlight	11/93	Harlequin	Superromance
637	Adam Then And Now	03/95	Harlequin	Superromance
9	Mingled Hearts	05/84	Harlequin	Temptation
25	Promise Me Sunshine	09/84	Harlequin	Temptation
92	An Impractical Passion	01/86	Harlequin	Temptation
113	The Fix-It Man	07/86	Harlequin	Temptation
137	When Angels Dance		Harlequin	Temptation
140	As Time Goes By	01/87	Harlequin	Temptation
155	Cupid's Caper	05/87	Harlequin	Temptation
192	The Flip Side	02/88	Harlequin	Temptation
217	Impulse	09/88	Harlequin	Temptation
240	Be Mine, Valentine (Editor's Choice)	02/89	Harlequin	Temptation
256	Full Coverage	06/89	Harlequin	Temptation
278	' Tis The Season	12/89	Harlequin	Temptation
288	Forever Mine, Valentine (Editor's Choice)	02/90	Harlequin	Temptation
344	Your Place Or Mine (Lovers Apart)	04/91	Harlequin	Temptation
374	It Happened One Weekend	12/91	Harlequin	Temptation
395	Anything Goes	05/92	Harlequin	Temptation
410	Ask Dr. Kate	09/92	Harlequin	Temptation
439	Fools Rush In	04/93	Harlequin	Temptation

AUTHOR/TITLE INDEX

Thompson, Vicki Lewis

484	Loverboy	03/94	Harlequin	Temptation
502	Wedding Song (Weddings, Inc.)	08/94	Harlequin	Temptation
516	The Bounty Hunter	11/94	Harlequin	Temptation
555	The Trailblazer	09/95	Harlequin	Temptation
559	The Drifter	10/95	Harlequin	Temptation
563	The Lawman	11/95	Harlequin	Temptation
600	Holding Out For A Hero	08/96	Harlequin	Temptation

Thompson, Victoria

Beloved Outcast			
Blazing Texas Nights	03/92		
Winds Of Promise	06/93		
Rogue's Lady		Avon	
Fortune's Lady	01/90	Avon	Romance
Playing With Fire	11/90	Avon	Romance
Sweet Texas Surrender		Zebra	
Wild Texas Promise		Zebra	
Texas Triumph		Zebra	
Texas Treasure		Zebra	
Angel Heart		Zebra	
Bold Texas Embrace		Zebra	
Texas Blonde		Zebra	
Texas Vixen		Zebra	
Wild Texas Wind	10/92	Zebra	
Winds Of Destiny	03/94	Zebra	
To Love And To Honor	05/95	Zebra	Anthology
A Christmas Kiss	12/92	Zebra	Christmas Anthology
Winds Of Promise	05/93	Zebra	Lovegram

Thorne, Alexandra

Desert Heat	01/92	Bantam	Fanfare
Intimate Strangers	08/92	Bantam	Fanfare
Past Forgetting	/91	Doubleday	
Lawless	06/94	Pinnacle	Denise Little Presents
Boundless	12/94	Pinnacle	Denise Little Presents
Fearless	08/95	Pinnacle	Denise Little Presents
Seasons Of The Heart	09/96	Pinnacle	Denise Little Presents

Thorne, April

50	Forgotten Promises	05/84	Silhouette	Intimate Moments
75	Winner's Circle	11/84	Silhouette	Intimate Moments
106	Foolish Pride	08/85	Silhouette	Intimate Moments
60	Once And Forever	11/82	Silhouette	Special Edition
111	Make-Believe Magic	08/83	Silhouette	Special Edition

Thorne, Avery

677	A Splendid Passion		Harlequin Presents
679	A Ruling Passion		Harlequin Presents
693	No Other Chance		Harlequin Presents

Thorne, Belle
532 Passionate Summer   Dell Candlelight
Thorne, Nicola
     Sisters And Lovers   Bantam
     Champagne   Harper Collins
     Pride Of Place   Harper Collins
Thornton, Carolyn
144 A Class Above   Harlequin American
204 To Ask Again, Yes   Harlequin American
248 The Search For Mr. Perfect   Harlequin American
 19 The Heart Never Forgets   07/80   Silhouette Romance
229 For Eric's Sake   06/83   Silhouette Romance
 11 Love Is Surrender   03/82   Silhouette Special Edition
 57 Pride's Reckoning   11/82   Silhouette Special Edition
 81 Looking Glass Love   03/83   Silhouette Special Edition
138 Smile And Say Yes   12/83   Silhouette Special Edition
146 By The Book   02/84   Silhouette Special Edition
168 Male Order Bride   05/84   Silhouette Special Edition
182 Changing Seasons   08/84   Silhouette Special Edition
202 Promises To Keep   11/84   Silhouette Special Edition
222 Haven Of Tenderness   02/85   Silhouette Special Edition
Thornton, Elizabeth
     Dangerous To Love   07/94   Bantam
     Dangerous To Kiss   03/95   Bantam
     Dangerous To Hold   05/96   Bantam
     My Guardian Angel   02/95   Bantam Anthology
     Cherished   09/93   Pinnacle
     Velvet Is The Night   Zebra Historical
     Scarlett Angel   Zebra Pinnacle
     Tender The Storm   Zebra Pinnacle
     Bluestocking Bride   Zebra Regency
     Fallen Angel   Zebra Regency
     The Passionate Pride   Zebra Regency
     A Virtuous Lady   Zebra Regency
     The Wordly Widow   Zebra Regency
Thornton, Helene
     Scarlet Ribbons   /84   Nal Signet
     Passionate Exile   /84   Nal Signet
     Journey To Desire   Nal Penguin
     Passionate Exile   Nal Penguin
Thorpe, Kay
1237 The Last Of The Mallorys   /68   Harlequin
1272 Devon Interlude   /69   Harlequin
1355 Rising Star   /69   Harlequin
1504 Curtain Call   /71   Harlequin
1583 Sawdust Season   /72   Harlequin

Thorpe, Kay

1609	Not Wanted On Voyage	/72	Harlequin	
1661	Olive Island	/73	Harlequin	
1756	An Apple In Eden	/74	Harlequin	
1909	The Shifting Sands	/75	Harlequin	
1967	Sugar Cane Harvest	/76	Harlequin	
1990	The Royal Affair	/76	Harlequin	
2046	Safari South	/77	Harlequin	
2079	The River Lord	/77	Harlequin	
2109	Storm Passage	/77	Harlequin	
2151	Timber Boss	/78	Harlequin	
37	Worlds Apart	08/96	Harlequin Presents	
81	The Iron Man	/75	Harlequin Presents	
93	Opportune Marriage	/75	Harlequin Presents	
237	Lord Of La Pampa	/78	Harlequin Presents	
242	Caribbean Encounter	/78	Harlequin Presents	
299	Bitter Alliance		Harlequin Presents	
311	The Man From Tripoli		Harlequin Presents	
336	This Side Paradise		Harlequin Presents	
360	The Dividing Line		Harlequin Presents	
378	Chance Meeting		Harlequin Presents	
394	No Passing Fancy		Harlequin Presents	
425	Floodtide		Harlequin Presents	
455	Copper Lake		Harlequin Presents	
491	Temporary Marriage		Harlequin Presents	
534	The New Owner		Harlequin Presents	
573	A Man Of Means		Harlequin Presents	
597	Master Of Morley		Harlequin Presents	
646	Land Of The Incas		Harlequin Presents	
678	Never Trust A Stranger		Harlequin Presents	
710	The Inheritance		Harlequin Presents	
789	No Gentle Persuasion		Harlequin Presents	
822	Double Deception		Harlequin Presents	
853	South Seas Affair		Harlequin Presents	
902	Dangerous Moonlight		Harlequin Presents	
941	Win Or Lose		Harlequin Presents	
973	Jungle Island		Harlequin Presents	
1084	Time Out Of Mind		Harlequin Presents	
1141	Land Of Illusion		Harlequin Presents	
1204	Tokyo Tryst		Harlequin Presents	
1261	Skin Deep		Harlequin Presents	
1301	Steel Tiger		Harlequin Presents	
1356	Against All Odds		Harlequin Presents	
1397	Initmate Deception	09/91	Harlequin Presents	
1446	Night Of Error	03/92	Harlequin Presents	
1501	Trouble On Tour	10/92	Harlequin Presents	
1534	Lasting Legacy	02/93	Harlequin Presents	

Thorpe, Kay

1556	Wild Streak	06/93	Harlequin	Presents
1571	Left In Trust	07/93	Harlequin	Presents
1603	Past All Reason	11/93	Harlequin	Presents
1619	The Alpha Man (Postcards From Europe)	01/94	Harlequin	Presents
1667	The Spanish Connection	07/94	Harlequin	Presents
2232	The Wilderness Trail		Harlequin	Romance
2234	Full Circle		Harlequin	Romance

Thorpe, Sylvia

The Reluctant Adverturess	Ballantine	Historical
Romantic Lady	Ballantine	Historical
The Scandalous Lady Robin	Ballantine	Historical
The Scapegrace	Ballantine	Historical
The Silver Nightingale	Ballantine	Regency
The Scarlett Domino	Ballantine	Regency
Captain Gallant	Ballantine	Regency
Torrington Chase	Ballantine	Regency
Mistress Of Astington	Ballantine	Regency
The Highwayman	Ballantine	Regency
The House Of Bill Orchard	Ballantine	Regency
Devil's Bandman	Ballantine	Regency

Thum, Marcella

Marguerite		
Mistress Of Paradise		
Wild Laurel		
The Thorn Trees	Ballantine	
The White Rose	Ballantine	Regency
Abbey Court	Ballantine	Regency
Fernwood	Ballantine	Regency

Thurlo, Aimee

109	Expiration Date		Harlequin	Intrigue
131	Black Mesa		Harlequin	Intrigue
141	Suitable For Framing		Harlequin	Intrigue
162	Strangers Who Linger		Harlequin	Intrigue
175	Night Wind	12/91	Harlequin	Intrigue
200	Breach Of Faith	10/92	Harlequin	Intrigue
217	Shadow Of The Wolf	03/93	Harlequin	Intrigue
246	Spirit Warrior	01/94	Harlequin	Intrigue
275	Timewalker	05/94	Harlequin	Intrigue
304	Bearing Gifts	12/94	Harlequin	Intrigue
337	Fatal Charm	09/95	Harlequin	Intrigue
377	Cisco's Woman	07/96	Harlequin	Intrigue
312	The Right Combination	06/88	Harlequin	Superromance
	Second Shadow	12/95	Tor	

Thurlow, Kathy

	A Brand New Life	03/94	Zebra To Love Again

AUTHOR/TITLE INDEX

Tracy, Pat
887   Wild Streak   09/92   Silhouette Romance

Tracy, Susan
159   Yesterday's Bride   06/82   Silhouette Romance

Travis, Jessica
1143   The Groom Wore Blue Suede Shoes   03/96   Silhouette Romance

Tremaine, Jennie
      Sally   Dell Candlelight Regency
      Susie   Dell Candlelight Regency
      Poppy   Dell Candlelight Regency
      Katy   Dell Candlelight Regency
      Maggie   Dell Candlelight Regency
527   Kitty   Dell Candlelight Regency
542   Daisy   Dell Candlelight Regency
562   Lucy   Dell Candlelight Regency
573   Polly   Dell Candlelight Regency
587   Molly   Dell Candlelight Regency
596   Ginny   Dell Candlelight Regency
660   Tilly   Dell Candlelight Regency

Trench, Caroline
412   Nurse Trenton   /58   Harlequin
419   In And Out Of Love   /58   Harlequin
467   Nurse To The Island   /59   Harlequin
486   Nurse Caril's New Post   /59   Harlequin
636   The Home At Hawk's Nest (Nurse Candida)   /62   Harlequin
850   The Other Anne   /64   Harlequin

Trent, Brenda
122   Without Regrets   03/84   Silhouette Desire
56   Rising Star   01/81   Silhouette Romance
74   Winter Dreams   04/81   Silhouette Romance
110   A Stranger's Wife   10/81   Silhouette Romance
161   Run From Heritage   07/82   Silhouette Romance
193   Runaway Wife   12/82   Silhouette Romance
245   Steal Love Away   09/83   Silhouette Romance
266   Hunter's Moon   12/83   Silhouette Romance
423   Bewitched By Love   03/86   Silhouette Romance
488   A Better Man   02/87   Silhouette Romance
506   Hearts On Fire   05/87   Silhouette Romance
540   Cupid's Error   11/87   Silhouette Romance
563   Something Food   03/88   Silhouette Romance
620   A Man Of Her Own   12/88   Silhouette Romance
638   Someone To Love   03/89   Silhouette Romance
667   Be My Baby   08/89   Silhouette Romance
715   A Woman's Touch   04/90   Silhouette Romance
757   The Southern Man   11/90   Silhouette Romance
778   For Heaven's Sake   03/91   Silhouette Romance

AUTHOR/TITLE INDEX

Trent, Brenda

816	Dance Until Dawn	09/91	Silhouette Romance
51	Stormy Affair	10/82	Silhouette Special Edition

Trent, Danielle

121	Winter Roses		Harlequin Superromance

Trent, Lynda

	Wyndfell		
	The Master's Touch		
	The Tryst		
427	Follow Your Heart	02/92	Harlequin American
	Christmas Yet To Come	/91	Harlequin Hist. Christmas Stories
59	Heaven's Embrace		Harlequin Historical
75	The Black Hawk	05/91	Harlequin Historical
119	Rachel	04/92	Harlequin Historical
154	Beloved Wife	02/93	Harlequin Historical
232	Thornbeck	08/94	Harlequin Historical
314	The Fire Within	04/96	Harlequin Historical
348	The Gift Of Summer		Harlequin Superromance
430	Words To Treasure		Harlequin Superromance
504	Jordan's Wife	06/92	Harlequin Superromance
536	Reflections Of Becca	02/93	Harlequin Superromance
569	Starlit Tomorrow	10/93	Harlequin Superromance
583	If I Must Choose	02/94	Harlequin Superromance
291	Another Rainbow	03/90	Harlequin Temptation
	Everlasting		Harper Collins
	A Valentine Sampler	01/93	Leisure Contemporary
	Opal Fires	08/93	Leisure Contemporary
	Yesterday's Roses		Nal Penguin
	Embrace The Storm		Pocket
	Embrace The Wind		Pocket
	Willow Wind		Pocket
	Shining Nights		Pocket Richard Gallen Books
	Opal Fires		Pocket Richard Gallen Books
	Yesterday's Roses		Pocket Richard Gallen Books
201	The Enchantment	04/85	Silhouette Desire
223	Simple Pleasures	08/85	Silhouette Desire
36	Designs	01/84	Silhouette Intimate Moments
68	Taking Chances	09/84	Silhouette Intimate Moments
134	Castle In The Sands	03/86	Silhouette Intimate Moments
378	High Society	04/87	Silhouette Special Edition
409	A Certain Smile	10/87	Silhouette Special Edition
443	Heat Lightning	03/88	Silhouette Special Edition
457	Beguiling Ways	06/88	Silhouette Special Edition
504	Like Strangers	01/89	Silhouette Special Edition
534	Repeat Performance	06/89	Silhouette Special Edition
	Summerfield		Zebra Historical

Tresillian, Richard

Tresillian, Richard
   1 The Bandmaster   Warner
   2 Blood Of The Bondmaster   Warner
   3 The Bondmaster Breed   Warner

Trevor, June
  88 Winged Victory   09/83 Silhouette Desire
  11 Until The End Of Time 07/83 Silhouette Intimate Moments

Trevor, Meriod
      The Wanton Fires   Ballantine Historical
      The Sun With A Face   Ballantine Historical

Triner, Jeanne
 267 By Any Other Name   Harlequin Superromance
 319 Make No Mistake   Harlequin Superromance

Troy, Amanda
  63 Double Deception   /82 Berkley Second Chance At Love

Truesdell, June
  39 Be Still My Love   /50 Harlequin

Tucker, Elaine
   4 They Said It Wouldn't Last /84 Berkley To Have And To Hold
  12 Strange Bedfellows   /84 Berkley To Have And To Hold

Tucker, Helen
      The Halverton Scandal   Ballantine Historical
      A Curious Proposal   Ballantine Historical
      Bold Imposter   Leisure
      Bound By Honor   Pocket
      Ardent Vows   Pocket

Tucker, Joy
      Wild Card Bride   10/91 Avon
      Traitor's Kiss   01/93 Avon

Turner, Barbara
 281 The Blond Chameleon 05/86 Silhouette Desire
 350 Cassie Come Home   03/85 Silhouette Romance
 410 The Catnip Man   01/86 Silhouette Romance
 465 Las Vegas Match   10/86 Silhouette Romance
 490 Satin And White Lace 03/87 Silhouette Romance
 608 True Bliss   10/88 Silhouette Romance
 641 Sister Wolf   04/89 Silhouette Romance

Turner, Elizabeth
      Forbidden Fires   /88 Avon
      Inside Paradise   04/96 Avon
      Midnight Rain   06/94 Avon Historical
      Fortune's Captive   04/91 Diamond
      Sweet Possession   /86 Tapestry

Turner, Joan
 772 Chloe Wilde, Student Nurse /63 Harlequin

Turner, Linda

AUTHOR/TITLE INDEX

Turner, Linda

65	A Persistent Flame		Harlequin	Superromance
220	A Glimpse Of Heaven	07/85	Silhouette	Desire
653	Wild Texas Rose	07/91	Silhouette	Desire
701	Philly And The Playboy	03/92	Silhouette	Desire
802	The Seducer	08/93	Silhouette	Desire
929	Heaven Can't Wait (Spellbound)	05/95	Silhouette	Desire
238	The Echo Of Thunder	05/88	Silhouette	Intimate Moments
263	Crosscurrents	11/88	Silhouette	Intimate Moments
298	An Unsuspecting Heart	08/89	Silhouette	Intimate Moments
316	Flirting With Danger	12/89	Silhouette	Intimate Moments
354	Moonlight And Lace	10/90	Silhouette	Intimate Moments
448	The Love Of Dugan Magee	09/92	Silhouette	Intimate Moments
523	Gable's Lady (American Heroes)	10/93	Silhouette	Intimate Moments
553	Cooper (The Wild West)	03/94	Silhouette	Intimate Moments
572	Flynn (The Wild West)	06/94	Silhouette	Intimate Moments
590	Kat	09/94	Silhouette	Intimate Moments
649	Who's The Boss? (Heartbreakers)	07/95	Silhouette	Intimate Moments
673	The Loner	11/95	Silhouette	Intimate Moments
709	Maddy Lawrence's Big Adventure	05/96	Silhouette	Intimate Moments
350	Shadows In The Night	12/86	Silhouette	Special Edition

Turner, Lynn

45	Mystery Train		Harlequin	Intrigue
210	Deadly Secrets	01/93	Harlequin	Intrigue
268	The Woman In The Mirror	03/94	Harlequin	Intrigue
893	Forever		Harlequin	Presents
1205	Impulsive Gamble		Harlequin	Presents
134	A Lasting Gift		Harlequin	Superromance
203	Double Trouble		Harlequin	Superromance
8	For Now, For Always	04/84	Harlequin	Temptation
56	Another Dawn	04/85	Harlequin	Temptation
75	Up In Arms	09/85	Harlequin	Temptation
107	Hook, Line And Sinker	05/86	Harlequin	Temptation
	Dreamer's Heart	08/96	Pinnacle	Denise Little Presents

Turney, C. Dell

	Danger At Bell Tide	/91	Avalon
	The Killing Tree		Avalon Mystery Romance

Tyler, Alison

99	A Glimmer Of Trust	/86	Dell Candlelight Ecstasy
109	Perfect Chararde	/86	Dell Ecstasy Supreme

Tyler, Antonia

303	This Shining Hour	/85	Berkley Second Chance At Love

Tyre, Robert

437	Saddlebag Surgeon	/58	Harlequin

Ullman, Albert E.

335	Hoodlum Alley	/55	Harlequin

Van Nuys, Joan

Beloved Pretender	10/93	Avon
Beloved Deceiver	11/94	Avon
Forever Beloved	05/96	Avon
Beloved Intruder	11/92	Avon Romance
Beloved Avenger		Leisure
Unwilling Betrayer	05/92	Leisure
Beloved Enchantress		Leisure Historical

Van Vogt, A.E.

177	The House That Stood Still	/52	Harlequin

Van Wieren, Mona

630	Rhapsody In Bloom	02/89	Silhouette Romance
783	A Prince Among Men	12/92	Silhouette Special Edition

Van Wormer, Laura

Any Given Moment	11/95	Mira

Van-Loon, Antonia

For Us The Living	Bantam

Vandergriff, Aola

Daughters Of The Storm	Warner
In This Sweet Land, Inga's Story	Warner
Daughters Of The Wild Country	Warner
Daughters Of The Far Islands	Warner
Duaghters Of The Misty Isles	Warner
Daughters Of The Opal Skies	Warner
Daughters Of The Southwind	Warner
Daughters Of The Shining City	Warner

Vann, Suzette

534	His Other Mother	11/93	Silhouette Intimate Moments

Vargas, Deborah

Red Hawk's Return	/91

Varner, Linda

625	Heart Of The Matter	01/89	Silhouette Romance
644	Heart Rustler	04/89	Silhouette Romance
665	The Luck Of The Irish	08/89	Silhouette Romance
698	Honeymoon Hideaway	01/90	Silhouette Romance
734	Better To Have Loved	07/90	Silhouette Romance
780	A House Becomes A Home	03/91	Silhouette Romance
835	Mistletoe And Miracles	12/91	Silhouette Romance
851	As Sweet As Candy	03/92	Silhouette Romance
868	Diamonds Are Forever	06/92	Silhouette Romance
906	A Good Catch	02/93	Silhouette Romance
943	Something Borrowed	06/93	Silhouette Romance
966	Firelight And Forever	10/93	Silhouette Romance
1036	Dad On The Job	10/94	Silhouette Romance
1051	Believing In Miracles	12/94	Silhouette Romance
1068	Wife Most Unlikely (Mr. Right, Inc.)	03/95	Silhouette Romance

Vasilos, Freda
231	Moon Madness	09/85	Silhouette Desire
286	Summer Wine	01/86	Silhouette Special Edition

Vasilos, Tina
68	Unwitting Accomplice		Harlequin Intrigue
101	Wolf's Prey		Harlequin Intrigue
132	Past Tense		Harlequin Intrigue
235	Cry Of The Peacock	07/93	Harlequin Intrigue
274	Lost Innocence	05/94	Harlequin Intrigue
341	Killing Her Softly	10/95	Harlequin Intrigue
351	Echoes On The Wind		Harlequin Superromance
467	Black Night, Amber Morning	09/91	Harlequin Superromance

Vaughan, Carter A.
	Yankee Rascals		Historical

Vaughan, Vivian
	Reluctant Enemies	05/95	Zebra
	No Place For A Lady	/95	Zebra
	Silver Surrender	06/92	Zebra Jarrett Family
	Sweet Autumn Surrender	10/91	Zebra Jarrett Family
	Sunrise Surrender	09/93	Zebra Jarrett Family
	Secret Surrender	06/94	Zebra Jarrett Family
	Reluctant Enemies	04/95	Zebra Lovegram
1	Texas Gamble	01/90	Zebra Texas Star Trilogy
2	Texas Dawn	08/90	Zebra Texas Star Trilogy
3	Texas Gold	04/91	Zebra Texas Star Trilogy
	Heart's Desire	05/87	Zebra Heartfire Silver Creek
	Runaway Passion	11/88	Zebra Heartfire Silver Creek
	Sweet Texas Nights	03/89	Zebra Heartfire Silver Creek
	Texas Twilight	12/87	Zebra Heartfire Silver Creek

Vaughn, Dona
	Rivalries		Harper
	Chasing The Comet	/86	Walker

Vaughn, Evelyn
8	Waiting For The Wolf Moon	05/93	Harlequin
39	Burning Times	09/94	Harlequin Shadows
52	Beneath The Surface	05/95	Harlequin Shadows
66	Forest Of The Night	07/96	Silhouette Shadows

Vayle, Valerie
	Mistress Of The Night	/86	Dell
	Night Fire		Dell
	Lady Of Fire	/83	Dell
	Seaflame	/83	Dell
	Orianna	/83	Dell

Vendresha, Vita
	Ride The Eagle	10/87	Worldwide Libr.

Verge, Lisa Ann

AUTHOR/TITLE INDEX

Vickery, Katherine

	Flame Of Desire	/86	Nal Onyx
	Tame The Wild Wind	/88	Nal Onyx
	Flame Across The Highlands	/90	Pocket
	Desire Of The Heart	/91	Pocket

Victor, Cindy

60	An Intimate Oasis	05/85	Harlequin Temptation
138	Kindred Spirits	01/87	Harlequin Temptation

Victor, Vanessa

70	Dinner For Two	06/83	Silhouette Desire

Vincent, Joan

570	Thomasina	Dell Candlelight Regency
586	The Education Of Joanne	Dell Candlelight Regency
595	A Bond Of Honour	Dell Candlelight Regency
604	A Scheme For Love	Dell Candlelight Regency
604	A Scheme For Love	Dell Candlelight Regency
632	Rescued By Love	Dell Candlelight Regency
650	The Curious Rogue	Dell Candlelight Regency

Vincenzi, Penny

	Wicked Pleasures	09/94	Bantam
	Old Sins	04/92	Ivy Books

Vincer, Rachel

117	Hot Copy	12/92	Meteor
146	Prim And Improper	05/93	Meteor Kismet

Vine, Kerry

264	Alpine Idyll	12/83	Silhouette Romance

Vinet, Lynette

Love's Golden Promise	01/93	Leisure Historical
Passion's Deep Spell	11/91	Zebra Heartfire
Pirate's Bride		Zebra Heartfire
Wicked, Wild Eden	/90	Zebra Heartfire
Emerald Desire		Zebra Heartfire
Emerald Enchantment		Zebra Heartfire
Emerald Ecstasy		Zebra Heartfire
Love's Golden Promise		Zebra Heartfire
Midnight Flame		Zebra Heartfire
Savage Deception	/89	Zebra Heartfire
Pirate's Bride	06/89	Zebra Heartfire

Vinton, Anne

407	The Hospital In Buwambo	/57	Harlequin
439	Hospital In Sudan	/58	Harlequin
477	Hospital Blue	/59	Harlequin
519	Doctor Pamela	/60	Harlequin
530	Dr. Daring's Love Affair	/60	Harlequin
534	Doctor's Wife ... In Secret	/60	Harlequin
559	The Time Of Enchantment	/60	Harlequin

Wagner, Kimberli

56	Encore	08/84	Bantam	Loveswept
96	Enchantment	06/85	Bantam	Loveswept
175	Expose	01/87	Bantam	Loveswept
567	A Cowboy's Touch	09/92	Bantam	Loveswept
623	The Doctor Takes A Wife	06/93	Bantam	Loveswept
679	Lord Of The Island	04/94	Bantam	Loveswept

Wagner, Nancy

	Two Sisters	09/93	Avon

Wagner, Sharon

26	Strangers Who Love		Nal	Rapture Romance
	The Lost Lilacs Of Latimer House		Zebra	Gothic
	Dark Cloister	01/94	Zebra	Gothic
	Black Bayou	07/93	Zebra	Gothic
	Moonglow	02/95	Zebra	To Love Again

Wainscott, Tina Ritter

	Shades Of Heaven	10/95	St. Martin's Romantic Suspense
	On The Way To Heaven	04/95	St. Martin's Romantic Suspense

Wake, Vivien Fiske

The Secret Shadows Of Ravensfall	Zebra	Gothic

Wakefield, Maureen

Accessory To Love	Warner

Wakley, Dorothy

Sweet Revenge	Berkley

Walden, Luanne

Bitter Sweet Destiny	Diamond
Tides Of Splendor	Diamond
Tides Of Ecstasy	Zebra

Walker, Constance

The Lost Roses Of Ganymede House	Zebra	Gothic
The Shimmering Stones Of Glendower Hall	Zebra	Gothic

Walker, Dorothy Pierce

319	Woman Doctor	/54	Harlequin
365	Doctors Are Different	/56	Harlequin

Walker, Elizabeth

	The Loving Seasons	04/89	Nal Regency

Walker, Elizabeth Neff

	A Curious Courting		Ballantine Regency
	The Nomad Harp		Ballantine Regency
	Heart Conditions	12/94	Signet
122	Antique Affair	10/83	Silhouette Special Edition
176	That Other Woman	07/84	Silhouette Special Edition
251	Paternity	07/85	Silhouette Special Edition

Walker, Irma

104	Sonata For My Love		Harlequin Superromance
147	Through Night & Day		Harlequin Superromance

AUTHOR/TITLE INDEX

Wallace, Edgar

361	Clue Of The Silver Key	/56	Harlequin
378	The Ringer	/57	Harlequin
387	White Face	/57	Harlequin
395	The Angel Of Terror	/57	Harlequin
418	The Feathered Serpent	/58	Harlequin
420	The Squeaker	/58	Harlequin
428	The Strange Countess	/58	Harlequin
444	Double Dan	/58	Harlequin
447	The Crimson Circle	/59	Harlequin
456	The Yellow Snake	/59	Harlequin
466	The Traitor's Gate	/59	Harlequin
475	The Mind Of Mr. J.G. Reeder	/59	Harlequin
484	The Northing Trap	/59	Harlequin
493	The Man At The Carleton	/59	Harlequin

Wallace, Pamela

	The Fires Of Beltane		Harlequin	Historical
16	Promises	08/82	Silhouette	Desire
13	Come Back, My Love	10/83	Silhouette	Intimate Moments
24	Fantasies	04/84	Silhouette	Intimate Moments
48	Cry For The Man	07/84	Silhouette	Intimate Moments
58	Promises In The Dark	02/85	Silhouette	Intimate Moments
83	Scoundrel	12/82	Silhouette	Special Edition
63	Love With A Perfect Stranger	06/83	Silhouette	Special Edition
102	Dreams Lost, Dreams Found	08/85	Silhouette	Special Edition
255	Tears In The Rain	05/86	Silhouette	Special Edition
311	All My Love Forever	09/86	Silhouette	Special Edition
334	Forever And A Day			

Wallace, Pat

4	Sweetheart Contract	05/83	Silhouette	Intimate Moments
53	Objections Overruled	06/84	Silhouette	Intimate Moments
100	Love Scene	06/85	Silhouette	Intimate Moments
116	Star Rise	10/85	Silhouette	Intimate Moments
56	Silver Fire	11/82	Silhouette	Special Edition
104	My Loving Enemy	07/83	Silhouette	Special Edition
145	Shining Hour	02/84	Silhouette	Special Edition

Walsh, Alida

273	This Business Of Love	11/85	Silhouette	Special Edition

Walsh, Kelly

248	Cherished Harbor		Harlequin	Superromance
286	Of Time And Tenderness		Harlequin	Superromance
336	A Place For Us		Harlequin	Superromance
360	A Private Affair		Harlequin	Superromance
415	Starlight, Star Bright		Harlequin	Superromance
445	Russian Nights		Harlequin	Superromance
475	Nightshades And Orchids	11/91	Harlequin	Superromance

Walsh, Penelope

968	Sweet Brenda	/65	Harlequin
1755	School My Heart	/74	Harlequin

Walsh, Sheila

The Arrogant Lord Alastair		Nal
The Golden Songbird		Nal
A Highly Respectable Marriage		Nal
The Incomparable Miss Brady		Nal
Madelena		Nal
The Notorious Nabob		Nal
The Rose Domino		Nal
The Sergeant Major's Daughter		Nal
The Wary Widow		Nal
Lord Gilmore's Bride		Nal Regency
Lady Aurelia's Bequest	09/87	Nal Regency
Minerva's Marquess	05/88	Nal Regency
Bath Intrigue	10/91	Nal Regency
The Perfect Bride	10/94	Nal Regency
A Regency Summer	06/92	Nal Super Regency
Tokens Of Love	12/92	Nal Super Regency
The Incorrigible Rake		Nal Penguin Regency
The Diamond Waterfall		Nal Penguin Regency
The Runaway Bride		Nal Penguin Regency
The Pink Parasol		Nal Penguin Regency
Lady Avalon's Request	09/87	Nal Penguin Regency
Minerva's Marquis		Nal Penguin Regency
A Suitable Match		Nal Penguin Regency
A Fine Silk Purse		Nal Penguin Regency
Tokens Of Love: Five Regency Love Stories	01/93	Penguin Super Regency

Walters, Jade

211	Greek Idyll	03/83	Silhouette Romance

Walters, Janet Lane

The Best Medicine	07/93	Zebra To Love Again

Walters, Linda

60	Dragon's Eye	Harlequin Intrigue
82	Dead Reckoning	Harlequin Intrigue

Walton, Bobbie

Rapture's Rage	Zebra

Walton, Kay

479	Over The Horizon	12/91	Harlequin Superromance
517	Message From Magens Bay	09/92	Harlequin Superromance

Walz, Jay And Audrey

157	The Bizarre Sisters	/52	Harlequin

Warady, Phylis Ann

Scandal's Daughter	09/90	Walker
The Earl's Comeuppance	12/91	Walker

AUTHOR/TITLE INDEX

Warady, Phylis Ann

The Persistent Suitor	12/91	Walker
The Golden Swan	/94	Walker
Flowers For The Bride	04/95	Zebra Anthology
Delightful Deceiver	05/95	Zebra Anthology
The Persistent Suitor	03/95	Zebra Regency
Breach Of Honor	10/95	Zebra Regency

Ward, Lynda

317	Race The Sun		Harlequin 1 Welles Family Trilogy
321	Leap The Moon		Harlequin 2 Welles Family Trilogy
325	Touch The Stars	09/88	Harlequin 3 Welles Family Trilogy
3	The Music Of Passion		Harlequin Superromance
33	The Touch Of Passion		Harlequin Superromance
89	A Sea Change		Harlequin Superromance
119	Never Strangers		Harlequin Superromance
162	Vows Forever		Harlequin Superromance
402	Precious Things		Harlequin Superromance
491	Morning Has Broken	03/92	Harlequin Superromance
141	Love In Tandem	02/87	Harlequin Temptation

Ward, Rebecca

My Lord Lion	04/95	Avon Regency
Cinderella's Stepmother		Ballantine
Lord Longshanks		Ballantine Regency
Lady In Siver		Ballantine Regency
Fair Fortune		Ballantine Regency
Lady In The Shadow	03/94	Fawcett Regency
A Monstrous Secret	05/96	Fawcett Regency
Enchanted Rendevous	10/91	Fawcett Crest Regency
Madam Mystery	03/92	Fawcett Crest Regency
Grand Deception	09/92	Fawcett Crest Regency
The Wild Rose		Fawcett Crest Regency Romance

Ware, Ciji

Island Of The Swans		Bantam
Wicked Company	11/92	Bantam Fanfare

Ware, Edouard

Mortal Sins		Bantam

Ware, Joyce C.

Bayou Dreams		Bantam
The Lost Heiress Of Hawkscliff		Zebra Gothic
White Roses Of Brambeldene	02/92	Zebra Gothic
And Be My Love	09/93	Zebra To Love Again
Homefires	11/94	Zebra To Love Again
Colorado High	03/95	Zebra To Love Again

Ware, Sandra

Sacred Lies	05/93	Bantam

Warfield, Teresa

AUTHOR/TITLE INDEX

Warfield, Teresa

A Touch Of Heaven	05/94	Mother's Day Novella
Summer Storm	08/93	Berkley Historical
A Heart So Wild		Diamond Great Lake Series
Prairie Dreams	10/92	Diamond Homespun
A Homespun Mother's Day	05/94	Diamond Homespun
Country Sunshine	09/94	Diamond Homespun
Cherokee Rose	10/93	Jove
A Matter Of Honor	06/94	Jove
Cherokee Bride	06/94	Jove
Make Believe	05/95	Jove Homespun
Heaven Made	12/95	Jove Homespun

Warren, Betsy

2770	Song Without Words		Harlequin Romance

Warren, Beverly C.

The Haunted Heiress Of Windcliffe Manor	09/92	Zebra Gothic
Lost Ladies Of Windswept Moor		Zebra Gothic
The Lost Locket Of Windbrace Hall	07/91	Zebra Gothic
The Midnight Heather Of Bridee Castle		Zebra Gothic
Bride Of Hatfield Castle	07/92	Zebra Regency

Warren, Linda

533	Branded	03/92	Bantam Loveswept
616	Swept Away	05/93	Bantam Loveswept
677	Body And Soul	03/94	Bantam Loveswept
699	Down And Dirty	07/94	Bantam Loveswept
737	After Midnight	03/95	Bantam Loveswept
761	On The Wild Side	09/95	Bantam Loveswept
780	Under The Covers	03/96	Bantam Loveswept

Warren, Pat

2	Bright Hopes	04/92	Harlequin Tyler
6	Sunshine	08/92	Harlequin Tyler
	' Til Death Do Us Part	02/92	Pinnacle Suspense
	Michael's House	09/96	Silhouette Intimate Moments
	Keeping Kate	10/96	Silhouette Intimate Moments
288	Perfect Strangers	05/89	Silhouette Intimate Moments
605	Only The Lonely	11/94	Silhouette Intimate Moments
6	Outlaw Lovers	01/95	Silhouette Montana Mavericks
553	Season Of The Heart	01/88	Silhouette Romance
	One Love, One Life	/96	Silhouette Special Edition
375	With This Ring	04/87	Silhouette Special Edition
410	The Final Verdict	10/87	Silhouette Special Edition
442	Look Homeward, Love	03/88	Silhouette Special Edition
458	Summer Shadows	06/88	Silhouette Special Edition
480	The Evolution Of Adam	09/88	Silhouette Special Edition
514	Build Me A Dream	03/89	Silhouette Special Edition
548	The Long Road Home	09/89	Silhouette Special Edition

AUTHOR/TITLE INDEX

Warren, Pat

582	The Lyon And The Lamb	02/90	Silhouette Special Edition
610	My First Love, My Last	07/90	Silhouette Special Edition
632	Winter Wishes	11/90	Silhouette Special Edition
659	Till I Loved You	03/91	Silhouette Special Edition
678	An Uncommon Love	06/91	Silhouette Special Edition
731	Under Sunny Skies	03/92	Silhouette Special Edition
758	That Hathaway Woman	08/92	Silhouette Special Edition
797	Simply Unforgettable	02/93	Silhouette Special Edition
815	This I Ask Of You	05/93	Silhouette Special Edition
841	On Her Own (That Special Woman!)	10/93	Silhouette Special Edition
893	A Bride For Hunter	06/94	Silhouette Special Edition
974	Nobody's Child (Man, Woman And Child)	08/95	Silhouette Special Edition
1048	A Home For Hannah	08/96	Silhouette Special Edition
	Forbidden	04/95	Warner
	Beholden	05/96	Warner
	No Regrets	/97	Warner
	Hurricane (Tentative Title)	/97	Warner
	Murder Under The Tree	11/93	Zebra Christmas Mystery
	Nowhere To Run	04/93	Zebra Suspense
	Shattered Vows	05/95	Zebra Suspense

Washburn, Jan

	Finders, Keepers	04/94	Bantam Sweet Dreams

Watson, Ken

442	Curling With Ken Watson	/58	Harlequin
635	Curling Today	/61	Harlequin

Watson, Margaret

45	Personal Best	06/91	Meteor
636	An Innocent Man	04/95	Silhouette Intimate Moments
708	An Honorable Man	04/96	Silhouette Intimate Moments

Watson, Mary

	Race Against Time	07/95	Pinnacle Denise Little Presents

Watson, Will

396	Double Cross Ranch	/57	Harlequin

Watters, Patricia

	Come Be My Love	04/93	Avon

Waverly, Shannon

	Father Knows Last!	05/94	Harlequin Anthology
	A New Lease On Love	06/92	Harlequin Romance
3074	Trust Me, My Love		Harlequin Romance
3150	No Trespassing	09/91	Harlequin Romance
3204	New Lease On Love	06/92	Harlequin Romance
3259	Temporary Arrangement	04/93	Harlequin Romance
3292	Christmas Angel	12/93	Harlequin Romance
3316	The Baby Battle (Kids & Kisses)	06/94	Harlequin Romance
3319	Expectations (Weddings, Inc.)	07/94	Harlequin Romance

Waverly, Shannon

3380	The Best Man	10/95	Harlequin	Romance
660	Three For The Road	09/95	Harlequin	Superromance
703	Under One Roof	08/96	Harlequin	Superromance

Way, Margaret

1446	The Time Of The Jacaranda	/70	Harlequin	
1470	King Country	/71	Harlequin	
1500	Blaze Of Silk	/71	Harlequin	
1530	The Man From Bahl Bahla	/71	Harlequin	
1571	Summer Magic	/72	Harlequin	
1603	Ring Of Jade	/72	Harlequin	
1687	Noonfire	/73	Harlequin	
1766	Storm Over Mandargi	/74	Harlequin	
1785	The Love Theme	/74	Harlequin	
1815	Wind River	/74	Harlequin	
1840	Return To Belle Amber	/74	Harlequin	
1863	Mc Cabe's Kingdom	/75	Harlequin	
1880	Sweet Sundown	/75	Harlequin	
1889	Reeds Of Honey	/75	Harlequin	
1974	A Lesson In Loving	/76	Harlequin	
2016	Flight Into Yesterday	/76	Harlequin	
2060	The Man On Half-Moon	/77	Harlequin	
2074	Swans' Reach	/77	Harlequin	
2111	One Way Ticket	/77	Harlequin	
2132	Black Ingo	/78	Harlequin	
2145	Portrait Of Jaime	/78	Harlequin	
2174	Mutiny In Paradise	/78	Harlequin	
2188	The Wild Swan	/78	Harlequin	
2203	The Awakening Flame	/78	Harlequin	
78	A Man Like Daintree	/75	Harlequin	Presents
82	Copper Moon	/75	Harlequin	Presents
94	Bauhinia Junction	/75	Harlequin	Presents
102	The Rainbow Bird	/75	Harlequin	Presents
134	Storm Flower	/76	Harlequin	Presents
154	Red Cliffs Of Malpara	/76	Harlequin	Presents
270	Ring Of Fire		Harlequin	Presents
549	Broken Rhapsody		Harlequin	Presents
	Marry Me, Cowboy!	04/95	Harlequin	Promotion
2258	Wake The Sleeping Tiger		Harlequin	Romance
2260	Marriage Impossible		Harlequin	Romance
2265	The Winds Of Heaven		Harlequin	Romance
2276	White Magnolia		Harlequin	Romance
2291	Valley Of The Moon		Harlequin	Romance
2328	Blue Lotus		Harlequin	Romance
2346	Butterfly And Baron		Harlequin	Romance
2357	The Golden Puma		Harlequin	Romance
2387	Lord Of High Valley		Harlequin	Romance

Way, Margaret

2400	Flamingo Park		Harlequin	Romance
2429	Temple Of Fire		Harlequin	Romance
2435	Shadow Dance		Harlequin	Romance
2448	A Season For Change		Harlequin	Romance
2454	The Mc Ivor Affair		Harlequin	Romance
2476	North Of Capricorn		Harlequin	Romance
2490	Home To Morningstar		Harlequin	Romance
2537	Spellbound		Harlequin	Romance
2539	The Silver Veil		Harlequin	Romance
2556	Hunter's Moon		Harlequin	Romance
2591	Girl At Cobalt Creek		Harlequin	Romance
2609	House Of Memories		Harlequin	Romance
2634	Almost A Stranger		Harlequin	Romance
2639	No Alternative		Harlequin	Romance
2658	Place Called Rambula		Harlequin	Romance
2700	Fallen Idol		Harlequin	Romance
2724	Eagle's Ridge		Harlequin	Romance
2784	The Tiger's Cage		Harlequin	Romance
2820	Innocent In Eden		Harlequin	Romance
2832	Diamond Valley		Harlequin	Romance
2958	Devil Moon		Harlequin	Romance
2976	Mowana Magic		Harlequin	Romance
2999	The Hungary Heart		Harlequin	Romance
3012	Rise Of An Eagle		Harlequin	Romance
3295	One Fateful Summer	01/94	Harlequin	Romance
3331	The Carradine Brand	10/94	Harlequin	Romance
3381	Once Burned	10/95	Harlequin	Romance
3391	A Faulkner Possession	01/96	Harlequin	Romance

Wayne, Joanna

288	Deep In The Bayou	08/94	Harlequin	Intrigue
339	Behind The Mask	09/95	Harlequin	Intrigue

Wayne, Rochelle

Ecstasy's Dawn	
Loving Torment	
Sweet Ecstasy	
Midnight Angel	Zebra
Rebellious Heart	Zebra
Savage Caress	Zebra
Texas Ecstasy	Zebra
Untamed Heart	Zebra
Midnight Slave	Zebra
Frontier Flame	Zebra
Surrender To Ecstasy	Zebra
Reckless Passion	Zebra
Elusive Enchantment	Zebra
Savage Abandon	Zebra

AUTHOR/TITLE INDEX

Weale, Anne

504	Passage To Paxos		Harlequin Presents
511	A Touch Of The Devil		Harlequin Presents
541	Portrait Of Bethany		Harlequin Presents
565	Wedding Of The Year		Harlequin Presents
613	All That Heaven Allows		Harlequin Presents
622	Yesterday's Island		Harlequin Presents
670	Ecstasy		Harlequin Presents
846	Frangipani		Harlequin Presents
1013	Girl In A Golden Bed		Harlequin Presents
1061	Night Train		Harlequin Presents
1085	Lost Lagoon		Harlequin Presents
1133	Catalan Christmas		Harlequin Presents
1270	Do You Remember Baby		Harlequin Presents
2411	Last Night At Paradise		Harlequin Romance
2436	Rain Of Diamonds		Harlequin Romance
2484	Bed Of Roses		Harlequin Romance
2940	Neptune's Daughter		Harlequin Romance
3108	Thai Silk		Harlequin Romance
3132	Sea Fever		Harlequin Romance
3216	Pink Champagne	08/92	Harlequin Romance
3257	The Singing Tree	03/93	Harlequin Romance
3318	The Faberge Cat	06/94	Harlequin Romance
	All My Worldly Goods		St. Martin's
	Antigua Kiss		Worldwide Lib.
	Flora		Worldwide Lib.

Weaver, Ingrid

570	True Blue	05/94	Silhouette Intimate Moments
660	True Lies	08/95	Silhouette Intimate Moments

Webb, Peggy

	Where Dolphins Go	01/94	Bantam
	Witch Dance	07/94	Bantam Fanfare
	From A Distance	10/95	Bantam Fanfare
	Indiscreet	09/96	Bantam Loveswept
106	Taming Maggie	08/85	Bantam Loveswept
112	Birds Of A Feather	10/85	Bantam Loveswept
137	Tarnished Armor	04/86	Bantam Loveswept
143	Donovan's Angel	06/86	Bantam Loveswept
157	Duplicity	09/86	Bantam Loveswept
170	Scamp Of Saltillo	12/86	Bantam Loveswept
178	Disturbing The Peace	02/87	Bantam Loveswept
192	The Joy Bus	05/87	Bantam Loveswept
203	Summer Jazz	08/87	Bantam Loveswept
216	Private Lives	11/87	Bantam Loveswept
275	Sleepless Nights	08/88	Bantam Loveswept
301	Hallie's Destiny	01/89	Bantam Loveswept
328	Any Thrusday	05/89	Bantam Loveswept

AUTHOR/TITLE INDEX

Webb, Peggy

AUTHOR/TITLE INDEX

Weger, Jackie
89	The Wings Of Morning	01/86	Harlequin Temptation
159	The Way Of Destiny	06/87	Harlequin Temptation
181	Eye Of The Beholder	12/87	Harlequin Temptation
207	On A Wing And A Prayer	06/88	Harlequin Temptation

Weinbaum, Stanley G.
205   The Black Flame   /53   Harlequin

Weir, Theresa
Amazon Lady
One Fine Day   02/94   Bantam Contemporary
Forever   11/91   Bantam Fanfare
Long Night Moon   03/95   Bantam Fanfare
339   Iguana Bay   06/90   Silhouette Intimate Moments
576   The Forever Man   05/88   Silhouette Romance
650   Loving Jenny   05/89   Silhouette Romance
761   Pictures Of Emily   12/90   Silhouette Romance

Weldon, Susan
Heart's Honor   09/95   Avon
Tempt A Lady   10/94   Avon Historical
Summer Nights   09/95   Zebra

Welks, Alyssa
Dragon Flower   Nal Penguin

Welles, Caron
13   Raven's Song   Harlequin American

Welles, Rosalind
575   Entwined Destinies   Dell Candlelight

Wellington, Kate
22   A Delicate Balance   /84   Berkley To Have And To Hold

Wells, Angela
267	Dishounourable Seduction	02/96	Harlequin
192	Golden Mistress	07/94	Harlequin Direct
1164	Love's Wrongs		Harlequin Presents
1181	Errant Daughter		Harlequin Presents
1462	Tattered Loving	05/92	Harlequin Presents
1581	Reckless Deception	08/93	Harlequin Presents
1691	Viking Magic (Postcards From Europe)	10/94	Harlequin Presents
2790	Sweet Poison		Harlequin Romance
2844	Moroccan Madness		Harlequin Romance
2845	When Love Flies By		Harlequin Romance
2903	Desperate Remedy		Harlequin Romance
2921	Fortune's Fool		Harlequin Romance
3006	Still Temptation		Harlequin Romance
3054	Rash Contract		Harlequin Romance
3143	Summer's Pride	08/91	Harlequin Romance
3246	Torrid Conflict	01/93	Harlequin Romance

Wells, Robin

Wells, Robin

Welsh, Jeanette

Wender, Ruth

Wendt, Jo Ann

Wentworth, Sally

AUTHOR/TITLE INDEX

Wentworth, Sally

1220	The Devil's Shadow		Harlequin Presents
1237	Strange Encounter		Harlequin Presents
1278	Wish On The Moon		Harlequin Presents
1309	Echoes Of The Past		Harlequin Presents
1334	Fire Island		Harlequin Presents
1357	Lord Of Misrule		Harlequin Presents
1390	Taken On Trust	08/91	Harlequin Presents
1453	Illusions Of Love	04/92	Harlequin Presents
1494	Broken Destiny	09/92	Harlequin Presents
1517	The Devil's Kiss	12/92	Harlequin Presents
1550	The Golden Greek	04/93	Harlequin Presents
1572	Stormy Voyage	07/93	Harlequin Presents
1605	The Wayward Wife	11/93	Harlequin Presents
1634	Mirrors Of The Sea	03/94	Harlequin Presents
1668	Yesterday's Affair (Postcards From Europe)	07/94	Harlequin Presents
1701	Practice To Deceive	11/94	Harlequin Presents
1738	Shadow Play	05/95	Harlequin Presents
1764	Duel In The Sun	09/95	Harlequin Presents
1787	To Have And To Hold	01/96	Harlequin Presents
1810	One Night Of Love	05/96	Harlequin Presents
1832	Chris	08/96	Harlequin Presents
2254	Rightful Possession		Harlequin Romance
2262	Liberated Lady		Harlequin Romance
2310	The Ice Maiden		Harlequin Romance
2361	Garden Of Thorns		Harlequin Romance

Werner, Patricia

	The Secret At Orient Point		Harlequin Gothic
26	If Truth Be Known		Harlequin Intrigue
	Stolen Bride Of Glengarra		Zebra
	Velvet Dreams	05/94	Zebra
	Island Of Lost Rubies	08/92	Zebra Gothic
	Mistress Of Blackstone Castle	10/91	Zebra Gothic
	The Swirling Mists Of Cornwall		Zebra Gothic
	Bride Of Blackstone Castle	10/91	Zebra Gothic
	Cherokee Bride		Zebra Heartfire
	Cimarron Seductress	11/91	Zebra Heartfire
	Treasured	08/95	Zebra Lovegram

Wesley, Caroline

	King's Castle	/87	Walker

West, Angela

3167	Endless Summer	12/91	Harlequin Romance

West, Cara

9	Guitars, Cadillacs	11/93	Harlequin Crystal Creek
259	Now There's Tomorrow		Harlequin Superromance
299	There Is A Season		Harlequin Superromance

AUTHOR/TITLE INDEX

West, Cara

410	Jenny Kissed Me		Harlequin Superromance
471	Thy Heart In Mine	10/91	Harlequin Superromance
526	Lone Star Drifter	02/93	Harlequin Superromance
674	Can't Forget Him	01/96	Harlequin Superromance

West, Chassie

	Sunrise	10/94	Harper Monogram

West, Frances

496	Honky Tonk Angel	05/89	Silhouette Desire
604	White Heat	11/90	Silhouette Desire

West, Jennifer

82	Passion's Legacy	06/91	Harlequin Historical
10	Season Of Rainbows	07/83	Silhouette Intimate Moments
31	Star Spangled Days	12/83	Silhouette Intimate Moments
71	Edge Of Venus	10/84	Silhouette Intimate Moments
99	Main Chance	06/85	Silhouette Intimate Moments
262	Earth And Fire	09/85	Silhouette Special Edition
283	Return To Paradise	01/86	Silhouette Special Edition
339	Moments Of Glory	10/86	Silhouette Special Edition
366	Object Of Desire	02/87	Silhouette Special Edition
383	Come Pride, Come Passion	05/87	Silhouette Special Edition
404	Sometimes A Miracle	09/87	Silhouette Special Edition
432	Greek To Me	01/88	Silhouette Special Edition
476	Tender Is The Knight	09/88	Silhouette Special Edition
552	Last Stand	09/89	Silhouette Special Edition
594	Suddenly, Paradise	04/90	Silhouette Special Edition

West, Nicola

102	Forgotten Love	01/92	Harlequin Direct
116	Enigma Man	08/92	Harlequin Direct
128	A Heart Set Free	02/93	Harlequin Direct
154	Devil's Dream	09/93	Harlequin Direct
589	Lucifer's Brand		Harlequin Presents
998	Unfinished Business		Harlequin Presents
2526	Devil's Gold		Harlequin Romance
2592	No Room In His Life		Harlequin Romance
2610	Wildtrack		Harlequin Romance
2640	The Tyzak Inheritance		Harlequin Romance
2646	Carver's Bride		Harlequin Romance
2669	Tormented Rhapsody		Harlequin Romance
2718	A Rooted Sorrow		Harlequin Romance
2771	Comeback		Harlequin Romance
2884	Hidden Depths		Harlequin Romance
3089	Snow Demon		Harlequin Romance
3101	A Woman's Place		Harlequin Romance
3168	Last Goodbye	12/91	Harlequin Romance

West, Sara Ann

Weston, Sophie

957	Yesterday's Mirror		Harlequin Presents
980	Beyond Ransom		Harlequin Presents
1014	Challenge		Harlequin Presents
1246	A Matter Of Feeling		Harlequin Presents
2362	An Undefended City		Harlequin Romance
3186	Gypsy In The Night	03/92	Harlequin Romance
3262	No Provocation	04/93	Harlequin Romance
3274	Habit Of Command	07/93	Harlequin Romance

Westwood, Gwen

1333	Keeper Of The Heart	/69	Harlequin
1396	Bright Wilderness	/70	Harlequin
1463	The Emerald Cuckoo	/71	Harlequin
1531	Castle Of The Unicorn	/71	Harlequin
1638	Pirate Of The Sun	/72	Harlequin
1716	Citadel Of Swallows	/73	Harlequin
1843	Sweet Roots And Honey	/75	Harlequin
1948	Ross Of Silver Ridge	/76	Harlequin
2013	Blossoming Gold	/76	Harlequin
2081	Bride Of Bonamour	/77	Harlequin
150	The Last Safari	08/93	Harlequin Direct
2363	Forgotten Bride		Harlequin Romance
2417	Zulu Moon		Harlequin Romance
2477	Dangerous To Love		Harlequin Romance
2586	Secondhand Bride		Harlequin Romance
2736	Wilderness Bride		Harlequin Romance
2796	Safari Heartbreak		Harlequin Romance
2885	Bitter Deception	/87	Harlequin Romance

Weyrich, Becky Lee

	Night Magic	09/93	Avon Anthology
	Hot Winds From Bombay		Ballantine Historical
	The Thistle And The Rose	/87	Bantam
	Forever, For Love	/89	Bantam
	Silver Tears	/90	Bantam
188	Detour To Euphoria	04/87	Bantam Loveswept
	Rapture's Slave	/80	Fawcett Gold Medal
	Captive Of Desire	/82	Fawcett Gold Medal
	Rainbow Hammock	/83	Fawcett Gold Medal
	Tainted Lilies	/84	Fawcett Gold Medal
	Summer Lightning	/85	Fawcett Gold Medal
	Gypsy Moon	/86	Fawcett Gold Medal
	Hot Winds From Bombay	/87	Fawcett Gold Medal
	The Scarlet Thread	/89	Fawcett Gold Medal
	Sands Of Destiny	05/96	Kensington
	Through Caverns Infinite	/78	Manor Books
	Image In A Golden Circle	/78	Manor Books
	Contents For Sale	/78	Manor Books

Weyrich, Becky Lee
    A Dream Come True   03/94   Penguin Topaz Man Presents: Anthology
    Once Upon Forever   03/94   Pinnacle
    Forever, For Love   Pocket
    Silver Tears   Pocket
    Almost Heaven   04/95   Zebra
    Sweet Forever   Zebra Historical

Wheeler, Amanda
    Arms Of The Magnolia   07/95   Fawcett

Wherlock, Julia
    The Beloved
    The Fire Bride   Richard Gallen

Whisenand, Val
  655   Treasure Hunters   06/89   Silhouette Romance
  695   Giveaway Girl   01/90   Silhouette Romance
  802   For Eternity   07/91   Silhouette Romance
  890   Molly Meets Her Match   09/92   Silhouette Romance
  926   Daddy's Back   03/93   Silhouette Romance
 1042   A Father Betrayed (Fabulous Fathers)   11/94   Silhouette Romance
 1165   Temporary Husband   07/96   Silhouette Romance

Whistler, Mary
 1151   Enchanted Autumn   /67   Harlequin
 1194   Sunshine Yellow   /68   Harlequin
 1228   The Young Nightingales   /68   Harlequin
 1550   Pathway Of Roses   /71   Harlequin
 1965   Escape To Happiness   /76   Harlequin

White, Ann Howard
  134   All But Love   03/93   Meteor Kismet
  948   The Mother Of His Child   03/95   Silhouette Special Edition

White, Tiffany
    Valentine Bachelors   02/95   Harlequin Anthology
  274   Open Invitation (Editor's Choice)   11/89   Harlequin Temptation
  318   Cheap Thrills   10/90   Harlequin Temptation
  367   Forbidden Fantasy (Editor's Choice)   10/91   Harlequin Temptation
  407   A Dark And Stormy Knight   08/92   Harlequin Temptation
  442   Bad Attitude   06/93   Harlequin Temptation
  465   Naughty Talk (Lovers & Legends)   11/93   Harlequin Temptation
  490   Love, Me   05/94   Harlequin Temptation
  514   A Kiss In The Dark   11/94   Harlequin Temptation
  550   Naughty By Night (Secret Fantasies)   08/95   Harlequin Temptation
    3   Male For Sale   09/95   Silhouette Yours Truly

White, William C.
   53   Pale Blonde Of Sands St.   /50   Harlequin

Whitehead, Barbara
    Quicksilver Lady   Bantam
    Ramillies   St. Martin's

Whitehead, Barbara
  The Quade Inheritance   St. Martin's
Whitfield, Donna
  Sweet Spanish Bride   06/94   Avon Historical
Whitfield, Isabel
  105   Silver Fury   12/91   Harlequin Historical
  140   Bodie Bride   09/92   Harlequin Historical
Whitiker, Gail
  A Promise To Return   04/94   Harlequin Regency
  78   Bittersweet Revenge   07/92   Harlequin Regency
  92   The Blade And The Bath Miss 02/93   Harlequin Regency
  106   Letters To A Lady   09/93   Harlequin Regency
  Regency Romps   05/94   Harlequin Regency Anthology
Whitmore, Cilla
  515   Manner Of A Lady   Dell Candlelight Regency
  537   His Lordship's Landlady   Dell Candlelight Regency
  613   Mansion For A Lady   Dell Candlelight Regency
Whitney, Diana
  31   The Raven Master   05/94   Harlequin Shadows
  530   Midnight Stranger   11/93   Silhouette Intimate Moments
  603   Scarlet Whispers   11/94   Silhouette Intimate Moments
  673   O' Brian's Daughter   09/89   Silhouette Romance
  703   A Liberated Man   02/90   Silhouette Romance
  745   Scout's Honor   09/90   Silhouette Romance
  874   The Last Bachelor   07/92   Silhouette Romance
  940   One Man's Vow   06/93   Silhouette Romance
  491   Still Married   04/93   Silhouette Special Edition
  508   Cast A Tall Shadow   02/89   Silhouette Special Edition
  559   Yesterday's Child   11/89   Silhouette Special Edition
  644   One Lost Winter   01/91   Silhouette Special Edition
  702   Child Of The Storm   10/91   Silhouette Special Edition
  874   The Secret   03/94   Silhouette Special Edition
  934   The Adventurer   01/95   Silhouette Special Edition
  984   The Avenger   09/95   Silhouette Special Edition
  1019   The Reformer   03/96   Silhouette Special Edition
Whitney, Phyllis A.
  Daughter Of The Stars   08/95
  Black Amber   Ballantine
  Columbella   Ballantine
  Domino   Ballantine
  Dream Of Orchids   Ballantine
  Emerald   Ballantine
  Feather On A Moon   Ballantine
  The Flaming Tree   Ballantine
  The Golden Unicorn   Ballantine
  Lost Island   Ballantine

Whitney, Phyllis A.

The Moonflower		Ballantine
Poinciana		Ballantine
Rainsong		Ballantine
Sea Jade		Ballantine
Seven Tears For Appollo		Ballantine
Silversword		Ballantine
Snowfire		Ballantine
Spindrift		Ballantine
The Stone Bull		Ballantine
Thunder Heights		Ballantine
The Trembling Hills		Ballantine
The Turquoise Mask		Ballantine
Vermillion		Ballantine
Rainbow In The Mist		Ballantine
Silverhill		Ballantine
Snowfire		Ballantine
Hunter's Green		Ballantine Gothic
The Singing Stones	07/91	Fawcett Crest
Woman Without A Past	06/92	Fawcett Crest
Listen For The Whisperer	08/93	Fawcett Crest
The Turquoise Mask	08/93	Fawcett Crest
The Stone Bull	08/93	Fawcett Crest
The Ebony Swan	08/93	Fawcett Crest
Woman Without A Past	08/93	Fawcett Crest
Star Flight	08/94	Fawcett Crest
Window On The Square	11/91	Harper
Blue Fire	08/91	Harper
Skye Cameron	05/91	Harper
Thunder Heights	07/91	Harper
Black Amber	09/91	Harper
Seven Tears For Appollo	01/92	Harper
Sea Jade	03/92	Harper
Moonflower		Harper Collins
Quicksilver Pool		Harper Collins
Trembling Hills		Harper Collins

Whitneyy, Phyllis A.

Daughter Of The Stars	09/95	Fawcett Crest

Whittal, Yvonne

1915	East To Barryvale	/75	Harlequin
2002	The Slender Thread	/76	Harlequin
2077	Devil's Gateway	/77	Harlequin
2101	Where Seagulls Cry	/77	Harlequin
2128	Price Of Happiness	/77	Harlequin
2162	Handful Of Stardus	/78	Harlequin
2198	Scars Of Yesterday	/78	Harlequin
318	The Broken Link		Harlequin Presents

AUTHOR/TITLE INDEX

Whittenburg, Karen Toller

621	Million-Dollar Bride	03/96	Harlequin	American
630	The Fifty-Cent Groom	05/96	Harlequin	American
303	Only Yesterday	06/90	Harlequin	Temptation

Whittington, Harry

120	Slay Ride For A Lady	/51	Harlequin	
140	The Lady Was A Tramp	/51	Harlequin	
366	The Brass Monkey	/56	Harlequin	

Wibberley, Mary

1717	Black Niall	/73	Harlequin	
1739	Beloved Enemy	/73	Harlequin	
1790	Laird Of Gaela	/74	Harlequin	
1802	The Benedict Man	/74	Harlequin	
1827	Logan's Island	/74	Harlequin	
1836	Kyle's Kingdom	/74	Harlequin	
1879	Dark Viking	/75	Harlequin	
1903	Country Of The Vine	/75	Harlequin	
1924	The Dark Isle	/75	Harlequin	
1935	That Man Bryce	/75	Harlequin	
1968	The Wilderness Hut	/76	Harlequin	
1994	The Whispering Gate	/76	Harlequin	
2031	The Moon-Dancers	/76	Harlequin	
2059	The Silver Link	/77	Harlequin	
2085	Dark Venturer	/77	Harlequin	
2105	Wildcat Tamed	/77	Harlequin	
2136	Daughter Of The Sun	/78	Harlequin	
2147	Wild Goose	/78	Harlequin	
2177	Lord Of The Island	/78	Harlequin	
2221	The Taming Of Tamsin	/78	Harlequin	
89	The Snow On The Hills	/75	Harlequin	Presents
129	The Man At La Valaise	/76	Harlequin	Presents
348	Savage Love		Harlequin	Presents
390	Debt Of Dishonour		Harlequin	Presents
419	A Dream Of Thee		Harlequin	Presents
432	Gold To Remember		Harlequin	Presents
486	Devil's Causeway		Harlequin	Presents
526	Law Of The Jungle		Harlequin	Presents
2245	Witchwood		Harlequin	Romance
2267	Love's Sweet Revenge		Harlequin	Romance
2277	The Dark Warrior		Harlequin	Romance
2298	Runaway Marriage		Harlequin	Romance
2316	With This Ring		Harlequin	Romance
2340	Dangerous Man		Harlequin	Romance
2364	Dangerous Marriage		Harlequin	Romance
2388	Man Of Power		Harlequin	Romance
2418	Fire And Steel		Harlequin	Romance
2664	Golden Haven		Harlequin	Romance

AUTHOR/TITLE INDEX

Wibberly, Anna
    Were This Wild Thing Wedded   Ballantine Regency

Wicker, Amberlina
    Made In Heaven   02/95 Pinnacle Arabesque

Widmer, Mary Lou
    Lace Curtain   /85 Berkley
    Night Jasmine   /80 Dell

Wiete, Robin Leanne
    So Bright A Flame   11/91 Nal Onyx
    When Morning Comes 01/93 Nal Onyx
    Fortune's Lady   02/90 Nal Onyx
    Freedom Angel   10/90 Nal Onyx
    Rebel's Desire   02/89 Nal Onyx

Wiggs, Susan
    Moonshadow   Avon
    Briar Rose   10/93 Avon
    Winds Of Glory   Avon
    This Time Marriage:"The Borrowed Bride" 04/96 Harlequin Anthology
    The Mist And The Magic 01/93 Harper
    Embrace The Day 01/93 Harper
    The Raven And The Rose 11/91 Harper
    The Lily And The Leopard 01/91 Harper
    A Purrfect Romance 08/95 Harper Anthology
    Lord Of The Night 10/93 Harper Historical
    Circle In The Water 08/95 Harper Monogram
    Jewel Of The Sea 04/93 Tor
    October Wind 10/91 Tor
    Kingdom Of Gold 06/94 Tor
    Texas Wild Flower   Zebra Heartfire

Wilbee, Brenda
    Sweetbriar   /93 Harvest House Historical
    The Sweetbriar Bride /93 Harvest House Historical
    Sweetbriar Spring /93 Harvest House Historical

Wilby, Jane
    1 Eleanor And The Marquis   Mills & Boon
    22 Man Of Consequence   Mills & Boon

Wilde, Hilary
   875 Doctor David Advises /64 Harlequin
 1011 The Turquoise Sea /66 Harlequin
 1044 Paradise Island /66 Harlequin
 1077 The Golden Valley /67 Harlequin
 1143 Journey To An Island /67 Harlequin
 1173 Red As A Rose /68 Harlequin
 1243 The Isle Of Song /68 Harlequin
 1282 The Shining Star /69 Harlequin
 1356 The Man At Marralomeda /69 Harlequin

Wilde, Hilary

1496	The Blue Mountains Of Kabuta	/71	Harlequin
1546	The Master Of Barracuda Isle	/71	Harlequin
1591	Operation - In Search Of Love	/72	Harlequin
1624	The Golden Maze	/72	Harlequin
1642	The Fire Of Life	/72	Harlequin
1685	The Impossible Dream	/73	Harlequin
1735	Temptaions Of The Moon	/73	Harlequin
1768	The Palace Of Gold	/74	Harlequin
1786	Sweeter Than Honey	/74	Harlequin
1824	A Handful Of Dreams	/74	Harlequin

Wilde, Jennifer

Dare To Love		
Love Me Marietta		
Master Of Phoenix Hall		
Wherever Lynn Goes		
Angel In Scarlet		Avon
When Love Commands		Avon
Once More, Miranda		Ballantine
The Slipper		Ballantine
They Call Her Dana	/89	Ballantine
Master Of Phoenix Hall	07/91	Dell
Betrayal At Blackcrest	09/91	Dell
Come To Castlemoor	11/91	Dell
Whisper In The Darkness	12/91	Dell
The Lady Of Lyon House	03/92	Dell
When Emmalynn Remembers	05/92	Dell
Midnight At Mallyncourt	07/92	Dell
Room Beneath The Stars	08/92	Dell
Susannah, Beware	09/92	Dell
Wherever Lynn Goes		Dell

Wilde, Jocelyn

The Bride Of The Baja	Richard Gallen

Wilde, Lauren

Captive Love	
Creole Temptress	Zebra
Nebraska Fire	Zebra
Passion's Thunder	Zebra
Rebel Heart	Zebra
Sweet Betrayal	Zebra
Sweet Texas Wildfire	Zebra
Tender Betrayal	Zebra
The Texan's Lady	Zebra
Rapture's Revenge	Zebra

Wilder, Quinn

265	Dream Man	01/96	Harlequin

AUTHOR/TITLE INDEX

AUTHOR/TITLE INDEX

Wilkins, Gina

309	After Hours	08/90	Harlequin	Temptation
337	A Rebel At Heart	03/91	Harlequin	Temptation
353	A Perfect Stranger	07/91	Harlequin	Temptation
369	Hotline	11/91	Harlequin	Temptation
392	Veils & Vows: Taking A Chance On Love	04/92	Harlequin	Temptation
400	Veils & Vows: Designs On Love	06/92	Harlequin	Temptation
408	Veils & Vows: At Long Last Love	08/92	Harlequin	Temptation
445	When It's Right	06/93	Harlequin	Temptation
458	Rafe's Island	09/93	Harlequin	Temptation
470	As Luck Would Have It	12/93	Harlequin	Temptation
486	Just Her Luck	04/94	Harlequin	Temptation
501	Gold And Glitter (Lost Loves)	08/94	Harlequin	Temptation
521	Undercover Baby	01/95	Harlequin	Temptation
539	I Won't! (Grooms On The Run)	05/95	Harlequin	Temptation
567	All I Want For Christmas	12/95	Harlequin	Temptation
576	A Valentine Wish	02/96	Harlequin	Temptation
592	A Wish For Love	06/96	Harlequin	Temptation

Wilkins, Gina Ferris

	Three Mothers & A Cradle	05/95	Silhouette	Anthology
955	A Man For Mom	05/95	Silhouette	Special Edition
967	A Match For Celia	07/95	Silhouette	Special Edition
980	A Home For Adam (The Family Way)	09/95	Silhouette	Special Edition
1006	Cody's Fiancee	01/96	Silhouette	Special Edition

Wilkinson, Lee

118	Hong Kong Honeymoon	09/92	Harlequin	Direct
201	Adam's Angel	09/94	Harlequin	Direct
21	Lost Lady	12/95	Harlequin	Presents

Wilks, Eileen

1008	The Loner And The Lady	06/96	Silhouette	Desire

Williams, Ann - #2

302	Devil In Disguise	09/89	Silhouette	Intimate Moments
335	Loving Lies	05/90	Silhouette	Intimate Moments
358	Haunted By The Past	11/90	Silhouette	Intimate Moments
384	What Lindsey Knew	05/91	Silhouette	Intimate Moments
408	Angel On My Shoulder	11/91	Silhouette	Intimate Moments
436	Without Warning	06/92	Silhouette	Intimate Moments
468	Shades Of Wyoming	12/92	Silhouette	Intimate Moments
585	Wild Horses, Wild Men	08/94	Silhouette	Intimate Moments
615	Sam's World (Spellbound)	01/95	Silhouette	Intimate Moments
487	Cold, Cold Heart	04/93	Silhouette	Special Edition

Williams, Ben Ames

152	Great Oaks	/52	Harlequin	
247	Dark Surgery	/53	Harlequin	

AUTHOR/TITLE INDEX

Williams, Bronwyn

3	White Witch	08/88	Harlequin Historical
23	Dandelion		Harlequin Historical
47	Stormwalker		Harlequin Historical
67	Gideon's Fall	03/91	Harlequin Historical
99	The Mariner's Bride	11/91	Harlequin Historical
	Dream Catchers	01/96	Harlequin Two Novels
	The Warfield Bride	06/94	Penguin Topaz
	Slow Surrender	12/95	Topaz
	Bedeviled	02/95	Topaz Historical

Williams, Cathy

20	Unwilling Surrender	11/95	Harlequin Presents
28	Shadows Of Yesterday	03/96	Harlequin Presents
1413	A Powerful Attraction	11/91	Harlequin Presents
1502	Caribbean Desire	10/92	Harlequin Presents
1829	Beyond All Reason	08/96	Harlequin Presents

Williams, Claudette

A Daring Deceit	07/94	
Lacey		Fawcett Crest
Lady Madcap		Fawcett Crest
Lady Bell		Fawcett Crest
Regency Star		Fawcett Crest
Sassy		Fawcett Crest
Song Of Silkie		Fawcett Crest
Sweet Disorder		Fawcett Crest
Cassandra		Fawcett Crest
Blades Of Passion		Fawcett Crest
Spring Gambit		Fawcett Crest
Lady Runaway		Fawcett Crest
Lady Sunshine		Fawcett Crest
Heart Of Fancy		Fawcett Crest
Lord Wildfire		Fawcett Crest
Desert Rose, English Moon		Fawcett Crest
Passion's Pride		Fawcett Crest
Lady Barbara		Fawcett Crest
Jeweline		Fawcett Crest
Lady Brandy		Fawcett Crest
Hatspun Of Taffeta		Fawcett Crest
Lady Magic		Fawcett Crest
Cherry Ripe		Fawcett Crest
Fire And Desire		Fawcett Crest
Lady Velvet	07/94	Zebra Regency

Williams, Frances

223	Easy Target	01/88	Silhouette Intimate Moments
287	Night Secrets	05/89	Silhouette Intimate Moments
378	The Road To Forever	04/91	Silhouette Intimate Moments
455	Shadows On Satin	10/92	Silhouette Intimate Moments

AUTHOR/TITLE INDEX

Williams, Mary
    Gypsy Legacy /86 Dell
    Stormswept /86 Dell
Williams, Patricia
    Warrior's Prize 09/94 Diamond Historical
    Freedom's Song 06/95 Jove Historical
Williams, Paula
    A Case For Love 11/88 Crown Pageant
Williams, Roseanne

34	Mail Order Man	08/96	Harlequin Here Come The Grooms
237	How Sweet It Is!	02/89	Harlequin Temptation
306	The Magic Touch	07/90	Harlequin Temptation
350	Love Conquers All	06/91	Harlequin Temptation
384	Under The Covers	02/92	Harlequin Temptation
401	The Bad Boy (Rebels & Rogues)	07/92	Harlequin Temptation
431	Seeing Red	02/93	Harlequin Temptation
443	Mail Order Man	06/93	Harlequin Temptation
459	Just Another Pretty Face	09/93	Harlequin Temptation
460	Hot Date	09/93	Harlequin Temptation
504	A True Blue Knight	08/94	Harlequin Temptation
531	Secondhand Bride	03/95	Harlequin Temptation
588	Stranger In The Night	05/96	Harlequin Temptation

Williams, Stephanie
  1168 Highland Turmoil Harlequin Presents
Williams, Wynn
   649 Starry Nights 05/89 Silhouette Romance
   756 One Breathless Moment 11/90 Silhouette Romance
   858 Bewitching Nights 04/92 Silhouette Romance
Williamson, Penelope
    Beloved Rouge Avon
    Hearts Beguiled 07/89 Avon
    A Wild Yearning 04/90 Avon
    Heart Of The West /94 Avon
    Keeper Of The Dream 05/92 Dell
    A Reckless Yearning Dell
Willingham, Bess
    The Vigilante Viscount 12/95 Zebra Regency
Willis, Kathy
    Southern Surrender 04/94 Zebra
    Tropical Thunder Zebra Heartfire
Willis, Ted
    The Bells Of Autumn 09/91 St. Martin's
Willman, Marianne
    The Court Of Three Sisters 07/94
    Once Upon A Castle 12/96 Berkley Anthology
    1993 Keepsake Christmas Stories 11/93 Harlequin Anthology

AUTHOR/TITLE INDEX

AUTHOR/TITLE INDEX

Wilson, Mary Anne

523	Could It Be You?	02/94	Harlequin	American
543	Her Bodyguard	07/94	Harlequin	American
570	The Bride Wore Blue Jeans	02/95	Harlequin	American
589	Hart's Dream (Heartbeat)	07/95	Harlequin	American
609	The Christmas Husband	12/95	Harlequin	American
637	Nine Months Later...	07/96	Harlequin	American
45	False Family	12/94	Harlequin	Shadows
230	Hot-Blooded	03/88	Silhouette	Intimate Moments
267	Home Fires	12/88	Silhouette	Intimate Moments
292	Liar's Moon	06/89	Silhouette	Intimate Moments
304	Straight From The Heart	09/89	Silhouette	Intimate Moments
336	Dream Chasers	05/90	Silhouette	Intimate Moments
350	Brady's Law	09/90	Silhouette	Intimate Moments
374	Child Of Mine	03/91	Silhouette	Intimate Moments
410	Nowhere To Run	12/91	Silhouette	Intimate Moments
438	Echoes Of Roses	07/92	Silhouette	Intimate Moments
472	Two For The Road	01/93	Silhouette	Intimate Moments
574	Jake's Touch	06/94	Silhouette	Intimate Moments
489	Two Against The World	04/93	Silhouette	Special Edition

Wilson, Patricia

934	The Final Price		Harlequin	Presents
1062	A Lingering Melody		Harlequin	Presents
1086	The Ortiga Marriage		Harlequin	Presents
1110	A Moment Of Anger		Harlequin	Presents
1125	Impossible Bargain		Harlequin	Presents
1150	Beloved Intruder		Harlequin	Presents
1174	A Certain Affection		Harlequin	Presents
1198	When The Gods Choose		Harlequin	Presents
1221	The Gathering Darkness		Harlequin	Presents
1238	Temporary Bride		Harlequin	Presents
1262	Guardian Angel		Harlequin	Presents
1286	Dangerous Obsession		Harlequin	Presents
1310	A Secret Understanding		Harlequin	Presents
1398	Passionate Enemy	09/91	Harlequin	Presents
1430	Stormy Surrender	01/92	Harlequin	Presents
1454	Curtain Of Stars	04/92	Harlequin	Presents
1469	The Gift Of Loving	06/92	Harlequin	Presents
1518	Perilous Refuge	12/92	Harlequin	Presents
1547	Forbidden Enchantment	04/93	Harlequin	Presents
1564	Jungle Enchantment	06/93	Harlequin	Presents
1564	Jungle Enchantment	06/93	Harlequin	Presents
1578	Intangible Dream	08/93	Harlequin	Presents
1602	Walk Upon The Wind	11/93	Harlequin	Presents
1644	Dark Sunlight (Postcards From Europe)	04/94	Harlequin	Presents
1685	Dearest Traitor	09/94	Harlequin	Presents
2856	Bride Of Diaz		Harlequin	Romance

Wilson, Patricia

3102	Bond Of Destiny		Harlequin Romance
3298	Out Of Nowhere	01/94	Harlequin Romance
3346	Passionate Captivity	01/95	Harlequin Romance
3354	Dark Illusion	03/95	Harlequin Romance
3364	Tender Deceit	06/95	Harlequin Romance
3372	Sense Of Destiny	08/95	Harlequin Romance
3405	A Dangerous Magic	04/96	Harlequin Romance
3417	Coming Home	07/96	Harlequin Romance

Wilson, Sandra

	Jessica	/80	Fawcett Regency
	A Woman Of Property	/81	Fawcett Regency
	Wife To The Kingmaker	/75	St. Martin's English Medieval
	Alice	/76	St. Martin's English Medieval
1	Less Fortune Than Fair	/73	St. Martin's English Medieval Trilogy
2	The Queen's Sister	/74	St. Martin's English Medieval Trilogy
3	The Lady Circle	/75	St. Martin's English Medieval Trilogy

Wilson-Harris, Crystal

	Dark Embrace	09/91	Odyssey Books

Wimberly, Clara

	Kentucky Thunder	07/93	Harper Monogram
	Primrose	07/94	Harper Monogram
	Nanchez Moon	09/93	Pinnacle
521	Ryan Blake's Revenge	09/93	Silhouette Intimate Moments
612	Georgia On My Mind	12/94	Silhouette Intimate Moments
718	You Must Remember This	06/96	Silhouette Intimate Moments
	Bride Of Sea Crest Hall	12/93	Zebra
	The Jeweled Heart Of Rosemont Castle	12/92	Zebra
	Home For Christmas	11/92	Zebra Anthology
	To Mother With Love	04/93	Zebra Anthology
	The Emerald Tears Of Foxfire Manor	04/90	Zebra Gothic
	The Ghostly Screams Of Stormhaven		Zebra Gothic
	Lady Of The Mists	03/91	Zebra Gothic
	Moonwatch	10/90	Zebra Gothic
	Lady Of Seven Emeralds	06/93	Zebra Gothic
	Tomorrow's Promise	08/92	Zebra Special Over 45 Release
	Angel Unaware	08/94	Zebra To Love Again
	Christmas Anthology	11/94	Zebra To Love Again

Wind, Ruth

	Lavender & Thyme	/92	Silhouette
587	Breaking The Rules	08/94	Silhouette Intimate Moments
555	Strangers On A Train	10/89	Silhouette Special Edition
588	Summer's Freedom	03/90	Silhouette Special Edition
635	Light Of Day	11/90	Silhouette Special Edition
742	A Minute To Smile	05/92	Silhouette Special Edition
785	Jezebel's Blues	12/92	Silhouette Special Edition

Wind, Ruth

881	Walk In Beauty	04/94	Silhouette Special Edition
977	The Last Chance Ranch	08/95	Silhouette Special Edition
1031	Rainsinger	05/96	Silhouette Special Edition

Windham, Susannah

| 207 | More Precious Than Pearls | 02/83 | Silhouette Romance |

Windsor, Kathleen

| | Forever Amber | | Historical |

Windsor, Linda

31	Wings Of Love	02/91	Meteor
	Wild Tory Rose	02/92	Pinnacle Historical
	Delta Moonfire	11/92	Zebra
	Bride's Passion	06/93	Zebra Anthology
	Midnight Lovestorm	03/92	Zebra Heartfire
	Pirate's Wild Embrace	02/90	Zebra Heartfire
	Hawaiian Caress	11/90	Zebra Heartfire
	Hawaiian Temptress	04/91	Zebra Heartfire
	Texas Lovestorm	11/91	Zebra Heartfire
	Island Flame	05/95	Zebra Lovegram
	The Knight And The Raven	04/94	Zebra Lovegram
	Hawaiian Flame	12/94	Zebra Lovegram
	Mexican Caress	07/93	Zebra To Love Again
	Ransomed Heart-Bride's Passion	06/93	Zebra Wedding Anthology

Wingo, Helen

| | The Restless Heart | /91 | Avalon |
| | While The Heart Fails | 12/92 | Avalon |

Winn, Bonnie K.

	Summer Rose	07/92	Diamond Wildflower
	Reckless Wind	06/93	Diamond Wildflower
	The Forbidden Fire	02/94	Diamond Wildflower
624	The Newlywed Game	03/96	Harlequin American
	Hearts Of Gold	02/94	Jove Anthology
	Reckless Hearts	05/95	Jove Wildflower

Winship,

| | At Summer's End | | |

Winslow, Betty

| | The Lady And The Lawman | 05/95 | Harper Monogram |

Winslow, Ellie

25	Painted Secrets		Nal Rapture Romance
39	A Distant Light		Nal Rapture Romance
54	Red Sky At Night	/84	Nal Rapture Romance

Winslow, Laurel

| | Heart Songs | | Avon |

Winsor, Kathleen

| | Forever Amber | /44 | Mac Millan |

Winspear, Violet

AUTHOR/TITLE INDEX

Winspear, Violet

	House Of Storms	10/88	Harlequin
	The Honeymoon	10/86	Harlequin
593	Lucifer's Angel	/61	Harlequin
884	Nurse At Cap Flamingo	/65	Harlequin
921	Desert Doctor	/65	Harlequin
1008	Bride's Dilemma	/66	Harlequin
1032	Beloved Tyrant	/66	Harlequin
1080	The Viking Stranger	/67	Harlequin
1111	The Tower Of The Captive	/67	Harlequin
1208	Tender Is The Tyrant	/68	Harlequin
1267	Court Of The Veils	/69	Harlequin
1318	Palace Of The Peacocks	/69	Harlequin
1344	The Dangerous Delight	/69	Harlequin
1399	Blue Jasmine	/70	Harlequin
1434	The Cazalet Bride	/70	Harlequin
1472	Beloved Castaway	/71	Harlequin
1514	The Castle Of The Seven Lilacs	/71	Harlequin
1555	Raintree Valley	/72	Harlequin
1580	Black Douglas	/72	Harlequin
1616	The Pagan Island	/72	Harlequin
1637	The Silver Slave	/72	Harlequin
1658	Dear Puritan	/73	Harlequin
1680	Rapture Of The Desert	/73	Harlequin
5	Devil In A Silver Room	/73	Harlequin Presents
6	The Honey Is Bitter	/73	Harlequin Presents
9	Wife Without Kisses	/73	Harlequin Presents
12	Dragon Bay	/73	Harlequin Presents
15	The Little Nobody	/73	Harlequin Presents
18	The Kisses And The Wine	/73	Harlequin Presents
21	The Unwilling Bride	/73	Harlequin Presents
24	Pilgrim's Castle	/73	Harlequin Presents
27	House Of Strangers	/73	Harlequin Presents
30	Bride Of Lucifer	/73	Harlequin Presents
33	Forbidden Rapture	/74	Harlequin Presents
36	Love's Prisoner	/74	Harlequin Presents
39	Tawny Sands	/74	Harlequin Presents
42	The Strange Waif	/74	Harlequin Presents
50	The Glass Castle	/74	Harlequin Presents
70	The Chateau Of St. Avrell	/74	Harlequin Presents
90	The Noble Savage	/75	Harlequin Presents
98	The Girl At Goldenhawk	/75	Harlequin Presents
114	Palace Of The Pomegranate	/75	Harlequin Presents
122	The Devil's Darling	/75	Harlequin Presents
130	Dearest Demon	/76	Harlequin Presents
138	Satan Took A Bride	/76	Harlequin Presents
142	Darling Infidel	/76	Harlequin Presents

903

AUTHOR/TITLE INDEX

Winters, Rebecca

3162	Rescued Heart	11/91	Harlequin Romance
3192	The Marriage Bracelet	04/92	Harlequin Romance
3210	Both Of Them	07/92	Harlequin Romance
3228	Meant For Each Other	10/92	Harlequin Romance
3265	Hero On The Loose	06/93	Harlequin Romance
3280	The Rancher And The Redhead	09/93	Harlequin Romance
3312	The Mermaid Wife	05/94	Harlequin Romance
3325	Bride Of My Heart	08/94	Harlequin Romance
3340	The Nutcracker Prince	12/94	Harlequin Romance
3362	The Baby Business	05/95	Harlequin Romance
3390	Return To Sender	12/95	Harlequin Romance
3409	The Badlands Bride	05/96	Harlequin Romance
3419	Kit And The Cowboy	08/96	Harlequin Romance
636	The Wrong Twin (9 Months)	03/95	Harlequin Superromance
650	A Man For All Time (Dreamscape)	07/95	Harlequin Superromance
697	Not Without My Child	06/96	Harlequin Superromance

Winwood, Eileen

	So Reckless A Love	03/95	Diamond Historical
	Noble Deception	03/92	Jove Regency
	Words Of Love	09/92	Jove Regency
	A Worthy Engagement	01/93	Jove Regency
	Garden Of Secrets	09/94	Jove Tea Rose Romance

Wisdom, Linda

	Love Has Many Voices		
643	Sudden Impulse	10/93	Bantam Loveswept
670	Midnight Lady	02/94	Bantam Loveswept
695	O' Hare Vs. Wilder	06/94	Bantam Loveswept

Wisdom, Linda Randall

	Ms. Scrooge Meets Cupid	01/93	
	Sudden Impulse	04/93	Bantam Loveswept
196	Guardian Angel	/83	Dell Candlelight Ecstasy
250	We Give Thanks		Harlequin American
284	Lady's Choice		Harlequin American
293	Appearances Are Deceiving	03/89	Harlequin American
310	Code Of Silence		Harlequin American
325	Sins Of The Past		Harlequin American
350	A Man For Maggie		Harlequin American
372	O' Malley's Quest		Harlequin American
382	Voices In The Night		Harlequin American
401	Free Spirits	08/91	Harlequin American
422	Sometimes A Lady	01/92	Harlequin American
443	This Old House	06/92	Harlequin American
457	Under His Spell	10/92	Harlequin American
470	A Man For Mom	01/93	Harlequin American
487	The Countess And The Cowboy	06/93	Harlequin American
515	No Room At The Inn	12/93	Harlequin American

AUTHOR/TITLE INDEX

Wolf, Joan

	A London Season	01/86	Nal Regency
	A Difficult Truce	03/88	Nal Regency
	The American Duchess	06/88	Nal Regency
	The Rebellious Ward	07/88	Nal Regency
	The Scottish Lord	08/88	Nal Regency
	Lord Richards's Daughter	10/88	Nal Regency
	Margarita	11/88	Nal Regency
	Fool's Masquerade	12/88	Nal Regency
	A Kind Of Honor	11/91	Nal Regency
1	The Road To Avalon		Nal Onyx Arthurian Trilogy
2	Born Of The Sun		Nal Onyx Arthurian Trilogy
3	The Edge Of Light	/94	Nal Onyx Arthurian Trilogy
	The Rebel And The Rose		Nal Penguin
	Highland Sunset		Nal Penguin
	New Orleans	/94	Nal Penguin Onyx
	His Lordship's Mistress		Nal Penguin Regency
	The Counterfeit Marriage		Nal Penguin Regency
	A Fashionable Affair		Nal Penguin Regency
	A Double Deception	06/93	Penguin Regency

Wolfe, Bronwyn

	Longer Than Forever	/95	Leisure

Wolfe, Lois

	The Schemers	05/91	Bantam Fanfare

Wood, Barbara

	The Dreaming	/92	
	Green City In The Sun	/91	
	Childsong		
	Yesterday's Song		
	Soul Flame		
	Night Trains		
	Curse This House	/77	Dell Gothic Romance
	The Magdalene Scrolls	/77	Doubleday Gothic Romance
	Hounds And Jackals	/76	Doubleday Romantic Suspense
	Virgins Of Paradise Street	01/93	Random

Wood, Deborah

	Gentle Hearts	04/93	Diamond Homespun
	Summer's Gift	05/94	Diamond Homespun
	Heart's Song	03/95	Diamond Homespun
	Maggie's Pride	03/96	Jove Historical

Wood, Nuria

7	The Family Plan	/84	Berkley To Have And To Hold

Wood, Sally

2155	Island Masquerade	/78	Harlequin

Wood, Sara

981	Passion's Daughter		Harlequin Presents

Wood, Sara

1070	Pure Temptation		Harlequin Presents
1102	Wicked Invader		Harlequin Presents
1134	Savage Hunger		Harlequin Presents
1166	The Count's Vendetta		Harlequin Presents
1182	Tender Persuasion		Harlequin Presents
1206	No Gentle Loving		Harlequin Presents
1302	Threat Of Possession		Harlequin Presents
1318	Love Not Dishonour		Harlequin Presents
1382	Nights Of Destiny	07/91	Harlequin Presents
1414	Desert Hostage	11/91	Harlequin Presents
1470	Sicilian Vengeance	06/92	Harlequin Presents
1573	Cloak Of Darkness	07/93	Harlequin Presents
1606	Dark Forces	11/93	Harlequin Presents
1628	Mask Of Deception	02/94	Harlequin Presents
1692	The Vengeful Groom (Weddings, Inc.)	10/94	Harlequin Presents
1715	Southern Passions (Too Hot To Handle)	01/95	Harlequin Presents
1765	Shades Of Sin	09/95	Harlequin Presents
1790	Tangled Destinies	01/96	Harlequin Presents
1796	Unchained Destinies	02/96	Harlequin Presents
1802	Threads Of Destiny	03/96	Harlequin Presents
1817	Second-Best Bride	06/96	Harlequin Presents
2814	Perfumes Of Arabia		Harlequin Romance
3066	Master Of Cashel		Harlequin Romance

Wood, Tonya

477	Gorgeous	06/91	Bantam Loveswept
587	Sneak	12/92	Bantam Loveswept

Woodbury, Leonora

	Game Of Hearts	Diamond Regency

Woodiwiss, Kathleen E.

Three Weddings & A Kiss	/95	Anthology
Ashes In The Wind		Avon
Come Love A Stranger	04/94	Avon
The Flame And The Flower		Avon
Rose In Winter		Avon
Shanna	10/93	Avon
So Worthy My Love		Avon
Forever In Your Embrace	09/92	Avon
The Wolf And The Dove	11/93	Avon
A Rose In Winter	03/94	Avon Historical

Woods, Eleanor

92	Just For The Asking	/86	Dell Candlelight Ecstasy
174	Tempestuous Challenge	/83	Dell Candlelight Ecstasy
199	Sensuous Persuasion	/83	Dell Candlelight Ecstasy
408	Mystery Lady	/86	Dell Ecstasy Romance
307	Second Time Lucky		Harlequin Superromance

Woods, Sherryl

1009	The Cowboy And His Baby	02/96	Silhouette Special Edition
1016	The Rancher And His Unexpected Daughter	03/96	Silhouette Special Edition
	A Bridge To Dreams	07/90	Silhouette Summer Sizzlers
	Jamaican Midnight		Velvet Glove
	Ties That Bind	/91	Warner
	Body And Soul		Warner Amanda Roberts Mystery
	Reckless		Warner Amanda Roberts Mystery
	Stolen Moments		Warner Amanda Roberts Mystery
	Wages Of Sin	10/94	Warner Amanda Roberts Mystery
	Ties That Bind		Warner Amanda Roberts Mystery
	Bank On It		Warner Amanda Roberts Mystery
	Hide And Seek		Warner Amanda Roberts Mystery
	Deadly Obsession		Warner Amanda Roberts Mystery
	Temptation	12/96	Zebra

Woolf, Victoria

2273	Sweet Compulsion		Harlequin Romance

Worley, Dorothy

376	Blake Hospital	/57	Harlequin

Worth, Susan

580	Commitments	03/96	Harlequin Temptation

Wren, P.C.

223	The Wages Of Virtue	/53	Harlequin

Wright, Cynthia

	Fireblossom	11/92	Ballantine
	Natayla	10/91	Ballantine
	Caroline	10/91	Ballantine
	Spring Fires		Ballantine
	Surrender The Stars		Ballantine
	A Battle For Love		Ballantine
	Silver Storm		Ballantine
	Touch The Sun		Ballantine
	You And No Other		Ballantine
	Brighter Than Gold		Ballantine
	Wild Blossom	07/94	Ballantine
	Barbados	07/95	Ballantine
	Natalya	10/91	Ballantine Historical
	Caroline	10/91	Ballantine Historical

Wright, Don

	The Last Plantation		Gray Stone Pres

Wright, Watkins E.

381	Doctor Joel	/57	Harlequin

Wrighton, Antoinette

	When I Give My Love	05/96	Pocket

Wulf, Jessica

	The Mountain Rose	08/94	Zebra Historical

AUTHOR/TITLE INDEX

AUTHOR/TITLE INDEX

York, Vickie

231	Abandoned	06/93	Harlequin	Intrigue
279	Moon Watch	06/94	Harlequin	Intrigue
333	The Eyes Of Derek Archer	08/95	Harlequin	Intrigue

Yorke, Erin

58	American Beauty		Harlequin	Historical
94	Forever Defiant	09/91	Harlequin	Historical
124	Heaven's Gate	05/92	Harlequin	Historical
152	Dangerous Deceptions	02/93	Harlequin	Historical
176	Bound By Love	06/93	Harlequin	Historical
202	Counterfeit Laird	01/94	Harlequin	Historical
239	The Honor Price	10/94	Harlequin	Historical
285	Desert Rogue	09/95	Harlequin	Historical
	Scadalous Spirits	01/88	Worldwide Libr.	

Yorke, Katherine

	The Enchantress		Richard Gallen

Young, Brittany

	Silent Night	/89	Silhouette	Christmas Stories
165	Arranged Marriage	07/82	Silhouette	Romance
297	A Separate Happiness	05/84	Silhouette	Romance
308	No Special Consideration	07/84	Silhouette	Romance
336	The Karas Cup	01/85	Silhouette	Romance
357	An Honorable Man	04/85	Silhouette	Romance
375	A Deeper Meaning	07/85	Silhouette	Romance
388	No Ordinary Man	10/85	Silhouette	Romance
424	To Catch A Thief	04/86	Silhouette	Romance
454	Gallagher's Lady	09/86	Silhouette	Romance
484	All Or Nothing	02/87	Silhouette	Romance
537	Far From Over	10/87	Silhouette	Romance
550	A Matter Of Honor	01/88	Silhouette	Romance
574	Worth The Risk	05/88	Silhouette	Romance
597	The Kiss Of A Stranger	08/88	Silhouette	Romance
622	A Man Called Travers	01/89	Silhouette	Romance
640	The White Rose	04/89	Silhouette	Romance
658	A Woman In Love	07/89	Silhouette	Romance
700	The Ambassador's Daughter	02/90	Silhouette	Romance
729	The Seduction Of Anna	06/90	Silhouette	Romance
759	The House By The Lake	11/90	Silhouette	Romance
807	One Man's Destiny	07/91	Silhouette	Romance
831	Lady In Distress	11/91	Silhouette	Romance
885	A Holiday To Remember	08/92	Silhouette	Romance
941	Jenni Finds A Father	02/95	Silhouette	Special Edition
996	Brave Heart	11/95	Silhouette	Special Edition

Young, Cassandra

387	Wish Upon A Star	09/85	Silhouette	Romance

Young, Karen

AUTHOR/TITLE INDEX

Young, Karen

	My Valentine 1994	02/94	Harlequin Anthology
341	All My Tomorrows		Harlequin Superromance
371	Compelling Connection		Harlequin Superromance
453	Debt Of Love		Harlequin Superromance
472	Beyond Summer	10/91	Harlequin Superromance
500	The Silence Of Midnight	05/92	Harlequin Superromance
532	Touch The Dawn	01/93	Harlequin Superromance
602	Roses And Rain (O' Connor Trilogy)	07/94	Harlequin Superromance
606	Shadows In The Mist (O' Connor Trilogy)	08/94	Harlequin Superromance
610	The Promise (O' Connor Trilogy)	09/94	Harlequin Superromance
681	Having His Baby	02/96	Harlequin Superromance
212	Yesterday's Promise	03/83	Silhouette Romance
284	Irresistible Intruder	03/84	Silhouette Romance
380	A Wilder Passion	08/85	Silhouette Romance
433	Darling Detective	05/86	Silhouette Romance
481	The Forever Kind	01/87	Silhouette Romance
517	Maggie Mine	07/87	Silhouette Romance
575	Sarah's Choice	05/88	Silhouette Romance

Young, Marie Selwyn

369	Forever Mine	08/87	Silhouette Desire

Young, Maryann

	The Shimmering Stones		Dell Candlelight
197	A Dream Of Her Own		Dell Candlelight
16	Beseiged By Love		Dell Candlelight Ecstasy

Young, Rena

2670	Catch A Falling Star		Harlequin Romance

Young, W.J.

391	How To Get More From Your Car	/57	Harlequin

Zach, Cheryl

	Hearts Divided	06/95	Bantam Southern Angels 1
19	Twice A Fool	07/84	Harlequin Temptation

Zane, Carolyn

1011	The Wife Next Door (Celebration 1000!)	05/94	Silhouette Romance
1035	Wife In Name Only (Hasty Weddings)	09/94	Silhouette Romance
1063	Unwilling Wife (Sister Switch)	02/95	Silhouette Romance
1082	Weekend Wife (Sister Switch)	05/95	Silhouette Romance
1093	Bachelor Blues	07/95	Silhouette Romance
1127	The Baby Factor	01/96	Silhouette Romance
1170	Marriage In A Bottle	08/96	Silhouette Romance
21	Single In Seattle	06/96	Silhouette Yours Truly

Zaroulis, Nancy

	The Last Waltz	Zebra Historical & Family Sagas

Zide, Donna Comeaux

	Chelaine	Tapestry

Zimlich, Jan

ABOUT THE AUTHOR

PEGGY J. JAEGLY is an active member of the Romance Writers of America (RWA) and has served as president and in other board positions for local chapters in both Ohio and New Jersey. She recently founded and served as first president for the Mystery/Suspense Subgenre Chapter of RWA which draws an international membership. She is multi-published in various newspapers and trade and city magazines on a wide variety of topics. She co-authored the booklet *Miscarriage: A Book For Parents Experiencing Fetal Death,* which was first published by Centering Corporation in 1983 and continues to be used nationwide. Currently, she is working on a series of romantic suspense novels and a young adult mystery series. *Romantic Hearts: A Personal Reference For Romance Readers* is a labor of love for her fellow romance readers and is the third edition of her collection of reference material regarding the romance genre.